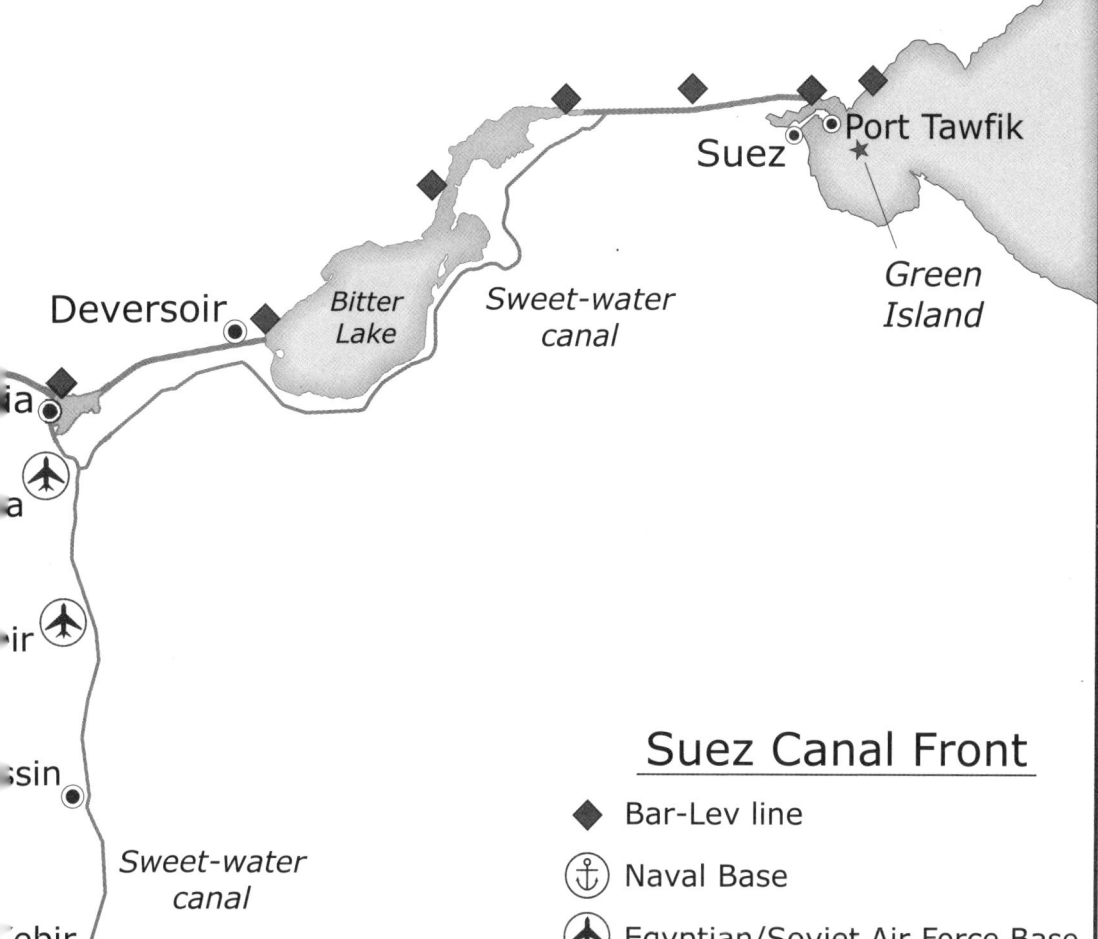

THE SOVIET–ISRAELI WAR, 1967–1973

ISABELLA GINOR
GIDEON REMEZ

The Soviet–Israeli War, 1967–1973

The USSR's Military Intervention in the Egyptian-Israeli Conflict

OXFORD
UNIVERSITY PRESS

Oxford University Press is a department of the
University of Oxford. It furthers the University's objective
of excellence in research, scholarship, and education
by publishing worldwide.

Oxford   New York
Auckland   Cape Town   Dar es Salaam   Hong Kong   Karachi
Kuala Lumpur   Madrid   Melbourne   Mexico City   Nairobi
New Delhi   Shanghai   Taipei   Toronto

With offices in
Argentina   Austria   Brazil   Chile   Czech Republic   France   Greece
Guatemala   Hungary   Italy   Japan   Poland   Portugal   Singapore
South Korea   Switzerland   Thailand   Turkey   Ukraine   Vietnam

Oxford is a registered trade mark of Oxford University Press
in the UK and certain other countries.

Published in the United States of America by
Oxford University Press
198 Madison Avenue, New York, NY 10016

Copyright © Isabella Ginor and Gideon Remez 2017

All rights reserved. No part of this publication may be reproduced,
stored in a retrieval system, or transmitted, in any form or by any means,
without the prior permission in writing of Oxford University Press,
or as expressly permitted by law, by license, or under terms agreed with
the appropriate reproduction rights organization. Inquiries concerning
reproduction outside the scope of the above should be sent to the
Rights Department, Oxford University Press, at the address above.

You must not circulate this work in any other form
and you must impose this same condition on any acquirer.

Library of Congress Cataloging-in-Publication Data is available
Isabella Ginor and Gideon Remez.
The Soviet–Israeli War, 1967–1973: The USSR's Military Intervention
in the Egyptian-Israeli Conflict.
ISBN: 9780190693480

Printed in India on acid-free paper

For our children and grandchildren

CONTENTS

Acknowledgments — ix
Abbreviations — xi
Foreword — xiii
  I. *Un-Rewriting History* — xiii
  II. *The Tyranny of Vested-Interest Sources* — xviii

PART 1
"WE WILL NOT LEAVE EGYPT IN THE LURCH"

1. Rescuing and Rearming the USSR's Allies in June 1967 — 3
2. Holding the Line on the Suez Canal — 17
3. The Soviet Presence Is Formalized and Expanded — 33

PART 2
OPERATION *KAVKAZ*

4. Framing the Cross-Canal Goal and the Attrition Strategy — 53
5. The Nuclear Non-issue — 67
6. "Yellow Arab Helmet, Blue Russian Eyes" — 73
7. Facing the Bar-Lev Line — 91
8. A New Phase from March '69? — 101
9. What Triggered *Kavkaz*? Refuting Heikal's Version — 113
10. Dr Chazov's "Vacation in Egypt" — 125
11. The Soviet Regulars Move In — 135
12. Operation *Kavkaz* Is Formally Organized — 151
13. The Soviet–Israeli Battle Is Joined — 161
14. "A Famous Indiscretion" as the Air War Peaks — 173
15. An MIA Mystery and Soviet Intelligence Methods — 183
16. SAM Successes and a MiG Debacle — 189
17. Ceasefire Violation Seals a Strategic Gain — 199

PART 3
A DECEPTIVE END

18. Sadat Proves His Stability and Loyalty — 213

CONTENTS

19. Return of the Foxbats	223
20. Trial Balloons from Both Sides	231
21. Flexing Muscles while Offering a Pullback	241
22. Jockeying and Posturing	255
23. The Deal at the Summit and the "Expulsion" Myth	263
24. Withdrawn Regulars Conceal "Banished" Advisers	275
25. Deception-on-Nile, July 1972	281
26. The Soviets "Return" in October	293

PART 4
"WE PREPARED THE WAR"

27. "We Can't Control the Arabs but Must Support Them"	305
28. "We Will Be Two Ismails"	315
29. The Ultimate Test of Ashraf Marwan	327
30. In the Thick of the Yom Kippur War	337
31. The Soviet Nuclear Threat and Kissinger's Defcon-3	347
Epilogue: So What Went Wrong, and When?	355
Notes	361
Bibliography	467
Index	485

ACKNOWLEDGMENTS

This book was mostly researched and written during our continuing tenure as associate fellows of the Harry S. Truman Research Institute for the Advancement of Peace at the Hebrew University of Jerusalem. We are immensely grateful to the Institute, its leadership, fellows and staff for the stimulating and convivial ambience that we have enjoyed there, as well as funding for the publication costs.

We owe heartfelt thanks to Hurst Publishers, and in particular Alasdair Craig, Michael Dwyer, Jon de Peyer, Tim Page, Lara Weisweiller-Wu, Daisy Leitch, Kathleen May, and Alison Alexanian, for their interest, enthusiasm and patience in steering us through the publication process. Our gratitude is also due for the invaluable recognition and head start that we were granted by the editors of the scholarly journals and edited volumes where the papers that are partly incorporated into the present text (and are listed in the bibliography) first appeared.

The reservations expressed in our foreword about exclusive reliance on archival sources detract nothing from the essential input of this material. For their indispensable support and advice, we are much indebted to innumerable staff members at the Israel State Archive, Israel National Library, Israel Intelligence Heritage Centre, US National Archives and Records Administration, Lyndon B. Johnson Library, UK National Archive, Churchill Archive Centre at Cambridge University, and the Liddell Hart Centre for Military Archives, King's College, London. No less important were the online and published resources of the Cold War International History Project at the Woodrow Wilson Center and of the National Security Archive, George Washington University.

Several Internet resources were instrumental for reviewing contemporary media coverage of the events. Most of the Israeli press items were located through the Historical Jewish Press Project of the Israel National Library and Tel Aviv University. The frequent quotes from otherwise obscure North American local newspapers, as sources for news agencies and syndicates, were mostly gathered from Thomas M. Tryniski's outstanding website fultonhistory.com and from the now-defunct search facility of Google News Archive.

Our personal thanks go to the following individuals for their contributions to this book in more ways than can be detailed here (those marked * are, sadly, deceased): Yael Artzi, *Me'ir Amit, *Yo'el Ben-Porat, Dave Brog, Mark Clark, Craig Daigle, Lynn

ACKNOWLEDGMENTS

Gamma, *Hermann Eilts, Adi Frimark, Nicholas Hagger, Norman Kass, *Yury Khripunkov, Jacob Kipp, Konstantin Kikoin, Harvey Klehr, Michael Klosson, Roland Lajoie, Stefan Meining, Dee Mortensen, Michael Oren, Jeff Peer, Uri Ra'anan, Denis Sellem, Danny Shalom, Mark Stout, Elena Suponina, Ilan Troen, Boaz Vanetik, Helena Vilensky, *Valery Yaremenko, Ilan Ziv—as well as those who requested anonymity or whose privacy we prefer to protect. Our sincere apologies to anyone we may have omitted.

David A. Korn and Ambassadors Yossef Govrin and Aryeh Levin kindly read the manuscript and offered expert advice.

And finally here but firstly in our hearts: our children and grandchildren, who had to share our time and attention with this inanimate sibling, and rewarded us with affectionate forbearance. The book's dedication to them is but a token of our love.

ABBREVIATIONS

AC	Agranat Commission
AFP	Agence France-Presse
AP	Associated Press
APR	(Agranat Commission) Additional Partial Report
ASU	Arab Socialist Union
CC	(CPSU) Central Committee
CDE-IHC	Captured Documents—Egypt collection (Hebrew translation by IDF Unit 550), Intelligence Heritage Center Library, Herzliyya, Israel
CPSU	Communist Party of the Soviet Union
CSIS	Center for Strategic and International Studies, Georgetown University, Washington
CSM	*Christian Science Monitor*
CWIHP	Cold War International History Project, Woodrow Wilson Center, Washington
DR	*The Rise of Detente: Document Reader*
DRG	*diversionnye-razvedyvatelnye gruppy* (sabotage-intelligence groups)
EAF	Egyptian Air Force
EW	Electronic Warfare
FCO	Foreign and Commonwealth Office, UK
FOIA	Freedom of Information Act (US)
FRG	Federal Republic of Germany (West Germany)
FRUS	*Foreign Relations of the United States*
GRU	*Glavnoye razvedyvatel'noye upravleniye* (Russian military intelligence agency)
HSU	Hero of the Soviet Union
IAF	Israel Air Force
IDF	Israel Defense Forces
ISA	Israel State Archive
JTA	Jewish Telegraphic Agency
LBJ	Lyndon B. Johnson Presidential Library, Austin, Texas
MA	The Vasili Mitrokhin Archive, Churchill Archives Centre, Churchill College, Cambridge

ABBREVIATIONS

MENA	Middle East News Agency (Egyptian, "semi-official")
MER	*Middle East Record*
MI	Israeli [IDF] Military Intelligence
MiG	Mikoyan-and-Gurevich (Soviet fighter aircraft)
MOD	Ministry of Defence, UK
NA(PRO)	National Archive (formerly Public Records Office), London.
NARA	National Archives and Records Administration, College Park, MD
NPT	(Nuclear) Non-Proliferation Treaty
NSC	National Security Council
NYT	*New York Times*
NVO	*Nezavisimoye Voyennoye Obozreniye* (*Nezavisimaya Gazeta* military supplement)
PFLP	Popular Front for the Liberation of Palestine
SAM	surface-to-air missile
SAR	*Soviet–American Relations: The Détente Years, 1969–1972*
TASS	Telegraph Agency of the Soviet Union (central news agency)
UAR	United Arab Republic (Egypt only, 1961–71)
UNGA	United Nations General Assembly
UNSC	United Nations Security Council
UPI	United Press International
USAF	United States Air Force
WSAG	Washington Special Action Group
WSO	Weapons System Officer
VKO	*Vozdushno-Kosmicheskaya Oborona*

FOREWORD

I. UN-REWRITING HISTORY

A. The hottest front of the Cold War

It was clear that we were actually fighting against Russia.

Maj.-Gen. Yisra'el Tal, Hearing of the Agranat Commission, 2 January 1974[1]

This book's title encapsulates its purpose: to describe how, between the Six-Day War of June 1967 and the Yom Kippur War of October 1973, the USSR conducted a direct military campaign against Israel along the latter's front with Egypt, at varying levels of intensity. What has conventionally been regarded as a conflict among regional actors, with the superpowers' backing for their respective clients, was actually a front of the Cold War itself—indeed, the hottest. In 1969–70, when it was *called* a war—the "War of Attrition"—this became the largest commitment of Soviet troops outside the Warsaw Pact until Afghanistan: up to 20,000 men at a time, for a total of over 50,000.[2] This phase saw the climactic, and bloodiest, head-on clash between Soviet and Israeli forces. In military terms, the Soviet servicemen then posted in Egypt largely accomplished their mission, while suffering considerable casualties.[3] They were instrumental in creating the preconditions for a Soviet-supported Egyptian offensive across the Suez Canal to regain the Sinai Peninsula that Egypt lost in '67.

But both before and after its acme in 1969–70, the Soviet role exceeded even the greatly expanded capacity of "advisers" and "technicians," and extended into combat operations or direct support thereof. A continuum was thus created between the two better-known wars that bracketed the period in question, and in which the USSR planned—and partly implemented—direct interventions. Our previous book, *Foxbats over Dimona: The Soviets' Nuclear Gamble in the Six-Day War* (2007), was the first—at least in Western academic historiography—to reveal the USSR's deliberate instigation of the crisis in May 1967 and its plans to intervene in the war that the crisis was intended to provoke. This disputed the bulk of existing literature, and has therefore been termed "truly revisionist."[4]

The same applies all the more to our present findings, not least because previous studies were much fewer. Commonly held perceptions of this period seldom acknowledged high drama; the term "war of attrition" speaks for itself. It settled into

FOREWORD

a violent but monotonous routine, and the three years after this war's ostensible end with the ceasefire of August 1970 seemed even duller, as diplomatic maneuvering toward a settlement stagnated. Those Middle Eastern developments that made front-page news were mostly from other arenas, such as the newly prominent (and newly Soviet-supported) Palestinian organizations and their clashes with both Israel and Jordan. Then the lull was punctuated by the thunderbolt of the Egyptian–Syrian offensive in October 1973.

As a result, while the spectacular events of 1967 and 1973 have been the subject of countless academic works, the intervening years have received a relative dearth of scholarly attention. For the most part, they are briefly included as a foreword, afterword or *entr'acte*.[5] Conversely, the handful of studies that did focus on this period tended to confine their treatment between the accepted dates for the War of Attrition's beginning (March 1969) and end (August 1970), downplaying the connection with its antecedents and, especially, its consequences—as well as the Soviet input.[6]

Likewise, this period in the Egyptian–Israeli or even the broader Arab–Israeli theater received cursory mention at most in general Western works on Soviet foreign and military policy, or on worldwide processes such as the Cold War and détente. This was not the view from the USSR. In the latest example, in 2014, it was announced that the Soviet casualties from Egypt would at last be memorialized among other Cold War losses at "Victory Park" overlooking Moscow. The report referred to their having fallen during "six years of war" from 1967 *through* 1973—that is, a single, unbroken campaign that was part of the global confrontation.[7] Egyptian President Gamal Abdel Nasser hardly needed to convince the Soviet envoy in Cairo that "the Arab–Israeli conflict is in truth a Soviet–American conflict."[8]

B. Challenging the myth of Soviet restraint

During almost twenty years of research into this Soviet campaign, we were surprised to find, in case after major case, that previously unquestioned assumptions were no longer tenable. Moving along the 1967–73 timeline, this book aims to demonstrate (among other points) that:

- The USSR not only undertook a massive rearmament and retraining of Egyptian forces while the Six-Day War was still in progress; regular Soviet personnel took up positions opposite Israeli forces to hold the Suez Canal line and man anti-aircraft defenses around Cairo until Egyptian formations could recover. The first Egyptian counteroffensive moves in the summer and autumn of 1967 were made upon, not against, Soviet advice, and almost certainly with direct Soviet participation. In the following year, Soviet advisers were central to the preparation, launch and conduct of Egypt's War of Attrition.
- According to conventional chronology, the massive deployment of integral Soviet units to Egypt came in response to Israel's "depth bombings" in the Egyptian hin-

FOREWORD

terland, which began on 7 January 1970. Specifically, the Soviet intervention was requested by Nasser during an urgent, secret visit to Moscow later that month, and granted only then by the Soviet leadership. We will show that the Soviet commitment preceded this Israeli move, and that Nasser's visit—if it took place at all—at most accelerated its implementation. The direct Soviet military intervention developed as a Soviet initiative; its peak extent was decided upon and set in motion during the summer of 1969 at the latest, following smaller precedents that began immediately after Egypt's 1967 defeat.

- The Soviet expeditionary force, using the USSR's most advanced and sometimes still-experimental systems, was highly successful in countering Israel's US-supplied weaponry. Contrary to the legend fostered by Israeli claims that the ceasefire of August 1970 represented a striking victory over Soviet as well as Egyptian forces, it was actually imposed upon Israel by the superiority of Soviet arms, the unsustainable human and material losses they caused to the Israelis, and the deterrent effect of the Soviet presence.
- Israel—and the United States—were therefore incapable of challenging the ceasefire's immediate and continuing violation by the Soviets and Egyptians in advancing the air defense system to the bank of the Suez Canal. This created an essential precondition for the Egyptian offensive across the canal in 1973.
- The hitherto unquestioned notion of an "expulsion of Soviet advisers" by Egypt in 1972, because of a rift between Cairo and Moscow, was certainly erroneous and most probably the result of a deliberate deception. What occurred was in fact a withdrawal of the integral Soviet formations, which was agreed not only between the USSR and Egypt but also with the United States. The advisers attached to Egyptian units continued to play a vital role in preparations for the canal crossing. Supply of Soviet offensive weapons—the denial of which was purportedly a cause of the rupture—also went on unabated.
- While tensions existed between Cairo and Moscow before the 1973 war, the USSR was party to determining the date and operational outline of the Egyptian–Syrian onslaught on 6 October, and the Arab side enjoyed full Soviet support throughout the hostilities as well as limited Soviet military involvement.

In sum, we found the Soviet input at all these junctures to have been proactive, purposeful and even aggressive in encouraging and supporting Egypt's military challenge to Israel, rather than a moderating and restraining influence as it was almost universally characterized. It was assumed that Moscow held back *any* Egyptian offensive out of preference for a political settlement and reluctance to risk a clash with the United States. The Soviets, it was held, kept fostering Arab military aspirations in order to preserve their regional standing, but always intended to block the fulfilment of these aspirations so as not to harm the USSR's global interests and its declared détente policy.

FOREWORD

Time and again, we encountered the opposite: Soviet motivation to reverse the 1967 debacle was just as strong as the Egyptians', and to achieve this peacefully—even if it had been possible to do so—would not rectify the damage. A Russian commentator was hardly exaggerating when he wrote, at the height of anti-Communist backlash in 1992:

> this war too is on the conscience of the [State Security] Committee. The KGB persuaded President Gamal Abdel Nasser to wage the War of Attrition to the bitter end. Nasser trusted the KGB men but did ask for help, and Big Brother, the best friend of oppressed nations, did help—first with military gear, and when it became clear that the Arabs could not do it on their own, by sending in its own forces.[9]

Likewise, we found that previous studies laid excessive stress on the diplomatic history of the period. While stalemate in peace efforts may have helped to justify the use of force, for Egyptians and Soviets alike winning a military rematch against Israel was from the outset both a means and an end in itself. A negotiated accord might have reversed the results of Israel's victory in June 1967 by gaining a return of lost territory. But it could not undo the humiliation of Soviet weaponry and doctrine, or reassure the USSR's other allies of its support, any more than it could redeem Egyptian valor. There is no indication that both parties' joint determination to achieve these goals was diminished at any point by the prospects for a peaceful resolution. On the contrary, as Egyptian propagandist Mohamed Hassanein Heikal not only admits but boasts, "the deception plan" for the ultimate offensive included instructions to diplomats to "speak in pacific terms (without, it must be added, knowing the purpose)."[10]

Likewise, the Soviets' immense military operation, once prepared and launched, assumed a logic of its own, which was at most modified or rescheduled to accommodate UN assemblies or US–Soviet summit meetings. At least as frequently, such linkage cut the other way. Several examples follow in which the parallel timelines show that diplomatic activity served as a diversion for military strategy. Moreover, persuasive cases have been made that military action in the Middle East was occasionally timed to suit Soviet purposes elsewhere, such as the unleashing of artillery barrages across the canal to coincide with the Warsaw Pact intervention in Czechoslovakia. But it was also perceived as essential to protect the USSR's own self-defined security interests. Vladimir Vinogradov, the Soviet ambassador in Cairo from October 1970 to April 1974, still maintained twenty-eight years later that the Soviet presence in Egypt was necessary in order "to oppose the United States' military machine and its advance guard approaching ... the southernmost approach to our own country, and ... possessing an anti-Soviet springboard on our very frontier."[11]

FOREWORD

C. Obviating the need for harmonization

> It may ... be better to disregard those patterns of behavior which Western Sovietologists have invented and in which they have sought to confine the fluidity of Soviet foreign policy.
>
> James Cable, 1971[12]

When the most glaring instances of Soviet support for, and participation in, Egyptian offensive initiatives appeared to contradict the prevailing concepts of Kremlin moderation, this was described most honestly as "a puzzling pattern" or "contradictions in Soviet strategy" that had to be "minimized."[13] But most Western scholarship tended to paper over the inconsistency with such formulations as "Soviet policy was dualistic ... providing the wherewithal for hostilities while nonetheless urging the Arabs to forego their war plans."[14] Other glosses reached near-Orwellian proportions: "escalated Soviet military involvement need not be interpreted as incompatible with a peace-seeking strategy."[15] When all else failed, resort was made to what might be called adverbial harmonization: the Soviets did what they did reluctantly, or (after a desperate reach for the thesaurus?) "adventitiously."[16]

Even the study of the War of Attrition that was rightly considered definitive waffled: "Soviet policy ... was a curious mixture of adventurism and prudence." But the author, David Korn, did touch the nub of the issue: "not that they had strong objections in principle to another war; their main concern was that Egypt not launch itself into one *prematurely*."[17] Indeed, we found that this was the Soviets' perennial argument for "restraint": that the Egyptian military was not *yet* ready. This was not an excuse for temporizing; constant and often costly tests were made by probing the envelope both of Egyptian capability and of Israeli or US response. When these proved to be ripe—first for various stages in the War of Attrition, then for launching the Yom Kippur War—the Kremlin gave its approval and support. In many of the cases that we explored, the Soviets actually exhorted their advisees to more aggressive, courageous and decisive action—and set personal examples.

The Kremlinology approach of the Cold War era left a lasting mark by ascribing the perceived contradictions between Soviet policy and practice to rivalries within the Soviet leadership: hawks v. doves, conservatives v. reformers, military v. civilian, in addition to shifting personal cliques. In contrast, we found that Soviet operations on the ground were on the whole consistent, purposeful and single-minded. Debates and struggles may have occurred in Moscow, but as the Soviet diplomat and propagandist Leonid Zamyatin put it, "major foreign policy initiatives always required something of a consensus in the Politburo. Without one, there would be no decision."[18] Once such consensus was reached or imposed, its implementation in the field was unequivocal.

The Middle Eastern intervention, before and during the period under examination, did coincide with—indeed, both exemplified and facilitated—the consolidation of CPSU General Secretary Leonid Brezhnev's supremacy in the Soviet power struc-

FOREWORD

ture. To cite one telling example: in the 1967 crisis, when the hotline to Washington was first used, it was Premier Alexey Kosygin, the formal counterpart of US President Lyndon Johnson as head of government, who signed the Soviet messages, even if they were formulated in the Brezhnev-dominated Politburo. This was still the case in January 1970, when Kosygin issued the threat of direct Soviet intervention. But by the outbreak of the Yom Kippur War in October 1973, this pretense was dropped: though both Soviet leaders still held the same titles, it was Brezhnev who signed the hotline messages to President Richard Nixon.

Again, to explain seeming inconsistencies, a dualistic harmonization has been offered. The same analysis of Brezhnev's leadership can describe him on one page as "completely in charge," "at the height of his powers," and on the next as "disorganized," "blowing with the wind" and exhibiting "a shambles" of a decision-making process.[19] Some key stages in Brezhnev's ascendancy and his defeat of challenges within the Party indeed paralleled developments in the Middle East (such as the CPSU Central Committee plenum of 20 June 1967). But these processes had at most a marginal effect on shaping Soviet action in the region, which was determined by Brezhnev and his allies before and outside the formal Party organs' convocations that ratified it. As David Kimche perceptively put it in an exceptional analysis twenty-five years ago, the War of Attrition was first and foremost "Brezhnev's War."[20]

We did discern marked variance in the effectiveness and style of implementation that stemmed from differing levels of competence and charisma among Soviet officers and diplomats. Though these had a significant effect on the outcome of Soviet activity, they were completely overshadowed in previous historiography (and in such intelligence reports as have come to light) by concentration on the top political echelon. Try, for instance, to google "Petr Lashchenko"—one of those whose very names, not to mention their momentous input, will be presented here for the first time to the Western reader. In this as in the other aspects just discussed, this book does not presume to create a new reading of history, but rather to restore the *scriptio inferior*, the underlying content that has been obscured in a heavily overwritten palimpsest.

II. THE TYRANNY OF VESTED-INTEREST SOURCES

A. *Exclusivity of open sources in contemporary historiography*

By this point, the reader must be asking: If the present authors are right, how could generations of analysts and historians have been so wrong? For us, too, our research has provided insights on how the accepted accounts were created and established, which was no less intriguing than setting the factual record straight. These two strands are intertwined throughout this book.

Ideological slant, political correctness or sloppy scholarship can occasionally offer a very partial explanation for unfounded claims that became nearly unassailable axioms.

FOREWORD

But it has never been our intent to accuse our predecessors of such flaws. On the contrary, the bulk of their research was made and published when accessible source material was so limited in scope and character that we can but admire, and build upon, the use that many of them made of it. This is especially true of those who qualified their conclusions, when appropriate, as reasoned speculation—which we too have sometimes had to do at the outer fringe of whatever certainty our new sources permitted.

Our only reservation is about the refusal of some established authorities to recognize that the emergence of new evidence may require a revision, and their consequent rejection of our studies out of hand only because of incompatibility with their theoretical models. We, on the other hand, believe that Soviet actions, as they are gradually being exposed, ought to serve as the basis of the historical record, and it is the theories that must be reconciled with the emerging facts. As we also anticipate a similar reaction to this book, we are permitting ourselves an introductory essay on sources and their evaluation.

The paucity of abiding interest in the relatively uneventful years of 1967–73 meant that most historiographical treatment of them occurred fairly soon after, when the available material was still largely limited to official statements, media reports and similarly open sources. This not only led to an exaggerated emphasis on diplomacy, in comparison to military or covert operations. Even within the public-policy sphere, and despite a historian's training to the contrary, speeches, communiqués and so on were too often taken at face value—not only in respect of the actual events but in particular as to intentions and expectations. Declared peace plans were seldom interpreted as anything but genuine policy goals; threatened moves were rarely exposed as having already been made.

Even more treacherous was reliance, for lack of official documentation, on the contemporary media. The Soviet and Egyptian media were usually and correctly treated as just a slightly less binding channel for official statements. But on the other side of the front, the Israeli press differed more in degree than in substance, and the issue of Soviet involvement was very much a case in point due to its political sensitivity. Military censorship excluded certain entirely untouchable areas (such as nuclear policy or new weapons systems); consensual restraint covered a much wider range, and the authorities provided much of the information as well as the terminology for presenting it. This was only partially mitigated by transparent codes differentiating bulletins that were literally dictated to the newsroom from those that a reporter actively obtained—often from the same sources.[21]

But while most historians allowed for these limitations, Western news outlets and particularly "newspapers of record" were relied upon for objective if not entirely accurate factual reports and authoritative commentary. This trust we found to be almost as unjustified as in the Soviet case. For most of the period in question, there was no American and little Western press presence in Egypt; none of either in the combat zone. Tight censorship was enforced, but was rarely necessary as local stringers were easily manipulated. Visiting foreign correspondents and even the few resident ones, who seldom spoke the local language, could be fed the desired information through confidential leaks from "knowledgeable circles." Back at the American or British newspapers' or networks' home base, analysts and commentators were similarly dependent on the officials and/or politicians that they had mutually cultivated, or whose agenda they shared.

After reading hundreds of examples, their content and bias became almost comically predictable; but in the absence of other sources for early historiography, they were treated as authentic reflections of what actually happened. Our own approach differed from this not in discarding the contemporary media as a source—on the contrary, following its coverage of events proved essential—but in constant reference to the context, purpose and origin of the information. Reports are cited, when possible, from the original print or broadcast media, often as a means of tracking a story in the daily news cycle or the hourly evolving "takes" of the news agencies, whose impact has rarely been adequately appreciated.

B. *The impact of early memoirs: Heikal and Kissinger*

Most historians, and certainly the best of them, were well aware of at least some of these pitfalls. But they were unavoidably susceptible to the inculcation of stretched or utterly false notions that was made over the following fifteen to twenty years by the handful of central figures who staked early claims with memoirs and other publications. This is hardly unique to the present subject and period: Churchill too, among many more or less iconic figures, "wrote a widely read multivolume account of the [second world] war to make sure that contemporaries and future generations would see the conflict and his role in it the way he preferred."[22] What stands out in the present instance is the degree of pervasive influence that these writers enjoyed. Since they were at or near the top leadership level, they gained wide attention and were ascribed the authority of possessing "inside information," which ensured their predominance in setting the factual record (*what* happened) in addition to its interpretation for causality (*why* it happened)—even though these actors obviously had the strongest vested interest in enshrining their versions.

The following chapters will demonstrate how a handful of these writers, and particularly newspaper editor and politician Mohamed Hassanein Heikal and Henry Kissinger, succeeded in establishing self-serving and highly misleading versions about pivotal events in the Soviet intervention: the former as to when and how it began, the latter as to when, how—and, indeed, *whether*—it ended.[23] It was no less than astonishing to follow the track of footnotes from one scholarly or popular publication to another, and to find how many of them originated mainly or exclusively from these two sources. Their shared celebrity status and media skill helped; the front cover of Heikal's *The Sphinx and the Commissar* (1978) features an endorsement from

Kissinger, which contrasts with his own evaluation of Heikal at the time of the described events: "I don't even know who Heykal is. Of course, I know his title, but I don't know what he stands for."[24]

Kissinger's and Heikal's respective vantage points, however, are still inadequate to explain why objections that were obvious even at the time did not call their narratives into more question than they actually met. The extra ingredient was, metaphorically, a perfect storm: a confluence of interests and constraints, on the personal as well as national level, that <u>discouraged *any* of the parties involved</u>—both contemporaneously and retrospectively—from pointing out the misstatements and spelling out what actually happened.

Readers will soon find that the following pages make extensive use of many subsequent memoirs by prominent political and diplomatic figures, as well as the very same books by Kissinger and Heikal. In the Soviet case, first *glasnost*, then the demise of the USSR, added a raft of former *nomenklatura* members to the already swollen ranks of US, Israeli and Arab figures for whom

> the genre of memoirs has become not a bad means for improving one's own biography ... if it is unknown and unremembered how much was left out of these autobiographical memoirs, one might think that the world had never seen a better, more decent, more honest man than the writer.[25]

This does not mean such literature is useless—only that it must be subjected to the same adjustment for context and purpose as the contemporary open sources. Except when verified by cross-checks against sources with clearly differing motivations, these VIP memoirs must be treated as what their writers sought to establish, not necessarily what actually took place. Reminiscences of rank-and-file participants, whose use is one of our main innovations, called for other tools and tests that will be discussed presently.

C. Archival documentation: worth the wait?

Historians who were rightly dissatisfied with the available sources often ended their presentations with the caveat, and on the hopeful note, that better-founded conclusions would have to await the opening of the relevant archives. Well, forty years or more have passed since the events in question; developments in both the political sphere and information accessibility have been no less than revolutionary, and the result has been mainly to undermine confidence in official records as the ultimate arbiters of factual truth.

First of all, the very notion that comprehensive—or even fairly representative—archival documentation is ultimately bound to emerge has proved to be illusory. When we mention our use of newly available sources from the former USSR, the response is almost always: "Ah, you mean the Soviet archives that have been thrown

FOREWORD

open." We then encounter disbelief or worse when we reply that this opening was largely mythical even at its height during the chaotic and corrupt heyday of Boris Yeltsin's administration.

There were several joint initiatives with Western countries to publish selected documents of the respective foreign ministries on their mutual relations; the Soviet entries were selected by Russian officialdom, but nonetheless were occasionally revealing, intentionally or otherwise. The same applies to document collections that were published unilaterally (though with Western sponsorship) by the Russian Foreign Ministry or other official institutions.[26] Disorder and economic hardship in the disintegrating USSR itself combined to make it possible for well-connected and well-heeled Westerners to obtain entire, but random, *fonds* of archival material.[27] Regime change in former Warsaw Pact member states enabled access to Soviet documents that had been shared with them.

But the declassification of Soviet archives, which was decreed by law soon after the transition from the USSR to the Russian Federation, "ran into political resistance as soon as 1992."[28] The archives that might be most essential for our purposes—such as those of the military General Staff and GRU (military intelligence), the Politburo and the KGB—were never made accessible in any systematic fashion. Occasionally, Russian researchers were granted a peek, or defectors made off with copies they had accumulated.[29] But even officially sanctioned writers who in theory should have enjoyed full access (from foreign intelligence chief, foreign minister and premier Evgeny Primakov through researchers of the Military History Institute and on down), often had to resort—admittedly or not—to citing Western studies on some key issues and to leaving others completely undocumented. So a good deal of material did emerge, and there was a good deal to be learned from it, but the opening was nowhere near exhaustive enough to permit drawing conclusions from *absence* of evidence.

Again, the situation in the United States and Israel differs mainly in degree, and it appears that even if full release does occur someday it may produce far less than all the answers. In the most recent Israeli example, when after forty years large batches of testimonies before the Israeli Commission of Inquiry on the Yom Kippur War (the Agranat Commission) were at last declassified in 2012, the potentially most revealing features were still withheld. Other records in the IDF archive are for the most part accessible only selectively and to officially authorized researchers.[30]

In the American case, from the accession of the Nixon administration in January 1969 through the Moscow summit, we initially had only limited US documentation to compare with the memoirs of Kissinger and others. These documents were mainly transcripts of formal Soviet–American talks, which, though made by the US side, presumably recorded the conversations verbatim or almost so.[31] This period, like the Johnson administration before it, was gradually covered by successive volumes of *Foreign Relations of the United States* (*FRUS*). These were immensely useful and are extensively cited here, as the editors can certainly be trusted at least to have omitted

FOREWORD

most of the insignificant underbrush that would have taken any individual researcher years to plow through (the handful of documents that we obtained laboriously through the FOIA process exemplified this difficulty). Therefore, the main problem here is not that the *FRUS* volumes are necessarily selective. Rather, the editors themselves have protested the continuing and sometimes gratuitous *exclusion* of highly relevant papers. They did this by listing in *FRUS* the mere existence of documents whose contents remain classified, in major part or even entirely.[32] How many more there are, or were, can only be guessed.

Still, these documents alone were adequate to prove that Kissinger was rather sparing with the facts, to say the least. More recently, a joint US–Russian publication of the parallel reports submitted by Kissinger and Soviet Ambassador Anatoly Dobrynin on their '"back channel" meetings has filled in a lot of the blanks and confirmed our hypotheses.[33] This collection is not only as entertaining as an epistolary novel, thanks to the authors' comments about each other; it also underlines the risks of relying even on archival documents from a single side of any process, as the two interlocutors' versions of a conversation often hardly appear to describe the same event. From the back channel, by definition, there are and will be no transcripts, so piecing together what actually was said and agreed is tricky. Yet even the most charitable reading for Kissinger shows up his memoirs as hardly worthy of the trust that historians have put in them.

D. *The four filters between events and accessible archival documents*

As we compared the Soviet archival papers that did surface with other newly available sources, it became increasingly apparent that political decisions and military operations that hardly squared with the USSR's declared principles would never be intentionally, directly and authentically revealed in official documents. Indeed, declassification and accessibility are only the last of a series of filters that such decisions and operations had to pass before being so disclosed.

First, the matter had to be put to paper to begin with. Both testimonies about the Soviet decision-making process, and the failure even of latter-day Soviet and Russian leaders to locate documentation of key turning points, showed that these were routinely determined in informal and undocumented meetings. Rudolf Pikhoya, who was head of the Russian Archival Service (1990–6), wrote in 1998:

> The most important and responsible decisions were worked out not in Politburo sessions, but before them in what was known as "the Walnut Room" next to the Politburo's meeting hall in the Kremlin. ... The director of the General Department simply noted in the working journal: "this issue was discussed in the Walnut Room and was not recorded."

It was in such a meeting, at a dacha in Crimea, that the decision to invade Czechoslovakia was made in August 1968—a move that was mutually related with

FOREWORD

some of those discussed below, and considered of equal magnitude.[34] These decisions were simply officially ratified in such formal organs as the Central Committee and the Politburo, where compartmentalized orders for implementation were issued.

Second, when relevant documents were composed—including those operational directives—we showed in *Foxbats* that their formulation was often designed (with the prospect of future exposure in mind) to obscure rather than to record the actual substance, cause and purpose of a decision.[35] This was hardly by way of a new revelation, though the maxim that Hugh Trevor-Roper "mercilessly taught" has been honored more often in the breach than the observance: "before plunging into a public archive, it is first essential to discover just why and how the records were kept, and what they signified to their authors."[36]

But since *Foxbats* appeared, the frequency and importance of yet a third filter has been increasingly highlighted: in order to be someday discovered, a document must be preserved. The eminent historian Col.-Gen. Dmitry Volkogonov pointed out in 1992, after a search made at his request in the KGB archive failed to turn up evidence of a case from the 1950s, that even if the documents had been honest and exhaustive "there are no guarantees that [they] all survived."[37] Pikhoya was more explicit: "there was a thorough 'purge of *fonds*' in the Party and State archives. During the 1960s and 1970s, more than 25 million files were destroyed there." One of the last resolutions of the Central Committee Secretariat, in March 1991, was entitled "Ensuring the Preservation" of Party documents but actually mandated their partial destruction.[38]

There are explicit testimonies that these processes specifically affected the area of this study. Even in the heady days of 1992, a Russian writer complained that "documents about the participation of Soviet forces in Egypt's war with Israel are not being publicized more than before; *many of them were destroyed.*" He was still hopeful that "after the army, maybe the KGB too will repent."[39] But fifteen years later, little of this had materialized.

A former counterintelligence officer who took part in the deliberations that led to the Soviet initiation of the Six-Day War applied to the KGB's successor agency for the release of his own memoranda from those days for his present work as a media commentator. His request was not simply denied,

> I received a letter from the FSB Central Archive to this effect: "Unfortunately ... a number of files from 1967, including those of the subdivision for which you worked, were destroyed in 1978 *in situ* and were not deposited in the archive." That is how the state security agencies treated their own history, and in the 20 volumes that I handed over at my retirement there were even more serious matters.[40]

Numerous examples follow to illustrate that for authentic documentation of the events here in question, surviving *all* these first three tests was the exception rather than the rule even before declassification became an issue.

FOREWORD

In this respect, as in those already listed, the Soviet setting (not to mention the various Arab countries) differed from the Israeli, American and other Western cases only in degree, though definitely to a considerable degree. But in the case of the former USSR, another perfect storm provided—in a window of opportunity that lasted about fifteen years—a remarkable alternative and complement to the historian's conventional fare of archival documents.

E. "Resurrected from oblivion": the Soviet veterans' narrative

> The secrecy covering us has been lifted. Our purpose is to tell the truth about these magnificent young men, who did not spare themselves and accomplished their combat missions successfully, for the greater glory of their fathers and grandfathers.
>
> Gen. Alexey Smirnov, Commander of the Soviet 18th Air Defense Division in Egypt, 1969–71.[41]

The appearance of this alternative was presaged even by the official Soviet media in its waning years. In one of its last numbers, the monthly *Sputnik* admitted:

> For most of our country's citizens, the wars in which their own country took part remain unknown. ... Even less is known about the regular units who took part in local conflicts. One of them is the Egyptian–Israeli one. Only 20 years later, the opportunity appeared to tell the truth about those days.[42]

The Soviet Union's final tailspin, and then the chaotic initial period of the Russian Federation, created an economic crisis, and one of the groups worst affected were those subsisting on state pensions. Many veterans of the Middle East operations in the 1960s and '70s were already in this group, or were now joining it. For them, the difference in benefits between war veterans and ordinary discharged soldiers became financially vital. Most of all, they demanded recognition—both for their fallen comrades and for themselves—as fighters in, indeed heroes of, a full-fledged though undeclared foreign war. As retirees, they had the leisure to pursue this goal and little to lose by way of jobs or status.

"We considered ourselves the heirs of those who had fought in Spain," writes one of the operation's commanders. "We were proud of the title 'internationalist.' ... Later, when praise for Egypt in the press gave way to frosty alienation, many things were remembered in a different light. The media began discussing our military personnel's role in Egypt only in November 1988."[43] As a former political officer put it, they were only then "resurrected and brought back from oblivion."[44]

Those of the "Egyptian" veterans from 1967 to 1973 who remained in active duty ten to fifteen years later, usually by then as ranking officers, and were posted to Afghanistan remembered this lesson well. As an admiring interviewer wrote about one of them, before Afghanistan

FOREWORD

his destiny included another, unknown page: participation in the Egyptian conflict, which no one ever mentioned. The internationalist soldiers ... found themselves completely forgotten. To prevent this injustice from happening again, many [such] officers rallied to defend the rights and interests of the *Afgantsy* combatants. Among them was our general.[45]

The mass of long-discharged Middle East "internationalists," which followed the example of the younger and even more numerous *Afgantsy*, mounted an organized struggle for their rights. Clubs and councils of Middle Eastern veterans sprang up in major urban centers, and a main channel for promoting their cause was to retell, and in effect unveil for the first time, their battlefield experience. This was enabled by the other prevailing winds that created a second perfect storm. One was the relaxation of censorship, surveillance and enforcement in the interregnum. Another was the prevailing *Zeitgeist* to pillory the communist regime as both criminal and antithetical to the authentic Russian spirit, which peaked in the Yeltsin administration's drive to outlaw the Communist Party. A third contributing factor was the advent and rapid spread of the Internet in Russia.

As a result, an extensive literature flourished and persisted even after one of the original purposes—recognition as combat veterans—was achieved, at least in theory, on 16 December 1994. The State Duma (lower house of parliament) then amended the "Federal Law on Veterans" to recognize as combat veterans participants in forty-six "local" military conflicts in various countries, including Egypt.[46]

However, proving one's eligibility was problematic, as the veterans' own papers provided no evidence. Although the Soviet presence in Egypt was too big and active to conceal entirely, US reluctance to decry it and pressure on Israel not to do so helped Moscow to keep up the pretense that it was limited to a few advisers. Even after the 1994 law, obtaining confirmation from military archives was difficult when at all possible—especially for those who now resided in the non-Russian republics of the former USSR.[47] In 2006, even a retired officer in Russia was still trying to claim "the financial allowance" he deserved for service in the Middle East.[48]

So the veterans' struggle continued, and their literature appeared in a variety of genres and media. The veterans' clubs, in the main cities and provincial towns, initiated and sponsored the publication of newsletters, monographs and book-size anthologies. A panoply of websites appeared, sponsored by the veterans themselves or their branches of the Russian armed forces. These were dedicated to memorializing the dead, as well as conserving the survivors' memoirs, backed up with photos and documents from their private scrapbooks. A quintessentially Soviet tradition was perpetuated by "bards" who composed and sang their own ballads to express both sentiment and protest:

> No one knew, nor knows till now
> About the awful heat and scorching sands;

FOREWORD

> How in the fiery Arabian desert
> We suffered thirst and yearning.
>
> We defended the *fellah*'s home and life
> But no one ever thanked us.
> No one but Allah knew
> How it was there and what happened.
>
> And there, in the sands on the Suez Canal
> It was as any war is:
> Fate did not spare my comrades,
> But commanded me to remember them.
>
> And to my last day I'll recall them
> Whose life they gave for the struggle
> Let the *Afganets*, my friend and heir,
> Sing about their fate and his.
>
> Vasily Murzintsev, "No One Knew"[49]

Interviews with the veterans or articles they contributed appeared in a wide range of print, broadcast and online news media ranging as far as corporate house organs and obscure regional papers. This was often in order to highlight local heroes on such military-oriented occasions as Army Day or the commemoration of victory in the "Great Patriotic War."

Even the books—which usually had print runs as small as a few hundred copies—and certainly the newspaper and electronic platforms were often ephemeral. It is only because we monitored this literature as it developed that we managed to assemble what we believe is one of the largest collections, and to introduce it as a source into Western scholarship. Its value was soon recognized: as Fredrik Logevall wrote in 2008, "Admittedly, key archival documentation remains under lock and key and will be inaccessible for a long time to come ... But enough material is available, in the form of declassified documents, memoirs, oral histories and journalistic treatments, to begin to piece together the story."[50]

The following pages will further illustrate what a wealth of insights and detailed information this reservoir of material offered, as well as the criteria we had to develop for evaluating its reliability, while allowing for such inherent risks as self-glorification, selective memory and hearsay. Thanks to their sheer number, overlapping descriptions from unrelated writers bear out their overall authenticity. They are most reliable in respect of what the writers actually did or witnessed; their perceptions of the overarching political or strategic considerations and decisions are less trustworthy in factual terms, but are noteworthy in themselves as reflections of what was rumored among the troops or was imparted to them by their *politruks* (political officers).

As a rule, the higher the writer's rank at the time, the stronger his knowledge of and commitment to the official line, though some of the senior officers are remarkably critical—even discounting for the benefit of hindsight. Often this is explained by the officers' subsequent careers: whether they remained in uniform and how high they eventually rose. As another yardstick, diaries that were written at the time (in violation of explicit orders) rate higher on the credibility scale than recollections that were recorded decades later. But all these measures defy precise definition and had to be adapted to each individual case; sometimes the decisive hurdle was a sense, refined by experience, of whether a narrative had "the ring of truth."

We then verified and complemented these post-Soviet sources by means of interviews and/or correspondence whenever possible, and compared them with whatever documentary record that emerge from Soviet archives. Next, we cross-checked them against official Israeli and US statements, military and intelligence documents, and similar alternative sources. There are parallels to the Soviet veterans' literature on the Israeli side as well: privately issued personal memoirs and memorial publications initiated by various military formations, often compiled, written or edited by noted authors. Although subject in theory to military censorship and often even published by the Defense Ministry, these first-hand testimonies feature a surprising number of deviations from the official account.

Likewise—though less often relevant to the present topic—the websites of US veterans from various units in the Mediterranean and Middle East, while usually limited to travelogues and descriptions of everyday service and off-duty adventures, occasionally give away operational information that has otherwise never been released. Since Arab archives remain inaccessible and memoirs by anyone below senior-officer status are nonexistent, we had to rely for comparison with the Soviet versions mainly on Egyptian documents captured by Israeli forces in "Africa" (west of the Suez Canal) in 1973.

In sum, the veterans' literature not only provided the human dimension and color that is usually associated with oral history; it enabled—indeed, demanded—our aforementioned challenges to the most established assumptions about the overall dateline and contours of the Soviet role. The extent of this innovation is exemplified by the absence, in any Western research before ours, of the Soviet codename for the massive intervention in Egypt, Operation *Kavkaz*.[51] Like the identity of its architect Lashchenko, this term was never so much as mentioned even in such Western intelligence reports as have so far come to light. In respect of the Yom Kippur War, too, Vladislav Zubok's authoritative Cold War history acknowledges that "the Soviet role in this war has long been the subject of great controversy. Today, this story can be analyzed with much more clarity, thanks to the recollections of ex-Soviet veterans."[52]

F. Putin's Russia: back to the USSR—for historians, too

What we call the "golden age" of the veterans' literature (*c*.1988–2003) did not endure for long. Under Vladimir Putin, a profound reversal began in respect of dis-

FOREWORD

closures about Soviet involvement in the Arab–Israeli conflict, as a corollary of Russia's domestic backslide toward authoritarian rule and its reversion to a pugnacious bipolar foreign-policy orientation. The change was soon felt in the area of archive opening. As one expert put it, "the collapse of the Soviet Union ... after a breath of fresh air in the mid-1990s, left Russian records firmly shut to public scrutiny."[53] What had not been opened before is not going to be opened, and a lot that had been opened has been locked anew.[54] Putin ensured the enforcement of this clampdown when in 2016 he assumed direct formal control of all state archives.[55] Even the controlled process of publishing bilateral collections of diplomatic papers has come to a halt.[56] By 2008, it could again be stated that "the history of combat operations in Egypt from 1956 till 1975, when the USSR assisted a friendly nation ... is to this day full of blank spots and many things still 'cannot be declassified.'"[57]

What is worse, Russia has gradually been gripped again by fear of incautious talk and writing, after dozens of politicians, activists, journalists and others who dared to flout the approved line met sticky ends. Veterans, academics and other sources who once communicated with us freely now decline to be interviewed without permission "from higher up," which they assume will not be granted.

Furthermore, the official line itself has changed radically. The element of Russian national pride has been greatly reinforced, but the earlier dissociation from the Soviet past has given way to identification with it. Not only is Russia perceived as the linear heir of the USSR; there is nostalgia for the latter's redoubtable superpower status, truculent resentment at its loss, and determined aspiration to regain it. Putin has repeatedly demonstrated this tendency in the Middle Eastern arena, most recently in the Syrian crisis, with almost the same assertiveness as toward the former Soviet fiefdoms of Georgia in 2008 and Ukraine in 2014. Any exposure of lies, aggression or crimes in the Soviet past has become an insult to, if not subversion of, Russia's resurgence—and is punished accordingly.

The formalization of this process began in May 2005, when the State Duma adopted a declaration condemning "attempts to falsify history."[58] In early 2009, the minister for emergencies, Sergey Shoigu (since promoted to defense minister), proposed a law against such "distortion."[59] In May of that year, Dmitry Medvedev, who had temporarily taken Putin's place as titular president, appointed a state commission to combat "distortion of history *to the detriment of Russian interests*."[60] In February 2012, the commission was disbanded, but in May 2014, Putin—now reinstated as president—signed its main project into law: a statute imposing up to five years in prison and a stiff fine, with heavier penalties if the falsification is backed up with "fabricated" evidence and/or spread through the mass media.

The law was passed in the context of the Russian–Ukrainian crisis, which was cast by Moscow as a renewed fight against Nazism. Like the preceding initiatives, it was painted mainly as being aimed against negative presentation of the USSR's role in the

FOREWORD

Second World War, and thus received some positive notices in the West and Israel as a measure against Holocaust denial.[61] But the law actually applies the prohibition to *any* "reports ... that express disrespect for society, or public profanation of symbols of Russian military glory."[62]

The veterans had already got the message. Their organized activity continued—the Moscow Council of Veterans of the War in Egypt held a public celebration of its twenty-fifth anniversary in January 2014.[63] But in retelling their memories, caution now dictated a change. The overall number of overtly factual accounts appears to have declined, but the change in their character and thrust is often a matter of nuance and cumulative effect. The pledges of secrecy that the servicemen were required to sign had been largely disregarded as inoperative since the demise of the USSR. Now, as one of the earliest and most outspoken among them wrote as early as 2001, this again became a concern: "In 1973, I gave a written commitment to the state security organs that I would never divulge their involvement in those events. Who knows, maybe that signature of mine is still binding."[64]

The transition is most starkly exemplified by a tendency to abandon documentary publications altogether in favor of supposed fiction: stories, novellas and full-length novels that can always be disavowed as imaginary. On the one hand, this enabled the authors to feature some of the most startling claims and to deal with events and areas that remained off limits even at the height of the "golden age." On the other hand, it posed a methodological question: How far can a text be trusted as a historiographical source if its author will not or cannot affirm its authenticity? The criteria that we had employed for the veterans' memoirs had to be applied with greater rigor, but even under such scrutiny this "fiction" did yield some significant disclosures that had never appeared before.

As in the earlier phase of documentary publications, an outsize role in the new genre of supposed fiction (and in the following pages) was played by the former military interpreters, who according to their professional supervisor at the peak of Soviet involvement in Egypt numbered up to 1,000 at a time.[65] Many of them

> "got to sniff the smell of gunpowder." It was said that injured students, and even dead ones, were sent back from Egypt ... the sad part was that none of these "interns," who fulfilled their "internationalist duty," was credited for this mission even as part of their military service—let alone [nominated] for decorations—nor received any documentation that they had fulfilled this duty in Egypt.[66]

Resentment that they were denied even the combatants' limited recognition added to these linguists' motivation to tell their stories. The alumni club of the Military School of Languages even started a competition for "amusing and edifying narratives."[67] As they were drawn from military and civilian academies, the interpreters had both better training and stronger inclination to write than other servicemen, especially after many of them resumed their careers in academe, journalism or related

FOREWORD

domains. Most of them specialized in Arabic and therefore were also more knowledgeable about the culture and politics of the region. Since they accompanied higher-ranking officers, they were exposed to more privileged information than ordinary lieutenants or captains, and thus ranked high on one of our credibility tests: the likelihood that the writer might have had first-hand knowledge in real time.

The reader must have concluded by now that what follows can hardly be pigeonholed into any rigid sub-discipline of history; rather, it combines, and moves among, military, diplomatic, social and even cultural historiography. For the most part, it forgoes any presumption to "magisterial sweep" in favor of cumulative detail. We trust that an overview will emerge from our blend of blow-by-blow chronology, thumbnail biography and forensic investigation. Purists may disapprove, but we consider that this eclectic approach has brought us a step or two closer to fuller and deeper comprehension of the long-past chapter in our own lives that we have relived vicariously through the eyes of our sources/protagonists.

Finally, readers of *Foxbats* may notice some fine-tuning of our argument. Since we completed that book, further evidence has emerged which—most gratifyingly—in nearly every case confirmed our overall thesis. Several factual errors required correction, which we completed in a follow-up essay. But our overall concept has also continued to evolve, and to the extent that this book differs from its predecessor, the exposition here reflects the present—but not necessarily final—state of our research. We were flattered and encouraged when the validity of both our methodology and our findings was recognized by citations in the most authoritative new surveys of regional arenas and Soviet foreign policy in the Cold War.[68] Retaining this trust demands that we constantly reappraise our own work, and any constructive critique that may help us improve it will be gratefully welcomed.

PART 1

"WE WILL NOT LEAVE EGYPT IN THE LURCH"

PART I

"WE WILL NOT LEAVE BRITAIN IN THE LURCH"

1

RESCUING AND REARMING THE USSR'S ALLIES IN JUNE 1967

Now Nasser is flagellating himself, but we are not feeling any better.

Leonid Brezhnev[1]

A. Fighting back: Soviet perception of June 1967 as a replay of June 1941

The pattern for future Soviet military involvement in Egypt was set even before the end of the Six-Day War. Subsequent chapters of this book will address the question of when and how the USSR's deployment of regular military formations in Egypt (Operation *Kavkaz*) was determined and began. But a detailed review of Soviet moves in June–July 1967 shows that commitment of various Soviet units actually occurred at this stage, to meet tactical as well as political demands that the war's results created. Moreover, the types of Soviet forces involved mostly correspond with those that had already been allotted for the intervention that Moscow had planned to exercise in the Six-Day War itself.

We described in *Foxbats* how the unexpected devastation of the Egyptian Air Force (EAF)'s craft and bases by Israel's preemptive strike on 5 June 1967 not only doomed the Egyptian army in Sinai. It also obviated most of the original Soviet plan to intervene directly in favor of an Arab counteroffensive once Israel had been provoked into an "aggressive" preemption. This setback delayed and redefined the assignments that Soviet units were tasked to perform but did not require new approval at the Politburo level. When such authorization did become necessary for a major expansion of the Soviet combat presence, both precedents and experience had been created, and expanding on them was already a matter of degree rather than principle. Among various dates that are given in post-Soviet sources for the onset of *Kavkaz*, the earliest is in late 1968.[2] But the operation's origin can be traced as far back as the initial Soviet–Egyptian war planning in mid-1966, and certainly to the plan's partial implementation in June–July 1967.

THE SOVIET-ISRAELI WAR, 1967-1973

Most previous accounts of the Soviet Union's response to the Arab rout assumed that Moscow had been surprised not only by its allies' defeat but by the very escalation of the crisis in May 1967 into full-scale war. Although it was widely accepted that a false Soviet warning of Israeli troop concentrations ignited the crisis, this was held to have been a routine disinformation exercise that got out of hand. But the comparisons that within days became ubiquitous in the Soviet media, between the Israeli attack and the Nazi onslaught on the USSR, appear to have bespoken more than mere propaganda. For the politicians and generals who had been commanders or commissars during "the Great Patriotic War" and the mid-ranking officers who had been young soldiers, the impact of the Egyptian fiasco was evocative and emotional. This comparison reflected an almost-instinctive Soviet response to regroup and counterattack, as a linear continuation of the June war rather than a new and distinct chapter. As a future commander of Soviet fighter pilots in Egypt recalled, "everyone was waiting for what was to come next ... Far-sighted commanders understood this was to be continued."³

Deputy Foreign Minister Vladimir Semenov had played a key role in the run-up to the Six-Day War. When it began on 5 June, he was summoned to a Politburo meeting that lasted till 3 a.m. He recorded in his diary that "SOS signals coming in from Cairo" were "both tragic and comic. The first days of war in the Soviet Union, 1941, were repeating themselves."⁴ Air Force Maj.-Gen. Aleksandr Vybornov had been sent to Egypt before the war to study the feasibility of Soviet air intervention.⁵ The scene he witnessed at an Egyptian airbase under Israeli attack "reminded him of the Russian defense of Moscow in 1941."⁶ Sympathy for the Egyptians' plight was partly due to the Soviets' sad memories of their own country's unpreparedness: Vybornov was struck by the "utter chaos," Semenov by "the illiterate Egyptian peasants, who were incapable of mastering technology and scattered at the sound of the first shot." Veiled equation of Israel with Nazi Germany by means of code words like "treacherous attack" soon gave way to explicit comparisons in the official press.⁷ Newspaper editors were reprimanded for running photos of a medallion struck in Germany with Moshe Dayan's portrait, or of an admiring Danish actress wearing the Israeli defense minister's trademark eyepatch.⁸ Recriminations were rife in the CPSU's own rank-and-file and even within the Soviet leadership. As Ukrainian Communist Party leader Petro Shelest noted in his diary, "everyone is in a kind of depressed state. ... there was confusion, apprehension, and uncertainty."⁹

B. *The airlift creates new definitions for Soviet military presence*

The Soviets' war experience and doctrinal preconditioning disposed them to expect that Israel would maximize its triumph by resuming air attacks, ground advances or both across the Suez Canal. This dictated an immediate response to prevent an even worse debacle. The first manifestation of Soviet resolve to up the ante in Egypt—the

RESCUING AND REARMING THE USSR'S ALLIES IN JUNE 1967

massive airlift of military materiel to Moscow's Arab allies—began as soon as the dimensions of the latter's defeat became apparent. On 20 June, addressing the first Central Committee session after the war, Brezhnev stated that the Politburo resolved "to provide the UAR [Egypt] and Syria assistance in renewing their armed forces" only after the cessation of hostilities on 10 June. Even as regards Syria, where the ceasefire had taken effect on that day, this date for the start of the resupply effort is questionable; in respect of Egypt, which acceded to a ceasefire on 8 June, Cairo's first request to replenish its war losses was received and approved as early as the 5th—that is, within hours of the Israeli strike. On the same day, Kosygin sought and received permission to overfly Yugoslavia, and the first flights took off on the 7th.[10]

This was as soon as the Egyptian runways could be cleared and patched up. A Soviet serviceman who made several round trips on the airlift relates that on the first, at night, Cairo International Airport and the adjoining Cairo-West airbase were still blacked out. On his second landing, in daylight, tow trucks were still moving some forty wrecks of Egyptian warplanes. There was a pause when Nasser declared his resignation, but flights resumed once he retracted it.[11] Indeed, it was the sight of Soviet transport planes over Cairo, pointed out by Soviet Ambassador Dmitry Pozhidaev to Nasser, that caused the latter to call off demonstrations against the Soviets' perceived inaction. These protests were staged on 8 June and ended on the 9th, so that by then the airlift was in full swing.[12] By the 14th, Nasser told Pozhidaev that his children, playing in their backyard, were counting Soviet planes landing every ten minutes.[13]

If indeed the Politburo formally approved the airlift only on the 10th, as Brezhnev claimed, then (as would recur in subsequent cases) this resolution either rubber-stamped an operational order that had been approved in a smaller, informal council and was already being implemented; or it was one in a series of continuing adjustments that were made as the Politburo's marathon session went on throughout the war; or it was simply a gesture to satisfy Arab demands and to reassure edgy Warsaw Pact leaders who gathered in Moscow on 9 June. Andrey Kirilenko, a key Brezhnev ally and Politburo member from 1965, is described in 1972 as "in charge" of a "committee for the Middle East" (apparently of the Central Committee Secretariat), directly overseeing the General Staff in this area.[14] According to a 1969 CIA analysis, Brezhnev himself as chairman of the Defense Council, "the supreme military–civilian consultative body attached to the Politburo," by then controlled "the Defense Council as fully as the Secretariat."[15] This was presumably the case by 1967. The transition from planned intervention to damage control to redoubling the stakes was almost seamless, rather than a single, deliberate turning point—which led to underestimates of its scope and significance by the adversaries. Israeli sources contended even four months after the war that Egyptian losses could not have been ascertained so soon, and therefore discounted the airlift as mainly a morale-boosting exercise.[16]

5

The materiel, in whole or in part, may have indeed been pledged to Egypt before the war, as some US sources pointed out to downplay the airlift's importance.[17] The declared purpose and outcome of the talks held in Moscow on 25–8 May by an Egyptian delegation led by Minister of War Shams Badran was to bring forward the delivery of weapons whose sale had already been agreed for the following year, and to have them shipped by the end of 1967. Although we have shown that the talks actually dealt primarily with Egypt's demand for clearance to strike first at Israel, the accelerated arms deliveries may have been concluded too. Some airlift effort may also have been prepared to replenish losses that were expected even if all went as planned.

But marshalling and transporting additional hardware, sooner and faster than foreseen, was still a prodigious undertaking and required large-scale improvisation. As early as 1974, one of the first Western studies estimated that the airlift's "promptness and efficiency ... must be regarded as one of the most decisive great-power acts since World War II."[18] And that was written before its full extent, and the dislocation it caused in the Soviet military, were fleshed out by the participants' own accounts as well as newly available Soviet documentation. These have shown how this operation effectively launched the presence of Soviet regulars in Egypt and the establishment of *de facto* Soviet bases there.

Replacements for the aircraft that Egypt and Syria had lost—by all accounts, the airlift's first priority—had to be collected from Soviet stockpiles or active squadrons as far afield as Kaliningrad on the Baltic and Tbilisi, Georgia.[19] For lack of Soviet aircraft carriers in the Mediterranean or other refueling options, flying the fighters from an East European base to Egypt was impractical. Instead, formations of An-12 transports (the Soviet look-alike of the C-130 Hercules) were used to carry disassembled MiGs. As the fighter's empty weight was around 5 tons, over one-quarter of the An-12's maximum payload, at most two crated MiG-21s could be carried by each transport plane.[20] On 11 July, Brezhnev reported to a gathering of Socialist bloc leaders in Budapest that 544 An-12 sorties had already been flown and 336 fighters delivered, as well as small arms, anti-aircraft guns and even tanks.[21]

The An-12s were hastily painted over with Aeroflot markings and the guns were removed from the tail turrets, though the overall green color easily gave away their military identity. In case of a forced landing, the pilots wore civilian clothes or Aeroflot uniforms. As one of them, Boris Dikusarov, admitted retrospectively to a Belarussian newspaper, they were well aware that this "conspirative" delivery of weapons in civilian airliners violated international law.[22] This made communications especially sensitive; while their route down the Adriatic and Ionian Seas would not enter the airspace of Italy and Greece, they would pass through the air traffic control zones of these countries—and the Soviet military pilots were not trained to communicate in English. The problem was addressed by pressing into service, in the middle of final-exam season, the entire student body of the Military Institute for

RESCUING AND REARMING THE USSR'S ALLIES IN JUNE 1967

Foreign Languages. In the first month of the airlift alone, Brezhnev listed 302 of them as dispatched to the Middle East, mostly to Egypt.

The first group of these linguists had, before the war, been "sent to Crimea and was on alert at airfields there."[23] The rest were recruited so hastily that "we were in motley civilian clothes and looked like partisans. Only later were civil-aviation uniforms issued, as well as service passports. We made the first foreign flights with the kind of papers that were used by Soviet forces in Socialist countries." Fortuitously, some of the interpreters had prior experience. As one of the recruited students, Vitaly Sochnev, relates: "two years before enrolling in the institute I had served in a special-forces unit as a *mikrofonshchik* [radio monitor] eavesdropping on radio communications of the USAF and NATO. I knew the terminology as a priest knows his liturgy." The others had to make do with a single briefing from "a lieutenant-colonel, who dictated abbreviations and terms, some of them exotic ... advised how to answer questions in flight, and listed the signal codes of air controllers in Italy, Greece and Egypt ... which later was very useful."[24]

The necessity to overfly Yugoslavia (where controllers still spoke Russian); the stopovers that the nominal head of state Nikolay Podgorny later made there on his way to Egypt and back; and particularly the first exposure of the airlift in the Yugoslav media, created the lasting impression that the Soviet transports landed there for refueling.[25] The interpreters' recollections were the first to clarify that the airlift's main staging point and refueling stop was actually the Soviets' airbase at Tököl, Hungary. From here, according to Sochnev, they took off for Egypt in formations of twenty to twenty-five aircraft each. As Tököl is located on the southern outskirts of Budapest, the delegates to the 11–12 July conference there were doubtless aware of this traffic's extent, even though Brezhnev only told them that the flights went "over Yugoslavia."

Moscow had good reason to distrust the Yugoslavs' confidentiality, and President Josip Broz Tito had every interest in maximizing his passive and inexpensive contribution to Nasser, his longtime partner in the leadership of the Non-Aligned Movement. Barely a week after the airlift got underway, "informed but unofficial Yugoslav sources and reliable Western diplomats ... confirmed a report that the Soviet Union has flown approximately 100 MiG fighters to Egypt."[26] This was even before the Israeli ambassador in Rome learned from "informed sources in the Prime Minister's office" that Italian air traffic controllers reported overflights by forty-five Soviet planes a day.[27]

The crated MiGs had to be accompanied by crews of mechanics to put them together, which—along with the onboard interpreters—partly accounts for the fifteen men on each transport (at least in the first rounds), while the craft's normal complement was five. Additional passengers were connected with other Soviet materiel, which was being sent by sea. As witnessed by a Soviet correspondent in Cairo, "the equipment from the USSR was no longer directed to training bases, but went directly to the surviving Egyptian units." This urgency dictated a substantive upgrade in the status of the Soviet personnel who accompanied the hardware. "Together with the technical materiel, our officers were sent to these units as advisers (*mustasharun*) who were intended to improve the fighting morale and combat capability of the Egyptians opposite the enemy dug in on the eastern bank of the Suez Canal."[28]

The transition from "specialists" (*hubara*) to "advisers"—that is, from technical services to operational supervision—would prove as significant as the addition of a third category, *askaryun Suvyet* (Soviet soldiers) would become two years later.[29] With the airlift still in progress, Brezhnev already referred to a *fait accompli*: the advisers were being directed "to all sub-units," that is, they would function at the field level and not only at headquarters or training facilities. On 11 July, Brezhnev already gave their number for Egypt, Syria and Algeria as 1,069, "plus 261 other specialists." The separate number of "military specialists for aircraft assembly" alone came to 514.

The Soviet ground crews reassembled the fighter planes on the runway, a process that took six hours per craft. Then the planes had to be test-flown, and Soviet pilots were on hand to do it. Even when the larger intervention plan backfired, pilot-instructors who were supervising the induction of newly supplied Su-7s apparently flew them on several combat missions during the war. Vybornov's team was also still in Egypt when "Podgorny visited us," that is, at least until 21 June. In addition, Soviet pilots were tasked at Algeria's request to ferry the fighters that it loaned to Egypt as a stopgap in the first days after the Israeli raids.[30]

"Working day and night, from 8 June to 26 July 1967 our officers assembled and test-flew some 200 combat aircraft that arrived from the USSR in kits."[31] Cairo-West's location adjoining the international airport meant that the test flights took place in full view of any observer in town. This was the origin of reports from Western newsmen, such as a UPI correspondent who flew out of Cairo on 16 June, when non-Egyptian airliners were first allowed in to evacuate foreigners.[32] His Greek plane "was one hour late because five brand-new MiG fighters, apparently flown in from Russia, landed on the main runway. The new Soviet MiGs have been flying in over Cairo since Thursday [15 June]."[33] His AP colleague, who also left for Athens, was closer to reality: "Soviet Antinov [*sic*] transports have been flying into Cairo airport since the end of the war. They are believed to have delivered between 50 to 80 MiG jets ... In ones and twos [the MiGs] make almost daily flights over the capital." Besides test flights, he considered that "Egypt is getting the maximum propaganda out of the MiGs ... probably in a bid to convince Egyptians their air force is intact."[34]

The suggestion that the MiGs flew in on their own power exemplifies the widespread misconceptions in the Western press, most of whose reporters were sent to Cairo only after the outbreak of the crisis in mid-May. It also accentuates this press corps' subsequent departure from Egypt. Nearly all the US correspondents had been rounded up along with hundreds of other Americans when Egypt severed diplomatic relations on 8 June and were shipped out of Alexandria the same night.[35] Most of the

RESCUING AND REARMING THE USSR'S ALLIES IN JUNE 1967

remaining Western reporters, such as Europeans and Canadians, left as soon as they could after the war, having been intimidated and even assaulted.[36] They then published retrospective reports stressing that these were now "uncensored"—by implication, unlike their previous dispatches from Cairo.[37] By-lined stories filed from Egypt virtually disappeared from the Western, and especially American, press after 18 June. The staff correspondents were replaced by wire-agency dispatches from unnamed local stringers. Their cables were augmented with "think pieces" by home-base commentators that reflected their own sources' spin. The imprint this left on historiography will crop up repeatedly as the Soviet involvement is reviewed.

US intelligence capabilities in Cairo and Damascus were also crippled by the closure of American embassies—as admitted by CIA Director Richard Helms (1966–73) when he was unable to assess the Soviet intervention threat that came over the hotline on 10 June.[38] US estimates of the airlift's scale lagged behind its actual pace. As Brezhnev spoke of 325 planes already delivered, "US intelligence information indicates Communist European nations have sent Egypt about 50 MiG jet fighters ... they disputed claims of Israeli military sources here [Washington] that ... the Soviets, Czechs and others have sent 150 to 200 MiGs."[39]

As the Arab disaster began to unfold, Moscow renewed the jamming of Voice of America (VOA) and BBC broadcasts, which had been suspended four years earlier. This was interpreted in the West as reflecting concern about social and economic discontent, rather than resentment of political or military defeat:

> it was too much to let the public know that anywhere from a billion to two billion dollars of war materiel supplied by the Soviet Union was being destroyed on the Sinai desert. Such a total waste hardly squared with the repeated pledges out of the Kremlin to raise the level of living ... in the 50th year of the Russian revolution.[40]

In Washington, there were hopes that highlighting the effect on Soviet consumers (rather than on domestic defenses) might restrain the reconsolidation of the USSR's Middle Eastern influence. In a paper on "propaganda issues" presented to White House adviser McGeorge Bundy on 15 June, a "joint State/USIA/CIA group," proposed "*for the Soviet Union*, hammer home the point that the Soviet military investment ... has cost the individual Soviet and Czech citizen consumer goods, automobiles, refrigerators etc."[41]

Actually, the increase in defense spending trickled down to quite a number of Soviet consumers, particularly the servicemen themselves and their families. "I don't know whether this should be written about," a former "Egyptian" officer told an interviewer in Latvia as late as 2008, "but ... many wanted to take part in local wars because they were paid well."[42] When Soviet regular formations followed the advisers, the reward for enlisted men was relatively even higher. Aleksandr Kon'kov, a private who served in Egypt in 1970–1, earned 130 rubles a month—equal to or better than a doctor or teacher—whereas domestically stationed soldiers were normally paid 3.8

rubles. Most of an "internationalist's" pay was credited to his account and paid upon his repatriation in "yellow checks"—certificates that could be redeemed at *Beriozka* foreign-currency stores. "Dazed by the windfall," Kon'kov "wanted to fill a taxi with cognac and speed home to Yaroslavl'," but his sober grandmother made sure he went by train.[43]

Pilots and other officers did even better. Out of their pay in Egypt, advisers "could save enough for a Soviet-made car in 7–8 months"—even a Moskvich 412, "the *dernier cri* of Soviet fashion."[44] A colonel was paid 100 Egyptian pounds, at an official exchange rate of 6 rubles; but felt that for "combat officers who risked their lives daily, this was low. We knew that specialists bringing in weapons from other countries got three times as much."[45] As a naval-aviation engineer recalls, "Our pilots' patriotism also had a material basis." In addition to standard salaries of 300 to 500 rubles, they received a special allowance of up to 1,000 rubles "which was terrific money. When they returned to the Soviet Union they bought cars and smashed them up for lack of [driving] experience."[46]

Even had US propaganda successfully presented aid for Egypt as depriving Soviet consumers, this was a basic misreading of Kremlin priorities. The economic cost of Moscow's vastly expanded presence in Egypt was acutely realized; as Shelest noted: "this is not going to come cheaply for our people and state."[47] But even at the height of détente five years later, with the USSR in its worst recorded drought and desperate for US grain supplies, a Soviet official would note derisively:

> perhaps Kissinger and Nixon really adhere to the concept so widely promoted by the *New York Times* and the *Washington Post*, who believe that the best way to establish universal peace on earth, or at least prevent nuclear war, is to raise the Soviet people's standard of living to American levels.[48]

The US "control group" went on to a forecasting error: "The Soviets, disappointed with Nasser's performance, may wish to make Algeria their major tool for their troublemaking in the area."[49] In fact, the involvement of Algerian President Houari Boumedienne was already being seen in Moscow as a hindrance to the main Russian effort in Egypt.[50] Within a year, Algeria would rebuff Soviet requests for the use of its main naval base at Mers-el-Kébir; in 1970, even the personal intercession of Soviet Navy Commander Sergey Gorshkov failed to obtain this concession, as well as joint naval maneuvers and use of a military airfield—all of which (as US intelligence confirmed) the Soviets had by then achieved in Egypt.[51]

Overall, the control group memo recommended that the United States "be careful about our Soviet relations and not force the Soviets into a corner. We must not fall into the Soviet trap which seeks to tie us with Israel. We must not gloat over Soviet discomfiture [*sic*]." In order to "prevent a new military buildup in the area," this inter-service group suggested "not [to] focus for the time being on the Soviet military resupply. This is not yet of alarming proportions and to focus on it would be wrong

RESCUING AND REARMING THE USSR'S ALLIES IN JUNE 1967

... It could get the Soviets off the hook."⁵² But it was in fact the United States that got itself off the Middle Eastern hook. Washington returned to its preoccupation with Vietnam, and it took a change of administration, as well as a serious challenge to Israel's US-supplied hardware by the Soviet presence in Egypt, to activate any American response.

As for the control group's concern for the "Czech" consumer, Czechoslovakia had served as a proxy for Soviet arms deals and security cooperation with Egypt since their beginning in the mid-1950s. But while US reports still credited it with a major role, Moscow now largely dispensed with this pretense. A former top defense official in Prague has stated that after the 1967 war the Soviets "took over from the Czech intelligence service, which had already comprehensively penetrated the Egyptian War College and had recruited valuable agents in the civil service and the armed forces."⁵³ Direct Czechoslovak involvement was now limited mainly to technical assistance: a staff officer of the Soviet force that was later stationed in Egypt states that Czechoslovak engineers supervised a program to house the resupplied aircraft in hardened underground hangars in order to forestall another Israeli attack as on 5 June, with dummy hangars and aircraft providing additional protection. The project cost, by this officer's accounting, the equivalent of 100 million pounds sterling and was completed by the end of 1967. But it was the Soviets themselves who put "our experience from the defense of Moscow" in the Second World War to use in stationing barrage balloons around the airbases, which required precise coordination to lower them for takeoff and landing of friendly planes.⁵⁴ Later, balloons were also used, at Soviet advice, to block approach routes through *wadi*s (ravines) leading up from the Red Sea coast.⁵⁵

While attention was focused on the freight that the An-12s flew *in* to Cairo, few if any noticed what they took *out*: dependents of Soviet advisers who had been stationed in Egypt before the war (but not the advisers themselves). The transports' human engineering was hardly designed for such long-haul missions, and certainly not for civilian passengers; one of the interpreters recalled how onlookers were impressed by the huge puddle that the crew left on the tarmac after landing. A toddler being flown out was overheard asking his mother to make sure she had brought the potty.⁵⁶

C. Damage control, military and political

The evacuation of Soviet dependents suggests that in the summer of 1967 Moscow's apprehension of renewed Israeli attacks was more than mere propaganda. Just as the Soviets considered their continuing involvement as another round of the same war, they expected Israel to make good on its success for further gains. At the global level, Soviet ICBMs that had been armed with half-megaton warheads during the May–June crisis remained in readiness for two months, as attested by a former officer of the Strategic Missile Forces in the Far East.⁵⁷ In October, Israeli Foreign Minister Abba

11

THE SOVIET–ISRAELI WAR, 1967–1973

Eban "recalled that in July, Israel had received [a] message from [the] Sov[iet]s, through Swedes, that if Israelis crossed [the] Canal [the] Sov[iet]s would no longer consider this merely an Arab–Israeli matter."[58]

This message was brandished by Soviet combat aircraft that, unlike the MiGs, did fly into Egypt under their own power: on 14 June, a squadron of Tu-16 bombers landed at Cairo-West. About thirty TU-16s had been readied on the eve of the June war, and some had been flown to a forward base in the Caucasus, for the putative intervention against Israel; they had been disguised in Egyptian air force markings.[59] Now the bombers arrived in full Soviet colors, "for moral support." They stayed only briefly, but set a precedent for such an overt presence of integral Soviet forces.[60]

Two days after their arrival, Chief of Staff Marshal Matvey Zakharov "slipped into the [Egyptian] capital unannounced" with a delegation numbering dozens of officers, and with a clear brief as stated by Brezhnev: "after analyzing the lessons of the war … [they] launched the re-arming of the Egyptian Army." The Air Force deputy chief of staff, Lt-Gen. Nikolay Ostroumov, recalled his urgent summons: "Late one evening," his superior "ordered me to go the following morning to one of the airfields near Moscow, but wearing civilian clothes and, he emphasized, without any documents … There I met … Col.-Gen. [Afanasy] Shcheglov and some other air defense generals and officers." Later, Zakharov arrived with Col.-Gen. Petr Lashchenko, whose assignment would soon be clarified. Even the senior officers in the delegation were informed of their destination only en route, though Ostroumov recalled that he had already guessed after hearing the news. "We flew to Cairo in the dark. The lights were never switched on because the Egyptians feared that this would lead to an attack on the aerodrome."[61]

Because word about Zakharov's presence spread only after Podgorny's much-fanfared arrival on the 21st, it was and still is widely assumed that the marshal was just part of the president's entourage.[62] But the future Soviet deputy chief of mission in Cairo, Pavel Akopov, who was in Podgorny's delegation, has confirmed that the marshal was already in Cairo when they landed.[63] In fact, his visit was more closely connected with the military resupply effort. It lasted much longer and had far more important and immediate practical consequences than the head of state's.

A diplomatic damage-control effort was undertaken along with the military one. In Budapest on 11 July, Brezhnev assured his allies that "since your departure from Moscow [on 10 June] there has hardly been a day or night without a meeting of the Politburo. We have been putting aside other matters and focusing on … the Middle East." The limits of disclosure about Soviet involvement in the war and guidelines for presentation of the Soviet response had indeed been adopted by the Politburo within a few days of the war's end. They were already circulated by Foreign Minister Andrey Gromyko to Soviet missions abroad on 13 June, a week before they were brought before an urgent, closed meeting of the Central Committee.[64] By 16 June, when the entire Politburo saw Kosygin off to Paris and New York, his brief had been determined both

RESCUING AND REARMING THE USSR'S ALLIES IN JUNE 1967

for the UNGA and for the subsequent Glassboro summit with Johnson.[65] The Soviet premier frustrated the US president repeatedly when "each time I mentioned [intercontinental] missiles, Kosygin talked about Arabs and Israelis."[66]

The next day—17 June—Brezhnev, "very concerned and much affected by the events," informed Shelest by telephone to Kiev that it had already been decided to send Podgorny urgently to Cairo, as "the situation has to be saved; everything must be done to shore up support for and trust in Nasser."[67] On 19 June at 11 a.m., when yet another Politburo meeting began about the "Near Eastern issue," Shelest still recorded that

> everyone was in a depressed mood. After Nasser's warlike and boastful declarations, we had not expected the Arab army to be routed so quickly ... Everything had been staked on [Nasser] as the leader of the "progressive Arab world," and this "leader" was now on the brink of an abyss. Political influence was lost. ... Most of the military equipment had been captured by Israel.

However, Shelest added, Brezhnev had already resolved that "'one battle in the campaign is lost but the political struggle of the Arab people against the US and Israel will continue.' We apparently will have to start everything from scratch: policy, tactics, diplomacy, arms ... this was not going to be inexpensive."[68]

This—19 June 1967—was the same day that the Israeli cabinet, also in secret, adopted a far-reaching proposal to return nearly all of the territory it had captured in exchange for peace and recognition.[69] The staff of the Soviet embassy in Tel Aviv, which was formally closed when Moscow broke off diplomatic relations on 10 June, had left Haifa on a Soviet ship on the 18th, and the Israeli proposal could not be presented formally to the USSR. In retrospect, this was the only point in the entire 1967–73 period when a proactive peace initiative might have had any chance of altering the Soviet or Egyptian course, before it was firmly cemented in both declarations and actions. But even at this early stage, the prospect was slim: Moscow had already moved in both principle and practice toward containment, then reversal of the Israeli gains by military means. In an analysis that runs counter to most conventional Western accounts, David Kimche stressed that whereas for Nasser, "the Six-Day War had become a national disaster which had to be overcome, for Brezhnev it was a personal humiliation which had to be avenged."[70]

The course had been set before the Central Committee convened in closed session on 20 June, and its propaganda cover had already begun. The same day, after analyzing foreign media reports, the retired "dean of Israeli military historians," Col. El'azar Galili, felt it was his duty to alert Foreign Ministry Director-General Arye Levavi. His conclusion ("*not* certain but *very* possible") was that

> the Soviet government has *resolved* to prepare a "fourth" Arab–Israeli war—and is already *acting* toward this purpose; not only by reestablishing the political and mental starting

point that would make such a war inevitable, but also by rebuilding a background of military numbers that would make it possible.⁷¹

His prognosis was based, among other things, on a report from Moscow by the veteran Indian correspondent Dev Murarka:

> The Russians are determined that in the next round Israel must not be the winner. For one thing the Russians are likely to persuade the Arabs to be better prepared and to undertake more intensive training of their troops. ... Soviet energy in the coming months will be directed toward coming closer to the Arabs, rather than in the quest of an elusive Middle East settlement.⁷²

Galili was right in ascribing more weight to Murarka's report than mere speculation. In 1985, the Indian newsman was listed by a former KGB operative who specialized in recruiting "cooperation from professional foreign journalists stationed in Moscow" via the Novosti news agency. "Murarka was in fact 'our man.' ... Mr Murarka's 'freelance' status was a fake."⁷³ The well-placed leak eagerly published as an "exclusive" would be widely employed by all the parties to the conflict.

D. Brezhnev ascendant: domestic repercussions in the USSR

Later accounts described the Central Committee plenum of 20 June 1967 as the climactic clash in a protracted struggle between Brezhnev's allies and his rivals, but the general secretary's authority was in fact challenged openly just by Nikolay Egorychev. The party boss in the city of Moscow had visited Egypt shortly before the war and had actually recommended all-out support for Nasser, so that Egorychev may have expressed genuine concern for his bailiwick's security, or acted for unrelated motives, when he now questioned Brezhnev's Middle Eastern policy.⁷⁴ He "infringed on the General Secretary's personal jurisdiction by asking whether the defeat of the USSR's Arab allies did not cast doubt on its own capability to defend its own territory."⁷⁵ Shelest confided to his diary that Egorychev "spoke the absolute truth, also addressing Brezhnev as Head of the Defense Council. What 'politician' likes such criticism?" But Shelest himself and others did not join in, the purportedly moderate Kosygin was absent, and such opposition as Egorychev's speech represented was swiftly quashed.⁷⁶ By the end of the session, he was deposed; the recently appointed KGB chief Yury Andropov, who had supported the intervention plan, not only retained his post but was promoted to candidate membership of the Politburo.

The Central Committee classified the Middle Eastern crisis as "a confrontation between progressive Arab regimes and the vanguard of world imperialism, Israel" and ruled out any accommodation in this "clash of ideologies."⁷⁷ The region was singled out specifically by the Soviet military as a theater for the "liberating mission of the Armed Forces" according to the nascent "Grechko Doctrine", named for Defense

RESCUING AND REARMING THE USSR'S ALLIES IN JUNE 1967

Minister Andrei Grechko: "the Soviet state actively and purposefully opposes the export of counterrevolution and the policy of oppression, supports the national liberation struggle, and resolutely resists imperialist aggression in whatever distant region of our planet it may appear."[78] Grechko himself was well known for his anti-Israeli, indeed anti-Semitic disposition; he was quoted as declaring, as early as 1963, "within 15 years the Israelis will be glad if we just permit them to live."[79] Together with his Egyptian counterpart Abdel Hakim Amer, he had hatched the plan to provoke a war against Israel, and its failure in May–June 1967 could hardly have moderated his attitude.[80]

Brezhnev's own speech to the Central Committee developed the key elements of the authorized narrative in detail. He left a telltale clue to be discovered only when the text came to light thirty-five years later: an offhand confirmation that the warning to Egypt and Syria about purported Israeli aggressive intent and preparations was made under a Politburo decision, in expectation that the Arabs would take "appropriate measures."[81] But at the time, the speech remained secret; speaking with a member of the Polish Politburo on 24 June, Brezhnev blamed "many mistakes, both political and military" on the part of "Arab friends," as well as a murky reference to "treason," for "the very complicated situation" in the Middle East, while crediting the Soviet Union's influence only for the fact that "the fight was interrupted" when it went against the Arabs.

Brezhnev did carry out a "changing of the guard" in the Soviet diplomatic team, especially in Middle Eastern capitals.[82] But the ambassadors who had handled the crisis were neither demoted nor otherwise penalized. Dmitri Chuvakhin, the envoy to Israel, was approaching retirement age when the closure of his embassy left him without a post; until the collapse of the USSR and even afterward, he was held to have been ousted from the diplomatic service and exiled to Siberia.[83] Western researchers who sought to interview him were falsely told, as late as September 1990, that he had died.[84] In fact, he was not only rewarded with an adviser's sinecure at ministerial-rank pay but was charged by Brezhnev with compiling a detailed report on the crisis, which included recommendations for the next conflict.[85] In Cairo, Pozhidaev was replaced after the war by Sergey Vinogradov, but interpretations that the former had been sacked for failure disregarded the fact that he too was approaching retirement age and his successor had already been designated in May 1967.[86] At that time, there were rumors in Moscow about dissatisfaction with Pozhidaev's performance. But as he was considerably outranked by Sergey Vinogradov after the latter's twelve-year tenure in Paris, his appointment in itself may just as plausibly have reflected the heightened importance that Moscow ascribed to the Cairo post in the run-up to the 1967 crisis.[87]

The plenum's deliberations, having been kept under wraps, could not silence all skepticism. To ensure grassroots backing, as Shelest noted, "a series of political moves began—assemblies, meetings, reports, speeches—all in support of the Arabs and condemnation of Israel." Brezhnev and his associates who had elaborated the war strategy had to point to their own domestic solidarity in order to assuage concerns and rebut accusations among the USSR's embittered and disturbed clients worldwide. Brezhnev saw need to reassure his Polish guest that "we did not have any panic. Rallies are being held in many plants and institutions. There were only isolated Zionist statements."[88]

Shelest was less optimistic: "in the [Ukrainian] republic, 2% of the population is Jewish, but they display organization and unity. Attempts are made to find Jews who will come out with condemnations for Israel. There is some success, but it is not convincing." The upsurge in Jewish national sentiment was addressed immediately: "following a submission by the KGB that was approved by the Central Committee in June 1967, the departure of Soviet citizens of Jewish nationality for permanent residence in Israel was stopped."[89] It would be restarted only in order to be used for planting agents, when other means proved inadequate. Persecution of "Zionist activity" was stepped up to levels that had not been approached since the death of Stalin. But at the Budapest conference three weeks later, speaking extemporaneously after his prepared remarks, Brezhnev admitted: "in terms of morality and prestige, we suffer[ed] a defeat. Not every one of our workers understands why 2 million Israelis defeated so many Arabs, equipped with our weapons. It is not easy to explain."

Indeed, insubordination to Moscow was now being rewarded: Romania was the only Warsaw Pact country that refused to follow the Soviet lead in severing diplomatic relations with Israel on 10 June 1967. Soon, Shelest complained: "Romania was buying captured tanks from Israel, which were of our manufacture." Farther afield, as the CIA reported, "since the Middle East crisis the Castro regime has been very critical of the USSR for not supporting its friends … The Cuban leaders [fear] the USSR will not come to the aid of Cuba in case of an attack." From Glassboro, Kosygin hastened to Havana to reassure Castro that "the USSR had been prepared to aid [Egypt] in the struggle against Israel" and offering the dubious pretext that this aid had been obviated only by Amer's message "that [Egypt] intended to stop fighting within several days."[90]

2

HOLDING THE LINE ON THE SUEZ CANAL

A. Podgorny's visit obscures military moves

On 21 June 1967, a Soviet flight that did refuel in Yugoslavia brought Podgorny to Cairo, after overnight talks with Tito. The brief for his mission in Egypt had, then, been determined before the plenum was convened, and as Brezhnev confirmed, he departed before the session concluded. The version propagated by Mohamed Hassanein Heikal in his memoirs, and reiterated as late as 1990, described the Soviet head of state's "heavy-handed efforts to get Nasser to agree to give the USSR naval and airbases in Egypt," against the principles of the Non-Aligned Movement. This supposedly left Nasser with "a bad taste in his mouth" from the "disastrous" visit.[1]

This was the politically correct version in Egypt at the time of Heikal's writing, after the Soviet–Egyptian alignment had deteriorated. Contemporary Soviet documents paint a different picture: Nasser recognized that Egypt's "armed forces in their present state cannot guarantee the defense of the country." In particular, its "aerial forces and other air defense means were incapable of it."[2]

In June 1967, only a small part of Egypt's SAM-2 (surface-to-air missile) array had been deployed in Sinai. At least one battery was captured intact (the first to fall into Western hands); it had apparently scored the single kill attributed to Egyptian missiles during the war.[3] Elsewhere, although the Egyptian batteries expended a large number of missiles, they proved completely ineffectual (unlike anti-aircraft cannon).[4] In Western analyses, and apparently in the USSR too, this was blamed on incompetent operation or on the poor quality of locally assembled missiles, though the main reason was probably the system's ineffectiveness against the IAF's low-flying tactics, as well as disruption by electronic countermeasures.[5]

To remedy this, Nasser "as a supremely urgent request ... brought up the question of direct Soviet participation in the restoration, reorganization and reequipment of the UAR's [Egypt's] air defense array." In return, he offered not only Soviet use of all his country's ports but also an overt political realignment:

> He posed to us the question of new forms for the mutual relations ... including the military sphere; a formal withdrawal from the nonaligned policy, because in effect—he said—the

17

THE SOVIET–ISRAELI WAR, 1967–1973

UAR was long since not a nonaligned country, that for over a decade it was in step with the Soviet Union.[6]

Relating this in Moscow to his Polish visitor even before Podgorny returned, Brezhnev quoted the Egyptian president more bluntly: "Nasser ... would like to forsake the policy of disengagement and reach a direct military agreement with the socialist countries." Like Podgorny's delegation in Cairo, the top leadership in Moscow was unprepared for this ostensible triumph. As Brezhnev put it,

> One cannot naturally announce it, but one must attend to it ... The Politburo ... has discussed a number of times ... what position we should take towards Nasser's proposal. ... we responded: we welcome with satisfaction his position ... but we do not consider it proper for the UAR to deviate from the policy of nonengagement. ... Nasser recognized the correctness of our position.[7]

A CIA report in 1971 quoted with some reservation a source (whose identity was still withheld when the document was declassified in 2007) as being told by "Egyptian leaders":

> Soon after the 1967 war the Egyptians had asked the Soviets to take over responsibility for the war-shattered Egyptian air defense; an elaborate agreement was supposedly worked out ... but the Soviets then "got cold feet" and backed away ... It seems unlikely that the USSR would have even considered such a suggestion in the immediate aftermath of the dangers run during the June 1967 war, but this story may nevertheless have some validity as a garbled reflection of Egyptian–Soviet arguments on the subject in 1968 and 1969.[8]

However, the evidence now available *does* indicate that in June–July 1967 the Soviets, while balking at a declared political alliance with Egypt, not only contemplated Nasser's specific military request but complied. "Nasser's attention was called to the necessity to address the solution of this issue not only from the viewpoint of military efficacy but also with weighty consideration of the political aspect, while taking into account the international resonance and domestic reactions."[9]

The Soviets had their own tactical concerns to address: their airlift's main terminal at Cairo-West had been exposed. This heightened the perceived urgency of defending this and other points of Soviet presence. According to a member of Podgorny's entourage, future KGB *rezident* (station chief) in Egypt Vadim Kirpichenko, Nasser was promised "much more active assistance in organizing Egypt's air defense."[10]

The internal Soviet report about Podgorny's talks in Cairo (released thirty-five years later) stopped just short of specifying that Egypt had requested, or Moscow had approved, the manning of newly supplied SAM batteries by integral Soviet crews, as distinct from individual advisers: "Consent was given to supply military equipment, armaments, and military advisers. In respect of organizing the air defense service, the degree and form of the Soviet side's participation" was theoretically subordinated to the aforementioned political considerations.[11] But in practice, deployment of Soviet air defense detachments had already begun before Podgorny's talks ended.

B. Creating precedents: Soviet air defense units dispatched to Egypt

In a July 1967 session of the Ukrainian Communist Party's Politburo, Shelest encountered blunt criticism: "we took up the question of air defense in Ukraine," and General A[leksandr] Pokryshkin reported on its "grim" state. "It is simply criminal that … in our republic, many vital objects are vulnerable, unprotected and undefended, while at the same time equipment *and crews*, … combat aircraft and SAM batteries are being dispatched to 'cover' Cairo." Shelest noted that after hearing Pokryshkin's "very disturbing and important question, I took [it] up with L. Brezhnev." The general secretary heard him out "in Olympic serenity" and replied: "don't interfere in this issue. There is an overall plan and we are following it."[12]

At the Budapest conference on 11 July, Polish Party Chief Władysław Gomułka reported that "Nasser also approached us about delivery of anti-aircraft machine guns and radar equipment, but at the same time he demanded sending people to service this equipment, as it turns out that he doesn't have such people."[13] Brezhnev confirmed that by then 182 anti-aircraft cannon and 300 AA machine guns had been dispatched by air, along with 334 "military advisers." As the latter are listed separately from "officers-advisers," this figure clearly referred to the weapons' operators. As Brezhnev explained,

> with regard to the participation of Soviet forces in their anti-aircraft defense, etc.—for which they asked us—we thought … it is more advisable to send an unlimited number of Soviet advisers, *even to form here and there complete advisory units*, but not to take the entire air defense into our hands.[14]

Vladimir Shirin, a SAM *divizyon* commander "on active duty defending our [Soviet] airspace," was ordered in late July 1967 to prepare for a mission to a "hot, arid climate."[15] He was kept on hold for some time; "later we learned that the question was being discussed whether to send military 'experts' or 'advisers' to Egypt, and the government decided on 'advisers.'" Shirin and three colleagues from his outfit were rushed through five days of briefing, and their yet-undefined status was reflected by a last-minute change: "first we were told that we were going for a year's mission without our families. Two days before departure, this was changed to two years and documents could be arranged for the families."[16]

The Soviets' presence was indirectly detected by Western journalists who left Cairo as soon as civilian flights were resumed: they noticed that "anti-aircraft guns bristle from dunes around the airport."[17] By 21 June, "gun placements appeared in Cairo and new antiaircraft gun trenches were being built on the outskirts."[18] It was the Yugoslav party organ *Borba* that first reported from Cairo that "the Soviet Union is providing *crews* for the new radar system, missiles, planes and other complex systems."[19]

Since this deployment was kept under wraps, and since Israeli planes did not actually challenge Cairo's defenses for another two years, the exact scope and duration of these crews' stay in Egypt cannot yet be determined. They may have been repatriated once fear of an imminent Israeli attack subsided, but there are indications that at least some stayed and formed the vanguard for the full division that arrived in Operation *Kavkaz*. By January 1968, IAF Commander Mordechai "Motty" Hod told USAF officers in Washington that "some 2,000 technicians ... are manning the control centers" of two new SAM sites at Alexandria and Port Said—a much larger number than could be ascribed to advisers alone. Hod described these missiles as "SAM-3 sites (navy version)"—the first source to specify that this new system, designed to overcome the SAM-2's weakness against low-flying aircraft, was deployed in Egypt at this early stage; even two years later, SAM-3s were operated in Egypt only by Soviet crews.[20] Soviet Navy diver Yury Bebishev related that while he served in Alexandria in 1968 "the sky was protected by our *raketchiki* from the Kiev Air Defense District"—Pokryshkin's men.[21]

There is sketchier evidence that fighter jets supplied in the airlift were operated by Soviet pilots beyond the initial test flights. Aleksandr Bezhevets, by then a senior air force officer, held forty years later that after the Six-Day War, "by decision of the Soviet government, a regiment of MiG-21 interceptors and a squadron of Su-7B attack bombers were sent to Egypt. They took part in battles with the IAF from 1967 through 1969."[22] Though there is no other explicit confirmation for this, several incidents are cited below in which Soviet operation of such aircraft was suspected.

When Soviet bloc leaders met in Warsaw in December 1967, "East European" sources claimed that "the Soviet Union wants the military staff of the Warsaw Pact to make ... a special planning section to which Egyptian and other Arab staff officers would be invited." The main idea was "to shift attention away from ... naked Russian imperialism" and to spread the cost and effort.[23] The closest thing to such a Soviet demand that has surfaced in documentation from this conference is a Bulgarian report whereby Gromyko promised "the Soviet Union will back any endeavor of ours to further develop bilateral relations with the Arabs, and most importantly ... the UAR. ... As a result, our bilateral contacts have intensified."[24]

The Soviets could not push too hard for satellite participation, as the meeting was disrupted by Romanian and Yugoslav objections. Gromyko's first deputy Semenov wrote that he got no sleep during the conference out of concern over the Pact's own future, and no evidence has emerged that the Soviet proposal was implemented.[25] Expectations of military aid from Bulgaria to Egypt were among the many Western speculations in the summer of 1967 that never materialized.[26] Direct Bulgarian military involvement in the Middle East never exceeded limited sale of small arms, and though other Warsaw Pact partners did make minor contributions in training and materiel, the USSR continued to bear the brunt of the effort.²⁷ While the question of formalizing Egyptian adherence to the Soviet bloc would recur periodically in coming years, the presence of Soviet troops on Egyptian soil was already an accomplished fact.

C. Marshal Zakharov and Soviet marines stabilize the canal defenses

While the political significance of overt Soviet presence may have preoccupied Podgorny in Cairo, it had little bearing on Zakharov's military activity. Anatoly Egorin was in Egypt long before the June war, officially as a correspondent for the Novosti news agency, but his detailed memoirs clearly indicate this was a cover for intelligence work.²⁸ Egorin, now deputy director of the Institute for Oriental Studies of the Russian Academy of Sciences, was mightily impressed by the sixty-nine-year-old, diabetic marshal.

> Zakharov developed, in Egypt, activity that would have befitted the peak of World War II. ... The marshal, always wearing the same green shirt and white beret, did his own reconnaissance by visiting units in the canal zone, where he approved neither of the forces' overall disposition nor of the hastily dug, shallow trenches. At one point he took a sapper's spade from an Egyptian soldier, and in short order dug a "full-profile" foxhole with his own hands, all in 40-degree [Celsius] heat.²⁹

This personal example was more than symbolic, and would be inculcated as part of the doctrine for future offense as well as present defense. After the Yom Kippur War, Israeli General Ariel Sharon described a major problem that Israeli tanks faced while confronting masses of Egyptian infantry: "Every soldier who reaches any point, no matter how long he is to stay there, immediately digs in. It was most impressive to see the aerial photos, when one sees the advance of the Egyptian divisions: the area is full of ... round holes"—which increased the effectiveness of their shoulder-held anti-tank weapons.³⁰

"Zakharov's headquarters [staff] in Cairo ... got no sleep for days on end but still could not keep up with all its commander's orders. No one knew how many hours per day the marshal himself slept."³¹ This mystery was cleared up forty years later by Zakharov's interpreter: the marshal lay down in his car's back seat between stops.³² He was clearly planning a complete overhaul not only of the Egyptian armed forces but of the Soviet presence within them. The existing "*kollektiv* of Soviet military advisers," which was now associated with Egypt's debacle, quickly felt his displeasure. As Egorin recalls,

> I heard vivid legends about the work of the military attaché's staff. Its chief, V.I. Fursov, was instructed to report to the marshal and present a briefing every day at 0400. Every night, the subordinates of Vladimir Ivanovich (who was called "Vi" for short) worked all night

21

to prepare reports ... and then they would wait for the attaché's return. Often, Vi would come back flushed and irritated, lock himself in his office and let no one in ("plugged himself into the lightning rod," they would say of him in these moments). Then, close to 0700, Vi would conduct an analysis of what had taken place and assign new tasks.

Fursov had cause for concern; when toward the end of 1967 the first round of decorations was proclaimed for service in Egypt, "the list included neither V.I. Fursov nor several others who really had devoted part of their lives to those events in June"— another allusion to the Soviet role in precipitating the crisis. "Fursov did get promoted to major-general ... but his mission in Egypt was nearly over. Many were replaced."[33]

Lashchenko replaced Fursov as chief adviser; this post would henceforth be separate from the military attaché, and feuding between them would ensue. A hands-on commander in the marshal's own mold, Lashchenko recalled twenty years later "we lost no time: we not only engaged in talks but helped the Egyptians restore order in their devastated military establishment, and our practical efforts ... were more effective than mere words in agitating for formalization of the advisers' *apparat*."[34] This would be no fast or easy task, but Lashchenko accomplished it with distinction that would leave a lasting mark. The total absence of his momentous input and even his name from Western intelligence reports and subsequent historiography alike is a striking testimony to their deficiency for lack of Soviet sources.

Unlike the anti-aircraft crews' deployment, the introduction of Soviet combat units into the actual war zone was flaunted as a response to resumed Israeli "aggression." The same rationale had been prepared for the intervention that was planned a few weeks earlier for the same Soviet forces—warships and marines. To assess whether their high-profile entry into Port Said on 9 July 1967 was likewise premeditated, the timeline of events has to be closely scrutinized.

Post-Soviet Russian accounts state that the Soviet Mediterranean *Eskadra* (squadron) had units, including a command post on the missile cruiser *Dzerzhinsky*, "based" in Port Said from 1 to 30 or "31" June. The specific ships so listed correspond with some of those whose "arrival" was trumpeted on 9 July—particularly two large landing vessels (BDK, *bol'shoy desantny korabl'*, the Soviet equivalent of an LST—landing ship, tank), *Voronezhsky Komsomolets* and *Krymsky Komsomolets*, and two medium-sized ones (*sredny desantny korabl'*, SDK), numbers 34 and 64, with a marine detachment. This formation, the 309th OMBP (independent marine battalion), had been assembled in 1966 from elements of the Black Sea, Baltic and Northern Fleets, as well as amphibious tanks and mobile artillery from ground forces in southern Russia.[35]

Israeli records appear to contradict this claim of consecutive Soviet presence: on the night of 5 June, IDF naval commandos penetrated Port Said but could not locate any targets as the harbor was empty. This, of course, means that no *Egyptian* ships were found either, and these were definitely present before the outbreak of war. They evidently put to sea after Israel's initial air strike in order not to present an immobile

HOLDING THE LINE ON THE SUEZ CANAL

and closely grouped target.³⁶ The Israeli frogmen's mother ships indeed encountered enemy craft outside the harbor, which delayed their rendezvous. Any Soviet ships in Port Said would have done the same, if they had not done so already to prepare for their landing operation on the Israeli coast.

The suspiciously "round" dates (especially "31 June") might indicate a generalization from unspecified dates in June—possibly after the war—to the entire month. Other sources are more precise. Aleksandr Kharchikov was a seaman on a Soviet destroyer that sailed from the Baltic in late May 1967 but reached a refueling rendezvous off Libya only on 11 June. He recalls being told that

> Black Sea Fleet ships entered the Suez [Canal] and along with Arab ships took up positions along the canal from Port Said to Ismailia and Qantara ... there was talk that the cruiser *Dzerzhinsky* had put a full stop to the war when, at the entrance to the canal it shot down an Israeli Skyhawk.³⁷

The *Dzerzhinsky* had indeed been converted to an anti-aircraft platform, carrying the naval version of SAM-2s, but the feat attributed to it was obviously magnified in retrospect. In June 1967, the IAF did not yet have any Skyhawks, which would become its first US-supplied jets only in December, and regardless of model no Israeli records of planes shot down on the Egyptian front match this claim. Also, if any Soviet warships had sailed up the canal to Ismailia, they would have become stranded there. Still, the *Dzherzhinsky*'s mere presence in Port Said could hardly have been utterly falsified.

The naval historian Aleksandr Rozin specifies that on *10* June the *Krymsky Komsomolets* was in Port Said with marines of the 309th on board.³⁸ This agrees with a unique but authoritative testimony from an officer of this outfit, which appeared in 2003 in an organ of the Belarussian Defense Ministry, but was then removed after we inquired for more details. Lt-Col. Viktor Shevchenko related how at least part of these marines came ashore and attempted to cross the Suez Canal eastward as the Egyptian army was fleeing westward from Sinai—that is, between 6 and 8 June. The unit he commanded was, however, decimated by an Israeli air strike; seventeen marines were killed and thirty-four injured, including Shevchenko himself, who thirty-five years later was still nicknamed "the Egyptian."³⁹ His narrative remains the only testimony to an actual clash of Soviet and Israeli forces in the Six-Day War.

That this engagement took place no later than 9 June is confirmed by the subsequently published account of another marine officer who was then based in Baltiisk, near Kaliningrad. At 4 a.m. on 10 June, then-Lieutenant Valery Mallin relates, his battalion was ordered into combat readiness, and the next day it sailed for Port Said—minus one *rota* (company), presumably Shevchenko's, which together with a number of PT-76 amphibious tanks had already been sent there on 26 May on board its usual operational platform, a BDK. This may have been either the *Krymsky* or the *Voronezhsky Komsomolets*, which had been attached to the Baltic Fleet since its completion in Kaliningrad in 1966 and is also listed as "based in Egyptian ports from June 1967."[40] Shevchenko's engagement appears to be reflected in the latter ship's combat record: "its name was glorified in Port Said during the Arab–Israeli conflict: the ship gave internationalist support to the armed forces of Egypt ... in repulsing Israeli aggression."[41] Mallin's detachment, it thus appears, had to be sent urgently in relief, and since no BDK was available it had to sail in a destroyer.[42]

D. The Soviet Navy moves in (again?)

It appears, then, that at least the greater part of the Soviet flotilla whose entry into Port Said (and Alexandria) was announced with great fanfare on 9 July was already there, and involved in combat operations, a month earlier. How could this have gone unnoticed, which permitted the second "visit" to be billed as unprecedented? One explanation is that the US consulates in both Egyptian ports were sacked by mobs and evacuated on 6 June. But even if the Americans had an inkling of the Soviet Navy's move, they preferred to play it down—as they would when it became a permanent deployment. The ships may have left port and returned, or even stayed and just had their "arrival" announced belatedly. Even then, all reports were from Alexandria; none bore a Port Said dateline, so there was no verification of exactly when the Soviet ships first anchored there.

Why bother with such an exercise? As with their planned intervention in what became the Six-Day War, the Soviets put a premium on the legitimacy of defending "victims of aggression." But they also preferred that their move look like a successful initiative to rehabilitate Egypt's sovereignty and strength, rather than a costly and doomed rear-guard action as Shevchenko's became.

According to an Egyptian admiral quoted by Kimche, as early as 18 June a delegation of his Soviet counterparts presented to Nasser a detailed, "ready-made schedule" for Soviet use of Egyptian ports. This account puts the naval delegation's arrival three days ahead of "the Podgorny–Zakharov mission," and "it was no accident that the admirals came first ... for in Soviet eyes it was the Mediterranean and the domination of the US Sixth Fleet that were of prime concern." But as it was since established that Zakharov came on 16 June and separately from Podgorny, it rather appears that the naval officers were part of the marshal's large group. Their program indeed stressed Soviet-controlled facilities for air and sea surveillance of the Mediterranean. One of their key demands was for monthly eight-day visits by the squadron's ships.[43] For this, and for the formalization of the Soviet naval presence, they were handed—or helped to create—the opportunity of the battles around Ras el-Ish.

While the 8 June Egyptian–Israeli ceasefire line was clearly defined along the Suez Canal from Qantara south to Suez City, the northernmost sector remained an unstable flashpoint. The marshes east of the canal had obstructed an Israeli advance to, and permanent stationing on, the canal bank. Port Fuad, east of the canal's northern end opposite Port Said, remained the only Egyptian foothold on its eastern side.

HOLDING THE LINE ON THE SUEZ CANAL

In August 1972, two Soviet officers were taken on a tour of the defenses at Port Fuad and told that it had remained in Egyptian hands in June 1967 thanks to a determined local governor who had rallied the local home guard and held off the Israelis with shotguns and hunting rifles. The Russians doubted this and considered that a legend had already developed, which certainly was the case about the subsequent events.[44] With the issue of control and navigation on the canal still unresolved, the importance of its northern gateway was obvious, and on 1 July 1967 it became the scene of the first pitched battle after the Six-Day War.

According to the contemporary Israeli version, it was the Egyptians who violated the ceasefire by crossing the canal to reestablish an emplacement at Ras el-Ish, some 6 miles south of Port Fuad on the narrow causeway between the east bank and the swamp. The IDF sent in an armored force to displace them. Egypt claimed that an Israeli tank column advancing on Port Fuad was halted by a thirty-man special-forces platoon that had been there all along, bearing only small arms. Even at the time, a CIA report was hard put to choose between the "conflicting Israeli & Egyptian versions." The report concluded that due to the terrain,

> it seems highly unlikely that the Egyptians chose [this] as the site of a major penetration ... It seems more probable that the Israelis stumbled on a pocket never evacuated by the Egyptians and decided to clean it out, or that the Egyptians were engaging in a gesture for propaganda purposes.[45]

Twelve years later, however, the memoirs of Yitzhak Rabin appeared to confirm part of the Egyptian version: as IDF chief of staff in 1967, he had ordered an advance to secure the east bank up to the outskirts of Port Fuad, against the opinion and obstruction of Defense Minister Dayan.[46] During the war, Dayan, more than anyone in the Israeli leadership, had consistently feared provoking the Soviets into direct intervention. He had tried to stop the IDF's advance before it reached the canal bank, though in his testimony before the Agranat Commission, he belittled this as mere "advice."

While it receives but passing (if any) mention in foreign histories, the Ras el-Ish incident took on heroic proportions in Egyptian lore as proving that "the defeat of June 1967 had not blunted the will of the Egyptian warrior, who could win if given an equal chance. The battle also showed that the Israeli soldier was no legend as presented by malicious Zionist propaganda."[47] On the twenty-fifth anniversary of the massive canal crossing in 1973, this minor cross-canal operation was still listed first among the milestones toward restoring Egyptian self-confidence.[48]

The new Israeli aggression that was needed to justify a Soviet intervention was thus provided. Was the Israeli probe toward Ras el-Ish deliberately provoked by the Soviets and Egyptians in a scaled-down replay of the plan that had failed in June? On 11 July, Brezhnev told the Budapest conference that the Soviet leadership had been "suddenly" alarmed into action on the evening of 8 July. But besides the speed of the ensuing Soviet naval action, a number of circumstantial indications point at least

THE SOVIET–ISRAELI WAR, 1967–1973

toward prior coordination of the response to the Israeli move. On 29 June, it was officially announced that the Soviet consulate was among the few remaining foreign missions in Port Said (as well as Suez City) that were ordered by Egyptian authorities to close "until traces of Israeli aggression are erased."[49]

The flare-up began the very day that Zakharov left Cairo, after concluding his inspection of Egyptian forces on the canal front. His final meeting with Nasser to present a detailed report began with a half hour of commiseration and mutual advice on their other common problem, diabetes.[50] Zakharov's departure provided some deniability for Soviet connivance in the following day's action.[51] But having pleaded for and obtained his agreement in principle to enhance the presence and role of Soviet advisers, the Egyptians would hardly have flouted it so quickly by launching an uncoordinated operation. Indeed, Lashchenko, who accompanied the marshal back to Moscow, returned immediately after the Ras el-Ish engagement.[52]

Egypt's crack commando forces had not been stationed in Sinai in the run-up to the war, so they hardly would have already garrisoned a pre-existing defensive position east of the Canal.[53] According to the Israeli account, on 1 July the Egyptians ferried not only some 100 commandos but several armored vehicles across the canal, an unprecedented feat for them; in the summer of 1968, Egyptian officers still had trouble floating tanks across a water obstacle even under staff-exercise conditions.[54] Encouraging and training the Egyptians to mount raids across the canal became a regular feature of the Soviet advisers' program. On 17 July, Pozhidaev told his Swedish counterpart in Cairo that "*if* Israeli forces try to cross the canal, the USSR will intervene directly"; but the Soviets frequently threatened moves that they had already made.[55] The Egyptian narrative does not credit the Soviets with any role, but as the advisers soon found out, such thanklessness would be par for the course.

Rabin admits that his troops, hemmed in on the causeway, soon found themselves in "a severe situation." On 8 July, they lost five killed and thirteen injured under a sudden and concentrated barrage from the west bank (Egorin states that Soviet servicemen played a direct role in "artillery duels on the canal front" in the immediate postwar period, but does not give a precise date).[56] Rabin sidestepped Dayan (who was characteristically incommunicado when a difficult decision had to be made) to order air strikes across the canal. Cairo confirmed that the Israeli planes knocked out several batteries of Egyptian artillery that had been shelling the Israeli sitting ducks. As the EAF chief later recalled, the Soviet airlift of fighter jets now enabled the local ground forces commander, Gen. Ahmed Ismail Ali, to call in an air counterstrike that ranged deep into Sinai.[57] Even though one Egyptian MiG-21 was shot down and Israel denied any losses, the boost to Egyptian morale was considerable.

For Soviet consumption, the Egyptians described the situation less optimistically—as Brezhnev told Socialist Bloc leaders in Budapest on 11 July:

> On the evening of July 8 we suddenly received from Nasser a disquieting letter ...: "This morning at 10:30 Israeli forces began an offensive in direction of ... Port Fuad. ... It is clear

HOLDING THE LINE ON THE SUEZ CANAL

they want to conquer it, to move military operations west of the Suez Canal ... to abolish the regime. At this difficult moment I turn to the Central Committee and Soviet government to undertake urgent measures in defense of ... the UAR, the urgent expedition of planes *together with pilots* ... to take over not only the anti-aircraft command but also the Egyptian air forces while they are still not destroyed ... we are ready to make available to you all airports." Very fast, at 3:00 a.m., we convened the Politburo. We called our embassy in Cairo ... but there were no grounds to send out our troops ... However, taking into account the moral-political factor, we decided to render support to Nasser and we gave orders to our military navy and submarines to call at the Arab ports under the pretext of a friendship visit. ... The next day, on July 9, Nasser said to our ambassador that he had already given orders to his air force to attack and destroy the Israeli armored units and only bad weather, clouds, had prevented it.[58]

Was this a pre-planned gambit? Even if Soviet complicity in initiating the Ras el-Ish clash cannot yet be conclusively demonstrated, there can be little doubt that it was quickly and effectively followed up on to legitimize a major Soviet objective: an overt and permanent naval presence in Egyptian ports. Besides the strategic significance of this goal, it offered an immediate political benefit. The mutual complaints lodged at the United Nations by Egypt and Israel spurred negotiations for the posting of UN observers to monitor the ceasefire. If the Soviet force intervened first to deter an Israeli advance and determine the ceasefire line, this would go a long way toward redeeming the USSR's reputation in the Arab world.

Cairo's first communiqué about the 8 July battle was issued within half an hour of the first shelling, and when the Israeli air strike began the Egyptian and Soviet delegates at the UN had already discussed and implemented the diplomatic response. Israel reported that the shore batteries at Port Said, normally mounted facing north at the Mediterranean, were swung around by 180 degrees to pound the IDF force, a maneuver that required some time and preparation in addition to technical expertise.[59] A Soviet adviser who later emigrated to Israel related in a debriefing that he had witnessed these batteries firing at Israeli craft during the failed raid on Port Said harbor on 5 June; he thus was certainly present when these guns were activated a month later.[60]

E. *The Fifth* Eskadra *is formally created—while in action*

The Soviet Mediterranean flotilla had been greatly reinforced in the lead-up to the Six-Day War, in which it was slated to take an active part. But it was still formally designated as a makeshift "combined *eskadra*" of ships from the Black Sea, Baltic and Northern fleets. We have demonstrated that its incorporation as a permanent *eskadra* was delayed in order to downplay its preparation for a central role in the Soviet intervention plan. The magnitude of this mission is highlighted by the arrival, on 11 May, of the Black Sea Fleet's deputy commander, Vice-Admiral Viktor Sysoev, to take command of the "combined *eskadra*." He personally delivered sealed orders for the operation to several of the captains involved.[61] Only on 14 June, after the war had ended, did Navy Commander Gorshkov promulgate a formal decree to create the permanent, independent Fifth *Eskadra*, subordinate directly to his headquarters.[62] On 27 June, operational orders were issued to implement the squadron's formation; it was to be inaugurated on 14 July, when the designated commander, Rear-Admiral Boris Petrov, was to be saluted by a regatta at the squadron's main anchorage, Antikythera off Crete.

However, the renewed fighting at the northern end of the canal changed the plan even before Petrov, along with Gorshkov's first deputy, Fleet Admiral Vladimir Kasatonov, sailed from Sevastopol on 9 July. Sysoev had already been recalled to Sevastopol, where he would take command of the Black Sea Fleet in December 1968. Now the squadron's interim commander, Rear-Admiral Igor' Molodtsov, was dispatched to Egypt, with its flagship and ten other vessels. The regatta had to be cancelled, but the operational mission fulfilled its purpose even better—to lift spirits in the squadron, after the frustration that most of its crews felt when their landings in Israel were aborted. In Kiev, Shelest noted: "our Black Sea Fleet was almost entirely gone to the Mediterranean. A combative attitude permeates all units, with many offering to volunteer for *desant* formations."[63]

And so, on 9 July, the day after the trap set for its forces at Ras el-Ish led Israel to send its warplanes across the canal, an imminent "visit" of Soviet warships to Port Said and Alexandria was announced in Moscow—rather unusually for a Sunday.[64] While this was reported in Monday papers in the eastern United States, the actual arrival of eight ships in Port Said and four in Alexandria was announced early enough the same day to make the late editions of West Coast papers. Molodtsov made headlines around the world by declaring, in an extraordinary press conference with the governor of Alexandria, that "among units of the visiting fleet are missile carriers ready to cooperate with your forces to repel any aggression." The visiting ships were led by two missile cruisers, including the *Dzerzhinsky*, now Molodtsov's flagship and the *Eskadra*'s forward command post.

How meager foreign, and especially American, press representation in Egypt was at this point is illustrated by the almost universal, identical misspelling of the officer's name as "Molochov," which traces back to a single AP item.[65] Only agencies catering mainly to Australia and Europe, where the event came too late for the same day's papers, noticed on the following morning that Molodtsov's statement went unreported in the Egyptian press, and quoted "informed sources" whereby the Soviet consulate in Alexandria had asked to suppress it.[66] Nonetheless, AP's follow-up story related that

> many Egyptians interpreted the promise of help from Adm. Igor' Molochov as a major change. ... There has been no sign in Moscow, however, of any change in the Soviet Union's policy of confining its aid to the Arabs to political moves and replacement of some of the arms lost.[67]

HOLDING THE LINE ON THE SUEZ CANAL

Did Molodtsov, carried away by his fleeting moment in the limelight, really exceed his instructions? That would be highly atypical of such a veteran Soviet officer, who had already commanded a ship in the celebrated landing behind Nazi lines at Novorossiisk during the Second World War. He had been promoted from captain first class to rear admiral just before the crisis of May–June 1967, and was put in provisional command of the "combined *eskadra*" until Sysoev took over on 11 May. But soon after his star turn in Alexandria, he was transferred to a teaching position at a naval academy. This might have been considered a kick upstairs had Petrov not just vacated the same position. Reluctance to stress the Soviet role in the signal victory at Ras el-Ish might be as plausibly attributed to the Egyptians—who also had the final say in censoring their own press—as to the Russians.

The day after Molodtsov's threat, his ships took no immediate action when Israeli naval craft sank two Egyptian torpedo boats 75 kilometers northeast of Port Said.[68] But the Soviet Navy's mission to deter Israeli land and air "aggression" into Egypt was accomplished. When on 15 July air battles resumed along the canal, "Cairo sources said Israeli planes stayed well clear of Port Said ... where eight Soviet ships have been moored since Monday at Egypt's invitation."[69] As General Hod told his USAF colleagues in January 1968, "Russian ships are tied in with the Egyptian air defense system."[70] The Soviets later took credit for deterring Israel from any air raid on Alexandria, even when Cairo itself was buzzed and bombed in 1969–70.[71]

In New York, it was noted that "while the United Nations Security Council sought a formula to station UN truce observers in the troubled Suez Canal zone, Soviet sea power was already there."[72] Only after the flotilla had anchored on 9 July did Soviet Ambassador Nikolay Fedorenko retract a threat to veto the observers' dispatch; the resolution was passed the next day, and the observers took up their positions only on the 17th.[73] Novosti's Egorin visited Ismailia as soon as the Egyptian authorities permitted, "at the end of July," and already met, in the sandbagged front-line trenches, a Soviet adviser to the local battalion commander with an interpreter. Their arrangements to write home had not yet been set up, indicating that they had been posted recently and hurriedly. But as the adviser told Egorin that Israeli fire had increased "when it became known that UN observers were to be sent in," the adviser evidently was there earlier—during, if not before, the Ras el-Ish engagement.[74]

The Soviets' coup was instantly and correctly recognized by leading analysts, such as the veteran UN correspondent William Frye:

> the Kremlin was conveying a clear message to Israel ... Thus far, and no farther ... Bluff or not, the positioning of Soviet striking power within easy range of Israeli front lines readjusted the balance of power in the area. It inhibited the use of Israeli air power against Egyptian artillery in the Port Said–Port Fuad region.

Frye's conclusion, though, was still by way of understatement: though he says "the move was as close as the Soviet Union has come to an open threat of physical interven-

29

tion,"[75] inserting regular Soviet forces, even in a tripwire function, *was* already more than a mere threat. As recognized by 1971 in James Cable's classic study *Gunboat Diplomacy*, this was "a clear-cut case of the purposeful use of limited naval force" which achieved its objective. "Whether or not the Israelis had ever intended a further advance none was made, and some of the credit earlier lost by the Soviet Union in Arab eyes was regained. Indeed, this seemingly trivial intervention probably had more immediate impact than the intrinsically more important deliveries of arms."[76]

Meanwhile, the commotion around the Soviet ships in Egypt provided a perfect diversion from the Fifth *Eskadra*'s formal inauguration on 14 July. Gorshkov himself joined Kasatonov to preside over the ceremony at Antikythera.[77] Future Admiral of the Fleet Ivan Kapitanets, who ferried Kasatonov back to Sevastopol on board his destroyer *Nastoychivy*, noted that the admiral stressed among the *Eskadra*'s missions "cooperation with the Egyptian and Syrian navies and the [Soviet] advisers' *apparat*."[78] If the Sixth Fleet picked up any signals or other indications of this portentous event, it was kept under wraps and went unmentioned in the Western media, which routinely reported every passage of Soviet warships through the Turkish straits. Likewise, although Molodtsov charged that aircraft of the US Sixth Fleet had shadowed his ships as they moved toward Egypt (a complaint more often voiced by the Americans), Washington apparently did not relay any warning to Israel.

This may explain Dayan's departure from his previous caution: the day before the *Eskadra*'s ships arrived in Egypt, he stated to *Frankfurter Allgemeine Zeitung* that

> he would not hesitate to advise his government to fight Russia if Soviet troops were ever used against Israel ... it was possible Soviet troops might fight with the Arabs in a future war because the recent crisis had shown them that Arab soldiers were of little use. ... Russia is using Arab dependence on it for arms to obtain complete influence in the Middle East.

This was mainly a symptom of internecine political sniping: Prime Minister Levi Eshkol, smarting from Dayan's glorification for the June victory, was openly favoring Rabin.[79]

But Dayan's bravado aroused genuine concern among his colleagues, who forced him to issue a clarification:

> The commotion ... reverberated in the cabinet session. Several ministers severely criticized [his] frequent statements ... which even if misinterpreted might have caused grave damage ... Mr Dayan clarified that the reporter, while discussing the continued supply of Soviet arms to Egypt, asked what Israel would do if Soviet *crews* took part in the fighting? In such a case, the Defense Minister noted, he would recommend to the government to fight those crews, too.[80]

Dayan's semi-retraction was published on the day that Molodtsov sounded his threat, which appeared to vindicate the Israeli minister's earlier apprehension about provoking the Soviets. The Israel mission in New York had already warned of

HOLDING THE LINE ON THE SUEZ CANAL

American resentment at "Dayan's remarks about a war with the USSR" and reported US demands "for us to act out of national unity, self-confidence, in a low key while maintaining proportions."[81] Now Jerusalem urgently directed its embassy in Washington to "ask US Government for their opinion on the declaration of the Soviet flotilla commander in Alexandria."[82]

But at least in public, there was little US verbal reaction, and even less in the theater of operations. State Department spokesman Robert McCloskey declined to comment on the Russian Navy's new presence in Egypt or on Molodtsov's statement. Instead, he continued to stress "increasing concern [about] reports of continued shipments of aircraft and other arms to the UAR ...," hinting darkly that "we do [have details on the volume of deliveries] but I am afraid that is classified ... It is significant enough to warrant the comment that I just made."[83] The same recurred on 20 July when British sources reported "Soviet marines sighted in Port Said and Ismailia," from among the "thousands of marines" on nine Soviet warships and landing craft in Port Said. Both "British and US officials ... said that positioning Soviet naval commando units outside the USSR is an innovation for Russia and if true, this fact might be a very significant event on the way to dangerous confrontation in areas of tension worldwide." But on record, McCloskey said that the State Department "cannot even check whether there indeed *were* marines on board" the Soviet ships.[84]

The next day, these ships, which were "originally scheduled to remain a week ... extended their stay indefinitely at Egypt's invitation as renewed Arab–Israeli fighting sullied the Suez truce line."[85] Port Said and Alexandria thus became Soviet naval bases in all but name. This formality allowed NATO experts even a year later to insist that "the Soviets as yet have no naval base in the Mediterranean and ... the Egyptians will not be prepared for such a possibility."[86] But US naval circles were soon concerned that "a preemptive landing by even a small force of Soviet naval infantrymen from one of the two LSMs [landing ships, medium] they normally keep in the Mediterranean *could* seriously restrict the use of superior US naval power because of the risk of direct confrontation"—a preliminary step toward Soviet aspirations "to *control* ... the Mediterranean."[87]

The continuous presence of warships and marines, with increasing control of shore facilities, would last through 1972. Alexandria, farther from the war zone and shielded from Israeli air attack by the Soviet presence, assumed the main function of the *Eskadra*'s maintenance, repair and supply. Its commerce and nightlife, whose continuing vibrancy despite the war astonished the Soviets, also provided their recreation.[88] Port Said, on the other hand, was a combat station, and the Soviets' role there remained holding the line against the Israelis' perceived intention to complete their occupation of the canal's east bank. "We sat there and looked at each other," Capt. Yury Khripunkov recalled a quarter century later.

> There were the Israeli forces on one side, and on the other—astern of us—were ours, that is the Arabs', and I was in the middle. Every morning at 0345 I would go out on the bridge,

the sailors would load the cannon and train them onto the Israeli trenches ... we were 2–3 km from the Israeli-occupied territory and I could see them.

Khripunkov's frigate remained at Port Said at least through October, when he "witnessed the Israeli navy's tragedy" in which Soviet advisers "did all but press the button."[89] This incident, the sinking of the Israeli destroyer *Eilat*, would coincide dramatically with the formalization of the Soviet military presence in Egypt.

3

THE SOVIET PRESENCE IS FORMALIZED AND EXPANDED

A. Lashchenko Hammers Out an Agreement

At the Budapest conference, Brezhnev announced that "at Nasser's request," on 10 July—that is, at the height of the Ras el-Ish clash—a delegation of senior Soviet officers was dispatched to Egypt "to restore the fighting capacity of the Arab army so that it will be able to repel imperialist attack." As its leader—Petr Lashchenko—clarified, it was also tasked with working out a formal agreement about the advisers' status. Besides Lashchenko, whom Brezhnev already described as "our chief adviser," this group included top officers from all the services, including the deputy commander of the Soviet Air Defense Forces, Air Marshal Evgeny Savitsky, as well as marine and tank commanders.[1]

Seconded from his post as commander of the Ciscarpathian military district (which title he retained), Lashchenko had earned a reputation as decisive and determined, not to say ruthless. He took part in the suppression of the uprising in East Berlin in 1953, and in 1956 led the Special Army Corps in Hungary, where he drew up and implemented the plan for putting down the revolt.[2] He had also honed his political skill as a member of the Supreme Soviet and of the CPSU Control Committee since 1966.[3] In Egypt, he soon earned, among the Soviet officers, the sobriquet "our Montgomery"—another example of comparison with the Second World War, with the canal front equated to El Alamein.[4]

The agreement had yet to be negotiated, but Lashchenko was not disposed to wasting time. In his only known memoir, he defined his team's mission as "*rapid reconstruction of the [Egyptian] armed forces and organization of a reliable defense … to establish the dimensions of the defeat, and assist the Egyptian command in liquidating the consequences of aggression.*" The CIA was, then, quite correct in concluding, at the end of July, that the USSR would no longer support an Arab effort to eliminate Israel entirely but would sponsor a limited offensive to regain the territories lost in the June war.[5] As Lashchenko's longtime associate Maj.-Gen. Evgeny Malashenko relates, while awaiting the arrival of his advisers' full complement, he directed the work of the experts already in Egypt for rehabilitation of the Egyptian army. ... the work of Lashchenko's group for setting up the defense of the Suez Canal was meanwhile convincing the Egyptian military leadership of the necessity to have Soviet military advisers.[6]

Talks to formalize the Soviets' expanded role dragged on all summer, with a constant traffic of delegations between Cairo and Moscow.[7] Despite Nasser's express request, the advisers' standing was a major point of contention. Evgeny Primakov, *Pravda*'s Cairo correspondent during the June war, was widely considered an intelligence operative, and this was soon confirmed when he was formally attached to the Soviet embassy.[8] He wrote on 10 August to his editor, who passed the report on to the International Department of the Central Committee: "For the present critical moment, the UAR [Egypt] would appear to need a large group of our instructors on the west bank of the Suez Canal *who could participate directly* in repelling new attempts at aggression by Israel." The advisers, he noted, would also "facilitate the consolidation of all healthy elements."[9]

There were, then, *un*healthy elements who objected to enhancing the Soviets' status. As Lashchenko reminisced in 1991,

> we found out that Egyptian generals and officers were in those days conducting a polemic in their own circles about the advisers. Some of them completely shared the president's position that [the advisers] were necessary for the army; others opposed it vehemently. Typically, members of the senior command were categorically against the advisers. Junior officers supported the president's decision.

As Malashenko put it,

> Certain Egyptian political and military activists did not desire Soviet advisers among their troops. ... They feared that the Soviet advisers would exert a certain influence on the personal makeup of the Egyptian army, would supplant its commanders and undermine their authority, and would also increase the UAR's dependence on the USSR ... The Egyptian side opposed granting the chief military adviser the right to report ... directly to the president, and to set up a staff; equipping the advisers with radio equipment, and many other issues. ... They even tried to avoid using the term "adviser" and instead used "specialist, expert, consultant."[10]

The latter point would remain contentious for years, and the confusion caused by the alternating terms would help to mask both the arrival and the withdrawal of regular Soviet formations.

Lashchenko stressed the ideological motivation, or excuse, for this resistance: "we soon were convinced that many Egyptian generals were as frightened of [our] 'communist spirit' as of fire—the ideological influence that the advisers might have on junior officers and enlisted men." But more specifically, he pinpointed the hard core of opposition in a group that he called retrospectively "the most reactionary generals

THE SOVIET PRESENCE IS FORMALIZED AND EXPANDED

and officers," led by Amer and Badran. Amer had until recently been a Soviet favorite. Before he and Grechko authored the failed war plan against Israel, he had been appreciated for his hard line on Yemen, and like Nasser was made a Hero of the Soviet Union (HSU).

But now he was a liability for the Soviets, as was Badran, who had conducted crucial talks in Moscow in the run-up to the war. They were foremost among the officers who were embittered at the USSR's failure to implement its promised intervention, and though they were scapegoated for the June debacle they still embodied a constant threat to expose the now-embarrassing Soviet role. Amin Howeidy, the former officer turned politician and diplomat whom Nasser brought back as a civilian defense minister after the Six-Day War, recalled before his death in 2009 that "the commanders who had been responsible for the defeat ... fought fiercely to deny responsibility. I became convinced that all [of them] had to resign."[11]

Malashenko singles out a central target of Howeidy's purge, Lt-Gen. Salah Mohsen, who "constantly found excuses to block the negotiations," resorting even to charges that there were spies for Israel among the advisers.[12] This obstacle was, however, abruptly removed in August, when in Lashchenko's words "an event occurred that facilitated the advisers' introduction. This was the arrest of a group of conspirators" led by Amer and Badran, who allegedly attempted a coup against Nasser.[13] On 14 September 1967, Amer reportedly poisoned himself in prison.[14]

A direct Soviet role in removing Amer appears unlikely, in view of the Kremlin's initial caution in taking sides and reporting the plot. Rumors that Nasser was again about to resign were taken seriously enough to bring forward Sergey Vinogradov's dispatch to Cairo.[15] It took several weeks and a visit to Moscow by Foreign Minister Mahmud Riad before Soviet media hailed the coup's failure as "a blow to imperialism."[16] But the benefit for Moscow was immediate: all at once, Lashchenko recalled, "unfriendliness and overtly slanderous statements toward the USSR almost ceased. Egyptian generals no longer felt that the advisers were being imposed on them. At every opportunity the commander-in-chief, the war minister and even the president himself would ask Ambassador Vinogradov, 'why is the advisers' arrival being delayed?'"

Now, as Malashenko relates, came Moscow's turn to play coy. "After complex negotiations, the USSR delayed signature of the agreement in order to allow the Egyptian side to grasp the complexity of the situation and the results of the Egyptian army's defeat, and to prepare for accepting the advisers." Lashchenko adds, somewhat smugly, "ultimately, Nasser again submitted a formal request to expedite the advisers. After the change in the Egyptian leadership's outlook was appreciated, the Soviet government decided to accede."

Even at the height of Egyptian recalcitrance, "the Soviet defense minister ... decided ... to continue practical work," and Lashchenko's still-small team along the canal took credit for impressing the Egyptian command. The chief adviser had not delayed the selection of his *apparat*. In July, he had already recruited Malashenko, who had been his top aide in Hungary and now was his first assistant chief of staff in the Ciscarpathian district, to be his chief liaison to the Egyptians. Lower in the pecking order, G.V. Karpov, who headed the rocket and artillery units of a training division in the Transcaucasian military district, was "summoned one summer day and was offered to go the Middle East as a military adviser," but both were put on hold till October.[17]

Signing the agreement, the culmination of Zakharov's mission as continued by Lashchenko, would appear to explain the marshal's return to Cairo in October. But a recently published Soviet document confirms Lashchenko's own statement that it was another member of the Soviet top brass who went there for this purpose. Meeting Nasser late in the afternoon of 21 October, Vinogradov informed him "that tomorrow a special plane was flying in a delegation headed by the First Deputy Defense Minister of the USSR, General of the Army Sokolov, S[ergey] L[eonidovich], to sign an agreement for dispatch of Soviet military advisers." Sokolov, the commander of the Leningrad military district, had been promoted in April to his sub-ministerial post, creating the anomaly whereby in the government hierarchy he outranked Zakharov—an ordinary deputy minister—while the marshal held the higher military rank.[18] Nasser, who had (according to Vinogradov) broached the subject by again expressing "supreme interest in the quickest arrival" of the advisers, "voiced his satisfaction" at the news. He expressed hope "that financial questions would be no obstacle ... I said that for us the main thing was not the financial aspect but for our military advisers to be able to provide the maximum benefit."[19]

It was one thing for Nasser to tell Vinogradov in private that Egypt must emulate the Soviets' sacrifice in the Second World War in order to repel its own occupiers, and to claim that he had just contemptuously dismissed a conciliatory feeler from US Secretary of State Dean Rusk. It was quite another thing to acknowledge openly that the Egyptian military was to be even more thoroughly saturated with Soviet officers. Sokolov was closer in political rank to Howeidy, with whom he signed the treaty, but though his visit was mentioned in the Egyptian press—in such innocuous contexts as a tour of the Aswan Dam construction site—it received virtually no attention abroad, and the agreement was never published.[20] Something of a smokescreen was provided by the return of Zakharov: news of his arrival, "suddenly and unannounced," first emerged on 23 October.[21]

The extraordinary presence of *two* top Soviet defense officials in Egypt demanded some explanation. If Sokolov's visit was preplanned to handle the formalities of a treaty, Zakharov's dispatch was widely interpreted as an improvised damage-control effort. It was initially reported after four blasts that were heard around the world and restored the Middle East to the front pages. These were the Soviet-made ship-to-ship Styx missiles that were fired from Port Said and sank the Israeli destroyer *Eilat*.

THE SOVIET PRESENCE IS FORMALIZED AND EXPANDED

B. "All but pressing the button": the Soviets and the Eilat *sinking*

This exploit went down in naval history as the first sinking of a warship by missile. In the Egyptian narrative, alongside Ras el-Ish, it marks the beginning of the 1967 defeat's reversal. As in the land battle, the Egyptians were eager to claim exclusive credit, while the Soviets were torn between pride in their cutting-edge weapons technology and political reticence to admit igniting a new round of violence. Nasser decorated the commanders of two *Komar* missile boats that were credited for the sinking. This was the main basis for the now-established account that it was accomplished by two Egyptian boats of this smaller, older model, which had two missile launchers each, rather than a newer, four-launcher *Ossa*.[22] But since the missiles were spotted by the *Eilat*'s lookout only as they approached the ship, Cable correctly noted soon after: "no outside observer could be certain that the Styx missiles had actually been fired by Egyptians."[23]

The prevalent assumption, which would recur time and again in the years to come, held that the Egyptians disregarded Soviet calls for restraint. "Western diplomats in Moscow," ran the initial speculations, "believe the Kremlin is concerned about the possible consequences ... and Zakharov had gone to Egypt to look over the situation." Never mind that "Moscow Radio said the sinking ... taught the Israelis an appropriate lesson." A commentary in Arabic entitled "The Israeli Extremists Got What They Deserve" endorsed Cairo's claim that the Israeli destroyer had penetrated Egyptian waters.[24] Then, on 24 October, it was announced in Moscow that Zakharov had actually been in Cairo "on an unofficial visit since Saturday [21 October]"—whereas the first missile struck the *Eilat* only after 5 p.m. local time the same day.[25] So he could not have been sent in response, and no record has emerged of the Soviets' supposed disapproval.

Nasser told an American envoy on 2 November that he was notified about the *Eilat* incident at about 6:30 p.m., after it was over.[26] Vinogradov also reported that, when he met Nasser late that afternoon, the president "said he had just been advised by phone that at 1700 Cairo time, an Israeli destroyer had violated UAR territorial waters. Preliminary data stated [it] was sunk by Egyptian missile boats."[27] But several later accounts from Egyptian officers stated that the president personally authorized the attack at midday, when the *Eilat* was first detected.[28] Amid preparations at such a high level that included systems in which the vital presence of Soviet advisers has already been noted; with two Moscow VIPs on hand to finalize an agreement giving their men a say in any such operation, could the Soviets have been left entirely out of the loop? An Egyptian military spokesman appeared to protest too much when he not only called allegations of Soviet involvement "absurd" but added: "we have not a single foreigner in our armed forces."[29]

In Israel, recriminations soon began that the *Eilat*'s foray—undertaken against its captain's judgment—had been pointless and foolhardy. This still-unresolved controversy within the IDF recently led to the disclosure that Israeli intelligence intercepted (but allegedly withheld from the *Eilat*'s skipper) Egyptian signals indicating that Port Said shore batteries and naval units had been alerted, and later—but still two to three hours before the attack—that missile launches had been approved.[30] At the time, the Israelis, smarting at the heavy casualties and the blow to their newly enhanced prowess, were hard put to admit it was all the Egyptians' doing, but they were also apprehensive of a head-on clash with the Soviets. A leading Israeli commentator cautiously deduced that even in the absence of conclusive evidence of direct Soviet involvement, "clearly, the Soviets held at least some 'advisory' authority, [and] no local commander could by any means have made the decision."[31] Others went further: Israel's Navy commander, Shlomo Erell, declared explicitly that it was "Soviet missiles fired from Soviet ships" but admitted that these had been "supplied to the Egyptian navy." An "authoritative Israeli source" said "his government doubted Egyptian crews had time enough to be trained to fire the missiles." Former Prime Minister David Ben-Gurion, still kept abreast of developments by his many disciples in the military, "charged that the hands that fired the missiles ... were not Egyptian. He did not say Russians fired the missiles, but observers said he was referring to Russians."

In London, "unofficial defense experts held that such a successful missile firing was beyond the talents of Egyptian naval personnel. They said it bore the hallmark of Russian skill."[32] *France-Soir* reported that Soviet advisers based in Port Said had planned and supervised the *Eilat* sinking.[33] In confidence, some Western intelligence agencies soon claimed they had proof of this. A week after the event, West German officials still insisted to Israeli colleagues that "Zakharov came to express displeasure and to ensure future coordination and consultation."[34] But by mid-December, the Germans had reversed their initial assessment, and based on "an authoritative and reliable source," they were now sure that "the Soviets knew in advance about the Egyptian intention to fire the missiles ... and gave their full consent."[35]

An official Russian military history published in 2000 cited the affair as an example "that many of the Egyptian naval personnel had gained some experience in combat operations even before the arrival of Soviet specialists."[36] But as already pointed out, there were both Soviet naval craft and advisers present in Port Said all summer. Five years later, the Soviet military attaché in Cairo still "cited with some pride the sinking of the *Eilat*, which he claimed was achieved without assistance from the advisers"—but he did acknowledge that "some may have been present ... at the time."[37] The naval historian Aleksandr Shirokorad has named an adviser, V.A. Goncharov, who "was not even thanked for the world's first use of anti-ship missiles," and adds a quote from the poet Pushkin to the effect that everyone was lied to. He blames the Egyptian *Komar* skippers' incompetence for the long interval between the two missile salvos, which were meant to be simultaneous; the final missile exploded in the water after the *Eilat* had already gone down. Shirokorad claims that, afterward, one boat ran aground due to poor navigation and was refloated only after three days.[38]

THE SOVIET PRESENCE IS FORMALIZED AND EXPANDED

Likewise, one of the first naval advisers dispatched under Lashchenko's agreement, who arrived after the incident (on 2 November), gives the conventional attribution of the *Eilat* sinking to Egyptian *Komar* boats—but appears to contradict it with his description of the state in which he found the Egyptian Navy. Not only was morale at all levels abysmal but "combat readiness, technical condition of the equipment and the vessels overall, left much to be desired. Organization of everyday routine and combat readiness in general, tactical preparation of the officers and primarily ship and detachment commanders, were at a low level." Sorties out of harbor were rare, attempted only in daylight and for a few hours, and the crews—who did not live on board—brought along their own food from home because the galleys were used as storerooms.[39] As late as 1972, the Soviets still saw little improvement, particularly in respect of the skippers' reluctance to put to sea even for training.[40]

Besides the advisers, did the Soviet navy itself play a part in the *Eilat* engagement? Over six months later, an American report from Cairo held that the *Eilat* was sunk "during a rare period when no Soviet ships were at Port Said last fall."[41] The Egyptian press had reported that the Soviet ships' first visit finally ended on 18 August and another began on 3 September.[42] Despite the lack of any direct evidence, it became established as fact that *all* the *Eskadra*'s ships and men left Port Said several days before the incident, returned on 27 October, and only "thereafter maintained a constant vigil, thereby deterring the IDF from further reprisals."[43]

But Port Said, the obvious address for avenging the *Eilat*, was already spared when Israel retaliated on 23 October with an artillery strike that destroyed the oil refineries at Suez City instead. Testimonies from at least two Soviet warships recently indicated that they were in or near Port Said at the time. One of the *Eskadra*'s missions was, explicitly, to "gather information on Israeli forces."[44] The destroyer crewman Kharchikov, whose ship was on "permanent station" at Port Said, attested: "We stood watch around the clock with radio spotting of targets" entering territorial waters,

> and continually reported them to the Arab officer on duty at the naval base command ... on one such watch, a ship was detected still outside the ... zone, moving at over 18 knots—that is, of military significance. As it turned out later, it was the Israeli destroyer *Eilat*.[45]

This roughly corroborates sketchy evidence that the Israelis had at the time: an informant of the Israeli embassy in Washington "heard from an Indian diplomat at the United Nations who heard from an Arab source there" that "the Russians have cracked the Israeli code in the Suez region [and] our signals are being deciphered by them. This also applies to the movements of the *Eilat* before she was sunk."[46]

Kharchikov goes on: "a Soviet-made *K[omar]*-class boat ... *with a mixed crew* proceeded to attack" the *Eilat*.[47] More than a year later, French and US reports held that in the Algerian Navy, *Komar* boats were still operated by such "mixed crews. The Soviets justify this because part of the equipment on these boats is secret."[48]

Other recent testimonies ascribe to the Soviets an even more direct role, but their provenance and content arouse some skepticism; over time, taking credit for the celebrated exploit may have become a common, but often fanciful, boast. Among others, an anonymous posting on a Russian veterans' website claims to record the account of a Soviet missile-boat captain who with his crew was still breaking in their Egyptian successors. This officer related that he elbowed aside the boat's nominal commander and pressed the launch buttons, on his own authority. He and his crew were decorated only for successful transfer of the boat, while the Egyptians were credited for the sinking to avoid international repercussions. This account displays accurate knowledge of the systems involved, but it differs in many basic respects from what is otherwise known—for instance, it claims that the boat was based at Alexandria, and that it attacked the *Eilat* at close range while on patrol on the open sea.[49]

A retired Croatian naval officer, Kuzma Pecotić, has claimed that at least one of the boats involved was an *Ossa*, which had been only nominally handed over to Egypt in 1967 but was withdrawn by the Soviets the following year and sold to Yugoslavia, where Pecotić received it from a Soviet crew. Documentation that the Yugoslavs discovered on board stated that this boat, while still Soviet-manned, had sunk the *Eilat*, and Pecotić's Soviet counterpart confirmed this to him "after a lot of cognac."[50] Unlike the various Russian versions, this one is hardly suspect of self-glorification, but it remains unconfirmed. However, when more than two years later, in December 1969, two regular Soviet *divizyons* of shore-based anti-ship missiles were positioned to bolster Alexandria's coastal defenses, an expert still had to be dispatched to train Egyptian crews in the system's operation, even though some of them had already undergone training in the USSR.[51]

The United States, absorbed in negotiating what would on 22 November become Security Council Resolution 242, did not protest the sinking. The CIA actually endorsed Cairo's version that the *Eilat* had entered Egyptian waters. Israeli Foreign Minister Abba Eban told American interlocutors in Washington on the morning of 23 October that "the Israeli government found itself asking ... what is the extent of Soviet involvement? Do the Egyptians feel they are operating under the cover of Soviet protection?" but nonetheless, "Israel would prefer to deal with this incident as a matter between them and the Egyptians."[52] As Rusk said "off the record," he *felt* like telling Eban, "we're not anxious to come over there and fight the Soviets for you." Publicly, the State Department "steered clear of any comment other than an expression of regret, and spokesman McCloskey said: 'I am not assessing the blame.'"[53] A letter from Johnson to Kosygin deplored this act of war but did not mention even the Soviet provenance of the missiles, let alone any direct Soviet involvement.[54]

The Americans soothed the Israelis with a confidential assurance that the Sixth Fleet was sent toward the Eastern Mediterranean. But the editors of *FRUS* found no record that such action was in fact taken. Ten days later, Israeli diplomat Ephraim Evron suggested leaking the supposed naval move: "an unaccredited story in the

THE SOVIET PRESENCE IS FORMALIZED AND EXPANDED

[*Washington*] *Post* or [*New York*] *Times* would be helpful both with the Israelis and with American Jews." Planting stories was no monopoly of Novosti or *Al-Ahram*. But Johnson's response was "no, no, no! This starts trouble with Russia."[55]

However, the *Eilat* sinking was credited with driving home what the massive Soviet resupply effort had not quite achieved for Israel in Washington. The day after Eban's talks, McCloskey announced that the United States was lifting the arms embargo it had clamped on the Middle East—effectively, on Israel—since the June war.[56] This not only went a step further toward cementing the superpower alignment in the Israeli–Egyptian conflict; it would have a decisive impact on direct Soviet involvement. The first batch of A-4 Skyhawk attack planes, which had already been contracted for before the June war, was delivered on 29 December 1967 and would enable Israel's "flying artillery" campaign in the summer of 1969. It also opened the way for the crucial supply of F-4 Phantoms—the two main triggers for the massive intervention of Soviet forces.

C. Lashchenko overhauls the Egyptian military on the Soviet model

The agreement signed during Sokolov's visit in October 1967 formally created several thousand new slots for Soviet advisers. In practice, their gradual arrival had continued throughout the summer, as necessitated by weapons deliveries as well as operational demands. For instance, in September, six Tu-16Ts were transferred to Cairo-West, when "under supervision of Soviet instructors, Egyptian crews began training flights on them. By the beginning of the 1973 war the Egyptian Tu-16 crews were already adequately prepared for combat missions."[57]

The agreement now signaled the dispatch of advisers in larger numbers—1,200 by the end of November, for an estimated total of 2,500 by the end of 1967.[58] Karpov, the artillery expert enlisted by Lashchenko, finally reached Cairo with a group of the advisers' top brass on 4 November. He noted in his journal that several colleagues had arrived "some time before," including an HSU (Hero of the Soviet Union), Col. Pavel Afanas'ev.

This group's arrival had considerable symbolic value, as it included senior advisers to the Egyptian General Staff, corps and division commanders. It was led by Lt-Gen. Ivan Katyshkin, Lashchenko's deputy and eventual successor, and Maj.-Gen. Evgeny Malashenko, the designated adviser to the Egyptian Army's chief of staff.[59] They lost no time in demanding respect for their newly enhanced authority and—Soviet egalitarianism notwithstanding—living conditions commensurate with their rank. As Malashenko recalled,

> We were billeted at the Victoria Hotel, as houses and apartments earmarked for the advisers were not yet ready. The hotel was not of the best: dark, damp, and even the shower was shared and worked intermittently. There was a large service staff, but no cleanliness or order, and an amazing abundance of roaches even in the restaurant. We, the senior officers,

were already ... used to other standards in hotels. I was tasked to announce this to the military liaison, Lt-Col. Bardisi. He declared that the Soviet experts had always lived in this hotel, and were satisfied. I told him that we were not experts but advisers, and this should be internalized. ... He offered to move me and Gen. Katyshkin to another hotel, but we refused to go without the others.[60]

Either standards at the Victoria were quickly improved, or the lower-ranking advisers were less demanding. Lt-Col. Vladimir Serkov arrived on 24 November and spent two weeks at the hotel before taking up his post as adviser to the headquarters of the 2nd Infantry Division, II Army Corps, at Ismailia. His precise and revealing journal, published forty years later in his remote Ural Mountains hometown with a print run of 150 copies, mentions no dissatisfaction with the lodgings.[61] Meanwhile, additional groups were arriving in rapid succession. A first group of thirteen new naval advisers came on 2 November, headed by Vice-Admiral Boris Sutyagin, who became chief adviser to the commander of the Egyptian Navy. One of his subordinates, then-Capt. Vitaly Zub, states that their number ultimately reached more than seventy. An adviser was attached to every flotilla commander—Zub was the senior adviser to a "brigade" of nine destroyers and frigates—and, eventually, they were posted on board most individual ships.[62]

Though Sokolov's agreement was never published, subsequent references indicate that the Soviets won their main stipulation: ensuring the advisers' authority at the field echelon and their direct access to the Egyptian troops. As explained to Party cadres at home, the Soviet side had insisted on this point to prevent misuse of Soviet weaponry and a repetition of its wholesale loss in the June war. "In October or November 1967," a former *nomenklatura* member from Vilnius recalled, a lieutenant-general had given a lecture to the *partaktiv* (i.e., assembly of activists) of the Lithuanian Communist Party's Central Committee:

> He said that up to the Six-Day War, Nasser had not allowed Soviet experts into his army, preferring to send his own officers to study at Soviet military academies. But now the Egyptians had been persuaded to post an expert at each battalion; no expert, no arms. Moscow, however, set its target at deploying advisers down to company level, because "that way we can exert complete control over the Egyptian Army."[63]

A senior Soviet interpreter posted to Egypt claims that Nasser was compelled to accept advisers down to the *squad* level.[64] As their number never approached the figure that would be necessary for such saturation, this must refer to their new clearance to work directly with the smallest field units. In the various land formations, advisers' memoirs and captured Egyptian documents agree that the standard was four to five per brigade, with only one interpreter for them all—a shortage that would soon be felt acutely. At division headquarters, the linguists were not quite so thinly stretched, with three of them for seven advisers.[65]

THE SOVIET PRESENCE IS FORMALIZED AND EXPANDED

The day after their arrival in Cairo, Malashenko's group received a sober briefing from their boss at the "Ofis," the originally British term that stuck to their headquarters. It was still "a 6-room apartment that we all could barely squeeze into."

> Lashchenko ... laid out the operative-strategic situation and the state of UAR armed forces, which had in effect disintegrated ... All command echelons and headquarters had been shown up as incapable of directing combat operations. The most important reasons for the defeat were the low morale and combat quality of the troops and the defeatist attitude of the officer corps after the Israeli first strike. The Egyptian armed forces are at the rehabilitation stage.

Though Brezhnev had claimed in July that the Arabs had already received more hardware than they had lost, the chief adviser put the effective replacement figure at 30–60 percent, but "the manpower is incapable of using [even] the existing weapons and equipment, and the officers too are poorly prepared." The advisers, therefore, had to insist on their expanded capacity. "Lashchenko ... described in great detail the tasks and working methods for the advisers, based on the personal experience and work of our specialists, ... demanding that we study them and observe them strictly."

This, however, would not be a simple assignment. Nasser spent an unprecedented full hour at the Soviet embassy's Revolution Day reception on 7 November and went out of his way to welcome the top advisers; Ambassador Vinogradov was "overjoyed" at their arrival. But at the Egyptian General Staff's Operations Directorate, to which Malashenko was attached, he found only useless papers being produced. When the Soviets tried to improve procedures, the Egyptian officers "treated us suspiciously and in my view were not very friendly."

> The director, Major-General Talaat, answered all my questions evasively, knew nothing and was concerned only about being summoned to the chief of staff and facing his questions. ... he had to be told what to do every day ... the directorate had no approved war plan ... I tried to point out to Talaat the difference between the advisers and the previous specialists ... we ostensibly worked out our cooperation, but he tried to overload us with superfluous work.

Malashenko had to remind him of the new dispensation: "we're advisers, not white slaves that can be kept busy with unnecessary tasks and do all the work for you." There was a slight improvement only after Chief of Staff Abdel Moneim Riad intervened in favor of the Russians.

On the other hand, Riad stalled for two or three weeks before he let Malashenko inspect the canal front. In July, Zakharov had departed with a promise that "we will not leave Egypt in the lurch," and outlined a classic Soviet three-tiered defense array along the canal.[66] Malashenko specifies that by July Lashchenko had submitted the detailed plan to the Egyptian high command. But three months later, Malashenko was still "depressed by his first view of the desert" and the actual state of affairs.

43

THE SOVIET–ISRAELI WAR, 1967–1973

At Ismailia, he was dismayed by the laxity of discipline and readiness, with soldiers not even bearing arms except in the fortifications close to the canal bank. Artillery and tanks were positioned ineffectively and without proper camouflage, even though the units had been holding the line for half a year and there were already Soviet advisers attached to brigade and division commanders. "Numerous soldiers were idling, cooking or washing underwear in the canal instead of improving their emplacements." The officers needed advice even in trivial matters: "I was told that commanders do not update data, as they do not want to make out new graphs. I suggested using a pencil instead of an ink marker. They had not thought of that."

The Soviet glossary of military terminology gives the following definition for "adviser" (as distinct from "consultant"):

> a serviceman, usually drawn from the officer corps, who is sent by mutual agreement from one state to another to extend assistance in constructing armed forces, preparing military cadres, training troops, and implementation of weaponry and equipment purchased by the [assisted] state from the other; and sometimes *to assist in the organization and conduct of combat operations.*[67]

As imparted to Karpov's group of advisers, the agreement for their deployment included a clause that reflected precisely this aspect: quasi-command status and combat readiness. "The adviser bears the same responsibility as the commander for the troops' combat training." Lashchenko clarified to the new arrivals "that if a war began, the advisers would go into battle with their advisees." Karpov's diary—which is unusually critical both for its Soviet-era time of writing and for its publication date, 2009—reflects some resentment at this instruction. "Whoever wrote that into the agreement did not think about our people. This was not our war. We swore allegiance to *our* Motherland. They should have written that 'all the adviser's recommendations must be implemented without question.' That would have been more correct."[68]

As Lashchenko recalled, "news of the Soviet advisers' arrival spread quickly and aroused varying reactions. In the [field] units the Soviet forces were received courteously, with traditional Arab hospitality, and sometimes even cordially." But some officers treated them with increasing suspicion, especially in respect of sharing information that might expose their own incompetence, and resented having their errors pointed out—which some advisers did too bluntly. After understanding this motivation, the advisers tried to overcome it by exchanging information about the enemy and explaining that they were there voluntarily to help Arab friends repel aggression. This took a week or two, and afterward the relationship grew stronger as work continued. But Lashchenko's complaint that progress was hobbled by habits going back to British times was exemplified by the Egyptians' insistence on addressing the advisers as "Mister."

THE SOVIET PRESENCE IS FORMALIZED AND EXPANDED

D. First Soviet–Israeli air encounters

Lashchenko singled out the air force advisers' task of rebuilding the EAF from scratch as particularly challenging. Most of the air advisers carried out his instructions with ostentatious enthusiasm, risking—indeed, provoking—direct confrontation with the Israelis. When Egyptian pilots excused their poor performance by charging that their Soviet planes were inferior to Israel's French-made craft, "upon Lashchenko's orders, senior Air Force adviser Lt-Gen. S[ergey] Gorelov organized flights by our pilot-advisers who successfully carried out some special sorties from forward airfields into Israeli territory."[69]

By late November 1967, Karpov—now already posted at a division headquarters—witnessed such a flight from the ground:

> Today, an Israeli attack plane flew over the division ... The EAF scrambled 12 fighters; they reached the canal but only one [pilot] flew into the enemy hinterland in Sinai. He turned out to be our senior adviser. The Egyptian pilots still dared not fly over enemy territory, and our pilot demonstrated there was nothing to fear.[70]

The Soviets "recommended that [the EAF] fly back and forth [across Israel], using Syrian fields." As Malashenko remarks, "they promised to work on it, but were in no hurry to get into practical implementation for fear of IAF retaliation."

If the Israelis were aware of the Soviet pilots' overflights, they kept it very quiet. The IAF acknowledged "numerous incursions over IDF forces in the canal sector and inside Sinai by Egyptian photoreconnaissance planes, which quickly returned to their own territory." Four intruders were shot down by Israeli guns east of the canal. In one exceptionally deep penetration in August 1967, Israel claimed that one of two low-flying Su-7s was downed by anti-aircraft fire over the former Egyptian airbase at Bir Gafgafa in central Sinai. It crashed on the runway; the dead pilot was unidentifiable, but assumed to be Egyptian.[71] The range from Israeli airbases made it impossible to intercept brief incursions if IAF fighters were scrambled only upon the enemy's appearance, and the Mirage IIIs' limited fuel capacity made it impractical to keep them on constant patrol over Sinai. In response, Bir Gafgafa was rebuilt (as Refidim) and a wing of Mirages was stationed there on constant alert from March 1968.[72] By then, as Mossad chief Me'ir Amit described to White House staffers, the Soviet presence "had entered a new phase in which Soviet pilots are flying 'for their own purposes'—orientation to the terrain." He put their number at seventy, one-fourth of the EAF's own pilot complement.[73]

On 14 November 1967, Ambassador Vinogradov relayed to Nasser a proposal to comply with the president's repeated requests for air support by sending twelve naval MiG-21s on a "friendly visit of 5–6 days"—that is, to display the fighters, in full Soviet markings, over Egyptian soil. Flying the MiGs in would require refueling stops in Iraq and Syria, which Nasser agreed would pose no problem. But overflight permission would be needed from Iran, since Turkey had denied such a request in June 1967:

THE SOVIET–ISRAELI WAR, 1967–1973

Nasser actively supported the idea of a visit by a Soviet squadron to the UAR, and expressed his gratitude. ... Together with the entry of Soviet ships ... [this] would have resonance throughout the Arab world. ... but he expressed doubts about Iran, with which the UAR's relations are strained, and under US pressure might refuse ... still, he would try through the Iraqi government to obtain the Shah's consent, under the pretext that the planes were going [only] to Iraq.

As a backup, Nasser proposed reactivating the July airlift's flight path over Yugoslavia. Vinogradov's demurral reflected the Soviets' ulterior motive: exploring an equivalent alternative to crossing Turkish airspace. Besides, as in the airlift, the MiG-21 simply did not have the range to fly from Yugoslavia without refueling. "The route via Yugoslavia has already been used more than once, and so the Iranian route presents a certain interest." Nasser responded that he actually meant a return of the Soviet Tu-16s, "which would create a greater impression."[74] If he did put out feelers toward Iran, they were rebuffed, as the Tu-16 option materialized two weeks later—via Hungary. Somehow, West German experts interpreted the bombers' arrival as a demonstration of Soviet readiness to defend Egypt, "in view of the increasing *tension*" between them.[75]

Meanwhile, the Soviets repeatedly delayed the vote on a Middle East resolution at the UN Security Council, initially by floating their own draft that would demand an immediate Israeli withdrawal to the pre-5 June lines. Failing that, they held out for a statement that would define "territories" (which the intentionally ambiguous British draft required Israel to evacuate) as "*the* territories"—that is, *all* the territories—that were occupied by Israel in June. American efforts were focused on preventing this, which caused uncertainty to the last moment over whether the Soviets would support the resolution.[76] In the vote on 22 November, they did—but never conceded the "all territories" point; it would figure in diplomatic wrangling for years. Most notably, at the Moscow summit of May 1972, US acquiescence in the Soviet interpretation would be extracted as a concession in return for reducing the Soviet military presence in Egypt.

On 1 December 1967, one of two Israeli Vautour IIb jets was shot down while on a reconnaissance mission over the northeastern tip of the Gulf of Suez, where a new Egyptian SAM-2 site was under construction—undoubtedly under Soviet supervision. The Israelis attributed the loss to anti-aircraft gunfire, but a biography of Chief of Staff Riad states that he had decided to test the missile technology provided by the Soviets, and this success led to the subsequent effort to construct a dense SAM array along the canal.[77] The plane crashed into shallow water off the coast. The other Israeli pilot reported sighting a parachute, and *Al-Ahram* reported two.[78] But Israeli rescuers found no trace of the two crewmen on site, except for one of their helmets. During the night, the Israelis noted constant movement of vehicle headlights from the SAM site down to the beach. The Vautour had been jointly developed by France and Israel as a nuclear-capable bomber after the USSR threatened both countries with a missile

THE SOVIET PRESENCE IS FORMALIZED AND EXPANDED

attack during the 1956 Suez–Sinai campaign; a specimen and/or operators would have been prize trophies for the Soviets. No Russian claim has emerged that one or both of these airmen were captured, but since such a claim was made in a later incident, this case also merits further research.[79]

E. Cairo-West becomes a Soviet airbase

Two days later, the active-duty, late-model Soviet Air Force Tu-16s that Nasser had requested landed at Cairo-West. Although this had not been the Soviets' preferred option for an overt air presence, they made the most of it. This time, the ten bombers kept an intentionally high profile—keeping close formation "as in a festive flypast," which was indeed headlined in the West as "Russian H-Bombers over Cairo ... [for the] First Time outside East Bloc."[80] For the formation's leader, the "legendary" Lt-Col. Aleksandr Shmonov, this was by way of a homecoming: in 1962–3, he had led a group of fifteen Soviet pilot-navigator teams stationed at Cairo-West who flew bombing missions in Yemen and Saudi Arabia. In that little-noticed precedent for direct Soviet intervention in a Middle East conflict, "the crews were mostly mixed." Their formation was sometimes commanded by then-Col. Husny Mubarak, a graduate of the Soviet pilots' training center in Ryazan'.[81] A few days before Shmonov's squadron landed, Mubarak had been appointed head of the EAF Academy, and in 1969 he would be promoted to air force chief of staff. Soviet advisers who met him in the coming years noted both his "almost-unaccented" Russian and his friendly attitude, including personal gifts.[82]

This time, journalists were invited to witness the Soviet planes' arrival, including Novosti's Egorin, who recorded that General Riad delivered a welcoming speech. Shmonov—by now an Honored Pilot of the USSR—responded, and "a formation of our soldiers ... accompanied him with cheers of 'hurrah!'" This guard of honor highlighted the changes that since June had effectively transformed Cairo-West into the first of several Egyptian airbases under direct and complete Soviet control—as Nasser had promised. The visiting pilots were still impressed by the partial blackout at night and the runway patched from Israeli bomb damage, with wrecked planes still visible on both sides. But as Egorin noted,

> our transports and other planes took off and landed at will. Not far from the runways stretched military towns with their usual routines of reveille, morning calisthenics and so on down to evening jaunts, when their marching song echoed over the Sahara: "here's the military post box number for you, my dear!"

The Novosti writer also

> happened to visit the area earmarked for our advisers' quarters ... They acted as if at home, and had hung up a banner [in Russian] over the entrance: "Excellence in preparation for combat and in political action is your duty." The internationalist colonels and soldiers were

now Egypt's great hope. After being saluted, they would be fitted with [Egyptian] yellow helmets.[83]

The Soviet news agency TASS, too, trumpeted the "friendly" visit, stressing Riad's "warm welcome." *Krasnaya Zvezda* published a feature that the son of one of the Tu-16 co-pilots recently described as "written in the best Brezhnev tradition: the facts were accurate but it leaves a feeling of something unsaid." His father, then-Lt. Boris Mel'nik, helped him fill in the blanks: "the main mission was to demonstrate the capabilities of [our] aviation hardware ... [but] the flights in Egypt did not always go smoothly." One demonstration was carpet bombing by all ten planes in the desert near Cairo. Hulks of vehicles destroyed by the Israelis in the June air raids were used to mark the target areas, but the pilots had trouble identifying them. "The bombs were dropped [only] 2km from the UAR leaders' observation point, and the shockwaves from 54 250-kg bombs knocked them off their feet. Fortunately there were no casualties."[84] The mishap was not publicized, and it did not prevent EAF chief Shalaby el-Hinnawy from seeing off the guests on 8 December.

Within a few days of the bombers' welcoming ceremony so close to Cairo's international airport, alarmed "diplomatic reports" in the Western press reflected the innovation. "The Soviet Union is escalating its aid to Egypt in return for wider controls and base facilities." The latter (along with Egyptian cotton) were described as part payment for Soviet supplies of arms, food and an oil refinery to replace the facility just destroyed at Suez City:

> Moscow now is pushing all out for the penetration of Egypt ... Egypt has denied that she is granting "bases" to anyone. But no matter how these facilities are labeled, they amount to the same. ... The Soviet Union was said to have reserved the right to control the use of the new equipment. The Soviets retain a finger on the trigger, presumably to avert the danger of being involved against their will in any confrontation with the United States.[85]

By January 1968, IAF Commander Hod stated to USAF officers "in a free-wheeling ... candid and cordial manner" that "Russian pilots are flying, and working with Russian controllers."[86] This assessment not only contradicted public statements but was not endorsed by most levels of Israeli officialdom. Nitzan Hadas, the Israeli diplomat in Bonn who had been relaying the Germans' moderately pessimistic estimates about *potential* Soviet bases, was admonished by his regional desk officer in Jerusalem: "Nasser will not be enthusiastic to change his status as a nonaligned statesman, and will see no advantage to be in the Soviets' pocket ... the Soviets' achievements ... are being overestimated in the West."

The Israeli official emphasized that "declared Soviet policy is against bases in foreign countries. So far we have not heard of any change."[87] Soviet theoreticians, however, singled out the Middle East and Egypt in particular as an exception:

> obtaining bases on foreign soil—no matter how they are called, no matter under which flag—was fundamentally opposed to Soviet policy principles in the region ... [because] the

THE SOVIET PRESENCE IS FORMALIZED AND EXPANDED

Arabs aspired to eliminate British and American bases. ... [But] here the issue presented itself to establish Soviet military bases for "defense against Zionist expansion and imperialist intrigues."[88]

The Soviets were indeed encountering problems, but from other quarters. Attending a conference of Socialist Bloc foreign ministers in Warsaw on 19–21 December 1967, Semenov "did not sleep all night" after "difficulties" (caused expectedly by the Romanians and unexpectedly by the Yugoslavs) created "a critically severe situation ... A wedge might have been driven into the Warsaw Pact." Semenov was relieved when the Romanians finally relented and made a "businesslike result" possible. A Bulgarian report from the meeting shows that this clash was over the Middle East. Reporting that in addition to the massive replacement of weapons "a big group of Soviet military advisers were also sent to the UAR," the Soviets cautiously stressed that "the purpose of all the military assistance was to strengthen the *defense* capabilities of the Egyptian army." Still, they had to make a major concession by omitting a reference to "Israeli aggression" from the joint communiqué.[89]

PART 2

OPERATION *KAVKAZ*

4

FRAMING THE CROSS-CANAL GOAL AND THE ATTRITION STRATEGY

A. Plans and training for "crossing a water obstacle"

Traveling in January 1968 to Egypt, where he was impressed by chief Soviet military adviser Petr Lashchenko as "a profound and wise strategist," Semenov found "our advisers trying to restore fighting spirit in the [Egyptian] Army"—and this was no longer limited to defense.[1] On the eve of Sokolov's arrival in October, Nasser had reiterated to Ambassador Vinogradov that Egypt sought a peaceful resolution but would build "a strong offensive army capable of ousting the occupiers."[2] On 25 November—three days after the Security Council resolution on terms for a peace settlement—Nasser met with his military command and called for a five-year period of concentrated war preparations. Riad followed up with instructions to draw up training plans for "an attack across the Suez Canal and securing a bridgehead on its east bank."[3]

Despite the Soviets' declared commitment to Resolution 242, the advisers were soon put to work on preparing such an offensive. The makeup of the advisers' team was remarkably suited to the task: as Brezhnev had pointed out, "we have selected experienced people, who have gone through the last war."[4] The generals and senior colonels were almost all veterans of the East European theater in the Second World War, where the Red Army had to cross countless waterways. Lashchenko himself had been made an HSU in 1943 for "skillful command and personal valor" while leading a rifle division across four rivers.[5] Even though the first contingent of advisers was later replaced by younger officers, Israeli analysts would note after the Yom Kippur War that the Egyptian canal-crossing operation resembled Soviet practice in the 1940s more than the revised doctrine that had been introduced in the 1960s.[6]

The Egyptians' theoretical fervor for reversing the June defeat could be harnessed to overcome their endemic resistance to practical change and effort. "Many Egyptian officers," Maj.-Gen. Malashenko recalls,

> said that Sinai must be liberated, but they were not getting ready for it and did not even think about crossing the canal. It was recommended to begin training, assemble all crossing

equipment available, repair it since most items were defective, and improvise [the rest] with readily accessible means. ... Bridge and ferry assembly was rehearsed.

Lashchenko employed another argument to enable preparation of the main offensive ground force. While developing the defense plan for the Suez Canal, despite both Egyptian and Soviet fears that a renewed IDF offensive was imminent, Lashchenko cogently pointed out that it could not be mounted without warning as the Israelis had but a sparse presence on the east bank. In November 1967, he still estimated that the IDF kept an "insignificant" force of three to four infantry brigades on the front line, facing five Egyptian divisions. There were two more Israeli brigades, one of them armored, farther back behind the strategic mountain passes in Sinai, but "he argued that the main Israeli force was 200 miles away, and would take 24 hours to approach." Anyway, as Lashchenko reckoned (this time mistakenly), the main IDF assault force would be airborne, and so would bypass the Egyptians' forward defenses. He therefore suggested pulling two of the Egyptian divisions, in rotation, back from their static and indolent front line positions for intensive training in the rear.[7]

It took some time to move the Egyptians from rhetoric to practice. In mid-January 1968, Karpov wrote, "Lashchenko came in the morning with the II Army Corps commander, General [Ahmed] Ismail ... he conversed with the division commander about crossing the canal, digging in on the bridgehead ... etc."

Then the advisers took part in a staff seminar on "an offensive operation to include crossing of the Suez Canal." The discussion went on till 3:00 a.m. "It was stormy ... [General Abdel Halim] Abu Ghazala raised the question of fire cover for the crossing. His speech was followed by much argument, until the floor was taken by the senior adviser of the 2nd Division," Col. Afanas'ev.

Afanas'ev's authority on overcoming water obstacles could hardly be questioned: his citation as HSU was for leading, as a lieutenant in 1943, a company across the Dnieper under heavy enemy fire "with the means at his disposal" (makeshift rafts and requisitioned boats). His force secured a beachhead, held it against two enemy counterattacks, and thus ensured a successful crossing for the entire division. When ammunition ran out, they fought off a third attack with bayonets and bare hands. Afanas'ev personally killed nineteen "Fritzies" and was one of seven Soviet soldiers who survived out of over 120. Now, in Egypt, he coolly "answered questions and calmed everyone down."[8]

B. The need for more advisers despite a shortage of Soviet officers

Lashchenko was concerned that the agreed number and assignments of Soviet advisers would not suffice to bring Egyptian servicemen up to the standards that Afanas'ev personified. In the same meeting in January 1968, he asked the advisers' opinion about sending in more of their colleagues, to be attached permanently to individual battalions instead of visiting them periodically from brigade headquarters. "The

FRAMING THE CROSS-CANAL GOAL

Arabs," he confided, "are asking for it. On one hand it is tempting to have so many advisers. On the other hand, our advisers' blood will be shed"—indicating his expectation that hostilities would resume during their tenure.

Karpov—who was already breaking field-security instructions by keeping a diary—went further by entering his own irreverent reflections. Considering the prospect of battalion-level advisers, he had identified two chronic problems: communicating with the Egyptians, and the gap between the old guard of war-seasoned Soviet officers and the younger ones who would occupy the lowest echelon:

> From the [Soviet] state's viewpoint it's a luxury. What good would it do for them to come? Even now we don't have enough interpreters, and without them the advisers cannot do anything. Besides, I'm sure that those to be sent would not be genuine commanders, so we'd have an extra burden to teach *them*.

Few younger Soviet officers could match the authority of, for instance, Lt-Col. Yury Azovkin, the adviser to the II Army Corps' artillery brigade: he was made an HSU in 1945 for repelling repeated attacks on his surrounded detachment in Poland, personally killing thirty Germans.⁹ "Now," Karpov wrote, "at least the brigade commanders' advisers do work directly with the battalions, but when the [additional] advisers come they will not." A year later, however, he noted that such advisers did arrive. Malashenko puts this "in the summer of 1968" and specifies a group of 400 that included advisers at battalion as well as SAM (surface-to-air missile) *divizyon* and air squadron level, with more arriving later.

By early February 1968, from a "Soviet official," the CIA picked up

> the first information received [sanitized] regarding Soviet plans to participate in a limited Arab offensive against Israel ... Whereas previously Soviet advisors [sanitized] stayed in the background and played a limited role in shaping and organizing Arab armies, they are now actively engaged in reorganizing Arab forces and engaging in some command functions.

This corroborated reports from Beirut during the previous weeks whereby "when the fighting is resumed, the Soviets will actively aid the Arabs ... Soviet advisors would direct a limited attack against Israel." The Soviets were emboldened since "the [USS] Pueblo incident dramatically indicated that the United States ... will avoid a commitment of its forces ... The Soviets believe that the United States will not intervene on Israel's behalf unless the pre-June 1967 borders are crossed."

The CIA's sources, therefore, stressed that a Soviet-supported Egyptian offensive would be of limited scope—to drive the Israeli forces back "three or four miles" from the canal. It would be meant only to improve Egypt's bargaining position in respect of Sinai rather than to destroy Israel itself (in which the Soviets "would not acquiesce"). And it would be undertaken only if diplomatic efforts—the already forlorn mission of UN emissary Gunnar Jarring under Resolution 242—failed. Actually, the Soviets set little store by the Jarring mission, which he undertook while serving as

THE SOVIET–ISRAELI WAR, 1967–1973

Swedish ambassador in Moscow, and did little if anything to enable its success.[10] The CIA more realistically estimated that the *Egyptians'* "extreme pessimism" on this count led to determination on their part to launch the attack soon, with differences between Nasser and Defense Minister Muhammad Fawzy only about the date—the emotionally charged anniversary of 5 June or as early as "late March or early April."[11]

The Egyptians kept pressing to prepare a canal crossing sooner rather than later. In early March 1968, Riad invited Malashenko to attend a secret exercise of an infantry brigade and ranger detachment commanded by General Saad-el-Din Shazly, then chief of paratroops and special forces, which included a parachute and helicopter drop. Nasser was present and asked Malashenko: "Is it very complicated to ford the Suez Canal? Can Egyptian forces do it?" The Soviet officer gave the good news first: "a crossing is very complicated, but with meticulous preparation, artillery and air cover and a reliable defense against air attack, Egyptian forces will be able to do it. However, they lack combat experience as well as the requisite morale and fighting qualities."

Malashenko reported this exchange to Lashchenko, who met Nasser to discuss the issue. "After this, recommendations were formulated to prepare forces for attack across a water obstacle. This formed the basis for training at various levels," and Malashenko maintains that "combat operations of the UAR [Egyptian] armed forces in 1973 began roughly according to this plan."

Testifying before the Agranat Commission in December 1973, the head of research at Israeli Military Intelligence (MI) admitted that as late as 14 August 1968, an MI report still held "that the Egyptians had not at that time begun to tackle the problem" of a canal crossing. But he took credit for this paper's accurate prediction of the eventual attack's form.[12]

C. Soviet naval presence: shielding Port Said and the Dakar sinking

The destroyer crewman Kharchikov was again posted to Port Said on his second Mediterranean tour in January 1968:

> To our left was the pedestal of the monument to [Mr] Suez, the principal builder of the canal [*sic*], next to it the burnt-out US consulate, then the Palace Hotel casino, which was still operating night and day ... Port Fuad was in full view. Just beyond Fuad, 7km from our anchorage, [were] the Israeli positions, [where dug-in T-54 tanks taken from Egypt in the war] occasionally fired at the Arabs. The Soviet ships took no part in these skirmishes. Their task [was] to begin combat operations in case of a Jewish landing on the western bank of the Suez Canal, and to destroy it. The enemy knew... what they would risk, and therefore they did not venture into Port Said or even Port Fuad.

The Soviets took strict precautions, which indicates that they did not impute offensive intentions to the Israelis for propaganda purposes alone: "from sunrise to sunset, every 15 minutes, each military vessel would drop grenades to prevent underwater sabotage. The explosion of such a grenade could split a frogman's eardrums at 200 meters." Kharchikov's memoir also alludes cryptically to a major naval incident the same month: "... during this tour of duty, northeast of Crete ... the *eskadra* conducted training exercises with depth charges. In this region, an Israeli submarine that became too curious vanished without a trace ..." This passage begins and ends with ellipses, clearly hinting that all is not being said.[13]

The time and—as is now known—the location match the disappearance of the Israeli submarine *Dakar* while on its maiden voyage to Haifa after being bought and refitted in Britain. For years, searches focused north of the Egyptian coast (because the submarine's emergency buoy had washed ashore near Gaza). Only at the end of May 1999 was the *Dakar*'s wreckage indeed found on the seabed south of the midway point between Crete and Cyprus. Its conning tower was sheared off and lay 200 meters away from the rest. This suggested that the submarine, rather than being sunk by a depth charge or torpedo, may have collided with (or was rammed by) another vessel as it moved submerged at "snorkel depth" of less than 50 feet. The Israeli Navy has stated, however, that no evidence was found on the wreckage, including the part of the tower that was raised, to prove either a hostile attack or an accidental collision. To date, no definitive account has been offered. An unspecified "sudden event" remains the Israel Navy's preferred version, with one possibility being loss of control during an emergency dive to *avoid* a collision, after sighting a surface ship at very close range on a stormy night.[14]

Could this ship have been Soviet? The *Dakar*'s remains were located before Kharchikov's memoir was published, and he may have made the connection after reading about it—but his was not the only such veiled reference to some Soviet connection. Among others, just *before* the wreck's discovery was announced the present authors were offered, for sale, the logbook of a Soviet ship that was supposedly involved. Specifically, the source referred to the *Kashin*-class BPK (large anti-submarine ship) *Soobrazitel'nyy*, which was indeed spotted in the Mediterranean at the time and mentioned in the Egyptian press.[15] The deal did not go through, and we published nothing about the *Dakar*'s fate, but shortly afterward a Russian diplomat in Tel Aviv who was evidently aware of our confidential contacts startled us with an unsolicited statement that "we did *not* sink the submarine."

A first factual clue of hostile involvement in the *Dakar* sinking emerged in March 2013, when the Israel State Archive declassified a batch of documents (which again indicated that not all information on the incident has been released). It included the transcript of a cabinet meeting on 28 January 1968, in which Navy chief Shlomo Erell reported about the search effort: twelve hours after it began, a signal was received starting with the *Dakar*'s identification mark. The routine Q&A's were exchanged in the international maritime code, but contact was broken off at the point when they were supposed to switch to the Israeli code (and presumably to Hebrew). The Israelis' suspicions grew when the same pattern was repeated some twenty-seven hours later.

By then, the *Dakar* should certainly have been aware that its silence had raised the alarm, and would begin with a reassurance. The messages were not recorded nor their point of origin triangulated, but a veteran Israeli Navy signalman who monitored one of them opined that its rhythm differed from the *Dakar* radioman's usual speed. Anyone versed in naval signals could have done it, said Erell. Tracking the submarine according to its own signals and duplicating them would have been simple, "and I suspected that someone else was calling us instead of *Dakar* ... perhaps in order to delay the search, [or] mislead [us]."[16]

Egyptian officers, up to Fawzy, have claimed that *their* navy sank the *Dakar*, but taking credit for Soviet achievements was routine practice, and the location where the submarine was ultimately discovered was far afield for the Egyptians at the time.[17] Indeed, Erell ruled out Egyptian action, as "they have not put out to sea" from Alexandria. Elimination of all other candidates leaves only the Soviets as suspects for originating the mysterious signals. What for? Could this have been a ploy to let the *Soobrazitel'nyy* or other Soviet craft put distance between them and the *Dakar*'s course? The Israeli Navy, Erell reported, shared its suspicions with US colleagues and asked whether *they* had picked up any extraordinary radio traffic. No reply was received, "and I don't suppose that they will tell us whether they have such a suspicion, or if they know anything. It would be very unpleasant for them to admit that they knew someone had attacked an Israeli submarine, without saying what they were going to do about it."

Replying to explicit questions about a Soviet input, Erell stated there were several Soviet ships in the general area but the Israelis did not have their specific locations. However, according to other Israeli accounts, during the submarine's voyage Israeli naval units were constantly updated about Soviet movements in the Mediterranean, including a *Kashin*-class BPK that was "between [the Syrian port of] Latakiya and Cyprus" three days before the submarine went missing.[18] Erell allowed there was "a possibility that another submarine or a Soviet warship torpedoed" the *Dakar*. There was also "some possibility that it unintentionally encountered Soviet forces, and the Soviets may have feared that it was attacking them. [But] those are merely speculations."[19] A few days later, Defense Minister Moshe Dayan went as far as stating "it cannot be ruled out that an Egyptian or 'Russian' ship damaged [the *Dakar*] and captured its crew"—a statement criticized by his colleagues as raising false hopes for the crew's survival.[20]

The recorded efforts of the Soviet Navy to track five new Israeli missile boats on their way from Cherbourg two years later—with a view to intercepting them—confirm that the Fifth *Eskadra* might have been tasked with shadowing and even engaging the *Dakar*. The Soviet Navy's "radio-technic" capability, as already reported in the *Eilat* incident, would definitely have sufficed for the deceptive signals. Remarkably, it may have been assisted in this by the Israelis themselves. As Dayan informed a Knesset committee, after the *Dakar* first missed its scheduled signal, "we applied to the Russians," via intermediaries. "The Russians asked for various particulars, we gave them these particulars, and we never heard from them again."²¹ The newly disclosed false signals thus strongly buttress the still-inconclusive evidence of some Soviet role in the loss of the submarine with all its sixty-nine hands.

D. Grechko inaugurates operations against the US Sixth Fleet ...

On 30 March 1968, Soviet Defense Minister Grechko arrived in Egypt with no prior announcement. When he left Moscow ten days earlier, he was said to be headed only for Baghdad and Damascus. Even more unusually, the arrival of Foreign Minister Andrey Gromyko in Cairo on the same plane was never disclosed at all. It came to light only in the veterans' memoirs: Malashenko described sitting opposite Gromyko at a banquet that Nasser held for the two Soviet ministers. He also listed Vinogradov among the guests; the ambassador was officially in Moscow for a month of consultations.²²

Several *Eskadra* ships including two cruisers joined the eight already berthed at Alexandria for a special review in Grechko's honor.²³ His arrival, then, was not merely a last-minute whim to visit his daughter Tatiana, who was married to A.I. Kirichenko, a first secretary at the embassy in Cairo.²⁴ The marshal, however, cancelled the "entertainment" at Alexandria in favor of a "business" tour of the front-line naval units at Port Said. The Soviet servicemen there were still at such close quarters with the Israelis that he warned them not to be taken prisoner.²⁵ But Malashenko, with an army officer's typical contempt for his sea and air counterparts, wrote that the Egyptian naval commander and his Soviet adviser Sutyagin "were unable to give a clear description of the navy's mission in supporting defense."

Western reports put the focus of Grechko's visit on the Soviet pilot-instructors, the "spearhead of the Soviet aid mission," who were now "flying alongside" the Egyptians but "<u>with great caution not to get involved</u>, after one or more of their pilots were shot down in Yemen." The Soviet–Egyptian bombing campaign in this much less obtrusive Middle Eastern corner of the Cold War had provided a precedent for Soviet regulars' presence on the ground there too: the Foxbat missions over Israel in May 1967 <u>originated in a Soviet-built and Soviet-maintained airbase in Yemen</u>.²⁶ The number of Soviet pilots in Egypt was now given at "several dozen," which "would not have much consequence in case of a clash with the IAF"—a prognosis that would soon be disproved.²⁷ Malashenko confirms that one of the Egyptian demands that Grechko accepted called for 100 more aircraft, in recognition that air superiority would be essential for any offensive. "Fawzy said that for an effective counterstrike at the IAF, the UAR needs up to 300 volunteer aces from Socialist countries. Lashchenko replied that he doubted the Socialist countries would comply." Grechko too deemed that the dispatch of such "volunteer pilots was unreasonable." But Malashenko noted that a new contingent of Soviet advisers, who arrived that summer "at the request of the Egyptian command and according to the signed agreement," did include airmen.

According to then-Lt. Leonid Zakharov, a naval-aviation navigator, it was also in March 1968—probably on the same occasion as the Grechko–Gromyko visit—that another agreement was signed to formalize the "temporary" deployment of Soviet reconnaissance aircraft in Egypt, for operations over the Mediterranean "in the common interest." The Tu-16Rs were prepared at the Severomorsk-1 base in the arctic Kola Peninsula and flown to Cairo-West via Crimea, repeating the airlift's flight path. "Their range enabled direct flight, but this was rare. Usually they refueled in Hungary ... Yugoslavia, which was ostensibly a socialist country, unlike Hungary did not allow our planes to land in its air bases ... it was fortunate that Yugoslavia even let us use its airspace."[28] Yury Gorbunov, an English-language specialist who had already done a tour of duty in Egypt from 1962 through 1965, was summoned urgently to Severomorsk in March 1968, issued a three-page glossary for conversations with air traffic controllers and flown to Cairo-West, where hulks of MiG fighters destroyed by "the Israeli pirates" were still visible. He claims that the US Sixth Fleet did not detect the Badgers' presence until their first appearance in low-altitude passes over its ships. This corresponds with a CIA report that mentioned only on 16 May that "there have been recent instances of surveillance of a Sixth Fleet carrier by Tu-16 aircraft with UAR markings."[29] But afterward, Gorbunov credits the Americans for sending up carrier aircraft to fly under the Tu-16s in order to prevent them from descending too low.

Boris Kudaev, a GRU English linguist who was attached to the Tu-16R crews to interpret US signals, is one of the former servicemen who turned to "fiction" in the Putin years. However, his "novel," *A Bullet Needs No Interpreter*, agrees precisely with Gorbunov's memoir in describing the squadron's *modus operandi*: two crews flying pairs of aircraft for six-hour missions in three-day rotation, ranging from Sicily to the Arab Sea. If locating the US carrier groups required extension of the flight westward beyond their range, they would refuel at Tököl. They "sometimes buzzed the USS *Independence* so low we could see the bolts on the deck." Gorbunov specifies that the photos and reports were submitted both to the "Ofis" and directly to naval headquarters in Moscow. Kudaev adds that "for the Egyptians' benefit," on their way to and from assignments the Tu-16Rs would fly along the Israeli coast to pinpoint military radar stations, concealing their own radar signature in the morning rush of civilian airliners.[30] This was a continuation and expansion of existing activity: in late February, Mossad chief Meir Amit had already described Soviet advisers with the Egyptian Navy and Air Force as "mapping Israeli [naval] activities by means of electronic intelligence ... trying to get a fix on Israeli radar and ... participating with the Egyptians in the establishment of electronic countermeasures."[31]

The Badgers, attended by "small signals and logistics detachments," were followed by two An-12RR radio-intelligence aircraft, Il-38 anti-submarine warfare planes, and "in

FRAMING THE CROSS-CANAL GOAL

the second half of 1968," three Be-12 anti-submarine flying boats from the Black Sea Fleet.[32] The latter were soon moved to Mersa Matruh and assigned to "special missions for perfecting methods to detect US submarines."[33] L. Zakharov states that "the aircraft appeared in full Egyptian air force markings ... but were staffed and operated by Soviet Naval Aviation." By November, the Sixth Fleet's aviation chief listed the Egyptian-based Soviet aircraft, along with the *Eskadra*'s increased presence, as causing "certain concern" to NATO—specifically as a threat to its Polaris submarines.[34]

US sources specified that nine Tu-16Rs manned by Soviet Navy pilots and based at Cairo-West took part (with other Soviet aircraft and nine warships) in unprecedentedly close surveillance of NATO naval maneuvers in late September. Although NATO commanders claimed a benefit from the Soviet presence—enhanced verisimilitude for the US war games—they were concerned that the Mediterranean could no longer be classified as "secure" and that in the event of war in Europe large forces would have to be allocated "to protect this soft underbelly." Cairo-West—as was now belatedly recognized—had become "the Soviet Union's first permanent airbase in the Middle East. ... The Soviets have already accomplished what they had desired for generations."[35] French reports added that Soviet Tu-16Rs operating out of Algerian fields, where runways had been extended by Soviet personnel, also bore Egyptian marks; they were presumably Cairo-based planes refueling for missions over the Western Mediterranean. Another Soviet air activity in Algeria was to transport Algerian troops to Egypt, where they held a small part of the canal line.[36]

The US sources also alluded intriguingly to a "possibility that the Soviets might soon reinforce the ... squadron now based at Cairo-West with ... a number of excellent high-altitude reconnaissance aircraft that just entered service a short time ago."[37] The Americans had cause for concern: Iran, which had just received its first F-4s, tried unsuccessfully to use them for intercepting such Soviet planes that were overflying its territory.[38] This is the first contemporary reference, in an Arab–Israeli context, to the craft later known as the MiG-25 or Foxbat, which had first been shown to Western observers at a Moscow air show in July 1967. Four of these planes would indeed be stationed at Cairo-West—but only in 1971. It can only be speculated whether this early suggestion reflects at least retrospective awareness of the Foxbat's use over Israel in May 1967.

Meanwhile, the Soviet pilot-advisers in Egypt suffered their first recorded casualty: Aleksandr Voinov, who from November 1967 had been attached to an EAF "combat preparation battalion" at Beni Suef airbase south of Cairo. His daughter Elena recalled decades later: "we were with him in Cairo; everything was kept secret. Father was sent ... to Egypt as an 'agricultural worker.'" They were lodged in

> an enormous hotel with servants almost at every door. Father would come 'home' once every two weeks for the weekend. ... While taking part in the May Day celebrations, a few days before Father fell, my mother overheard a talk between him and his commander. It appears that not all of our planes were equipped with parachutes.

THE SOVIET–ISRAELI WAR, 1967–1973

After learning about Grechko's order not to be taken prisoner, Elena suspects this was intentional.

> I remember how our neighbor, an artillery man ... mentioned in passing that they had seen a plane of ours burning in the sky. Mama said right away "oy, that is Sasha." ... I remember how we were sent back with the coffin in the top commander's plane, the farewell at the officers' club.[39]

Unexplained accidents would also plague the Soviet airmen after regular squadrons were posted to Egypt: in the summer of 1971, a two-seat MiG-21U trainer crashed into Lake Qarun "five seconds after reporting they were on their way back" to nearby Qawm Ushim airbase.[40]

E. ... and endorses planning for a cross-canal offensive

During his tour in March 1968, Grechko was as usual reported to have counselled at all three Arab capitals not to undertake any offensive against Israel—*for the time being*. One reason "foreign diplomats in Paris" suggested for this was that "the problems now preoccupying the USSR in Czechoslovakia and Poland, which also have a military aspect, reduce the Soviets' ability to intervene forcefully ... in case of a Middle East conflict"—a linkage that would be partly borne out within a few months.

However, Malashenko holds that the minister's advice to delay any offensive ambitions stemmed primarily from his dissatisfaction at the state of Egyptian troops. Inspecting defenses on the canal bank on his way to Port Said, the marshal commented that it "should be easier to cross than the Dnieper was during [Soviet army] exercises the previous autumn"—but the Egyptians were clearly not up to it. "As usual, in some of the trenches soldiers were preparing their own food. Grechko inquired about their rations, which consisted of pita bread and onions." Visiting a brigade on the "third line" of defense west of Ismailia, he asked for a demonstration of a counterattack against an Israeli breakthrough. Malashenko witnessed how "after some delay, three tanks moved forward, followed by several infantry detachments of 20–30 men. The marshal said that such action should follow the order much more promptly."

Still, in order to address this weakness, Grechko endorsed Lashchenko's project to pull back front-line formations for intensive training, which was already being implemented. Karpov's 118th Infantry Brigade had been withdrawn to Qassasin, west of Ismailia on the Sweet Water Canal from the Nile, to drill an attack across a water obstacle. When Grechko himself recognized him, Karpov could remind the marshal that they had met before "while training on the Danube in Hungary. ... The army corps chief of staff attended [the exercise]." Later, the division chief of staff's adviser, Afanas'ev, returned from a council of senior advisers with the Soviet defense minister in Cairo and reported to his colleagues: "Grechko confirmed that if the attack should begin, we must be with the Egyptians and help them." To Karpov, this seemed easier said than done: "there are not enough interpreters, we know no Arabic, they [the Egyptians] will not carry out our orders, and whatever orders they give on their own we won't understand. We don't have [personal] weapons, either."[41]

Returning to Moscow, the two Soviet ministers recommended compliance with most of the Egyptians' material requests, including hardware for two new divisions, and intensification of the USSR's commitment to bring operational standards up to the level required for an offensive. "In the summer of 1968, a large group of advisers to battalion and *divizyon* commanders—some 400" arrived in Egypt, with more yet to follow.

Two weeks after Grechko inspected Karpov's outfit, it was the turn of Serkov's *podsovetnye* (advisees) from the 2nd Brigade to use the Sweet Water Canal as a training platform. After live-fire exercises of individual companies (which Serkov oversaw, demonstrating that the advisers were indeed operating down to this level), the Egyptians went on to maneuvers of an entire battalion to demonstrate an "attack in direct contact with the enemy, [after] crossing a water obstacle." Serkov marked this as "significant progress," even though "unfortunately, due to conditions in the field, the crossing has to be practiced separately." Within a year, this would be remedied by constructing a full-scale model of the Suez Canal in the Egyptian hinterland.

By the autumn of 1968, Lashchenko had already gone beyond training exercises to initiating actual small-scale raids across the canal to rehearse securing a bridgehead on the east bank. "This would," Malashenko wrote, "harden the troops, reassure them of success in the future operation, and weaken the enemy." Such raids, also aimed at taking prisoners and updating intelligence, would become a staple of the impending War of Attrition. If the Soviets had any reservations about an ultimate offensive across the canal, it was not relayed to their personnel on the ground. At Cairo-West on 9 May 1968, Gorbunov was among the Soviet officers who celebrated "Victory Day" (over Nazi Germany) with Egyptian counterparts. "We toasted the victory over Israel. The Egyptians drank to our meeting in Tel Aviv next year," and the Soviets made no objection even though this went far beyond Moscow's stated policy.[42]

F. Attrition adopted as a precursor to all-out offensive

So far as we have been able to establish, the term "war of attrition" was first applied to the Egyptian–Israeli conflict in a report from Moscow. A few days into the Ras el-Ish engagement in July 1967, the London *Spectator*'s Murarka predicted from Moscow that "the fresh flare-up in the Suez Canal zone is a pointer to what may now be going on. ... A phrase which has constantly occurred in Soviet public pronouncements refers to the need 'to liquidate the consequences of Israeli aggression.'"

> The Arabs as well as the Russians will now be thinking of fresh ways of bringing pressure on Israel. ... We could be in for a long war of attrition. The Russians would not be happy about such a situation, involving the risk of a greater confrontation; but it is difficult to see how they can either object to it or fail to support the Arabs.

63

This presaged what would become the stock Soviet line whereby Moscow preferred a political solution, but if it was not forthcoming would reluctantly support a war of attrition.⁴³

The War of Attrition is usually dated as beginning on 9 March 1969. However, several earlier dates have been proposed—some of them by parties closely involved, such as then-Vice President Anwar Sadat. This suggests a phased development coordinated with Moscow and with its advisers on the ground over the summer of 1968.

By the anniversary of the Six-Day War on 5 June, Malashenko's general estimate of the Soviet resupply effort as well as the advisers' work was that the Egyptian Army had been restored to combat form—quantitatively. Still,

> analysis of incidents indicates that despite the Egyptians' superiority, they cannot inflict significant casualties, and permit [Israeli] fire at cities and forces with impunity. Egyptian artillery takes too long to fire, and [hits] open areas rather than targets identified by intelligence. Division and brigade commanders do not direct the fire, and cannot see the targets beyond the rampart [on the Israeli-held bank]. The Israelis shoot more efficiently, make better use of mobile weapons, and change positions frequently.

Nonetheless, or indeed because of these Egyptian military shortcomings, Bar-Siman-Tov's perceptive study concluded as early as 1980 that "the Soviet leadership framed its decision for [military] intervention as a matter of principle even before the War of Attrition" and "the Kremlin gave Nasser this understanding" when he visited Moscow in July 1968.⁴⁴ To set the scene for this development, two digressions are now in order.

First, the "intelligence on Israeli targets" that Malashenko mentioned (and about Israel in general) was no longer as easy to come by as it had been a year before. The diplomatic rupture with Israel in June 1967 faced the Soviets with urgent damage control, as the "legal" *rezidenturas* in the embassies of the USSR and its satellites were obliterated at a stroke, which disrupted communication with their "illegals" as well. Some stopgap was provided by the "Red" Russian Orthodox Church mission; a series of incidents before the June war had already shown up much of its personnel as KGB operatives.⁴⁵ Within a year, Israel's security services warned: "the mission is increasingly becoming a substitute for the diplomatic representation at least in regard of observation assignments, and is using both overt and clandestine means for this purpose."⁴⁶

The urgent need to augment this capability demanded posting new undercover agents, and this was begun forthwith by short-term missions of such senior operatives as Mikhail and Elizaveta Mukasei.⁴⁷ However, rebuilding a full and permanent "illegal" infrastructure required some compromises with the increasingly harsh domestic repercussions of the clash with Israel. In June 1968, exactly one year after the Central Committee approved their own recommendation to halt emigration to Israel, Andropov and Gromyko requested and secured a resolution to "resume the emigration ... in a number limited to 1,500 persons this year." While one rationale given for this was to counteract Western accusations of anti-Semitism, the move was explicitly aimed at enabling the KGB "to continue the use of this channel for operative purposes"—that is, planting agents.[48]

Little is known about the flip side of this issue, namely Israeli espionage, if any, in the USSR. It too was undoubtedly hobbled by the closure of the Israeli embassy in 1967.[49] The repeated Israeli failures to predict Soviet actions do not bespeak an effective presence, but these failures were shared by US intelligence, which did have it. The fact that no Israeli agents or informants were exposed during this period could have stemmed either from their success or their absence. An extraordinary disclosure in an official IDF history, from still-classified MI documents dated 6 October 1973, refers to "a source in the Soviet Union" that transmitted "a report from Soviet sources." This appears to call for further inquiry—but the quoted content turned out to be false (that Syria had banished its Soviet experts on the eve of the Yom Kippur War).[50]

5

THE NUCLEAR NON-ISSUE

The other matter that calls for examination is the reduced impact of the nuclear factor on Soviet–Egyptian considerations, at this juncture and throughout the 1967–73 period. Nasser arrived in Moscow on 4 July 1968, three days after Egypt was among the thirty-six nations that signed the Non-Proliferation Treaty (NPT) there. Given the centrality of Israel's impending nuclear power for Egyptian and Soviet motivation to instigate the war a year earlier, the near-absence during Nasser's ten-day stay of any blast against Israel for *not* signing the NPT marked a noteworthy change—especially since this had just been a major issue between Israel and the United States.

The two superpowers had jointly tabled the treaty on 18 January. After a lot of informal US wrangling with Israel, US Secretary of State Dean Rusk relayed an appeal to sign the treaty from President Johnson to Israeli Foreign Minister Abba Eban on 28 April. Anticipating Israeli evasion, he promised "we will press every opportunity to achieve satisfactory limitation of [conventional arms] shipments from the Soviet Union. I can also repeat what the President said in January about our determination to keep Israel's needs [i.e. the Phantom fighter planes] under active and sympathetic review."[1] The Israelis stalled until 6 June, when Yitzhak Rabin (newly appointed ambassador in Washington) responded that "Israel believed it would be a mistake in present situation to make clear to Arabs that they faced no Israeli nuclear threat. ... Problem was therefore a psychological one rather than question of whether or not Israel should have nuclear weapons."[2] Israel did vote for a UN General Assembly resolution "commending" the NPT, but its formal reply—handed by Eban to the US Embassy the day *after* the treaty was signed—amounted to a diplomatic "maybe" that means "no." Eban directly blamed Moscow for Israel's recalcitrance: "the U.S.S.R.—one of the proposers of the non-proliferation treaty ... is supplying them [the Arabs], at nominal cost, with massive quantities of the most modern military equipment ... and has in the past threatened us with missile attack."[3]

The "threat" refers to then-Premier Nikolay Bulganin's letter to then-Prime Minister David Ben-Gurion in November 1956, which precipitated Israel's withdrawal from Sinai. The fact that Eban invoked no contemporary Soviet nuclear menace indicates that the Israelis were not aware of—or preferred not to acknowledge—the continuing assignment, from at least several months before the Six-Day War, of Israeli targets for Soviet nuclear-missile submarines in the Mediterranean, with orders to fire if Israel tried to use any WMD. Kosygin, visiting Egypt in May 1966, confirmed a pledge to this effect that was evidently given there by Defense Minister Grechko the previous December. The Soviets promised this guarantee in order to deflect Egyptian demands for nuclear weapons, after reports—including one from an authoritative Israeli source—indicated that Israel was resolved to acquire them, and was approaching this target.[4] The Soviets' apprehension that a nuclear-armed Israel might both weaken Moscow's ability to repeat the successful 1956 exercise in favor of Arab clients *and* endanger the southern USSR led to the Soviet initiative that sparked the Six-Day War, in a botched attempt to halt the Israeli project—the preemptive war that Nasser had repeatedly threatened since 1960.

According to most retrospective sources, including the leaders of the Israeli nuclear project, it did cross the weapons threshold on the very eve of the 1967 war. But the first CIA estimate that acknowledged Israel had produced at least four bombs was filed only in February 1968 and was based on a volunteered personal account from a visitor to Israel, rather than on the agency's own intelligence.[5] It was suppressed by order of the president, and a State Department study composed three months later still treated an Israeli "nuclear decision" only as a potentiality.[6]

If the Soviets had better data, they did not make much of it. As early as November 1968, the Russian-born Canadian UN delegate George Ignatieff stressed to an Israeli colleague that the Soviet Union was eager to reach a nuclear arms control agreement with the United States, without so much as mentioning an Israeli angle. He pointed to the Soviets' main motive being the "USSR's mortal fear of a renewed German menace" as the spearhead of a West European nuclear power.[7] When, in US–USSR talks to finalize the NPT, problematic countries were discussed one by one, Israel was not listed except as an accessory of West Germany, whose putative nuclear armament was the Soviets' overriding concern.[8]

Simultaneously with his nuclear guarantee to Egypt in 1966, the Soviet prime minister had promoted (unsuccessfully) a "Kosygin Initiative" for a clause in the nascent NPT. It would bar "nuclear" nations that acceded to the treaty from threatening "non-nuclear" ones, but only if the latter had no nuclear weapons stationed on their soil. This was generally interpreted as designed to exclude West Germany.[9] In Soviet perceptions, Israeli and German nuclear aspirations were closely connected, and were similarly suspected as part of a US plot to surround the USSR with nuclear-armed pacts. Then-Middle East correspondent Evgeny Primakov's 2006 book still charges technical cooperation between the German and Israeli nuclear programs in 1968, but the data is both questionable and derived from later Western literature.[10]

The alleged West German–Israeli connection—a Soviet concern more than an Egyptian one—accounted for the only allusion to nuclear weapons in the joint com-

THE NUCLEAR NON-ISSUE

muniqué after Nasser's talks in Moscow. Non-proliferation was listed among a range of topics on which Egypt and the USSR held an "identity of views." This referred specifically to Bonn, which unlike East Germany "offered and continues to offer assistance to Israel."[11] Otherwise, both parties' reaction to Israel's obduracy on the NPT was remarkably muted. Meeting US Undersecretary of State Eugene Rostow in Washington the day Nasser arrived in Moscow, Soviet Ambassador Anatoly Dobrynin "turned to the question of NPT" only as the last of ten items on his agenda, "asking why Israel had not signed." Rostow was constrained to mouth the same Israeli excuses that the Americans themselves had rejected. But Dobrynin responded calmly that "he believed Israelis realized they could not achieve security through nuclear weapons."[12]

Rusk warned the newly elected President Nixon in the transition process that "if the Israelis developed nuclear weapons ... the Soviet Union would respond by putting nuclear weapons into Egypt."[13] But this prediction did not materialize, and the Egyptians disclaimed any intent to obtain such arms from Soviet or other sources. According to Heikal, when Muammar Qaddafi made his first visit to Egypt as Libyan president and asked, "'do the Israelis have nuclear bombs?' Nasser said this was 'a strong possibility.'" However, when "two or three months later," Qaddafi's "second man," Abdel Salam Jalloud, came to ask for support for buying a "tactical" bomb from China, Nasser was cool to the idea and "Jalloud came back empty-handed."[14]

In February 1968, Henry Kissinger (on a foray into the Middle East as an adviser to Nelson Rockefeller's presidential campaign) saw little to deter a first strike by Soviet missiles. He warned Israeli academics that the Soviets were liable to "go to the brink" to aid an Egyptian offensive for recapturing lost territory, including use of intermediate range ballistic missiles (IRBMs) against Israeli targets in Sinai (such as air bases), and no US administration would risk a response. The sole testimony to this exchange, from Shlomo Aronson, does not specify whether Kissinger factored Israeli nuclear response into his calculations. He had made his reputation by contemplating the possibility of limited nuclear war, but when pressed by the Israelis, he clarified that the Soviet missiles he envisaged would be conventionally tipped and based in Egypt. Kissinger did not say whether his estimate was based on Soviet statements, US intelligence or theoretical speculation, but in 1973 it turned out to be fairly accurate.[15]

A year after the NPT signing, Kissinger (now as Nixon's national security adviser) submitted an excruciatingly convoluted report to the president about options for US action toward Israel on the nuclear matter. It quite correctly noted that "both Soviets and Arabs have been surprisingly quiet about this issue," although "the Soviets must be aware of the general state of Israel's nuclear weapons." US agencies at that point were divided as to whether Israel's "fissionable material" had already been used to produce "completed nuclear weapons" for ten of its French-supplied surface-to-surface missiles. The Americans saw little prospect of turning back the clock, and their half-hearted efforts to get Israel to accede to the NPT assumed US acquiescence with Israel's continued possession of weapons so long as it remained undeclared. Even the strongest opponents of Israeli nuclearization were most concerned about the results if Israel announced its possession of such weapons, or indeed even if the United States made its concern about the issue public, which might "spark Soviet nuclear guarantees to the Arabs, tighten the Soviet hold on the Arabs, and increase the danger of US–Soviet nuclear confrontation."[16] The latter warning was borne out in 1973, but the Soviet nuclear guarantee was long since in effect when Kissinger's paper was filed.

Returning from Moscow at the climax of the War of Attrition and Soviet involvement in the summer of 1970, Nasser made an extraordinary public statement at his party congress: "I am not sure whether conditions in the Middle East are ripe for a nuclear war. However, as is well known we have signed the NPT and this treaty commits the United States and the USSR to assist states that face nuclear danger." Even as he announced his acceptance of an American-brokered ceasefire, Nasser stressed that for such support "I am not referring to the United States, which will help Israel. But we will turn to the USSR and I have reason to believe that it will come to our aid."[17] Nasser, then, had given up any aspiration toward acquiring nuclear weapons.[18] The Soviet guarantee was evidently still in effect: in the early spring of 1968, before departing for a tour of duty in the eastern Mediterranean, the captain of submarine K-172 was instructed to prepare a launch of eight SS-12 nuclear missiles at Israel if the latter undertook "certain offensive action."[19] The reiteration of this commitment to Nasser in July 1968 was soon borne out overtly by the first visit of a Soviet nuclear attack submarine, K-181, to an Egyptian port.[20]

It could hardly be expected that any Soviet concern about Israel's nuclear prowess would be imparted by *politruks* (political officers) to rank-and-file advisers, much less to enlisted men of regular Soviet units—none of whom mention such instruction. But it would have had to constitute a major strategy factor at their command level— for example, in 1968, Lashchenko or Malashenko—and there is no evidence that their concept of an offensive into Sinai ever took the prospect of an Israeli nuclear response into account. The interpreter Gorbunov who, after his stint with the Tu-16R squadron and another on the canal front, served at the Egyptian military academy confirms that "what our generals never discussed in their lectures was that the Israeli generals had nuclear weapons." In 2013, he still wondered—or professed to wonder: "Nasser may have known about the Israeli nuclear bomb. But did Moscow know about it? And if it did know, why didn't it say anything?"[21]

Previous studies have indeed noticed, in the 1967–73 period, "the decrease of public Arab statements on the issue of Israel's nuclear capability." Several rationales were suggested, mainly attributing the change to Arab weakness or resignation, but the writers admitted that none were conclusive.[22] It now appears more likely that the cause was less the deterrent effect of Israel establishing its nuclear clout as a *fait accompli* than of its *failure* even to declare or test such arms—let alone use them—in the darkest days of May–June 1967.[23] This demonstrated a lack of political will to invoke the nuclear option except in the face of imminent existential threat to the Israeli heartland, and the Arab and Soviet perception was adjusted accordingly.

Though this was never formally stated by Moscow, its previous recognition of Israel only within the borders of the UN Partition Resolution of 1947 had become inoperative. In effect, the 1967 war moved the goalposts, and the Soviets were now committed only to restoring the "green line" of the 1949 armistice.[24] When the USSR endorsed and supported Egypt's aims of "eliminating the consequences of Israeli and imperialist aggression," this was limited to regaining Sinai, and Moscow sought to reassure Israel that this was its genuine as well as declared position. By February 1968, the CIA reported: "the Soviets made it very clear that Israel is here to stay and they will not ... facilitate its destruction."[25] Among other instances, Primakov—in Israel in August 1971 for secret talks on behalf of the Politburo—congratulated the Israeli leadership on its major achievement in the Six-Day War: universal recognition of the 1949 lines as the country's definitive borders.[26] Egypt, he asserted, no longer sought Israel's eradication, and—as he claimed, under Soviet influence—now recognized its existence.[27] The risk of triggering an Israeli doomsday scenario therefore seemed improbable enough to be canceled out by the deterrent value of the Soviet nuclear guarantee to Egypt—of which the Israelis were given periodic reminders. As IDF analysts noted, in theory Soviet doctrine held that "so long as the adversary ... has not been deprived of the capability to produce nuclear weapons and the means for their delivery ... the enemy will be able to resist and cause casualties."[28] But Soviet and Egyptian planning for their limited objective against Israel could disregard the issue.[29]

The NPT signing ceremonies, in Washington and London as well as Moscow, were overshadowed by the increasing tension over the "Prague Spring."[30] Even less interest was aroused by a Soviet government statement issued over the signature of Kosygin, the only member of the leadership *troika* who attended the Moscow event.[31] It recycled his 1966 proposal for denuclearization of the Mediterranean region. But Israeli commentators—among the few in the international media who bothered to analyze this text—saw more immediate significance in its call for "slackening of the [conventional] arms race in the Middle East ... only on condition of ... the full evacuation of Israeli forces."[32]

The Israelis considered that Kosygin's statement was intended to *exclude* the Middle East from any global conventional-disarmament process, in order to reassure Nasser that there would be no such regional accord with the United States before an Israeli withdrawal.[33] The operative significance was, then, an implied commitment "that if the USSR's conditions for Israeli withdrawal are *not* fulfilled, there will be no limit to Soviet weapons supply for the Arabs, while at least for the time being there is no parallel armament of Israel" by the United States.[34]

Moshe Dayan's recently declassified testimony before the Agranat Commission included a still heavily censored passage in which the defense minister listed the types of decision that would be in his purview, as distinct from those to be determined by the military on its own:

> I can come in at the moment that the matter becomes one of principle [one line sanitized], if they should be capable of attacking the Soviet Union ... or just the neighboring countries. I say: that's already a question of concept, and I would want to share it with the cabinet and so on [three lines sanitized].[35]

This appears to confirm Seymour Hersh's unsourced claim that Dayan considered Israel's nuclear deterrence as aimed mainly toward the Soviets rather than the Arabs, and that he took care to notify the Soviets so.[36] Knowing this Israeli posture would have reinforced Soviet determination to keep a nuclear deterrent poised against Israel, but need not have affected Moscow's support for Arab offensive plans that could be presumed insufficient to trigger a desperate Israeli move. The assumption whereby Israel would be adequately reassured that its heartland was not at risk would prove dangerously flawed in 1973, but for the time being it appears to have held.

6

"YELLOW ARAB HELMET, BLUE RUSSIAN EYES"

A. Nasser's Moscow talks and Georgian spa

Foreign reports about "friction" in Nasser's talks in Moscow claimed once again that Egypt was alarmed by Soviet reluctance to continue military aid.[1] West German experts shared with an Israeli counterpart their impression that "the visit was typified by disagreements ... Nasser tried to sound out the possibility of Soviet intervention on Egypt's side in a new outbreak of war with Israel. The Soviet reply was apparently no, with a recommendation that Nasser refrain from warlike initiatives." There were "persistent rumors among the diplomatic corps in Moscow that USSR is interested in resumption" of diplomatic relations with Israel. However, one perceptive German specialist added: "it is very likely that this data ... originated in deliberate Soviet disinformation, which is trying intentionally to display disagreement between Cairo and Moscow in order to camouflage coordinated operative decisions that may have been made during Nasser's visit."[2]

No major conflict between Nasser and his Soviet hosts was in evidence when it was announced that he was extending his stay from seven days to ten in order to spend 7–9 July "resting in the Moscow region." Again, various political speculations were made in the West as to the reason.[3] But Nasser's "rest" was actually a checkup, which began on 6 July, at the Kremlin clinic, a facility of the Health Ministry's Fourth Directorate—the VIP medical service for the Soviet elite. Its chief, Dr Evgeny Chazov, who would treat the *nomenklatura* for over twenty years, related in his memoir how Brezhnev called him within a day of Nasser's arrival, at the request of physicians attending "one of our close foreign friends."

Nasser's medical condition had deteriorated beyond the diabetes he discussed with Marshal Zakharov. His doctors reported that in the past year he had suffered steadily intensifying pain in his legs, which now would not allow him to walk any distance; the five-hour flight to Moscow was agonizing and he had to lie down most of the time. Nasser's own retinue was "panicky" even about holding the examination, as the very news that it was necessary might have disastrous domestic repercussions. At their demand, Brezhnev stipulated that the consultation with a Soviet medical team be held under total secrecy and be concealed even from others in the Soviet leadership.

Chazov and the specialists he assembled diagnosed atherosclerosis. When this was reported to Brezhnev, the latter urged that "every effort be made to restore Nasser's health," as "if he should leave the political scene it would be a major blow to our interests and those of the Arabs." No effort was spared to keep him on his feet—literally and figuratively. Chazov not only prescribed treatment at the Georgian spa Tskhaltubo but went there himself to make the arrangements while Nasser flew home via Yugoslavia (where Tito too reportedly lectured him on the inadvisability of provoking the Israelis—for the time being).

On 23 July 1968, Nasser, addressing the Arab Socialist Union (ASU) National Congress, "was lavish in praise of Soviet assistance and generosity: 'we took part of the Soviet weapons as a gift and concluded a contract for the remainder, for which we shall pay in the future in long term installments.'"[4] Once again, foreign interpretations, which are still echoed in Western historiography, had misread "not yet" as "never" in Soviet advice to Egypt.[5]

Chazov was waiting at Tskhaltubo when the Egyptian president came there on 26 July, and attended him until Nasser departed on 17 August for an equal period of recuperation at his villa near Alexandria.[6] Even before his return to Cairo, developments on the canal belied his purported dispute with the Soviets.

Israeli sigint monitors reported in August a "qualitative change in the Soviet presence in Egypt." They may have picked up the signals of an electronic warfare (EW) monitoring and jamming system with the permanent participation of a Soviet *spetsnaz* (special forces) "radio-technical" outfit at a level commanded by a major; a subsequent head of this unit dates its establishment to 1968.[7] The Israeli monitors warned of a possible "unprecedentedly active Soviet intervention," but were overruled by the MI authorities who were empowered to disseminate such estimates.[8]

B. Advisers prepare artillery duels and cross-canal raids

Anatoly Isaenko had returned from his service in the airlift of summer 1967 to complete his studies at the Military Institute of Foreign Languages, majoring in English. In July 1968, after his graduation, he was again dispatched to Egypt and attached to a SAM brigade that had been advanced to the canal front. He had to serve all five of the brigade's advisers and two more at division headquarters, so that "there was no lack of work." Within two weeks, he "got to tour the entire length of the front from Port Said to Suez without meeting any misadventure." But the quiet was misleading, and Isaenko's colleagues with the Egyptian ground forces were privy to the Soviet role in preparations for ending it.[9]

Yury Gorbunov and others from his English-linguists group were transferred in June 1968 from the Tu-16R squadron at Cairo-West (where they were replaced by

"YELLOW ARAB HELMET, BLUE RUSSIAN EYES"

students of the languages institute even before graduation) to the 2nd Division on the canal front—another reflection of the constant shortage of Arabic interpreters. He was attached to the revered Col. Afanas'ev, whom he describes admiringly as "like a father to us all." As Gorbunov was now told, an adviser like his boss

> differs from an expert in that his level of responsibility is higher. He issues advice and recommendations to his advisees and assumes part of their responsibility for accomplishing the mission ... He makes decisions and proposes them to the Arab commander, and together they take part in the implementation. He and his protégé together reconnoiter the terrain, and direct the firing. ... He pinpoints enemy positions during exchanges of fire, and supplies the coordinates to the division's artillery chief, who issues the firing orders.[10]

Valery Klimentov, another interpreter with the Soviet advisers to the Egyptian II Army Corps, retained a vivid recollection of such a preparatory reconnoiter on 14 August 1968—despite some drinking the night before:

> I remember the date well, as the 13th was my birthday, and after this event I had a mighty headache. I was ordered to go with the division commander's deputy in charge of artillery to a lookout post on the roof of the Suez Canal Administration building in Ismailia ... The parapet gave us only knee-high cover. Ahead, as far as the naked eye could see ... stood [Israeli] tanks and other guns, and Star-of-David flags waved ... Young Israeli soldiers in unfamiliar olive drab were walking around; some of them were presumably my countrymen till not long ago, [as] at the brim of the trenches were boards with slogans in Russian such as "*Sovki*, isn't it time to go home?" or "Have you forgotten the wars in 1948, 1956, 1967?" or "Welcome to hell!" Here and there, young Israeli women from auxiliary units sunbathed in bikinis. It was sad to think that a few days later they would all simply become targets for the Egyptians' powerful artillery, which was already being deployed in its firing positions.

> "We'll show them soon enough," said our artillery man—an Armenian by extraction—and flashed his gold-crowned teeth. Fearing the Israeli snipers, who knew how the Egyptian officers adored gold [dental] crowns whether needed or not, I advised the gloating adviser to talk less. It was no coincidence that the Egyptian officers escorting us kept silent, and presciently removed their starred epaulets ... as well as their sunglasses, which enlisted men didn't wear ... True, the Armenian and I were both rather dark and could have passed for Egyptians, but there was [already] proof that Russians too were not insured against bullets. ... A few days later the Egyptian artillery struck forcefully and accurately.[11]

The accuracy was ensured as "intelligence had been collected" on the Israeli targets. "In infantry brigades," Serkov wrote—that is, no longer only in elite ranger units:

> *diversionnye-razvedyvatelnye gruppy* [DRGs, sabotage-intelligence groups] were prepared for activity east of the canal. ... Their missions are locating and assessing Israeli positions, headquarters, manpower and armament; taking prisoners; and mining access routes. These groups of 4–6 men are sent almost every week, cross [the canal] after nightfall on rubber dinghies, and return before dawn.

In late August, two such raids killed three Israeli soldiers, captured one and set a record for depth of penetration into Sinai.[12] An Egyptian deserter told a news conference in Tel Aviv that at least one of these, on the night of 26 August, was carried out by Karpov's 118th Brigade. He confirmed the format of the Soviet presence: the advisers still were not stationed permanently at battalion level, but made regular visits there.[13]

The Soviets' part in processing the raiders' product into combat-useful data is illustrated by a Hebrew-language interpreter, Janis Sikstulis, who as his former classmate Klimentov attests, took part in interrogating prisoners at the intelligence department of II Army Corps headquarters.[14] Reminiscences of Israeli POWs bear this out: in December 1969, a paratroop officer who was badly injured and captured in an ambush east of the canal recalled "blue-eyed Russians" among the officers who crowded around his stretcher after he was carried across. In February 1970, two Israeli operators of a mobile canteen were captured by an Egyptian raiding party that came "on four rubber boats." They were subjected to preliminary interrogation in a front-line bunker, in the presence of "six big Russian guys" (as one of the prisoners retold it) or (according to the other) "two Russians in the corner of the room ... with pale skin and blue eyes." An IDF paratrooper, captured in the major Egyptian raid of 30 May 1970, was also taken for interrogation "to a place where I saw some Russians."[15]

C. The guns of September: the Soviet role

It was under the Soviet advisers' supervision, Klimentov writes, that the raiders' data was put to use when on the afternoon of 8 September 1968 Egyptian artillery landed a massive bombardment on Israeli positions. In contrast with previous local engagements, this one encompassed nearly the entire length of the canal. Isaenko and "his" SAM advisers were returning from an exercise on the coast south of Suez City when sirens sounded. They just made it to headquarters in an old British-built bunker when "'the earth started rearing up' all around. After an hour, Egyptian 130mm guns entered the fray, and then silence suddenly reigned."[16] The Israelis charged that Egypt had twice violated a UN-brokered truce and continued the cannonade, while the Egyptians boasted that Israel had "begged" for the ceasefire.

Despite admitting ten soldiers killed—a devastating loss by the Israelis' standards—they claimed that while "the Egyptians fired more than 10,000 shells over three hours and a half, this caused negligible damage to the IDF's forward defense array."[17] But the Israelis were clearly outgunned, and their forward outposts on the canal had but flimsy protection. Briefing a reporter after Israel constructed the strongpoints that would become known as the Bar-Lev Line (for Chaim Bar-Lev, Rabin's successor as IDF chief of staff), an Israeli colonel reckoned that "Soviet connivance and assistance" had enabled the Egyptians to reach an advantage of 25:1 in guns and 13:1 in manpower along the canal before they launched their barrage. The Hebrew version of this interview added, apologetically, that this Soviet assistance had been "clandestine."[18]

"YELLOW ARAB HELMET, BLUE RUSSIAN EYES"

The 8 September clash thus clarified Egypt's estimation that it had regained enough of its military capability to start the second phase of Nasser's strategy—"deterrence" or "active defense," as termed by Defense Minister Muhammad Fawzy. In retrospect, Sadat would date the onset of the War of Attrition here, and this chronology has been increasingly accepted in recent studies.[19] Previously, attention was focused mainly on the period after consecutive hostilities began the following March. As a result, the preceding events were dealt with briefly and superficially, even though they largely determined the course and character of subsequent developments.

The Soviets in Egypt tended to agree that the events in the autumn of 1968 ushered in a new stage, even though their *podsovietnye* (advisees) were not yet ready to play it out fully. In the trenches with the II Army Corps, Serkov, whose specialty was firepower management, noted in his journal that "the last 10 months were not spent without benefit for the Egyptian Army":

> Full rearmament was completed, as well as refreshing command cadres with higher-quality personnel. The artillerymen's readiness has been qualitatively improved. A lot of toil and energy was invested by the divisional artillery commander's adviser, Varenko, and the artillery brigade adviser, Azovkin. ... Egypt [now] held the advantage over the Israelis in all the duels, not only in respect of gun numbers but in the quality of shooting ... Hundreds of guns along more than 60km of canal unleashed a hurricane of fire.

The preplanning of the cannonade on 8 September—denied by Egypt at the time—was also indicated by the designated cue to open fire "simultaneously along the entire front": the Israelis' detonation of a mine near Port Tawfik. Serkov's account agrees in this with the Israeli version, whereby the mine had been laid by an Egyptian "commando detail" very shortly before the incident, as the road in question was combed daily. This use of a raiding party was in itself a major achievement for the Soviets and especially Lashchenko, who had been stressing its importance for over a year. He and Malashenko had visited the site several months earlier. At a range of 200 meters, they had observed the Israeli flag flying over the Port Tawfik jetty, "even though the [IDF] garrison was no more than a platoon and could easily be overwhelmed."[20]

Karpov noted after the 8 September engagement that the Egyptians at the front "rejoiced; their bosses were going through the formations and distributing medals ... Dayan and his chief-of-staff came to Sinai to see *our* work." The Soviet adviser took pride in what UN observers disclosed that their chief had heard from the Israelis: Egyptian artillery "was shooting very effectively and accurately, and this could only be accomplished by Russian artillerymen. [Israeli] radio told the Egyptians: 'don't jubilate—the Russians aim your guns and you only pull the trigger.'"[21]

Israeli assessments for domestic consumption admitted that the achievements of the Soviet advisers, now estimated at over 3,000, "should not be underevaluated." But the Israeli media were told that although Egypt's weaponry had been restored beyond its 1967 strength, "a substantive change in Egyptian combat standards will require not a year or two, but a generation. A Russian expert, who comes for a few years, ... cannot change an Egyptian's character and mentality." When Mohamed Hassanein Heikal crowed that now "we will have to cross to the other side where the enemy is dug in, to fight him there and to enjoy the advantage of offensive," Israeli officials warned Nasser that "this would of course be a fatal error, as this time too they will be dealt a severe defeat by the IDF."[22] Such arrogance hardly led the IDF to promptly draw the lessons from its sobering unpreparedness on 8 September, and the results of this failure would become evident in a matter of weeks.

The Soviet advisers, too, readily admitted—indeed, warned—that despite the Egyptians' marked progress in artillery fire and small-scale raids, they were still unfit for the ultimate offensive. Lashchenko's training plan called for conducting staff exercises of large formations, and the first had been held in the II Army Corps—which then held the entire canal front—in the summer of 1968. Malashenko prepared the blueprint and presented it to Fawzy, but had to tone down the war minister's enthusiasm that "this is almost the plan for the reconquest of Sinai!" Yes, Malashenko confirmed, but the exercise merely comprised a single army corps; "the navy and air force are included only schematically." Even so, and although "the exercise was more like a game on the map," as actual forces on the ground were not involved, the simulation's purposes of "advancing a field army with the crossing of a water obstacle, establishing a beachhead, repelling a counterattack, and further advance ..." was a complex matter, and doubly so for the Egyptian officers because they had never studied it or dealt with it before.

The interpreter Gorbunov listed a typical Soviet adviser's tasks in June 1968: "he guides the Egyptian units in the field about the practical construction of pontoon bridges, until they reach adequate proficiency for crossing the Suez Canal in the event of hostilities."[23] The staff exercise, however, showed that such proficiency was still far from achieved. The participants were entirely unable to progress from generalizations to practical execution:

> The timetables they drew up for ferrying forces across the canal had not taken into consideration the capacity of fording equipment, and had to be revised. Provisions had not been made to surmount the concrete wall of the canal and the rampart behind it. ... The gathering of situation reports was conducted slowly and only over the telephone ... due to unpreparedness of the signalmen and officers, and also for fear of using the radio. The Egyptian generals and officers worked willingly in daytime, but as soon as night fell their working capacity diminished. ... Contrary to the preset rules for the exercise, at night only a duty shift remained and all the others went to rest.

"Before the exercise began," Malashenko recalled, "Lashchenko told me that if I could get the army corps' headquarters to work and relocate at night, he would recommend me for a decoration. [But for] lack of communications, the army corps' headquarters failed to relocate, so there was no reason to recommend me." Lower down in the command chain, Serkov registered similar concern that "from bitter experience of the previous war, many—though unfortunately not most [Egyptians]—understood that not much has been done yet to improve capability." Presciently, he added that the weakness remained "especially in air defense." This was now addressed by reorganizing Egypt's air defense forces as a separate command from the Air Force, on the Soviet model and presumably at the advisers' behest, but it would not much improve their performance for a year to come.[24]

What, then, had motivated the Soviets to approve and support the 8 September action, with the attendant risk of escalation into a full-scale conflict that they knew the Egyptians were still likely to lose? Varied and even contradictory rationales were suggested by Western and Israeli analysts. The most far-fetched among them was that the bombardment had been intended (but failed) to launch the decisive Egyptian attempt to cross the canal in force, retake its east bank and open it to shipping—an aspiration that at this point would have been dismissed by the advisers.[25]

D. The specter of Soviet action to open the canal

In January 1968, a UN-brokered attempt to free the merchant ships trapped in the Suez Canal was blocked by Egyptian demurral at Israeli use of the waterway once reopened, and by Israeli suspicion that Soviet naval vessels based at Port Said would be the first to enter the canal. A unilateral probe by Egyptian boats northward from Ismailia ended in a major firefight on 30 January.[26] According to Capt. V.I. Popov, Soviet marines were landed again, in response to an Israeli attempt to capture the northern entrance to the canal.[27] In early July, ahead of Nasser's visit to Moscow, a "mysterious Soviet dredge" went through the Turkish straits—fueling speculation that the Soviets were preparing to *force* the canal or at least to clear the waterway from Port Said to Ras el-Ish, the stretch held by Egypt on both sides.[28] "The Russians," it was suggested, "could send [the dredge] into the canal with a destroyer escort, daring the Israelis to shoot."[29] Conversely, it was rumored that "the next Soviet step [would be] a *political* initiative to open the canal."[30] Word was spread from "diplomatic sources" in Cairo "that the United Arab Republic [Egypt] would permit Israeli cargoes [as distinct from Israeli ships] to pass through the Suez Canal if Israeli troops evacuated a strip of desert just east of the canal"—which could be interpreted as a bid to justify a forcible move into the canal if Israel, as expected, rejected the deal.[31]

Both variants of the canal-opening scenario were backed with estimates that "no country has felt the pinch of the Suez shutdown more than Russia, which must send its ships around Africa ... in order to keep Hanoi supplied."[32] Such theories persisted despite observations that shipments to Vietnam were already being made mainly from the Soviet Far East.[33] Indeed, NATO had concluded by the beginning of 1968 that the Soviets had overcome any difficulty caused by the canal closure in respect of Vietnam, and air transport had proved sufficient for their needs even in Yemen—so that the USSR "was unlikely to risk an explosion" on this account. But an alternative hypothesis was that "opening up the canal" would enable the Soviets to link up with their putative "new Indian Ocean fleet."[34]

In 1969, authoritative US estimates still held that only the closed canal was preventing the formation of a Soviet fleet that would dominate the Indian Ocean.[35] Iran too reportedly had "fears about Soviet domination of the Persian Gulf ... should the Suez Canal eventually be opened."[36] US naval commanders continued for years to claim that reactivating the canal would be more advantageous to the Soviets than to the Americans, both in order to maintain new bases in Yemen and Somalia and in order to facilitate pressure on oil supplies.[37] But by 1971, the US admirals conceded that "on balance, the relative disadvantage of an open canal should be accepted in the interest of promoting peace and regional stability. If, as a part of reopening the canal, Soviet presence in the UAR were reduced, this relative disadvantage to the United States would tend to be offset."[38]

Even that was an overstatement. Soviet and post-Soviet literature on and from the period reflects no pressing interest in reopening the canal beyond supporting Egypt's obvious economic gain. Certainly none was reflected in the mission purposes that were imparted to Soviet commanders and servicemen in Egypt. During the India–Pakistan War of 1971, with the canal still closed, Soviet ships from the Pacific Fleet moved in fast enough to effectively counter a US carrier task force, and it appears that afterward Moscow relied on a friendly, Soviet-supplied Indian Navy rather than attempting a permanent presence of its own.[39] When the canal did open in 1975, no Indian Ocean fleet or even *eskadra* materialized, and it was recognized that the canal's closure had actually rewarded the USSR, especially in respect of its oil trade.[40] As will be seen, the Soviets did move to block alternative routes for Middle East oil to the West, such as Israel's Red-Med pipeline, which in 1968 began a major upgrade. In retrospect, Western sources even identified "among the ships which had been stationed permanently at Port Said ... minelayers intended to *mine* the Suez Canal if the Israelis should attempt a crossing."[41] In early 1973, Secretary of State William Rogers was quite correct in telling King Hussein of Jordan that "opening of Suez Canal ... would be [of] some advantage to [the] Soviets but we feel that advantages to US would be even greater."[42]

But in the summer of 1968, scare-mongering about a canal reopening to Moscow's benefit was the order of the day. The new helicopter carrier *Moskva*, the Soviet Navy's largest ship and the symbol of its revised operational doctrine, caused a stir by passing through the Turkish Straits on 24 August. It was described to the Sixth Fleet's press corps in Italy as "narrow enough to pass through the canal" and as slated to remain in the Indian Ocean, when it would be replaced in the Mediterranean by its even newer sister ship, *Leningrad*. This turned out to be as imaginary as the "vertical-takeoff fighter planes" that were supposedly stationed on these carriers.[43]

"YELLOW ARAB HELMET, BLUE RUSSIAN EYES"

In confidential briefings, US officials were less concerned. The day after the September 8 duel on the canal, responding to concerns in the Senate about "increasing activity of the Russian Fleet" in the Indian Ocean and the Persian Gulf, Rusk assessed that its "importance ... is more on the political side than it is on the military side. ... They just are not in a position to support fighting units out in that part of the world." But Rusk was somewhat overoptimistic when he suggested the same about the Mediterranean: "with NATO air power along the entire northern coast of the Mediterranean, and with the 6th Fleet, their fleet in the Mediterranean ... is almost as exposed as our forces are in Berlin."[44]

The *Moskva* was only the largest of twenty-four Soviet ships that entered the Mediterranean in August 1968 alone, raising the Soviet presence to a peak of at least sixty-five units, by US count.[45] Preoccupation with the "large Soviet naval presence in the Middle East" was seen as distracting attention from other concerns.[46] Briefing the Sixth Fleet's press corps after the 8 September incident, Chief of Naval Operations Thomas Moorer called the *Moskva* "visible evidence of Russia's announced intention to become a modern major offensive sea power ... which we must assume is capable of landing Russian naval infantrymen." Off the record, the admiral evidently inspired "speculation the *Moskva*'s deployment was timed to give Egypt moral support during a period of new tension with Israel."[47] But the *Moskva* ranged no closer to the canal than the Aegean, where it concentrated on training exercises for anti-submarine warfare. Its practical connection with Egypt was only through the Tu-16Rs from Cairo-West, which took part in these maneuvers.[48]

The dredge did reach Egypt but never showed up in the canal. It was put to continuous work improving the Mediterranean harbors used by the Soviet fleet.[49] In October, it was joined by a floating drydock, which was pulled through the straits to Alexandria by two Soviet tugs.[50] Soviet Navy divers were tasked with guarding the drydock, ships and other installations against Israeli frogmen. They also performed underwater welding and inspection on submarines that made port calls every three to four months for maintenance and refueling.[51] Shortly after, an incredible number of 4,800 Soviet shipyard workers was reported by the *Sunday Telegraph* as manning the facilities. More plausibly, Polish diplomats disclosed the dispatch of 200 workers from the Gdansk shipyards, in an unusually large non-Soviet input.[52] By "the end of 1968," Alexandria was able to accommodate what naval historian Shirokorad describes as the first visit by a Soviet nuclear-powered submarine to a foreign port.[53]

The K-181, of the Kit or November attack-sub class, was routinely armed with nuclear-capable torpedoes designed for use against coastal targets, though there is no direct evidence that it carried them on this port call.[54] The visit was intended to "raise morale" among the Egyptian Navy's seamen, but it surfaced in the press only the following March. "Well-placed informants" in Cairo then revealed that it had taken place "unpublicized"—which conforms with the *Telegraph*'s claim that Alexandria port, like Cairo-West airbase, was by now under full Soviet control and was closed to

Egyptian civilians.⁵⁵ When the Israeli diplomat Nitzan Hadas's German contacts told him "the Soviets do not yet have naval and air bases in Egypt fully manned by Soviets," this time his home office pointed out:

> they hardly need it. All the equipment in these ports is Soviet, there are Soviet experts everywhere serving the Soviet ships, the USSR has its own stores in Port Said and Alexandria where it keeps all that its naval forces need—in a sovereign fashion, even if it has not signed a territorial lease agreement.⁵⁶

By mid-October, the initial reports of discord in Nasser's Moscow visit were reversed: "United States officials" now viewed "with growing concern ... a long-term military and political pact" that had been reached with Nasser in July. The time frame for enabling Egyptian forces to retrieve territory lost to Israel was set "within two to five years," but meanwhile military pressure against Israel would be kept up by "long-range guerilla penetration, sabotage and espionage."⁵⁷

Both the *Moskva*'s tour and the *Eskadra*'s peak strength ended by December, and thus could be attributed to routine rotation as much as to temporary prepositioning for the clashes on the Suez Canal in September and October. As a forcible canal opening was never attempted and no evidence has emerged that it was ever planned, this theory appears to have been by way of Soviet disinformation, Western guesswork or a combination of the two. At any rate, it distracted attention from the lasting upgrade of Soviet presence in Egypt.

E. Czechoslovakia and Egypt: diversion or multitasking?

Another line of speculation about the cause, and mainly the timing, of the 8 September cannonade was that the lack of a firm Western response to the Soviet invasion of Czechoslovakia had emboldened Egyptian commanders. These, it was suggested, "are now pressing their Soviet allies not to restrain them too much in warlike activity toward Israel, and not to be overly apprehensive that local incidents might cause [global] deterioration and a superpower clash ... The Soviet military advisers ... are very influenced by this pressure."⁵⁸ Israeli Deputy Prime Minister Yigal Allon told Johnson the day after the Egyptian bombardment that "the trouble along the Suez is serious. ... After the Czechoslovakia affair where the West had been incapable of responding ... the UAR might well consider that it has greater freedom of action."⁵⁹ The Americans understood this to mean that "the Czech experience ... had (a) made the Russians anxious to ... take the light of world publicity off them, and (b) possibly encourage the Egyptians to start probing across the Canal because of the passivity of the Western reaction."⁶⁰ A converse theory held that the Soviets themselves were making the best of global attention being focused on Czechoslovakia to make hay in other arenas.

But it can also be argued that the artillery duel at Suez served as a diversion when global outrage over Czechoslovakia peaked. Either way, there are several indications of a connection between the two theaters. The artillery adviser quoted by Klimentov predicted the artillery barrage a week before Soviet tanks moved toward Prague. Western observers discerned coordination between "several politically and psychologically significant activities of Soviet fleets," including the Mediterranean squadron, "before the invasion of Czechoslovakia."[61] The destroyer crewman Kharchikov recalls being sent again, "urgently" to the Mediterranean, with extended calls at Port Said and Alexandria, in the second part of August '68 (he noted that Port Said was now a far cry from his first tour of duty there, devastated by shelling and with most of its population gone).

Nasser, who returned to Egypt from the Georgian spa three days before the invasion of Czechoslovakia, was informed about it within hours.[62] The Soviet chargé d'affaires came to his villa near Alexandria on 21 August at 4 a.m., which means the diplomat was either poised nearby in advance or left Cairo as soon as the Warsaw Pact armies began the operation.[63] On 9 October, Lashchenko and his chief *politruk* (political officer) visited the advisers of the II Army Corps. Karpov asked them a characteristically provocative question, "'what is our policy?' He [Lashchenko] stated: 'the tension that we created here is justified. The entire world's attention must be drawn away from the events in Czechoslovakia. But the Egyptian army is not yet ready for decisive action.'" When Soviet military intervention in Egypt became overt and direct, Israelis would frequently compare their situation with the Czechoslovaks'.

Such calculations may indeed have affected the precise timing of military moves, as did the endless maneuvering and posturing about a political settlement in the Middle East. But as already exemplified, at least on the Soviet side the shoe was more often on the other foot. To the extent that the two were connected, it was the diplomatic contacts that were strung out or accelerated to accommodate, obscure or legitimize the military initiatives, which once set in motion took on dynamics of their own.

However, the invasion of Czechoslovakia was studied seriously in the IDF. Yo'el Ben-Porat, the head of IDF sigint, held that the Soviets were the best in the world at deception. They had fooled the West's "good intelligence agencies" by launching the invasion out of a supposed maneuver, and the same might happen in the Middle East. At his behest, a committee was formed that formulated a directive whereby any major Arab maneuver should be treated as a potential offensive. For reasons he could not explain, this procedure was not observed in early October 1973.[64]

F. The advisers counter new Israeli weapons

The relatively free rein that the advisers' staff had in directing operations is illustrated by Malashenko's account of a typical incident:

> Moscow would get on our nerves whenever an exchange of fire began. The military attaché, Fursov, would report it immediately, without checking the data. Sometimes he would report that Israeli amphibious tanks had appeared on the canal, floating on ordinary rub-

ber life rafts. Demands would come in right away from Moscow to file a report for the chief of staff: where [this occurred], how many guns were firing, how many shells, and what the Egyptian and Israeli casualties were.

Ultimately, "a group of officers from our General Staff arrived, led by Maj.-Gen. S.G. Krivoplyasov"—one of those who had badgered the advisers for detailed reports. "He wanted to convene the senior advisers, but Lashchenko advised him to go to the canal zone instead, and there to get acquainted with the advisers' work and lifestyle. ... He wanted to use a radio transmitter, but under the agreement the advisers had none, nor any car" to transport him. As long as they worked within the mandate received directly from the Defense Minister and higher up, the advisers were evidently able to pay little more than such contemptuous lip service to the armchair generals.

Unlike the casualty-conscious Israelis, the Soviets from Lashchenko down saw the engagements on the canal as live-fire exercises, an essential and routine component of a long-term program, rather than the start of its ultimate fruition. Malashenko recorded Lashchenko's candid report to Nasser that according to conventional criteria Egypt already had the necessary numerical advantage to take the offensive, but it was still unfit to do so. The greatest weakness of the Egyptian military—despite some improvement in 1968—was its "low level of moral and psychological conditioning, its lack of the fighting spirit essential for combat operations." Defense alone left the Egyptian troops passive; many officers preferred classroom to field study; they had to be "battle hardened." Every round of actual hostilities was, then, a deliberate object lesson.[65] Once an Israeli provocation was claimed, as it always was, the advisers did not require high-level authorization to support the response that had been approved in advance—and was periodically modified to meet new challenges. On the Israeli side, it was belatedly realized that "the artillery 'incidents' of September–October 1968 were apparently a sort of trial run, a preliminary to the utilization of a limited military option" that was decided upon shortly after the Six-Day War.[66]

One such aspect of the 8 September duel was ignored in previous studies, even after a few details about it emerged in the 1970s: the appearance of what seemed to be a formidable new weapon on the Israeli side, and the Soviets' effort to counter it. One of the advisers' regular tasks was to obtain and examine specimens of advanced enemy hardware—both for use in refining the Soviets' own arsenal and in order to devise responses on the ground. At the end of June 1968, artillery expert Karpov was summoned to inspect an unexploded Israeli rocket of a hitherto unfamiliar 216mm model, which had "left a big crater" when it was first used a few days before.

In respect of the access granted to the Soviets, this invitation in itself marked a considerable improvement since the Six-Day War. In June '67, the GRU *rezident* in Cairo had barely persuaded the Egyptians not to "saw up" a state-of-the-art Israeli air-to-air missile which had landed intact, but rather to hand it over for immediate shipment to

"YELLOW ARAB HELMET, BLUE RUSSIAN EYES"

the USSR.⁶⁷ After Soviet MiG-21 units were deployed in Egypt, pilot "Oleg Tsoy intercepted an enemy reconnaissance drone flying at low altitude. He attacked the tiny machine and brought it down in the desert. The Egyptians collected the wreckage and found that the drone carried top-secret equipment whose information was recovered almost undamaged" and presumably made available to the Soviets.⁶⁸ But experience ultimately motivated the Soviets to trust their own personnel for such procurement, sometimes from behind Israeli lines. The Russian military historian Col. Valery Yaremenko states that "special units were established ... during the War of Attrition, in 1969–70, for the sole purpose of crossing the Canal and capturing any booty of equipment, in order to load it quickly onto aircraft and send it to Moscow."⁶⁹ However, the only account that has emerged so far of Soviets actually crossing the canal before the 1973 war—a boast from a veteran in Kazakhstan that he took part in twenty such forays with a "special operations" unit—remains unconfirmed.⁷⁰

Egyptian and Soviet statements indicate that the new Israeli rocket was a major concern for them.⁷¹ For the Israelis, the new weapon, codenamed *Ze'ev* (wolf) was a makeshift and yet-experimental attempt to offset their numerical inferiority in artillery pieces. This "flying bomb" was inaccurately aimed from a primitive pipe-frame launcher, and Israeli soldiers soon learned that it was prone to boomerang. Still, at virtually point-blank range it could cause a good deal of damage to positions that were hardened only against smaller shells. The intended effect of its blast was what would be called, a half-century later, "shock and awe." Even Israeli soldiers, from whose outposts the *Ze'ev* was launched by specialists but who were not permitted to handle the top-secret weapon themselves, judged by its impact across the canal that it must deliver a half ton of high explosive.⁷²

Faced with this challenge, Karpov began working out a response. He calculated or gathered from field observations that the rocket had a 90 kilogram payload, at the expense of very short range—4 kilometers—which would put the launch sites within easy reach of Egyptian cannon.⁷³ The matter was presumably addressed by Chief of Staff Riad, who accompanied Nasser to Moscow a few days after the weapon's appearance and had two days of "important talks" with Grechko. For years, Israel did not officially confirm the *Ze'ev*'s existence, let alone its use—even after one such rocket killed Riad himself on 9 March 1969.⁷⁴ In the summer of 1968, and even after UN observers reported at least three rockets fired on 8 September, Egypt too did not publicize their introduction.⁷⁵

The battle on 8 September showed that the Israelis could still use the rockets despite the Egyptians' heavy shelling—and this may have been one reason for the Soviets' dissatisfaction with their clients' performance. Maj.-Gen. Vladimir Ryabukhin, the former logistics chief of the Volga military district, was since December 1967 the adviser to his counterpart in the Egyptian II Army Corps. He registered that in the three hours of artillery fire, "our side used up 415 tons of ammunition," but considered that the Egyptians' estimate of the casualties on the Israeli side

85

was exaggerated. At headquarters in Cairo, Malashenko explicitly discerned "failures of the Egyptian forces during the exchanges," and instructed the senior artillery adviser to prepare recommendations for correcting them.

Meanwhile, "as combat engagements were not continuous ... the Egyptian forces were able to hold a series of training exercises at various levels from battalion to division, including one at division level that included a parachute drop, from 4 to 8 October."[76] This was evidently the occasion for Lashchenko's review on the 9th, and the "next missions" he assigned were carried out two weeks later. But in Washington, though Secretary of State Rusk told a Senate committee that the "artillery duel ... this time apparently was started by the Arabs," he remained cautiously optimistic about diplomatic prospects. "We would be, I think, somewhat surprised if there were a resumption of any large scale military action."[77]

G. 26 October, the "rocket incident" and Israel's airborne raids

The surprise came within six weeks. In the interim, Rusk had come away from two days of talks with Foreign Minister Gromyko with little prospect of agreement to advance the Jarring mission. Under increasing pressure from Congress as well as the newly nominated Republican candidate Nixon, Johnson publicly approved negotiating the Phantom fighter plane sale.[78] As the deal's opponents in the US administration feared, this cemented identification of the United States as Israel's sponsor, enabling an escalation of Soviet propaganda. Although one of the main arguments of the deal's proponents was to deter Soviet and Egyptian action, the reverse was achieved: it encouraged preemption before the much-feared F-4s were delivered.

By 26 October, at least some of Chistyakov's recommendations appear to have been implemented. When "the Egyptians unleashed a storm of fire and under its cover landed *desantniki* (landing troops) on the Israeli east bank," Serkov noted that the results were "even more significant" than on 8 September. On this point—that the Egyptians initiated the duel—the Soviets' memoirs differ from Soviet declarations at the time and conform to the Israeli version. Malashenko writes explicitly that the cannonade was planned in advance. UN observers agreed with Israel's charge that the Egyptians shot first; to prove it, the IDF pointed out that Egypt's triumphant announcement of its artillery barrage came only a few minutes after it claimed that Israel had opened fire.

This "provocation" consisted, according to Cairo, of two 216mm rockets that destroyed houses in Port Tawfik.[79] Out of the fourteen rockets the Egyptians accused Israel of launching that day at civilian targets, they produced one unexploded specimen, which they claimed was shot down by their anti-aircraft guns—quite a feat given the missile's short trajectory. Or was it the same one that had been shown earlier to Karpov? Cairo also claimed that its big guns—clearly following Karpov's instructions—destroyed ten "newly constructed" rocket-launch sites.[80] Malashenko also confirms that the Egyptians' firepower in this incident was "concentrated on the Israelis' 216mm [rockets]." The IDF, as before, denied using any missiles at all, but in Egypt the entire engagement was henceforth referred to as "the missile incident" and would later be described as "one of their major achievements."[81] When the one-eyed Dayan came again to inspect the battlefield, he was jeered by Egyptian soldiers across the canal as "Musa the blind man."[82]

Israeli "observers" told military correspondents that "the numerous Soviet advisers posted in all Egyptian units took an active part in directing the artillery fire." "Experts in Paris" agreed that "the enemy that Israel must defend against is the Russian enemy. In artillery too, there are many Soviet experts even at the lower echelons."[83] But in the Knesset, Allon—Dayan's perennial rival—"surprisingly" rejected suggestions that Soviets were behind the bombardment. Allon admitted an oxymoron: Moscow was encouraging a moderate faction in Egypt to reach a political settlement—while also abetting warlike elements with arms supplies.[84] This would become the standard "dualistic-policy" gloss for those who insisted on presuming a cautious Soviet posture even when it did not conform to actual Soviet moves.

In Cairo, as usual, no public credit was given to the Soviet advisers, and their deprecation of the vaunted Egyptian success was unlikely to evoke much gratitude. Karpov pointed at "incorrect technique" against the Israeli rocket array, due to faulty implementation of his plan. Although Ryabukhin's figures showed that on 26 October the Egyptians used up less ammo—only 320 tons—analysis at the Soviet advisers' headquarters still found "a great waste of 16,000 rounds." Noting improvement in Egyptian performance, Malashenko's headquarters still detected residual flaws, such as the DRGs' failure to bring back prisoners or documents. Yet Serkov noted correctly that "the Israelis suffered even greater casualties" than on 8 September.

This was again largely due to their unpreparedness: most of the fifteen Israeli fatalities were caused when the first Egyptian volley hit soldiers playing soccer in the open, a fact so embarrassing that it was suppressed by military censorship. So was the enemy's apparently having observed that IDF troops holding the canal line had been rotated just two days before the incident.[85] Even if this was a fortunate fluke for the Egyptians, Serkov was astonished that the Israelis did so little in the six weeks since the previous cannonade had shown up the frailty of their positions. "They had observation posts along the canal with Star-of-David flags waving over them ... The reason for [their] casualties was mainly the lack of secure shelters."

The Israelis were also surprised when, evidently thanks to Karpov's skill, a battalion headquarters that was supposed to be out of Egyptian artillery range did come under fire.[86] Here luck was on the Israelis' side and no casualties were caused, though legends spread about female soldiers fleeing naked from the shower shed.[87] On the other hand, two Israeli fatalities were caused by three simultaneous *desantnik* raids across the canal. Perhaps in order to excuse what they saw as an Egyptian success, the Israelis stressed correctly that the raids were "obviously initiated and planned by Soviet advisers," but also overstated the raiders' numbers: on 8 September, each party's strength had been put at thirty to fifty.[88] Raids on such a scale were recorded by the advisers themselves only a year later. Israeli reports on the October clashes mentioned an Egyptian soldier who was killed in one encounter. His comrades carried his body back with them part way to the canal, but then had to abandon it and took only his weapon—which appears to indicate there were only four to six raiders as described by Serkov, rather than a platoon-size force.[89] But Israeli "observers" warned that the latest incidents might be "a prelude to a Russian–Egyptian attempt to cross the canal in force."[90] This Israeli assessment was echoed in Western reports.[91]

The exaggerated Israeli description was in effect a backhand compliment to the Soviets' training and morale-building program, which was described in Israel as being conducted "on the Panfilov model" of baptism-by-fire.[92] Analyses by "authoritative western sources" held as usual that "by heating up the canal Nasser is trying to draw the USSR into intervention. Certainly the duel improved home-front morale and Nasser's political position. It also provided training."[93] But there were now opposite readings too, whereby "Nasser had been put up to it by his Russian advisers," and these again suggested that the Soviets did so "as a warm-up for an attempt to clear the Suez by force."

In fact, despite the improvement in Egyptian performance, Malashenko recommended that the exercise *not* be repeated—by implication, until the shortcomings were corrected. Indeed, no initiative on such a scale was undertaken by the Egyptians for the following five months. In Israel, this was attributed to the IDF's forceful response. The Suez refinery—rebuilt with Soviet aid after its destruction a year earlier—had been spared in September, reportedly for fear of harming Soviet personnel.[94] Now it was again struck and damaged by Israeli artillery, using Soviet-made multiple rocket launchers that had been captured in Sinai in 1967.[95]

The IDF's predictable response came in for unusual press criticism, some of it apparently inspired by dissent within the military. Besides recriminations that the IDF had *twice* been caught off guard, doubts were expressed about its knee-jerk retaliation in kind. "There is nothing wrong with shelling economic targets, but it is not very effectual in stopping attacks, as Egypt is willing to pay the price, whereas the casualties are too heavy for Israel. It is Egypt that needs to be surprised by a new form of Israeli response."[96]

The new tendency in IDF thinking was exemplified five days later, when heliborne Israeli troops carried out the first raid of its kind in the Egyptian hinterland. Unlike official Egyptian announcements that admitted only an air raid, the Soviet advisers confirmed a "well planned and executed" commando operation that struck at Nile bridges and an electric installation at Nag Hammadi, midway between Cairo and Aswan.[97] Serkov noted that this "delivered a serious warning to the Egyptian leadership," but the effects were felt more on the home front than along the canal. There was a

"YELLOW ARAB HELMET, BLUE RUSSIAN EYES"

wave of domestic unrest ... especially [among] students ... the government made an urgent decision to raise a home guard, and the students were called to enlist. We soon saw a company of young men in uniform with shovels digging trenches. Three days later, after experiencing life at the front, they were sent back to Cairo.

Most Western studies still reflect the Israeli narrative at the time, and credit the IDF raid with "freezing any Egyptian military activity" for several months. This inaction is, in turn, conventionally portrayed as a major failure that enabled the Israelis to construct, almost unhindered, the array of strongpoints (*ma'ozim*) that would become known as the Bar-Lev Line. But the Russian aviation historian Mikhail Zhirokhov sees the Nag Hammadi operation as the first impetus for *Kavkaz*, even if acting on it took some time: "it was precisely this raid that faced the Egyptian military and the Soviet advisers with the issue of reinforcing air defense of the canal ... Through all of 1968, [Egyptian] SAMs had shot down only one Israeli Piper [Cub]."[98]

7

FACING THE BAR-LEV LINE

A. The lull that enabled the strongpoints: lapse or reorganization?

It is generally accepted that the bombardments of 8 September and 26 October 1968, and the casualties they caused, settled a year-long debate within the IDF top brass. Between proponents of "static" and "mobile" defense strategies along the canal front, the decision now went in favor of the former (or, as its supporters would claim after its failure in 1973, a hybrid formula that only leaned toward their approach). Despite domestic criticism of unpreparedness for the "second surprise," work to harden the outposts did begin after the first—as proved by a civilian worker who was among the fatalities in October.[1] But the formal decision was finalized, and large-scale construction was begun, only afterward.

Some accounts hold that the Egyptians failed to notice or fully appreciate the substantive change in the Israeli defense concept until January. On 12 November, Serkov did observe that "capital fortifications" were beginning to replace the Israelis' ramshackle observation posts on the canal. Soviet thinking, however, still held that "the Israelis' main defense fortifications and forces are deep inland, in order not to expose them to artillery fire, and consist of mobile formations capable of providing sufficient time for main forces to arrive and deploy"—the very strategy that Israel had now altered if not abandoned. So Soviet-Egyptian initiated "heavy artillery exchanges were less frequent."[2] This also reflected Malashenko's recommendation, based on his staff's critique of the 26 October operation, that it should not be repeated on the same scale.

Previous studies suggested that the Egyptians delayed action against the Israeli fortification effort as they were "awaiting vital shipments of Soviet equipment."[3] Malashenko clarifies that this refers to materiel for two entire new divisions, which had been requested during the 1968 Grechko–Gromyko visit and approved in Moscow soon after.[4] They were to form the nucleus of a new III Army Corps, as part of a reorganization that the Soviet team had outlined. The advisers had found that entrusting the entire canal front to the II Army Corps alone was unwieldy and inefficient. Preparations for this restructuring had begun "a few months" before the

8 September flare-up, but the transition was problematic. Staff exercises held for the officers of both formations produced dramatically unsatisfactory results when they went beyond the improvement of static artillery warfare and small-scale raids.

"The [new army corps'] commander, General Hassan, had been present at the II Army Corps' [staff] exercise," Malashenko noted. "When it came to criticism he exhibited correct judgment." But when his own new formation was put to its first test,

> at the start of the exercise it became clear that the commander and headquarters of the III Army Corps are very poorly prepared, ... incapable of organizing and preparing an offensive operation. We had to teach and advise them on elementary matters. For a long time after the crossing, the headquarters could not establish communications and control. Toward the end of the exercise, as usual, our material was submitted to Riad.

But the advisers were excluded from the final debriefing, to prevent embarrassment. Afterward, Riad told his Soviet adviser: "if we conduct an offensive operation and liberate Sinai ... I will ask the president to give you a villa in a nice place on the Mediterranean. We will both retire and be neighbors." But, Malashenko concluded wistfully, this was not to happen during his tenure in Egypt.

When the offensive did materialize in October 1973, either the Soviets' idea to divide the front between two army corps or its still-faulty implementation would produce calamitous results. The cusp between the two formations would become the corridor for the Israeli counterthrust across the canal that reversed the course of the war.[5] The advisers, Malashenko claims, foresaw an Israeli counter-crossing almost as early as the II Army Corps' staff exercise in the summer of 1968:

> When I described an episode in which Israeli forces beyond the Mitla Pass, despite the Egyptian forces' superiority, hold back [the Egyptians'] advance, land a counterblow and send a force across the Bitter Lake to the west bank, Riad said that this episode was not so realistic as the Egyptian forces would have superiority in numbers. They would be attacking and the enemy retreating. I reminded him that during the fighting in Sinai [in 1967] the enemy, though it lacked overall superiority, scored a success by massive use of air power and skillful maneuvering. ... Many Egyptian generals and officers, [including Generals Ahmed Ismail and Gamasy] could not understand the character of modern operations and reduced everything to calculations of numerical proportions.

The scenario that the advisers tried to rehearse would actually transpire in '73: "the enemy outflanked them, penetrated the rear and threatened to surround a numerically superior force."

Organizing the III Army Corps and transferring the southern sector to its control required yet another group of advisers, and even reducing qualification requirements for younger officers did not suffice to fill the quota. Those old-timers that were recruited now were also not as gung-ho as the first contingent. Col. Mikhail Filonov, who had served with the Syrian Army before and during the Six-Day War and returned home in January 1968, was recalled in early 1970—at age fifty-two—to spend two years in a bunker on the canal as engineering adviser to the new formation. In 2003, he recalled the experience with little relish. Neither of the Arab armies he had advised was anything like his Soviet comrades in the Second World War in respect of motivation, and the living conditions "turned my hair completely gray."[6]

In late 1968, the reorganization offered another reason—or pretext—to limit combat operations. According to Serkov, "directly aimed cannon were used ... *sparingly* to disrupt the [Israeli] fortification work, which compelled most of it to be done at night." The Egyptian military history of the '73 war claims that Israel's use of air power prevented Egyptian artillery from fully interdicting the construction, but this hardly applies before the summer of 1969.[7] Egyptian officers told David Korn of the US Embassy in Tel Aviv that they repeatedly begged Defense Minister Fawzy for permission to use small arms against the Israeli construction crews, and he granted it only in February. Indeed, Malashenko faulted the Egyptians for not keeping up *some* pressure on the Israelis, particularly by firing at the latter's roads and firebases and by seizing beachheads across the canal, which would oblige the Israelis to increase their presence there and thus enable the Egyptians to inflict more casualties. In retrospect, the same result was caused by the lull in Egyptian shelling that facilitated the construction of the Bar-Lev Line, because the Israelis' reinforced presence on the canal bank enabled the Egyptians' attrition strategy that would be explicitly declared a few months later. But there is no indication that this was foreseen or suggested by the advisers. They were only methodically continuing their test-and-improve program.

B. Lashchenko's legacy and his succession

If the advisers' progress with their trainees was unnecessarily slow and an ambivalent hiatus did set in, it can be partly ascribed to Lashchenko's departure in November 1968. There is little reason to suspect that the official explanation of "health reasons" (a heart attack) concealed dissatisfaction on either side with his performance. Malashenko—Lashchenko's townsman (from Chernigov, Ukraine) and longtime aide—does not appear to exaggerate in stating that his boss "commanded universal respect" in Egypt. In his farewell meeting with Nasser, Lashchenko again presented a candid report that included, besides the flaws already noted in the two autumn clashes, a realistic appraisal not only of the Egyptians' "somewhat improved" capability but of the Soviets' readiness to assist them. He listed a litany of problems that would remain sore spots for some time, such as weakness of air defense and poor intelligence management. In respect of his centerpiece project, preparations for a canal crossing, he still lamented that "the [Egyptian] command and [its] forces have not dared to take a single beachhead on the east bank."

Still, Lashchenko recommended providing the Egyptians with a list of new weapons, some of which would indeed play pivotal roles in the coming stages: *Grad-2* rocket systems, whose upgraded multiple and mobile launchers would help to balance the heavier but shorter-range *Ze'ev*; two brand-new shoulder-fired missiles, the antitank *Malyutka* (Sagger) and anti-aircraft *Strela-2* (SAM-7), as well as fording equipment. But he frankly told Nasser that the Egyptian military should be reinforced "in useful proportions," and ruled out certain requests such as replacing tanks with newer models. As is, Lashchenko warned, the aid to Egypt cost the USSR heavily and tilted its industry excessively toward military production.

That Nasser nonetheless decorated Lashchenko indicates the esteem the general had earned. Although the Egyptians had trouble spelling his name (which helps to account for his total neglect in Western studies), and resented his rejection of their complaints about Soviet weapons based on combat experience, they remembered him gratefully.[8] In Moscow too, Lashchenko's subsequent assignments attest that he was not recalled from Egypt due to perceived failure there or excessive support for Nasser's offensive ambitions. He was promoted to general of the army, made deputy commander of ground forces, and remained on call as an authority on Egypt in general and the canal crossing plan in particular.

Lashchenko introduced Nasser to his successor Ivan Katyshkin, who in a portent of things soon to come was now, in addition to chief adviser, designated "head of the Soviet operational group in Egypt."[9] But despite this upgraded status, Katyshkin did not retain the same access to the Egyptian leader—perhaps because he did not keep up his predecessor's constant drive for action and results. Malashenko does not hide his contempt for the new chief adviser: as Lashchenko's deputy, Katyshkin

> had not shouldered much work and had not visited the troops on the canal. Now he did develop activity—[but] with special attention to preparing reports for Moscow, which he amended to enhance the actual situation, the results of the advisers' work, and the improvement of Egyptian forces under his leadership. Sometimes he would personally write coded cables to this effect.

Despite Malashenko's admitted bias, at least some of his disdain was evidently well founded. Lower-ranking advisers also describe Katyshkin as coarse, blustering, and mainly ineffectual.[10] After he was replaced in September 1970, Katyshkin—unlike Lashchenko—was kicked upstairs to head the training institute for military linguists, at whom he had openly and gratuitously sneered in Egypt. One of them spitefully recalled the general's frequent remark: "we have two adversaries, the Israelis and the interpreters."[11]

Besides his trouble with Katyshkin, Malashenko needed surgery. He soon requested a reassignment, and with Lashchenko's support obtained it—after the major artillery duels resumed in March, when the Bar-Lev Line was already approaching completion. Meanwhile, the Soviet advisers, at least those posted with the land forces, appear to have had a dysfunctional leadership that hardly kept up their former dedication to proactive input.

• In the short term, however, the relative successes of the autumn of 1968 were reflected in the tone of an Egyptian directive issued in January '69 on "organization [and] method of advisers' activity." "The Russian experts," as declared in the preamble, were there "at the request of the UAR in order to benefit from their practical specialization for improving combat capability." They were assigned to "units and sub-units" and would enjoy the same privileges as these outfits' own officers. Egyptian commanders were instructed to treat them with "mutual respect" and to "ensure an atmosphere of creative cooperation"—while eschewing any political or ideological discussion. They were to "remove all obstacles" and provide all information and documentation needed for the advisers' functioning so that the latter could elaborate "realistic" recommendations. Disagreements were not to be debated in front of the troops.[12]

C. Air activity intensifies, and accelerates the Phantom deal

If intensity of ground activity subsided, the air advisers showed that this was not due to any radical change in Egyptian or Soviet intentions or plans. Here too, the advisers could be described as emulating Panfilov. As early as July 1968, an Israeli commentator close to the intelligence community reported that the Soviet pilot-instructors were leading formations of Egyptian planes on operational missions, to demonstrate both air combat and ground attack techniques.[13] By 13 October, Israel's "official commentator" Chaim Herzog stated that the Soviets were "presumably" flying in Egypt as well as Syria, and were "very deeply involved in the EAF's electronic infrastructure."[14] Authoritative Western sources in Paris stated as a fact that "the Russian pilots are making joint flights with the Egyptians."[15]

The result became evident on 22 October, when the *New York Times* reported, from Washington sources, a substantial rise in both the sophistication and the audacity of Egyptian air sorties into Sinai. Several plane models were now being deployed simultaneously, with MiG-17s and Su-7s coming in low for photoreconnaissance missions and MiG-21s covering them higher up over the canal. The Egyptian Air Force (the *Times*' sources said), under the management of Soviet advisers, had been dispersed to a number of new airstrips, even taking off from straight sections of highway. The use of such improvised fields close to the canal, rather than the permanent and closely monitored bases, for one-time "ambushes" would be perfected by regular Soviet squadrons before too long. Soviet technicians, the *Times* reported, were manning Egyptian radar stations, and Soviet pilots were actually carrying out certain reconnaissance flights.

This item obviously represented a tendentious leak from US elements interested in aircraft sales to Israel: it stressed that Israel's strategic situation had worsened, with its greatest inferiority being in the air. A US official pointed out that Israel had yet to replace the forty to fifty supersonic craft that it had lost since 1967, and its sixty-five Mirages were vastly outnumbered.[16] The context was obvious: the subsonic Skyhawks that Israel had already received did not complete the bill, and the request for two squadrons of F-4 Phantoms that Prime Minister Eshkol had submitted to President Johnson in January 1968 had not been formally approved (though Israeli airmen were already involved in technical preparations for their purchase). After the 8 September clash, Israeli Deputy Prime Minister Yigal Allon reiterated to Johnson that "agreement to supply Phantoms might be a helpful reply to the Soviets." With a Democratic loss in the US November election increasingly likely, intense lobbying was under way to get the deal signed before a presidential transition delayed it further.

The *Times* report was almost prophetic: the very next day, Egypt claimed with great fanfare that its MiG-21s, after completing a sortie across the canal with impunity, had shot down three Mirages, at least one of them over Sinai. Malashenko's comment that the Egyptian success "obviated the need to send in *our* MiG-21s" confirms that Soviet pilots were in readiness to do so, and may have done it in other cases. Israel denied any plane losses, or indeed any contact with the intruding planes (which did not prevent the IAF from also claiming that it had "beaten them off"). But Western media followed the Egyptian line in calling this the first dogfight since the Six-Day War.[17] The Egyptians had already pulled off a similar incursion on 23 September, though without claiming any kills, and its recurrence confirmed that using the forward airstrips permitted the Egyptians to penetrate Sinai deeper and longer than in previous attempts, without Israeli interceptors overtaking them even by taking off from Refidim.[18]

Israeli accounts admitted only that the Egyptians' air activity had been increasing for several weeks and they were "willing to take somewhat greater risks than before."[19] As to the claims of Mirages shot down, the Israelis asserted derisively that fuel tanks jettisoned by their planes were presented by the Egyptians as wreckage of downed aircraft. But retrospective accounts of the next encounter—this time, undisputedly a dogfight—that took place on 3 November 1968 illustrate that the Egyptians' claims, while exaggerated, were not entirely fabricated. Two Israeli Mirages that were scrambled from Refidim to intercept an intrusion in the northern sector of the canal were outnumbered and—as the lead pilot admitted—outmaneuvered by at least ten MiG-21s. Both of the Israeli planes missed all their shots at the Egyptians, though the official IDF version hinted that one of the latter had been hit. It did not disclose at the time that both Mirages were themselves damaged by the MiGs' Atoll missiles, which gave some basis to Egyptian claims that one IAF plane was shot down and the other possibly hit.[20] The disparity between Egyptian claims and Soviet records as against actual Israeli losses would recur frequently, as discussed below.

Yiftah Spector, the lead IAF pilot in this incident, glimpsed one of the MiG-21 pilots (who was wearing a leather cap rather than a helmet), and suspected that he was Russian. Cairo identified by name and as Egyptian only the first four pilots who drew the Israelis into the fight, which does not exclude the possibility that Soviet pilots joined the fray later. Both at the time and in retrospect, the engagements of

23 October and 3 November went almost unmentioned in Israel.[21] In Egypt, they were hailed at the time and later canonized as a turning point in the air war, similar to Ras el-Ish on land and the *Eilat* at sea. The Soviets, as usual, were not explicitly credited but the Egyptian "victories" were attributed to "modern tactics" as well as accurate directions to the pilots from the radar system and control center, which were clearly the Soviets' work. In another incident on 10 December, Israeli interceptors managed to shoot down only one of the slower MiG-17s–the IAF's only kill in air combat for all of 1968.[22]

Either the tangible change in the air balance finally tipped the scales in Washington, or—as the Israelis presented it, and recently released documents confirm—Johnson was already resolved to keep his promise before leaving office, and overruled the near-unanimous objections of administration officials. On 1 November, the Americans had requested yet another memo from Israel about "provisions" for the Phantom sale. On the morrow of the 3 November clash, Israeli Ambassador Rabin quoted "current Israeli intelligence appreciation of the build-up of Soviet aircraft in Egypt. ... The inventories ... projected ... by 1970 had in fact already been exceeded on November 1."[23] Assistant Secretary of Defense Paul Warnke reluctantly notified the Israelis that "the President agrees in principal [*sic*] to the sale. It is a difficult decision," he added, and the United States would have preferred continued Israeli reliance on European suppliers as this had "lessened the risk of US–USSR confrontation."

Warnke made a final try to extract a quid-pro-quo: assurances that Israel would not "develop, manufacture, or otherwise acquire" strategic missiles or nuclear weapons, and that it would accede to the NPT.[24] Rabin balked, and Johnson settled the issue: "the President ... said that he had promised the F-4s without any conditions, and that was his position."[25] The deal was leaked to the press on the morning of Nixon's election victory, and formally announced on 27 December, with delivery to begin "in late 1969."[26] All the elements for the climactic phase of the War of Attrition were now in place—as well as a major rationale for direct Soviet intervention.

D. *The Phantom deal as impetus for Kavkaz*

After the EAF's relative success on 24 October, and in marked contrast to previous Soviet and Egyptian warnings, the War Ministry in Cairo sneered that acquisition of F-4s by Israel would make little difference because the EAF's Soviet-built planes outclassed them anyway.[27] The Soviets did not join in this braggadocio; if Heikal is to be believed, Brezhnev admitted that "they had nothing to match the Phantoms."[28] The F-4 was not only the leading US model in Vietnam; for years to come, it was considered by the USSR to present—by virtue of its range, payload and performance—a potential threat to the Soviet Union itself, if only on a one-way mission. As Gromyko said in an arms-control discussion in September 1977, the Phantom was "capable of reaching the territory of the Soviet Union and strike [*sic*] targets thereon."[29]

It is hardly coincidental, then, that the earliest date given for the dispatch of integral Soviet formations to Egypt is "soon after" the finalization of the Phantom deal, and in the air defense context: the Soviet response went beyond the supply of late-model SAM-2s—the S-75 *Dvina* system—"in 1968."[30] Egorin, the Novosti correspondent in Egypt, likewise asserts that

> about the end of 1968, the first Soviet *units* began arriving in Egypt together with the advisers, initially for defense against attack from the air. Our military men now began to be called *askaryun Suviet* (Soviet soldiers). At headquarters in Moscow the whole operation was called *Kavkaz*. ... Not one line appeared in the contemporary Soviet press about this ... someone decided to send our boys into war, but without giving the fathers, mothers or public any inkling of it.[31]

A recent, semi-official history of the Russian Air Force dates the formation of two fighter squadrons, earmarked for Egypt as the 283rd Division, in the autumn of 1968—although the aircraft arrived there only a year later.[32] Simultaneously, Soviet surveillance outfits (whose equipment the Soviets were reluctant to let the Egyptians handle, even if they had been qualified to operate it) were deployed in Egypt; they "could monitor the conversations between pilots and air controllers throughout Israel."[33] "The Russians," Egorin writes, "deployed as though the enemy was within 120km not of Cairo but of Moscow."[34]

This, in addition to the stalled Jarring mission, was the context when, on 24 November 1968, First Deputy Foreign Minister Semenov met Israel's UN Ambassador Yosef Teko'a—the first such contact since June 1967. Teko'a's preliminary report describes an ostensibly random encounter at a diplomatic reception. But he had already requested and received urgent instructions from Jerusalem, which indicates a prior Soviet approach.[35] Subsequent disclosures show that this was carefully planned by the Soviets, after Moscow began to realize that "the more we alienated Israel, the closer Israel got to the United States." Semenov was specially dispatched to New York for the purpose, as the UN representative Yakov Malik was considered too hardline (and anti-Semitic) to effectively deliver what the few Soviet diplomats in the know described as a conciliatory signal.[36] It was to be kept secret from the Arabs, even though an optimistic message that "Russia doesn't desire a new war but is interested in peace and stability" had already been transmitted by Dobrynin a few days earlier through the notoriously indiscreet Zionist leader Nahum Goldmann.[37]

Media reports of the Semenov–Teko'a meeting evidently caused Arab remonstration, as resentful Soviet accusations of Israeli obduracy stressed the talk's broken secrecy rather than its substance. Semenov himself charged even more than two years later that "he was interested in a dialogue with Israel, but the Israelis were not and therefore leaked his meeting."[38] In October 1971, the Soviet delegate of the moment for secret feelers toward Israel, Primakov, still complained that the Semenov–Teko'a meeting "within a few days was leaked to the Israeli press. I don't mean to say that Teko'a is not a decent man, but this leak ... burdened our relationship."[39] Teko'a, for his part, was not much impressed with Semenov's supposed moderation, and began his report with the Soviet's warning that "Israel is liable to exacerbate the USSR's attitude."[40] What stuck in the Israelis' mind was a thinly veiled threat: "Israel may regard Egypt as a backward country in military terms, but the USSR is not backward and knows how to use weapons."[41] No Soviet–Israeli rapprochement resulted, the Jarring mission went nowhere and the Phantom deal went through.

In a Knesset statement, Allon held there was "no use in guesswork under what circumstances the USSR might attack Israel with its own forces," as so far this had been done nowhere outside the Warsaw Pact. In any event, "Israel would not stand alone as the United States would stand up for us."[42] But even before the 26 October flare-up, Israeli commentator Chaim Herzog had dismissed as moot the question "Soviet Intervention in Our Region—Yes or No?" The intervention—he stated—was already in progress, and its expansion might not necessarily ensure a US response:

> It would be a mistake today, after the events in Czechoslovakia and in view of the increasingly obvious Russian military psychosis, to state that there is no risk of Soviet intervention in the Middle East. ... True, the USSR has no interest in a confrontation with the West ... [but] the USSR already has intervened in the Middle East and is still doing so. Further intervention may come in various forms, such as posting naval vessels in certain areas, or stationing forces on or along the canal, on the assumption that the IDF will be afraid to respond.[43]

8

A NEW PHASE FROM MARCH '69?

A. Soviet initiative or smokescreen?

In hindsight, beginning immediately after the Yom Kippur War, Egyptian historians neatly divided the 1967–73 period into four phases, and their colleagues elsewhere have largely adopted their chronology.[1] This is most evident in marking the transition, in March 1969, from "active defense" to "war of attrition"—so much so that most studies of this war begin here.[2] The prevailing concept, then, holds that on 8 March 1969 Egypt not only launched a mighty artillery strike at the Bar-Lev Line, but Nasser also abruptly abrogated the ceasefire with Israel and declared the start of this new stage.

Actually, the transition was not so clear-cut. Nasser's two declaratory steps were taken only some time later. The military action, which did break a relative lull of some four months, still followed virtually the same format as the engagements in September and October 1968: air incursions at midday on a Saturday, followed by a cannonade and coordinated with raids across the canal. The main innovation was that these strikes were henceforth kept up almost consecutively.

One pivotal development between November 1968 and March 1969 was the inauguration of the Nixon administration, and Kissinger's rise to a dominant position in US foreign policy. To appreciate the impact of his input on Soviet military involvement in Egypt, it has to be tracked from the outset, which predated Nixon's election.

In retrospect, probably in order to deflect responsibility for permitting the Soviet buildup in Egypt to occur on his watch, Kissinger equivocated on the date when the Middle Eastern arena was first transferred to the unofficial and confidential "back channel," that is, to his stewardship. According to his memoirs, this occurred only two years after the election, on 20 September 1971, when before a visit by Gromyko to the White House, Dobrynin "forewarned" Kissinger that "the [foreign] minister would propose putting the Mideast issue into the special channel," which had been established the previous December.[3]

Actually, Kissinger's involvement started much earlier. He began to dabble in Middle Eastern affairs while still advising Rockefeller. It was at the same stage that

Boris Sedov, a KGB political operative at the Soviet embassy in Washington working under the cover of a Novosti correspondent, began to cultivate the professor with frequent meetings.[4] Oleg Kalugin, Sedov's superior at the *rezidentura*, asserts "we never had any illusions about trying to recruit Kissinger; he was simply a source of political intelligence."[5] Still, the Soviets would be astonished by the sensitive information that Kissinger volunteered.

Kissinger was invited to join the White House team two days after Nixon took office, and accepted a week later.[6] By then, Sedov had operated what his boss would call in retrospect a "back channel" with Kissinger for over a month. Dobrynin was "not thrilled" with this activity so long as Nixon had no official status. Once the new administration was installed, he protested the meetings with Kissinger, and Sedov was "relegated to background"—but developed an alternative contact with National Security Council aide Richard Allen. This as well as Sedov's previous link with Kissinger may explain the latter's quite accurate comment, after only one meeting with Dobrynin, that the ambassador's reports "probably do carry weight in Moscow, but his bosses also seem to run a check ... through the sizeable KGB establishment in their embassy."[7]

On 30 December, Nixon's yet-informal status did not prevent the Soviet leadership from presenting him (as well as the outgoing administration) with a Middle East settlement initiative. Although Israel rejected it within days, Soviet emissaries, including a TASS correspondent at the UN, still tried to pitch the plan to Israeli diplomats—presumably to minimize Jewish pressure on Nixon against it.[8] Simultaneously, Moscow made sure, by such habitual means as an article by Primakov in *Pravda*, to denounce and deny "rumors in the West" that the Soviet Union was about to reach a settlement with Israel "behind the Arabs' back."[9]

On the day of Nixon's inauguration, after his address promised a change from confrontation to negotiation, the Soviet leadership also presented him with a proposal to discuss strategic arms limitation (SALT). Kissinger impressed on the president his theory of linkage between this and other global issues. Nixon listed the Middle East first when, a week later, he declared to the press that he was willing to hold strategic arms talks "in a way and at a time that will promote ... progress on outstanding political problems."[10]

Dobrynin—already a candidate member of the CPSU Central Committee and soon to be promoted to full membership—rushed to Moscow to discuss this with the *troika*, and returned by special plane. He received Kissinger for their first talk while in bed with the flu. Dobrynin's report of this meeting stresses two points that Kissinger omitted in his. First, that the American suggested "to actively utilize a confidential channel" between them, in order to sidestep the leak-prone State Department. Second, when Dobrynin voiced Soviet suspicions that the new concept of linkage was "a political game for pressuring the USSR in the hope ... of unilateral Soviet concessions," Kissinger "immediately began to justify himself" and suggested Nixon meant that talks on the

A NEW PHASE FROM MARCH '69?

Middle East and Vietnam—in that order—could proceed "*in parallel and simultaneously*" with SALT, rather than as a precondition.[11]

Kissinger had judged condescendingly that Dobrynin's "comprehension is imperfect; consequently, important points must be made in simple words and relatively slowly."[12] Dobrynin's comprehension was, however, acute enough to deduce rapidly that "relations between him [Kissinger] and Nixon are indeed very close," and that Kissinger was "quite vain ... not averse to boasting ... without excessive modesty."[13] KGB *rezident* (station chief) Kalugin likewise concluded, based on wiretaps of Kissinger's phone calls, that he was "vain and boastful."[14] The following chapters will outline how, for the coming years, the Soviets would exploit both Kissinger's vanity and his linkage concept by holding Vietnam, SALT and other elements of his signature détente as hostages to press *him* into concessions on the Middle East.

Remarkably, in his foreword to the collection of their parallel reports, Kissinger admits in effect that he misrepresented the president's approach to Dobrynin:

> Nixon ... did *not* think it possible to conduct simultaneous negotiations with the Soviet Union, China, the Vietnamese and the Middle East parties. He had made up his mind to make the Middle East a centerpiece of his foreign policy in the second term ... During Nixon's first term, my role on the Middle East in the Channel was largely a watching brief.[15]

"This"—Kissinger states—"was accomplished by confining the channel to elaboration of principles to guide the substantive negotiations being carried out by the State Department." He is correct that these "efforts to stabilize the region proceeded desultorily." Through the initial months of the administration, both he and the Soviet ambassador repeatedly dismissed, as "talks for talk's sake" and "windowdressing," the two-power talks, the four-power talks, the attempts to revive the Jarring mission and so on—the fine points of which make up the bulk of the period's historiography. But it is only one of Kissinger's many retrospective stretchers that "Dobrynin correctly conveyed the White House's reluctance to use the Channel for detailed Middle East negotiations."

Actually, by 21 February Dobrynin reported that Kissinger saw their exchange on the Middle East as important—and, in the Soviet ambassador's first meeting with the president, he was told clearly that Nixon "would like to further develop ... confidential channels ... designating Kissinger, his chief aide, for such contacts."[16] This was after Dobrynin had delivered to Nixon a note from the Soviet leadership, which, though referring to all of Israel's neighbors, reflected particular Soviet concern that the incipient Bar-Lev Line might become a permanent border.[17] The note deplored that "Israel continues to follow aggressive and expansionist aims," and warned that "the Arabs and their supporters cannot agree." As there was still "not much progress" in the "consultations" begun at the United Nations by Ambassador Charles Yost with his Soviet counterpart Yakov Malik, Kissinger now explicitly proposed that the matter be handled through "the Kissinger/Soviet ambassador channel."[18]

103

Dobrynin quickly obtained approval from Moscow—with a directive to highlight the issue of Israeli withdrawal. Kissinger promised to propose a "mechanism" for the new channel within a week—and demanded to keep it secret from Secretary of State William Rogers, Assistant Secretary Joseph Sisco (who had just been formally put in charge of Middle Eastern affairs) and Yost. Dobrynin inferred from this that Kissinger "himself intends to play an active role."[19] Kissinger thus intended the channel to supplant, if not undermine, the diplomatic process rather than to "guide" it.

Kissinger requested a delay; he reckoned the back-channel talks could begin within a month. The Americans sensed no urgency: in a talk with French President Charles de Gaulle, Nixon had already interpreted the all-but-overt threat in the Soviets' message as a sign that they "might be as alarmed about the situation in the Middle East as we."[20] For the first time but not the last, Kissinger would be blindsided by the Soviets and Egyptians.

B. 8–9 March: did the Soviets initiate or just join in?

On 8 March, "around noon Egyptian MiG-21s crossed the canal. ... After 6 hours ... Egyptian artillery opened fire all along the canal in order to wipe out the Israeli line of fortifications."[21] Since 1967, Egyptian spokesmen had been pointing out Israel's relative vulnerability to casualties and to protracted disruption of its economy by the mobilization of reservists that would be required for major hostilities. Heikal had introduced the term "attrition strategy" in late February 1969 to describe concerted pressure on Israel from several Arab fronts.[22] He wrote again in his Friday column on 7 March that Egypt could withstand 500,000 fatalities better than Israel could take 10,000.

The cannonade was not initially recognized in Israel as a substantive turning point. Foreign Minister Eban, on his way to the first high-level discussions with the new US administration, predicted that "the exchanges of fire ... will not lead to a major flare-up, because Egypt knows well that it cannot sustain one. It was a grave violation of the ceasefire, but no more." Still, he warned Nixon that "the Arabs are trying to stir up a war psychosis with active Soviet support." Israeli correspondents were concerned that the president had actually been impressed by "Soviet readiness to reach an accommodation"; pundits opined that his fear of confrontation with the USSR was excessive, as Moscow was focused on border clashes with China, which had escalated into pitched battle on 2 March.[23]

If current events had anything to do with the timing of the barrage, Egypt was probably more mindful of a brief interregnum in Israel. Egyptian officers claimed to David Korn that Nasser had in mid-February issued "battle orders," after hearing pleas from low- and mid-level commanders while visiting the front line. Egyptian soldiers were now permitted, and in effect encouraged, to fire at will at any Israeli they spotted.[24] In the first week of February, sniping across the canal reached such intensity that the Israelis suspected a special unit of sharpshooters had been brought

A NEW PHASE FROM MARCH '69?

in. UN observers determined that the shots, which initially injured two IDF soldiers, were unprovoked. Cairo Radio confirmed this by quoting foreign agencies to gloat that Egypt had launched a "war of nerves."[25] Dayan and other Israeli leaders threatened retaliation, but they had more pressing concerns: Prime Minister Eshkol had just suffered a heart attack (on 3 February). The Israelis responded only with small-arms fire.

After Eshkol died from a second attack on 26 February and his country was plunged into uncertainty over his succession, Egyptian sniping increased dramatically along with mining of roads on the Israeli side of the canal by raiding parties. On the 28th alone, over twenty incidents were registered, exchanges of fire went on for over twelve hours, and the observers had to arrange a truce. Israeli commentators suggested the Egyptians were attempting to back up Soviet and French pressure on Nixon to demand an Israeli withdrawal.[26] The bombardment on 8 March came the day after Golda Meir was confirmed as the candidate for prime minister in order to avert an open contest between Dayan and Allon. In an interview for the *Washington Post*, she deemed that the USSR would never accept, or lead Nasser into, any settlement acceptable to Israel.[27]

The Egyptians' new aggressiveness and initiative could be—and was—attributed in large part to the advisers' efforts, though as usual they were less than satisfied. In January, a meeting of the CPSU members among the advisers at II Army Corps headquarters (referred to as "the trade union" to sidestep the Egyptian ban on political activity) concluded that "some successes had been scored in combat readiness, [but] many problems are still unsolved." Although they had progressed to "command staff exercises and tactical training in brigades and divisions and live-fire exercises at company and battalion level, which had not been done before, ... due to late and inadequate assignment of missions by officers, sessions become lectures rather than practical training." In one case, "Arab officers burned plans for two staff exercises that had taken the advisers two weeks to prepare." Despite—or because of—these difficulties, the problematic step of attaching advisers directly to Egyptian battalions and *divizyons* was finally made. The first of the new battalion advisers arrived in Serkov's sector on 9 March, in the midst of the fray, and "got their baptism of fire." Their comrades had to postpone a welcome party due to the "circumstances," and finally held it on the 11th, under fire and by kerosene lamplight, as their power line had been cut after the Israelis began to respond with heavy shelling.[28] The exchanges now continued daily.

So, was the gradual escalation and then the massive bombardment done at the Soviets' bidding, or with their passive knowledge, or against their advice? Bar-Siman-Tov's conclusion, a decade later, was "there is nothing to indicate that the Egyptian decision to start a new war was agreed upon beforehand with the Soviet leadership," but "it is possible that the Soviets knew of Egypt's intentions."[29] Newer evidence is no less ambiguous. In the front-line ground units, Serkov sensed a tightening of regime that appeared to reflect preparation for renewed fighting: for one thing, fishing in the canal was forbidden. "Not long ago furloughs were reduced in duration and frequency," to counteract officer absenteeism that reached as high as 30 to 40 percent. This initially aroused resentment: "the [Egyptian] officers are blaming us. ... Even the division commander hinted that this was at the advisers' behest."

The Soviets received specific notice when two SAM-2 batteries were advanced into the canal zone on 3 March, along with their advisers.[30] But several testimonies indicate that at least the precise timing of the cannonade was not known in advance to the higher-echelon advisers—possibly to avoid their predictable demand for even better preparation.

Serkov and some other advisers were absent when the bombardment began—as usual, on a Saturday. They were in Cairo, attending a celebration of International Women's Day, presumably in honor of their wives. Malashenko's memoir appears to suggest deliberate Egyptian evasion: Riad, he writes, usually took him along on all his inspections of the front. But this time, on Sunday, "we learned that an exchange of artillery fire was being prepared on the canal. The same day, I called Riad to coordinate our departure ... to check preparedness and observe results of the duel." But that night the Soviet headquarters' duty officer reported that the Egyptian chief of staff had been killed two hours earlier, on the road to Port Said, when his car was struck. "It was only by chance that I was not in the same car."

This seems an almost excessive effort to dissociate from the Egyptian action: it was highly unusual for no Soviet adviser at all to be in Riad's retinue.[31] In particular, since this was the second day of heavy fighting, Malashenko could hardly have just "learned of preparations for a duel" that had already begun. And contrary to this initial version that Malashenko received, the Egyptian general was killed when a *Ze'ev* scored a direct hit on a front-line outpost that he was visiting.

Whether or not they colluded in setting the zero hour, once the shooting began there is little evidence to back Israeli claims at the time that Soviet opposition caused "clashes and arguments between the Soviet advisers and the Egyptian officers ... the advisers' situation is pretty difficult. They are caught between loyalty to the Soviet line of awaiting a political settlement and the aid that the Egyptian army expects."[32] Actually, it was again enthusiastic advisers who pressed hesitant Egyptians for more aggressive action.

Serkov and his colleagues reported immediately back to "their" units. As the artillery duel continued, at "a SAM *divizyon* deployed very close to the canal north of Suez City," the interpreter Isaenko "arrived with an adviser surnamed Sharashkin, who—it must be said—was a wise and determined man. ... He would not only advise but demonstrate how things should be done." Isaenko describes the scene that ensued in the missiles' control cabin:

> The SAM *divizyon*'s radar detected a target flying low over the east bank. It turned out to be an artillery observer flying along the canal with impunity. Our adviser suggested to the

divizyon commander to destroy this aerial spy. The Egyptian officer vacillated and stalled. The adviser pressed me: "you must be translating too softly. You have to be tougher and more decisive." Finally the *divizyon* commander answered: "Mister Sharashkin, it's forbidden to shoot down a plane. There's high politics involved." But he agreed to contact his superiors at headquarters ... and the politics changed right away. Sharashkin shouted to me: "run out of the cabin and watch—we're firing a missile!" ... Yellow smoke billowed into the sky and the plane's fragments fell to the ground. Behind me I could hear applause ... Soon a second target was detected. The *divizyon* launched another [missile], but after it had gone halfway it suddenly turned its nose downward and hit the ground, so that this Israeli pilot was lucky ... the artillery duel stopped forthwith.[33]

In *Pravda*, Primakov's eulogy of "the progressive-minded" Riad hardly reflected any misgivings about his last decision. "The battlefield death of this great Egyptian soldier ... symbolizes for the people of the UAR that the war against the Israeli aggressor continues ... the Arabs will step up their 'active defense.'" Primakov distinguished this term from full-scale war, and asserted that "Egypt will not be provoked into any adventure ... much has yet to be done to improve the morale of the Egyptian Army."[34] For his part, Nasser betrayed no disagreement with the Soviets but rather lavished praise on the advisers, "who left their families to devote themselves day and night to training the Egyptian army." Israeli monitors noticed that he even departed from his standard-Arabic text and switched to Egyptian vernacular to stress that the advisers' work was essential. This was interpreted as being aimed at "convincing those who dispute the presence of so many Soviet technicians."[35]

Even Riad's death by a new Israeli rocket was not enough to clinch an agreement for supply of Soviet *Luna* (Frog) short-range missiles to Egypt. As this weapon was as unsophisticated and inaccurate as the *Ze'ev*, but with a much longer range, the *Luna* would have been a suitable riposte, especially since its sale had ostensibly been approved already. According to an Egyptian general captured by Israel in the Six-Day War, this had been agreed in principle as early as 1965 and he had been among the officers sent for a training course. But actual delivery was delayed due to a dispute over which version of the *Luna* would be provided. On the anniversary of Riad's death, reports appeared that the system would finally make its appearance on the canal front.[36] The deal would be finalized by Nasser in Moscow only in June 1970, and the missiles' arrival was reported that December.

C. The Soviet advisers are reinforced for protracted fighting

As could be expected, the advisers were less than entirely pleased with the outcome on 8–9 March. Serkov was at first misled by the dust and smoke on the Israeli side to believe that "the strongpoints are not as hardened as was thought, and are easily destroyed by direct-aim fire" (the Egyptians later claimed to have destroyed about 80 percent of the Israeli fortifications).[37] In fact, the Israelis suffered fewer casualties during two days of shelling than the Egyptians did in the Riad incident alone. This even though "the Egyptian artillerymen were shown to be better prepared" and despite the disparity in guns and in ammunition expended. Serkov counted a total of only 120 rounds fired from the Israeli side at Ismailia on the 9th, presumably including the *Ze'ev*s, but this was enough to cause "the worst damage yet." He observed "big explosions, which darkened the city with smoke. Fires broke out. Our artillerymen fired quite intensively but could not silence the enemy."

Indeed, the Bar-Lev Line's bunkers were now stronger than the Egyptians' fortifications—as proved by Riad's fate. Within a few days of the first barrage, Serkov saw "papers being drawn up urgently for improving the defenses." By the fourth day of dueling, the II Army Corps alone had used up 25,500 shells, and "the results were effectively very minor." Such damage as was inflicted on the IDF was mostly on convoys and other exposed targets between the strongpoints. The latter—as the Israelis now disclosed—had been reinforced with rails dismantled from the Qantara–El-Arish track as well as layers of rock-filled wire cages.[38] When on 13 March the firing went on and Egyptian "official data reported that up to 30 tanks were disabled" as well as Israeli strongpoints damaged, Serkov considered the figures to be inflated.

Civilian evacuation of Ismailia, Port Said and the other canal cities was accelerated; the market where the advisers used to shop emptied. "One can't show oneself in the frontline positions for fear of snipers." At Serkov's own villa, "hiding in our flimsy shelters made no sense." A larger and safer shelter was built, "but it still will not hold up against a direct hit." They decided to remain there anyway and fortunately suffered no casualties—for now.

Major artillery exchanges continued unabated, but neither side yet acknowledged a substantive change. Nasser himself did not use the Arabic word for "bloodletting"—the term usually translated as "attrition"—in two speeches at his party conference on 27 and 28 March, which (as Serkov and his colleagues were informed) were otherwise quite warlike. He did not announce a new phase, but promised quite truthfully that "we are doing all we can, and even more, [to prepare] for the campaign. Rest assured, we will not start it one day too early, but also not one day too late." Addressing workers on May Day, Nasser still claimed only that the second stage, "active operations and acquisition of combat experience," had begun—with no mention of "attrition." Although Nasser had preceded the 8 March attack with a declaration that, due to Israeli violations, he would no longer be bound by the ceasefire, both sides continued to complain about violations and the UN observers kept on adjudicating them. Only on 23 July would Nasser even predicate the ceasefire on Israeli withdrawal, and call to "*prepare* for a long war of attrition" before the liberation phase could begin.[39]

A Russian historian—then a correspondent in the Middle East—who dates Nasser's unilateral abrogation of the ceasefire at 1 April 1969 suggests that the dynamics of events on the ground overcame any political misgivings in the USSR about the timing: "the Soviet interest was actually in perpetuating a status of 'no war,

A NEW PHASE FROM MARCH '69?

no peace,' even though formally Soviet diplomacy spared no effort to settle the conflict." Nonetheless, "in Moscow, after some hesitation, no opposition was raised to these steps. Possibly, during those months, a feeling of 'brotherhood-in-arms' was generated between Russians and Egyptians."[40]

Meanwhile, the new arrivals brought the advisers' complement in Serkov's division to thirty-two, but some chronic problems remained: "there are not enough translators to go around, and transportation is insufficient." Worse, among the fresh crop of advisers not all were up to the level of the first contingent; several had come from desk jobs:

> One major ... previously worked for five years at a recruitment office, then spent three filming the movie *War and Peace* ... we had to send him back to the USSR. Another, a lieutenant-colonel who was appointed adviser to an artillery *divizyon* commander, had served for a long time as acting commander of a city garrison. Here he had to work long and hard to fill the gaps in his knowledge.

The Egyptians too were not satisfied. In "Africa" (west of the canal) in 1973, Israeli forces captured a copy of the highly sympathetic instructions for work with the advisers that were issued in January 1969, with a sample report attached that is dated almost a year later. It sums up the work of Andrey Drugatin, an adviser who began his tour in the 336th Infantry Battalion shortly after the procedure was formulated. The battalion commander admitted there had been some benefit from Drugatin's experience, but his knowhow was "poor," he evaded preparation of a training-exercise plan at the company level, and twice declined on various pretexts to deliver lectures. "I believe that he is [merely] a reserve officer, and I recommend not to extend his contract."[41]

Faced with this decline in the quality of new candidates, and with the original two-year hitch of Lashchenko's first recruits approaching its end, the chief adviser's "Ofis" in Cairo urged the old-timers to volunteer for one more year. But even the doughty Serkov confided to his diary that he was beginning to feel his age, and found it "understandable" that few others came forward: "defying fate in the interest of defending a country that has dubious prospects for social and political development—is this worthwhile? I put down my replacement time as November–December '69.'" Afanas'ev, true to his iconic image, did sign on for an extraordinary total of close to five years.[42]

"Truth be told," Serkov concluded, "these shellings are exclusively for moral-political gain. Indeed if evaluated so, they might be quite justified ... [But] for a long time we have been pointing out that from the military viewpoint, such shooting with no precise targets pinpointed by intelligence and with poor fire management achieves little purpose."[43]

D. Cross-canal raids improve

In order to obtain this intelligence data and gain combat experience, Serkov did note a further expansion of cross-canal raids:

THE SOVIET–ISRAELI WAR, 1967–1973

With our support, the division increasingly activates raids by DRGs. They operate at night, so far with little tangible outcome. For a year, they captured no one. We insist on increasing the scale of these raids, using 'ranger' special-operations units in collaboration with other forces … Whatever effect artillery fire may have, real success can be achieved only through proper operations by infantry formations.

Here too, the advisers were actually pressing for more aggressive action than their *podsovietnye* (advisees) were eager to undertake. "Resolve is lacking for more decisive operations. The officers say they will settle for no less than guaranteed success, but in war everything involves risk."[44] Heikal echoes this in judging that "the main military problem confronting Nasser … when the War of Attrition was just beginning" was "how to hold a bridgehead." Egyptian "commando patrols" had succeeded in "staying in Sinai for up to 24 hours," but "the Russian Military Mission was of the opinion that [they] ought to be kept there longer."[45]

Despite the Soviets' discontent, this was one of their greatest successes. Censored Israeli accounts tended to disparage the scale and efficacy of the cross-canal forays. The IDF "victory album" on the War of Attrition states that Egyptian raids and ambushes "although they score no success, require counteraction, safety measures and patrols." The album lists eight major incidents from 19 April through July, in which "the Egyptians made repeated attempts to capture and destroy" an Israeli strongpoint, but never achieved it. However, unnamed Israeli officers told Korn that by December '69, the Egyptians were crossing the canal almost every night to lay mines. "The road south of Deversoir was so heavily strewn with mines that the Israelis gave up trying to dig them out and simply stopped patrolling it." At the time, the service of conscripts and reservists on the canal line was euphemistically described as "the toughest days of their lives." Explicit accounts of increasing demoralization among IDF soldiers, due both to repeated attacks on patrols and prolonged bombardment and isolation in the strongpoints, began to appear in the Israeli media only long after the Yom Kippur War discredited the Bar-Lev Line concept.[46] Like the Soviets, but with better response, the IDF had to appeal to seasoned reserve officers to volunteer for extra stints as strongpoint commanders.

Lashchenko's objective of taking and holding a beachhead on the east bank was finally accomplished in December 1969. The Israelis ridiculed an Egyptian claim that a 250-man raid held one strongpoint for twenty-four hours, and that artillery fire prevented Israel forces from retaking it even after the Egyptians withdrew.[47] But Maj. Avraham Almog, the deputy commander of an Israeli tank brigade on the canal front from March 1969, confirmed in retrospect:

> bit by bit [we] gave up points where access was difficult. … We had a directive to enter one of the abandoned strongpoints at the northern end of our sector. We always found a reason not to go in there. We were afraid to have men killed or wounded. This particular strongpoint, on our side [of the canal], had an Egyptian flag flying over it all the time.[48]

A NEW PHASE FROM MARCH '69?

In testimony before the Agranat Commission that was released only in 2012, Maj.-Gen. Avraham Adan confirmed that the Egyptian raids were "successful" in laying ambushes between the strongpoints, as the planned electronic warning system did not work and manned lookouts were gradually discontinued. Several strongpoints

> were blown up by the Egyptians. They were just before completion in March [1969 and] ... were abandoned by the IDF because of the shelling. The Egyptians mined [them] and backed up the mines with anti-tank fire from the other side. So tank patrols there were stopped ... up to the ceasefire there were areas that were taboo [for us], that were not under our control.[49]

When the ultimate Egyptian offensive was launched, at least some of the soldiers in every Egyptian formation had already experienced a combat crossing, knew what obstacles to expect, and were not intimidated by the mission or the enemy. The Egyptian Army's history of the war attributes its success to this morale-boosting practice in steadily growing formations—as usual, with no mention of the Soviet input.[50] The Israelis did credit the Soviets, at least in retrospect—no doubt partly to excuse their own initial setback in the Yom Kippur War. Briefing Kissinger sixteen days into the fighting, MI (Military Intelligence) chief Maj.-Gen. Eliyahu Ze'ira pointed out that "the enemy armies prepared for this war for four years, and every unit rehearsed its mission countless times. ... The Soviets' influence is [also] very evident in improving confidence, communications, eavesdropping capability on the IDF, electronic warfare and deception."[51]

One of the weapons that Lashchenko had recommended supplying to Egypt was now delivered and soon made its debut. A team of four Soviet instructors arrived in the summer of 1969 to introduce the *Malyutka* (Sagger) shoulder-fired anti-tank rocket.[52] The Israelis identified its first launch on 7 July 1970, when the lead Israeli tank in a convoy evaded the missile but it struck the following tank, causing little damage. In November 1970, however, an Israeli tank was first destroyed by a Sagger.[53] The shock that would be inflicted by this weapon's devastating success against Israeli armor in October 1973 could hardly be attributed to unfamiliarity. More than forty years later, it was still cited by an Israeli general as an example of the surprise caused by a threat that was not unknown but not properly evaluated.[54]

In the short term, however, Serkov noted only a slow improvement in his *podsovietnye*'s ability to carry out routine staff work.

> Combat fire [is being drilled] now at platoon and company level, crossing exercises for battalions. ... Our demands have become more brazen. No room for diplomacy. Sometimes there's a feeling of incompetence when our efforts yield no return. ... There are officers who do not believe in their own capacities, in victory. They start up with talk that we are already fed up with—that the USSR is giving them only little materiel, and it too is unsuited for desert conditions, etc. Apparently they often talk so among themselves in order to justify the low level of their forces' preparedness and their own fecklessness. ... There's no use even

[giving] examples from the successful operation of Chinese, Korean or Vietnamese forces armed with Soviet weapons and equipment against the US Army. In everyday life it is sad and ridiculous to observe how under the tracks of a tank stuck in the sand, the crew clears it away with their bare hands. In the machine's kit there are no shovels ... not even a [towing] cable.

For a year and four months we have not managed to get, from the officers of the division's operations department, any independent development of plans for tactical training or staff exercises. ... The department's deputy commander declared that we will have to keep on preparing such papers for them. [Afanas'ev] explained to him in "popular" language ... that we were here temporarily. To me, Pavel Aleksandrovich said we should draw up one more plan for tactical training at the brigade level, but afterward they should do everything.

The plan was drafted, scheduled for 8 April, and training exercises proceeded despite the continued fighting. Serkov conceded grudgingly, "I would have graded the soldiers 5 [out of 5] for diligence, the officers 3-minus. ... More practical training is needed and less talk." Still, "we prepare such training carefully and the results are noticeable." A month after daily hostilities began, "even a copying table was set up at the operations department. ... This is our first victory. ... A good draftsman was transferred to the department—our second triumph." And yet "it is early to speak of a victorious war. They can carry out a single tactical operation, but only if their forces are reliably covered against the enemy's air force. This is the Egyptians' Achilles heel." He would soon be proved right.

9

WHAT TRIGGERED *KAVKAZ*?

REFUTING HEIKAL'S VERSION

A. How "Nasser's secret visit to Moscow" was canonized

By mid-1969, small-scale precedents had been created for the deployment of regular Soviet formations in Egypt as tripwires or even in deliberate combat assignments. But what was to follow within a year would be such a quantum leap, up to extended engagement with the Israelis, that by April 1970 it could no longer be ignored. At least in hindsight, it had to be accounted for: How, when and why did it start? To trace how an almost universally accepted narrative was created out of all-but-whole cloth, we must fast-forward to the point where the massive, direct Soviet intervention is conventionally held to have begun.

Nearly all histories state that this followed 7 January 1970, when the newly acquired IAF Phantoms began a campaign of "deep-penetration bombings" in Egypt's hinterland, which the latter was powerless to counter. A desperate Nasser flew secretly to Moscow on 22 January and threatened to resign in favor of a pro-American figure unless the Soviets undertook the defense of Egypt's skies. The Politburo reluctantly complied by passing a resolution to dispatch its most advanced SAM-3 missiles and MiG-21 fighters, along with the manpower to operate them until Egyptian personnel could be trained. On 31 January, Premier Kosygin warned the Western powers that if Israel's aggression were not halted, Moscow would provide the Arabs with the means to defend themselves. But the Israeli air raids continued, and the Soviets made good on their threat. By late March, the Soviet-manned missiles and planes appeared in the combat zone. This direct involvement of a superpower in a local conflict was then, by implication, the result of a gratuitous and bloody Israeli escalation, and indirectly of the United States' supplying the tools.

The above is often considered so axiomatic that no sources are cited. Where they are, the trail of footnotes usually leads to a single, retrospective assertion by Nasser himself and (mainly) to the writings of his propagandist, Mohamed Hassanein Heikal. Nasser mentioned "my January visit" to Moscow once, in a speech six months later, at the height of the Israeli–Soviet confrontation on the canal front.¹ Sadat, by then president, first referred to Nasser's request for SAM-3s with Soviet operators in a broadcast on 30 August 1971.² Heikal's detailed account of Nasser's secret visit to Moscow first appeared in the newspaper he edited, *Al-Ahram*, on 28 July 1972.³ Ten days earlier, Heikal had been handed another policy shift to justify: the end of Operation *Kavkaz* with the supposed expulsion of the Soviet advisers by Sadat. This will be addressed later as another egregious but successful falsification by participants with obvious axes to grind.

Heikal's version about both of these turning points—indeed, that they *were* turning points—was canonized in 1975 by his memoir *The Road to Ramadan*.⁴ This book established itself as the authorized version on the antecedents of the 1973 war—not only from the Egyptian side but (for lack of anything comparable) from the Soviet side, too.⁵ It was only in the 1990s that Heikal's account of the January 1970 visit was backed up by two other members of Nasser's entourage to the alleged Moscow talks.⁶

Walter Laqueur observed as early as 1974: "Heykal has been a fairly accurate barometer of the political climate in Cairo. ... [But] as a historical source his 'revelations' have to be read with the greatest of care."⁷ However, Laqueur himself endorsed Heikal's version about the genesis of *Kavkaz* despite the lack of any supporting evidence.

No Soviet or post-Soviet source has ever confirmed even the fact of a visit by Nasser in January 1970, much less identified it as the starting point for direct intervention.⁸ A recent chronology of the post-1967 air war by a Soviet military analyst does not even mention 7 January 1970 (nor any of the depth bombings) as the start of a new phase.⁹ Indeed, several statements by former Soviet officials and officers, which were made after Heikal's version was established, seem at pains to avoid denying it outright. The USSR's then-deputy foreign minister and future ambassador to Egypt, Vladimir Vinogradov, fudged the issue by speaking of a visit "in the winter of 1969."¹⁰ Other testimonies and official research publications, if they mention a visit at all, date it in December or specifically in *early* December—raising the possibility of confusion, intentional or otherwise, with another top-level Egyptian mission to Moscow that month.¹¹

The few weeks' discrepancy with Heikal's version about 22 January is much more than a technical detail. If the Soviet deployment was undertaken before 7 January, it could not be described as a response even to the first deep-penetration raid, let alone the bloodshed caused by subsequent bombings that struck civilian targets. But as the following analysis indicates, it must now be questioned whether Nasser was in Moscow *at all*, in either month. More importantly, there is now a compelling accumulation of mutually supporting testimonies that *Kavkaz* was not only undertaken and prepared, but actually was set in motion, in the summer of 1969 (if not earlier, as claimed by Novosti's Egorin and several others).

WHAT TRIGGERED *KAVKAZ*? REFUTING HEIKAL'S VERSION

B. The sonic-boom incident, 17 June 1969

Back now to the chronological timeline. Igor' Kubersky's 2011 "novel" *Egipet-69* typifies the "fiction" genre of the Putin years. Kubersky was an interpreter for the chief Soviet adviser to Egypt's air defense array, headquartered in the elite Cairo suburb Heliopolis, and his colleagues there have certified his account as factually accurate.[12]

> One morning, I awake to the sound of thunder shaking all the building as if the sky has fallen onto our roof, and I reflexively run out to the balcony. I see them in the dim light—two Israeli Mirages directly over the rooftops ... two afterburners, two orange flames. Belatedly ... from the rooftop where anti-aircraft machineguns were manned around the clock by Arab crews, came the dry rattle of a fire burst ... They had overslept ... But on this memorable morning of 17 June 1969, this blast of breaking the sound barrier woke up all of Cairo and President Nasser himself, over whose residence in Heliopolis the Mirages flew mockingly, flaunting the total helplessness of Egypt's air defense.

> During the morning, we discussed how easily we might have lost our workplace—it would have been nothing for the Mirages to fire a couple of rockets into our headquarters. ... Fortunately no one bombed Cairo, and apparently did not intend to—this was only a gesture ... to humiliate us.[13]

The Israeli intent was so described in proud retrospect by one of the pilots, the leader of one pair among the four Mirages that took off from Sharm el-Sheikh. Their primary mission was photoreconnaissance, but "the secondary purpose" was "to show the Egyptian political echelon that it could not rely on its air force ... to let them know that we were there and they couldn't stop us. There could be no telling of tall tales about it ... and Cairo of summer '69 was full of foreign reporters." All four Mirages turned on their afterburners in coordination upon signal from base, in order to break the sound barrier.[14] This version was taken up by most Israeli and Western histories.[15] But the most recent and authoritative chronicle of the IAF in the War of Attrition attributes the sonic boom to an "operational mishap" in "a fairly routine" sortie. The result was, according to this version, a classic case of unforeseen consequences. It broke several weeks of relative lull in air activity, though the ground fighting along the canal continued to rage with Israeli fatalities approaching an average of one per day.

The latter version, based on the pilots' debriefing immediately after the incident, holds that after the foursome split up, pilot number two of the pair tasked to overfly central Cairo lagged behind his leader, and turned on his afterburner to catch up. The resulting boom

> left a swathe of destruction as its rolling thunder passed through the streets of Cairo, waking the still-sleepy residents. Thousands of panes were shattered. The boom was heard everywhere—including the Egyptian President's residence in Heliopolis and the air defense HQ at Muqatem. ... The Egyptian air defense command was bewildered.

115

THE SOVIET–ISRAELI WAR, 1967–1973

From here, the aviation historian Danny Shalom also takes his own flight of fancy: "Foreign ... radio and TV stations broadcast live about the panic in Cairo's streets. The IAF could not understand the commotion that echoed in from Cairo," though its commander, Hod, was pleased with the outcome.[16]

As a check of contemporary media showed, the incident actually exemplified the paucity of Western news coverage from Cairo, the effectiveness of Egyptian censorship, or both. Not only were there no live broadcasts, but the first mention of the boom incident appeared in the foreign press only ten days later, in reports that were datelined elsewhere and highly exaggerated:

> four Israeli jet fighters flew an unprecedented reconnaissance mission over Cairo on June 17 and got away without being fired on, despite prompt radar warnings when they crossed into Egypt, according to reliable diplomatic reports from Cairo ... The Israeli Mirage planes crisscrossed over the Egyptian capital freely for six or seven minutes before a dozen Egyptian MiG jet fighters were scrambled to intercept them. But it was too late.[17]

By the time this emerged, a reshuffle of top Egyptian commanders had already been reported, in a variety of versions as to the officers involved and the reasons for their ouster or promotion.[18] Once revealed, "the failure ... to react to the Israeli penetration ... was said in Cairo to have been the decisive factor in the abrupt dismissal early last week of the Egyptian air force commander ... and the chief of air defense," and it was suggested that Nasser had replaced the former with "a Soviet-trained officer."[19] This rationale, and the very connection of the purge to the boom incident, was disputed even at the time; whereas the incoming appointees were clearly acceptable to the Soviets, so were their removed predecessors.

The outgoing EAF commander, Mustafa Shalaby el-Hinnawy, was a pioneer of Soviet orientation in the force: during the Suez/Sinai clashes of 1956, he was the only Egyptian pilot already qualified to fly a MiG-17, and led the force's first squadron of these aircraft into combat.[20] His replacement in June 1969, Ali Mustafa el-Baghdady, was of similar background. Moreover, he had headed Egypt's Air Defense Force since it was officially constituted as a separate service a year earlier, and had already been replaced there in May by Mohammad Ali Fahmy, who would remain at the post through the 1973 war and become a national hero. Baghdady, then, was actually *promoted* to command of a larger service, despite the failure of the air-defense system that he had built. The "air defense chief" who was reportedly scapegoated for the 17 June incident was in fact Hassan Kamel Ali, a "special assistant for air defense," through whom Baghdady had reported to the minister of war, and since no replacement for him was announced his post was apparently abolished.[21]

So the personnel changes that followed Nasser's humiliation did not necessarily reflect a shift toward greater reliance on the USSR. But another reminder was served on Egyptians and Soviets alike that restructuring along Soviet lines would not suffice

WHAT TRIGGERED *KAVKAZ*? REFUTING HEIKAL'S VERSION

to counter even Israel's existing aircraft, never mind the Phantoms that it was about to acquire. As Kubersky noted, at air defense headquarters

> it was now clear to everyone: our [SAM-2] missiles are powerless against low-flying targets. Against high-flying targets they work all right, but who would be stupid enough to fly high, where he would be overtaken not only by missiles but even by the antediluvian 85mm AA guns. ... And the Israelis are no fools. They appear instantly and suddenly, at 50–100m altitude—and you are done for.[22]

The lack of early warning on 17 June also emphasized the shortcomings of both Egyptian operators and their Soviet early warning systems: the Egyptian array had received some Soviet radar stations, but it still relied on antiquated telephone reports of visual sightings and on manually updated situation maps at headquarters.[23] The human lookouts were not phased out, but on Soviet advice they were equipped with radio communications and posted in a double ring so that IAF intruders would have to pass over at least two of them; a senior Soviet adviser lists this as an achievement rather than a problem.[24]

C. Israel's "flying artillery" tilts the balance

Worse was to come before the Egyptians and Soviets were jolted into more drastic countermeasures. On 8 July, Egyptian artillery routinely targeted an Israeli convoy moving between strongpoints of the Bar-Lev Line and pinned it down for hours. This time, the ranking officer in the convoy was former IAF Commander Ezer Weizmann, now the IDF operations chief. Weizmann had long since been pressing to involve the air force more actively in the worsening duels along the canal. He now prevailed over the reservations of his successor Hod, as well as the political leadership, who were apprehensive about the US response: Washington had stipulated that the Skyhawks should not be used for offensive operations. Planning began to use the IAF's jets as "flying artillery" to offset the Egyptian advantage in guns.

On 20 July 1969, the artillery and tank duel near Suez City reached a peak. That night, Israeli commandos attacked the Green Island fortress in the Gulf of Suez just off the city's waterfront. Egypt claimed to have repelled the landing and to have shot down no fewer than nineteen Israeli planes. It was announced that Nasser was "satisfied with the outcome ... and convinced it represented a turning point." But Israel, justifying the raid by Egypt's "total disregard" for the ceasefire, denied any aircraft losses at all.[25] The alarm in Cairo was reflected by other wild claims, such as the government spokesman's charge that the raid had been timed to coincide with the Apollo-11 landing on the moon in order to minimize media attention.[26]

Foreign studies have suggested that one of the Israelis' main objectives on Green Island was to knock out an air defense radar station in order to open a corridor for a bombing campaign across the canal.[27] Israeli accounts likewise connect the two operations, though the presence of a radar station on the island has been denied by the leader of the naval commando unit that led the raid.[28] The air offensive that started the next day—the IAF's largest ground-attack operation since the Six-Day War—actually began at the northern end of the canal (which had only sparse SAM coverage anyway) and was later expanded southward.[29] It has been argued that Israel's decision, at this point, to throw its air force into full-scale action was unforeseen by the Egyptians and caused their strategy's breakdown.[30] But Serkov's misgivings cited above are only one indication that such an effort by the Israelis was not entirely unexpected, precisely because of the Egyptians' relative success in the ground war. As a Soviet adviser put it, "Israel's patience snapped." The accelerated attempt to reestablish a SAM barrier along the canal indicates that counteracting the IAF offensive was attempted—for now, unsuccessfully.[31]

The relative immunity of Port Said thanks to the Soviet naval presence was now ended. Two days into the Israeli offensive, a Soviet marine lieutenant posted there, V.I. Dmitriev, witnessed an attack on Egyptian missile boats, even though they "nestled up to [his] BDK for shelter. One burst of aircraft [cannon] fire perforated a UAZ-452 ambulance that was on the upper deck."[32] The Israelis, while bannering the success of the IAF action, took care not to mention any damage to Soviet ships. However, it was noted that Nasser met Vinogradov the same day. *Izvestiya* reported that "for the first time since 1967, the Israeli military bombarded Port Said," and a subsequent Israeli document quoted a Soviet note, which was delivered "through the Finns, after Soviet ships were struck," protesting "this attack as a provocative act which may lead to very serious consequences."[33]

The entire IAF series of deep-penetration bombings that began on 7 January 1970 would comprise eighty-eight sorties in twenty raids spread over three months.[34] For comparison, between July and December 1969 the Soviet advisers along the canal sometimes counted over eighty Israeli sorties *per day* in a single sector. The bombardment was so intense that it forced the Soviet advisers posted to Egyptian front-line formations to move their living quarters underground, and several were killed nonetheless.[35] Once the Israelis had effectively wiped out the Egyptian SAM-2 batteries—as Serkov noted in his journal—Egyptian artillerymen became reluctant to fire lest they reveal their emplacements to Israeli planes, and Israeli tanks could venture out of their shelters to take direct aim at Egyptian positions.[36]

By August 1969, Israel's "flying artillery" had interdicted water-obstacle training in the canal zone, but a better facility had already been inaugurated northwest of Cairo. Vladimir Dudchenko was an interpreter with the Soviet advisers of an infantry brigade of the new III Army Corps. He witnessed how "in the Wadi Natrun area irrigation system, a training ground was set up simulating a section of the Suez Canal with fortifications of the Bar-Lev Line type, where sub-units of the Egyptian army conducted intensive training."[37] By 1973, statistics compiled by IDF intelligence showed that every Egyptian infantry platoon had rehearsed the crossing about fifteen times, with four to five of these exercises conducted at division level.[38]

If this activity was spotted by Israeli pilots during the subsequent "depth bombings," it might explain Israel's retrospective claim that these raids disrupted preparations for a major Egyptian land offensive in the summer of 1970. After the depth raids went wrong and were halted, an Israeli colonel claimed that they "effectively frustrated the Egyptian preparations for an all-out attack ... a possible war was prevented—or at least delayed."[39] But the scope of "depth bombings" could hardly have achieved such a result, and Wadi Natrun is not recorded as one of their targets. A senior Soviet interpreter confirms that already in the summer of 1969, it was Israeli air raids on the Egyptian II and III Army Corps *in the canal zone* that "disrupted their training exercises in preparation for liberating the occupied territories."[40]

So in military terms as distinct from morale and politics, the entire depth-bombing series—and certainly the raids before 22 January—was marginally significant compared to the main theater of war in the summer and autumn of 1969. On 21 July, the day after the "flying artillery" campaign commenced, Karpov, the Soviet artillery adviser posted near Ismailia, noted that in his sector alone, Israeli napalm bombs had destroyed an artillery battery and a SAM-2 *divizyon*. By 1 August, he recorded that two more SAM *divizyons* had been lost and the Egyptians had moved all available AA guns up to the front line to protect the remaining missiles.[41] Serkov, with a neighboring outfit, had already counted five *divizyons* knocked out on 24 July, out of seven then guarding the whole canal. "In effect, the country's entire front-line air defense" was eliminated in a "sudden, daring" IAF operation without losing any planes.[42] The Egyptians counted 15 tons of bombs dropped by Skyhawks in one raid on a single SAM battery, four times the quantity that they reckoned would have sufficed to take it out. The official Egyptian history of the 1973 war states that it was the "flying artillery" campaign (rather than the depth bombings) that led to a decision to remove the remaining SAM-2s from the front "temporarily" until SAM-3s could be procured from the USSR and Egyptian crews for them trained there.[43] Heikal himself puts the bulk of Egyptian civilian losses, which led to Nasser's request for Soviet intervention, among the laborers who were employed in 1969 to set up SAM-2 sites "in a 30-km strip west of the Suez Canal"—not at the heartland targets of the depth bombings.[44]

D. *The Soviets respond: the* Strela-2 *as the vanguard of Kavkaz*

Although the Egyptians claimed to have inflicted similarly heavy losses in air counterattacks on the Israeli side of the canal, the need for a quick fix had become even more pressing. The Israelis, Karpov wrote on 15 August 1969, "had convinced Nasser and his high command that the Air Force and Air Defense were very weak and it was too early to start a war." A writer more sympathetic than Malashenko toward

THE SOVIET–ISRAELI WAR, 1967–1973

Katyshkin credits the chief adviser with the initiative to address this weakness by sending in Soviet regulars:

> When in Moscow the issue had to be decided whether to comply with the Egyptian leadership's request and introduce Soviet military formations into the UAR, there were many doubts and discussions. Not the least part in the positive decision was played by Katyshkin's position. He was of the opinion that besides the nuances of international relations and diplomacy ... an example of combat skills and courage could be given to the Egyptians by Soviet soldiers.[45]

At the end of July, Marshal Savitsky returned to Egypt to inspect the effect of the Israeli air campaign. He "immediately asked to fuel up an interceptor and, in front of the astonished Egyptian pilots, executed some superior aerobatics to demonstrate the combat capabilities of our planes. Their generals don't fly, and the pilots are very poorly prepared—so that the IAF rules the air."[46] Another visitor at this "darkest hour for the air defense forces ...when it seemed that they could not hold out" was the radio-technics head of Soviet Air Defense, Lt-Gen. M.T. Beregovoy. "He listened attentively" to the advisers and made a helicopter tour of the units, "despite the risk of making such a flight in daylight under combat conditions. The results of this tour as reported in Moscow caused the formation of a military specialist group that arrived in Egypt under a separate contract. These were lower-ranking officers, the air-defense forces' repair experts."[47]

By then, at least a partial antidote for low-flying Israeli intruders was on the way. According to Kubersky, it was already in the works when its necessity was demonstrated by the sonic-boom scare:

> Two months before, I had been with one of our advisers when he was received by the Egyptian Army's counterintelligence chief. ... From us he needed only figures and dates, technical-tactical data—when and how many ... [we could supply of] the hand-held, self-homing *Strela-2* system that is effective from 50m to 1500m [altitude], with a range over 3km and a combat-ready weight of 14.5 kg—that is, shoulder-fired. ... The United States' Stingers were still under development, while our *Strela-2* was already being inducted.[48]

The *Strela*'s lead designer, Sergey Nepobedimy, confirms that its development had begun only in late 1967, in response to the IAF's success in the Six-Day War, and was completed in a crash effort "in the spirit of 'socialist construction'" under the personal supervision of munitions production boss Dmitry Ustinov.[49] Heikal states that the *Strela* was first promised to the Egyptians by Brezhnev's now demoted archrival, Aleksandr Shelepin, on a visit to Cairo in January 1969, and supplied during the same year while problems with the "primitive" initial production series were still being ironed out.[50] The decision to try it out in Egypt was thus made but a few weeks after Lashchenko, in his final report, had included it among the "new weapons" that he recommended sending there, and was further accelerated by Nasser's umbrage at the

WHAT TRIGGERED *KAVKAZ*? REFUTING HEIKAL'S VERSION

shattering of his windowpanes.[51] The high priority that the Soviets ascribed to Egypt in this project was noted a year later in a CIA report:

> The new Strela antiaircraft rocket would not be sold to Warsaw Pact countries because several years of production will be needed for the Soviets to meet their own needs ... [but nonetheless] the Soviets are providing the Egyptians with the Strela missile and training them in its use. ... Soviet personnel are almost certainly involved in this program as advisers or technicians. Initial training may have begun in mid-1969, enabling the Egyptians to carry out combat firings beginning in the fall.[52]

Multiple Russian sources, however, now clarify that the *Strela* was used in Egypt even earlier. A highly detailed article by a specialist at the Russian General Staff's Military Academy, Viktor Tkachev, describes an Israeli Skyhawk pilot who ejected and was captured on 19 August after being hit by a *Strela-2* in the missile's "first combat engagement." This confirms the incident's earlier and widely accepted identification by *Jane's* as the new missile's first known kill, attributed to "Egyptian soldiers." Tkachev adds that the *Strela-2* detachment in question had been deployed as early as 9 August to protect a SAM-2 *divizyon*.[53] Nepobedimy revealed in 2003 that his development team was involved in the *Strela*'s Egyptian debut: "We trained a crew in Alexandria and they shot down six out of 10 American [*sic*] planes flying at a low altitude. There was a report to Brezhnev and Grechko. The minister called me in and said 'I have good news for you' ... So I was in heaven with my team."[54]

The Israelis admitted only one Skyhawk lost, and attributed it to "ground fire"; when they first identified a *Strela* hit, on 15 October (as evidently reflected in the CIA report), the weapon's designation was still unknown. A circular from the IAF Operations Branch warned only that a Super-Mystère had been struck by "a surface-to-air missile of the US Redeye type." All squadrons were instructed to raise attack altitude to over 6,000 feet and to minimize their planes' "heat signature."[55] The Soviets soon noticed this, as Kubersky wrote:

> The IAF had used low altitudes and [now] it paid the price. The Arabs rejoiced—the Israelis were in shock. But their intelligence did its job and soon the reason for these casualties was discovered. For sure, they had agents within the top Arab officer corps, and IAF planes went up to high altitude again [where they were vulnerable to SAM-2s].[56]

This, according to the doctrine that is still being taught at the Russian General Staff's Military Academy, was precisely the purpose of deploying the *Strela-2* as a component of the SAM array.

Official Russian military historian Yaremenko gives an almost identical account of the *Strela*'s first use, but puts it at the end of December.[57] This might refer to an additional engagement, but Israel reported no aircraft of any model lost for all of December.[58] It seems, then, that in his 1998 lecture the military historian postdated the *Strela*'s deployment, and listed the six Israeli planes supposedly shot down as

Phantoms, in order to conform with the narrative about the outset of *Kavkaz* "a few days after Nasser's December visit" that was then the authorized narrative in Moscow. When confronted with the Israeli version, Yaremenko pointed out that inflated claims of aircraft shot down (six Phantoms would have been about one-fourth of all Israel had in December 1969) were reported by Soviet officers in the field:

> It's not impossible that they exaggerated. There was also a paradox: the rivalry between the Egyptians and our [men]. We shoot [a plane] down and the Egyptians take credit for the kill. So one plane gets shot down and two are recorded ... that was a game that did a bad job for the statistics, because now it's very hard to prove [the actual numbers].[59]

Another reason for this disparity is probably that the *Strela*'s impact was frequently less than fatal—but once the hit was sighted, or even if the flame of afterburner activation looked like a hit, the plane was reported as shot down. Soviet pilots would have bailed out in such situations, but IAF airmen, acutely aware of their force's numerical inferiority, went to extraordinary lengths to save and land their craft even when severely damaged. In the 19 August battle, for example, Tkachev lists three Skyhawks downed, even though the missile operators actually saw only one plane hit the ground. They reported that another "fell into the Suez Canal," some 10 miles away and therefore out of their sight, while the third was merely seen "turning back."

These discrepancies would recur throughout *Kavkaz* and would apply to the main SAM units too. Their commander, Aleksey Smirnov, mentions a promise from the Air Defense Forces chief that the first *divizyon* commander to shoot down an Israeli Phantom would be made a Hero of the Soviet Union. Glory was not the only motivation for inflated claims: a senior political officer, Viktor Logachev, attests that the commander of any missile crew credited for a kill received a bounty of 200 Egyptian pounds, more than two months' pay.[60] Smirnov's own figures for Israeli planes shot down by his missilemen also exceed Israel's confirmed losses, and he admits that some Soviet officers registered even wilder claims. "I don't know where they took these figures. Let them stay on their conscience."[61] But accurate or not, the claim on behalf of the SAM-7 was used effectively by the Soviets to promote the prowess of their weaponry and by the Egyptians to solicit further Soviet assistance: "The intensity of Israeli raids decreased drastically. The world learned of the appearance of a shoulder-fired, heat-seeking Soviet missile system."[62]

Was it Egyptians or Soviets who actually fired the newfangled *Strela*s in these early encounters? Since Tkachev mentions that "the [Egyptian] personnel had not yet completed the full training course," at least Soviet instructors were undoubtedly still present. Kubersky's "fictionalized" genre allowed him to describe the Soviets' role more openly: "that some teams of our experts reached the canal, ready to 'work' on the IAF, was a super-secret."[63] Yaremenko, lecturing in 1998, already hinted almost as broadly that the Soviet experts were directly involved: "the Egyptians were trained ...

WHAT TRIGGERED *KAVKAZ*? REFUTING HEIKAL'S VERSION

by test engineers from a military scientific institute who had been sent urgently to a friendly country ... a unique precedent in Soviet military co-operation."

More importantly, Tkachev's description clarifies that the SAM-7s were not merely an isolated stopgap, but the vanguard of an integrated array that in the Soviet Air Defense Forces routinely shielded all SAM-2 and SAM-3 batteries and also included mobile anti-aircraft cannon. Thus even if the first Soviet crews that brought the shoulder-fired rockets only trained Egyptians in their use, the Soviet SAM-3 division that was soon to deploy in Egypt certainly included Soviet-operated *Strela*s, possibly manned by the same crews, and they must have accounted for at least part of the kills claimed for these missiles until the ceasefire in August 1970. Being the most easily portable part of the array, the shoulder-launched missiles could be sent urgently in response to Egyptian concerns after the boom over Cairo and Israel's intensive bombing in the canal zone. The heavier cannon would soon join them.

E. MiG-21 squadrons are marshaled for Egypt, August 1969

In previous Israeli and Western studies, the earliest date given for the Kremlin's beginning "to contemplate sending pilots to Egypt" was October 1969.[64] That too contradicts Heikal's claim, but a commander in the air contingent has clarified that this operation was not only decided upon but set in motion more than two months earlier.

The first Israeli Phantom pilots completed their crash course in the United States ten days after the "flying artillery" was sent in.[65] On the morrow, the Soviet chargé d'affaires in Washington delivered a protest against these attacks and "attempts to take possession of Green Island," while stressing that the Soviets "are for restraint" and more "exchange of views."[66] But the same day, 1 August 1969, Lt-Gen. (then Col.) Yury Nastenko, the leader of a MiG-21 air reconnaissance wing, was summoned to a full meeting of the "military council" at the headquarters of his Air Army Corps. The commander, Lt-Gen. V.S. Loginov, asked him point-blank "what I would think about an offer to command a group of volunteer pilots to provide internationalist aid for the Egyptian people in repulsing the Israeli aggression." For Nastenko, "thus began the operation code named *Kavkaz*."

Nastenko had a personal score to settle: as a MiG-21 squadron leader in June 1967, he and his men had sat out the Six-Day War in their cockpits at Yerevan-West, the closest Soviet air base to the combat zone, waiting for an order that never came to intervene in favor of the Arab side. Now, when "offered" a second go,

> for twenty years I had been trained to answer in the positive. The next day ... we flew to a meeting with Minister of Defense A.A. Grechko and Chief of Staff Zakharov. When one of the unit commanders started declaiming the usual slogans about our being the strongest and most capable and our victory being assured, Marshal Zakharov (who had seemed to be dozing) lifted his eyes and ... said: "I don't know if you can beat this *supostat* [arch-

123

THE SOVIET–ISRAELI WAR, 1967–1973

enemy], but you owe the Motherland and the pilots' families to bring them back alive rather than in zinc coffins."[67]

Nastenko puts the force earmarked for Egypt at seventy MiG-21s (of the naval variant, which was better armed for interception of Israeli Mirage fighters than the Air Force version) and 102 pilots. According to aviation historian Zhirokhov,

> these Soviet pilots were ... selected from amongst the very best. They had been rated as 1st, or at least 2nd, class and some had an enormous number of flying hours to their credit. Before leaving the USSR they had to pass a theoretical examination and undertake special training flights at the Central Asian airbase of Mary [now Merv in Turkmenistan], where the desert climate was considered comparable to that of Egypt.[68]

This prior training went on for a month. Col. Boris Abramov, who would soon be assigned as a staff officer at the Moscow headquarters of *Kavkaz*, admitted retrospectively:

> The intention was excellent, but the implementation very poor. First it was decided to train the crews for flight at minimal altitude, but a catastrophe ensued when a pilot hit the ground. The lowest approved altitude was immediately raised, [but] another catastrophe [occurred]. The flights at minimum altitude were stopped completely. ... Our pilots arrived in Egypt and immediately encountered a severe reality, where they had to fly so low that the sand was blown [off the ground].

Abramov attributes both the combat and accidental losses that the Soviet air group would incur to this deficient training.[69] "One of the men who went through this procedure" is quoted by Zhirokhov as blaming a different problem: "those who trained them and tested their flying capabilities took the matter very seriously. Their briefings did, however, tend to emphasize the weaknesses rather than the strengths of the Israeli Mirages which the Soviet pilots would soon have to face."[70] At any rate, they were deemed ready for departure by mid-September 1969.

That month, the number of Soviet military interpreters in Egypt alone reached at least 430; since only top commanders had personal interpreters attached while others had to share them at a ratio of 4–5:1 at best, the number of advisers must have both grown in itself and been swelled by the arrival of *Kavkaz* officers ahead of their units.[71]

According to Lt-Col. Yossi Sarig, then head of research at IAF intelligence, in September or October Israeli sigint intercepted messages between Soviet MiG-21 units in the USSR and Egypt about equipment transfers that he interpreted as preparation for arrival of Soviet squadrons. MI chiefs, however, declined to spread the report beyond the Air Force, and it was largely overlooked.[72]

10

DR CHAZOV'S "VACATION IN EGYPT"

A. Superpower talks and Nasser's "flu"

Through the summer of '69, US–USSR discussions about "basic principles" for a Middle East settlement dragged on, in an apparent effort by Moscow to temporize until its regulars were in place. After meeting Kissinger on 11 June, Ambassador Dobrynin reported that the Middle East was next on Kissinger's agenda after Vietnam and SALT. But Kissinger said that Nixon thought a settlement could be "accomplished only through an *unpublicized* exchange of opinion between the USSR and USA, who ... need not be under the thumb of their clients ... it would be necessary for both sides (the Arabs and Israel) to 'swallow the bitter pill of certain compromises.'"

This was a clear jab at the talks that Dobrynin had been holding regularly with Assistant Secretary of State Sisco. The Soviet ambassador, despite his earlier disparagement of Kissinger's character, now noted that they had developed a "fairly good personal rapport." Since "Kissinger's influence on ... Nixon's foreign policy remains predominant," Dobrynin considered "it would be advisable to develop and utilize the Kissinger channel ... where publicity is undesirable, something that very often cannot be achieved by working through the State Department."[1] Still, Dobrynin continued to meet almost weekly with Sisco. A blow-by-blow analysis of their wrangling over minutiae of phrasing and procedure thus might offer a fascinating exercise in diplomatic history, but would be relevant to developments on the ground mainly as a diversion.[2]

In early September, as the groundwork for Soviet intervention was being laid, Nasser suffered a heart attack and (as informants close to the Egyptian president disclosed long after his death) he "received medical care from the Soviets. ... Soviet doctors told Nasser he had one year to live."[3] At the time, it was reported that he postponed a trip to Moscow that was originally scheduled for September on the pretext of a bad flu, which actually disguised this heart attack.[4] Heikal retained this fiction in his story of a secret visit to Moscow in January 1970: Nasser supposedly decided to go even though "he was ill—an attack of the flu on top of all his other complaints."[5] But the memoirs of Nasser's Soviet physician call into serious question not only his purported flu but whether the president was in the USSR at *any* time during this period.

THE SOVIET–ISRAELI WAR, 1967–1973

Dr Chazov relates that he took a "vacation" in Egypt "several months" after Nasser left Tskhaltubo in August 1968, and found him "feeling well, walking a lot and even playing tennis." Nasser repeatedly put off another trip to take the Georgian waters, but an Arab summit in early September 1969 "exhausted him." On 10 September, then-KGB Chairman Yuri Andropov informed Chazov that Brezhnev had received a request from Cairo to send the doctor there urgently and in strict confidence (as it turned out, this was at the suggestion of Sadat and Heikal).

Andropov estimated that the arrival of a special plane would draw the attention of Israeli intelligence "which operated well in Cairo." So Chazov, in shades and hat, was put on an Aeroflot flight, sharing the entire first class cabin with a single military adviser. Within twenty minutes of arrival he was rushed to Nasser, who on the 10th had felt weakness and chest pain. Chazov could only confirm the Egyptian doctors' findings: symptoms of myocardial infarction—a heart attack.

Nasser would not hear of resting for a month or longer, which (he feared) might disrupt the rehabilitation of his military. They settled on an initial ten days of rest and medication, during which Chazov was cloistered in a cordoned-off section of Shepheard's Hotel except for daily house calls after dark. His presence was successfully concealed: no Soviet physician was named among the three doctors that the foreign press reported as treating Nasser. It was at Chazov's suggestion that the medical bulletins stated Nasser had caught the flu "which was going around in Cairo"; this euphemism had been used frequently for Soviet and other communist leaders. Heikal and other Egyptian flacks perpetuated the flu story, extending it as far as January, and it became firmly established as fact even though Nasser never actually contracted the disease.

As his patient improved, Chazov relates, their nightly talks extended beyond mere medical matters:

> At the end of the visit, when he gave me a personal letter for Brezhnev ... I understood that Nasser was dissatisfied with the supply of outdated weapons, that he needed SAM-3s instead of SAM-2s, and MiG-25s to cover Egyptian skies, and to train an adequate number of Egyptian military experts in the USSR. He spoke of Israel's impending attack and of Alexandria's vulnerability. All this was stated indirectly and diplomatically.[6]

The defense of Alexandria, for instance, was brought up by suggesting that Chazov should take a seaside break there, which he accepted. But the message he relayed is yet another proof that the main element of *Kavkaz* was at least under discussion no later than mid-September. Even if Nasser did go to Moscow in December *or* January, the visit's purpose and outcome was at most to accelerate the Soviet intervention that had already been undertaken.

After Nasser's agreed ten days of rest, Chazov flew home concerned that his patient would not maintain the prescribed regimen, and indeed a week later the

DR CHAZOV'S "VACATION IN EGYPT"

Egyptian president resumed his routine workload. Chazov states that he was kept abreast of Nasser's condition but was able to see him again only in July 1970 in Moscow.[7] *Nasser death 28 Sept. 70.*

Nasser's seclusion produced a plethora of rumors, leaks, wishful thinking and disinformation, which the Western press—lacking direct sources in Cairo—headlined almost daily, overshadowing the intense ground and air fighting that continued on the canal front. The story broke on 16 September, after Jordan's prime minister related, on his return from Cairo, that the president "was too sick with a cold to see him." The greatest play was given worldwide to an exclusive report by the "independent" Beirut paper *Al-Jarida*. It claimed that Nasser had purged "several top pro-Soviet colleagues" to forestall a Soviet plot to depose him. Front-page stories claimed that "the Kremlin planned to engineer Nasser's overthrow while he was in Russia for medical treatment" later in September. "The Soviet Union wants to topple Nasser because of widening conflicts with him on the issues of armaments for Egypt, Russian influence in Egypt and the overall Middle East problem."

When this did not occur, it had to be reported that the Soviet coup was foiled. The best-known pro-Moscow figure in Egypt, Arab Socialist Union (ASU) Secretary Ali Sabry, whom the Soviets had supposedly groomed to supplant Nasser, was reportedly ousted and put under house arrest. "Relations between Nasser and Sabry have been tense, and the situation became further inflamed recently when Sabry returned from Moscow with a load of expensive furniture."[8] Two days later, "diplomatic sources" in Beirut claimed that "Nasser has demanded the recall of Soviet Ambassador Sergey A. Vinogradov … Nasser is trying to emphasize his annoyance with what he considers Soviet interference … the Soviets are believed to have been alarmed at what they consider Egypt's increasing belligerence."[9]

As Cairo officially denied that Nasser was scheduled to go to the USSR in the first place, a prominent Israeli commentator later suggested "one of the most plausible" among many speculations: that not only the flu was fictitious but that Nasser had never been sick at all. Rather, he had used the imminent trip to Moscow to excuse, in advance, his absence from the first Muslim summit conference, which was scheduled for the Moroccan capital Rabat on 22–5 September. The Saudis, taking advantage of the fire at the Al-Aqsa Mosque in Jerusalem on 21 August, had outsmarted Nasser by expanding the *Arab* summit (which he had envisaged to press for more money from the oil-producing states) into an all-*Muslim* conference.[10] But

> Moscow was not particularly interested to have Nasser there and [to] be obliged to promise him further large quantities of arms at a time when Mr Gromyko hoped to present his best peace-loving face … There are mounting indications that friction between Egyptian officers and officials, on the one hand, and Russian military advisers and Soviet diplomats in Cairo, is attaining critical proportions … Nasser is in a bigger mess that at any time since he lost the June 1967 war.

So—this optimistic Israeli reading went—Moscow postponed the invitation, Nasser saved face by claiming he never intended to go there anyway, and the flu was invented merely as an excuse to stay away from Rabat.[11]

Still, reports from diplomatic sources in London held that "Soviet leaders and ... Nasser are preparing for a face-to-face meeting within the next few weeks ... there has been a marked cooling off in Egyptian–Soviet relations recently, which necessitates a policy review."[12] Even after Nasser resumed a partial workload on 24 September,[13] a well-connected Washington columnist was told that "President Nasser sent a message to President Nixon asking what the United States would do for his country if Soviet influence should be reduced. Apparently, the suspicious Nasser had been listening to rumors" whereby Sabry "had been dealing behind his back with Moscow. Nasser might even have feared that Moscow was conspiring to install Sabry in his place."[14] After a "lengthy" session with Rogers at the UN General Assembly, Egyptian Foreign Minister Mahmoud Riad had indicated that "his country may, at long last, be willing to sit down at the same table with representatives of Israel," and this was explained by "the apparent withdrawal of Egypt's President Nasser from the public scene, lending support to a belief that his pro-Soviet advisors also are out of favor."[15]

None of this had any basis. Any innovation in Riad's offer was soon dispelled when he clarified that it was predicated on a prior Israeli withdrawal. The reports of tension or worse between Nasser and the Soviets proved to be another judicious deployment of the Cairo "chattering class" to plant disinformation. Sergey Vinogradov was out of Cairo at the time, but he was never removed and would die at his post there a year later—shortly before Nasser's own death disposed of any doubt that his illness had been both real and worse than flu. While Sabry's downfall was being proclaimed in the Western media, he was in fact one of the few confidants allowed into Nasser's residence during the president's indisposition, where he met Chazov and, at Nasser's behest, invited the doctor home for dinner.[16] Sabry remained in prominent positions; he was later appointed air defense adviser to Nasser and thus his liaison with the Soviet military in Egypt, with a brief for bimonthly trips to Moscow. He would be considered the favorite to succeed Nasser, and would become vice-president when Sadat surprised everyone by getting the top job. As late as January 1971, Sadat even declared, after one of Sabry's Kremlin visits, that Egyptians had "nothing to worry about" in respect of continued Soviet aid.[17] Sabry would be deposed only several months afterward.

The only ostensible fulfillment of "the prediction by *Al-Jarida* ... that Nasser had begun a purge of pro-Moscow officials" was his decision to replace Chief of Staff Ahmed Ismail (Gen. Riad's successor, an alumnus of the Frunze military academy) with Mohammed Ahmed Sadiq.[18] But this followed an unprecedentedly daring Israeli raid on 9 September 1969, when a force of Soviet-made tanks and armored personnel carriers (APCs) that had been captured in 1967 met no effective resistance as it swept for dozens of miles along Egypt's Red Sea coast. A Soviet-supplied radar station was among the targets that were overrun.

Kubersky's "novel" relates how he encountered the Israeli column while traveling to Cairo on leave from an Egyptian SAM-2 battery at Hurghada, where he had been transferred after the sonic-boom incident. He was the only soldier in a civilian bus, and the driver quickly turned him in when the Israelis demanded, at the point of a tank cannon, the surrender of any military personnel. But after an exchange with a Russian-speaking member of the tank crew, he was allowed to proceed with the other bus passengers—bearing a message to the Soviet command to "go home." Continuing north, he saw the remains of vehicles destroyed by the Israeli column, including the flattened American car of the Egyptian general in command of the sector.[19]

If Kubersky's account of his own escape is factual, he was lucky. In the car were probably also the remains of a Soviet colonel, the Egyptian general's adviser, who was unaccounted for after the raid.[20] So was the adviser to a SAM battery at Ras Zaafrana that was attacked by IAF planes supporting the armored incursion before the tanks overran it.[21] The latter was recently named in a regional Russian newspaper as Major Pavel Karasev.[22] But Israeli accounts include no such incident as Kubersky describes, and indicate that the tanks destroyed every moving target they encountered, civilian as well as military.[23] In the absence of corroborating evidence, this part of his "novel" must be considered as fictitious embroidery around the reports he read or heard about the raid.

However, this was another case of Soviet casualties long before the "depth bombings." The Arab media stressed, and neither Israeli nor US spokesmen denied, that Israel's newly received Phantoms had provided some of the operation's air cover, which would hardly have disposed Nasser to initiate any gesture toward Washington.[24] The weak Egyptian defense so enraged Nasser that it was reported to have caused a relapse of his diabetes—actually the heart attack of 10 September.[25] Ahmed Ismail was indeed Soviet-trained and considered pro-Moscow, but he was only the highest-ranking among a large group of officers who were cashiered after the Israeli raid—all of whom were directly connected with the failure to repel it.

The Egyptian president's real standing in Moscow was demonstrated when, soon after Chazov's return home, the doctor was awarded the Order of Lenin—officially for "developing medical science and public health." When he protested to Andropov, "I didn't earn it," the KGB chief replied "what you did for Nasser, you did for our country. You cannot imagine how great a political asset his health is today."[26] In a 2010 interview, Chazov embellished the story by adding to Andropov's "surprised" answer: "you have to understand that ... your work in Egypt meant more than if we had sent in two divisions."[27]

THE SOVIET–ISRAELI WAR, 1967–1973

B. The Shilkas *arrive as the next component of* Kavkaz

One division was already on its way. Nasser was back on his feet in time to greet the first seaborne elements of a Soviet Air Defense division, which would be formally constituted only later. Gennady Shishlakov, a former noncommissioned officer, related in 2006 that as the crew leader of a state-of-the-art *Shilka* (ZSU-23–4) self-propelled anti-aircraft cannon, he was sent to Egypt in the vanguard of *Kavkaz* in October 1969. When their ship docked in Alexandria, "because we were the first among the entire Soviet forces group ... there was a small ceremony, and Abdel Nasser spoke." As Shishlakov relates that his outfit was fielded only after the crewmen were screened by the KGB and underwent specialized training, the process must have begun considerably earlier.[28] "October 1969" is also the starting date for "Soviet combat operations" in Egypt, according to an official military publication in 1989.[29]

A Politburo decision enabling the SAM division's dispatch thus had to be made long before January. It was impossible to pretend that this was a gesture to placate Nasser, as he had already witnessed its implementation. The post-Soviet history of the Russian Air Force states that in December 1969, Grechko issued the formal order to activate operation *Kavkaz*, under a *previous*, secret Politburo resolution that was "based on understandings with the Egyptians to establish in UAR territory an operational group of Soviet forces."[30] As already seen about the Fifth *Eskadra*, the formal incorporation of the command structure followed, rather than preceded, the formation's practical creation and even its deployment.

Nasser was not always present, but the Soviet regulars were routinely welcomed—and indoctrinated—by the top Soviet brass in Egypt. Chief military adviser Katyshkin "personally met every ship that brought Soviet personnel, told them confidentially about the situation" and warned that "in the Egyptian armed forces, up to the very top echelon, Israeli and US agents were operating. He also informed his compatriots that among the IAF personnel there were more than a few originating in the United States and Europe, as well as mercenaries"—one of the earliest appearances, and possibly the source, of this tenacious canard.[31]

Was the "mercenaries" fabrication originated by the Soviets or the Egyptians? In June 1967, the Egyptian "big lie" that US and British carrier-based aircraft took part in Israel's preemptive air strike was echoed by the Soviet media. It was dropped (but not denied) after the Fifth *Eskadra*, which was monitoring the Sixth Fleet, reported that there had been no such US activity.[32] As Katyshkin's statements are not precisely dated, it is hard to determine whether they preceded or followed an interview that Egyptian Defense Minister Fawzy gave to a Polish newspaper on 9 December 1969. He charged there that some 120 Americans, including electronics and radar experts as well as airmen, had changed their names and come to Israel.[33] Badry's 1974 book on the war of the previous October, written while criticism of the United States was still politically correct in Egypt, alleges that US support for Israel included "numer-

DR CHAZOV'S "VACATION IN EGYPT"

ous volunteers to operate sophisticated electronic equipment."[34] Whether or not the Soviets had suggested this propaganda line, they continued to repeat it, both to their own forces and outwardly, and pounced on any fact that seemed to confirm it.

Fawzy's charge appeared on the day that Egypt claimed to have shot down a first Phantom in a big dogfight over the Gulf of Suez. The encounter did take place, though at the time the Egyptian claim was dismissed in Israel as "fairy tales." IAF Phantoms were used for the first time to cover Mirages and Skyhawks attacking Egyptian SAM batteries. An Egyptian MiG-21 did get into position behind the lead F-4, and fired two Atoll missiles, one of which "exploded near the plane." The Egyptian pilot stated "I *think* the F-4 crashed on its way home." The Phantom, however, flew again the next day.[35]

Meanwhile, the *Shilka*s had taken up positions. Shishlakov's recollection of their arrival in October 1969 checks out against Israeli observations. A year earlier, after the IDF's heliborne raid at Nag Hammadi, on the northern fringe of the Soviet-built Aswan Dam complex, the Soviet ambassador pledged to defend the dam, and "air defenses subsequently built up around it were partially Soviet-manned."[36] In April 1969, the Israelis carried out an air bombardment of the same site. The pilots reported that the region was brightly lit up, and that again they met no resistance. But when the IAF tried to repeat the exercise on 26 October 1969, the Nile valley was blacked out and the attackers ran into heavy, effective flak. Two planes sustained considerable damage and barely managed to return to Sinai.[37] The Soviet *Shilka*s had evidently arrived, for their first deployment outside the USSR.[38]

On the canal front too, the Israelis noticed that

> the AA cannon can be a greater nuisance [than the SAM-2s] ... One squadron leader noted: "... I must say to their credit that they don't stop shooting. They don't get scared. Once they used to flee at the very sound of [our] planes and bury their faces in the ground. Now they shoot even as the bombs are falling."[39]

As there is no evidence that the Soviet-manned *Shilka*s had already been posted on the canal, the air defense advisers may have begun to achieve results even with the Egyptians' older-model guns.

So did their naval counterparts: on the night between 9 and 10 November, Soviet advisers led an Egyptian naval bombardment of Israeli forces on the northern Sinai coast.

> Our directives were clear: "the Soviet military advisers should not participate directly in military operations." We used to go to sea incognito, in seamen's blue fatigues with no insignia or documents. ... Only six months later, when they returned to the USSR, three advisers were decorated for "bravery and valor while carrying out a mission for the Soviet government."

They were the only naval advisers to be decorated during 1967–9.[40]

For lack of long-range bombers, the IAF had used its French-made Nord Aviation Noratlas transports for the Nag Hammadi raids, dumping the bombs through the rear cargo doors. After their narrow escape on the second try, the Israelis no longer had to resort to such improvisation. On 5 September, the first four Phantoms had flown in from the United States. More arrived at the rate of four a month, and by 22 October they were sent into action on the canal front, even before technical adjustment and crew training were complete.[41] This was a matter of some concern for the first squadron's commander, Shmu'el Hetz. He flew the plane that the Egyptians claimed to have downed on 9 December, together with Menahem Eini, the squadron's senior WSO (weapons system officer, the US term; "navigator" in IAF parlance). Hetz and Eini would really be shot down only in July 1970.

C. Whose mission to Moscow in December 1969?

On 8 December, after another attempt to reestablish an Egyptian SAM-2 array in the canal zone was thwarted by the IAF, an Egyptian delegation to Moscow was led by Sadat, Fawzy and Riad.[42] Premier Kosygin was officially quoted as promising them "active measures to strengthen the defense potential of the UAR."[43] The advisers in Egypt were briefed by 14 December that "in Moscow, Soviet–Egyptian talks have concluded. We hope that some cardinal measures are to be implemented in respect of the inadequate condition of the air defense and air force."[44]

Others were told about a "personal request" by Nasser without mentioning any Egyptian mission to Moscow at all; they too describe the preparations for dispatching the SAM division as already in full swing by December.[45] Riad later quoted Brezhnev as stating to Sadat's party that sixty Soviet pilots were ready to leave for Egypt within a month, and promising to send SAM-3 detachments—almost precisely the commitments that supposedly were obtained by Nasser only in January.[46] Indeed, multiple Russian sources still describe the Egyptian delegation in December as led by Nasser himself. This version was most recently reiterated by the deputy head of the Russian Defense Ministry's Military History Institute, Valery Vartanov.[47] Post-Soviet journalists who interviewed veterans about their service in the Middle East, and evidently consulted standard Russian reference works for background, dated Nasser's visit in December as a matter of fact.[48]

If that was the case, the official Egyptian announcement that Sadat, Fawzy and Riad only *reported* to Nasser after returning from Moscow on 12 December was fabricated to disguise a secret trip by the president himself.[49] But Nasser would hardly have passed through Moscow, even under the strictest secrecy, without being examined by the trusted Chazov. The latter, however, not only mentions no such visit, but positively states that he did *not* see Nasser until the following summer. The doctor only notes disapprovingly that Nasser disobeyed his orders from September. This occurred when Nasser visited the new revolutionary regime in Libya on

DR CHAZOV'S "VACATION IN EGYPT"

27–8 December, on his way back from the finally convened Rabat conference. Chazov confirms Heikal's version that Nasser was rebuked by Brezhnev—and adds that this reprimand was made at the physician's behest: "Dr Chazov has learned that you spent five hours standing up in a jeep, and followed this by making a speech lasting an hour. This is absolutely contrary to his instructions and a grave danger to your health."[50]

The persistent Russian version about a visit to Moscow in December by the Egyptian president in person may thus reflect rumors intentionally spread at the time within the Soviet military in order to highlight the urgency of Nasser's plea, which was actually transmitted by his emissaries, and thus to justify the unprecedented nature of the nascent intervention. In any event, the talks with Sadat's delegation—or Nasser's, if he led it after all—could not have caused the initiation of *Kavkaz* but at most speeded up its implementation.

The overwhelming evidence that integral Soviet formations began to arrive in Egypt no later than October 1969 not only contradicts Heikal's version that their dispatch was approved only late in January 1970; it also casts in a rather pathetic light the preliminary presentation of Rogers's peace plan to both Egypt and the USSR on 28 October (it was publicly unveiled on 9 December 1969).

The earlier date for activation of *Kavkaz* is corroborated by testimonies from all echelons of the SAM division, up to its commander, Col.-Gen. Aleksey Smirnov (then a major-general), who dates Nasser's visit in "*early* December." The same month, he was urgently summoned to meet his superior, Air Defense Commander Marshal Pavel Batitsky. In Smirnov's account, one of the first to emerge about the Soviet involvement, Batitsky is said to have been told by Brezhnev two months earlier "Pavel Fedorovich, the Arabs must be helped," and to have responded "why not? We helped them before, and will do so again."[51] Then, as Smirnov relates, Batitsky asked him: "'What do you think—should Israel be punished for launching aggression against the Arabs?' Being a military man, I answered briefly 'It should.' 'Are you ready to go?' 'I am.' And so I left for Egypt, to punish Israel."[52]

In later versions, Smirnov toned down the language and added detail. Batitsky "advised me of top-secret information regarding preparations for Operation *Kavkaz*, and ordered Col.-Gen. V.D. Sozinov to brief me on the particulars." Secrecy was tight: "Sozinov warned me that no one should know about this. I signed a document without having time to properly consider what my subordinates and I would be expected to carry out."[53] In a 1998 interview for *Al-Ahram*, also giving the December date, Smirnov stressed: "Our mission was, of course, undertaken on the orders of the Soviet government and the Politburo of the Soviet Communist Party, in execution of the agreement between us and the Egyptian leadership."[54] When he was briefed, not only had the codename *Kavkaz* already been assigned, but the manpower too—for the SAM-3 batteries as well as their *Strela* and *Shilka* outriders. *Divizyon* commander Konstantin Popov dated his own attachment to the operation in November.[55]

133

THE SOVIET–ISRAELI WAR, 1967–1973

Smirnov's new command, the 18th Air Defense Division, was formally created on 13 January 1970, ten days before Nasser allegedly requested it.[56]

Even before its official incorporation, by the end of 1969, 10,000 officers and men had been assigned to the 18th Division, out of a total of 32,000 who had been selected for service in Egypt. The division's manpower would be rotated to keep it at a constant level of over 10,000.[57] A staff officer of the *Kavkaz* "operational group" states that the Soviet–Egyptian agreement set a figure of 15,000.[58]

"No one was forced to go to Egypt," writes Col. Boris Zhayvoronok, who would command an air defense brigade on the canal front:

> It was possible to refuse. You won't believe this, but the only one who was afraid to go was a colonel. ... He took me aside to ask that I say something to disqualify him—muttered something about pains in his legs that prevented him from running fast. I didn't blame him, but it's better not to go into battle with such people.[59]

11

THE SOVIET REGULARS MOVE IN

A. Screening and training

"Selection was very meticulous, [by] health, combat morale and political characteristics," relates a political officer who was posted to Egypt. "Anyone who had relatives overseas, who had two children, who had been married more than once, or who tended to drink or 'veer to the left' [carouse and womanize] was disqualified."[1] In this screening, "the 'fifth rubric' [ethnicity] played a role too, because for the war against Israel a certain nationality was unsuitable."[2] A former intelligence officer states this explicitly: "Jews ... weren't taken. The Arabs didn't like them, and their special services saw to it zealously. If anyone's face looked 'suspicious' they demanded his exclusion."[3]

The process, then, was not overseen by the Soviets alone, and this was not the only Egyptian presence: K. Popov relates that when the missilemen went for training in desert operations, at Ashuluk north of Astrakhan', the first Egyptian crews had already arrived there too. "In the morning, the Soviet officers taught the Egyptians ... and in the afternoon, they would repair the equipment that the Egyptians had damaged." In January, Popov recalled, the Soviet Air Defense top brass visited the training ground, were shocked by the Egyptians' ineptitude, and made the final decision that Soviet personnel had to be dispatched instead.[4] The designation of the Russian deployment as temporary, until it could be replaced by Egyptians, was taken seriously—but it would take over two years to prepare.

V. Rakovsky, an An-12 flight engineer, describes how the destination of their transport mission was kept secret, and the senior political officer of his unit even misled them by recommending they read a book about Japan. "But another *politrabotnik* [political officer] explained why 'members of the Jewish nationality were not being included in the crews.' The obvious meaning was the Middle East."[5] Jews were even asked by others to help them evade the mission. A Jewish senior official at Radio Vilnius at the time recalled that "colonels ... from units based in Lithuania who had been 'offered' postings in Egypt but didn't want to go came to Jewish civilian doctors to consult how they could simulate some disease that would get them exempted from the mission without being discharged from military service."[6]

THE SOVIET–ISRAELI WAR, 1967–1973

A typical story is that of Aleksandr Pechenkin, who was conscripted in May 1969 and sent to Baku for training in air-defense radio technology. In December, shortly after he finished the course, "rumors spread that 'volunteers' were being selected for service 'overseas.' ... All the *zenitchiks* [anti-aircraft weapons operators] had their photos taken for special documents, and later it turned out that a *divizyon* was being assembled in each Air Defense district."[7] Sent back to Baku, Pechenkin and his comrades were joined by "mysterious Arabs" to train for cooperation. Their SAM-3 outfit was later augmented with *Shilka* and *Strela* crews. After live-fire exercises, they loaded their hardware onto a train for an undisclosed destination, but were informed on the way by a railroad worker that they were going to Nikolaev, and that "you're not the first shipment going there, nor the last." At the closed Black Sea port, they spent three days loading the gear onto a freighter; after sailing, though dressed in civvies, they were kept below deck except "when they needed the heads." Surprised by the luxury of several long movie screenings in the ship's hold, Pechenkin was told that this was intended to discourage the men from going topside while their ship went through the Turkish straits.[8]

B. A new airlift

The Soviet fighter squadrons that had been readied since August were finally dispatched to Egypt following the December talks, and so arrived before the SAM division's deployment was complete. The MiG-21s were dismantled and flown to Egypt, in An-12 transport planes as in the 1967 airlift—but this time, together with a full complement of pilots and ground crew, "after a hasty farewell from their families." Despite the lengthy preparations, the squadrons' actual dispatch was mounted hurriedly, or staged to appear so even to the Soviet rank-and-file. "Suddenly, on the double, we had to repaint the [transport] aircraft—or rather, their identification marks," relates a flight engineer. "Over the [military] stars and aircraft numbers we painted the emblem of Aeroflot and the national flag."[9] There were, however, some marked changes from the 1967 airlift. According to Evgeny Poluektov, this time the civilian disguise was so perfunctory that the transports' tail turret was not removed, and its gun was brandished to ward off US carrier-based planes that approached his An-12 en route. Likewise, the disassembled MiG-21s were not crated, and the fuselage merely rested on blocks.

Poluektov was one of an entire class at the military language school who were pressed into service for this massive operation—a takeoff every thirty minutes—before completing their studies. Again, their main function was to handle English communications with Italian and Greek, as well as Egyptian, air traffic controllers. But this time the Yugoslav controllers at Dubrovnik also refused to speak Russian. The Soviet invasion of Czechoslovakia had put them on edge, fearing that the supposedly civilian An-12s might be used to ferry an airborne landing.[10]

THE SOVIET REGULARS MOVE IN

Nastenko arrived at Cairo-West with his dismantled planes on 20 December 1969:

> As we prepared to unload our aircraft from the cargo bay, we heard sporadic fire from all sorts of weapons. A few seconds later we saw two unfamiliar aircraft overfly the base at 15–20 meters. These were two Phantom F-4s. Immediately we saw two SAMs being launched from a battery nearby. After a while the shooting stopped. We had no time to be frightened, even though there was no shelter. A technical crew came and told us that one of the enemy planes had been shot down by a missile, but later it transpired that the downed plane was an Il-28 [target-]towing craft belonging to the EAF.[11]

IAF Phantoms had indeed begun buzzing Cairo at low altitude on 4 November.[12] But remarkably, even a year after the ceasefire of August 1970, an IDF tabulation of the Soviet presence in Egypt listed "Soviet-piloted planes" only as late as 31 March.[13]

As related to Zhirokhov, in Egypt the combat pilots were still, like the previous advisers, called *habir* (singular for *hubara*, as the term was usually rendered in Russian):

> They were housed in comfort but also in silent isolation, their barracks seeming more like an oasis than part of Egypt proper. ... They reported for duty at 0500 hours each day. ... All EAF bases had been alcohol-free since the early 1960s, but the base where the Soviet personnel were working was relatively new and did not even include a restaurant. A large number of such new airbases had been built in Egypt in the aftermath of the 1967 war. ... But for the Soviet officers in Egypt these rather rudimentary conditions came as a shock. ... They, like their Egyptian colleagues, not only ate together but had to cooperate in the purchase and preparation of meals. ... Plenty of food was, of course, available including any meat except pork. Once a meal had been prepared, the officers sat on carpets to eat, since there were not many tables and chairs. Those that could be found were mostly used in the offices. ... As a result meals were rather relaxed.[14]

Within a few weeks, the Soviet airmen had to refine the flight pattern for continuing supply transports. This was also necessitated by the start of Israeli bombings around Cairo on 7 January—another indication that *Kavkaz* was already under way when they commenced. Petr Stavitsky, an English major at the Moscow linguists' institute, was drafted in January for one of the transports flying Su-7s and -9s, which were loaded at Komsomolsk-on-Amur in the Soviet Far East (and required *two* An-12s for each warplane). He and his colleagues boarded the planes at Tököl, also to communicate with English-speaking traffic controllers. "We set course to Cairo International [Airport], with which we spoke in English, but at the same time the crew was talking in Russian with our own controllers at Gianaclis airbase near Alexandria ... to mislead the overseas intelligence services." After making a sharp turn, landing at Gianaclis and "unloading the merchandise," the planes continued to their official destination and the crews were given two days' leave in blacked-out, "sullen" Cairo.

Stavitsky was horrified when later in January, at home in Kiev, he listened in—"on a rare occasion when there was no jamming"—to a Radio Canada broadcast in Ukrainian that spoke of Soviet planes landing at Gianaclis "every half hour" with disassembled MiGs and Sukhois. The deception, then, hardly worked, but his account is among the first of an additional Egyptian air base—besides Cairo-West—coming under effective Soviet control.[15]

Though the Soviet squadrons were already in Egypt, in December 1969–January 1970 Israeli intelligence still dismissed even an "important" report that they "might arrive." As the head of MI sigint told the Agranat Commission, "these reports were received with mixed feelings, because there was an established thesis that Soviet intervention was improbable."[16]

C. Effects felt on the canal front

Meanwhile, several more attempts were made by the Egyptian Air Defense Command to reestablish the SAM-2 array west of the canal. This was met by another wave of intensive Israeli bombing throughout December, enhanced by the Phantom's greater payload. This climaxed in ninety-eight sorties against eight missile batteries on 25 December alone, after their overnight reconstruction was detected a day earlier. Although the Israelis claimed the entire array was once again destroyed, they also reported much more effective defense by both cannon and missiles: at least twenty-four SAM-2s were fired, in volleys rather than singly as before; damage to one Skyhawk was admitted. This improvement was attributed to closer involvement by Soviet advisers. Still, the Egyptian missiles had actually shot nothing down since the artillery observer's light plane in March. But help was on the way: the Israeli pilots also reported massive earthworks under excavation but yet unoccupied, which at least in hindsight were identified as intended for Soviet-manned SAM-3s. Col. Yeshayahu Bareqet, IAF intelligence chief at the time, states that they were identified as such upon detection, but Military Intelligence overruled this finding at the General Staff level until American analysts concurred. This failure would be the subject of continuing recrimination and investigations in the IDF.[17] The new missile shelters were heavily bombed anyway, and by counting the improvised graves of the soldiers and laborers killed in these attacks, IAF reconnaissance estimated them at many hundreds; Nasser and Heikal admitted 4,000.[18]

The Soviets' anxiety was heightened when on 26 December an Israeli heliborne force literally lifted a Soviet-made P-12 radar station from Ras Gharib on the Red Sea coast. The rear-echelon infantry brigade that, along with one from the new home guard, had been tasked with securing the vicinity was fully manned with Soviet advisers, one of whom had been killed in an Israeli bombardment a few weeks earlier. Arriving at the station with a replacement adviser a month before the spectacular heist, the interpreter Igor' Kulikov noted that it was "defended by barely 10 soldiers, who didn't even have foxholes." The Egyptian officer in charge preferred to concentrate his main force around a dummy station, which the Soviets considered crude and unlikely to fool anyone—but they were quartered there too. This, along with the Egyptian's rejection of the Soviets' proposal to hold a defense exercise on the night of the raid, kept the advisers out of the line of fire.[19] Major Mikhail Antonov, the Soviet adviser to the Egyptian armored battalion charged with protecting the sector, arrived on the scene too late, and found that the nearest tanks had been hidden uselessly in a ravine. When he began to draw up plans for their more effective emplacement, the Soviet higher brass who came to inspect the "disaster" scene advised him "not to work too hard as they [the Egyptians] are fighting here, not we."[20]

The Egyptian media did not mention the Ras Gharib caper for nearly a month, and the Soviet media never did. But the US embassy in Moscow reported that an official speaker had discussed it at an unspecified gathering—presumably of Party activists—which was taken to indicate that foreign broadcasts about it had "been received" and necessitated some response.[21] It remains an open question whether this trauma was magnified, and the silence deepened, by capture of Soviet technicians at the station itself. Given the P-12's advanced technology (as Kulikov mentions, the same model was in use in the USSR's own air defense), it would be remarkable if there were no Soviet personnel operating or overseeing the facility.[22] The Israelis confirmed taking four Egyptian technicians who had been trained in the Soviet Union. The senior "radio-technical" adviser to the 5th Egyptian Air Defense division based in Cairo, K.M. Molodtsov, wrote in 2005 that the Israelis took two unidentified "members of the combat crew."[23] Antonov mentions only "the station's crew" being captured, without specifying their nationality.

The senior interpreter Zardusht Alizadeh related how "we were relieved that our people returned safely," which might refer either to their release by the Israelis or to their successful escape before the station's capture. Before leaving Cairo, Kulikov and the adviser he accompanied had been warned by a senior *politrabotnik* "don't dare to be taken prisoner by the Jews."

D. Was there a Soviet ground-forces presence?

It was widely reported that Israel let US experts inspect the P-12 station, like other captured Soviet hardware. The interpreters in Egypt heard that the Soviets had to alter their identification codes worldwide as a result.[24] In Washington, Sedov relayed a warning through a Jewish journalist that the radar hijacking was "a very grave matter. Henceforth we will *make sure* that valuable and up-to-date equipment *will be guarded by us*, so that the Israelis will think twice."[25] Guarding the Soviet-manned SAM array against "possible Israeli paratroop raids like the radar station" was given as the motive when, in April 1970, the Soviets were reported as having dispatched "an estimated five battalions of troops" to Egypt.[26]

THE SOVIET–ISRAELI WAR, 1967–1973

Later, when Soviet-piloted MiG-25s were stationed in Egypt, a *Spetznaz* (special ops) detachment escorted the yet-experimental planes to ensure security, and such special forces also saw action during the Yom Kippur War. But the only testimony so far to the presence of a sizable Soviet ground force "in late 1969 or early 1970" comes from a naval adviser, Vladimir Kryshtob, who had just been posted to Alexandria:

> An armored division came into Alexandria. It was unloaded in the space of one night ... That night they woke up the entire Alexandria beach promenade ... They were driving around without insignia, all fair-haired and smiling. They got into the tanks and drove 80 km south into the desert. By dawn they had spread barbed wire fences around them, dug trenches, set up headquarters, a signals network and all the infrastructure for defense. This was a real, complete Soviet armored division, but somehow it was outside any plan. No supplies were allotted for it. ... Collections began to be taken up among us ... soap and cigarettes for the tank crewmen. ... They were [living] under terrible conditions in the desert ... Apparently this was to economize with foreign currency. ... A month later, supplies for the new division were taken care of. They got fresh underwear and other necessities.[27]

We have only one other, second-hand, testimony about an integral Soviet armored force in Egypt at this stage, and no indication what became of it afterward.[28] Kryshtob's account still requires verification, but it appears to reflect genuine apprehension that Israel's success against the SAM array might presage larger-scale incursions and expose the main Soviet naval base, as well as the Gianaclis air base, to direct threat.

Even though the regular units were formally subordinated to a separate headquarters in Moscow rather than the advisers' "Ofis," Katyshkin now had to lead them both. "He studied previous interventions of Soviet forces from Spain onwards, of which he knew some of the veterans, and also in Korea and Vietnam."[29]

On the eve of the new year 1970, the SAM array was quickly taking shape: the division's designated commander Smirnov was in a group of about ten generals led by Air Defense chief Batitsky for a reconnoiter of Egypt.[30] In one of the first veteran accounts to be published outside the USSR, *divizyon* commander K. Popov stated that he reached Egypt as early as December 1969—apparently with this advance tour of the command group, to return with his outfit afterward.[31] According to Smirnov, at this stage "our only form of communication with Egyptian soldiers was sign language; there were no interpreters available." He related that Nasser was on hand both to welcome them and—flanked by Sadat—to receive, "on January 2 or 3," their deployment plans. "This young general," Batitsky introduced Smirnov, "will solve the problems of repulsing the Israeli Air Force."[32]

In Alexandria, Kryshtob watched Batitsky's party drive along the beach promenade to pinpoint locations for SAM emplacements. Soon after, "amid the civilian yacht anchorages, kiosks and sunshades there appeared missile launchers with purely Soviet crews. Their commander visited us very often, but his personnel were camped next to their launchers and not allowed to leave the sites." He describes several incidents similar to the one that Nastenko witnessed in Cairo:

> one missile was launched without authorization. Thank goodness, it fell into the sea. Later, the entire Fifth *Eskadra* and all the available divers searched for it. It turned out to be very secret. But it was never found. Afterwards these missilemen fired a hand-held *Strela* at an Il-28 of ours. They hit it successfully, one engine blew up and part of the wing came off, but somehow it managed to land—it was, after all, flown by Soviet airmen.[33]

E. The Cherbourg fiasco

A diversion was created when on Christmas Eve five newly completed fast missile boats—Israel's ultimately successful response to the *Eilat* sinking—evaded the French arms embargo by sneaking out of the shipyard in Cherbourg and heading for Haifa. They were unarmed, and although reportedly escorted by two submarines once they entered the Mediterranean, the boats were ostensibly vulnerable. While Israeli Navy headquarters considered an Egyptian "ambush" unlikely, and a Soviet one even more so, the government in Jerusalem was edgy.

The mentions of this affair by Soviet veterans are uncharacteristically apologetic. V.M. Pak, an interpreter at Egyptian Navy headquarters in Alexandria, recalls that the Soviets' "preliminary calculations showed the Egyptians still had enough time to intercept [the boats]. Since they were unarmed, our advisers proposed to take them as booty." The Fifth *Eskadra* must have had a good idea of the boats' whereabouts: after passing Gibraltar, the Israelis sighted (and were presumably sighted by) several Soviet ships, which they described as freighters. When on 28 December 1969 they stopped to refuel from an Israeli car ferry that had been prepositioned south of Malta, a Soviet intelligence trawler "bristling with antennas" came within 300 meters and stayed there for hours, pointing a telephoto lens at the boats.

Was it monitoring a target for an armed naval force? The first opportunity, Pak writes, "was spotted in the Gulf of Tunis, and a destroyer was sent there along with several other craft masked as civilian. But before they could reach the projected interception point, salt water started leaking into the destroyer's boiler and it had to return to base for extended repairs."

As a precaution, the Israeli flotilla split up to circumnavigate Crete, and the two boats that sailed north of the island passed near if not through the *eskadra*'s Antikythera anchorage; the Israelis reported "evading two unidentified ships."[34] At Pak's headquarters, it was concluded on New Year's Eve that

> one more chance remained: to dispatch missile boats based in Port Said. I remember well that this question was discussed at the Navy commander's [office] in the first part of the day, in an ambience of strict secrecy. ... But by that evening, I went to the market ... [and] heard one butcher tell another that Egyptian missile boats had been sent from Port Said toward the Israeli ones.

That night, Pak heard on the radio that the Israeli boats had entered Haifa; it was later explained, he writes, that the Israelis were helped by strong back winds and got home faster than expected.[35] The submarine adviser Kryshtob also recalls a joint Soviet–Egyptian effort on 31 December, and cites the weather to excuse its failure:

> the Egyptians and the Fifth *Eskadra* wanted to intercept them. ... But such a winter storm broke out here that all the Arabs were scattered. Our Mediterranean *eskadra* came to their assistance, but to no avail. The storm washed nine men overboard off the Arab ships. So they caught nothing, neither the ... boats nor their crews [who would soon be tracking Kryshtob's own submarine].[36]

Leonid Zakharov of the Soviet 90th Naval Aviation Reconnaissance Squadron recorded that on the same day their Tu-16Rs were dispatched to locate the "hijacked" boats east of Crete—exactly as a *Daily Telegraph* reporter was tipped off two days earlier that the Soviet-manned Badgers at Cairo-West might do.[37] The Soviet airman goes on wistfully: "it was no simple mission. Pairs of recce craft left all day at intervals," including his own in the late afternoon. "The crews were highly motivated but had no luck. This was probably the only case in which the squadron did not accomplish its mission."[38] The boats were, however, located and tracked even by media-chartered light planes, not to mention French naval aircraft. It rather seems that by the time Zakharov's squadron was launched to search for the boats, it was too late to block them: they arrived off Haifa early that day but were ordered to enter port after dark, to minimize media coverage. It can only be speculated whether the Soviets were really as feckless as the memoirists felt, or their leadership intentionally avoided a high-profile incident that might disrupt the progress of *Kavkaz*.

Between 5 and 7 January 1970, that is, still before the first "depth bombing," Smirnov submitted his detailed air defense blueprint to Defense Minister Grechko. Two days before Christmas, with *Kavkaz* already in full swing, Moscow had finally stopped the diplomatic charade and rejected US Secretary of State Rogers's peace plan. Nasser publicly rebuffed it in a speech in Tripoli on 27 December, and again in Khartoum on New Year's Day. Vladimir Vinogradov, then a deputy foreign minister, claims that "in the beginning of 1970" he was sent by the Politburo to discuss with Nasser a possible end to the War of Attrition, apparently in the context of the Rogers Plan's "second version." However, he recalls that one of Nasser's arguments for Soviet troops to man the anti-aircraft defense was "that the Egyptian forces are not ready yet for big offensive operations ... Israeli [air] raids are becoming more and more destructive ... in order to prepare the Army there is a need for reliable air defense."[39]

F. Diplomatic stalling and a pretense of outrage

It was only after the rejection of the Rogers Plan that Assistant Secretary of State Sisco finally warned Congress he had serious doubt about Russia's "willingness to play an

THE SOVIET REGULARS MOVE IN

actively constructive role," and another month passed before he "advised [Ambassador] Dobrynin ... there was no point in continuing the two-power talks."[40] These had anyway been overtaken by Dobrynin's back channel with Kissinger—of which Rogers and Sisco were deliberately not informed.

Kissinger either sought some detour to salvage US influence after the failure of Rogers's diplomacy—or spotted an opportunity to horn in on the handling of Middle Eastern policy. The new collection of back-channel reports confirms that the Middle East was put high on the channel's agenda on 29 December 1969—when Kissinger and Dobrynin each told his boss that the other had suggested the idea.[41] The subject would come up for specific discussion soon enough and Kissinger would discover that the Soviets had played him, too, for time until their military move was completed.

On 10 January, only three days after the IAF's Phantoms staged their first raids around Cairo, a Supreme Soviet delegation arrived there for a ten-day visit, headed by Politburo candidate member Dinmukhamed Kunaev. He was greeted in Alexandria by a KGB operative at the Soviet consulate, whose tour proposals illustrate that *Kavkaz* elements were already present: "'What would you like to see?' I asked politely. 'We have our naval base, *rocket base, air base, army base* ... our shipyard—any of those?' Kunayev turned his head rigidly from side to side." He was interested only in shopping for jewelry.[42]

Officially, his party "was briefed by Nasser on the situation and given an urgent message for Brezhnev."[43] It now appears, however, that this political delegation—like Podgorny's in June 1967—served also, if not mainly, as a foil for yet another large group from the Soviet Ministry of Defense and General Staff. The latter party arrived on board two planes during the night between 9 and 10 January. One of its members was Lt-Col. Aleksey Zhdanov, the Soviet Union's leading expert on construction of SAM sites. As this specialist recalled, a few days after its arrival the military group was transferred from a downtown hotel to the Soviet advisers' compound in "Nasser City" in order "to minimize attention of the local population and foreign tourists." The product of this mission—the disposition of the expeditionary force—was submitted to Nasser by Air Defense Commander Batitsky at the beginning of February; though this formality took place after Nasser's purported visit to Moscow, Zhdanov's account demonstrates that the planning was accomplished well before.[44]

Implementation also began before 22 January: the 18th Division's newly appointed chief, Smirnov, was evidently in the same delegation, as he relates that he returned to Egypt in "mid-January." The missile sites, he writes, were under construction, and although they were still unfinished, he was surprised and annoyed to learn that the force he was slated to lead was already en route to Alexandria. He rushed to the "Ofis" to send a coded message to Grechko, protesting the dispatch of his outfit before preparations were complete and calling for its delay. But Batitsky's deputy Shcheglov "smiled and said, 'Alexey, you're a big boss and have to use your head. If the force has left without your approval there's a reason for it, a decision has been made, and we must do everything to accomplish our operational mission successfully under these circumstances."⁴⁵ Although the first "depth bombings" should ostensibly have been a major concern for Smirnov, he does not mention them at all—much less as the trigger of his division's deployment.

The IAF codenamed and numbered its depth-bombing raids *Priha* (Blossom) no. 1, no. 2 and so on, with no. 1 on 7 January 1970. So it is easy to determine that only two more took place before 22 January, and all three targeted distinctly military installations.⁴⁶ Heikal cited among the motives for Nasser's supposed flight to Moscow to plead for Soviet intervention the "heavy loss of life" from two of the "depth bombings": one on a factory and one on a school. But these occurred, respectively, on 12 February and 8 *April*.⁴⁷ Despite calling Heikal's overall credibility into question, Laqueur's seminal work adopted the Egyptian propagandist's anachronistic version in this matter: "In the bombing of a factory at Abu Zaabal on February 12th, 1970, 88 workers were killed. There were frantic calls for Soviet help, and on January 20th Nasser went to the Soviet capital."⁴⁸ So the trip in January is claimed to have come in response to an attack in February.

There is no doubt that the *Priha* operations ultimately had a political and psychological effect in Egypt. But most of the "depth" raids were made, and their effect came into major play, *after* the date when Heikal claims they caused Nasser's plea and the Soviets' compliance. Likewise, in respect of Soviet considerations: at the beginning of February US intelligence intercepted a conversation between Brezhnev and Grechko, in which the general secretary was "bitter about the Israeli raids and especially ... the strike on the house of the Soviet advisers, which he implied was deliberate."⁴⁹

Brezhnev's outrage at these Soviet losses has been held to explain his acceptance of Nasser's demands. But his comment in the intercepted talk referred explicitly to the first Soviet casualties from an Israeli bombing in the Egyptian hinterland, which occurred only *after* Nasser allegedly got what he wanted in Moscow. This was on 28 January, when among several targets of *Priha*-5, an Israeli bombing destroyed the three-story building that housed the advisers of the 6th Motorized Division in a suburb of Cairo. Reports from the Egyptian capital later spoke of over 100 fatalities, rather than the three civilians that were killed according to the first official statements. Among the dead were the division commander's adviser, Col. Ivan Ogibenin, its air defense commander's adviser, Col. Nikolay Vlasenko, and an interpreter, Lt Ziyaddin Yusubov from Azerbaijan; five others were injured.⁵⁰ Sadat, according to some versions of a speech he gave in January 1971, referred to six Soviet missilemen who were killed the same day, evidently referring to another *Priha*-5 objective, a SAM complex at Dahshur, south of Cairo.⁵¹

But the Soviets had begun to suffer casualties before the "depth bombings" even began. On 7 January, Mikhail Kalchenko, the adviser to an infantry brigade commander, was indeed killed in an Israeli raid, but although the IAF included it in the same day's *Priha*-1, unlike the other objectives of the operation this target was the headquarters of the Egyptian II Army Corps at Tel el-Kebir. This was only about 35 kilometers from the canal; whereas the new "depth targets" were tackled exclusively by Phantoms, this one was attacked by the shorter-range Skyhawks, which together with older IAF craft continued the intensive bombing of the canal line simultaneously with the deep-penetration raids.[52] Tel el-Kebir was no new target; a Soviet adviser had died there in a previous Israeli "flying artillery" raid, among the significant Soviet casualties during the summer.[53]

Closer to the front at 2nd Division headquarters in Ismailia, Gorbunov dates the first Soviet casualties to 1969, when the IAF bombardments obliged the Soviet advisers and interpreters on the canal front to "take part in combat operations." During one artillery exchange, their chief Afanas'ev's foresight in changing positions saved their group from a direct hit, but on other occasions "fatalities and injuries occurred. Our wives stayed with the bereaved womenfolk" at their Cairo hotel billets.[54] An anti-ship missile specialist, Viktor Vasilenko of the Northern Fleet, who was sent to Alexandria in December 1969, recalls seeing "numerous" posthumous citations for advisers who had already lost their lives, "and I understood there was a real war going on there."[55] On 4 November 1969, while Kryshtob was waiting to leave for Egypt, he encountered at his Moscow hotel the widow of an air defense adviser killed about a week earlier. He was asked to contribute to a collection for her travel expenses to Egypt. "I learned afterward that this was usual for the period ... at the outset, we had to bury our dead at our own expense. Special funding for keeping the bodies in Egyptian morgues, obtaining coffins and transportation to the Soviet Union had not been foreseen by the General Staff." Ultimately, "because of the large number of fatalities ... the problem came into the open," and after repeated protests, this "disgrace" ended.[56]

Still, as *Kavkaz* continued, at least some of the casualties among enlisted men were buried where they died in Egypt; their families were informed only that they had "fallen in the course of duty," and received no financial benefits.[57] At least some of the Soviet missilemen who won Egyptian bounties for shooting down IAF planes donated the money to the bereaved families of their comrades.[58] Moscow's callous attitude toward these casualties hardly bespoke genuine alarm or outrage. A monograph on the subject twenty years later found that "the Soviets are less ready to tolerate massive sacrifices than has hitherto been supposed," but admitted that "this position stems as much from utilitarian-military logic as from any altruistic compassion." If indeed it was Soviet losses in Egypt that precipitated the Soviet intervention, it was because they represented a military setback rather than a human tragedy.[59] These casualties began much earlier, and reached significant proportions later, than the first "depth bombings" or Nasser's purported appeal.

If not in Moscow, the losses on 28 January definitely caused some shock among the advisers. Gennady Goryachkin, a military interpreter who was posted to Egypt in August 1969, was attached in January to the advisers of an Egyptian mechanized division near Giza.⁶⁰ He relates that in two Israeli air raids on its command post, three Soviet advisers and a senior interpreter were killed. Upon arrival, Goryachkin inherited the hotel billet of a fallen colleague, and sleeping in the dead man's bed troubled him. "I had a recurring nightmare of myself crawling with a wounded leg under the barbed-wire fence of an Israeli concentration camp, dragging some girl with me."⁶¹ Others were worse affected: V.P. Povelko, an adviser who shared a Cairo hotel with Serkov, was "urgently sent back to the USSR due to a nervous-psychiatric breakdown." But Serkov—who took time off to visit his wounded comrades in hospital—relates that, nonetheless, he and the other advisers "continued to develop the training plan for an infantry division attack ... across a water obstacle, which was drilled the following week with the 4th Division." He had already overstayed his tour of duty despite his refusal (at the insistence of his wife) to extend it, and went home only on 19 February 1970.⁶²

G. Heikal's admitted propaganda function

Let us now revisit Heikal's account of Nasser's supposed talks in Moscow. The Soviets were well aware of the propagandist's function, and took care not to contradict him explicitly. Vladimir Shagal', a GRU "Arabist" who spent thirty years from the early 1960s analyzing Middle Eastern affairs, relates that Heikal's columns in *Al-Ahram* were carefully parsed to monitor trends in the Egyptian leadership and were interpreted as his master's voice.

Remarkably, in his description of the alleged talks in January, Heikal himself defines the role he was tasked to perform:

> At one point Brezhnev ... came round and sat beside me. "*Gospodin* Heikal," he said, "all this is secret ... Of course one day the Americans and Israelis are bound to know, but before that happens, we come to your domain. How can we present it to the world? I want you to work out a scheme." ... I said: "Mr Secretary, it is up to the statesmen to make the big decisions. We can always find ways and means by which we can present their decisions to the world."⁶³

One could hardly better phrase a caveat for the evaluation of vested-interest sources.

The Russians, of course, were very capable of keeping their moves secret: if Brezhnev indeed spoke to Heikal in late January 1970, the Soviet pilots and planes were already operating in Egypt and the SAM division was being deployed—still utterly unbeknownst to the Americans and the Israelis. So Heikal's story looks more like an excuse for a deliberate *Egyptian* leak—or fabrication—about the visit, which was effected within a few days.

As in other cases, NBC reporter Wilson Hall had to fly to Beirut in order to file the story on 29 January, as censorship in Cairo at least made a show of suppressing it—which lent it all the more credibility.⁶⁴ The item made the afternoon papers in Israel, a few hours after the morning papers headlined that Nasser had summoned Ambassador Vinogradov for the second time in as many days to *demand* "Soviet action to stop Israeli air strikes."⁶⁵ The question of why this demand was necessary if Nasser had just received the desired commitment from Vinogradov's Kremlin superiors has been rendered moot by the new evidence that the actual operation began long before, but at the time no one appears to have asked it.

On 31 January, the day Kosygin's threatening messages went out to Western capitals, US papers picked up the NBC story.⁶⁶ But Israeli intelligence was tipped off about Nasser's "secret visit" even before it was leaked to the press. A day before Kosygin's missive was received, Sisco and Israeli Ambassador Rabin "exchanged assessments [about] reported Nasser['s] Moscow trip":

> Sisco ... [stated] USG has no hard intelligence that visit in fact occurred or if it did, what might have been discussed. ... Rabin said Israeli intelligence lacks clear cut piece of information proving Nasser was in Moscow, but all intelligence indications show he did go. Israeli intelligence ... comes from Arab sources in Cairo.⁶⁷

H. Ashraf Marwan's first deception?

Rabin's reference to "Arab sources in Cairo" was elucidated in a book published in 2004 by two Israeli writers specializing in intelligence. It featured an unsourced claim that this was one of the first reports submitted by a newly volunteered spy in Egypt, codenamed "Bavel" (Babylon).⁶⁸ Several months before, he had offered his services to the Israeli embassy in London for a hefty price, which the astonished Israelis gladly paid when they ascertained that he was Nasser's son-in-law, Ashraf Marwan.

When Marwan, by then a wealthy expatriate businessman, fell to his death from a high-rise balcony in London in June 2007, the mysterious circumstances rekindled a controversy that had roiled the Israeli intelligence community for decades. It focused on his role as the trusted Mossad informant who, in the wee hours of 6 October 1973, warned that Egypt and Syria were about to launch a concerted offensive the same day, Yom Kippur.

This story has been widely retold, in versions reflecting the writers' position in the bitter internecine Israeli feud. Marwan's handler in 1973, then-Mossad chief Zvi Zamir, led the camp who considered this warning the crowning achievement of their greatest-ever recruited spy. Zamir blamed his counterpart at Military Intelligence, Eli Ze'ira, for causing Marwan's death (presumably at the hands of vengeful Egyptians) by revealing his identity. Ze'ira's disclosure came after years of struggle to clear his name; he had been cashiered as the main scapegoat for Israel's disastrous unpreparedness in 1973. As Ze'ira and others claimed, Marwan was a sophisticated double agent who transmitted his message just in time to maintain credibility with the Israelis, but actually served the Egyptians well by temporizing until it was too late to do much about it, especially to mobilize and effectively deploy vital reserve forces.[69] The dispute was settled by arbitration in Zamir's favor, but in July 2012 Israel's attorney-general dropped criminal charges that Zamir pressed against Ze'ira, and further official investigation or pronouncements were precluded.[70]

The Marwan saga concerns this study only insofar as his input dealt with the Soviet involvement. His report on Nasser's "secret talks in Moscow" was the first in a series that show this aspect's centrality in his activity, and the evidence we have assembled in this regard strongly supports the double-agent thesis.[71]

Dudchenko's "novel" *Kanal* claims that following "Mirwan Hassan's" first contact with the Israelis (after the arrival of the IAF's first Phantoms, that is, after 5 September 1969), Soviet surveillance cameras recorded him *entering* the embassy in London.[72] But Uri Bar-Joseph's more recent book—the strongest academic presentation of Zamir's case—clarifies that Marwan never physically visited the embassy.[73] This detail in Dudchenko's story may, then, have originated in a too-literal reading of Marwan's frequent description as a "walk-in."

On the other hand, the evidence bears out Dudchenko's claim that after detecting Marwan's dealings with the Israelis, the Soviets checked with his boss—a veteran Soviet agent, Nasser's *chef de cabinet* Sami Sharaf.[74] Once the Soviet military attaché and GRU *rezident* in Cairo, "Ivanov" (in real life, Rear-Admiral Nikolay Ivliev) ascertained that Marwan was under control, he was authorized to "put [him] into operative play," that is, to supply the Egyptians with material intentionally prepared for him to feed to the Israelis (and, as will appear presently, to others as well). But the Soviets' subsequent attitude toward Marwan indicates that they did not recruit him directly; he did not sell out to them, or to anyone else. Besides feathering his own nest, he consistently served Egypt's interests through its changing orientations—including its policy toward Moscow.

The specifics of Marwan's report on Nasser's "crucial meetings with ... Brezhnev in January 1970" remain murky.[75] The only details that Bergman and Meltzer give about this first product are that the Egyptians demanded long-range bombers and Scud missiles as a prerequisite for launching a war.[76] Retrospectively, Ze'ira described this as one of the origins of Israel's notorious "Concept," whereby Egypt would be unable to launch a war so long as the USSR supposedly denied it this offensive weaponry.[77] The Bergman–Meltzer book, however, also ascribes the same content to "a secret message from Sadat to Brezhnev on 30 August 1972," which Marwan reported too, and indeed it appears more appropriate at that point.[78] But even without a negative assessment of Nasser's mission, reporting the dubious mission itself might well qualify as Marwan's first plant of disinformation—and if Rabin relied on it, it worked.[79]

More will be said about the Egyptians' and Soviets' subsequent use of the "chattering classes" in Cairo, including Marwan, to mislead Western as well as Israeli monitors at critical junctures. As Ahron Bregman—who knew Marwan personally and has

THE SOVIET REGULARS MOVE IN

taken responsibility for first exposing him—concluded in his latest assessment: "If Marwan was planted by the Egyptians to fool the Israelis, then he did his job extremely well"—in respect of the Soviet involvement.[80]

In European capital cities, Israeli diplomats received similar tips about a visit by Nasser to Moscow in January, which were notably numerous and uniform for mutually unrelated intercepts of a genuinely guarded secret.[81] Within a few days, it was firmly—if not yet unquestionably—established in Western perceptions, even though it was denied by both officials in Cairo and the Egyptian embassy in Moscow, and no comment at all was forthcoming from the Soviets. Alvin Rubinstein's observation in 1975 that "the trip has never been discussed in any Soviet source," still holds true in respect of official documents.[82] The same applies to US documents after the Sisco–Rabin exchange: following a report by the US ambassador in Moscow Jacob Beam on a talk with Soviet Foreign Minister Gromyko on 11 February, Kissinger estimated to Nixon that the Soviets "may already have made some new commitment" to Egypt but made no mention of a visit by Nasser.[83] In a 1978 memoir, Beam himself accepted the version that "Israel's deep bombing raids in Egypt ... invited the Soviets to interpose their own force," but still made no mention of Nasser's arrival in the Soviet capital despite the information that Sisco had received about it.[84]

The leaks about Nasser's visit, true or false, provided background and justification when Kosygin wrote to Nixon (as well as the leaders of Britain and France) that "if Israel continues its adventurism to bomb the territory of the UAR and other Arab states, the Soviet Union will be forced to see to it that the Arab states have means at their disposal with the help of which due rebuff to the arrogant aggressor could be made." Richard Parker attests that "the almost universal reaction among the Soviet specialists in the Department of State and the CIA was that the Soviets were bluffing and would not in fact go beyond supplying more equipment to Egypt."[85]

Kissinger's National Security Council (NSC) deputy Helmut Sonnenfeldt discerned "an emotional reaction to the killing of Soviet officers." Based on the intercept of the Brezhnev–Grechko talk, he suggested (correctly, but for the wrong reasons) that the general secretary was personally involved in drafting the premier's letter. Sonnenfeldt headlined a memo to Nixon, which he drafted for Kissinger, with the assessment that Kosygin's message was "an inept performance."

Sonnenfeldt was a veteran State Department Kremlinologist who was transferred to the NSC at Kissinger's request. Typically, his main concern was that, in Moscow, the Middle East situation would again be "used by a rebellious faction in an indictment against the present leaders," who in turn might "do something brave to recoup." Still, Sonnenfeldt did not foresee—nor did Kissinger—that the Soviets would do more than "merely sending more equipment, [which] even if it is more advanced is unlikely to accomplish anything."[86] Given this US attitude, it is hardly surprising that Israeli accounts claim there had been at least tacit or even "indicated" US acquiescence with the start of the "depth bombings" on 7 January, even if it was later disavowed.[87]

The Soviets were indeed bluffing—but not by brandishing an empty menace. On the contrary, they were once more threatening a move that they had already decided upon and had begun to implement, in order to blame their adversaries for causing it by refusing a reasonable Soviet demand. Without ever confirming Nasser's visit and desperate appeal, they enabled the Egyptians to succeed brilliantly in depicting the direct Soviet intervention that the visit supposedly obtained as a direct outcome of Israel's "depth bombings." By the time Heikal's version was published in 1972, the Egyptian propaganda line had changed. The line was now that the massive Soviet presence was unwanted and had to go—but it remained expedient to portray this intervention as a last-ditch necessity that Nasser was constrained to accept because of the humiliation and bloodshed inflicted by Israel's "insolent" bombings.

At the time, in early February 1970, Israel was buoyed by its Phantoms' exploits as well as the Cherbourg escapade. In Jerusalem as in Washington, both Nasser's purported visit and Kosygin's actual letters were dismissed almost flippantly. An alarm that the Soviet threat might be serious was raised by the French—but by now they were considered almost as hostile as the Soviets. On top of the missile-boat affair, Paris had just announced the sale to Libya of Mirages that were ordered by Israel but stranded by the French embargo. In his Khartoum speech, Nasser had listed France along with the USSR as "friends of Egypt," and rumors were even floated that he too was considering the replacement of inferior Soviet weaponry with French arms.[88]

So Israeli Foreign Minister Eban told a reporter he was relieved when the British ambassador did not even mention Kosygin's letter in a long conversation. "Western sources" were quoted to estimate that Nasser had indeed "run" to the USSR for help, but "Nasser asked for radar and missiles—Moscow [merely] sent three letters." The main apprehension in Jerusalem was now that Washington had acquiesced in the depth bombings in the hope that they might boomerang politically: a helpless Nasser would be compelled to endorse the Rogers Plan, which in turn would put US pressure on Israel to follow suit.[89]

12

OPERATION *KAVKAZ* IS FORMALLY ORGANIZED

A. Nasser offers—again—to join the Warsaw Pact

The new Russian versions, even together with the back-channel reports, fall just short of absolute proof that Heikal invented "Nasser's secret visit to Moscow in January" *ex nihilo*. Such a conclusion would be seductive, as in view of the way this story was propagated, it would stand as a rare masterpiece of disinformation. But it cannot be utterly refuted unless a clear sighting emerges of Nasser elsewhere than Moscow on 22–6 January, and so far none has. Heikal just *might* be conflating several visits, or misdating Nasser's crucial talks or correspondence with Brezhnev over several months. But the genesis of *Kavkaz* in January 1970, as a response to Israel's new offensive strategy, can now definitely be discarded.

It is likewise intriguing though still inconclusive that the Russian military historian who disputes Heikal's January date for Nasser's visit also describes the *content* of the Egyptian president's message as the opposite of Heikal's version. Western accounts have hitherto echoed the latter's claim that Nasser threatened "to resign and hand over power to someone who would seek a settlement through the Americans, unless he received immediate effective help against the Israeli air attacks."[1] But according to Yaremenko, not only did Nasser make no such threat; on the contrary, he—who had suppressed communism at home—once again "stressed insistently that if his suggestion 'might embarrass the Russians,' Egypt was prepared to join the Warsaw Pact 'even tomorrow'" in order to secure the deployment of integral Soviet formations.[2]

In a 1998 lecture, Yaremenko noted that until then his team had found no official documentation of the Kremlin's response.[3] Senior Soviet officials of the period replied vaguely when asked about what must have been a momentous decision: to reject a proposal for formal extension of the Warsaw Pact outside Europe. "I heard about it but never saw any document on the subject. I think it's apocryphal but I can't rule it out," said Karen Brutents, who was at the time an adviser to the International Department of the CPSU Central Committee.[4] "Those are rumors," Dobrynin told the present writers. "I don't know whether they're true or not. Such information did not reach Washington. I read something in the papers, but I can't say yes or no."[5]

151

However, when Sadat (by then president) signed, in May 1971, a five-year Friendship and Cooperation Treaty with the USSR, Western analysts were surprised to note that "the provisions of the treaty bore a remarkable resemblance to those of treaties between the Soviet Union and other Warsaw Pact nations."[6]

Furthermore, according to Yaremenko, Nasser insisted that the entry of Soviet forces be overt:

> At worst, it could be explained to the world that only volunteers were involved. Brezhnev opposed this, arguing that no one would believe the Soviet leadership because it was impossible that so many volunteers could be recruited in a few days for a war in a foreign country. Finally it was agreed that the operation would be top secret and without unnecessary "noise" [which does conform to Heikal's account of Brezhnev's position].[7]

B. *The back-channel reports cast further doubt on "Nasser's visit"*

On 10 February 1970, Kissinger and Ambassador Dobrynin took up Kosygin's message in the confidential back channel. In his memoirs, Kissinger maintained that he warned the Soviets against making good on the premier's threat by inserting troops into Egypt.[8] Writing in 1992, David Korn, then of the US Embassy in Israel, found no record or recollection that Kissinger had informed the State Department of such a warning. But presumably because keeping the diplomats in the dark was par for the course, Korn concluded: "Whether Kissinger did actually foresee" the Soviet move "and to what extent he in fact acted to try to prevent this, will only be known once the archives are opened."[9]

The reports by both back-channel protagonists are now available, and just as expected it depends whom one believes. Both of the interlocutors attest that despite Kosygin's threat ten days before, they discussed only a *theoretical prospect* of Soviet servicemen being deployed to Egypt. No visit by Nasser to Moscow was so much as mentioned. Dobrynin disclosed no Politburo resolution authorizing a direct intervention—let alone that it was already well under way. Kissinger did report to Nixon that he had warned "the introduction of Soviet combat personnel to the Middle East *would* be viewed with the gravest concern ... we want to make sure that the Soviet leaders are under no misapprehension about the possibility of grave consequences." Dobrynin, he noted, "was extremely affable. ... He wanted to assure me that the Soviet leaders had no intention of exacerbating tensions."[10] The Soviet ambassador, for his part, wrote home that "Kissinger did *not* explicitly say they are concerned about the direct participation of our military in combat operations," but nonetheless Kissinger "made it clear that this is primarily and precisely the crux of the matter."

Commenting to Moscow, Dobrynin did not foresee better progress with Kissinger than with Sisco toward a settlement, and suggested "to exploit *to a somewhat greater extent* ... the paragraph of A.N. Kosygin's message that made Nixon uneasy." The president, he opined, wanted only to prevent direct Soviet involvement while out-

[handwritten: Soviets don't understand American setting.]

OPERATION *KAVKAZ* IS FORMALLY ORGANIZED

wardly maintaining his hard line. Therefore, informing the Americans confidentially about "the *possibility* of our pilots appearing in the UAR" might be the best way to press Nixon, since sending American pilots to Israel in response would be politically untenable (the obvious reason why the Soviets and Egyptians would repeatedly complain that this was being done). "We are playing a new political card," Dobrynin wrote.[11] But Moscow evidently preferred operational secrecy to diplomatic pressure. This recommendation of Dobrynin's was not adopted, and if Kissinger thought the Soviets were more candid with him than with Rogers or Sisco, he was in for a shock.

C. Stretching Soviet logistics and maintaining secrecy

The Soviet expeditionary force's command structure was formally incorporated only after Heikal's version about its origin had been propagated. Air Force Colonel Abramov dates the formal organization of the "*Kavkaz* operational group" on 30 January "by order of the Defense Minister." It was headed by Lt-Gen. Sergey Krivoplyasov, whose investigative mission to Egypt in 1968 the advisers had ridiculed. He is never mentioned as reaching Egypt with the *Kavkaz* formations, but ran the operation's rear headquarters in Moscow, bypassing standard channels with direct reports to Defense Minister Grechko and Chief of Staff Zakharov. Officers who were tapped to represent the various services in this combined outfit were forbidden to inform their formal commanders about its activities, even when these pertained to their own services. Abramov recalls the resentment of his Air Force superior, Lt-Gen. (and twice HSU) Pavel Taran, when he was denied such information, and an ensuing row with Krivoplyasov. The latter cited orders from Grechko and warned that even if Abramov were replaced, his successor would be bound by the same strictures.

Conversely, *Kavkaz* staff officers were referred directly to top-level political figures when the latter's authorization was required for specific moves. They were generally "received cordially, with understanding for our requests." The exception was the military's own Political Command (Glavpur), which "considered itself an *imperium in imperio* responsible only to the Central Committee." Abramov derisively relates the top *politruks*' demands that the Soviets in Egypt uphold and spread Marxist–Leninist doctrine, while *Kavkaz* chiefs stressed the need to understand and allow for Islamic custom and the military constraints of confrontation with Israel. "We never found common ground on this."[12] But experience in the field soon changed the outlook of many political officers.

In Moscow, *Kavkaz* staffers "were quartered separately next to the central command post and were issued the latest signal equipment that enabled direct communication with Cairo. The overload on the group's officers was boundless. The working day was unlimited. Every task had to be accomplished 'by [the next] morning.'" Abramov himself had been attached to the group to replace this regimen's first heart-attack victim.

THE SOVIET–ISRAELI WAR, 1967–1973

Whether or not he said so to Heikal, Brezhnev may have insisted on secrecy for domestic as well as external considerations: deployment to Egypt was highly taxing for the USSR's conventional capability, which was already stretched from Czechoslovakia to the Chinese frontier. To form the 18th Division, experienced cadres had to be withdrawn from units defending the Soviet heartland, including Moscow and Leningrad—exactly what regional leaders and commanders had resented in 1967.[13] A few days after their initial tour of Egypt—that is, a few days into January 1970—the Air Defense officers were joined by Air Force and Navy bigwigs in a meeting at Grechko's office. Air Force Commander Marshal A.N. Yefimov requested a larger number of aircraft to be sent to Egypt. Grechko cut him short, expressing dissatisfaction with the report just presented, and told him that results must be achieved through capability rather than numbers: "think not only of yourself but of our country and its own defense."[14]

The secrecy measures that were applied to the vanguard of *Kavkaz* were maintained when the main units were shipped to Egypt. Even after the Soviet presence became common knowledge, it was camouflaged both en route and on the ground. The personnel "merely had to pass a medical examination to confirm that they were fit for service 'in a country with a hot climate,' and it was not until the very last minute that they learned where they were going."[15] They were stripped of Soviet uniforms and identification papers before leaving the USSR, and their hardware was painted with Egyptian markings; their operations were never officially acknowledged. Lt Ivan Mishchenko, a "*spetsnaz* radio-intelligence technical officer," relates that when he was posted to Egypt in May 1971, this pretense was still maintained:

> At Nikolaev they dressed us in mufti, issued us smart foreign-tailored suits (from Socialist-bloc countries). The enlisted men got berets and the officers, hats. We turned in all our personal effects and military documents and boarded the cruise liner *Admiral Nakhimov* as tourists. My surveillance station was masked as an ambulance.[16]

One of the interpreters, however, remarked that the standard-issue civvies were so uniform and distinctive that all American intelligence had to do was to count the suits and hats.[17] So possibly in order to vary this routine, in time other guises were introduced. Lt Vladimir Presnukhin, whose SAM unit was pulled from the Chinese frontier in October 1970, relates that in Nikolaev they were kitted out as a sports team en route to a training camp; thirty years later, he still kept a jacket with football-shaped buttons.

On duty in Egypt, the Soviet regulars—like the advisers who preceded them—wore tan Egyptian fatigues with no insignia. Officers could be distinguished only by tunics worn outside their trousers, while enlisted men had shirts tucked in.[18] These uniforms' quality and condition prompted a visiting general to comment, "I have never seen such a motley crew since '45, when we liberated POW camps in Germany." He urged officers to maintain their dignity by making their own repairs, for which he promised a shipment of needles and thread that never arrived.[19] Strictures were eventually relaxed somewhat at the top level and away from the front. In 1971, an interpreter who had spent a year on the canal was delighted at his transfer to a Soviet general at headquarters in Cairo, with whom he "could ride a Volga [car] in civvies."[20]

The Soviet soldiers "were not allowed to mention their places of service in the letters they wrote home."[21] Even in 1972, Danakan Nurgaliev, a sergeant in a SAM unit from the Far Eastern Amur region, was not told of his destination until his group embarked, disguised as "sports instructors." If when writing home they mentioned their top-secret location, "censorship would return the letter."[22] The return address given to their families was "Moscow 400," and some parents thought it was a military prison.[23] The photos they now display of their activities and outposts in Egypt—unlike the formal group portraits of the Egyptian and Soviet brass—were taken surreptitiously, against orders, and smuggled back home—as one serviceman describes, "under the lining of a suitcase."[24]

This denial was never formally abandoned. The appellation of "advisers" or "experts" stuck to the SAM crews and other regulars in part because "officially, Moscow was declaring that there were advisers present in Egypt, but not troops."[25] In his initial briefing to the commanders of *Kavkaz*, Grechko warned the airmen: "if you fly across the Canal or Gulf [of Suez] you're no longer ours." As events would prove, this did not mean that no such operations would be undertaken—only that any captured pilot would be repudiated.[26]

Such situations, however, would occur only later. By the end of January 1970, the entire MiG-21 contingent had been deployed in underground shelters at five air bases in Egypt, and on 1 February they were first assigned to operational but distinctly defensive duty. The mission for Nastenko's unit was initially to cover the naval bases and industrial centers along the Mediterranean coast from Alexandria to Mersa Matruh and south as far as Cairo. The other regiment was to defend Cairo from the east, as well as industrial centers down to the Aswan Dam.[27]

An unsourced version by a reputable IAF pilot and historian holds that "in early February," US intelligence agents in Turkey were surprised to spot Soviet naval vessels hauling SAMs and MiGs through the Bosporus. This account appears to have been embellished in transmission, as the agents supposedly made out through binoculars not only the ships' cargo, under camouflage nets on deck, but also "many officers wearing pilots' wings and Air Defense insignia." Such disregard for secrecy would have contravened the Soviets' strict instructions. Likewise, Israeli and Western accounts, presumably in order to explain the Soviet anti-aircraft formations' appearance so soon after Nasser's purported visit, describe their arrival as another massive airlift. But "the noise of a simultaneous Soviet airlift" could not have been heard "over the [US] agents' heads," since the routine Soviet flight path to Egypt did not overfly Turkey. At any rate, if "a few hours later word spread through CIA corridors that a

THE SOVIET–ISRAELI WAR, 1967–1973

Soviet expeditionary force was on its way to Egypt," it did not spread outside Langley for a quite a while yet.[28]

D. The SAM-3 sealift

The "early February" date is apparently correct at least for the first SAM-3 shipment. A British visitor was arrested in *mid*-February for "wandering too near a Soviet SAM-3 missile site" near El Alamein; "these were among the first to be delivered."[29] As the initial postings of Soviet personnel were for one-year periods, Smirnov's account of leaving Egypt with the first group of his subordinates when they were rotated in mid-February 1971 appears to confirm the first arrivals a year earlier.[30]

The main body of the Air Defense division left Nikolaev in the first days of March, on board sixteen freighters whose captains were given sealed orders as to their destination. The civilian cover was identical to that used for the missile shipment to Cuba in 1962. "Dates and places of embarkation were kept secret, even from family members," says the division's deputy commander. "We sailed under the pretense of transporting agricultural equipment. Everyone stayed below. ... Going through the straits we declined Turkish pilots."[31] According to the official military historian's account, the Turkish pilots were actually bribed to stay off. "There was an *osoby otdel* [field security] officer supervising each captain ... there was a strict order to shoot anyone who tried to jump overboard."[32]

Interpreters were again too scarce. Upon arriving in Egypt, operations officer Anatoly Podalka was surprised to discover that his group of twenty-six had only two interpreters. Instead, they were issued a four-page Russian–Arabic glossary, which they called *matyugal'nik* (phrasebook of obscenities). On the other hand, he was impressed by the young Egyptian women who were pressed into service, along with "freshly graduated schoolboys," to prepare the SAM emplacements by manual labor under whip-cracking overseers. The women, Podalka noted, were astonishingly obedient and could even carry a sack of cement balanced on the head.[33]

E. Kissinger blindsided

Fighting on the canal front continued unabated. On 10 March, Kissinger again discussed the Middle East with Dobrynin, who gave not the slightest inkling of a Soviet military move (he would later deny to Kissinger that he knew about it). On the contrary, the Soviet ambassador came with what his American interlocutor considered "significant concessions," including a new offer for a ceasefire along the canal. Such a ceasefire was exactly what the head of the US interests section in Egypt, Donald Bergus, had recommended that Washington propose after the Israeli "depth" raid on 28 January came uncomfortably close to the American School in Cairo. The Washington columnists Rowland Evans and Robert Novak—on a still-unusual visit

OPERATION *KAVKAZ* IS FORMALLY ORGANIZED

by US journalists to Egypt—had strengthened Bergus's hand at home with an alarming report that the school's windows were blown out and the Israeli bombing "was a threat to the school itself." Their headline reflected another deception coup by the Cairo "chattering class": "Egypt Turns Westward: Nasser's Arms Search." No one had told *them* about Nasser's real or fictitious rush to Moscow that week.[34]

Discussing his ceasefire initiative with Korn in 1988, Bergus still thought it was a "non-starter," as the administration had decided after the Dobrynin–Sisco dead end "not to work with the Soviets any longer."[35] But in the back-channel discussions that had (unbeknownst to Bergus) superseded the overt talks, Kissinger welcomed the idea when it came from Moscow. He noted proudly that the United States could now "show the Israelis we have achieved something for them with ... our policy of relative firmness" on the Kosygin letter. Was the timing of Dobrynin's offer merely coincidental? Did the Egyptians and/or Soviets learn of Bergus's initiative, which was perhaps even leaked to them intentionally to give it greater force? At any rate, once it was proposed by the Soviets, the issue was taken up with the Israelis and, despite their apprehensions that the truce would be used to rearm the Egyptians, after a week of discussions they acceded.

Meanwhile, US airmen had a close call in an encounter with Soviet counterparts, though the latter were the long-established Tu-16Rs at Cairo-West rather than the newly arrived MiGs. On 11 March "an F-4 from the USS *Roosevelt* ... experienced a mid-air collision with a Soviet medium bomber ... Both aircraft experienced only minor damage." The event was deemed serious enough to warrant an immediate, secret memo to the president via Kissinger.[36] But whether or not it was considered an indication of emboldened Soviet behavior, the near-disaster—which would be repeated a year later—was never publicized.[37]

Then, on 20 March, Kissinger demanded a meeting with Dobrynin and told him furiously—as even the dry language of the American's report reflects:

> Within 24 hours of calling them [the Israelis] in to make it [the Soviet-proposed ceasefire] final ... we learned about the introduction of Soviet SA-3 missiles and Soviet combat personnel. I had warned Dobrynin about the serious consequences of such a step. The move was reminiscent of such tactics employed ... [in] the Cuban crisis. The Soviet Government had to learn that the President could not be dealt with on this basis. As a result, the President had canceled his request to the Israelis for a ceasefire.[38]

Kissinger, then, was as surprised as the rest of the US establishment by the appearance of the Soviet missilemen (and the Americans had not yet learned at all about the MiG squadrons, which had already been in Egypt for three months). Once again, diplomacy had served as a smokescreen for military moves. As his subsequent steps indicate, Kissinger resented this enough to let pique get the better of him. This in turn would set in motion his own manipulation of the historical record about the end of *Kavkaz*, just as Heikal did with the operation's beginning.

THE SOVIET–ISRAELI WAR, 1967–1973

F. "Better than the Hawk!"

The Soviets' strict secrecy could now be relaxed somewhat, though they never confirmed their regulars' presence: Heikal relates that when a shipment of missiles arrived in Alexandria "a few days" after 18 April, the Egyptians tried to unload it clandestinely but the *Soviets* insisted on a festive motorcade through the streets. Heikal suggested (from his viewpoint in 1976) "that the Russians had told the Americans in advance." But either he misdates the event or—more likely—his reference to it as the *first* SAM-3 shipment is intentionally misleading, to support his account of Nasser's visit and agreement in January.[39]

By early March 1970, Israeli pundits who had previously dismissed any prospect of direct Soviet intervention were conceding retrospectively that it had been on the cards since Moscow approved Nasser's declaration of the War of Attrition. They now held that although the "Sovietization" of the conflict would probably be limited by its predictable consequences, the Kremlin's brinkmanship had to be met resolutely.[40] This line, however, was hard to market in Washington. Very little materialized out of the "grave consequences" for the Soviets that Kissinger had threatened. Instead, on 21 March, Nixon upstaged a scheduled statement by Secretary of State Rogers to announce an "interim decision" *not* to supply Israel during 1971 with the additional twenty-five Phantoms and 100 Skyhawks that it had requested. This, he asserted, had been determined before the stationing of Soviet missiles in Egypt was detected.[41]

According to Smirnov, the first of his division's SAM-3 batteries became operational on the night of 24–5 March. The first missile it launched brought down another Egyptian Il-28 with an "Arab" crew flying at 200–250 meters. The Soviets were aghast and considered repatriating the officers responsible. They were amazed when an Egyptian air defense division chief, Maj.-Gen. Mohammed Bassiouny, joyfully described it as a success, presumably as it proved the system's much-awaited efficacy against low-altitude incursions. "All the hundreds of Egyptian officers and men who witnessed the plane being shot down cheered: 'better than the [US-supplied Israeli missile] Hawk! Better than the Hawk!'" When Smirnov offered his condolences to Egyptian Chief of Staff Muhammad Sadiq, the latter rejected any apology and instead praised the Soviet units that had come to Egypt's aid.[42] Recalling the incident to *Al-Ahram*, Smirnov blamed the Egyptian airmen: "The pilots did not give the necessary signals and so we shot them down. We wanted to reprimand the Soviet officer [who fired the missile], but the Egyptians said, 'No, it was the pilot's mistake.'"[43]

Smirnov confirms contemporary reports that Israel avoided clashes with the Soviet air defense system as long as it was limited to protecting targets deep in Egyptian territory. IAF chief Hod proposed to the General Staff "to attack one of the Soviet batteries, and thus to signal Israel's displeasure. ... Hod's proposal was not adopted at this stage, and the IAF was instructed not to go near the area manned by Soviet units."[44] The Israeli reconnaissance flights, Smirnov recalls, approached only Egyptian

OPERATION *KAVKAZ* IS FORMALLY ORGANIZED

formations, and the Soviet SAMs registered little success when fired at targets at the outer fringe of their range.⁴⁵

"Shortly after" Hod's suggestion was rejected,

> the Egyptians began digging new T-shaped emplacements close to the canal sector. The IAF estimated that the Egyptians intended to advance the SAM-3 batteries to the front line, and thus to threaten the Israeli planes that continued to operate along the canal. The same day, it was decided to prevent the Egyptians from bringing the missiles closer to the canal than their 30-km range. ... The battle began to prevent the advance of the missile batteries, while also hitting Egyptian radar systems. ... Heavy casualties did not deter the Egyptians from keeping up construction, which was held up significantly so long as Israeli fire continued.⁴⁶

After the 1973 war, Allon recalled that in March 1970 "we had a cabinet discussion about the first appearance of SAM-3s in the Egyptian array near the canal. ... There was an argument about the operational significance of this weapon [for] a crossing." Suitably for the Russian context, Allon cited the "Chekhov's gun" principle: once positioned to cover a canal crossing, the missiles would eventually *have* to do so.⁴⁷

G. *US acquiescence in "unacknowledged" Soviet presence*

In a back-channel meeting on 7 April, Kissinger vented his annoyance at being "tricked by the Soviet introduction of SAM-3s." Dobrynin countered that the missiles were "purely defensive," and insisted (according to Kissinger) that the ceasefire offer still stood. "He then asked tentatively what we would say if the Soviets promised to keep their deployment confined to Alexandria, Cairo and the Aswan Dam." Kissinger reported that he agreed to consider the offer—thus effectively acquiescing in the Soviet intervention so long as it remained "defensive," despite his previous remonstration.

Dobrynin's report quotes Kissinger as admitting that the United States "can understand that the deployment ... is defensive, but it agrees with Israel that placing such systems in the Suez Canal zone is quite different." Kissinger promised to consult Nixon without delay, but Dobrynin "sensed from his confident tone that his remarks ... had already been approved by Nixon himself"—who, as Kissinger admitted in his own report, "did not take the same active interest in the Middle East negotiations as he did ... on Vietnam and SALT."⁴⁸

Their next meeting, two days later, was marked mainly by Dobrynin's pleasant surprise at Kissinger's proposal to schedule a US–Soviet summit conference, which would focus mainly on the latter issues, though "the agenda could also include preliminary discussions of ways to reach a Middle East settlement." Kissinger indicated—in his own words—that "the key to our attitude on the Middle East" would be the Soviet stance on Vietnam, since Nixon was elected without the Jewish vote and did not depend on it. The impact of this US "attitude" would be felt in due course; meanwhile, Dobrynin left for Moscow, and the back-channel talks resumed only two months later.[49] The issue of SAM-3 deployment in the canal zone was left unresolved. In view of the Americans' failure to fulfill their warning of "grave consequences" for *any* direct Soviet intervention, it could evidently be disregarded.

13

THE SOVIET–ISRAELI BATTLE IS JOINED

A. First air encounters

Once again, a Soviet move had been threatened when it was already being implemented. On 12 April, IAF reconnaissance reported that several of the "T emplacements" had been occupied, and although it was assumed that they were manned by Soviet regulars, Israel now abandoned its previous caution not to engage them. Two Phantoms were dispatched on a bombing raid, and reported that the Soviets appeared to be unprepared as no missiles were fired. This marked the first direct clash of the Soviet–Israeli war in which both sides were aware of each other's identity.[1] It ushered in the pitched battle between Soviet and Israeli forces, which was to last just under four months.

The United States gave scant support for Israel's effort to prevent the Soviet SAM shield from reaching the canal bank and extending its range into Sinai. For the Nixon administration, highlighting this Soviet advance was undesirable, and Israel's alleged role in provoking it was resented. If the Soviet military presence in Egypt could no longer be averted, at least the political damage could be limited by not advertising it. In Washington, the view remained the same as before the Soviet SAMs were detected: "*unacknowledged* Soviet involvement in the defense of the UAR does not directly affect US interests," whereas "forcing the USSR into *open* support would be forcing the extension of the Brezhnev doctrine into the Middle East and extending the area of dominant Soviet influence."[2]

Despite the Soviet MiG squadrons' initial assignment to the Egyptian rear, Nastenko anticipated that their clash with the Israelis was also just a matter of time. He took chief military adviser Katyshkin's indoctrination seriously: "We had to prepare for dogfights with Israeli pilots of American origin, with rich experience, who had been trained at a war school in Vietnam." Training for such encounters was facilitated after Nastenko noticed, on the desk of the Egyptian base commander, a thick manual graphically describing previous dogfights against Israeli aircraft. He persuaded the Egyptian to share this vital material only after agreeing that the latter would read it to him and he would take no notes. "For two weeks, for no longer than an hour per day, I listened to

THE SOVIET–ISRAELI WAR, 1967–1973

this sparse but very important information. After each session or lesson I would return to my bunker to write and sketch from memory everything I could retain and understand."[3]

Even before this data could be put to use, Nastenko notes proudly—and correctly—that the Soviet air presence persuaded Israel to discontinue the deep-penetration bombing raids.[4] After Operation *Priha-21* on 13 April, the Israelis stopped flaunting their domination of Egyptian skies, even though no *Priha* raider was ever brought down by the Soviet interceptors or missiles. This was five days after the school bombing caused forty-seven immediate fatalities, "one of the greatest tragedies of the War of Attrition," but the official IAF account holds that this second disaster was not the main motivation for the Israeli climbdown. Rather, "the Israeli Cabinet resolves *at this stage* to avoid provoking the combat squadrons manned by Soviet pilots, in the hope that the Soviets would not intervene in the fighting."[5]

Shortly afterward, an Israeli colonel, while claiming that the depth raids had prevented an all-out Egyptian attack, also admitted "now the situation has changed again. With Soviet pilots and rocket technicians actively protecting the interior of Egypt, we have been forced to curtail our activities."[6]

When exactly did "this stage" end? As already seen, the arrival of Soviet-manned SAM-3s was detected on 17 March, but according to Heikal the Soviet-piloted MiG-21s were successfully camouflaged—as Brezhnev had demanded—until 18 April, when they had their first brush with Israeli planes. "The Russians pursued [the Israelis], all communications between them going out ... in Russian." This led the Egyptian editor to question the Soviets' aversion to publicity. "Nasser ... was puzzled. How did this square with all the talk about the need for secrecy? My own theory was that ... it was a signal to the Americans that the Russians had arrived."[7] One of Egyptian Vice-President Sabry's visits to Moscow, in April 1970, has been credited with persuading Brezhnev and Defense Minister Grechko to send Soviet pilots into combat in the canal zone.[8] However, as Sabry was officially in Moscow to attend the celebration of Lenin's centennial, which took place on 22–3 April, and his return was reported on the 26th, this attribution is uncertain at best.[9]

Intentionally or not, the 18 April incident did give the Israelis, and through them the Americans, their first indication that Soviet-flown aircraft had entered the fray. A new IDF sigint unit, codenamed *Masregah* (knitting needle) and staffed with Russian-speaking servicemen and women, was created early in 1970. It was based at MI's main listening post, next to the IDF Southern Command's forward headquarters at Umm-Hashiba, on a ridge overlooking the canal. The unit's initial assignment was to track the Soviet advisers. During the initial phase of *Kavkaz*, the "Grechkos"— as the monitors were nicknamed—picked up nothing that betrayed the appearance of Soviet regulars. At a recent reunion, they recalled a lot of free time that permitted vodka-and-music parties and practical jokes such as fabricated intercepts of complaints by Soviet naval advisers about the quality of Port Said women (the earlier,

THE SOVIET–ISRAELI BATTLE IS JOINED

unheeded intercept that forewarned of the Soviet squadrons' arrival occurred before *Masregah*'s formal organization).

Then, on 18 April, a pair of Phantoms was sent again on a deep-penetration sortie—but for reconnaissance rather than bombing: the mission was to monitor Egyptian canal-crossing exercises in the hinterland (presumably Wadi Natrun). The lead pilot (and second F-4 squadron commander) Avihu Bin-Nun let his subordinate take the lead to gain practice, and the latter flew back slower than the planned 600 knots in order to conserve fuel, eliminate the refueling stop at Refidim, and return earlier to home base in northern Israel. This permitted Soviet pilots to overtake them. "They were right over us," Bin-Nun related. "Apparently they didn't spot us because of the cloud shadows ... We got out of there without even seeing them. When we got back, we first understood there were Soviet combat pilots in the region."

The *Masregah* eavesdroppers—as retold by one of them, identified only as Lt-Col. David—noticed the difference in tone and style between the new pilots' signals and those of the veteran advisers. "The discovery was so astonishing that a three-hour shouting match ensued with Tovia [Feinman, the unit's commander]." After initially responding to this "nonsense" with some Russian obscenities, Feinman was persuaded, and sent a helicopter to pick up the tapes. That very evening they were delivered to Prime Minister Meir, who presented them to Nixon, correctly claiming that "no one but us had spotted the transfer of Soviet forces to Egypt."[10]

The Soviets gave a different explanation of the first encounters' indecisive outcome. According to Colonel Konstantin Korotyuk, one of the MiG-21 regiment commanders,

> to stop the Israelis from striking at Egyptian targets ... our fighters had to take off when any Israeli aircraft which had been discovered were still at least 200km away. ... By the time the latter had penetrated 30 to 40km inside Egyptian territory our fighters would be 25 to 30km from them, but at that point the enemy turned away and headed home. We were only allowed to pursue them as far as the Suez Canal but not to cross it.

This, said Korotyuk, recurred daily with as many as five such interception sorties. His colleague Nastenko added:

> we were in a constant state of stress and our nerves were frayed to the limits. ... The pilots would be sitting in ... their fighters which were standing in the shelters ... wearing partially pressurized high altitude suits, and there was not even the slightest breeze into the shelters. It was often over 40 degrees centigrade outside, and waiting for sorties like this often took many hours.

As such constant stress exhausted the pilots and slowed up their reactions, they were ordered to do a full sequence of aerobatics before landing at the end of each sortie, as well as mock dogfights.[11]

B. The United States blames Israel

Though *Masregah*'s David has claimed his intercepts showed the Americans that Israel was their strategic asset, at the time the Israelis were blamed for this sea-change in the global balance of the Cold War. They were unable to refute the already widespread account that Nasser's flight to Moscow, his desperate appeal for help against Israeli aggression, and the resulting Soviet intervention had been caused by the depth bombings. The Israelis had to sidestep the question with ambiguous formulations that acknowledged a visit to Moscow by Nasser in January, but still contended that the Soviet deployment had begun previously.[12] The latter claim has now been vindicated, but at the time it came too late for Israel's advocacy purposes and would not stick. "Whatever the truth of the Egyptian–Soviet arms negotiations," insider William Quandt wrote a few years after the events, "few officials in Washington were prepared to accept the Israeli version." They "thought that Israel had brought on the Soviet response by a reckless bombing campaign and irresponsible rhetoric aimed at the Nasser regime's existence."[13]

By January 1971, a report by no less than the chief of the Soviet Division at the CIA's Office of Regional and Political Analysis stated as established fact that Nasser "made an emergency visit to the Soviet Union in the third week of January [1970] to demand help [and] the Soviet leadership consented." The report conceded the minor point that "this decision was not prompted but was reinforced by news received by the Soviet leadership soon *after* Nasir's visit that important Soviet advisers in Egypt had been killed and wounded." But it dismissed any claim that the Soviet deployment was initiated earlier:

> Some Israelis—sensitive to the implication that their deep-penetration raids had proven unwise—have since argued that the Soviet intervention ... had been planned for months before those raids began. This argument is not credible in view of the evidence suggesting that the Soviet Ministry of Defense and the Soviet leadership were galvanized to action and to decision-making during and shortly after Nasir's visit.[14]

Eventually, the Americans relented from Nixon's declared freeze of aircraft supply, but only to the extent of restoring Israeli losses when the Soviet SAMs began taking a heavy toll, and that too with no publicity.[15]

At the end of April, even the sympathetic US ambassador in Israel, Walworth Barbour, in a talk with Israeli Foreign Minister Eban, still "repeated the US position about the IAF bombings deep in Egypt, which in the US opinion had caused the Soviet deployment of the SAM-3s." When Eban told Barbour that Israel intended to publicize the Soviet intervention, and appealed for a "forceful and clear American response," the ambassador coolly "thought aloud that there might be some advantage in keeping the presence of Soviet pilots secret, so as not to engage their prestige."[16] Against his advice, on 29 April Israel went ahead with a highly unusual cabinet dec-

THE SOVIET–ISRAELI BATTLE IS JOINED

laration that bannered the Soviet intervention.[17] In retrospect, Israeli officials claimed rather unconvincingly that this was done to signal to the Soviets that Israel did not desire a confrontation.[18] However, the main target was clearly American: the communiqué was backed up, confidentially, with *Masregah*'s "daily recordings of Russian operational conversations" relayed by the Mossad to "contacts in Washington." But even this failed to force the US hand in respect of public diplomacy or accelerated arms supply.

When this Mossad initiative was leaked to, and broadcast by, the Israel Radio correspondent in Washington, it did little to promote Israel's case but caused internecine feuding that further shackled its advocacy: Mossad chief Zamir "stopped sending sensitive information" to all diplomatic missions. Israel's ambassador in London (a former IAF commander), frustrated that "I am not getting even a minimum of trust" with evidence that might help his efforts, reported that the British too were "blaming this [Soviet intervention] on our deep-penetration policy."[19]

The chastised Israelis never again tried to rub American noses in the presence of Soviet regulars. Subsequent Israeli statements referred only to Egyptian planes and missiles. It remained the elephant at the tea party, very much present but rarely mentioned, hidden behind such euphemisms as "experts" or "technicians," which then became interchangeable with "advisers," despite the substantial difference. Approved Israeli versions featured the oxymoron that "Russian 'advisers' stationed in Egypt" then numbered more than 10,000, "and they alone were to man and protect the top-secret SAM-3 installations."[20] This, in turn, helped vested-interest sources to shape mainstream historiography when the Soviet regulars were withdrawn.

In later years, as the Israelis were unable to disprove the link between their depth bombings and the Soviet intervention, their publications tried to harmonize it with the Israeli position while accepting Nasser's January visit as fact. Here is one such gloss from early 1973, which in retrospect came closest to an accurate assessment:

> the Russians decided at the end of 1969 to supply Egypt with SAM-3s. The Israeli bombings deep inside Egypt, which came after this had already been decided, convinced the Soviets all the more of this matter's urgency. This was added to by Nasser's appeal during his secret visit to Moscow at the beginning of 1970, when he succeeded in persuading the Soviets to accelerate increased military aid and Soviet units.[21]

An official IDF publication in late 1971 tried to reconcile the two versions: Nasser's "secret" visit to Moscow and his appeal for Soviet help are described as caused by the devastating Israeli air counteroffensive along the canal, before the depth bombings. But only after *another* appeal from Nasser, in March 1970, did the USSR "begin the construction of a new AA array, manned by Soviet crews."[22]

After Heikal's memoirs gained currency, the Israeli line became that

> the closed character of both countries ... makes it very difficult to get a clear picture of that critical meeting between Nasser and the Soviet leadership. Detailed descriptions were

165

given by Heikal and Minister of War Fawzy, both of whom are of course suspect of distortion, but in the main the report seems *prima facie* reasonable ... [though Fawzy] blurred, apparently on purpose, between the discussions in late December and the situation that was created after the depth bombings.[23]

Even such reservations were gradually dropped or limited to footnotes—in Israeli studies and all the more so in foreign ones—as the Egyptian–Israeli clash faded from the news after 1973, and Heikal's version became the standard. Korn's long-definitive study of the War of Attrition reproduces the Heikal–Fawzy account of Nasser's visit after describing the *entire* depth bombing campaign, implying that it drove Nasser to this move.[24] Fifteen years after his aforementioned endorsement of the Egyptian version, Quandt's subsequent, broader history added only in a footnote that there were opposing views.[25] As late as 2000, a detailed timeline and analysis of the Egyptian–Israeli confrontation gave the January–visit version as undisputed, resting only on the Egyptian sources.[26] The official military history published in Egypt soon after the 1973 war also put the "start of intensive work" on the SAM array at January 1970, and in one of its few allusions to any Soviet role, admits that "our engineers had at their disposal the useful knowhow of our friends in the Warsaw Pact."[27]

If the main objective of Operation *Kavkaz* was to block IAF deep penetration into the Egyptian heartland, it was achieved by mid-April 1970. Nasser had supposedly requested the stationing of Soviet personnel in the first place only for this purpose, and as a stopgap until sufficient Egyptian crews could be trained. He reportedly envisaged a two-year transition. But even the originally defined mission of protecting the skies over Cairo and the delta necessitated blocking Israeli penetration through the canal zone, and the dogged preparation of SAM-3 sites there—which began before the missiles' own arrival—confirms that this was the original plan. There are several indications that the Soviet presence in Egypt was intended from the outset also to advance the long-term goal of a cross-canal offensive. Moreover, the Soviet troops' dispatch was accompanied in the Soviet military press by calls for maintaining permanent bases in the Mediterranean arena as necessary for defense of the USSR itself.[28] The number of men screened and selected for the expeditionary force in the summer of 1969 was adequate for several tours of duty.

An eyewitness account describes Grechko as initiating the SAM's advance into the canal zone. A staff officer who accompanied Air Defense Commander Batitsky when he reported to the defense minister on 10 May about the progress of *Kavkaz* relates that Grechko was satisfied with the exclusion of IAF planes from the Egyptian hinterland, but pointed out "a weakness in the canal area." He reckoned that another four to five *divizyons* would have to be posted there. When Batitsky protested that he had no more units to dispatch without dereliction of his duty to protect the USSR, Grechko overruled him, and a tense confrontation ensued. The upshot was evidently to send the batteries already in Egypt forward, rather than to send additional formations.[29]

THE SOVIET–ISRAELI BATTLE IS JOINED

C. An increasingly active naval role

The Soviet naval presence was also drawn into the confrontation with Israel. After the Abu Zaabal bombing, Nasser had threatened to spread the war into the naval arena, and in early April Egypt again declared that "it would seize the initiative at sea."[30] This coincided with Israel's formal unveiling of the Cherbourg boats and, more significantly, their armament with home-developed *Gabriel* missiles, the first Western answer to the Styx.[31]

In the last week of April, submarine adviser Kryshtob was summoned to his Egyptian superior and told of an impending mission to "strike at the Jews." He was ordered not to tell other Soviets about it, but the three top advisers were present when the operational order was handed to him and his boat's captain, Bagir. The Soviet officers had no problem with the mission—to sink enemy shipping off the Israeli coast—but they clarified to Kryshtob that he must not execute it without rising at least to periscope depth to verify the targets' identity. In other words, the Soviets were not trying to restrain offensive action, but to ensure its legitimacy. The risk involved was brought home to Kryshtob by the crewmen, who went to pray and wrote wills.

During an eleven-day cruise, the submarine twice identified large targets by means of sonar alone. Kryshtob managed to persuade Bagir to surface before attacking the first, off Tel Aviv, which turned out to be a 20,000-ton freighter. Checking it out exposed the submarine because its diving systems were slow due to poor maintenance, and three of the "Cherbourg boats" gave chase; "now they were already hunting me." Shaking them off demanded more than ten hours at maximum depth. Another technical fault, with the air compressors, caused some of the crewmen to faint. When a second target appeared, off Haifa, Bagir ordered torpedoes readied. Kryshtob insisted on surfacing first, prevailed—and was horrified to see that the Egyptian had almost sunk a Greek car ferry. He needed to use his strongest language, Bagir lodged a complaint, and Kasatonov himself chaired an inquiry that reprimanded Kryshtob for disgracing the Navy. The adviser was so upset he could not eat for five days. Not having sunk anything, for him "it would have been a routine cruise, [but] for them it was heroism. All their training had been done while moored at the pier."

On the night of 13–14 May, returning to Port Said on the surface, Kryshtob logged strong flashes and explosions. Soon after, the submarine was buzzed by Israeli Mirages. After putting into harbor, he learned that the Egyptian "missile boats on duty" had attacked and sunk an unidentified target without the knowledge of their Soviet adviser. Again, Kryshtob was shocked that it *might* have been a civilian vessel. In fact, it was—the 75-ton Israeli fishing boat *Orit*, which was blown out of the water by two Styx missiles with the loss of half its four-man crew.

The Soviet officer comforted himself with a retrospective Egyptian claim that the *Orit* was a large freighter converted to an intelligence-gathering ship with a complement of 116—but having witnessed the incident, he denied that it had penetrated Egyptian waters. The latter version was supposedly gleaned from foreign sources but was so fanciful that it was never officially announced. Kryshtob's account indicates that previously (as in the *Eilat* sinking), Egyptian naval craft only operated under Soviet guidance, with the adviser in effect overseeing the nominal skipper. Whether he was indeed uninvolved in the *Orit* sinking is called into question by a statement from the usually cautious military historian Zhirokhov, hinting broadly that Egyptian naval commandos who "sank an Israeli patrol boat the same night" in Eilat port "might quite reasonably have been Soviet *spetznaz* [special ops]."[32] Port Said, not to mention Alexandria, was still relatively protected by the Soviet presence, and Israel retaliated for the *Orit* with an air raid on the Red Sea base of Ras Banas that sank an Egyptian destroyer and *Komar* boat.

D. Direct hits on the Soviets in Port Said

On 30 May 1970, the Egyptians staged an enhanced replay of the Ras el-Ish raid. Fawzy later claimed that this time the canal crossing was at battalion level—which meant certain involvement, at least in the planning, by the Soviet advisers. Israel claimed it had defeated the incursion but admitted an extraordinarily heavy loss of fifteen soldiers. Fawzy stressed that building up the entire army for a cross-canal offensive was continuing, and this objective was already within reach. Israeli commentators could only quibble with the numbers.[33]

The magnitude of this blow was reflected in the IAF response: an unprecedentedly intensive bombing campaign on the Port Said area, in which—reporters were told—more bombs were dropped on Egypt than in the entire Six-Day War. Soviet ships had been spotted before in the harbor "and occasionally fired on Israeli planes"; this time, one of the pilots reported sighting three.[34] Although the Israelis claimed they had steered clear of them, on 7 June Eban confirmed to the Knesset that a warning from Moscow had been relayed via the Finnish embassy after shrapnel hit a Soviet ship—a fact that was deliberately omitted in IDF communiqués. Dayan later confirmed that some Soviet naval crewmen were killed.[35] The Israeli bombardment cut off road transport and water supply to the city—whose remaining population of 20,000 was mostly employed in services for the Soviet base—and auxiliary ships of the *Eskadra* took over supplying the inhabitants' necessities.[36] Nonetheless, an Israeli air raid across the canal several days later reported that the Egyptians had not fled as on earlier occasions, but were holding their positions.

E. Kissinger presents Soviet withdrawal as a policy goal

Returning from Moscow almost two months after the 9 April meeting in which Kissinger had suggested a summit, Dobrynin met first with Rogers and Sisco. Despite

THE SOVIET–ISRAELI BATTLE IS JOINED

the disdain he professed to Kissinger for "the petty legalism of Sisco's approach," Dobrynin told the State Department chiefs that he was authorized to continue talks on the Middle East with *them*, and presented "new formulations" of previous Soviet proposals on a peace settlement. Rogers responded with a written protest of the Soviet military involvement in Egypt. Dobrynin not only was unfazed, but reported to Moscow that the talk had "demonstrated the efficacy of ... conducting a 'constructive dialog' with the United States while strengthening the 'defensive capability' of Egypt"—in other words, that the best way to prevent a forceful US response was to keep on playing the rivals within the administration against each other.[37]

Six days later, Rogers invited Dobrynin for a "secret, unofficial conversation"—precisely what Kissinger's back channel was supposed to provide. The secretary indicated that the Americans were "seriously considering" a ceasefire and indirect talks to be conducted by Jarring (what was to become the "Rogers Plan II"). A delighted Dobrynin reported that at last the Nixon administration was coming around, and "the most important factor in this was our military presence in the UAR, first of all Soviet pilots and missiles."[38]

Kissinger sensed that the Soviet ambassador was avoiding him and initiated a restart of the back-channel talks.[39] They met on 10 June, and Nixon joined them for part of their lengthy talk. Dobrynin pointedly dismissed much of what Kissinger had to offer on the specifics of a settlement, saying that Rogers had already made the proposal to him. Kissinger did, however, have something entirely new. In his memoirs, he would relate telling Dobrynin that it was "crucial for us to know whether the Soviet Union would be prepared to withdraw its military forces as part of a negotiated peace."[40] Kissinger's contemporary report differs only slightly: "I told him that for us the presence of Soviet combat personnel in Egypt was a matter of the very gravest consequences. ... I therefore wanted to know whether, assuming that there was a peace settlement, the Soviet Union would be prepared to withdraw its combat personnel."

After making sure that this meant the withdrawal would come only after the agreement, Dobrynin said the idea was "conceivable" and—according to Kissinger's report—promised a reply at their next meeting.[41]

Nixon and Kissinger congratulated each other, with the latter indulging in characteristic flattery for the president.[42] But as usual, the parallel Soviet document reflects Kissinger's inquiry somewhat differently:

> Wouldn't Moscow consider it possible to somehow tell them—in any form and on a strictly confidential basis—that it has no intention of maintaining its military presence in the UAR even after a *final* settlement and the withdrawal of Israeli forces, i.e., that at that time there will be no Soviet pilots there carrying out combat missions, or Soviet personnel of anti-aircraft missile systems or infantry units ("we know that they are not there now, but who knows what may happen tomorrow"). In that case, it would be easier

for the US Government, despite all the domestic criticism and Israel's objections ... to start looking for specific compromise recommendations that Jarring needs in order to organize talks ... even before the midterm elections ... although that "may involve certain domestic policy costs."

The latter costs, Kissinger specified, might include the much-feared electoral damage of limiting arms sales to Israel.

Dobrynin reported that he sensed—and warned against—a US attempt to take over any Israeli–Egyptian talks and exclude the USSR.[43] He did not report promising, nor did he recommend that Moscow give, an urgent answer on the withdrawal question. He had little reason to do so. Kissinger had in effect accepted the Soviet presence in the canal zone too for the foreseeable future. Activity of both the Soviet fighters and SAMs was intensified, and as much as declared. Radio Moscow in Arabic warned that just as Israel's deep-penetration raids had been halted, IAF activity in the canal zone would also not remain beyond reach.[44]

F. Soviet MiG-21s engage the IAF

On 17 May 1970, Nastenko's MiG-21s were assigned a forward "reserve" base at Katameya, an enlarged stretch of highway 40 kilometers from the Suez Canal. Six planes were stationed there, in camouflaged underground bunkers, to "ambush" Israeli attackers. By the beginning of June, each Soviet pilot had logged 100 flight hours or more, but no dogfights had occurred. On 22 June, a pair of Soviet pilots claimed the first kill from such ambush tactics.[45] Nastenko's detailed account claims that early in the morning Egyptian radar at Gianaclis spotted a formation of Skyhawks heading toward Ismailia:

> Other marks also briefly flashed on the radar and these were quickly identified as the Mirages of a covering group which were flying at lower altitude. Immediately some MiG-21s took off, climbed and lured the Mirages. A swirling dogfight then began. Meanwhile a pair of Soviet MiG-21s led by Captain Sal'nikov flew at only 10m altitude towards Ismailia and was soon on the tail of the Israeli Skyhawks. Next day the Soviet squadron was sent some wreckage from a Skyhawk which had come down on the western bank of the canal.[46]

This was never confirmed by the IAF, whose bulletin for that day's action was entirely routine: MiGs had approached the Skyhawks, but no contact was made.[47] However, Israel's suppression of similar incidents a month later—in which a Skyhawk *was* badly damaged—indicates that in this respect its official accounts may not be much more reliable than the Soviets'. Nastenko might be suspected of conflating two events, or simply confusing June with July, except that the particulars differ substantially. The 22 June incident is reported in detail by multiple Russian sources. Nastenko first mentioned it publicly as early as the 1980s. In addition, one of the pilots describing engagements in July notes that a Skyhawk had already been shot

THE SOVIET–ISRAELI BATTLE IS JOINED

down earlier.[48] As this is of some importance, it calls for further inquiry: if true, it would qualify as the only Soviet kill in air combat against Israel. Even if it reflects as in other cases a hit that did not bring down the Skyhawk but left some debris on the ground, it marks the start of the Soviet–Israeli air war earlier than previously acknowledged, and considerably enhances the Soviet airmen's hitherto inglorious record against the IAF.

14

"A FAMOUS INDISCRETION" AS THE AIR WAR PEAKS

A. The origin of the "expulsion" misnomer

> In the Cold War, when our enemies lied, they lied to conceal the wretchedness of their system. Whereas when we lied, we concealed our virtues.
>
> David Cornwell ("John le Carré")[1]

Here, another fast-forward digression is called for in order to introduce the first antecedents of another spectacularly successful falsification that this study aims to rectify. Just as Heikal's version as to the origin of the Soviet intervention became—and largely remains—unchallenged, so did and does the dating of the operation's end on 18 July 1972. This is when Sadat, by then Nasser's successor as president, announced his decision "to terminate the mission of the Soviet military advisers and experts, who came here in compliance with our request."[2] Sadat's measure was immediately dubbed, and is still termed, the "expulsion of Soviet advisers,"[3] frequently with the added modifier "surprising." The number of Soviet "advisers" who were "expelled" is variously given as 10,000–20,000,[4] and they are explicitly or implicitly described as "all," or at least the bulk, of the Soviet military personnel in Egypt.

This "expulsion" is described by Western historiography as the first step toward Egypt's eventual rupture with its Soviet patrons, and therefore (to quote one recent study), "the single greatest Third World success for the United States during the entire Cold War."[5] Its direct motive is held to be that "under the guise of Détente, the United States had persuaded the Soviets to reduce their support for the Arabs."[6] Specifically, Moscow purportedly refused to supply Egypt with the advanced offensive weaponry that first Nasser and then Sadat desired as a precondition for an all-out offensive against Israel.

Even more than Heikal's version about the start of *Kavkaz*, the "expulsion of advisers" concept was—or ought to have been—suspect at the time. The glaring inconsistencies will be pointed out as they crop up in the timeline of events. Suffice it to mention here that the number of genuine advisers never approached the figure for Soviet manpower that was known to leave Egypt in 1972. Conversely, in October

THE SOVIET–ISRAELI WAR, 1967–1973

1973 the dependents of Soviet advisers who had ostensibly been expelled over a year before were evacuated in preparation for war. It is, however, the genesis of the term "expulsion" that can be traced back to the stage now under discussion, spring–summer 1970, and to the main purveyor of the entire misnomer, Henry Kissinger.

It has already been noted that in early June 1970, Kissinger tried to sound out Dobrynin about an agreed withdrawal from Egypt of the newly discovered regular Soviet formations, and that Moscow was in no hurry to respond. When the back-channel interlocutors met again on 23 June, Dobrynin only noted briefly at the end of his report, without even specifying the troop-withdrawal issue: "Kissinger interjected that the President would also like to receive a response to the views he had expressed on the Middle East issues. However, [he] did not elaborate."[7] Kissinger reported that he found the Soviet ambassador "noticeably more businesslike and less cordial than before ... Dobrynin did not take the bait about the suggestion of Soviet troop withdrawal in case of a settlement." He had little reason to; three days before, Rogers had presented him with "proposals on securing a Middle East peace settlement," which included a ceasefire that would bar *Egyptian* missiles from further advance toward the canal, but made no mention at all of Soviet missiles or other forces.[8] Dobrynin thus denied Kissinger even the token achievement of commitment to a future withdrawal. Instead, he accused the Americans of failing to respond to a "significant concession" that the USSR had offered—bilateral talks—and instead coming back with Rogers's "unilateral overture. It is your problem now, and we are out of it."[9]

Three days later, at the conclusion of a presidential media briefing in the "Western White House" at San Clemente, Kissinger vented his frustration in what has been called "a famous indiscretion."[10] In the 1979 installment of his memoirs, he wrote: "I took the initiative of challenging the Soviet military presence in Egypt ... We are trying to *expel* the Soviet military presence, *not so much the advisors*, but the combat pilots and the combat personnel."[11] A very uncharacteristic indiscretion indeed it was, and not only because it overstated the Americans' actual effort. It undermined US public diplomacy, which was doing its best to downplay the Soviet combat presence in Egypt. Moreover, Kissinger had promised confidentiality as the basic purpose of the back channel.

In the 1982 volume of his memoirs, Kissinger admitted that "'expel' was the word I used in a *much criticized* briefing on June 26, 1970."[12] The criticism began after the briefing's transcript became public, within a month. "Kissinger's anonymity was violated with unfortunate consequences," wrote one Washington columnist. "This did not contribute to the peace initiative, and Kissinger sent Rogers a telegram apologizing for the slip." It was an excruciating humiliation for Kissinger, which could hardly have been extracted if his move had proven as effective as he later claimed. The same column—clearly sympathetic to the secretary of state—cast the incident as marring Kissinger's otherwise rapid ascent at Rogers's expense.[13] But more importantly for the

"A FAMOUS INDISCRETION" AS THE AIR WAR PEAKS

long range, the term "expulsion" was coined. Kissinger had displayed a policy objective for which he might be willing to make tradeoffs, and the idea endured even though he did not repeat the indiscretion.

B. The last Israeli airborne raid and the first Phantom shootdown

Meanwhile—even if the Soviet pilots' claim to have downed an IAF Skyhawk on 22 June is discounted—their presence was impressed on the Israelis again a week later. On the 29th, an IDF force flown in on five helicopters attacked an "administrative" facility near "the Soviet-operated Bir Arida airbase," and ambushed an Egyptian ground patrol. *Masregah* reported that Soviet-piloted MiG-21s were scrambled to intercept the intruders. Dayan personally ordered in a Phantom to distract the Soviets, but it was instructed to avoid engagement. Chief of Staff Bar-Lev told the returning raiders: "this was in an area under Russian air control, and we did it under their noses. The Russians came pretty close, but the situation wasn't serious enough to put a plane of ours into actual combat."[14] He pronounced the raid a complete success—but it was the last ground-forces landing that the IDF would attempt in the Egyptian hinterland. As on 18 April, the very presence of the Soviet squadrons achieved a deterrent effect.

Nasser arrived in Moscow the same day (29 June), with an entourage that again included Riad, Fawzy and Heikal (newly appointed as information minister). Most of his eighteen-day sojourn was devoted to medical treatment. Dr Chazov finally saw him and was shocked by his state, which again indicates that the Egyptian president had not been in the USSR in December, January or any time since his previous examination in Cairo in September 1969.[15] The main political talks with the Soviet leadership took place on 30 June and 1 July, with both sides getting constant updates about momentous developments on the canal front.

In retrospect, a watershed was marked when the Soviet-manned SAM-3s and Egyptian SAM-2 batteries, along with independent *Strela* and *Shilka* detachments besides those attached to the missile *divizyons*, were incorporated into a unified command in the canal zone, with overlapping coverage and improved detection systems and communications. The Soviet units were now encouraged to initiate engagements with the IAF craft that were struggling to prevent the entire array's renewed eastward progress. As Smirnov described it, until then "the enemy conducted active air reconnaissance, but as a rule Israeli aircraft did not enter the range of our *divizyons*. Several Arab *divizyons* suffered hits. [But] the Phantoms had time to turn around and get out of [our] range. Operational tactics had to be changed."

Israeli reconnaissance concluded on 30 June that the IAF's success in bombing out the newly dug missile emplacements had failed to stop the SAMs' advance eastward. The Soviets had overcome the setback by dispensing with the protection of concrete shelters, and instead began "ambushing" IAF attackers within hours of taking up improvised positions. Speed and mobility, which the Soviet advisers had been drilling with the Egyptians for almost three years, were now essential. This new method involved considerable risk, Smirnov noted, and "demanded outstanding coolheadedness as well as moral and psychological preparation. ... The commander had to be certain that his manpower and equipment alike would function, otherwise the enemy might strike [our] *divizyon* itself, which would result in death of personnel and loss of hardware."[16] Both the Soviet and Egyptian batteries did suffer losses, but their aggressive tactics paid off.

The Israelis quickly felt the change. "Recently the Egyptians have been trying to infiltrate missiles into the canal zone at night. ... They prepare them for operation by 'primitive' methods, as they cannot operate complete electronic systems. Then, they fire at IAF planes." Hours after the IAF detected this innovation on 30 June, the Soviet-manned SAMs claimed their first Israeli F-4—the second of *two* that Israel confirmed lost that day to "Soviet-*advised* Egyptian" SAMs.[17] The first Phantom was indeed downed by Egyptian SAM-2s. Its pilot was the one who had caused the 18 April incident with his slow flight home. He and his WSO were now captured. The second Phantom, also struck by two SAM-2s, was finished off by a Soviet SAM-3. Smirnov cautiously—and unusually for the Soviets—took credit only for the latter success, for which his outfit had physical evidence: a helmet attributed to the pilot of the first Phantom shot down by the Soviets is kept in the Russian Air Defense Corps museum.[18]

This, however, is when Smirnov noted that some colleagues had gone on record with wilder claims, which were reflected immediately in the Moscow talks. Heikal reported in *Al-Ahram* that on 1 July, Nasser told the Soviet *troika* that four Phantoms had been downed the day before. "His remark caused great surprise. After a moment of silence, Grechko said: 'no, Mr President. According to our information, *six* planes were shot down yesterday.'" The defense minister pointed out the sites on a map.[19]

Even according to Smirnov's modest version, 30 June was of immense significance to the Soviets' morale as well as their operational doctrine: "these new tactics proved themselves. The first Phantom was shot down by the first missile that Capt. Valeryanos Prano Malyauka's *divizyon* launched." A political officer went further in Malyauka's praise: "after identifying the target, the captain did not betray his excitement to his subordinates but continued to issue orders as clearly and confidently as in training." After seeing that the pencil of a staff officer, Lt Gurov, was rattling on the plotting table, "he said: 'calm down, comrades, relax, we'll have a shootdown right away.'" He held up the missile launch until the last moment, Gurov recalled, "and we were all gripped by fear: why don't we shoot? Only after the commander's calm order was given ... we understood: the enemy was thus denied the time for evasive action."[20] Smirnov summed up the day: "this first Israeli Phantom—one of those American-made super-aircraft, whose invincibility was legendary—fell on Egyptian soil. ... To learn from the experience of this successful first engagement, that very night all *divizyon* commanders as well as missile-guidance and radar officers were assembled in Malyauka's *divizyon*."[21]

"A FAMOUS INDISCRETION" AS THE AIR WAR PEAKS

The Soviets' special interest in the Phantom, and in the knowhow possessed by its pilots, was demonstrated when they took part in the interrogation of the downed airmen. Yitzhak Pe'er (Jeff Peer), the pilot of the second plane shot down on 30 June, was captured by the Egyptians but told the present authors that several of the officers who questioned him were Russian. He identified them by appearance, accent, and—in one case—the Cyrillic letters on a wristwatch dial.[22] Pe'er volunteered his American birth early in his interrogation, and was told "you are ... a mercenary. We'll hang you in public in Cairo to show the whole world that American pilots are flying for Israel."[23] The threat was not carried out, but Pe'er's origin appears to have reinforced the fabrication that Israeli planes were being flown by Vietnam-seasoned USAF pilots—American Jewish volunteers or, in a version widely circulated among Soviet personnel, highly paid mercenaries.[24]

Pe'er was the only US-born IAF pilot who took part in combat missions during the War of Attrition, but he arrived in Israel as a boy of fourteen and had never served in any US force. Several former USAF pilots did serve at various times with the IAF, including in this period at least one Vietnam veteran, but he was barred from combat missions precisely to avoid any risk of capture.[25] There were also contrasting rumors among the Soviets that "many of the Israeli pilots are believed to have been emigrants from the Soviet Union."[26] This may have been more plausible, given the Israelis' ability to intercept and even imitate Soviet signals. But while such immigrants were common in other functions—including intelligence and signals—none are known to have served as pilots.

For Smirnov and his men, the 30 June triumph ended on a sour note. He wrote thirty years later:

> when P.F. Batitsky issued the combat orders for Operation *Kavkaz*, he notified me that the first missile *divizyon* commander to shoot down a Phantom would be nominated for Hero of the Soviet Union. He said this had been arranged with the defense minister. Of course I did not share this with anyone, but when the first Phantom was shot down we officially submitted Malyauka's nomination.

The Lithuanian officer received, however, only the lower-ranking Order of the Red Banner, which was understood as discrimination against a non-Russian. His dismayed superior could only console himself in retrospect that "later we had 'heroes' too." Malyauka's certificate of internationalist service was signed only in December 1988, by General Secretary Mikhail Gorbachev; it mentions neither Egypt nor his feat there.[27]

C. A ceasefire initiative masks intensified Soviet involvement

In Moscow, the overstated good news evidently reinforced Soviet–Egyptian agreement to press on with the military buildup. After returning to Cairo, Nasser told his party conference that the *troika* had promised him full military as well as political support. The detailed accounts of the Kremlin talks that were later published by Heikal and Fawzy reported full agreement to intensify preparation for the ground offensive, and meanwhile to accept the ninety-day ceasefire, which now had become a US initiative—in order to exploit it for advancing the missile array. This would indeed be carried out when the ceasefire ultimately came into effect on 7 August.

Nasser was promised new weapons, including a Soviet-manned SAM-6 mobile array, which was positioned in August around the Aswan Dam, releasing Egyptian SAM-2 formations for stations closer to the front. Even sooner, three frigates armed with the SAM-6's naval version took up positions off Port Said to remedy the perennial weakness of land-based anti-aircraft defense at the northern end of the canal and to protect the Soviet naval base, whose vulnerability had been demonstrated three weeks before the Moscow talks.[28] The long-delayed deal for supply of *Luna* missiles was also finalized, to be discovered only when "several battalions" appeared on the canal front in December.[29] They saw limited actual use on the Sinai front in the first days of the Yom Kippur War, when Syrian forces—unlike the Egyptians—were close enough to fire multiple *Luna*s at targets inside Israel.[30]

The Soviets reportedly balked at basing ten more Tu-16s in Egypt, of the C variant armed with air-to-ground Kelt missiles. They suggested that this might motivate the Americans to provide Israel with the newly developed Lance ground-to-ground missiles. But the Soviets did agree to preposition the Tu-16 squadron's missiles and other equipment at bases in Upper Egypt, where the planes would be flown on six hours' notice from the Egyptians and operated under joint command.[31] Before long, the Soviet-manned planes were stationed there too, and in greater numbers. Lt Evgeny Lashenko, a radar engineer with the Northern Fleet at Severomorsk, relates that his regiment of missile-bearing Tu-16s, in Egyptian markings, was ordered to Upper Egypt in 1971 and his tour of duty there was slightly over a year. When they arrived, the field still had not been fully cleared from the Israeli bombing in 1967 and the aircraft hulks were shunted aside from the runways to enable routine operation.[32] Lashenko's detachment, whose mission included "teaching the Egyptians the art of war," was the first in what became a continuing rotation.

Of more immediate significance was the Egyptian version that credited Nasser with selling the ceasefire-smokescreen idea to the reluctant Soviets—much as he had supposedly persuaded them in January to intervene militarily in the first place. In 1989, based on a comparison of the published Egyptian transcripts with the practical outcome, Dan Schueftan concluded that it was actually the Soviets who pressed Nasser to accept Rogers's proposal, and either this was agreed tacitly or the transcripts were doctored.[33] Three years later, Korn provided further indications that the Soviets were already inclined toward the idea.[34] The Dobrynin–Kissinger reports have now proved that the USSR actively promoted the proposal.

"A FAMOUS INDISCRETION" AS THE AIR WAR PEAKS

So for US consumption, the Soviet leadership's talks with Nasser had produced a very different line from the one he proclaimed in Cairo. Meeting Kissinger on 7 July, Dobrynin—who had already complained that the back-channel talks were producing little more substance than those with Rogers and Sisco[35]—was quick to take Kissinger to task for the "expulsion" remark. As Kissinger reported, "he couldn't understand why we made the statements. ... [he said] it would have been better for us to keep quiet." Still, Kissinger found Dobrynin "obviously taken aback by the various comments that had been made about the Middle East," for which Kissinger took implied credit.[36] Speaking with Nixon the same evening, he described Dobrynin as "frightened."[37]

D. The SAMs turn the tide; a limited US response

If this reliably described Dobrynin's behavior rather than Kissinger's wishful thinking, the Soviet diplomat must have put on a convincing charade, as there was little cause for such fright. On the ground, Smirnov's SAMs had just scored another kill. The Soviets' newly mobile tactics made it difficult for the Israelis to determine whether emplacements previously spotted as occupied would—if attacked the next day—still contain real missiles, dummies, or nothing at all, while still being protected by cannon and *Strela*s. On 5 July, a massive IAF strike was partly wasted on decoys, and was aborted after paying dearly for meager results. "A second Phantom crashed into the Egyptian ground like a flaming torch. It was shot down by the *divizyon* of Maj. S.K. Zavesnitsky. A third Phantom was luckier that day, and though leaving a trail of fire and smoke it managed to get across the canal." The latter claim was not confirmed by the IAF, and possibly was another case of afterburner activation being described as a missile impact.

As for the Phantom that was downed, Israeli versions still vary over whether it was struck by missile or cannon fire.[38] Both crewmen were captured, and told after their release in 1973 that they landed in an Egyptian emplacement. After an officer rescued them from "hysterical" soldiers, they were taken into a shelter and were surprised to encounter "a Soviet crew. Till then it wasn't known in Israel that the Russians were fighting in the actual war." The pilot, Amos Zamir, recalls that the Soviet officer took special interest in his WSO (weapons system officer), Amos Levitov, "because [the Soviet] decided that [Levitov] had Russian facial features. The atmosphere was relaxed. The officer never stopped talking on the telephone and sounded pleased with himself." As Levitov remembers it, "two big Russians were sitting there, in Egyptian military uniforms. A small Egyptian major was sitting between the two, talking on the phone excitedly." As the pilot related, "we were treated decently" and handed over to the Egyptians.[39]

The next day, US officials rejected the Israelis' claim of Soviet involvement, and still insisted that "the Soviets clearly were impressed by the American warnings and have not advanced the SAM-3 missiles up to the canal, in order to avoid a direct clash with Israeli

179

planes."⁴⁰ But within a week, Israel had lost an alarming chunk of its Phantom fleet. It had received a total of forty-four, one had already been shot down on 2 April in a dogfight over Syria, and at least one was lost in a training accident.⁴¹ According to a former squadron commander, an average of only thirty were serviceable at any given time during the War of Attrition.⁴² Worse, even a greater part of the IAF's few airmen qualified for the F-4 were lost to a markedly effective and proactive Soviet air defense effort.⁴³ IAF chief Hod admitted there were only twelve F-4 crews, and the effort demanded of them was "sublime."⁴⁴ Col. Rafi Harlev, who joined the first F-4 squadron on 4 June, recalled that "the feeling was we didn't know what to do. ... Pilots felt they were being sent to die for no purpose."⁴⁵ Henceforth the casualty rate among Phantom-trained crewmen became an even greater concern for the IAF than aircraft losses, as the personnel would take longer to replace even if more planes were readily available.

But the decision whether to supply additional Phantoms was still pending—indeed, on 19 June Donald Bergus had delivered in Cairo a US commitment that no more would be sold.⁴⁶ On 12 July, *Newsweek* reported that Nixon authorized the resumption of Phantom supply at the rate of two per month, including two from the original contract and six more. Together, this would not bring the total up to the fifty specified in the original 1968 agreement and so could not be held to constitute an additional sale. But as US officials hinted, the rate of supply would in any case be "flexible" and pegged to the military balance. Still, as the magazine reported, the order had been kept secret to avoid inflaming Arab opinion. When the news broke, Rogers confirmed that the announcement had been "purposely withheld" and Sisco declined any comment. The decision was now presented as compensating for Israel's losses, but the extra six Phantoms, to be taken from "US production quotas," were still on the assembly line, and the first two would be delivered only in August. By then, Israel would already lose two more, and only the ceasefire would stop this unsustainable attrition.

A more tangible compensation was the disclosure, in the same *Newsweek* story, that Nixon had approved the dispatch of advanced, active electronic-warfare systems for Israel's existing Phantoms.⁴⁷ Israeli pilots felt that "the SAM-3s had caught us with our pants down as low as they could go," and American solutions were sought for lack of anything else.⁴⁸ US concern about the field-security risks that supplying the EW (electronic warfare) gear entailed was soon confirmed by "American military and civilian sources" when they dismissed a report by *Al-Ahram* that "Egyptian military experts had discovered some of the Phantom's secrets while examining the fragments of the planes that were shot down." Dozens of fully-equipped F-4s had been shot down in Vietnam, the Americans pointed out, whereas the Israelis had not received the latest, secret USAF systems—so the Egyptians could not find out anything new for the Soviets.⁴⁹ Events would soon prove the opposite.

Neither of these US decisions had yet emerged when the back-channel partners had another long talk on 9 July. Dobrynin was now convinced that "Kissinger has a predominant, or at any rate much greater, influence on Nixon ... than Rogers does. ...

"A FAMOUS INDISCRETION" AS THE AIR WAR PEAKS

We should occasionally use this in our own interests." But, he concluded, "it might be useful to simultaneously provide our response to the US proposals on the Middle East ... through Kissinger *as well*."[50] So the back channel was placed on the back-burner for the time being, and Kissinger—whether embarrassed by his "indiscretion" or, more likely, sensing another debacle in the works for Rogers's diplomacy—did not press Dobrynin for the replies he still owed. Judging by both their reports, the Middle East was mentioned only in passing (as an item on the agenda of a proposed summit). Neither side's reports reflect any detailed discussion in the back channel throughout the coming, crucial month.

Instead, Kissinger left to the State Department the thankless task of dealing with the Soviets. Meeting Foreign Minister Gromyko on 11 July, with Nasser still in the USSR, Ambassador Beam protested that Nixon's conciliatory response to Kosygin's threat, and particularly his politically risky withholding of planes from Israel, had been snubbed. "Soviet support of the UAR in the Canal combat zone has led to a major qualitative change in the military balance ... contributing to a serious escalation of the conflict." Gromyko "was non-belligerent and avoided giving offense," but rejected US accusations that "Soviet military personnel have in fact moved into close proximity to the Suez Canal. New deployments of Soviet surface-to-air missiles make this conclusion inescapable." The Soviet foreign minister insisted:

> The USSR has a certain number of advisers in the UAR. ... Their number represents a threat to no one. ... Even if something along the lines of what [Beam] said had taken place, ... they would be purely defensive actions. He went on to stress that he had not used the conditional tense accidentally.

Although Beam hadn't even mentioned it, Gromyko volunteered that "Israel ... is spreading tendentious information ... and if one should believe them, then one would think that Israeli and Soviet pilots are clashing. This is totally absurd." Beam's reply was diplomatic: "We do not have precise, accurate information from the Soviet side regarding its military activity in the UAR. This situation may engender exaggeration and speculation, but the evidence available to us is impressive and very disturbing."[51]

Despite the urgency of Israel's request for the latest EW systems, two USAF officers and several technicians delivered them only eight days after Nixon's approval, on 12 July—the day after Gromyko's evasion. Like their Soviet counterparts, the American experts traveled in civvies, on a commercial flight. Their dispatch was—incidentally or intentionally—camouflaged by the overt arrival, on a USAF Boeing, of a twenty-one-man "fact-finding mission" from the Air Force Strike Command, led by the command's deputy chief, Lt-Gen. James Edmundson. It "heightened speculation that the Nixon administration is planning some sort of gesture as a partial counter to the growing Soviet involvement in Egypt. There have been unconfirmed reports that ships of the US 6th Fleet or a US Air Force squadron might visit Israel to demonstrate American support."[52] This would never materialize; the "gesture" would consist of the EW crew already in Israel. It had five days, before the IAF's schedule for the next major assault on the SAM array, to install the new pods and instruct the Israelis in the system's operational doctrine, which had been developed in the Vietnam arena. No training flights were held, and the haste was to prove fatal.

Meanwhile, addressing air crews and their families on Air Force Day (16 July) after meeting Edmundson, Dayan (who was usually the most cautious in the Israeli leadership in respect of provoking Moscow), demonstrated his unpredictability by issuing an explicit threat to attack Katameya and Salahiya, two of the forward airstrips the Soviets were using west of the canal. To his surprised spokesman, he explained that this was necessary to boost morale, though in practice "there's no point in escalating the situation and losing more pilots." Dayan was undoubtedly aware of continuing preparations for a major strike at Soviet targets—but at the SAMs rather than the airbases.[53]

On Saturday, 18 July, two formations of four Phantoms each, fitted for the first time with the new EW pods, flew into what became the climactic engagement of their duel with the Soviet SAMs. The first foursome was led by Shmu'el Hetz, Israel's top F-4 pilot and a brilliant officer who was widely considered in line for command of the IAF. His colleagues and subordinates recall Hetz's misgivings about the instructions of the leading USAF expert, Maj. Dave Brog, which called for flying in at high altitude and trusting the system for protection. Versions still vary as to whether the Israelis ignored Brog's guidance, or implemented it imperfectly—or the pods simply didn't work.

15

AN MIA MYSTERY AND SOVIET INTELLIGENCE METHODS

The battle of 18 July 1970 has gone down in the history and "combat heritage" of both the opposing forces. The Soviet Air Defense Corps, which analyzed and charted all the engagements of that summer, memorialized this one in particular detail both for its signal achievement and due to the Soviets' own heavy losses. The corps' museum displays, along with fragments of an Israeli F-4, a heroic painting of the battle (which, perhaps to assist younger or uninitiated viewers in locating the scene, fancifully adds the pyramids in the near background).[1] So the episode was not brought back from total oblivion when a postscript to this event appeared suddenly thirty years later, and opened a Pandora's box of unresolved missing in action (MIA) cases in the Cold War context.

Flying in high—at 18,000 feet—like "ducks in a shooting gallery," Hetz's Phantom was quickly disabled by a missile launched from his designated target, a SAM-3 *divizyon* near Ismailia. One of the other three pilots in the leading Israeli formation saw the F-4 "emit a trail of white smoke, turn left—eastward—and reduce altitude. Hetz's plane vanished from my sight. ... There was not a word from him over the radio."[2] After he failed to return, the IDF put out word that "pilots who operated in the same sector reported seeing both crewmen parachuting."[3] This version might have come from the second formation of F-4s, led by future IAF Commander Avihu Bin-Nun, which struck the same SAM battery successfully one minute after Hetz's attempt. Bin-Nun's own plane was also badly damaged by a missile, but he managed to crash-land at Refidim. The Egyptians and Soviets, as usual, scored this too as a kill, this time with some justification: Bin-Nun's F-4 was stricken from the IAF roster for over a year.[4]

The Israelis' two-parachute version, however, was most likely a fiction aimed at putting pressure on Egypt to disclose the fate of Hetz and his WSO (weapons system officer) Menachem Eini. The Egyptians had uncharacteristically delayed any announcement of the engagement. The next day, the two-parachute claim disappeared, after Egypt stated that Eini had been captured, and that the Phantom had exploded in air after he bailed out. In Israel, it was assumed that the plane did hit the ground—but that either way Hetz had perished, and he was declared dead, resting place unknown.[5]

THE SOVIET–ISRAELI WAR, 1967–1973

Eini's account was received only after his release from captivity in Egypt more than three years later. In a published memoir and several interviews, he stated that Hetz had been conscious and in control after the missile exploded, trying to fly back across the canal at 600 knots and 100 feet. "No more than 15 seconds' distance from the canal ... the plane went out of control. ... To this day I don't know whether I bailed myself out or Hetz pulled his lever a split second before I pulled mine."[6] Eini lost consciousness after ejecting, and came to only on the ground, seriously injured. There were, then, no Israeli eyewitnesses of the Phantom's last moments and its actual crash.

In an effort to clear up the mystery, Eini and several other comrades of Hetz organized a search party on the west bank of the canal while it was still held by Israel after the 1973 war. They reported finding fragments of an F-4, shreds of flight overalls and parachute straps, and the remains of Hetz's body. "We held a funeral for him in February 1974." Hetz's name is inscribed on a headstone in a military cemetery near Tel Aviv. So the matter stood until 1998, when Soviet and Egyptian veterans held a joint conference in Moscow to mark the twenty-fifth anniversary of the Yom Kippur War.

The proceedings, entitled *Shaking Hands after a Quarter-Century*, were distributed in 300 copies. It was in this mimeographed text that the present writers read the following statement by Col. Yaremenko, delivered in his capacity as official military historian:

> On 18 July [1970] the Israelis tried to destroy a Soviet anti-aircraft gun and missile formation ... 24 Phantoms took part ... Lt-Col. V[asily] Tolokonikov's *divizyon* was attacked from several directions. In a fierce battle, the missile operators destroyed two enemy planes and damaged one ... One of these Phantoms was "special." ... The plane, which fell into deep sand, remained intact—which immediately drew the attention of the Soviet experts. In short order, the plane and pilot were sent to Moscow.[7]

The IAF pilots that we consulted considered it impossible that a disabled and abandoned Phantom could have landed in one piece. But photos published by Soviet veterans show them posing proudly next to such hulks. Yitzhak Pe'er, who'd been shot down on 30 June, related that though he bailed out at about 10,000 feet, his F-4 "came down next to me, full of fuel and ammunition, and I was afraid it would explode."[8] Eini denied to us ever being removed from Egypt during his captivity or even encountering Soviet personnel. So the only candidate for transfer to Moscow was Hetz.

We contacted Yaremenko in Moscow. He reaffirmed his claim, and volunteered "Shamuel" Hetz's name. It appeared in 2001 in an official book of the Military History Institute, of which Yaremenko was a co-author.[9] "If I hadn't been sure the story was true I'd never have published it," he said, and attributed it, among others, to eyewitness testimonies of two Soviet officers, one of whom "saw an Israeli pilot being put on the plane" to Moscow and the other flew there with him. "Ever since I told this, I have been waiting for someone to refute it, but no one has."

184

AN MIA MYSTERY AND SOVIET INTELLIGENCE METHODS

We then located Tolokonikov at his home in Zhukovsky near Moscow. A Second World War veteran, he was the most experienced among the *divizyon* commanders in Egypt, and was still embittered that instead of a decoration and reward for shooting down Hetz's Phantom, he was reprimanded for the casualties and damage that his outfit sustained.[10] When asked about an Israeli pilot being captured alive, Tolokonikov replied twice: "I do know something, but I don't want to talk about it. ... I was not personally on scene, being too busy with my men," but he said the *divizyon*'s political officer, K.B. Chervinsky, did speak with the downed pilot, who was "pulled away" from something—the plane?

How, then, to account for Hetz's remains being interred in Israel? When informed of the Russian version, Eini still insisted: "Hetz is dead and buried. That's that." This was also the response of Hetz's family members. Out of consideration for their wishes and emotions, we are withholding the details that we have established about the actual findings of the search party. We can, however, state with certainty that nothing was found that could provide conclusive evidence of human origin or death, much less definite identification by the methods available at the time (fingerprints or dental records; DNA testing was still a thing of the future). Of Hetz's plane, all that was found amounted to parts of its landing gear and fragments of the canopy.

In November 2000, we submitted a detailed questionnaire to the IDF spokesman—who took over two months to concede that the identification was "circumstantial." Still, the spokesman's response ruled out any prospect that Hetz had survived, let alone been transferred to the USSR. But it contained several glaring contradictions and ignored some central questions, to which—when we reiterated them—the spokesman replied only: "we have nothing to add."[11]

Heavy pressure was exerted on the present authors and our media not to publicize the new information from Russia, and strong criticism was leveled at us when we went public with the new evidence on Israel's Memorial Day in April 2001.[12] But then-Prime Minister and former Maj.-Gen. Ariel Sharon, who as head of the Southern Command in 1970 knew Hetz, surprisingly confirmed in response that the ace's body had *never* been found and his fate was still unknown.[13]

Israeli discomfiture at the Russian disclosure was, however, minor compared with that of the Russians themselves once its significance was clarified. The head of the Military History Institute and the editor-in-chief of both publications that mentioned Hetz's deportation, Maj.-Gen. Vladimir Zolotarev, was also the Russian co-chairman of the Joint Commission on POWs and MIAs (USRJC) that had been set up with the United States in 1992. The US co-chairman of USRJC, Maj.-Gen. Roland Lajoie, and the executive secretary of the US team, Norman Kass, took a keen interest in the Hetz case: here was an unprecedented, unsolicited official Russian statement that a POW from a regional arena of the Cold War had been transferred to the Soviet Union. At the USRJC, the Russians had not confirmed so much as one of the multiple testimonies compiled by the Americans about sightings of US servicemen in Soviet prison camps

THE SOVIET–ISRAELI WAR, 1967–1973

and other localities, where some were said to serve as a "brain trust" for countering US technology and training personnel for service in English-speaking environments.[14] Some of this was confirmed by a defecting Soviet fighter pilot.[15]

The US delegation proceeded to confront Zolotarev with his own publication at the USRJC's Fourth Meeting of Principals in Moscow on 12 November 2001. He declined immediate response and returned the next day with an unsigned reply on plain paper, stating that "the fact concerning the transfer to Moscow of Israeli pilot Sh. Hetz and his aircraft to the territory of the former USSR cannot be supported. The ultimate fate of the pilot is unknown."[16] Zolotarev was then dismissed as co-chairman of the joint commission. Later, as the US side reported, "the Russians disbanded their side of the commission in 2006 and as a result, suspended archival access."[17]

In both the Institute and the USRJC, Zolotarev had succeeded Dmitry Volkogonov. Up to his death in 1995, Gen. Volkogonov had reported finding no trace of American Cold War POWs in the USSR. In his posthumously published memoirs, he admitted: "We ... helped the Americans to clarify the fate of their compatriots during the Korea and Vietnam wars. ... But I am not sure we have found out everything. I know that not a few documents were destroyed." Most significantly, he revealed a KGB directive that was issued shortly before Hetz's disappearance:

> One sensational document was preserved, and a copy is in my possession. Its essence: in the late 1960's the KGB, the First Directorate for foreign intelligence, was tasked "to bring informed Americans to the USSR for intelligence purposes." When I discovered this sensational paper in the "special file," I immediately went to E.M. Primakov (head of foreign intelligence). He called in his men. They brought a copy of this plan ... [but] I was told: the directive was not implemented. What actually happened? The regime then was such that the wildest versions can be assumed. The answer to this question remained a secret, which I never managed to penetrate.[18]

Volkogonov's claim was also denied by Russian officialdom. However, this KGB policy in respect of "informed Americans" is confirmed by a Middle Eastern case detailed in the Mitrokhin Archive: a few weeks before the Hetz affair, then-KGB Chairman Andropov sought and obtained Brezhnev's approval for tasking Palestinian proxies with abducting a CIA operative in Beirut for transfer to the USSR.[19] The repeated description of Hetz as American thus gains special resonance.

Our voluminous dossier on the Hetz case has produced a series of tantalizing leads, none of which has yet developed into evidence solid enough to publish. The most recent example, however, merits cautious mention. Dudchenko's "novel" *Kanal* includes a detailed account of the 18 July engagement, and focuses on the capture of the Phantom pilot "Sha'ul Katz." It offers an explanation of how Katz/Hetz wound up in Soviet custody while his WSO was captured and kept by the Egyptians: "Katz" *pretends to be Russian* in an attempt to escape lynching by the Egyptian soldiers who surround him.[20] If true, his fear was not unfounded: one of Hetz's subordinates was murdered barely two weeks later.[21]

AN MIA MYSTERY AND SOVIET INTELLIGENCE METHODS

Dudchenko's alter ego, the "novel's" hero Aleksandr Polishchuk—a military interpreter who has the author's proficiency in both Hebrew and Arabic—is called in to verify the prisoner's identity. He quickly dismisses "Katz's" pretense, as the pilot refuses to talk and knows only two words in Russian ("vodka" and "Dostoevsky"). But this alerts the Soviets to the capture of a US-trained Israeli squadron leader who can provide privileged information on the advanced systems of his plane, which itself is recovered almost intact. The ranking Soviet officers in Cairo exercise every diplomatic effort, and soon

> instead of horrible torture in an Egyptian prison [Katz] found himself in an uncomfortable seat on board a Soviet air force transport, which brought him to Kubinka near Moscow. Sha'ul Katz understood well that his illegal deportation to Moscow was related to his Phantom, and he was tormented by thoughts about what faced him [which the "novel" does not go on to relate].[22]

Dudchenko has admitted that some real figures served as "prototypes" for his "imaginary" characters.[23] Most of his story might have been embroidered around Yaremenko's original account or (given Dudchenko's command of Hebrew) our own publication in 2001. But his narrative features some accurate particulars about Hetz that were not previously published and could hardly have been invented. This appears to confirm some first-hand knowledge of the case.

Finally, it bears mention that one of the last feature films produced in the USSR describes a case that mirrors Yaremenko's account of Hetz's: a Soviet pilot stationed in Egypt is shot down, survives, and is captured. The film goes on to depict his recruitment, and eventual dispatch on mission back to Moscow (where he is long since "buried") as a CIA agent.[24] The factual inspiration, if any, for this plot can only be speculated about.

For us, then, the Hetz case remains unresolved. The Russian publication in itself cannot be taken as incontrovertible, but neither has the Israeli military or anyone else produced proof that can refute it. The best—but most improbable—scenario was hinted at by Yaremenko: that Hetz not only survived and was brought to the USSR but still lives there today after pledging to renounce his former citizenship, accept restrictions on his movement, and refrain from any foreign contacts. Several such cases have been discovered in the former USSR, dating back to the Second World War. These ex-POWs were even allowed to start new families, sometimes under their original names.[25] But in the remotely possible eventuality that the same happened with Hetz—not only the IDF, the Russian authorities, and Hetz's Israeli family would have no interest in his being found; the pilot himself, now approaching eighty, would hardly desire it. A former IAF subordinate described him as "a champion at human relations, politics; a man who could ingratiate himself with anyone"—another "perfect storm" for suppressing the facts.[26]

16

SAM SUCCESSES AND A MIG DEBACLE

A. Was there a "standstill" commitment?

The 18 July engagement registered strongly with the Soviet servicemen: Lt Ivan Skobanev, an electronic-warfare specialist, recorded in his diary on 21 July that his brother Valery, who was serving at division headquarters, informed him of the battle and casualties the next day, and at taps "we observed a minute of silence in their memory." Kon'kov, a driver with a *Shilka* detachment on the canal front, heard vivid stories about the SAM-3 crew leader "who visibly went gray" after losing all his seven men (the eighth Soviet fatality was an officer in charge of the radar antennas, who ventured out to fix them in the midst of the attack). Afterward, when combat was expected the troops were issued a 50-gram ration of alcohol "to counter shock and fear."[1] But although Tolokonikov's *divizyon* was due to be relieved, "the boys asked to stay on duty. Their mood was very combative."[2]

Valery Skobanev had a special interest in the incident due to the electronic warfare (EW) pod that came down with Hetz's Phantom. As head of a *spetsnaz* (special ops) "radio-technical intelligence center," he was charged with countering Israeli systems. In April 1970, the Soviets' experimental and "super-secret" *Smal'ta* jammer was brought to Egypt for battlefield tests, particularly for suppression of the Israelis' Hawk missiles, which were considered roughly analogous to the SAM-3. The Hawks had since May '69 shot down at least four Egyptian planes, some of them over the canal or east of it, from mobile launchers near the east bank. In order to monitor the Hawks' parameters at close range, Valery was put in command of a joint Soviet–Egyptian group that included factory experts and KGB operatives; the latter were not even listed in the group's complement, and the others also carried no papers. Their orders were to blow up their hardware if Israeli raiders tried to capture them—which they feared might happen mainly because of leaks from Egyptian quarters. On one occasion, they mistakenly took up a position at some distance from the planned location, and claimed witnessing Israeli helicopters land at the other spot. Returning to base, Skobanev found a report already prepared with a list of the Soviets captured or killed, omitting the KGB agents.[3]

THE SOVIET–ISRAELI WAR, 1967–1973

The Soviet EW systems' failure to protect Tolokonikov's *divizyon* aroused sufficient concern to reinforce these *spetsnaz* radio-technical intelligence crews in Egypt. On the morrow of the 18 July battle, Sgt Viktor Rogozhinsky's unit in Crimea was called urgently onto the parade ground to announce a *spetskomandirovka* (special mission) to an unidentified friendly country, for which six officers and five servicemen were to be selected. One officer refused to go; he was not punished, but his promotion was halted. The group was sent to Nikolaev, where it joined an assembled complement of 350 for dispatch to Egypt.[4]

But in sum, the SAMs' success against the Phantoms could only buttress Egyptian and Soviet conviction that Israel would be powerless to resist further advance of the missile shield toward the canal. On 23 July Nasser announced his acceptance of the US ceasefire proposal. The Soviet media indicated that in his Moscow talks he had received approval for this move.[5] But Nasser served notice that the SAMs would be advanced regardless of the ceasefire, even though the same day Dobrynin confirmed to Rogers that both the Soviets and the Egyptians accepted a contrary provision of the US proposal: "[Rogers said:] we assume that a military standstill as part of the cease-fire is also acceptable to the Soviet Union. Dobrynin responded affirmatively, adding, 'Yes, of course.' It was his understanding that Foreign Minister Riad's statement to the Secretary covered this point."[6]

Dobrynin may not have been personally aware of it, but this "understanding" proved to be disingenuous, and its violation would doom the Rogers Plan. Kissinger would then reportedly deny, in a promptly leaked off-the-record briefing, that there had been a full Egyptian "commitment" to the standstill and confirmed only an "understanding." Other sources attributed it merely to tacit Egyptian acquiescence in an unsigned paper that Donald Bergus, head of the US interests section in Egypt, had left on Foreign Minister Riad's desk.[7]

Nasser declared that failure by Israel to accept full withdrawal from Sinai within the ceasefire's three-month duration would restart his military efforts to regain the territory. To critics in Egypt, he explained that accepting Rogers's proposal was the only way to deny Israel the additional Phantoms that would suffice to prevent a canal crossing.[8] Fearing the same, Israel balked at Rogers's proposals. The direct Soviet–Israeli engagements continued.

B. Inter-service rivalry draws the Soviet MiGs into picking a fight ...

Envy of the *zenitchiki*'s achievement, however costly, motivated more aggressive tactics on the part of the MiG-21 squadrons. Aleksandr Akimenkov—then among the youngest pilots in the Soviet force—described in his memoir the resentment his superiors felt that no one gave the Soviet squadron at Beni Suef credit for deterring Israeli raids in the Nile Delta. They felt pressed for time to score a tangible achievement comparable to the SAMs', as they were told that "talks had begun about a ceasefire."

SAM SUCCESSES AND A MIG DEBACLE

Our daredevil group commander started to demand combat results. Just accomplishing the mission that he had been assigned, preventing Israeli attacks, was no longer enough. There was a demand to shoot down enemy planes. By this time we had already shot down one Skyhawk, and our superiors liked this precedent. The atmosphere was burdened by the successes of the missilemen, who by this time had exceeded ten kills. ... At noon on 21 July our "young" squadron relocated to El-Mansura airbase, near the canal. That same evening, the Israeli radio broadcast the entire list [of the pilots].[9]

But the Hebrew media, on the same day, still referred to "activation of Soviet pilots over the canal" only as a potentiality.[10]

Other veterans' accounts also mention that they used to tune in to "Jerusalem" for the Israeli accounts of their engagements.[11] The memoir of "radio-technical expert" Boris Krokhin clarifies that the program the Soviets heard daily at 8 p.m. was broadcast on a separate wavelength from Israel Radio's domestic and foreign Russian services. It evidently emanated from *Masregah*'s station in Sinai, which in the case mentioned by Akimenkov might have picked up the pilots' names from signal intercepts.

The program began with a Russian song as theme tune, followed by the sound of whistling wind and a male announcer intoning "the wind blows from the sands of Sinai ... a program for Soviet servicemen and their families on the other side of the front." Krokhin regretted not having risked the political officers' wrath by recording some of these programs, as he correctly reckoned they would be of historical value; nothing about them has so far emerged in Israel. Along the canal, he was told, "special television programs for future adversaries" could be picked up too. They featured, together with the IDF's weaponry, military troupes in Russian-style song and dance routines that the Soviets accompanied with clapping and stomping, to the disapproval of their Egyptian advisees.[12]

Besides such psychological warfare, the Israelis' advantage of having Russian speakers with perfect accents—which even the Soviet schools' excellent Hebrew training could not match—was also used for operational deception. Misleading signals beamed on the Soviet squadrons' radio network, along with EW disruption of the Soviets' own transmissions, would be credited for drawing them into a fatal trap in the war's biggest dogfight on 30 July.[13]

A week earlier, though, the Soviets still appeared to have the upper hand in matchups with Israeli pilots. Korn, then chief of the political section at the US embassy in Tel Aviv, had until recently been the only source—from his own notes—for two incidents, on 21 and 25 July, in which Soviet pilots pursued IAF planes up to the canal line. In the second case, they even crossed into Sinai airspace and badly damaged a Skyhawk with an air-to-air missile. "The Israelis told the Americans of these encounters but kept them secret from their public."[14] The second incident was disclosed by *Aviation Week* in January 1971, and recently confirmed by Danny Shalom from Israeli sources.[15] IAF command was infuriated. The force's website mentions

Soviet pilots chasing Skyhawks across the canal on 25 July as the final provocation that triggered the assembly of twelve Israeli aces to initiate a clash with the Soviets.[16]

A year later, Dayan would ask a Soviet emissary:

> why did your airplanes try to shoot ours along the Suez Canal, just one month or three weeks before the ceasefire? ... We tried all the time to avoid ... any clash with your airplanes, but ... we were faced with the situation either to be shot or to run away.[17]

This was said in hindsight; after the 21 July incident, Dayan had in fact balked at forcing a showdown with the Soviets, and insisted on bringing IAF chief Hod's proposal to "lay a trap for the Russians" before the entire cabinet. To the IAF command's surprise, the cabinet approved the idea on 25 July—the very day of the second Skyhawk incident.[18] The same day, an Israeli military correspondent was already told by "military observers" that since "the Russians have ... decided to take an active part in air battles in the canal zone ... dogfights between Soviet and Israeli pilots are just a matter of time."[19] Detailed planning began, expanding on tactics that had been tried against Egyptian pilots, most recently in April.[20] Meanwhile, according to Akimenkov, the Soviets and Egyptians attempted the same entrapment idea. The first time around, the Israelis declined the gambit—or just responded more slowly than expected:

> A pair of Arab MiG-17s was to bomb Israeli positions across the canal. ... The expectation was that the Israelis would scramble the [Mirage] detail on duty, which would give chase to the Arab pair across to our side of the canal, and we would engage them over Egyptian soil. We were categorically forbidden to cross the canal. On the morning of 27 July we flew according to the rehearsed scheme. The Arabs completed their attack, but the Israeli planes took off too late.

On the second try, the Soviet tactic was foiled by the incompetence of the Egyptians—for whom Akimenkov barely hides his contempt.

> The Arabs, inspired by their success, forced us to include a formation of their MiG-21s in order to relay signals [to the MiG-17s]. ... On the runway they staged such a bazaar that it disrupted the entire planned timetable. In sum, we were late and got aloft only when the Israeli Mirages were already on the way home, having shot down the two MiG-17s. ... The only consolation was that the Arab pilots bailed out successfully. Credit must be given them when due. They had learned to get out of planes in time.[21]

C. ... and losing it

Close to midday on 30 July, Akimenkov was scrambled and directed south. "Soon we were over the Sokhna valley, where charred remains of MiGs littered the ground. We got the explanation at Beni Suef. The Israelis had got fed up with our air-ambush exercises and they set up a similar operation against us." He had just missed a historic air battle, which ended with four MiGs shot down for no Israeli losses (as in other cases, one Israeli fighter was damaged but managed to land).

Israel imposed a blackout on the MiG pilots' Soviet identity, which had been learned from their radio communications. As an Israeli official said to a Soviet envoy a year later, "we don't want a flareup with your forces."[22] IDF communiqués and the first reports in the Israeli media either referred to Egyptian planes or stated archly that the pilots' nationality was unknown, while pointedly mentioning the first reports of the Skyhawk downed by Soviet airmen, which had just appeared in the foreign press.[23] Two days later, *Time* reported that Soviet pilots had possibly died in the battle—and Israeli papers gleefully quoted this as fact.[24] Since then, the IAF's "trap for the Russians" became a hallowed centerpiece of its heritage, recounted in minute detail in Israeli literature.[25]

Akimenkov's account of the 30 July dogfight is one of notably and understandably few among the dozens of memoirs by Soviet airmen. Not surprisingly, another exception appeared outside the former USSR and from a Soviet naval officer.[26] The official Russian military history admits that Soviet pilots were shot down, and even adds the tragic note that some of them were devoured by sharks in the Red Sea.[27] If true, this must refer to additional, so far unknown incidents: on 30 July 1970, all the Soviet planes were downed over land and the bodies of at least three of the pilots were recovered.[28] One of them, Capt. Vladimir Zhuravlev, was recently described as buried in Novosibirsk, near his native village. Typically for the veterans' literature, this fact was published in a local newspaper to protest that Zhuravlev was still not included in a memorial list of the region's casualties in foreign wars, although he had posthumously been awarded an Egyptian decoration.[29]

Honoring the fallen Soviet pilots could hardly mask their Egyptian colleagues' *Schadenfreude* after being so often sneered at. Mustafa Hafez, who had commanded an Su-7 squadron at Beni Suef before this airbase was handed over to the Soviets, recalled his efforts to overcome the lack of full radar coverage of the Red Sea coast, especially after the P-12 hijacking:

> The biggest problem was the mountains between Beni Suef and the Red Sea. ... This meant that the Israelis could come in low and hidden by the mountains before sending up another flight to lure the Egyptians into the air. Then the first unit would pounce on them from below. This was why I told my controller never to send aircraft east of the mountains, but to wait for the Israelis to come to us. A Russian unit took over at Beni Suef after I and my squadron left, and very soon fell into the same Israeli ambush."[30]

Israel's triumph overshadowed its daunting losses, and enabled its government to accept the ceasefire the next day (31 July) without excessive loss of face. Israeli spokesmen and media alike claimed for years to have scored a total victory in the War of Attrition against the combined forces of Egypt and the USSR, pointing to the latter's

THE SOVIET–ISRAELI WAR, 1967–1973

greater losses in air combat.³¹ More than a year later, briefing a US counterpart, Hod acknowledged the Soviet pilots' gallantry but disparaged their skill, as demonstrated in the 30 July engagement. As the American general reported, Hod dealt the unkindest cut when he judged that

> [the] Egyptians are the best pilots in the Middle East ... Soviet pilots are rotated every six months and they are not up to the quality of Israeli pilots. The first air engagements convinced him of the lack of Soviet training in "dog fighting." He states Egyptians were better at handling the MiG-21s than the Soviets in a dog fight, until IAF pilots got on the tail of the Egyptians and they ejected sometimes without a shot being fired. This is not the case of the Soviet pilots, ... [but] the Soviet fighter pilot has much to learn.³²

The Soviet pilots ached for revenge, especially after Air Force Chief Marshal Pavel Kutakhov rushed to Egypt to investigate their defeat. Or so Akimenkov and his comrades may have been told. "Western defense experts" also considered that this was the direct cause of the marshal's trip.³³ But a journal kept by one of Kutakhov's deputies shows that he was about to depart for Egypt "with a group of generals" when the news came in. July had already become his force's worst month since 1964 in respect of losses. From Egypt, Kutakhov instructed this deputy, Nikolay Kamanin, to prepare six replacement MiG-21s.³⁴

The IAF—while continuing its bombardment along the canal—did not give Akimenkov another chance. "Up to the ceasefire, we tried to draw the Israelis into a rematch, but the Israeli code of honor does not include such chivalrous duels. ... [The IAF's] mercenaries squandered their bounty money at bases in the rear."³⁵ Another Soviet pilot, Oleg Tsoy, was likewise frustrated:

> Oleg saw an Israeli Mirage on the tail of an Egyptian MiG-17. Tsoy rushed to help but the Israeli saw him coming and turned away towards the Suez Canal. In the excitement of the chase Tsoy forgot about the orders banning Soviet pilots from crossing the canal. So he flew on into Sinai and launched a missile at the Mirage, but the Israeli pilot evaded it.³⁶

D. *The* zenitchiki *score again*

The Soviet pilots' scorn for the Egyptians was shared by the SAM crews. During the action of 18 July, Zhayvoronok was inspecting a battery commanded by Major Midskhat Mansurov, where the crew members in charge of plotting the paths of incoming planes included Egyptians—apparently trainees:

> Our battery was shaking from the explosions ... the Arabs' nerves failed, they took off their earphones, threw off their helmets and began running out of the cabin. You had to be there to know how horribly hot it was, everyone sitting there in underpants, helmets and gas masks and giggling nervously. So one of ours grabs [the fleeing Egyptian] by the underpants and hits him on the head with a helmet while hurling some untranslatable expres-

SAM SUCCESSES AND A MIG DEBACLE

sions at him—to the effect of "you bastard, we who have come all the way here stay at our stations, and you run away?" ... There was not a single instance where one of ours gave in to fear.³⁷

Divizyon commander Konstantin Popov, who had taken up "ambush" positions at the same time as Tolokonikov, was among the next to see action: "On 29 July I was ordered: on 31 July, lay the ambush ... there was a Party-Komsomol assembly, in which 100% of the communists and most Komsomol members declared they were ready to carry out the combat mission."³⁸ This commitment was more than merely feigned for the benefit of party minders. Throughout their deployment, "bards" among the advisers and regulars alike composed and performed songs celebrating their mission, which were even applauded by Israeli soldiers when blared by loudspeaker across the canal:

> Here the firing is no warning shot
> A military storm is thundering.
> From under the yellow Arab helmet
> Gleam blue Russian eyes.
>
> Imagine us for a moment
> Marching under a rain of steel:
> How for a few Egyptian pounds
> We risk our very heads.³⁹

Indeed, it was sometimes the Soviet political officers who, as they later admitted, were dismayed by the disparity between the servicemen's dedication and Moscow's official position, and did their best to hide it from the men. "Judging by the statements of the [Soviet] press, radio and television we weren't there at all," the *politruk* (political officer) Logachev lamented:

> Once, in the midst of our battles against the Israeli Air Force, here comes the latest edition of *Pravda* with a front-page editorial headlined "falsifiers." It's all about the bourgeois liars and their claims that Soviet soldiers are stationed in Egypt, heatedly demolishing all the western arguments—obviously aimed at people who didn't know the truth. But how was I to explain to the soldiers that ... the main organ of the CP Central Committee was, to put it mildly, not telling the truth? On my own authority, I burned all fifty copies.

But even in this 1998 memoir, which could have appeared only under the relatively freewheeling, anti-Soviet spirit of the time, Logachev maintained the other Soviet canard whereby "nearly all the Israeli pilots had combat experience in Vietnam."⁴⁰ It was repeated by Maj.-Gen. Aleksandr Bezhevets, an ace pilot and Hero of the Soviet Union (HSU), as late as 2007.⁴¹

In the summer of 1971, the *zenitchiki* were told that their success had so intimidated the IAF "mercenaries" that the latter "began refusing to go up, even when offered more than $1,000 per sortie."⁴² But it was actually the Soviets who dispatched some Vietnam veterans to Egypt. One of the SAM-3 brigade commanders, then-Maj. Vladimir Belousov, admitted in retrospect: "the Israeli pilots fought more bravely and skillfully than the Americans [whom] I fought in Vietnam."⁴³ Smirnov's replacement from February 1971, Maj.-Gen. Yury Boshnyak, invoked his year's experience in Vietnam to improve SAM-3 and *Shilka* performance.⁴⁴

Also fresh from Vietnam was the political officer Nikolay Streletsky, who served with a SAM-3 brigade protecting the Helwan steel works. His account about the men's ideological loyalty—published in Belarus, 2007—contrasts sharply with Logachev's in respect of credibility. Especially suspect is his story about the outfit's obligatory "Lenin Room" (a combined library, clubhouse and briefing hall) whereby the Egyptians would fall on their knees to pay obeisance to the bust of the "proletarian leader, whom they associated with Allah himself."⁴⁵

Popov's SAM-3 *divizyon* took up its ambush position on the night of 31 July, flanked by Nikolay Kutyntsev's to the south and an Egyptian one to the north with overlapping missile ranges. As Popov noted proudly, that night his men accomplished a 150-kilometer relocation two and a half times faster than the standard requirement. The Israelis were fooled: in 1973, the IDF still attributed the ensuing shootdown to a new mobile weapon, probably the SAM-6, which they were not yet able to track.⁴⁶ Before dawn, under total blackout, the Soviets set up and effectively hid their missiles in plantations near the canal. Even the trucks' diesel exhausts were extended with rubber hoses so that the fumes would rise at some distance. A dummy array was concealed just enough to suggest a genuine camouflage effort.

> By 0600 the *divizyon* was ready for battle. ... On 1–2 August the IAF made a lot of sorties in the canal zone but did not enter the *divizyon*'s range. It can be assumed that the Israelis knew something about our positions and tried to detect them, but we did nothing that could give us away. We sent out signals only for a few seconds at a time. The P-15 target identification system worked constantly. On 2 August, Maj.-Gen. Gromov came to the *divizyon* ... we concluded that if 3 August also passed quietly, we would relocate again.⁴⁷

The IAF attack did come on the 3rd, and the Soviets' meticulous preparations paid off. The Israeli pilots bombed the dummy missiles; they were surprised by the SAM-3 launches; one Phantom was hit by at least two missiles, possibly from different batteries. According to Popov, an outlying *Strela* crew of his outfit captured both crewmen and handed them over to the Egyptians. The pilot, Yigal Shohat, reported being shot at and injured while still suspended under his parachute, later losing a leg in an Egyptian hospital. His WSO Yoram Goldwasser reached the ground alive—as shown the next day in Egyptian media—but did not survive, and was reportedly lynched.

Phantom no. 2 in Shohat's formation was hit by another SAM-3 and the pilot, Ra'anan Ne'eman, was disabled. The WSO Yoram Romem assisted him to land it at Refidim.⁴⁸ As in previous cases, the Soviets scored this as a kill, and the overlap of

SAM SUCCESSES AND A MIG DEBACLE

divizyon ranges might account for both planes' being claimed twice. Dayan confirmed in 1973 that "we lost three Phantoms" in this action.[49] In addition, an upgraded Super-Mystère was hit by anti-aircraft gunfire on the night of Popov's move (31 July), and this time the pilot did abandon it over Israeli territory; this may be the Mirage that Popov claimed later.[50] Both Popov and Kutyntsev were first recommended for the Order of Lenin and ultimately made Heroes of the Soviet Union, even though the latter's battery had been responsible for the early shootdown of an Egyptian Il-28. Their commander Smirnov listed a total of 166 officers and men who received various decorations for combat in *Kavkaz*.[51]

By the time Popov's *divizyon* was relieved for rest and refitting at its base camp near Lake Qarun in the rear, the ceasefire had gone into effect and, as the brigade *politruk* Logachev relates, "UN checkpoints were posted on the highways. But officially we weren't present in Egypt at all. Therefore the *divizyon* pulled back not on the Ismailia–Cairo highway but over caravan trails."[52] The Soviets would be less reticent about moving other SAM units *into* the canal zone.

17

CEASEFIRE VIOLATION SEALS A STRATEGIC GAIN

A. U-2 flights come too late

Ten minutes before the ceasefire came into effect at midnight between 7 and 8 August, an Israeli pilot on patrol east of the Suez Canal saw multiple headlights go on beyond the Egyptian lines and move in convoys eastward.[1] Standstill provisions notwithstanding, the SAM belt was advancing into positions that would not only cover the canal itself but create a no-fly zone at least 20 kilometers to its east—the very outcome that the IAF had fought so hard to prevent.[2] Nasser was soon explaining publicly to critics of the ceasefire, such as the PLO's Yasser Arafat, that this had been his purpose in acceding to Rogers's proposal.[3]

This had not been unforeseen: in addition to concern over the losses on 30 July, a purpose widely imputed to Air Force Chief Marshal Kutakhov's visit was to work out a way to achieve this advantage even under a ceasefire regime—that is, to ascertain under what inspection procedures it might be accomplished.[4] Given the Soviets' continuing denial of their troops' very presence in Egypt, and hence of their collusion in the exercise, it is hardly surprising that an even higher-ranking visit was kept under wraps. It has come to light only in a memoir by K.A. Pirogov, a "cultural-educational officer" in the SAM division who attended a meeting with the high-ranking guest. He indicates clearly that this was after the ambush of 3 August but before the ceasefire began on the 7th:

> We learned from our interpreters that hostilities were about to end and that ... Grechko was flying out to visit us. Our meeting with the defense minister took place in Cairo, where he visited the *divizyon* commanded by Lt-Col. A.D. Galkin. ... [He] thanked the personnel for their excellent combat skills, for the job well done [and announced home leave for the officers and noncoms, while enlisted men could enjoy a new R&R facility in Alexandria]. I was tasked to go there, to ensure communal cultural activities.[5]

Grechko may have left before the missiles were advanced, but it would stretch the imagination to suggest that this might have been done without his foreknowledge.

THE SOVIET-ISRAELI WAR, 1967-1973

At an IAF gathering just before the ceasefire, Hod "squirmed" when Dayan demanded that he "propose a solution to overcome these missiles."⁶ The defense minister was so apprehensive of a SAM advance that once Israel had accepted the Rogers Plan—which brought down its national-unity governing coalition—he tried to put the ceasefire into effect as quickly as possible, while the Soviets and Egyptians temporized. Meeting the US ambassador on Friday, 7 August, Dayan pressed Barbour to apply the ceasefire immediately so as to prevent a last-minute advance of the missiles. The truce was finally declared only a few hours ahead of its entry into effect at midnight—so late that Israel's weekend papers did not report it.⁷

Despite its hasty finalization, the ceasefire had been under discussion for months and the standstill provision for weeks, with mounting US suspicion as to the Soviet and Egyptian commitment to observe it. Still, as the director of the US National Reconnaissance Office (NRO) admitted, "we did not have a good baseline on Soviet-provided emplacements in Egypt."⁸

How could this have happened? Although he had left the negotiation of the ceasefire itself to Rogers, Kissinger involved his own National Security Council (NSC) in setting up the verification procedures—perhaps to ensure the plan's success, but just as plausibly to blame the State Department and its chief for a predictable failure (which he and Nixon indeed went on to do).⁹ The tangled chains of command resulted finally in no monitoring at all when it counted.

Intelligence historian Norman Polmar credits Kissinger for initiating surveillance of the canal area and asking first for satellite photography. But a satellite was tasked only for 10 August—which had been the target date during the last phase of the ceasefire talks.¹⁰ The satellite use evidently was not (and probably could not have been) rescheduled when the ceasefire was brought forward at the last minute. At any rate, satellite imagery did not have adequate resolution for identifying individual vehicles or emplacements, and the Israelis objected to exclusive reliance upon it.¹¹ In response, the Americans floated an "open skies" proposal whereby each side could send unarmed observation sorties over the other's front lines. When that was rejected, it was replaced with "mutual verification" by each side's planes peering diagonally across the canal. Neither the mode of observation nor how complaints were to be adjudicated was adequately clarified.

Kissinger, meanwhile, approached the US Air Force for U-2 reconnaissance flights, but the USAF estimated that providing them would take several weeks. CIA Director Richard Helms stepped in and promised at an NSC meeting to mount such flights within one week of activation. Ambassador Beam in Moscow was advised to inform the Soviets of "our government's intention to police [the ceasefire] unilaterally by US observation flights. ... Foreseeing trouble, I suggested that this mission be given to the British, who had bases in the area and who wished to play some part in peacekeeping. This proposal was turned down."¹²

CEASEFIRE VIOLATION SEALS A STRATEGIC GAIN

But CIA sources hold that after Italy, Greece and Spain caused further delay by refusing to host the U-2s, Britain had to be "begged" for use of its base at Akrotiri, Cyprus, and British pilots did conduct some of the twenty-nine flights.[13] The agreement required intense negotiations with the Cypriot authorities too, and was obtained on condition that the flights not be made public, a constraint that hampered US exposure of the violations that the U-2s documented.[14]

If, as the CIA claimed in retrospect, despite all obstacles the two planes were transferred within seventy-one hours, and arrived on 8 August, then the operation was approved on the 4th or 5th. The NRO director proudly described them as "the only true crisis use of the IDEALIST [U-2] for national intelligence collection in the last four years."[15] But when finally, "on August 9 we flew the first IDEALIST mission," it was too late. The first reports could determine only that since 28 July (evidently the date of the latest previous US imagery) and as of *10* August, 23 Egyptian SAM-2 and four Soviet SAM-3 sites had been moved forward. US analysis suggested that this had been done mainly in the run-up to the ceasefire, though possibly completed afterward.[16] Other versions hold that this data was useless anyway, because the various parties to the conflict used differing sets of map coordinates.[17] Either way, for the first few days the Americans could produce little if any proof that they had been double-crossed.

B. *The Soviets laugh off US complaints*

By then, the Israelis had remonstrated with Washington on the basis of their own evidence, and US diplomacy followed up with a move that is so far known only from the Soviet side. Vladimir Vinogradov, the deputy foreign minister "in charge of the Middle East," recorded in his memoir that "on a Sunday in the summer of 1970 ... I was phoned from the ministry to inform me that the US chargé d'affaires was requesting an urgent meeting." This could only be Sunday, 9 August, when Boris Klosson, a Soviet-affairs expert and counselor at the embassy, was acting as chargé. By the 13th, Ambassador Beam was already back from summer vacation.[18]

Vinogradov prefaces this anecdote with a background note that is egregiously false on several counts:

> the Egyptians had reached an agreement for a ceasefire on the canal, on condition that Israel stopped its attacks on peaceful Egyptian cities. But the United States craftily inserted in the English-language document's title one more little word to which the Egyptians did not ascribe any significance. It could now be interpreted ... as a "standstill ceasefire."

Dobrynin had, of course, already pledged that the Soviets as well as the Egyptians accepted a ceasefire-in-place. The full Rogers Plan as presented to the Knesset on 12 August included not merely "one little word" but a detailed section (3) requiring both sides not to alter the military status quo within 50 kilometers of the canal.[19]

As the Soviets had been approached about the U-2 flights, they were aware that the Americans lacked conclusive evidence of this provision's violation. Vinogradov was confident enough to respond derisively when Klosson "began by submitting his government's protest at the Egyptians' behavior."

> "The matter is," the American diplomat fumed, "that the Egyptians are moving forces in their territory, which is not permissible under the agreement for a standstill ceasefire!" I rejected the chargé's pretenses, and declared that Egypt, like any sovereign state, could do as it pleased in its own territory. We were not aware of any commitment that Egyptian soldiers would stand still, and suppose some soldier had to go somewhere—would he have to ask permission from the Americans or Israelis? The expression "stand still" that the Americans used is known to mean "stand at attention," and it is not applicable to relations between states, regardless of whether for any reason it appeared in the agreement or not. This is legalistic nonsense.[20]

No US record of this exchange—or what instructions Klosson acted on—has yet surfaced. Subsequent reports of US–Soviet discussions, and even the meticulous notes of *FRUS* editors, do not mention it. But while Vinogradov's smug account may have been enhanced somewhat in hindsight, it conforms to his statements in later talks—none of which were on a Sunday—and there is no reason to suppose that he fabricated it entirely.[21] Some explanation for the apparent suppression of the episode may be provided by the infighting that ensued in San Clemente.

Craig Daigle has documented how the muddled US response—like the unhappy choice, by the State Department, of the codename Even Steven for the U-2 flights—stemmed from Rogers's insistence on demonstrating American impartiality and preventing any disruption of the Jarring talks, which were to resume under his plan. On the other hand, so long as the ceasefire appeared to hold, Kissinger could not resist voicing to the media his resentment at the very phrase "Rogers's proposals"—and claiming they had been worked out by his NSC over eight months.[22] But once the Soviet–Egyptian violations were established, he was quick, in consultations with Nixon, to pounce on the secretary's failure and demand a stiff response toward the Soviets.[23] The result was a deadlock.

Meanwhile, as Dayan put it in his memoirs, "The Egyptians, or to be more precise the Soviets, thumbed their nose at the agreement including its standstill provision. ... The United States, to which we turned to decry this, first tried to evade it."[24] He was apparently unaware of Klosson's abortive protest, and took out his frustration on the Americans. A day or two after the U-2 flights started, that is, on 10 or 11 August, the American deputy chief of mission in Tel Aviv (ambassadors everywhere were hard to find on duty in August) was told by a "furious" Dayan that the "U-2 had deviated from the 5-km flight corridor that the [defense] ministry had assigned it. The agreement between Israel and the US called for the U-2 to look only at dispositions on the Egyptian side ... If the deviation happened again, Israel would shoot down the U-2."

CEASEFIRE VIOLATION SEALS A STRATEGIC GAIN

When the incredulous diplomat asked how this could be accomplished, Dayan explained that a Phantom would be sent under the spy plane's flight path and fire a missile upwards—precisely the stratagem that would be tried, unsuccessfully, against Soviet MiG-25s two years later. Dayan's response to another question, whether he understood the consequences of such a shootdown, is not recorded.[25]

With no American reaction evident, the Israelis increased their pressure by leaking the detected violations to the press, with an emphasis on the Soviet role. British journalist Jon Kimche—whose brother and frequent co-author David was then a senior Mossad officer—reported on 11 August in the London *Evening Standard* from "Israeli sources" that the Soviets had, "recently" and especially on Friday night, brought into the canal zone new equipment that they had not risked introducing before, thus violating the standstill provision.[26] Israel's all-but-official commentator Herzog in effect confirmed the report.

Jon Kimche hedged his claim by explaining to an interviewer that the Soviet move was made "on the threshold" of the ceasefire.[27] But much greater commotion was created the next day, when the *Los Angeles Times* published a description closely resembling the Israeli pilot's account: how a convoy began under cover of the final Egyptian artillery barrage; how the SAMs were repositioned within four hours; how the violation was discovered on Sunday and immediately reported to the United States.[28] For another fortnight there was no US counteraction, not even a further diplomatic demarche, toward the Soviets. After the latest American EW pods failed on 18 July, USAF expert Brog had seconded the IAF's request for Shrike radiation-seeking missiles to counter the SAM radars. To placate the Israelis, on 14 August Ambassador Rabin was told that Nixon had approved the Shrikes among other new arms sales. But Washington still lacked, or professed to lack, hard proof that the Egyptians, let alone the Soviets, had broken their word.[29]

Dayan summed it up: "The Egyptians and Russians ... did not pull back the batteries and we did not send our delegate to the Jarring talks."[30] Continued Even Steven flights spotted more, undisputedly new SAM sites—that is, such that had been deployed after 10 August.[31] Besides the advance of Soviet *divizyons*, the massive forward movement of Egyptian batteries was facilitated by new Soviet transfers of both weapons and personnel: the SAM-6 batteries that had been promised to Nasser in June were deployed in August around the Aswan Dam, releasing Egyptian SAM-2 formations for positions closer to the front.[32] The introduction of ten Soviet-manned SAM-6 launchers "supported by anti-aircraft artillery crews and base security troops" was disclosed to the US press only after Sadat declared their "expulsion" two years later.[33] New EW systems were also supplied by August and installed, with Soviet operators, both in the canal zone and around Cairo.

THE SOVIET–ISRAELI WAR, 1967–1973

C. Advancing the missile shield dooms the Rogers Plan

On 22 August, Ambassador Beam finally took the matter up with First Deputy Foreign Minister Vasily Kuznetsov, but got little satisfaction. Nixon was prevailed upon only in early September to issue explicit instructions to the Moscow embassy for a firm response. Armed with these orders, Beam confronted Vladimir Vinogradov on Thursday, 3 September.

This was a few days after Sergey Vinogradov (no relation), the ambassador to Egypt, had died suddenly while on home leave.[34] Vladimir's appointment to succeed him would not be announced for another month, but he was fully prepared for what Beam would call in retrospect "a sarcastic but amusing interview." At the time, he was hardly amused: he reported getting a "lengthy, repetitive, and largely unyielding reply."

> I told Vinogradov that, while we were taking up [the] matter with UAR, we regarded the USSR as involved since Soviet weapons and personnel were there and that their people on the ground must have knowledge of developments which were contrary to the ceasefire agreement.
>
> He then said "there were no Soviet weapons in the UAR," although the UAR had bought Soviet weapons. There were no Soviet troops there; only advisers and technicians. Therefore ... the USSR was in no way involved in the Middle East crisis.

By now, the Soviet deputy minister could add an accusation that the US was covering up for Israel's walkout from the Jarring talks. He ignored Beam's "personal suggestion"—in fact a US climbdown—that if "quietly and without publicity ... the UAR would withdraw some—maybe not all—of its missiles as a gesture, this would be a small step toward ... returning Israel to the conference table."

Vinogradov also aimed a barb at the Americans' failure to determine the *status quo ante* by aerial photography. "Since US planes are flying over eastern side of Suez Canal and can see over both sides, USG should be able to determine accuracy of UAR charges" that *Israel* was actually violating the ceasefire. Beam recalled in his memoirs how Vinogradov "for my benefit ... acted out the steps which US pilots presumably took to 'pull down the window blinds when they flew over Israeli territory.'" Beam did not admit it to his interlocutor, but the Americans' position was weakened by their assessment that the Soviet accusations against Israel were not unfounded, in respect of fortification and weapons upgrading, though much less significant than the Soviet–Egyptian violations. Vinogradov's charge that the IAF was preparing to renew air strikes the very next day never materialized.[35]

Receiving Beam's report in Washington, Assistant Secretary of State Sisco angrily rejected Vinogradov's assertions in a return cable:

> we feel that USSR cannot take position [he] expressed ... There [is] no need to outline how heavily involved USSR is in UAR with its own personnel and equipment. USSR and US

CEASEFIRE VIOLATION SEALS A STRATEGIC GAIN

agreed on ceasefire/standstill in hope that it would lead to serious talks and political solution. Violations are serious, and both USSR and UAR would be taking on heavy responsibility if they should lead to breakdown in peace efforts.[36]

But Beam made no further attempt to press the issue in Moscow, and the breakdown had already occurred.

Kissinger, in stark contrast to his bravado in Nixon's presence, did not bring up the ceasefire violations at all in his few back-channel contacts during August and much of September (through the Soviet chargé Yuly Vorontsov; Ambassador Dobrynin too was on home leave). Sonnenfeldt went so far as to warn his boss on 16 September: "we may have (unwittingly) misled the Soviets to believe that cheating on the ceasefire was a matter of indifference to us and that we may have thereby contributed to a potentially much deeper crisis."[37] But by then, a flap over a suspected new Soviet base in Cuba had eclipsed the Middle East at the top of Kissinger's agenda.

Even within the region, American attention was distracted by the hijacking of four airliners to Jordan and the worsening crisis there, where Palestinian, Iraqi and finally Syrian forces challenged the Hashemite regime.[38] The direct Soviet backing for this effort is beyond the scope of this study, but it merits mention that Kissinger reported being told by Dobrynin: "we might not believe it but the Soviet Union had not known of the invasion of Jordan by Syria and ... in any event Soviet advisors had dropped off Syrian tanks prior to crossing the frontier. I [Kissinger] let this somewhat contradictory statement go."[39] This pattern would be repeated in October 1973. For the time being, the prime concern in Washington was whether an Israeli intervention in Jordan with US approval would send the Suez ceasefire "out the window," as Admiral Moorer expected. On 9 September, Sisco still spoke of this only as a hypothetical response to such Israeli action:

> Mr *Sisco*: ... The Egyptians would probably move some of the SAMs closer to the Canal. Also, Russian pilots would likely become more involved. ... Nasser would have to step up his campaign against Israel in some way—probably by small, showy raids.
>
> Mr *Helms*: He might undertake a bombardment of the Bar Lev line.[40]

So, Kissinger reported that when on 25 September he finally saw Dobrynin, "the Ambassador tried to discuss ... the Middle East ... I cut him off."[41]

Dobrynin, who had initiated the meeting in connection with the Soviet clients' ultimate defeat in Jordan's "Black September," reported that Kissinger actually made "lengthy arguments 'about the major Soviet share of responsibility' for ... moving missile launchers in the Suez Canal Zone." But Dobrynin claimed that he again "flatly rejected" these charges, and went on to protest the "slanderous anti-Soviet campaign" in this matter. "Kissinger," he reported, "in effect confirmed the correctness of my remarks, although he made all sorts of excuses."[42] By 6 October, Dobrynin was calling the violations "fabricated" and threatening damage to US–USSR relations.⁴³ NSC staffer Harold Saunders, after examining the U-2 photos, concluded that "activity is not leveling off ... [the] defensive missile complex means more to the Egyptians than peace talks."⁴⁴ Even Secretary Rogers had by then come around to the view that for the Soviets, improving their military position took precedence over restarting the Jarring mission. He attributed this to the situation in Southeast Asia.⁴⁵

D. Israel's hollow declaration of victory

While Israeli leaders decried the SAM move to the Americans, they tried to play its significance down for domestic consumption. An official "victory album" on the War of Attrition signed off on the note that the conflict "ends with an Egyptian rout. Egypt does not fulfill its obligations, but rather advances and reinforces its AA array in the canal zone. However, fighting does not resume. Israel is ready for a peaceful solution, but prepared for war."⁴⁶ Journalists well connected in the establishment were encouraged to write in a similar vein. Arnold Sherman, who for years had worked with the aviation and military industries, ended an English-language book that he published shortly after the ceasefire with a rather ominous epilogue. Giving the exact specifications of the SAM systems that were advanced after the ceasefire took effect (and even of the trucks used to move them), he wrote that "the ugly meaning was clear: by violating the ceasefire agreement, Soviet missiles had achieved a measure of control over Israeli air space. Israeli aircraft could be destroyed before they ever approached the border." A Hebrew version that appeared a few months later added "but Israel has sought—and also found—the appropriate solution for this, too."⁴⁷

The IAF's rationale for accepting the ceasefire was to gain time for developing countermeasures to the SAMs. The force's chief of operations at the time, Ya'aqov Agassi, relates that a plan for a massive attack on the SAM array was ready for implementation at the expected expiry of the ceasefire on 7 November.⁴⁸ He may have alluded to the plan for a Shrike missile barrage that was finally launched only a year later, with very disappointing results. In January 1971, *Aviation Week* reported that although Shrikes were being mounted on Israeli Phantoms and Skyhawks, IAF commanders were unsure of the missiles' effectiveness as they did not have the Soviet systems' frequencies, and therefore preferred that ground forces should strike the first blow at the SAMs.⁴⁹

IDF ops chief Weizmann, who had pressed to start the air war, conceded famously that "the missiles dented [our] planes' wings." IAF chief Hod repudiated this admission even as late as 1984.⁵⁰ But over time more candid assessments by his then-subordinates recognized that Israel had been defeated, mainly due to the Soviet SAMs' upper hand against the Phantoms. Even before the loss of its commander Hetz and senior WSO Eini, the latter felt that the first F-4 squadron "was indeed in a great crisis."⁵¹ An airbase commander at the time, Col. Aharon "Yalu" Shavit, admitted

CEASEFIRE VIOLATION SEALS A STRATEGIC GAIN

thirty-seven years later: "we ran into a wall of Russians and Egyptians. When a Russian is dug into a foxhole, you can't get him out unless you kill him. The IAF had no solution for overcoming the missiles."[52]

Phantom pilot Yiftah Spector, soon to be appointed commander of a new squadron, calculated that at the rate of loss the F-4s sustained—one for every 8.3 sorties against the missile array—the thirty serviceable craft that Israel had on average at the height of the war would have been exhausted within weeks (not to mention the crews).[53] The damage—he argued—might have been mitigated had the IAF fielded its entire order of battle, including older craft, against the missiles rather than put the entire burden on the F-4s. By the fortieth anniversary of the War of Attrition, a pamphlet issued by the semiofficial Air Force Association echoed Spector in assessing that "Israel lost the war." It had failed to achieve its main objective, whereas the Egyptians and Soviets had gained theirs: ensuring the precondition for an offensive across the canal.[54]

In any case, the air war was only "the last straw" in a confrontation that was unwinnable because of Israel's numerical inferiority and its social-political inability to sustain mounting casualties in the ground war as well. Losses on the Egyptian front alone for 1970 up to August were 124 killed (including four civilians) and 329 injured in 4,820 incidents.[55] Admitted Soviet fatalities numbered thirty-five between March 1969 and August 1970.[56] But even had they been publicized, they would have had no comparable effect, just as the thousands of Egyptian casualties put no pause to their leadership's resolve.

Shortly after the ceasefire, Ashraf Marwan again met his Israeli handler and satisfied the latter's demand for the Egyptian cross-canal offensive plan, indicating that it was still operative. At this stage, it had to be Lashchenko's blueprint. Bar-Joseph holds that this, along with a detailed list of the Egyptian order of battle that Marwan also provided, cemented his credibility with the Israelis.[57]

Even a genuine Israeli agent placed as close to Nasser as Marwan, and as aware of the president's failing health as his son-in-law must have been, could not have predicted the date—28 September 1970—of another heart attack, this time fatal.[58] Lashchenko and Chief of Staff Zakharov were both in the delegation that Kosygin led to Nasser's funeral three days later.[59] It also included Col.-Gen. Vasily Okunev, who had been appointed in "early September" to replace Katyshkin as chief military adviser in Egypt. He was listed with Lashchenko as signing the condolence book, in an implied message that no change of military plans was envisaged. According to the American Defense Intelligence Agency, the delegation numbered no fewer than seventy-two Soviet officers—who remained in Egypt with Okunev.[60]

Also in the Soviet premier's entourage was Vladimir Vinogradov, who on the morning of the delegation's departure was officially appointed to succeed his surname-sake Sergey as ambassador in Cairo. Skipping the formality of *agrément* by the Egyptian Foreign Ministry, Kosygin introduced Vinogradov to Nasser's vice-president and temporary successor, Sadat.⁶¹ The latter welcomed the appointment and promised regular weekly meetings with the new envoy.⁶² Together with Zakharov, Lashchenko and Katyshkin, Vinogradov took part in a military consultation with the Egyptian leadership. According to Heikal, Defense Minister Fawzy stressed to the guests that "Egyptian forces should have full confidence in the continued flow of Soviet weapons."

> Zakharov promised to do what he could, though he thought the shopping list ... was too big. He also said ... we should make every effort to get all Russians in Egypt replaced by Egyptians before the battle started. "Not that we are in any way afraid for our men here," he said, "but we think it is much better that you should take over completely."⁶³

Two years later, this handover to adequately trained Egyptians would be presented as a sign of the Soviets' disapproval for launching an offensive and their banishment by Egypt for withholding the necessary arms. But for the moment, neither the ceasefire nor Nasser's death signaled any downscaling, let alone termination, of the Soviet military presence or its commitment to preparing the ultimate "battle."

In late August, a State Department official shared with an Israeli diplomat reports that Soviet arms shipments to Egypt by air and sea had actually increased, including additional *Shilka*s and possibly 203mm cannon. The Americans, the Israeli reported, "are wondering what this considerable buildup is intended for. In his opinion, the Egyptians are incapable of crossing the canal and digging in on the other side, despite the amphibious equipment they received, unless this is done with the participation of Soviet forces in large numbers."⁶⁴

Sgt Rogozhinsky's *spetskomandirovka* (special mission) reinforcement had only reached Nikolaev when the ceasefire came into effect, and was delayed there for two months. On 13 October, the 350 *spetsnaz* men, in civvies but with weapons and ammo concealed in their luggage, boarded the liner *Armenia* for Alexandria and reported to Inshas air base, together with several replacement pilots. "Our main mission was to teach the Arabs to operate our technical equipment. ... Their officers were inferior to our privates. ... They couldn't cope with contemporary hardware. Our officers used to joke that if war were still conducted on horseback, the Egyptians could teach the Israelis a lesson."⁶⁵

Okunev formally took over from Katyshkin in early 1971. His previous post—commander of the Moscow Air Defense District—underlined the SAMs' continuing prominence in *Kavkaz*. As Kapitanets (newly appointed deputy commander of the Fifth *Eskadra*) was instructed, "in case of emergency" it too was to come under Okunev's command, stressing Egypt's centrality to the Mediterranean squadron's mission. At the ceasefire, by Kapitanets's reckoning, Operation *Kavkaz* included—besides the original Air Defense division—four Air Defense brigades, several independent battalions, eleven electronic-warfare units as well as "radio-technic," signals and intelligence detachments. The aviation component comprised two interceptor

CEASEFIRE VIOLATION SEALS A STRATEGIC GAIN

regiments, as well as transport aircraft, and would soon be further reinforced with—among others—a numerically small but strategically and symbolically important token of Soviet commitment: the return of the Foxbats.[66]

PART 3

A DECEPTIVE END

PART 3

A DECEPTIVE END

18

SADAT PROVES HIS STABILITY AND LOYALTY

A. Early mentions and field testing of the MiG-25, 1968–70

In March 1971, Popov's *divizyon* ended its year's stint in Egypt. It was relieved by a contingent that was drawn in November from the regional air defense formation at Mariupol, Ukraine, and like its predecessors underwent training at Ashuluk. Its commander, Col. Vasily Linkov, volunteered a detailed memoir to a Mariupol newspaper in 2008. As he describes their dispatch, secrecy was somewhat eased: sailing on board the liner *Ivan Franko* from Nikolaev, the men were still dressed in mufti but were allowed to go on deck and even to "dance with the women of the ship's crew." The ship was escorted by two submarines, which surfaced only off Alexandria. This was not divulged to the rank-and-file: on a similar voyage in December 1970, a *Strela* operator who was posted as a lookout on the bridge was alarmed when he spotted a periscope, and alerted the captain, who said "take it easy, son—it's ours and here to protect us."[1] Upon arrival, to prevent any Israeli attack, the Egyptian pilot boats that guided Linkov's steamer dropped depth charges as they progressed along the channel into the harbor.

Taking over from Popov near the canal, Linkov and his men already heard inflated legends about the *divizyon*'s exploits. Despite the "temporary peace," the SAMs' outer defenses of *Shilka*s and *Strela*s were posted daily before dawn up to 15–20 kilometers away "in the most dangerous directions," but at night the SAM crews took the risk of turning off their systems to let them cool. Israeli planes approached the missiles' range up to twenty times a day, and Linkov considered that even though they turned back when his radar acquired them, their purpose was to tire out the Soviet crews with constant alerts.[2]

The ceasefire-violation affair and the U-2 flights had emphasized the importance of high-altitude photo surveillance. The Soviets had a suitable, though yet experimental, counter for the US spyplane—with the added advantage that unlike the U-2 or the newer SR-71, it could be armed for combat missions too. The model that would later be known as the MiG-25, NATO reporting name Foxbat, had already been used in May 1967 for at least two sorties from Egypt over Israel that were designed for provocation no less than reconnaissance.³

There have been retrospective suggestions that selling MiG-25s to Egypt, or at least restationing them there with Soviet crews, was demanded by Cairo, envisaged by Moscow, and even implemented from the outset of *Kavkaz* or earlier. United Press International (UPI) reported on 30 November 1968 that in response to the finalization of Israel's Phantom purchase, "the Soviet Union ... began delivering 200 'MiG-23s' to Egypt. The MiGs were capable of carrying nuclear weapons and were more maneuverable than Phantoms."⁴ A similar but more plausible report actually appeared in *Time* magazine *before* Johnson's announcement, stating that the 200 planes were to include MiG-21s *and* "23s." Israeli commentator Chaim Herzog correctly pointed out that the USSR had very few of the latter. Besides the confused appellation, the model's specifications were described very inaccurately.⁵ According to Heikal's version of the commitments that Nasser received in Moscow in January 1970, the MiG-21 squadrons were to be "*preceded* by four high-altitude supersonic reconnaissance planes ... the West now knows them as MiG-25s."⁶ *Kavkaz* staff officer Abramov confirms that this was included in the agreement to launch the operation.⁷

On 14 February 1970, Nasser told the *New York Times*' James Reston that he "is pressing the Soviet Union for 'MiG-23' fighter planes ... to intercept the Israeli bombers," mentioning the option of "Soviet pilots."⁸ Soviet Foreign Ministry officials denied this to Ambassador Beam.⁹ But following Kissinger's rude awakening by the Soviet regulars' appearance in Egypt, Ambassador reported that Washington was less concerned about the SAM-3s than about their Soviet crews—and about the possible "introduction of Soviet pilots to fly the latest 'MiG-23' aircraft." He suggested that Moscow could use the issue to put pressure on Washington, which is exactly how the Foxbats' deployment was viewed when it became known, and permanent, a year later.¹⁰ V. Vinogradov, Soviet ambassador in Cairo, includes "MiG-25 aircraft ... with Soviet crews" in the air defense division whose arrival "sobered up not only the Israelis but also the Americans," implying that this brought about the ceasefire in August 1970.¹¹ Before Katyshkin's tour of duty in Egypt ended in September of that year, according to his colleague and biographer he "would frequently visit the deployment sites of Air Force personnel in Egypt in missile-bearing MiG-25 bombers, which for camouflage were referred to as M-500."¹²

A continuous Foxbat presence in Egypt this early seems unlikely, as the still-experimental model had suffered a major setback in April 1969 when an engine failure cost the life of the Air Defense Corps' aviation arm commander, Gen. Anatoly Kadomtsev, and the problem was still being addressed. The craft may have been sent to Egypt for short-term field trials combined with specific operational missions, just as it was in May 1967. According to Russian aviation writer Viktor Markovsky, based on interviews with "participants," this was precisely the purpose of an initiative by the deputy minister for the aviation industry, A.V. Minayev, who had been one of the MiG-25's designers. He suggested such trials in Egypt in "the summer of 1970," but implementation was delayed by the uncertainty following Nasser's death and resumed once Sadat confirmed the continuity of Egypt's policy.[13] The senior test pilot Bezhevets, who led the project from 1963 and would command the Foxbats in Egypt, has also related that "formation of the team for Egypt began in mid-June 1970" but was formalized only later.[14] The test pilot Aleksandr Lysenko is described as serving "*from December 1970 ... in combat activity in Egypt ... in a MiG-25 aircraft.*"[15]

B. Soviet doubts about Sadat dispelled

Even if a continuous MiG-25 presence would be established only in mid-1971, these preliminaries attest that there was only a brief suspension, if any, of Soviet military involvement due to uncertainty about Nasser's succession. Speaking in the post-Soviet 1990s, Akopov claimed that following Sadat's accession there already were Soviet views that "he is not our man—he is looking at the West." But the Soviet embassy staffer himself felt that the differences were mainly over Sadat's demands for economic aid that the USSR could not meet rather than over policy goals, and that agreement could be reached.[16] Sadat did put out first feelers toward US emissaries as early as Nasser's funeral, and entertained a series of senior American guests over the following six months—but any qualms the Soviets had about him were soon dispelled. His consultations with Kosygin's delegation to the funeral, as already cited, betrayed little dissent.

Among other reassuring moves, Sadat immediately reinstated the reputedly pro-Soviet Ahmed Ismail, though for now at a lower but politically influential post as chief of intelligence.[17] Sadat's rival and the Soviets' reputed favorite, Sabry, was kept on as vice-president and liaison with Moscow. If there was any discord, it was only over Sadat's overenthusiasm to praise and flaunt the Soviets' direct military involvement beyond what Moscow intended to disclose. A case in point was Sadat's speech at Tanta in January 1971, which the Soviet embassy reportedly hastened—and had sufficient clout—to suppress.[18]

In the military, reliance on the Soviet advisers was if anything stepped up: ahead of a conference on 30 December 1970 to "analyze the results of recent combat operations, Egyptian air defense formation commanders were instructed to avail themselves of assistance by the Soviet advisers in preparing reports and lectures."[19] Instructors from Soviet military academies organized study courses for senior Egyptian officers, such as Navy commander Fahmy who completed a thesis on *desant* (landing) operations (like Kapitanets's own, and under the same supervisor). A joint exercise of such landings, which Kapitanets and the chief naval adviser, Vice-Admiral Grigory Chernobay, had planned with Fahmy in early September, went ahead after Nasser's death. "On the surface nothing changed," Kapitanets wrote in retrospect. Nasser's approval for *Eskadra* ships to enter all Egyptian ports was not rescinded.[20]

THE SOVIET–ISRAELI WAR, 1967–1973

C. Ceasefire-extension brinkmanship

Sadat, once established in power, declared 1971 to be "the year of decision," and received full Soviet support in threatening war. The first ninety-day extension of the ceasefire was about to expire on 5 February. In the month preceding the deadline, there was intensive consultation between Cairo and Moscow. Sabry returned from a periodic visit to the USSR with promises of "unlimited military and political support for Egypt ... in its struggle against the United States and Israel."[21]

Sadat now transmitted to Washington through a "private channel" a proposal to open the canal after only a partial Israeli withdrawal. A month later, he would take care to assure Donald Bergus of the US interests section in Cairo "that his proposal was not in any sense a Cold War exercise. There had been no Soviet pressure on him." Overtly, Sadat declared that Egypt was ready for war, and issued an ultimatum for Israel to make a "positive step" as a condition for extending the ceasefire again. Israel, under heavy US duress, had already reluctantly agreed on 28 December to restart the Jarring talks. But Sadat soon clarified that this would not suffice. He "felt Jarring would not get anywhere and would take a long time doing so."[22]

In mid-January, Soviet head of state Nikolay Podgorny returned to Egypt, ostensibly for the festive inauguration of the Aswan Dam. However, he used this and other public opportunities to pledge support for another war with Israel. He told a cheering crowd of 5,000 shipyard workers in Alexandria that the USSR would "bear any material losses to help Egypt repulse Israel. We will furnish you with experts and money to enable you to achieve your aims." Sadat replied that Egypt "will be a faithful friend."[23] As the ceasefire expiry approached, the EAF resumed daily flights over the east bank of the canal, backed by electronic-warfare coverage from Soviet planes in Egyptian airspace. Israel complained to the UN observers that this violated the ceasefire but did not attempt interception, despite increasing fears of an imminent Egyptian–Soviet offensive.[24] During such incursions on 26 April (by a MiG-21) and 9 May (by two Su-7s), Israeli ground positions did open fire, but the intruders were not hit, the incidents drew little attention, and the flights continued.[25]

A week before the ceasefire extension was due to expire on 5 February, Dobrynin reminded Kissinger that no response had been received to Soviet proposals for general principles of a settlement. "Kissinger assured me that Nixon wants to resume the bilateral confidential dialogue ... but ... did not say anything more specific"—except that "a reliable and reputable Egyptian source 'had confidentially informed'" the Americans that opening the canal might be acceptable without a final settlement, but with a mutual 30–40 kilometer pullback of forces *except for the SAMs*"—a crucial element that Bergus had not mentioned.

Kissinger asked Dobrynin to verify this with Egypt. Dobrynin replied that he had heard nothing except for a similar Israeli proposal attributed to Dayan, which was rejected in Egypt as it included no commitment for an ultimate full withdrawal. But

SADAT PROVES HIS STABILITY AND LOYALTY

though he expected nothing from Kissinger except "general phrases and assertions," Dobrynin suggested encouraging the White House to play a more active role, in order "to exploit the advantage of [Nixon's] interest in the summit."[26] For the Soviets, the State Department's utility had been maximized, and there was now more to be gained by switching tracks. Kissinger reported only inquiring about the "Dayan plan's" acceptability to Moscow, adding "I had reason to believe ... Cairo was interested (I was thinking of the [Amin?] Channel)."[27]

Sadat waited until the last moment before extending the ceasefire—this time for only thirty days. On the same day (4 February), he sent the Soviet leadership a message calling for a "forceful riposte to the unholy alliance of the enemies of progress, liberty and peace."[28] But sidestepping Jarring on the very day that the UN envoy submitted questionnaires to both sides, Sadat also went public with his new settlement proposal in a celebrated interview for a US magazine.[29] This appeared to be an abrupt change: in his previous talk with a US correspondent at the end of December, Sadat had been unwilling to make the "concessions Israel wants in order to withdraw Israeli troops from Egyptian soil," and the interviewer concluded that he was merely saying "terrible things in a much nicer way" than Nasser.[30]

Bergus in Cairo had to profess "surprise" at Sadat's move—for "local [US] consumption," as he explained to Heikal, who now added the sweetener of resuming diplomatic relations with Washington if the deal went through.[31] Sadat's proposal would be remembered mainly for the offer to open the canal after only a partial Israeli withdrawal, but to the usual Egyptian demand for prior commitment to withdraw from all Egyptian territory, he now added the West Bank too, as well as return of Palestinian refugees. These elements had also by now been adopted by Soviet policy. A partial settlement on the canal had been broached by Dayan in one of his frequent turnarounds. But the new elements were non-starters for Israel's cabinet, which was now faced with a strident opposition after its right-wing component walked out to protest the ceasefire and the acceptance of the Rogers Plan.

In Washington, it was assumed that the Soviets had connived with Sadat's move, but still it was taken as a retreat achieved by Rogers's continuing efforts, and Israel came under increasing US pressure to reciprocate. "The Soviets have 'blinked' perceptibly in the Middle East," columnist Joseph Alsop was told. "There can be no doubt whatever that Sadat's offer was Soviet-inspired, and perhaps even Soviet-imposed" due to greater Soviet interest than Egypt's in opening the canal.

This was also the view of the US Embassy in Moscow. Reporting it to Kissinger, NSC staffer Saunders still held that US initiative leading to the ceasefire had scored a positive change by putting the focus on the Jarring talks "with the US as a not-too-veiled prime mover behind them. The USSR (except for the standstill violations) has been left in the wings."[32] The perceived diplomatic gain thus overshadowed the very real military setback. Not all in Washington agreed. Alsop's sources considered that two years of quiet could be foreseen. But he stressed "the terrible potential meaning of the Soviet military preparations in Egypt ... now complete in almost every detail ... for a Soviet-supported crossing of the Suez Canal by the Egyptians." This meant "important people in Moscow were thinking very seriously about winning the whole Middle East by beating the Israelis to their knees, or crushing Israel altogether."[33]

This alarmist view of Soviet acquiescence in, if not support for, total eradication of Israel was also gaining ground in Israel itself, due to Sadat's new Palestinian-related conditions. This elicited calls for a preemptive strike as in June 1967. But there is little evidence to indicate that in early 1971 the Soviets, or indeed Sadat, were on the brink of launching even a limited cross-canal offensive; their preparations were for the longer range. The ostentatious declarations contrasted sharply with the stealth and secrecy that would precede the ultimate attack in October 1973, and more resembled the intentional provocation of Israel to strike first in May 1967—as illustrated by the military moves that were soon to follow.

D. The agreed Soviet handover to Egyptians begins

A week before the new ceasefire expiry date on 5 March, Sadat arrived in Moscow for his first visit as president. A week earlier, Dobrynin reported that "the central objective of American policy in the Middle East remains ... above all else to 'eliminate' Soviet military presence there"—again a clear reflection of Kissinger's "indiscretion." He suggested skillful and deliberate use of "threatening various actions ... in the military-political realm. ... This is a very effective means for influencing the White House."[34] His advice was evidently followed. On the eve of Sadat's arrival, the Soviet press bannered a government statement supporting the Egyptian proposals and castigating the United States for failing to press Israel to accept them.[35]

Like Nasser's real or fictitious trip a year before, Sadat's "secret" visit became common knowledge within a few days, and US officials claimed a week later that they had known about it in advance.[36] But when Sadat announced on 7 March that Egypt would no longer be bound by the ceasefire, Dobrynin reported, with evident satisfaction, that the decision came as an "unpleasant surprise for the Nixon administration."[37] Kissinger had just a few days earlier treated a ceasefire extension as a foregone conclusion, now that "we could be on the verge of getting a real Egyptian–Israeli negotiation started." He considered this also an opportunity to approach the USSR "on the question of removing their combat forces from the UAR *if there is a peace agreement*."[38] Just the day before Sadat's statement, Nixon had agreed with Kissinger to "go for the partial solution," and they both considered that this would "give the Russians an added incentive for the Summit"—now the White House's premier objective.[39]

So the national security adviser was blindsided again, and the Soviets' military follow-up soon gave Democratic hawks good reason to judge that Sadat's Moscow visit was a repeat performance of Nasser's, "which led to the reinforcement of Soviet missiles, forces and tanks in Egypt." Sen. Henry Jackson charged "the USSR is running the Egyptian game."⁴⁰ The same conclusion—"the USSR is dictating Egypt's military and political moves"—was declared by the Israeli cabinet, in a meeting that was somewhat too blithely described as "totally calm!"⁴¹ The next day, Dayan famously stated in the Knesset that it would be better to forgo peace than to gain it by relinquishing all of Sinai, and on 11 March he rejected the opening of the canal in a partial deal, which according to earlier reports he had advocated.⁴² Heikal responded by publishing the Israeli and Egyptian order of battle, stressing that Sadat's strategy was now based on the SAM shield across the canal.⁴³

As usual, there were also reassuring interpretations, holding that Sadat's talks had exposed *differences* with the Soviet leadership.⁴⁴ This reading leaned, among other things, on reports that the Soviet crews of SAM-3 batteries on the canal had handed them over to Egyptians.⁴⁵ These in turn may have originated from observations of the first *Kavkaz* personnel being rotated, at the end of their year's tour of duty, with other *Soviet* servicemen. The reports were later denied.⁴⁶ However, the first Egyptian crews were really completing their training period in the USSR, for which the Soviet units had originally been intended as a stopgap. Sadat even boasted that Egyptian commanders at all levels, including electronic warfare, had ended their courses in the Soviet Union at a level "that surprised even their Soviet instructors."⁴⁷

E. Embarrassments in Egyptian cities, rearmament at the front

Akopov relates that Sadat "several times raised the issue of limiting the number of Soviet military specialists," and the Soviet leadership actually welcomed the suggestion. Akopov's boss, Ambassador V. Vinogradov, puts it only in 1972 that

> the embassy concluded that it would be desirable for the Soviet side itself to propose to Sadat a reduction of the number of Soviet military experts. ... It would be better, we thought, if our military men would begin a gradual "exodus" at our own initiative, than to have Sadat himself raise the question of their withdrawal.

But after Sadat's visit to Moscow in March 1971, Vinogradov (newly appointed a candidate-member of the Central Committee) was summoned to a Politburo meeting. Before it began, "Brezhnev told me that he was in full agreement with the embassy's well-reasoned and farsighted proposals" to initiate a withdrawal from Egypt—that is, the ambassador submitted this suggestion not long after taking office.

The first speaker at the Politburo was Defense Minister Grechko, who threatened that if the embassy's proposals were accepted, he "would disavow any responsibility for the state of the Egyptian armed forces." Grechko had been Brezhnev's commander in "the Great Patriotic War," and was his political ally. His resistance must have been awkward for the general secretary, who effectively ended discussion by referring the matter to a committee. Vinogradov's recommendation was in effect adopted. In retrospect, he wrote: "the embassy had looked into a crystal ball."

Vinogradov explains that one of his motives was to reduce the chronic problem of Soviet dependents' obtrusive presence in Cairo:

> The advisers' wives, the *oboz* [baggage train and camp followers] as we called them, filled the Egyptian bazaars. ... The presence of a big Russian *oboz* in the streets [was one of the reasons that] led the embassy to consider how essential the continued stationing of so many military men, with their wives, in Egypt really was.[48]

The exposure of several black-marketeering and smuggling attempts exacerbated this issue, and it was not limited only to noncombatants. The Soviet servicemen themselves, especially the regulars and junior advisers who were *not* allowed to bring their wives, were increasingly and sometimes embarrassingly visible too.

As described by an interpreter who was happily reposted to headquarters in Cairo after a year in "bombed-out" Suez City, anyone "on furlough from the desert with 10 Egyptian pounds in his pocket" could hardly resist "the hordes of pimps" in Cairo's main squares "who all but imposed" their merchandise. As the Soviets' liaison, "the tall dandy" Lt-Col. Bardisi, confided to interpreter Igor' Vakhtin, the regulars gave him an even harder time than the advisers had done. Bardisi could not understand why their superiors had rejected an offer to arrange a brothel staffed with carefully selected and monitored women, which besides the obvious intelligence advantage for the Egyptians might also "prevent venereal problems." In Upper Egypt, naval aviation engineer Lashenko recalls,

> we were very well treated—so well that prior to the Soviet friends' arrival, the Egyptians set up ... a bordello. But the moral fiber of Soviet officers proved itself as superior. The Arabs were surprised: "What's there to think about? When we studied in the USSR, we had your girls." But we didn't touch the Egyptian women.

Bardisi blamed this display of prudery for the series of scandals he had to handle, when Soviet officers tried to smuggle "love priestesses" into their quarters.[49]

According to Col. Logachev, the deputy chief political officer of the air defense division, even before the ceasefire, it was said that a returning officer's wife should welcome him with a glass of Russian vodka in one hand, black bread and herring in the other—all of which were not provided in Egypt—"and the hem of her skirt between her teeth."

> The military tribunal and Party committees stood guard over the Soviet warrior's morality, while the "special department" was more concerned lest he blab something unopportune during such encounters. ... For visiting nightclubs, four officers got Party and military reprimands. Nevertheless, curiosity sometimes trumps even the strictest prohibitions. After the battles ended, three of us [political officers] decided to visit such a nightclub, to see what it was and to witness belly dancing.

On this investigative mission, they went to a club near the pyramids. In 1998, Logachev described in graphic detail that would have been unthinkable under either

SADAT PROVES HIS STABILITY AND LOYALTY

Soviet prudery or Putin-era pride how a dancer "unexpectedly" sprang off stage onto his lap, and his discipline lapsed. "My entire essence came to life," as the girl "squirmed on my lap until she achieved her purpose. ... Thirty Egyptian pounds, a third of my monthly pay, went up the chimney" for French champagne, caviar and other delicacies that were foisted on him, "plus an unscheduled laundry of my underwear." He claims that the incident "taught me never to visit such places again, but [my] curiosity was satisfied."[50]

For enlisted men such binges were less frequent, and over time were limited even further—probably in order to reduce the Soviets' visibility, which became an increasing political problem. Sgt Nurgaliev, during eight months spent in a desert SAM base in 1972, never got to see not only the pyramids but even a bathhouse, though there were occasional visits to a local pool. "Living conditions were very bad. ... A plethora of crawling, jumping and flying insects. On parade, everyone was scratching—officers and men. Not everyone could stand it. Some had to be sent back to the Soviet Union." The food was still good, but monotonous; after eating rice three times a day throughout their internationalist service, he and his comrades were aghast when at a welcome-home banquet the main course was pilaf. "We begged for potatoes and herring."[51]

Arranging with contacts in Odessa for the donation and shipment of herring and black bread along with a "new year's fir tree" was one of the morale-boosting measures that the *politruk* (political officer) Artem Khandanyan—who arrived with the second "shift" of Soviet missilemen in February 1971—initiated that December. He credited the Soviets' presence for deterring any incursion by the enemy, but it was precisely "the absence of combat operations" that

> had a negative influence on the servicemen's mood. They did not understand: "why are we far from the homeland, in these tough conditions, if there's no war?" Besides, 85% of the division's manpower was now under age 30, a generation whose concept of war was drawn from books. The junior officers lacked adequate knowhow, as well as proficiency in psychology and pedagogy, while real life and the circumstances required this daily.

While they stood guard around the clock and lived in dugouts where even the relative luxury of air conditioners provided only "artificial air," in nearby Egyptian cities nightlife throbbed "for the affluent classes" (a complaint that mirrored similar discontent in the Israeli military). Despite increased interest in the political officers' information about world politics, "not everyone understood the need for our presence. Our primary mission was explaining, putting across to every soldier that our country's policy was peace-loving." Still, "a frame of mind developed that it was time to get out of here, that there wasn't going to be a war, and they were fed up with the desert."[52]

Akopov was among the Soviet embassy staffers whom Khandanyan and his colleagues enlisted for frequent visits to the troops. So there is little reason to doubt the diplomat's assertion that, shortly after the ceasefire, the Soviet regulars' "withdrawal was already in the air, but ... if we withdrew them ourselves, the world would profess that the Soviet Union is abandoning friends ... when the war is about to begin." The latter statement very much describes the atmosphere in March 1971, which after the "blink" in January soon returned to high suspense—while, as Akopov puts it, "Soviet–American relations at that period of time [began] to develop."[53] In sum, the conflicting demands of Moscow's position vis-à-vis other allies and its emerging détente policy toward the United States both suggested and necessitated a combined exercise: to offer a withdrawal, which it desired anyway, as a concession to the United States—but to do so secretly.

Toward the Soviet advisers on the ground, however, the Egyptian command's only complaint was again that the benefits of their advice were not being maximized. A circular to the elements of the 16th Infantry Division pointed out that the advisers' "output reports" had become perfunctory and routine, and did not reflect "ideas, suggestions and experiments worthy of study and dissemination." Field commanders were instructed to "take advantage of [the advisers'] full capability and experience, ... seek their advice and ask their opinion." A form was provided for this purpose.[54]

While interpretations of Soviet intent varied, the thrust of Soviet action soon became clear. Sadat's visit was immediately followed by a renewed sea- and airlift of munitions—or rather, the appearance of reports about these shipments, which had already begun. The Western media first identified additional MiG-21s, Su-7s and SAMs, and a new variant of *Shilka* (ZSU-23–4V1) with improved radar and firepower. The most prominent new arrival was the Mi-8 assault helicopter, which was described as suitable for commando raids (correctly, as their use in the Yom Kippur War would prove). Three shiploads of the helicopters were reported by US intelligence sources as unloaded during the month-long extension of the ceasefire, indicating that their supply was agreed before Sadat's visit.[55]

While even such distinctly offensive gear could be construed as part of a long-term program, there were signs of more immediate preparations. US intelligence reported that the USSR had undertaken an unusual effort to place a surveillance satellite over the Middle East and monitor its photography by direct transmission rather than delayed retrieval, the usual technique at the time.[56] Insufficient data received even by this means was one rationale proposed a few weeks later for the most dramatic new development, which was initially kept top secret: the dispatch to Egypt of an entire new Soviet unit, with the most advanced aircraft.

19

RETURN OF THE FOXBATS

Any suggestion that the Soviets frowned on Sadat's renunciation of the ceasefire is dispelled by the Soviet move, immediately after his talks in Moscow, to introduce a long-term presence in Egypt of the MiG-25, whose prime function was to prepare his promised cross-canal offensive. Precisely as Moscow and Cairo prepared to offer the United States a withdrawal of Soviet pilots from Egypt, several of their finest were dispatched there as the 63rd Air Group.[1]

As in previous instances such as the Fifth *Eskadra* and Operation *Kavkaz* headquarters, the high-profile gesture of creating a new formation followed the practical assembly of its components. Bezhevets, who had begun preparations in June 1970, was summoned from a furlough in February 1971 and told to get ready to lead a "special team for overseas deployment" in a "warm country." His associates all understood this was Egypt.[2] The handful of selected airmen included civilians (from the Mikoyan design bureau and the Ministry of Aviation Industry) and military officers. The latter were drawn from reconnaissance squadrons of the Moscow Military District—to which the 63rd was subordinated, with its home base at Shatalovo, near Smolensk.

While Bezhevets remained in charge of the pilots, overall command of the new group was entrusted to Air Force Maj.-Gen. (and Hero of the Soviet Union) Georgy Baevsky, the Moscow district's deputy commander for combat preparedness. He had been inducting new models including the MiG-25—in which his own first flight is dated on 18 May 1967, the day after the first Foxbat overflight of Dimona. Baevsky's command, including ground crews, electronic equipment operators, auxiliary personnel and a base-security *rota* (company), numbered a total of 450 men—and four planes.

Most of the MiG-25s already flying were of the original interceptor version, four exemplars of which had been displayed in July 1967. But from the outset, the Egyptians requested the model for reconnaissance use (as over Israel in May 1967) rather than for air superiority.[3] Of the two variants that would ultimately be sent to Egypt, the reconnaissance version was at an earlier stage of development than the interceptor. But its relative importance became more pronounced when the last flying prototype of the American B-70 Valkyrie, the mach-3 high-altitude bomber that the MiG-25 was originally designed to intercept, was retired in February 1969.

223

The reconnaissance-bomber version, MiG-25RB, was even newer. Bezhevets, at the test facility at Akhtyubinsk on the Caspian Sea, was tasked only in 1969 to begin urgent tests of high-altitude bombing that would utilize the MiG-25's advanced navigation systems. He reported very good results, and "understood that this was meant for the Middle East." His subordinate, Capt. Nikolay Borshchev—a pilot who doubled as the 63rd's political officer—stressed this newly developed feature when he reminisced that upon the Foxbats' arrival in Egypt,

> they were attentively observed. All the Egyptian personnel ran to the phones to report the first flight to someone. Now it is known with what alarm Israeli intelligence monitored the group's action, especially the RBs [reconnaissance-bomber version] which could also bomb any target in Israel or the occupied territories accurately and with impunity.

This was an exaggerated assessment of Israeli intelligence capability: six months later, the IAF still believed that all four of the aircraft were of the "reconnaissance type."[4]

Given that the 63rd had only two RBs, if they were readied to deliver only conventional bombs these would have to be aimed at exceptionally sensitive targets in order to pose a significant threat. Unlike the Foxbats' next appearance in the theater, during the Yom Kippur War, there is no mention in the numerous veterans' accounts from 1971 to 1972 either of nuclear weapons for them or of Dimona as their projected target. The IAF too was little concerned about, or even aware of, a possible bombing function for the Foxbats. To the extent that they were seen as increasing the Egyptians' offensive capability, it was in achieving air superiority.[5] But soon their small number became apparent; as late as October 1971, the Israelis still *overestimated* "the maximum figure" between six and twelve.[6] Even this number obviated the original concerns that Foxbats would be pitted against Phantoms for dominating the sky over the canal (which caused a flurry of comparisons between the two models' performance). Only later was attention focused on the 63rd's actual spying mission.

The Soviets' preparations took two weeks. Before their departure, Bezhevets (with Air Force chief Kutakhov) was summoned to a meeting with Grechko, indicating the importance attached to their deployment. Accounts from this briefing reflect only a reconnaissance mission, as well as the Marshal's perennial concern: while he approved flights over Israel at 20,000 meters and 2,800 kilometers per hour—calculated to outperform any IAF interceptor—Grechko "categorically" forbade any closer approach to Tel Aviv than 40 kilometers, as there would be "a lot of noise" if a plane or pilot fell into Israeli hands. Bezhevets, correctly foreseeing the tactic that the Israelis would devise, tried to suggest that the MiG-25s take off from Egypt, fly straight across Israel and land in Syria. If they doubled back to Egypt, he argued, even slower IAF planes could meet them head-on. Grechko swept this idea aside: "Colonel, [expletive], do I need to put another division in Syria to guard them?" No one ever dared to broach the idea again.

RETURN OF THE FOXBATS

Grechko demanded tight security on the ground in Egypt, which fell to pilot-*politruk* Borshchev. "The responsibility was great: 400 men under my supervision, both officers and conscripts. Personal documents were left in Moscow and everybody was dressed in civvies." The elaborate transport operation began on 16 March—the day a $376 million credit line for Egyptian development projects was signed in Moscow, and hailed in Cairo as a token of continued military support as well.[7] Both to supervise the planes' reassembly and to highlight the event's significance, the 63rd was accompanied by Deputy Minister Minayev and the Mikoyan bureau's deputy chief designer, P.G. Shengelaya, leading a group of experts.

Four An-22s carrying one crated MiG-25 apiece took off for Egypt. No fewer than fifty-six An-12 flights were needed for personnel and other equipment. Additional gear was sent by train to Novorossiisk and shipped on a merchant freighter to Alexandria. Tankers were henceforth dispatched regularly to deliver the special fuel necessitated by the Foxbat's extreme operating envelope.

After an overnight stop at Tököl that was dictated by a sandstorm in Egypt, the convoy landed at Cairo-West. It was met by the deputy to the chief Air Force adviser, Gen. Grigory Dol'nikov, who had headed the Soviet MiG-21 force since its arrival. Like others in the original *Kavkaz* leadership, he was a legendary Second World War ace (under Pokryshkin) and HSU, who was featured by Mikhail Sholokhov as the protagonist in the novel and film *Destiny of a Man*.[8]

Like their predecessors in *Kavkaz*, the MiG-25 crews were issued Egyptian fatigues without insignia. More noteworthy, and apparently indicative of an urgent dispatch, were the inadequate quarters. Bezhevets recalls that the entire complement lived for two or three weeks in barracks with no running water and only makeshift latrines in the desert, before the flight crews were moved to a renovated hotel, guarded by Egyptian soldiers. Baevsky and Minayev were quartered in a suburban cottage, and each of them was given a car with an Egyptian military chauffeur who—so they were told—did not speak Russian.

Baevsky recalls that "the day after arriving we were briefed by the advisers, which did not improve our mood—indeed, the opposite. An enemy offensive was expected shortly. ... War was expected to begin in 10 days." Bezhevets recalled the chief adviser, Okunev, warning him that "war will begin in a week." Signs of escalation increased from day to day: on 19 March, Egyptian anti-aircraft guns opened fire for the first time since the ceasefire at two Phantoms that penetrated Egyptian airspace. On the 20th, at a meeting of a "commission to prepare the nation for war," Sadat granted expanded emergency powers to regional governors.[9] On the 21st, military conscription in Egypt was extended to five years.[10] On 1 April, the Israeli Ambassador cabled from Washington that without a political breakthrough, Sadat was liable to restart hostilities.[11]

The MiG-25s had to be assembled fast, and thanks to the efforts of the technical experts, this was accomplished in three days. General Mahmut Gareev, who had succeeded Malashenko as the advisers' chief of staff, listened sympathetically to the 63rd's pleas for enhanced protection. He assigned one of the new *Shilka*s to each of the Foxbats, which were housed in the corrugated-iron sheds used previously by the Tu-16s (later they were moved to underground concrete shelters).

The Foxbats were painted with EAF markings, but the substandard paint obtained for the purpose would burn off from the heating at peak speed and expose the more durable red stars. The pilots came under enormous stress, and would be soaked with sweat under their G suits—one explanation for their relatively large number in proportion to the aircraft. The cockpit canopy too "got so hot that it could not be touched and the glass would begin to melt." This had required the design of a cooling system based on pure alcohol; periodic changes of this fluid would soon provide the crews at Cairo-West with occasions for revelry. Also, "a problem arose about heat-resistant bombs and missiles. It was solved quickly and thank goodness, our internationalists did not have to use the new developments"—another confirmation that the RBs were armed and prepared to attack Israeli targets.

Once assembled, the MiG-25s were to be tried out by test pilot Vladimir Gordienko, who had put them through their trials at the Gorky factory. However, a hitch was caused by the Soviets' penchant for secrecy. "We learned suddenly," Baevsky recalled,

> that the Egyptian SAM crews defending the base had never seen a MiG-25, and showing them one either in flight or in pictures was not approved. ... Every takeoff and landing had to be protected by our MiG-21s, and SAM crews had to be warned that "unidentified" planes flying in these formations must not be shot at.

Finally, the SAM crews around the field were replaced by a Soviet brigade, whose headquarters now doubled as the Foxbats' command post. When in November 1975 the Soviets were reported as "delivering Foxbat aircraft to the Libyans," Sadat was skeptical: "when four Foxbats were stationed in Egypt, the Soviets never let the Egyptian pilots near them."[12]

Gordienko made the first test flight on 26 March, six more within a week, and a total of nineteen test flights on the 63rd's four planes.[13] But before he had even begun, the secrecy was blown: Baevsky was called from Moscow to explain "who had authorized flights and how a photo, supposedly of our plane in air, got into a local [Cairo] newspaper with the plane's specifications." In this photo, it was labeled "Foxbat" and ascribed a speed of Mach 3.2—well over its top velocity at the time. "My reply was brief: 'We have not yet flown; the photo was evidently made during the demonstration at Domodedovo on 9 July 1967.'"

Still, it took a while for the 63rd's arrival to register with US or Israeli intelligence—or for their governments to admit it. It was only on 24 March that the daily reports in the Western press about the flow of Soviet munitions to Egypt first listed "crates of unidentified equipment" as part of "an accelerated Egyptian campaign to prepare a new war with Israel."[14] Ten days later, the *Daily Telegraph*'s John Bulloch, who would become a frequent channel for disinformation, reported from Beirut that the mysterious items were "apparently Su-11s," describing them as superior to the F-4.[15] It took another week for US officials to admit that the planes flown into Egypt *might* have included a small number of Foxbats or Floggers "capable of successfully facing the Phantom," and that these *might* be flown by Soviet pilots.[16]

The next day, the world press bannered definitive news of the Foxbats' deployment, and the Israeli media dealt with little else. "State Department sources" finally admitted that the Soviets "may have flown a few disassembled 'MiG-23s' to Egypt," implicitly blaming Israel that this was done "in view of the almost total standstill in diplomatic efforts." The officials maintained that there was no conclusive evidence yet—despite other reports the same day about "'MiG-23' test flights in the Middle East."[17] The US sources still held that although this development would intensify the Soviets' involvement, as only they would fly the Foxbats, the number of craft would be limited as few of them existed and had first been deployed in the western USSR only the previous year. The Pentagon reportedly saw this mainly as a gesture to highlight Soviet support for Egypt.

But the same considerations were seen by Israeli pundits as a cause for alarm rather than reassurance. They stressed the superiority of the "MiG-23" over the Phantom, and pointed out (correctly) that the F-15 was being developed to counter the Foxbat but would be ready only in the mid-1970s.[18] And most perceptively, the Foxbats were viewed as part of a coordinated Egyptian–Soviet response in case Israel reacted to Sadat's abrogation of the ceasefire with a preemptive attack.[19]

The reminiscences of the 63rd Air Group's pilots appear to indicate—though not yet to prove—that as in 1967, their flights were at least initially designed as a deliberate provocation to draw such an Israeli strike, with the RBs' bombing capability to be part of the response. But at the time, although the Foxbats' deployment "caused widespread concern in the West," this was mainly due to their spying function. Their possible combat role had already been discounted as "largely symbolic" and bombing missions were not taken into consideration at all.[20] As for the MiG-25's unequalled combination of armed reconnaissance, "the Israelis proposed an engine upgrade for their F-4E ... to increase altitude for an improved reconnaissance aircraft that could reach 78,000 feet [and Mach 3.2]. Known as Project Peace Jack, this aircraft could have carried air-to-air missiles ... In the event this so-called F-4X modification was not made," and the Foxbat remained unchallenged for more than another decade.[21]

On 12 April (the day that the Foxbats' appearance in Egypt dominated the Middle Eastern news), Rabin finally presented to Kissinger—pointedly sidestepping the State Department—an Israeli proposal for an interim settlement. It was still irreconcilable with Egyptian and Soviet demands, but its very promulgation represented a considerable shift after lengthy domestic debate.[22] Kissinger, however, was unimpressed and referred the Israeli ambassador back to the State Department, which took to it more kindly and began preparing another mediation tour by Rogers. Rabin, who was himself dissatisfied with the proposal, reckoned correctly that Kissinger preferred its failure to be blamed on the State Department.[23]

There is no record that Kissinger so much as mentioned Rabin's paper to Dobrynin until 23 April, when the latter brought up the Middle East as a possible agenda item for the proposed summit. Discussions about the conference, with a possible date in September, were then snagged on a crisis around Berlin. Asked for "details of the Israeli proposal," Kissinger reported that he said only "it had been essentially covered in the press."

> Dobrynin said that he couldn't understand the secretary's trip. The United States seemed to be mediating, negotiating, coming up with all the proposals ... but it wouldn't get anywhere. At some point, he said, you will have to wind up talking with us, but we will not propose it any further.[24]

According to Dobrynin, Kissinger did give him a précis of Rabin's proposal—notably, that "Israel was ready to pull back a certain distance from the Suez Canal, provided that the canal's eastern bank would not be occupied by Egyptian or Soviet troops." He added that Nixon had turned it down in order not to "associate himself" with ideas unacceptable to Egypt. Though US mediation efforts were continuing, the White House was "not fully certain the Rogers mission will succeed" and "did not want to associate itself too officially with the outcome."[25] It would be 9 October before Kissinger told Dobrynin about "a secret conversation" with Rabin, who complained about the State Department's "distortions." Dobrynin concluded that "it evidently suits him [Kissinger] for now that the activities of Rogers and Sisco provoke displeasure both among the Egyptians and in Israel, and impel both of them to appeal directly to the White House." This, Kissinger had said explicitly, would make it easier for him "down the road, when it becomes necessary to tell Tel Aviv about US–Soviet negotiations if they result in some agreement."[26] Once the agreement was reached, however, he did not inform the Israelis about its central provisions.

Meanwhile, by the time their presence was publicized, the Soviet MiG-25 pilots had completed a series of test and training flights designed to mirror their planned missions: flying north to the Mediterranean coast, they turned west over El Alamein rather than east toward Israel. The planes performed even better under desert conditions than they had in arctic tests, and approval for flight at top speed was extended from three minutes to eight and then to forty—long enough to perform the entire planned sorties at a velocity that could outpace any Israeli interceptor. Though Bezhevets had one serious landing-gear failure, by April most problems had been ironed out and Minayev's design team went home.

The 63rd's airmen were puzzled that neither the Israelis nor the Americans appeared to have taken notice of the "mirror" practice flights. Now, Moscow cabled clearance for operational sorties. The first flight, over Sinai, also appeared to go unnoticed by Israel. Bezhevets was summoned to Okunev: "Moscow is asking how you can fly without any response." They concluded that the Israelis simply could not believe the flight characteristics of the blips on their radar screens. Headquarters authorized more sorties in the same pattern. The second flight was sent over Israel proper, and from here on the Soviets knew their new trump card had been detected. Monitoring the flights from the ground, Bezhevets always saw the same picture: as soon as a Foxbat came over the Mediterranean, up to ten IAF planes and sometimes more would appear around Israeli airbases. "When you're flying in the MiG's cockpit you don't suspect that a hunt [is on] after you, but on the ground when you see the armadas chasing your comrade it gets very uncomfortable."

An elaborate technique for protecting the Foxbat's vulnerable stage—takeoff and landing—was now perfected, and soon detected by the Israelis too. In November, Rabin told Sisco that twelve Soviet-piloted MiG-21s were scrambled to create a cluster of radar blips around each MiG-25. The following month, IAF chief Hod spoke of three full squadrons performing this maneuver.[27] Pilot-instructor Petr Rubtsov, who began his *spetskomandirovka* (special mission) in November 1971, describes this exercise in detail but mentions only four MiG-21s taking off from his base north of Cairo at high speed toward the canal and swerving south at the last minute, while two MiG-25s continued into Sinai. Either additional MiG-21s took off from other bases, or the Israelis were overawed. Soviet accounts add that electronic-warfare platform planes were also used to obscure the Foxbats' activity, while the MiG-25s themselves observed radio silence throughout.

The Israelis' quick response despite this smokescreen rekindled the Soviets' security concerns. As Rubtsov describes, "whenever we developed a battle plan together with the Arabs, it quickly became known to the other side."[28] As the 63rd's personnel were proudly told, their audacity was even discussed in the Knesset "and an official declaration was published that *Soviet* pilots would no longer be permitted to overfly Israel." The Soviets suspected that their identity had been reported by Israeli agents in the Egyptian military. Baevsky's suspicions about the photo in the Cairo paper deepened: "we clearly were being watched constantly and attentively, by more than one person, and every day this was increasingly confirmed."

Bezhevets noticed that IAF scrambling in Israel began even before the time that had been given to the Egyptians for the MiG-25s' takeoff. Secrecy was tightened even further, and only a small group was informed at the last minute that a sortie was about to begin. Originally, on a concrete apron between the four plane shelters, a cross had been marked to calibrate the automatic navigation system before each flight. But rolling the plane out and positioning it over the cross could give away an impending flight, so instead a separate geodesic setting had to be made for each hangar. Various deceptions were tried out: mock engine tests were abruptly turned into takeoffs. The Soviets credited such tactics for making the IAF scramble several times a week for more than a year, even though the actual Foxbat flights were much less frequent.

THE SOVIET–ISRAELI WAR, 1967–1973

As war fever relaxed, bombing options were set aside—to be revived in 1973. But reconnaissance sorties, both for monitoring immediate Israeli intentions and for preparation of a future offensive, settled into a routine. They were made every other week with two Foxbats flying each time, in case of an equipment failure in one. Each pilot made at least two such flights before the group's deployment ended a year later. First Sinai and then Israel itself were covered in a tight grid, with high-resolution cameras that even at 20,000 meters showed the Israeli defense lineup such as radar installations, anti-aircraft sites and airfields in great detail. The planes were also equipped with state-of-the-art computerized mapping systems that could beam observations to the ground control center while the sortie was still in progress.[29]

Despite the Soviets' suspicion that the Israelis were getting early warning, all intercept attempts by Phantoms and Mirages failed; the 63rd's radar operators watched how the Foxbats shook them off. There was even an intelligence bonus for the Soviets when after one RB flight, the Egyptians near the canal found an unexploded US-made air-to-air missile and brought it to Cairo, where "our experts studied it meticulously." Israel's Hawk missiles were likewise ineffectual at the MiG-25's altitude. Soviet expectations that Israel would receive the US high-altitude Nike-Hercules missiles never materialized, and tactics developed against them proved unnecessary.

As it had with the initial Soviet intervention, Israel vacillated about making any disclosure that would confront the US administration publicly with a major Soviet advance. Tension with Rogers was bad enough already. The closest Israel came to an official comment was when Dayan called the Foxbats' presence in Egypt "burdensome." That, commented a US columnist, "sets a new ... record for one-word understatement in Tel Aviv by a man with an eye patch. 'Burdensome' is as inadequate as calling Hitler a 'spoilsport.'"[30] Okunev was but slightly exaggerating the Israelis' concern when he told Bezhevets that they had assembled three battalions of Arabic- and Russian-speaking commandos, and promised them a million-dollar bounty for every MiG-25 they destroyed on the ground. "But thank God, they never showed up."

20

TRIAL BALLOONS FROM BOTH SIDES

A. Sadat responds through Rogers to Kissinger's "indiscretion"

With Rogers making the rounds, war fever was at least temporarily cooled. In Cairo on 7 May—the day UPI again reported Soviet pilots flying Foxbats out of Egypt—he received an offer that was clearly designed in response to Kissinger's "indiscretion." Recordings of Nixon's Oval Office conversations show that Rogers reported to the president a promise by Sadat:

> if we can work out an interim settlement ... all the Russian ground troops will be out of my country at the end of six months. I will keep Russian pilots to train my pilots because that's the only way my pilots can learn how to fly. But in so far as the bulk of the Russians—the ten or twelve thousand—they will all be out of Egypt.

There was no mention of the new Soviet craft or personnel that had just been introduced.[1]

Rogers came to sound out Dayan on the defense minister's reputed proposal for an Israeli withdrawal. Dayan specified that in return for Egyptian "nonbelligerency" as a component of a "partial solution," he would agree to pull back as far as the Sinai passes—but with no further commitment. Prime Minister Meir and her other cabinet colleagues rejected even that.[2] In two days of stormy talks with Meir trying to reconcile the disparate concepts of an interim settlement, Rogers apparently did not disclose Sadat's offer of Soviet withdrawal. He only asked Meir (in vain) *whether* the departure of Soviet forces might soften her position. She retorted that the Soviets would not be moved by anything Israel did or didn't do. Even when Meir asked about the US response if Soviet forces crossed the canal after an Israeli pullback, Rogers only declined any guarantee of US action—without suggesting that the Soviet forces might no longer be there. The talks ended in acrimony, with a threat from Rogers that the Nixon administration would distance itself from the peacemaking effort; the threat was empty, as the secretary himself had in effect already been excluded.[3]

Still, Nixon went through the motions of instructing Rogers to follow up on Sadat's offer. But in an extraordinary directive a week later, the president so much as ordered him to desist. Nixon pointed out that the United States had more to gain from tilting its policy toward 100 million Arabs than two million Israelis. Maintaining Israeli military superiority was in the US interest so long as Soviet influence in Egypt and other Arab states remained strong. But *once Soviet forces left Egypt a radically different policy would be required.* Nixon stated that he would not support the State Department initiative until after the US election, and by that time Soviet arms shipments might make an Arab–Israeli war inevitable.[4] In other words, removing the Soviet presence remained a central and urgent aim, but it would have to be achieved directly with Moscow rather than by virtue of a US-brokered Egyptian–Israeli accord.

Sadat, then, had chosen the wrong messenger, and his offer went nowhere—for the time being. The Soviets would repeat it in September, and the fact that they made, almost verbatim, the same distinction between combat troops and advisers indicates that they too were responding, in coordination, to Kissinger's signal.

B. Sadat foils a "pro-Soviet" coup but signs a treaty with Moscow

On 13 May 1971, within two weeks of meeting Rogers, Sadat foiled a coup against him (or engineered a preemptive countercoup), and any remaining doubts about the stability of his government were removed. Vice-President Sabry, chef de cabinet Sami Sharaf and Defense Minister Fawzy topped a list of figures with pro-Soviet reputations who were ousted and jailed. Ambassador Vinogradov was even rumored to have engineered the attempted coup himself, which strengthened expectations for an anti-Soviet backlash in Egypt.[5] But he remained at his post, no mention was made of any Soviet context in public statements, and speculations that an anti-Moscow swing was the hidden agenda were soon disproved. One unrelated result was that Sharaf was replaced by his underling Marwan, about whose role in suppressing the conspiracy against Sadat there are wildly divergent versions; in any case, his promotion and heightened proximity to Sadat increased his perceived value for Israeli intelligence.[6]

The very day columnist James Reston was told in Washington that "Rogers established a good personal relationship with Sadat," US officialdom was "surprised" by the arrival of Soviet head of state Podgorny for another visit to Cairo.[7] It produced a friendship and cooperation treaty. According to Ambassador Vinogradov, the pact was requested by Sadat and the text was prepared by the Egyptians.[8] Western pundits were forced to conclude that the power struggle in Egypt had been personal or domestic—and in foreign affairs, connected to the newly announced federation with Syria and Libya rather than to relations with the USSR.[9]

Meeting Dobrynin on 8 June, Kissinger reported that the Soviet ambassador gloated: "We can always prevent a settlement if you push us to it. We got a 15-year treaty out of the Rogers visit." Kissinger had to backpedal: "I said it was not our policy to push the S[oviet] U[nion] out of the Middle East. Politically, though, some reduction in the Soviet military presence there had always been part of our program."[10] Most significantly, Dobrynin reported that after months in which the Middle East had hardly figured in the back-channel talks (compared with SALT, Vietnam and other issues), Kissinger said it "now moves to one of the top spots" in discussing the summit. Whereas he had previously discounted the issue's electoral impact, he now stressed the "great sensitivity of this problem in US domestic politics." Therefore, Rogers and Sisco were now to be left out of the loop, as "Nixon does not want to trust anyone from the State Department bureaucracy." Kissinger's previous argument about facilitating disclosure to the Israelis was superseded: "If a purely confidential agreement were reached with the Soviet leadership, the President would find ways without accounting to anyone ... to fulfill his part."[11]

C. A Soviet feeler toward Israel

Despite Dobrynin's bravado, not all in Moscow were convinced of Sadat's trustworthiness. In early June, Primakov (now officially at a desk job in a Moscow research institute) was summoned back from a vacation and dispatched by TASS boss Leonid Zamyatin for a month in Egypt. In Cairo on the 12th he met *New York Times* reporter Raymond Anderson, who told him that Sadat had relayed through Bergus to Nixon that the proposal made to Rogers about reducing Soviet military presence was still in effect, despite anything the Egyptian president might be obliged to declare.[12] The alarmed Primakov—evidently unaware that Sadat's offer was coordinated with the top Soviet leadership—rushed to Vinogradov, who angrily rejected his suspicions and even denied him the use of a secure line to report them. Like Western correspondents with stories that they couldn't cable from Cairo, Primakov flew to Beirut and sent a limited-circulation TASS "special file," which enraged Podgorny and was promptly censored. A Brezhnev aide later told Primakov that he had barely "saved your skin."[13]

Still, the Soviets were concerned that US diplomacy might produce, and take credit for, a canal deal—if only for lack of Soviet influence in Israel. Likewise in Jerusalem, means were being sought to counter US pressure. Briefly, there appeared to be a confluence of Israeli and Soviet interests in mending fences. On 28 May, a day after the Soviet–Egyptian treaty was signed, Meir, while attending a Socialist International conference in Helsinki, put out feelers through the Finnish foreign minister for contacts with the Soviets; the secretary-general of her party made almost as explicit an appeal from the rostrum.

Within less than three weeks, the London *Evening News* Moscow correspondent Victor Louis was in Israel—clandestinely, more at the Israelis' insistence than his own. When news of his visit emerged two weeks later, it was explained as "treatment of his lumbago," arranged by "his friend, a doctor" who happened to be a former Israeli ambassador to the Soviet Union.[14] Any official mission was denied by both the

Israelis and Soviets, but Louis had come with a "service passport" and was already famous for predicting Khrushchev's downfall, presumably based on inside information. The *Time* Moscow bureau chief who dealt with Louis to smuggle out Khrushchev's memoirs characterized him as a "KGB disinformation agent" and "authorized provocateur," who had carried out similar missions in Taiwan (where he was the first Soviet emissary) and China.[15]

He now claimed to have anticipated the Israeli feelers and the Soviet response, "even before Golda opened her mouth," by cabling his Israeli friend on the same day she approached the Finns. The Israeli Foreign Ministry, however, stated that Louis contacted the doctor only on 9 June, and his visa request was received later.[16] This is borne out by Primakov's memoir, which shows that Golda's message was reported to Moscow on 28 May and that on 3 June the Politburo tasked Andropov to follow up on her initiative. Louis's KGB handler and recent biographer, Maj.-Gen. Vyacheslav Kevorkov, states that KGB Chairman Andropov used to give Louis verbal instructions personally, and describes the latter's eager compliance when he was *offered*—rather than proposed himself—the mission to conduct "secret talks in Israel." Kevorkov claims that Louis was never on the agency's payroll but gladly accepted such assignments to maintain the insider's aura that enhanced his journalistic status, as well as for the sheer adventure.[17]

The KGB simultaneously continued its covert operations against Israel. On 11 June, PFLP gunmen on a speedboat out of South Yemen fired rocket-propelled grenades at the Israeli-operated tanker *Coral Sea* as it sailed, under a Liberian flag, through the Bab el-Mandeb strait into the Red Sea with a load of Iranian oil.[18] The PFLP declared that its operation was aimed as much at Iran and Saudi Arabia as at Israel and its Red-Med pipeline—which in 1970 had reached peak traffic—as a channel for their exports to the West to replace the Suez Canal.[19] Despite the organization's, and the South Yemenis', strong Soviet connections, there is no record that Soviet complicity was suspected at the time. But newly released documents from the Mitrokhin Archive describe in detail how KGB experts had given the PFLP "an authoritative recommendation to organize and implement" the attack, and provided the RPG-7 launchers.[20]

Israel first suppressed the news about the tanker attack and then played down any relevance to the *Egyptian* front; no mention at all was made of a Soviet input, even if one was suspected.[21] In contrast, the excessive secrecy around Louis's visit restarted, when it was exposed, the periodic speculation that he came "to examine the possibility" of rapprochement.[22] Even if the trip to Israel was his own idea, he already had the reputation of "the Soviet journalist who many people think is a Soviet government agent."

In Moscow, where he was hosting Egyptian Foreign Minister Riad, Soviet Foreign Minister Gromyko "brushed off the reports ... 'they don't even deserve to be refuted,' he said."[23] But when Israel imposed a similar news blackout on a visit by CIA Director Richard Helms and it too was broken, this only reinforced assumptions that following Louis's talks

234

TRIAL BALLOONS FROM BOTH SIDES

the CIA chief was acting on secret information ... that a renewal of diplomatic relations between Russia and Israel may be in the offing. ... Israeli officials also may be worried about the so-called phantom memorandum, a paper given Egypt in May by ... [Donald] Bergus ... for getting the Suez Canal reopened. It apparently prompted complaints by Russia of secret Cairo–Washington dealings.[24]

Helms's supposed dispatch to Israel was interpreted as another mark of decline for Rogers, whose State Department hastened to assert that the Bergus paper was "personal and unofficial" and had not been cleared in Washington.[25]

Helms's supposedly urgent, secret visit soon turned out to be only a "stopover" on a rather ostentatious "15-day swing around Europe" with his wife on board the CIA's converted jetliner.[26] Gromyko's belittlement of Louis's mission was fairly apt at least in terms of its results. He did not get the interview he sought with Meir or Dayan, despite his suggestion that even a brief photo opportunity—and "a bit of publicity"—would gain the attention of the top Soviet leaders for his purported initiative. The transcript of his talk with the only Israeli official he got to meet, Meir's adviser Simha Dinitz, shows that Louis described the renewal of full diplomatic relations only as a distant prospect, with a pointed warning that the Israelis should not seek to humiliate Russia or to extract any apology for the rupture in 1967.

His immediate purpose, Louis stated, was to suggest a Soviet–Israeli "back channel." To sweeten the proposal for Israeli ears, he sounded harsher about Sadat than Primakov's "special file" had, and even disclosed—though in a skewed version—Sadat's offer to Rogers about removing the Soviet military presence. This should have been a momentous discovery for the Israelis, but it appears to have slipped by them unnoticed as they were concerned more about Bergus's "phantom cable." Even more remarkably, Louis gave away that the Soviets either had the Egyptian president's office bugged, or had access to Sadat's own recordings:

> When this Rogers business came, the Russians were horrified—for heaven's sake look what is going on there with Sadat, almost embracing him! Sadat failed to say [to us] what he was saying to Rogers ... Rogers began to sort of lure Sadat and suggest ... that [Soviet] arms could be substituted by American arms, and Sadat said: but not the advisors. ... And when he was asked questions, he didn't mention this part of the private conversation [with Rogers] which was on tape.

Louis was likewise dismissive of the Soviet–Egyptian treaty:

> This treaty which the Egyptians were refusing to sign for five years ... [was] a kind of payment after they had been caught red-handed that they haven't been honest with us ... Who needs this treaty? What is the advantage for Russia? ... But Podgorny is proud that he brought the treaty [just as] Rogers came proud that he had done something.[27]

THE SOVIET–ISRAELI WAR, 1967–1973

D. Moscow approves an ambitious canal crossing—and sends an official emissary to Israel

Despite any mutual suspicion, it was after signing the friendship treaty that Sadat issued his formal order to start preparations for war. An Egyptian general who was to lead an infantry charge across the canal detailed, in a 1998 lecture to Soviet and Egyptian veterans, how "Egypt decided in favor of a military solution to the problem": Sadat's directive included military and political diversionary actions, which had evidently begun with his offer to Rogers and would climax in the summer of 1972.[28]

The Soviets not only endorsed and enabled the Egyptian offensive plan, which was based on their blueprint; the Egyptians later claimed to have secured Moscow's backing for a version that was much more ambitious than what the more sober-minded among them believed they were capable of achieving. General Shazly, chief of paratroops and special forces, was appointed chief of staff in the shakeup of May 1971. By July, he presented what he describes as his idea for the anti-Israeli offensive to his predecessor Muhammad Ahmad Sadiq—now promoted to minister of war to replace Fawzy. Sadiq was "convinced that when we did launch our offensive it had to be forceful and unlimited: a clean, swift sweep through Sinai and the Gaza Strip." Sadiq believed that "if the Soviet Union supplied us with what we needed … we could launch the offensive inside a year, perhaps less." Shazly was much less optimistic: "even if the Soviets did supply us, we would need several years to absorb it, especially into the air force and air defense system." The two supposedly anti-Soviet officers, while differing on the scope and timing of the operation, both considered Soviet support essential.

A double compromise was worked out: according to Shazly, Sadiq agreed to settle for a thrust reaching only as far as the key mountain passes between the canal zone and central Sinai, 30–40 miles into Israeli-held territory.

> This plan we called Operation 41. In reality, its only virtue was that it would need less equipment than a wholesale assault across Sinai, so the supplies list presented to the Soviets would be less traumatic. Therein lay the point. The preparation and development of Operation 41 was to be done in full collaboration with our Soviet advisers.

As the planes and mobile anti-aircraft weapons were insufficient to protect the advancing forces beyond the cover of the static SAM array east of the canal, Shazly claims he obtained Sadiq's consent that, in parallel with Operation 41 but in total secrecy from the Soviets, another operation was to be planned: the High Minarets. "This would be based more closely on the actual capability of our armed forces, as opposed to some notional capability after untold arms shipments. Its objective was the limited goal I had set of a five- or six-mile penetration."[29]

Soviet feelers toward Israel continued, whether as a parallel option or—more likely—as a diversion. Meir's adviser Dinitz had been skeptical about Victor Louis's standing in Moscow, and stressed that confidential contacts had to be at an "authorized level." Louis suggested that unofficial contacts—that is, through him—were preferable, because top-echelon talks would cause confrontation not only with the Arabs but between the Brezhnev and Kosygin factions in Moscow (implying that he spoke for the former).[30]

Louis's report to Andropov was soon seconded: on 22 July, Brezhnev's old rival Shelepin, now demoted to trade-unions chief, dutifully relayed a recommendation from his Australian counterpart, future Prime Minister Bob Hawke: "the USSR can and must seize the initiative from Nixon and take immediate steps to reestablish relations with Israel."[31] This was reported to Brezhnev the next day, which happened to be Egypt's Revolution Day. The Soviet delegate to the festivities in Cairo, Boris Ponomarev, cabled Sadat's comment: "It's bad that only the USA and not the USSR is speaking with Israel."[32] On 28 July, Primakov—at the request of the same Brezhnev aide who had frowned on his "special file" from Cairo—submitted a formal recommendation: "together with greater firmness in our course in the Arab countries, it seems that some initiatives toward Israel and the USA should be taken."[33]

On 5 August, the Politburo approved another mission to Israel, and this time entrusted it to Primakov. Whether or not he was strictly truthful when he told his Israeli hosts that Egypt was not informed in advance about *his* trip, it was thus clearly undertaken only after Sadat had signaled his overall agreement, and Primakov's memoir does state explicitly that Sadat was updated after the fact. Meanwhile, several global issues (Berlin, Kissinger's mission to China) had delayed an agreement on the summit for too long to hold it on the Americans' preferred date in September. On 16 August, it was fixed for May 1972 but a joint announcement, originally scheduled for mid-September, was only made a month later.[34] The timetable would henceforth largely determine both superpowers' Middle East agenda.

E. Primakov in Israel: seeking an alternative or playing for time?

Primakov needed no introduction to the Israelis: given the incendiary character and effect of his *Pravda* reports from Cairo on the eve of the Six-Day War, Jerusalem's very agreement to accept his good offices was a measure of the importance that Israel also attached to establishing liaison with Moscow. He set it up through—of all people—the head of Israel's Atomic Energy Commission, Shalhevet Freier, whom Primakov had met at a Pugwash conference—an international organization of scholars and scientists promoting nuclear and other disarmament, named for its first meeting at Pugwash, Nova Scotia, in 1957. If they discussed the once-crucial issue of Israel's nuclear program, Primakov did not disclose this in his memoir. The Israeli documentation of his subsequent talks in Israel—though top secret at the time—includes no such reference, and Freier's papers are still classified.

The only other source for the Primakov–Freier connection is Herbert York, a prominent US nuclear physicist and arms-control advocate who was a central

Pugwash activist. He too indicates that the nuclear aspect was merely an excuse for their meetings. York appears to have both misdated this link and exaggerated its significance when in 1998 he called it "one of the most important of those combinations" that Pugwash provided for "people to meet each other at a time when there were no other good places to do that. ... They were entirely secret, these meetings. They were fully sanctioned ... by both governments."[35]

Primakov arrived in Israel on 28 August 1971, was lodged in an anonymous Tel Aviv apartment, and unlike Louis's talks, his were never leaked. To his hosts, he described his visit as the first time the Kremlin had sent anyone to Israel since the rupture in '67, "not to name the lower journalist." He claimed a much higher status for himself, "close to the top leadership," and warned menacingly that he would not like to return with nothing beyond an Israeli demand to change Soviet positions.

Primakov's memoir contrasts markedly with the Israeli records of his talks. These include not only summaries but also transcripts from recordings, despite Primakov's demand that none be made (the verbatim quotes in his own memoir appear, however, to indicate that he did the same, or took copious notes). Indeed, the comparison is similar to Kissinger's and Dobrynin's contrasting accounts of their conversations, and illustrates the peril of relying on only one side's papers.

For example, Primakov denigrates his first meeting—with Eban, the day after his arrival—as a tiresome "lecture" read out by the foreign minister. But in the transcript, Eban hardly gets a word in for the first eight pages. Then, after a few diplomatic sentences about his difficulty to be polite in describing Soviet policies, Eban was brusquely interrupted by Primakov with a demand not to engage in "propaganda."

Despite his suspicions about Sadat, it was Primakov who started off with an ominous blast at the Israelis: any accord must be acceptable to the Arabs, he said, "because if they won't accept the arrangement ... they would be willing to sacrifice a lot of people, more than Israel could sacrifice." He charged that the Arabs had made steps toward Israel "under the influence of the Soviet Union," but these were not reciprocated. Most emphatically, he declared that "the Soviet Union will not assist in a political arrangement if it will involve the liquidation of the Soviet positions, our military positions, or if it will bring about an approach ... of our potential enemies nearer to our borders."

This came in response to a statement by the ever-unpredictable Dayan, which Primakov claimed to have read en route, describing Israel as part of NATO. Primakov pointedly said he was "happy that Israel is *not* a member of NATO, an organization that is to be used to destroy or limit Soviet positions in the Mediterranean."[36] Nowhere in the talks did he give away the proposal to withdraw Soviet troops from Egypt.

From the meeting with Meir that he expected to be climactic, Primakov came away disappointed—or so he told her adviser, Hanan Baron. Since it was she who had initiated an exchange with Moscow, he expected new ideas from her. Baron replied that

TRIAL BALLOONS FROM BOTH SIDES

the Israelis felt the same, since the guest's visit was at the *Soviets'* behest. Primakov's memoir highlights a military aspect of this talk. Meir, he writes, lost her calm demeanor in the heated conversation:

> "If there is a war, we'll fight that war," she said. "If any aircraft get in our way, we'll shoot them down" ... I asked her: "Could you clarify whose aircraft you intend to shoot down?" ... Meir could tell from my reaction that she had gone too far. Hurriedly, she reiterated the importance of Israel's dialogue with the Soviet Union.

If indeed Meir caught herself misspeaking, it may not have been due to Primakov's response but out of anxiety that she had given away a military secret. As the Soviet MiG-21s in Egypt had seen no action since the ceasefire, she almost certainly referred to the continuing Foxbat flights over Sinai and Israel, which remained a serious concern, and to the countermeasures that the IAF was close to perfecting (or so it believed). It would be another month before Israel confirmed that it was being overflown by Soviet pilots in advanced craft, and Meir did not press the issue—of which she was undoubtedly aware—as a test of Soviet goodwill.

Her outburst, however, elicited another barely concealed threat from Primakov, which he repeated twice to Baron over lunch: "This kind of expression is hard to accept. [You] must remember that the Soviet Union is a very mighty power and even the United States would not use such language." Primakov recounted it even more strongly in his memoir: "Baron got nervous when I mentioned" Golda's statement. "Doesn't she understand how we will respond, or does she think the United States will intervene at risk of nuclear war?" Baron could only admit "of course not." The centrality of the overflight matter to Primakov would be reflected in his next round of talks with Israeli officials in October.

The Soviet emissary then requested, and received, a meeting with Dayan. Besides the defense minister's aforementioned reference to NATO, this may have been connected with Dayan's reputed openness to an interim settlement, or—conversely—with his call, a few days before Primakov's arrival, for Israel to function as a "permanent government" in the occupied territories.[37] The Soviets may also have been testing an Arab trial balloon whereby an "Israeli-born Jew"—specifically Dayan, as distinct from his immigrant colleagues—might be acceptable as a negotiating partner.[38] Whatever Primakov's motives, the transcript of their talk shows that the emissary was much more solicitous than in his previous talks, not to say fawning. He flattered Dayan as "a man who says what he thinks," and repeatedly responded "that is very important" to the defense minister's clarifications of his cryptic or contradictory statements.[39]

Already briefed about Primakov's ire at Meir's aircraft-shootdown remark, Dayan soothed him that Israel "was anxious to avoid any kind of confrontation with Soviet military personnel in Egypt and that the Israeli air force have been given orders to that effect." However, when Dayan blamed the Soviets for the direct air clashes a year before, Primakov denied any knowledge and countered, "we have our positions in Egypt and frankly speaking, we can't give up all this." Dayan's response was as tough as Meir's: "if this continues—we must either retreat from [the] canal or defend ourselves in [the] air. We have no choice but the latter alternative."

There was little more progress on political issues. Pressed by Dayan about Egyptian readiness for any amendment of the pre-1967 border, Primakov said he could not speak for Sadat. When asked for the Soviets' own position, he obfuscated so effectively that the Israeli transcriber noted in the margin: "listen to this passage again." Primakov did suggest superpower guarantees for Israel after a full withdrawal (Dinitz, sitting in on the talk, noted that he had asked Meir about the same option). In response, Dayan returned to the Soviet military presence: "had it not been for your pilots there, your installations there, we wouldn't have to be worried about our security." Any expectations that Dayan might break ranks with Meir were dashed, and Primakov left Israel with little but a vague agreement to continue mid-level meetings.

A week later, in a letter to Nixon on 7 September 1971, Brezhnev still linked the summit in Moscow, which had just been agreed upon, with progress on the Middle East ("a region directly adjoining ... the Soviet Union") as well as Indochina. In particular, Brezhnev accused the United States of "losing interest" in an agreed settlement. "Can this leave Soviet–American relations unaffected? Obviously, not." Public announcement of the summit was postponed by another month.[40]

21

FLEXING MUSCLES WHILE OFFERING A PULLBACK

A. Countering Israel's Shrikes: the Stratocruiser affair

On 18 August 1971, the interpreter Viktor Yakushev was reposted to Egypt and assigned to Operations Headquarters, General Staff, where, he relates, "the future offensive" was being drilled, based on the plan developed by the Soviet advisers. Together with Egyptian generals and lower officers, the Soviets conducted exercises that included all branches of the Egyptian services. With Egyptian Army engineers, Soviet advisers were achieving bridge construction twice or three times faster than the Soviet standards, "which was hardly surprising, as the soldiers and sergeants had been serving for six or seven years."

One specific issue reflected a recent update:

> Crossing water obstacles was rehearsed, including [enemy] use of flammable compounds such as napalm. ... We came to the disturbing conclusion: so long as the napalm was not burnt out, not only would it be impossible to cross the obstacle; it would be impossible even to approach the water. Therefore, special units of Egyptian paratroops were tasked ... to guarantee the prevention of flooding the canal surface with napalm through pipes from deep in the Israeli defenses. Later, during the October war, these trainees of the Soviet advisers carried out the mission honorably, at the cost of their own lives.[1]

The IDF had indeed developed such a scheme to ignite the canal surface, codenamed *Or Yeqarot* (brilliant light), and even tested one system on site on 28 February 1971. Inflated reports in the Arab press about the resulting conflagration led the Israelis to set some store by the system's deterrent value, as Yakushev's account confirms. But it was considered impractical for defense of the entire canal length. Only two units were actually constructed, along with several dummy installations. Most of the latter were subsequently destroyed by earthmoving, and the idea was dropped from Israeli operational planning. A few hours before the outbreak of war on 6 October 1973 an engineering crew was sent to check the remaining systems, and found at least one of them in working order. But the team was pinned down by the Egyptian cannonade before it could receive authorization to ignite the fuel, and was later taken captive. The system was never activated, and the IDF dismissed Egyptian claims after the war that this was because their commandos disabled it.[2] But the Soviets' preparations do illustrate their constant refinement of canal-crossing plans.

The Soviets' commitment to maintaining and improving the SAM shield across the canal was demonstrated in the first major air incident since the ceasefire. On 11 September 1971, an "accurate machinegun burst" from an Israeli position on the east bank brought down a low-flying Su-7, the first such loss since such flights were resumed a half year before. The plane came down in the marshes of the northern sector and was not recovered, so that its pilot could only be assumed as Egyptian.[3] The Soviet personnel in Egypt were also informed "orally" that "one of our planes, flown by an Egyptian pilot" had been shot down.[4]

The same day saw a replay of the March 1970 mid-air collision between US and Soviet aircraft—this time closer to the Egyptian–Israeli front. Corporal Aleksandr Mitrokhin, an aircraft mechanic, was posted at the end of January 1971 to a squadron of Tu-16R electronic-warfare planes based at Aswan.[5] He recalls an incident reported by one of their crews, whose mission was to provide electronic interference "cover" for an Egyptian reconnaissance sortie into Sinai. "The crew of the Soviet Tu-16 waited for the Egyptian to return, but he did not reappear at the scheduled time, so ground-control ordered the Tu-16R to make one more pass."

> While turning around over the Mediterranean, their craft was intercepted by a US Sixth Fleet Phantom. Coming to very close quarters, the F-4 crew began photographing our machine—which, by the way, was done routinely. After banking on the left wing, [our] crew could not see the American fighter. But banking right, they felt an impact. The Phantom, after dropping a few hundred meters, leveled off and disappeared toward the sea.

After the Soviet plane returned to Aswan, "examination of the right wing flaps found a dent, scratches, and traces of paint." The incident can be dated to 11 September, as Mitrokhin added, "the unfortunate Egyptian reconnaissance pilot had not, in fact, returned because he was shot down by Israeli anti-aircraft fire."

The Tu-16's "minimal damage was carefully repaired, but the confrontation was to be continued. During the next sortie ... the situation was repeated. This time the F-4 crew seemed to be paying special attention to the right wing flap of our plane. Our crew had a few very unpleasant moments."[6] As in the previous case of a US–Soviet encounter, this incident was not publicized. Nor was another with the IAF, as described by Nikolay Bondarchuk, a former communications officer with the same Soviet squadron. He recalled that "his Tu-16R was intercepted by an Israeli F-4 Phantom which made what might have been a simulated attack. This was, however, driven off and there were no further Israeli interceptions."[7]

When Israeli officials met Primakov again in Vienna on 8 October, a month after the Su-7 shootdown, they pointed out that such a lucky shot could only have been scored point blank while the plane flew "right over our strongpoints." Primakov

FLEXING MUSCLES WHILE OFFERING A PULLBACK

insisted first that if the plane fell west of the canal it must have been flying there; then he quoted "our experts" that the plane had not crossed the *middle* of the canal.[8] This provided additional proof that Soviets were closely involved, but by then they had already initiated a spectacular retaliation. On 17 September, Ambassador Vinogradov met Sadat "to discuss a working paper drawn up by Soviet and Egyptian specialists on Egypt's military position," and Sadat, in a speech, reiterated that he would not be bound by the ceasefire. The same day, a SAM-2 brought down an Israeli Boeing 377 Stratocruiser transport converted into an advanced electronics platform, which was "executing angular photographic surveillance of the Egyptian missiles" from east of the canal. As the Soviets in Egypt were told, "on board were some 30 intelligence officers, captains or majors, half of them American."[9]

This coup is still cited by the Egyptians as proving how *their* "proper planning enabled the Air Defence Forces to shoot down" a prize target.[10] Chief of Staff Shazly, characteristically, claimed in his memoirs that "*I* determined to stop this [the Stratocruiser flights]. In early September 1971, *I* gave permission to prepare an ambush."[11] When his version appeared in Russian translation, several former advisers were outraged. Still, as one of them related,

> we kept silent both then and later. ... Only recently [in 2010], a group of veterans from the Egyptian war addressed the Speaker of the Federation Council (the upper house of the Russian parliament), and related the true history. At last the name was stated of the hero who commanded this audacious operation.

After an investigation by the speaker's aide, a statement in the official *Rossiskaya Gazeta* named the hero as Viktor Petrovich Kopylov, "who sadly died two years ago," and detailed his accomplishment. "The Stratocruiser was shot at from a location where in theory the Egyptians could not have had SAM launchers." Kopylov, who served from March 1970 as the adviser to a SAM-2 *divizyon* that "went on to shoot down a Phantom," was "a determined, resourceful man who was always ready to argue with his superiors if the cause required it." Under his guidance, "the missilemen managed, undetected by the omnipotent Israeli intelligence, to set up its radar" in a date-palm grove on the very bank of the Great Bitter Lake—in effect repeating Popov's feat a year earlier, but with an Egyptian outfit. Although Kopylov "received authorization" to attack the Israeli plane, his comrades complained that

> the Stratocruiser incident drew an ambiguous response from the leadership. Kopylov, after a conflict with the adviser to the commander of Egyptian Air Defense, was instructed to return to the USSR before the [scheduled] end of his tour, but ultimately he was decorated with the [Order of] the Red Star.[12]

Whether or not the Soviets approved of Kopylov's exploit, they were well prepared for the Israeli response. Once the Shrike radar-homing missiles had arrived in Israel, after the ceasefire, IAF chief Hod proposed to use them immediately against the standstill-violating SAMs "once and for all, to show them we are not putting up with it"—but he was overruled again.[13] On the morrow of the Stratocruiser incident, the Shrikes were put to their first test—and failed. Again, Shazly took credit:

> We had devised electronic means of countering [the] Shrike and were quite keen to test them. On September 18 Israel did as we had expected. The aircraft launched their missiles from six miles east of the canal. Shrike only has a range of ten miles. The missiles fell hopelessly short.

But as early as January 1971, *Al-Ahram* had credited the Soviets for promising "state-of-the-art electronic equipment" to counter the newly supplied US missiles.[14]

General Gareev, the Soviet advisers' chief of staff, took pride for decades in foreseeing the Shrike's appearance and devising "a dialectic approach to the practical problem." After analyzing the missile's performance in Vietnam—data hardly available to the Egyptians—"and the initial combat actions along the canal," he "simply packed the area with radars and turned them all on," which confused the missiles' homing systems. Gareev claimed that of seventy-two Shrikes launched that day, only one struck a Soviet-made radar.[15] "Lt Aleksey Smirnov," a "radio-technical" expert who was on a routine maintenance visit to a radar installation at Abu Suweir, witnessed this hit and reported only minor damage, mainly to the P-35 station's concrete pedestal. His group spent hours collecting Shrike fragments for study.[16] Primakov told his Israeli interlocutors that there had been only one fatality and one injury among the "Arabs," and commended the Egyptians for not striking back.[17] *Al-Ahram* even claimed that one Shrike hit an *Israeli* position.[18]

Although the Egyptians gave no more credit to the Soviet advisers for countering the Shrikes than for downing the Stratocruiser, their announcements were more truthful than the Israelis' about both incidents. The IDF insisted on describing the plane as a cargo-laden transport, even after Egyptian statements identified it correctly and noted that its advanced equipment made it the IAF's most costly craft—at $4 million, twice the price of a Phantom.[19] There remained little security justification to hide this from the Israeli public. Frequent censorship and occasional falsification were intended to protect American support and Israeli morale, but ultimately contributed to Israeli complacency.

A week after the Shrikes' failure, Bar-Lev "acknowledged indirectly" that these missiles had been used, by confirming for the first time that Israel had them while declining comment on the specific incident. Israeli statements only refrained from the usual claim of accurate hits.[20] A later history of the IAF admits that the damage was "inconsequential" but gave what appears to be a more realistic figure of twelve Shrikes fired. The writer, a former IAF officer, deplores the force's failure to address the missile's weakness. The Shrike remained the basis for IAF strategy in the Yom Kippur War, and only after it again fell short of expectations did development begin of an ultimately successful improved model.[21]

FLEXING MUSCLES WHILE OFFERING A PULLBACK

Meeting Hod barely a month after the missiles' failure, US Air Tactical Command chief William Momyer felt the IAF commander still "was putting too much confidence in the kill capability of the Shrike." Hod was certain that "he can handle the SA-2s and 3s but not the 4s"—probably a misidentification of the SAM-6 systems that had already been deployed in Egypt. He believed that "a concentrated series of strikes could neutralize the SAM belt."[22] As late as May 1973, a senior IAF officer, Rafi Harlev, told Hod in a staff meeting that "we don't know exactly what the SAM-6 is, but it's not a problem."[23]

Some in the IDF command gave up entirely on countering the SAMs from the air (they were proved correct in October 1973). The *New York Times* reported only in August 1971 that several months earlier, Washington had declined Israel's request for Lance tactical missiles—which would become operational with US forces only in early 1972.[24] The IDF deputy chief of staff, Yisra'el Tal, testified after the Yom Kippur War that he had pressed to procure the Lance as the only effective weapon against the SAMs. When the Americans refused, he urged "with all my might" to develop a home-made "artillery rocket" with a 70 kilometer range, the *Ivry*, for this purpose (the weapon's name, which means "Hebrew," stressed its indigenous origin, though it was based on the heaviest Soviet *Katyusha*). But Dayan and others were opposed, funding was held up, and although the weapon was tested successfully, by the outbreak of war only eighteen were ready. Tal estimated that two Lances would suffice to take out a SAM *divizyon*. The equivalent number of *Ivrys* is sanitized, but was clearly larger, and thus the supply available was insignificant against the SAM belt. The rockets were posted only on the Syrian front and were never fired.[25] Unlike the Shrike, which Egypt overcame thanks to Soviet technical capability and intelligence work, this was one of many cases where the Egyptians had the upper hand thanks to Israel's overwhelming numerical inferiority, economic limitations and strategic errors, as well as US reservations.

In September 1971, the Soviets' double success had far-reaching implications: expectations of the "political consequences if a plane were shot down" again by the SAM's cross-canal reach led to discontinuation of IAF photoreconnaissance sorties even over the east bank. Angular photography from flights outside the missile range would prove inadequate for detecting Egyptian preparations in the run-up to the Yom Kippur War.[26] Still, reporting from Tel Aviv in the week of the double fiasco against Soviet technology, Joseph Alsop prophetically noted:

> One of the more bewildering features of the present Middle Eastern lull is the plain cockiness of the Israelis. ... The weight of metal the Soviets have given to Israel's enemies is downright astonishing. ... If the Israelis did not believe there was no longer any real threat of active Russian support for the Egyptians, it would, of course, be very different.

But even with Alsop's usual suspicion of Soviet intentions, he too misread them: "with the Russians known to be urging the Egyptians to prolong the cease fire, the Israelis are firmly convinced that ... Sadat does not have any reasonable military option."[27]

Arriving at Inshas airbase in November 1971 to take over as chief adviser to the local EAF brigade commander, Col. Petr Rubtsov found that the Egyptian pilots had gained enough confidence to challenge their instructors to mock dogfights—but not yet quite enough capability: one pilot lost control and crashed. They also needed instruction in night flying. The language problem was still acute: no interpreter could help when Rubtsov took off with Egyptian trainees, including a squadron leader, in a two-seater MiG-21 trainer. Unlike the higher officers, they had not picked up Russian during courses in the USSR. "We were unaccustomed to such a situation: two pilots flying a supersonic plane cannot speak with each other in air." He also had to put up with delays when the squadron leader, before takeoff, spread a rug on the tarmac and knelt to pray.[28]

B. "Yeah, yeah, yeah": Nixon receives the Soviet withdrawal offer

Against the backdrop of this new power play, and with the summit all but formalized, the Soviets made *their* response to Kissinger's "expulsion" challenge. Besides the almost identical formulation of the offers, coordination with Sadat is confirmed by the preceding flurry of Soviet–Egyptian contacts. On 19 September, two days after Vinogradov met Sadat to discuss "Egypt's military position," the former, longtime Egyptian ambassador to the USSR (1961–71) Murad Ghaleb was promoted to minister of state for foreign affairs "as an explicit gesture of goodwill toward the Soviet Union."[29] On 21 September, Egypt's deputy defense minister, General Abdel Kader Hassan, arrived in Moscow.[30]

The agreed gambit, as shown by the ensuing developments, was again to offer what the Soviets intended to do anyway as a concession, for which the United States should have to reciprocate. The demanded quid pro quo would be to press the Israelis into a withdrawal from the canal as part of an interim agreement as envisaged by Egypt—that is, with a prior commitment to relinquish all of Sinai in a comprehensive settlement. There was, however, no expectation actually to achieve this outcome. Rather, the Americans' expected failure to deliver—as Kissinger had indicated—would let them be saddled with responsibility for a new war.

This time, Rogers was bypassed entirely. According to Kissinger's memoirs, on 20 September 1971 Dobrynin "forewarned" him for the first time about Gromyko's intent, in an imminent visit to the White House, to "propose putting the Mideast issue into the special channel." This of course had been proposed long before, and the difference now was mainly Kissinger's readiness to fill the vacuum in detailed negotiation that was created by Rogers's failure.[31] Gromyko came from the United Nations General Assembly in New York, where in a dinner with Rogers on the 24th the Middle East was hardly mentioned.[32] It did come up in an after-dinner *tête-à-tête*, and

FLEXING MUSCLES WHILE OFFERING A PULLBACK

Gromyko reported repeatedly mentioning "withdrawal"—but only of *Israeli* forces from all Egyptian (and Jordanian) soil as a key Soviet demand.³³

On the same day (24 September), the Politburo approved another meeting with Israeli officials in Europe, and entrusted it to the KGB. As Primakov was again the emissary, this removes any remaining doubt as to his subordination to the agency. According to his memoir, his instructions from the Politburo were to stress that Soviet influence had moderated the Arab position. Yet he was not to engage in propaganda.³⁴ Meanwhile, the Foxbat flights continued; but the next day, the IDF spokesman still denied a *Ma'ariv* report that Soviet-piloted "MiG-23s" were flying over Israel proper.³⁵

In a briefing that Kissinger prepared for Nixon before Gromyko's visit, not much of substance was predicted—except for Dobrynin's "foreshadowing" a shift of Middle East discussion to the back channel. Kissinger of course supported this, as "the State Department's negotiations ... have led Sadat to expect more than we can deliver from Israel."³⁶

The formal talk in the Oval Office (with Rogers present) was essentially a replay of Gromyko's discussion with the secretary himself. But afterward, in a "private chat" that was recorded by Nixon's taping device, Gromyko sprang his surprise. When the president stated that "the main thing" at the Moscow summit would be "to have some things that we can make progress on," Gromyko cited a discussion he had with Brezhnev before leaving for the States—that is, his instructions. In respect of the Middle East, this referred clearly to Kissinger's "indiscretion":

> *Gromyko*: ... Some time ago you expressed interest of, I don't know, Egypt, about our presence there—our military presence.
>
> *Nixon*: Yeah, yeah, yeah.
>
> *Gromyko*: ... In connection with understanding, full understanding on the Middle East, we are ready to agree not to have our military units there. ... We would leave a limited number of advisors for purely advisory purposes.

So Gromyko offered, almost in Sadat's very words, what eventually occurred: the advisers were to remain, while the presence of integral Soviet units was to be ended. His hesitation ("I don't know ...") in specifying Soviet "personnel" and "military units" was not coincidental: admitting the regulars' presence contradicted all previous Soviet statements. But in return he again stipulated the prior acceptance of the Arabs' major demands for a comprehensive settlement: "*some kind of paperwork ... which would provide [for] withdrawal of Israeli forces from all of the occupied territories.*"³⁷

The 1979 installment of Kissinger's memoirs confirmed that Gromyko "indicated a new approach to the Middle East; the Soviet Union would be prepared to withdraw its combat forces from Egypt in case of a final settlement (discussed more fully in

Chapter XXX)." Kissinger claims that he ignored this proposal when he met Gromyko for a follow-up talk on 30 September, and that he demurred at declaring the outlines of such a settlement at least until after the November 1972 elections, as this would inevitably outrage Israel and its US supporters.[38]

Kissinger's contemporary report from this talk shows, however, that he did "check with Gromyko whether the President had understood him correctly ... [that] the Soviet Union would withdraw all organized military forces from the Middle East ... as part of an interim settlement." Although this was more than the Soviet minister actually offered (withdrawal from *Egypt*), "Gromyko said correct—provided that the interim settlement contained provisions for ... a final settlement." And contrary to his memoirs, Kissinger did agree to continue discussing this deal, with the "aim to have the interim agreement by May," the target date for the summit. He only stipulated repeatedly that the Middle Eastern parties should not be informed—meaning mainly the Israelis, as

> this would produce an enormous outcry. ... Pro-Israeli groups control the US media to a significant extent, it would be difficult for the President to agree to measures that would seriously displease those groups during the election period. ... Once the election is over ... Nixon will be able to implement a solution ... without paying a great deal of attention to Jewish circles.

Gromyko's response (as Kissinger reported it), is in retrospect little short of comical: "The withdrawal of our air forces and other organized units will not be happily greeted by our allies," but Brezhnev, despite "some hesitation," was acting out of "global considerations." Sadat was about to visit Moscow again, and Gromyko asked Kissinger whether there was some possibility of both superpowers informing their respective allies, in strict confidence. "I said ... the Egyptians were incapable of keeping a confidence. Gromyko laughed and said this was generally true, but in this case it was to their interest to keep it, since if the agreement that might be reached at the summit should leak, it would be aborted."

Kissinger's report does not indicate that he explicitly ruled out telling Sadat. His only response was: "the more it [the agreement] was acceptable to Israel, the less concern one had to have about secrecy." Gromyko reported only "the intention is to talk to the top leaders of Egypt and Israel at some stage ... but for the time being not to inform them."[39] "At some stage" would be interpreted quite differently on both sides.

None of this appeared in Kissinger's memoirs, and they add little more on the matter for over 400 "numbingly long and stupefyingly detailed" pages covering eight months, including the preparations for the Moscow summit in May 1972 and the conference itself.[40] It was to be recorded, and credited to Kissinger, as the historic apotheosis of détente. From September 1971 through July 1972, the memoirs consistently downplay the importance of the Soviet withdrawal issue in the back-channel talks, as well as Kissinger's actual readiness to bargain over it, and the Middle East in general.⁴¹ Only when the events of July 1972 are recounted in Chapter XXX does Kissinger state (truthfully enough) that he balked at the demand to *openly declare* the outlines of the final settlement, at least until after the US presidential election.⁴²

But the chapter is entitled "Sadat *Expels* the Soviets," even though Kissinger was obviously aware that this was at best an exaggeration.⁴³ And the Dobrynin/Kissinger reports show that the Soviet withdrawal offer *did* remain under intense discussion throughout the preparations for the summit. Moreover, the American side in effect acknowledged the Soviet contention that Nixon and Gromyko had reached an understanding on the withdrawal offer and its conditions, and the Soviets constantly urged the Americans to deliver their side of the deal—which they knew Nixon and Kissinger would not or could not do.

C. Another round of threats from Primakov

Gromyko's report on his White House talks on 29 September was designated for circulation down to candidate members of the Politburo. In a paper for wider dissemination, the foreign minister stated only that Nixon "specifically had in mind what the US side had said regarding the presence of Soviet military personnel in Egypt," making it look as if Nixon raised the issue, and omitting Gromyko's own initiative.⁴⁴ So Primakov, arriving for his talks with the Israelis in Vienna on 8 October, was apparently not privy to the withdrawal offer, as indicated also by his flat rejection of any demand to relinquish Soviet "positions" in Egypt. Meeting Baron and an official from the Prime Minister's Office, Mordechai Gazit, Primakov again took elaborate precautions to ensure secrecy, such as demanding to move into another room from the one that was booked by the Israelis, and to turn on a radio.

Either Primakov's initially moderate instructions were altered after US receptiveness to Gromyko's proposal reduced the urgency of rapprochement with Israel—or he simply ignored them. According to Israeli minutes, Primakov actually resorted to almost-naked intimidation, using nearly the exact language that Brezhnev would use the next July: "It is a secret to no one that we do not wish to be involved and we want to avoid such a necessity. [But] it is entirely clear that ... such a situation may develop in which we cannot stand by." Repeating the charge that "we supplied Egypt with the air defense system only after your depth bombings," he alluded to continuing "Arab pressure for more procurement, especially offensive aircraft." Again referring to NATO, despite Dayan's clarification, he told the Israelis: "you are part of the military array of a country that—by its own definition—is in a state of war with us. ... Whatever your intentions may be, the results of your policy (and policy means deeds) are undoubtedly detrimental for us."

Primakov harked back to Meir's unguarded statement and responded with a counterthreat that hardly seems to refer to a merely theoretical conflict: "If such statements are repeated, ... to the effect that 'Israel wants peace but we'll shoot down any plane,' that is not a serious approach. You know that the balance of power between us is not equal. Better to not let such things develop, rather than to make threats." Primakov stressed that there was zero chance of a US–USSR confrontation over the Middle East, which Gazit understood as meaning the Americans would not respond even if Soviets did get involved in fighting. Gazit retorted, and reiterated the next day, "we will defend ourselves when attacked by Egypt, and clearly it will be hard to distinguish between [Soviet] forces and those of Egypt."

An opportunity to demonstrate Soviet influence on Egyptian policy arose when the Israelis brought up the plight of their POWs in Egypt and requested the release of four wounded prisoners, especially the seriously injured pilot Eyal Ahiqar. Primakov received a detailed list and promised to check it out. He relates that when Sadat was informed of the Vienna talks, this was included; Ahiqar was exchanged on 15 December.[45]

But with this exception, the talks again adjourned inconclusively—just before the IDF disclosed that on 10 October a Foxbat explicitly described as *Soviet* had come within 30 kilometers of Ashqelon, Israel's southernmost city on the Mediterranean coast. Israeli military correspondents were told that "IAF planes were unable to make contact"—that is, they failed to overtake the intruder. The matter was grave enough to top the cabinet's agenda.[46]

This coincided with the long-delayed public announcement that the summit would take place in May—and also with Sadat's arrival in Moscow on 11 October. Foreign Minister Riad noted Brezhnev's interest in the details of Egypt's contacts in Washington and his advice "to cultivate the American connection."[47] According to Shazly, even though the Soviet advisers had argued that Egyptian demands for weapons were excessive, and not all were met when "President Sadat and General Sadiq flew to Moscow," they nevertheless "concluded our biggest arms deal so far with the Soviet Union"—enough in Shazly's view to enable the Minarets plan if not a deeper incursion into Sinai.[48]

Ashraf Marwan provided the Mossad in record time with a transcript of the talks, which indicated only a partial acceptance of Egyptian demands. As he reported, Egypt's Tu-16s were now authorized to fire their Kelt missiles without prior consultation with the Soviets, and discussions were to continue about the supply of Scud tactical ballistic missiles. But in marked contrast with Brezhnev's recorded performance in talks with US leaders, Marwan depicted him as woefully uninformed on the basics (not knowing, for instance, where the Sinai passes were). The Soviet military specialists were even more incredibly described as ignorant of the Egyptians' existing Soviet-supplied armament (they supposedly believed the most advanced tanks to be T-34s).[49]

These Soviet-related clues may have been among those that initially aroused the suspicion of Lt-Gen. David "Dado" Elazar when, presumably, he was first informed about Marwan upon taking over as IDF chief of staff in January 1972:

FLEXING MUSCLES WHILE OFFERING A PULLBACK

About [sanitized] I had a period of hesitation. For months I suspected that he was double, and I had discussions about this with [sanitized; presumably Mossad chief Zamir]. Many times I had the sense that his report was almost a message. I was very, very skeptical and cast a lot of doubt on the credibility of [sanitized].

But over time, Elazar told the Agranat Commission, "his credibility grew when we began to receive [sanitized]. ... I never had absolute confidence, but I began to rely upon him very, very seriously."

Marwan became trusted as "a good source for warning within a range of days" before any Egyptian action. Indeed, he became the only intelligence source whose raw reports were always shown to the chief of staff.[50] Achieving such status was a major success in itself for Marwan as a double agent. In September–October 1973, this exclusive Israeli reliance backfired when warnings from other sources were disregarded until Marwan confirmed them—too late for an effective response.

While the Egyptian delegation was in Moscow, on 12 October 1971, the Israeli cabinet formally rejected the latest version of the Rogers Plan. Israel, then, was not about to volunteer the cover for a withdrawal of the Soviet forces, and it would have to be obtained by the Americans—that is, Kissinger. Primakov states that he had a final talk with the Israelis in Vienna on 15 October, when they in effect rejected the Soviet proposals too, though they had taken the extraordinary step of conducting business on Saturday. But it took another three weeks for the Israeli delegates to write Primakov, "we reported to the leaders whom you met here [in Israel] that our talks were useful; even though disagreement remains, it was important to learn each other's thinking." They suggested keeping up periodic exchanges. Andropov and Gromyko proposed only on 3 December, and the Central Committee approved with Brezhnev's knowledge, that Primakov be instructed to reply no more than "I too reported. The assessment here is analogous to yours"—with no provision for a follow-up. There things stood for nearly four months.[51]

On 27 October, meeting Tactical Air Command (TAC) Commander Momyer, Hod was adamant:

> Israel will never agree to the terms of negotiation set forth by the US. Israel's position is clear and unequivocal, as stated by Golda Meir. In the judgment of most of the military, war is only a matter of time and he is proceeding on that assumption. ... I asked if war broke out what would be the role of the Soviets. He said the Russians will try to hold their fighters in the Delta and along the coast, letting the Egyptians do the fighting over the canal and the Sinai. However, if the IAF penetrated the Delta, Cairo and Mediterranean bases or Soviet bases, the Soviet fighters would open up the entire area to combat.[52]

D. *A Foxbat over Tel Aviv while Sadat is "rebuffed" in Moscow*

By late October 1971, Israeli spokesmen were treating MiG-25 flights over Israel as an established fact, even though it had not been officially confirmed. Leaving for the

UN General Assembly on the 20th, Eban complained that this development was not getting adequate attention in the United States, where "a struggle still continues" for Israel to get more F-4s.[53] Meanwhile, the IAF was attempting to make do with what it had: Hod disclosed to Momyer a new stratagem that was being devised. It was just what Bezhevets, the Foxbat commander, had feared: coming at the MiG-25 head-on when it doubled back toward Egypt. As Momyer reported it:

> One F-4 attempts a head-on zoom pass, realizing it can't get up to the Foxbat, but tactic is designed to encourage Foxbat to make a turn to evade AIM-4 missile. If Foxbat turns, Hod claims it will loose [sic] five to ten thousand feet and three or four hundred knots. This would then give one of the F-4s best position to launch a zoom climb attack on advantage. [I] questioned the loss in performance of the Foxbat ... I suspect instructions to Soviet Foxbats are "to keep up the speed and altitude until over water or friendly land since nothing can get up to your altitude."[54]

Some of this apparently leaked, as there was soon discussion in the Israeli media of missiles that might allow IAF Phantoms to hit a Foxbat even from lower altitude.[55] But within a few days, on 6 November, the IAF still was unable to challenge a flight by two Foxbats down the middle of Sinai. This time, the IDF issued an official communiqué about the incursion. Again, it was considered important enough to discuss in cabinet the next day, "as the planes might have gathered much information on the IDF's disposition."[56] Renewed supply of Phantoms was still not forthcoming, and the Israelis resentfully stressed that the Foxbats' impunity posed a challenge to US technology as well as marking an escalation of the Soviets' regional role. In Congress, demands intensified to restore the military balance, which had been tipped by the Foxbats' appearance.[57] By 2 January 1972, a month after this item led a "shopping list" that Meir presented in Washington, Nixon confirmed in a television interview reports that eighteen more F-4s would be supplied, but as yet with no timetable.

On 17 January, Brezhnev reminded Nixon: "as before, we are prepared in real earnest to find concrete solutions on the basis of the principles set forth in that conversation [with Gromyko]. ... It is desirable to act without delay."[58] Four days later, Dobrynin reported that Kissinger "confirmed their readiness to try and prepare ... for the meeting in Moscow" the US thoughts on both the interim and the permanent settlement "in the spirit of what Nixon and A.A. Gromyko discussed."[59] Kissinger, on the other hand, reported to Nixon that he told Dobrynin in the same talk (which went on for four hours "in an atmosphere of effusive cordiality, buttressed by slugs of vodka and cans of caviar") that it had been impossible to continue discussing the Soviet proposal "without talking with the Israelis at least in general terms, because their intelligence was so good." Kissinger said he and Nixon had finally obtained from Meir "some concrete proposals" that permitted continuing discussion of an interim settlement, with a "good possibility" of concluding it at the summit if both sides took no military action. Dobrynin agreed and said Soviet influence was being applied in

FLEXING MUSCLES WHILE OFFERING A PULLBACK

that direction. He also said Moscow understood that the question of the permanent solution could not be broached with the Israelis before "well into 1973," that is, after the US election.[60]

A few days later, after student demonstrations in Cairo protested his supposed peace feelers, Sadat pointed to the renewed Phantom sales as one reason why the "inevitable" war with Israel would have to be postponed. But he promised to fly to Moscow again with his own shopping list for arms—and notified Sisco that Egypt was breaking off talks with the United States. It was at this stage, in late January 1972—recalls Abramov, the *Kavkaz* staff officer—that Bezhevets was tasked with photographing military targets inside Israel. He had done so once already, but this time he was to pass directly over the "capital" and IDF headquarters, Tel Aviv. Defense Minister Grechko's strictures had by this time apparently been relaxed, in view of the Foxbats' proven invulnerability. Still, this was considered a complex and risky operation, as the Soviets were uncertain whether the Israelis had received the Nike system. Preparations for the flight involved the entire *Kavkaz* staff.

As these preparations progressed, on 28 January, Dobrynin pressed Kissinger again for an answer, and reported that the latter complained the Americans "were encountering much greater difficulties than in the talks about West Berlin"—a situation that he blamed on Israel. Kissinger now claimed (according to Dobrynin), contrary to his statement a week before, that in their talks with Meir he and the president had "let her understand clearly that [at the Moscow summit] the Middle East question would be discussed ... regardless if Israel shares its thoughts or not."

By contrast, Kissinger's report to Nixon emphasizes Dobrynin's anxieties about the parallel efforts of the State Department:

> He was horrified by Sisco['s] ... compulsive tendency to talk ... There was also the danger that Sisco would complicate their problems with the Egyptians because the Soviets could not put forward a position that was softer ... Wasn't there some possibility that I could simply order Sisco to stop?

Dobrynin himself mentioned nothing like this in his report, relating only that Kissinger had assured him "Sisco (and Rogers) are unaware" of the back-channel exchanges. Kissinger thus appears to have exaggerated Soviet objections to State Department involvement in order to press Nixon for a monopoly, on the grounds that it would facilitate progress toward the summit.

It was also in the 28 January talk, with another visit by Sadat to Moscow approaching, that Kissinger finally agreed that the Soviets might inform the Egyptian president about "the idea that was discussed with Gromyko." According to Dobrynin, Kissinger's only proviso was that Washington be advised of such coordination. Kissinger reported that he left it up to Gromyko how much to tell Sadat, but warned against disclosing "substantive details."[61]

THE SOVIET–ISRAELI WAR, 1967–1973

Bezhevets's daring flight took place on 3 February—the day after Sadat arrived in Moscow for a visit that Heikal described as "one of the most important and delicate in the history of Arab–Soviet relations," after a public exchange of recriminations about the Soviets' purportedly lukewarm support for Egypt's war plans.[62] After it ended, Victor Louis was fielded again to spread word that "Russia is now evidently anxious to avert war in the Middle East," whereas China "is fomenting it in order to disturb President Nixon's visit." This was interpreted in "diplomatic quarters" in London to the effect that "Moscow has all but vetoed a major Egyptian military operation against Israel."[63]

The setting was thus similar to that of the Foxbat flight over Dimona on 26 May 1967, while Egyptian Defense Minister Badran was locked in negotiations in Moscow over whether Egypt should be cleared to attack Israel *first*, or should wait for an Israeli strike as the Soviets demanded. As it did then, an ostentatious overflight of the Israeli heartland again served as a gesture to prove Soviet support. It came a few weeks after the IAF magazine published a report belittling the Foxbat's performance and suggesting that even Mirages, never mind Phantoms, could overcome it—evidently based on the plans Hod had revealed to Momyer.[64]

Bezhevets, covered as usual with a dense formation of MiG-21s on takeoff, approached from the sea to within 29 kilometers of downtown Tel Aviv and then crossed Sinai unhindered, "upending all the Israeli defensive array." As always, two copies of his films were made, one for the Egyptians and one for immediate dispatch to the Soviet General Staff. "His photos showed every house. The Egyptians pointed out Prime Minister Meir's. The flight took only 50 minutes but made a lot of noise." Abramov writes that Bar-Lev was sacked as IDF chief of staff "for not having assured air defense of the capital. But what could he have done?"[65]

This claim is spurious, but the description of concern within the Israeli military was accurate enough: this time nothing about the flight was released in Israel or reported anywhere.[66] Since the US decision to supply more Phantoms had already been announced (and denounced by *Pravda*), decrying the Soviets' advantage in the air was no longer necessary for putting pressure on Washington, and the effect on domestic morale evidently was now the Israelis' overriding consideration for the news blackout.[67] So the reports about Sadat's disappointment in Moscow were not challenged by news of the continuing Soviet support for his war preparations.

22

JOCKEYING AND POSTURING

A. Kissinger and Dobrynin both give away some secrets

On 1 March 1972, Kissinger reported that Dobrynin again complained about US procrastination on the attractive deal that Moscow had offered: to trade the Soviet presence in Egypt for Israel's withdrawal to the 1967 borders. Kissinger claimed to have corrected him that the proposed US part of the deal was to promote a final settlement, not to delineate specific borders.[1] But this came to light only with the publication of the back-channel reports. In Kissinger's memoirs, the only talk in which the Middle East was discussed at all took place on *17* March 1972 (partly in Nixon's presence, so it hardly could be concealed). As for its substance, the memoirs claim that it was only at this stage that

> Dobrynin sought to engage me in a dialogue designed, in effect, to impose the extreme Arab program. This did not fit into our strategy as long as Soviet troops and advisers were so prominent in Egypt and as long as the Soviet Union was supporting the radical Arabs. When I countered with proposals related to Israel's security concerns, he quickly lost interest.[2]

Kissinger's own newly released summary of the 17 March talk is clearly at odds with this description, and Dobrynin's report is even more so:

> Underlying all of Kissinger's comments ... was the apprehension that the top-secret talks they are conducting with us about expediting a Middle East settlement, i.e., about the future status of Israel itself, could be made public in the US, especially at a time of heightened emotions during the election campaign. ... The "crazy fanatics" from the Jewish Defense League would accuse him of "betraying Jews" and might then even make an attempt on his, Kissinger's, life.

Dobrynin added another uncharitable appraisal of his back-channel partner who, "it must be said, is not notable for great personal courage." But for the Soviet ambassador, the most startling part of the exchange was when Kissinger—retreating from his previous reluctant agreement that Sadat be at least partially informed—seemed to give away a vital Israeli intelligence asset:

255

THE SOVIET–ISRAELI WAR, 1967–1973

Kissinger remarked ... with noticeable hesitation, that Israeli intelligence "has very good sources of information in the highest circles of the Egyptian government." If Sadat finds out ... from the Soviet side, he might share this information "with a certain circle of individuals, from where it could go further, to Israel" ... This is the first time Kissinger has mentioned Israeli agents in direct proximity to Sadat. It is hard for us to judge the reliability of this information here (it could also be some kind of disinformation), but we think it necessary to point out this remark.³

So it is rather rich that Kissinger's memoirs claim he stood up at this meeting for Israel's security interests. He was almost certainly referring to Ashraf Marwan, who by now had been passing information or disinformation to the Mossad for over two years. During her talks in Washington in early December, Meir had presented Nixon and Kissinger with the transcript of the Brezhnev–Sadat talks in October that Marwan had provided. Mossad chief had given another copy to CIA Director Helms, whose experts confirmed (or fell for) its authenticity. Congratulating Zamir on this achievement, Meir considered that sharing it helped move Nixon toward resuming Phantom sales. According to Israeli informants quoted by Bar-Joseph, the document's source was not named to the Americans, but it could only be a member of Sadat's entourage.⁴

Presumably, Dobrynin had not been informed previously about Marwan's activity; the "Center" in Moscow almost certainly was—but even if the Soviets relayed Kissinger's tip to Egypt it only confirmed Marwan's success. In any event, his continuing role in the crucial events of 1972 and '73 shows that he was not compromised by Kissinger's disclosure—another clue that Marwan's services for the Israelis were staged by Egypt. In March 1973, an expert visitor to Egypt still listed "Mirwan" first among "three men reportedly closest to Sadat."⁵

B. The SAM-3s' handover begins

In the meantime, the very discussion of an agreed withdrawal was kept *so* secret—or the disinformation campaign in Cairo, which would go into high gear after the deal's implementation, was launched so early—that even the CIA was taken in. A secret intelligence memorandum ten days after the Kissinger–Dobrynin talk still described "frictions" in Soviet–Egyptian relations, which "spawn recurrent reports that some or all Soviet personnel will be *expelled* from Egypt."⁶

There were indeed some frictions, and after Sadat's ultimate break with Moscow these could be interpreted retrospectively as omens. Vladimir Ivanov, then in charge of manpower on chief military adviser Okunev's staff, wrote a strongly anti-Egyptian memoir in 2001. In "early 1972," Ivanov claims, the Egyptians' command issued "order no. 200" proclaiming high alert in preparation for a cross-canal offensive. "Okunev, in my presence, discussed this with the EAF's commander ... and its chief-of-staff Mubarak" and stipulated that pilots should be confined to bases to ensure

JOCKEYING AND POSTURING

secrecy. "The Egyptians responded that this could not be maintained for more than 72 hours. Okunev was visibly dismayed, and the same was true in other Egyptian services. They listened to our advice but did as they pleased."

Ivanov sensed a "provocation" at an even higher level when Grechko stopped over in Cairo on 18 February 1972, on his way back from Somalia (where the Soviets were developing naval facilities despite the supposed disadvantage of the closed canal). The Soviet minister's plane was kept in a holding pattern for thirty to forty minutes, on the pretext that a formation of helicopters returning from a *desant* (landing) exercise in the desert was about to land. A large, high-level welcoming party was kept sweltering on the tarmac, "humiliated and uncomfortable. The minister himself was annoyed to the very limit of his forbearance." Speaking before the adviser *apparat* in Cairo, Grechko was so moody that a flustered Ambassador Vinogradov forgot to offer him tea.[7] However, when the defense minister visited a SAM-3 *divizyon* protecting the Helwan works, he was in high enough spirits to promise officers who completed a year in Egypt a ten-day furlough in Moscow—indicating that they would return to continue their service.[8] He went on to "tour the front line," and Sadat—at an ASU congress that was reportedly called to emphasize Grechko's visit as a token of Moscow's support—warned against "questioning Egyptian–Soviet friendship."[9]

Other frictions were caused by Egypt's reluctance, as in Nasser's day, to permit Soviet ideological indoctrination. Defense Minister Sadiq had already issued a sweeping ban on Egyptian military personnel of all ranks "to converse on political and religious subjects with the advisers and experts. ... Conversations should be limited to matters of instruction, or religious subjects pertaining to work."[10] Sadat's gestures toward the Americans were accompanied by a further warning to field units from the War Ministry to beware the advisers' "repeated attempts" to screen Soviet films, "military and civilian," for the Egyptian troops. Also, in what may have been a sincere effort to overcome the language barrier and shortage of interpreters, the Soviets were "proposing to reinforce the units with Russian-language teachers from the Soviet Cultural Center." Both initiatives were blocked.[11]

Not all the problems were ideological: on 8 May 1972, a major scandal erupted when Soviet servicemen who had invested their earnings in gold jewelry—a common practice, according to many veterans' memoirs—were detained while trying to take it onto a flight home. This was not illegal, as the Soviets protested, and ultimately they were allowed to export these "presents for their wives or girlfriends." Still, as the *politruk* Khandanyan recalled, "this left a bitter aftertaste and we stopped shopping for gold."[12] But it was only CIA ignorance of Kissinger's moves, and the agency's susceptibility to Egyptian spin, that led the agency to consider these "frictions" as leading to an imminent "expulsion," and Langley would soon resent being kept in the dark.

On the other hand, Kissinger's anxiety that the Israelis might get wind of the actual deal under discussion appears to have had some basis. Whetten, writing in 1973, mentions that "as early as March 1972, reports were circulating in Israel of an alleged collu-

257

sion whereby the Soviets agreed to accept a limited withdrawal ... in exchange for the resurrection ... of the Third Rogers Plan."[13] This may have been confirmed when the Soviets "left unanswered" an Israeli proposal at the end of March to renew the "useful" talks with Primakov.[14] At the same time—27 March—Kissinger discussed on the telephone with the president how to proceed in the back channel: "*K*: ... get it done before the election and brutalize them [the Israelis?] after the election. *P*: that secret deal still concerns me. ... *K*: we have got to get the Soviets out of the Middle East."[15] But meeting Dobrynin on 12 April 1972, Kissinger "temporized" on the Middle East and neither of them referred to it in their reports from a week of intensive discussions before Kissinger left secretly for the summit's "dress rehearsal" in Moscow.[16]

The transfer of SAM-3s and other Soviet-operated systems to Egyptian crews was well in progress before the summit, though it was running into some snags. Lt Presnukhin, whose missile unit was posted to Nag Hammadi in November 1971, lists among its main tasks imparting maintenance knowhow to the "Arab contingent"— who, he recalls, were not particularly enthusiastic or capable, and "frankly, they were ruining our equipment."[17] Air Force Maj.-Gen. Aleksandr Vagin, who had recently ended his service as second-in-command of a Soviet Air Force corps in East Germany, was dispatched "toward the end of 1971" to Egypt as chief adviser to EAF Chief of Staff Mubarak, initially for a two-year hitch. His main task was overseeing group and individual training of Egyptian pilots "to prepare the Egyptian Air Force for repulsing an Israeli attack." He recalled thirty years later that he was less than entirely satisfied with the results, blaming both the Egyptians' capability and their motivation.[18]

A recently published Russian account relates that on 13 April 1972, Grechko received a coded message from Okunev that a recalibration of the SAM-3 systems by a party of over 100 Soviet technicians had resulted in a complete disabling of Egypt's air defense array. "Several test launches failed, as the guidance center lost control of the missile in flight."

"An Il-18 left ... Moscow with a group of military and civilian experts," led by the deputy chief designer Yevgeny Nikiforov:

> The stakes were too high in the geopolitical game—the state's reputation and the honor of its factories had to be protected. Since their dispatch had been decided urgently, all the participants were issued passports but without visas. ... This fact would turn out to be a cruel joke at their expense.

At Cairo-West, the select team "quickly discovered that ... their colleagues had not recalibrated the [SAMs' radar] stations, because the agreement had somehow omitted this. Also, the Arabs were of the opinion that periodic maintenance was uncalled for," and even neglected to replace burnt-out indicator lightbulbs. After two weeks of corrections by Nikiforov and his team,

> special tents, armchairs and drinks were set up at Cairo-West for a big gathering of Okunev, air defense commander Fahmy, and the ranking officers and advisers. An Il-28 dropped a

JOCKEYING AND POSTURING

target and the *divizyon* fired a missile. It received its signal, but for some reason the target was missed by 200m—another debacle.

The humiliated Okunev blamed the designer, who protested that the missile must have been defective. "Another Il-28 was about to drop a target. Nikiforov was sure that Okunev would not permit another launch. ... So Nikiforov ordered a launch on his own authority, and the Arabs fired a missile at the parachuting target. This time they didn't miss." Altogether, by 10 May Nikiforov replaced bulbs and carried out successful test launches at six *divizyons*. After a two-hour briefing for Egyptian officers "to remedy their ignorance," a lavish banquet was held. But another delegation arrived from Moscow, led by a deputy minister for the aviation industry, Mikhail Il'in, to check the entire Egyptian SAM arsenal. It too found "many missiles were disabled due to dust and debris as a result of Egyptian negligence." A new agreement was signed for a further two months of upgrades, inspection, and training of Egyptian technicians, to prepare for the systems' scheduled handover.[19]

C. Kissinger and Sadat in Moscow as the summit looms

On 19 April, Kissinger did not even include the Middle East in a memorandum for Nixon on "issues for my Moscow trip."[20] Dobrynin too estimated before Kissinger's departure that the latter would "put his main emphasis on Vietnam," the crucial issue for Nixon's reelection. But in return for Soviet "understanding" on that front, the Americans might "somehow facilitate resolution or progress" on "issues primarily of interest to the Soviet Union," including "to some extent, the Middle East." Kissinger (Dobrynin estimated) was empowered to continue discussion "in the spirit of the understanding reached" with Foreign Minister Gromyko, but would probably resort to generalities such as "principles of conduct" for the superpowers. However, Kissinger had said that considering the "'particular sensitivity' of ... a Middle East settlement, he intends to discuss this alone [with the Soviet foreign minister], without any aides present," and asked that he be notified in advance, or taken aside, if the Soviets intended to bring it up.[21]

Describing his secret talks in Moscow on 20–4 April 1972, Kissinger's memoirs again belittle the "inconclusive discussion of the Middle East," blaming Gromyko

> who sought to commit me to some general principles. Rather than turn him down flatly, I replied soothingly with comments long on goodwill, sparse on specifics. ... My objectives here were modest: [in order] to gain time and ... an incentive for Soviet restraint, I suggested that a detailed discussion be deferred to the summit.[22]

But the transcript of Kissinger's conversation with Gromyko shows up the American's memory as highly selective, and confirms that the Soviet withdrawal offer remained under intense discussion.

259

THE SOVIET–ISRAELI WAR, 1967–1973

Dr Kissinger: What level of forces do you envisage for yourselves?

Gromyko: We will leave behind only a certain quantity of advisers and military specialists. All the rest will be withdrawn ...

Dr Kissinger: What number?

Gromyko: That is something we will tell you later, but ... I think you will applaud us when we tell you, and perhaps tell us to leave some more!

Dr Kissinger: I would not bet on the last.

The Soviets still demanded formulating "general principles" as a condition for their proposed withdrawal, but Gromyko, in a significant concession evidently prompted by the progress in handing over the SAM array, was now willing to settle for agreement even on *part* of the "principles"—the part that "maybe can be made public" before the US election. However, Kissinger's reluctance to frame the comprehensive settlement still precluded a compromise and endangered the entire détente package:

Dr Kissinger: ... The Mideast is the big unsolved problem.

Gromyko: [in English] Big, big, twice big. I tell you frankly, if it is not solved, it may poison the atmosphere ... at the summit.[23]

Sadat arrived in Moscow unannounced on 27 April—two days after Kissinger's secret visit was unveiled.[24] As recounted by Vinogradov, "he said that he wanted to make a secret visit ... To disguise himself, Sadat dressed in an old coat and soft hat! In Moscow, without any official ceremony, we went directly to the Politburo."[25] Although the secrecy was soon lifted and the visit reported on Radio Moscow, few Western reports, and none in the US press, noted that Sadat's delegation included Mubarak, who had just replaced Baghdady as EAF chief. He was met by Soviet Air Force Chief Marshal Kutakhov, and "air procurement" was listed among the visit's purposes.[26]

Several contemporary accounts of this visit vary from the now-conventional version, whereby Sadat was flatly denied the weaponry and support that he desired in order to attack Israel. Laqueur states cryptically: "in Moscow Sadat met twice with Brezhnev and received Soviet approval to go to war—if he really wanted to."[27] A lower-echelon member of Sadat's entourage related that he "asked for medium- and long-range bombers, offensive weapons and better tanks. The Soviets didn't think we were serious about going to war. Sadat insisted, 'I'm going to war.' They still didn't believe him."[28]

D. A military display for Grechko in Egypt

Grechko's presence at the talks with Sadat indicates that he had by now accepted the withdrawal idea. A "sensitive intercept" by US intelligence confirmed this on the eve of the summit: Brezhnev had fielded "his cronies and ... his friend Grechko to justify

260

his military policies" at a Central Committee plenum where the general secretary "maneuvered successfully to overcome" any opposition.²⁹ Based on unattributed records of the Sadat–Brezhnev–Grechko talks, Kimche holds that their purpose was "to complete arrangements … to 'expel' about half the Russian personnel," as "Brezhnev was particularly interested that nothing should interfere with the policy of Détente which he intended to finalize at a summit meeting."³⁰ At the time, analysts noted the first explicit, if "guarded," Soviet acknowledgment—in the joint communiqué—of the Arabs' right to use "other" than peaceful means to liberate the lands held by Israel.³¹ This was supposedly balanced by a new Soviet demand that arms shipments be paid for in hard currency, but a solution for the financial problem was already in the works as part of the "expulsion" exercise.

This corresponds with Heikal's version that Sadat and Brezhnev had "much negotiation" over an Egyptian demand (and supposed Soviet reluctance) to turn over the SAM-3 batteries to Egyptian crews that had already returned from training in the USSR—exactly what the Soviets, as already seen, were more than ready to do and had in fact begun.

A few days after Sadat's return, Defense Minister Sadiq issued a directive imposing strict and intricate procedures on visits by the Soviet "experts and advisers" to field units. Such visits now had to be requested by the "senior Soviet adviser," and transport had to be arranged, nine days in advance. The guests had to be escorted throughout, and a report about their visit submitted after its conclusion. These provisions could hardly apply to the field units' resident advisers. The order's language clarifies that it represented a tightening of supervision over the top, Cairo-based Soviet officers' activities—or a deliberate move to create such an impression.³²

This and other alleged disagreements were "papered over" during a "friendly visit" by Grechko, Navy Commander Gorshkov, Kutakhov and a bevy of Soviet officers to Egypt in mid-May 1972—that is, between Sadat's talks in Moscow and the summit. Heikal lists among the disagreements a demand by Gorshkov for naval "facilities" at Mersa Matruh, which the Egyptian military (and Heikal himself) opposed.³³ But Soviet sources state that "our ships were stationed" there already. Indeed, as in Alexandria, Soviet control of Mersa Matruh was such that "someone got it into his head to post [Soviet] sentries even in the desert, at the approaches to town. These sentries once barred Sadat and Qaddafi from entering … which touched off a huge scandal."³⁴

At any rate, the papering-over was quite ostentatious, particularly in the naval sphere: the Soviet minister and navy chief officiated at a ceremony in Sadat's residence, where the president decorated "for military achievements" twelve Soviet naval officers, including the captain and first mate of nuclear submarine K-313. The submarine was on port call in Alexandria, for what was now publicized as the first such visit—more than three years after such calls actually began. The veterans' accounts have added that the accolade was for a successful demonstration by K-313 and the cruiser *Grozny* of two naval missiles at ranges of 90–100 kilometers.³⁵ The Soviets did not spoil the show by informing the Egyptians that a leak had sprung—apparently from the cooling system of the submarine's reactor—and it was ordered to continue its Mediterranean patrol for another month, during which the crew was exposed to an amount of radiation "that remained secret for the rest of their lives."³⁶

Cairo Radio also announced that Grechko and Kutakhov attended a demonstration for Sadat and Sadiq of "aircraft flying at 24,000m and 3,000kmh," which were still identified in Western and Israeli analyses as "MiG-23s."³⁷ The communiqué described them as flown by Egyptian pilots, and the same was claimed of two such craft that made another sortie over southern Sinai on the same day, 16 May. This was allegedly in order to impress Grechko that the EAF could take charge of the advanced planes. All recent Russian testimonies contradict this claim.³⁸ In March, the test-pilot component of Bezhevets's original team had been replaced by regular Soviet Air Force pilots, indicating that the Egyptian deployment had completed the MiG-25's experimental phase. The R version was formally certified as operational in December.³⁹ But the Soviets never agreed to let Egyptians near the planes even in 1973; in mid-'72, this remained one of several genuinely contentious points, while the overall agreed withdrawal was being secretly coordinated. Otherwise, the Grechko visit looked then, and still does, like a show of continuing Soviet commitment on the very eve of the Moscow summit.

It was undoubtedly all the more convincing because the IAF's anti-Foxbat tactic that Hod had outlined to Momyer the previous October, and Phantom pilots had rehearsed for months, was now tried—and failed. After thirty-five years, one of the pilots, Uri Ya'ari, apologetically blamed a series of technical breakdowns and human errors for what he considers the Israelis' missed opportunity to score the first MiG-25 shootdown.⁴⁰ A slightly differing account was given by his squadron commander and formation leader, Spector, but they agree that both the F-4s and their pilots were stretched to the limit of their physical capability, in vain.⁴¹

23

THE DEAL AT THE SUMMIT AND THE "EXPULSION" MYTH

A. Kissinger blinks first on the conditions for Soviet withdrawal

Nixon and Kissinger arrived at the summit on 22 May, determined that the unresolved Egyptian–Israeli conflict must not "poison" the all-important goal of détente, which would reduce pressure on the administration in other arenas such as Vietnam. The Soviets were likewise eager for progress on economic issues, among others, as well as to secure a cover for the withdrawal they desired from Egypt. But as the talks began, the Middle East deadlock appeared unchanged. On Kissinger's advice, Nixon told Brezhnev: "when Mr Gromyko reported to me that ... the Soviet Union would be willing to withdraw its military forces—as distinct from advisers ... That was very constructive. But that requires something from Israel that they simply have not done." Nixon's mention of the troop withdrawal offer at a meeting attended by the entire Soviet *troika* indicates his understanding that all of them, and presumably the full Politburo, had endorsed this measure. He went on to say: "we have prepared a paper on this matter ... in response to the one that you have prepared."[1]

Kissinger's memoirs conspicuously omit any mention of such an American paper. "The culmination" of the summit, he wrote in 1982,

> was ... Gromyko's agreement ... to a paragraph in the final communiqué so anodyne that it permitted no other interpretation than Moscow was putting the Middle East negotiations on ice. ... The Soviets were willing to pay *some* price for Détente. That, in any event, was the perception of Anwar Sadat ... and it led to ... the expulsion of Soviet troops from Egypt.[2]

In an earlier installment of his memoirs, Kissinger stated even more flatly that "the upshot was a meaningless paragraph [in the final communiqué] that ... was practically an endorsement of the status quo and was bound to be taken ill ... in Cairo." Dobrynin concurred in *his* memoir: "The sides presented their positions ... But there were no concrete advances on this question."[3]

The communiqué, however, was not the main product of the summit in respect of the Middle East, and the record now shows that Kissinger too was willing to pay a price. On the last day of the conference, he finally gave in to the Soviets' demand to formulate a separate, secret agreement on "general principles" for the region. In the 1979 volume of his memoirs, Kissinger published the text of this document for the first time—but he relegated it to a footnote, and dismissed its importance almost as totally as that of the communiqué:

> inexplicably, Gromyko spent four hours with me trying to agree on "general principles" ... I conducted what was in effect a delaying tactic. ... They were so vague as to leave wide scope for negotiation. ... Their practical significance was to confirm the deadlock. ... The Soviets never pressed them. Neither did we.[4]

This is where Kissinger's memoirs go beyond mere omission and approach outright misstatement. William Quandt, writing in 1993, already questioned this version: "my impression is that Kissinger took the exercise somewhat more seriously, and almost certainly Nixon did. ... The principles did not simply parrot UN resolutions, as Kissinger implies."[5] Quandt's doubts have since been confirmed by the transcript of Kissinger's talk with Gromyko, in which the "general principles" were finalized. It clarifies why, if the principles were as bland as Kissinger claimed, he demanded to conceal them from Rogers, from the Egyptians, and most of all from the Israelis. "I can assure you this paper would create an explosion in Jerusalem," Kissinger told Gromyko.[6] Toward the end of two long bargaining sessions, he remarked again: "both of us are terrified of what our allies would do. This is the best guarantee of secrecy."

But Kissinger had already agreed that Sadat was to be informed, so he had no reason to expect an angry response from the Egyptians. He did have good cause to fear an Israeli backlash: among other points of the permanent settlement, the haggling ended with a major concession by Kissinger on the notorious ambiguity of Resolution 242, in its various translations, in respect of the withdrawal to be demanded from Israel.

> *Mr [Georgy] Korniyenko* [Head of US Department, Soviet Foreign Ministry]: The Foreign Minister is saying that the content of this phrase means *the* Arab territories.
>
> *For. Min. Gromyko*: "All."
>
> *Dr Kissinger*: "The." I understand the content the Foreign Minister is giving this principle, and I do not dispute it. ... When I go back, I will say there are no secret agreements.
>
> *For. Min. Gromyko*: We agree.[7]

The secret agreement that, of course, *had* been reached thus comprised—beyond the written "general principles"—some oral understandings. These were evidently completed when "the Foreign Minister and Dr Kissinger then adjourned ... for an extended discussion," which was not recorded. They presumably included the implementation of the Soviet offer of troop withdrawal, which for Kissinger had been the original purpose of the whole exercise.

THE DEAL AT THE SUMMIT AND THE "EXPULSION" MYTH

The withdrawal of regular Soviet formations from Egypt was, then, a done deal by the end of the Moscow summit. But its implementation was predicated on an interim settlement—and, Kissinger's memoir notwithstanding, the Soviets *did* call his bluff on the "general principles" by carrying out their part of the deal—as they had resolved to do anyway. There was no risk that an interim settlement would actually be reached: Kissinger had clarified that Washington would not press Israel for it before the US presidential election, and Primakov's talks had precluded any other prospect of reconciling the Israeli formula with Sadat's or the Soviets'. So Moscow's perennial priority of legitimacy for a military solution would be achieved, with the added attraction of a faked "expulsion" to reduce Israeli preparedness. Moscow and Cairo each had their own, overlapping though not identical, reasons to bring the withdrawal forward, which would be the subject of discussion that now intensified between them.

"The Center [Moscow headquarters] was regularly informed about the planned action against the military specialists," writes the KGB's Kirpichenko, who by 1972 had taken over as *rezident* (station chief) in Cairo. When the "expulsion" was announced "it baffled no one."[8] Confidentially to the few Americans who were aware of the agreement, the Soviets would present the withdrawal as a goodwill gesture symbolizing the spirit of détente, while the Egyptians could hold it up as a harbinger of their disengagement from Moscow—and both could ask for American reciprocation. Since Kissinger was not about to reveal his complicity, the Soviets and Egyptians could feign an irrevocable rift between them and mislead nearly all others—especially the only party where no one was informed, the Israelis.

B. Detection and rejection of the "expulsion" ruse

It is at this point that, even at the time and especially after the Yom Kippur War, several analysts—most notably, Uri Ra'anan—began to discern a concerted and successful Soviet–Egyptian deception effort. Some of these claims were advanced to back up charges that Sadat's postwar peace moves and his subsequent shift from the Soviet bloc to the American camp were also deceptive. When the latter changes turned out to be genuine, the analogous suspicions about the 1972 events were also largely but gratuitously discarded and even ridiculed. By 1981, an Israeli expert on the Soviet military, Amnon Sella, could write:

> commentators too often describe the ups and downs in Soviet–Egyptian relations as a feint in the best tradition of Communist devious practice. The worse the relationship appears, the craftier the feint. According to this sort of ratiocination, the expulsion of Soviet advisers from Egypt was carried out in connivance with Moscow in order to prepare for war.

Despite this derision, Sella actually listed a series of examples whereby all the "deficiencies" caused by the Soviet withdrawal "taken together did not inflict any lasting damage on the long-range plan for war." He concluded that "distorted as such a [deceptive] notion is, the expulsion did in fact partly serve to camouflage Egyptian war preparations." The USSR, Sella allowed in an elegant example of adverbial harmonization, "went along with this line willingly enough, in part adventitiously and in part deliberately."[9]

At the time, Kremlin announcements said "the Soviet military personnel in Egypt has completed its functions. ... After the exchange of opinions, the sides deemed it expedient to bring [it] back to the Soviet Union." This was interpreted as a gloss on a serious setback for the USSR.[10] For decades afterward, Egyptian boasts about the successful ruse could be dismissed as retrospective bragging. But as our account of the "expulsion" progresses, new evidence will show how this supposed "ratiocination" is borne out at every stage. As Egyptian Maj.-Gen. Adel Suleiman Yusry told a veterans' conference twenty-five years later, "the most effective part" of Sadat's deception moves was "his renunciation of Soviet advisors and experts. This deceived both Israel and the USA, which concluded that under the conditions thus created, a military solution to the Middle Eastern problem was hardly possible."[11]

The widespread post-summit expectation that global détente would limit Soviet action in regional arenas and particularly the Third World ignored both the language of the meeting's documents and their Soviet interpretation. The "Basic Principles" paper explicitly stated that it did not affect the parties' obligations toward their allies. Official Soviet commentary—over Brezhnev's signature—declared that the international class struggle would continue.[12] In an analysis of the summit that was evidently written before the "expulsion" but published later, an IDF officer correctly concluded that détente notwithstanding, "the violent struggle between the superpowers has not ended, but has been shifted to limited arenas ... in which their participation is indirect or unilateral." Still, he concluded that in the Middle East, the USSR, being militarily weaker than the United States,

> has no possibility of supporting an Egyptian military action ... as it would not only cause an Egyptian debacle but would also severely endanger the Soviet regional presence. Furthermore, the USSR has no capability to conduct direct military operations against Israel in aid of Egypt, as the United States aids South Vietnam.[13]

Kissinger for his part claimed that "Détente did help to split Egypt from the Soviets."[14] There was a concerted effort on all three sides to impress even their own constituencies, as well as the others' and Israel's, that this was the case.[15] Another benefit of the "expulsion" was to convince the fiercely anti-Soviet Arab oil states, such as Saudi Arabia and Kuwait, that they could safely underwrite the cash payments now demanded for Soviet arms. In the less plausible case that they were privy to the deception, this at least provided them with a pretext.[16]

Soon after the summit, Egyptian documents show a further and ostentatious increase in surveillance of the Soviet military advisers and enforcement of the limitations on their direct contact with Egyptian soldiers. On 17 June, the security officer

THE DEAL AT THE SUMMIT AND THE "EXPULSION" MYTH

of the 2nd Mechanized Infantry Brigade reported finding a copy of a Soviet youth magazine in the troops' quarters. It turned out to have been distributed, along with other Soviet publications, on a regular basis, by an adviser whose name was garbled into "Nualov, Fladimir." The Egyptian officer requested instructions whether this was permissible, and apparently was told that it wasn't, as Nualov's subsequent record indicates he was removed—temporarily.[17]

C. The timing of Sadat's "sudden decision"

Sadat is conventionally held to have first informed Vinogradov "on the spur of the moment" on 8 July 1972 that "effective 17 July, the services of the Soviet military advisers would no longer be required."[18] This rests almost entirely on Egyptian sources: a report in *Akhbar al-Yawm* on 22 July that Sadat's decision was made ten days before his public announcement on the 18th, and Heikal's detailed report about Sadat's move in *Al-Ahram* on 28 July.[19] This version was expanded in Heikal's books and endorsed in Sadat's memoirs.[20]

The date of 8 July was first approximately confirmed by a former Soviet source with the publication of the diary that was begun in 1972 by Anatoly Chernyaev, then Ponomarev's deputy at the Central Committee International Department. In the entry for 15 July, he wrote: "Last Sunday [9 July], Anwar Sadat demanded immediate withdrawal of Soviet specialists and all Soviet military from Egypt—to protest the fact that he wasn't given what was promised to him during his last meeting with Brezhnev in Moscow. Namely, offensive weapons and Su-17 fighter-bombers. There was a commotion."[21] This, however, only illustrates how such a mid-level official was not informed about the withdrawal negotiations before, during and after the summit: he equates the "specialists" with "all Soviet military," and—as will be demonstrated— the Su-17s (initially, the Su-20 export version) were already being delivered.

An authoritative, post-Soviet Russian history of Israel states that Sadat's "unexpected" decision was made only on 13 July—the day Egyptian Prime Minister Aziz Sidqi began "a friendly working visit" in Moscow.[22] The CIA estimated, after learning about Sadat's imminent announcement one day before it was made, that Brezhnev was informed about it when he met Sidqi on the 14th—that is, the day before Chernyaev heard about it.[23] To Chernyaev, the visit was described as a *Soviet* initiative following Sadat's move: "We persuaded Sedki ... to come to Moscow."

Sidqi would have been Sadat's natural choice for an extremely sensitive and confidential mission of coordination with the Soviets. The "shy," civilian, Harvard-trained prime minister had made his career in economic positions dating back to Nasser's day, focusing on industrialization and modernization of Egypt with Soviet aid but also developing ties with Western corporations.[24] Sidqi had been instrumental in bringing Sadat to power, thus gaining his trust.[25] As first deputy prime minister, he had led the economic aid negotiations in Moscow in March 1971, when in meetings with

Brezhnev and Kosygin he secured Soviet credits for a five-year plan stressing consumer products and rural electrification. But he was also trusted with a message to Sadat following up on the latter's talks, which preceded the ceasefire abrogation.[26] During the May 1971 power struggle in Cairo, Sidqi was the first to publicly support Sadat against the "sowers of division and conspiracy" and appealed to "the working masses," without mentioning the "plotters'" supposed Soviet sympathies.[27] In January 1972, he replaced Sadat's first prime minister, Mahmud Fawzy, who was shifted to vice president; Sidqi's promotion was interpreted as a reward for personal loyalty, and he was deemed "neutral" in foreign affairs.[28] But before long he was billed as heading a "war cabinet," and described as "Russia's man in Cairo, as Sabry used to be."[29]

His statements grew steadily more aggressive: while Sadat's other vice-president, Hussein Shafei, called for waging guerilla operations in Sinai, Sidqi initially held that war should be initiated only when Egypt was ready and as a last resort.[30] But by 31 March 1972, when Sadat declared war was inevitable and called the Americans liars, public statements pointedly named Sidqi as chairing a cabinet session on war preparations.[31] A week later, Sidqi declared "the day of war is close, and Egypt has all the necessary weapons."[32] He even incurred public US protest by praising the terrorist attack at Israel's Lod airport on 30 May.[33] None of this made Sidqi unwelcome in Moscow, which hardly conforms with its supposed opposition to Sadat's war plans. Moreover, his delegation also included foreign minister and former ambassador to the USSR Ghaleb, a longtime liaison with the Soviet leadership.[34] Ghaleb lost his post in August, but rumors that Sidqi himself would also be ousted never materialized, so that his mission was hardly considered a failure; he served until March 1973, when Sadat himself took over the premiership.[35] Upon returning to Cairo at 3 a.m. on 15 July 1972, Sidqi reported immediately to the president.[36]

Sidqi's visit has been accounted for in various and conflicting ways, depending on whether it was assumed to have taken place just before or just after the Soviets were informed of their purported ouster. He was initially assumed to have presented the Soviets with a final ultimatum to supply the weaponry that Sadat had demanded; its rejection was held to have led to the expulsion order.[37] One request attributed to Sidqi was indeed turned down (again): a renewed demand to buy the MiG-25s.[38] But these aircraft had never been promised to Egypt, much less contracted for.

A British embassy official (and MI6 operative) in Cairo, Alan Urwick, put the arms-denial theory to Adm. Ivliev after Sadat's announcement. As the Briton reported on 21 July, Ivliev—"relaxed and in good humour"—confirmed Sidqi had presented demands for weaponry "but he did not say that Sidky had delivered an ultimatum. The impression he gave was that only after Sidky's return to Cairo was the instruction to leave given." Urwick also quoted another ultimatum version, which was picked up by his Italian colleague: that Sidqi's visit resulted from an ultimatum given to Sadat "in the early part of July" by "a committee of senior army officers ... to get rid of the Soviet advisers," and that Sadat intentionally created the appearance

THE DEAL AT THE SUMMIT AND THE "EXPULSION" MYTH

that "the Soviets were refusing 'legitimate' demands."³⁹ The latter part of this theory now seems to have been closest to reality, but there was clearly an effort to spread the ultimatum version about Sidqi's trip in various forms.

However, once the Egyptian line was shaped whereby the decision had been made and communicated to the Soviets on 8 July, before Sidqi even left for Moscow, other explanations were called for. On 22 July, the day that *Al-Akhbar* so dated Sadat's move, the paper claimed that Sidqi's mission was "a confirmation of continuing friendship and cooperation."⁴⁰ This was disbelieved at the time by Western diplomats and subsequently by Western historians, who conjectured that Sidqi was "sent by Sadat to Moscow to … permit the Soviets some face-saving," but "the Soviets refused to cooperate"; the visit was "a total failure" and the joint communiqué was a "lie."⁴¹ However, this conclusion rested merely on the *absence* of "any mention of military aid or military cooperation" in Sidqi's farewell speech. No positive evidence was or is offered, except for the subsequent "expulsion" itself.⁴²

Indeed, in Moscow, Chernyaev was instructed to round up several bigwigs and another "200 people from the regional committee, to show enthusiasm during his [Sidqi's] departure." However, "the negotiations ran behind schedule and the guest was delayed for his flight. I allowed the people to go, because it was hot, they were sitting for four hours without lunch, and it was Friday." Chernyaev was anxious that "there could be some 'serious consequences' for me" from this failure—which indicates that no snub was intended. On the contrary, his impression was that "we gave them quite a bit of what they were asking. A week ago [Hafez] al-Assad, the President of Syria, was here. … He was able to get our guys to practically approve a 'military solution,' and got a great deal."⁴³

The rapid succession of conflicting Egyptian versions has been seen as a series of inept and increasingly transparent attempts to mask a genuine rift. But it could just as plausibly have been deliberately aimed to create the false impression of a badly concealed rupture. The latest Russian dating of the decision at 13 July appears to point in the latter direction, since if the Soviet withdrawal was finally determined in Sidqi's talks, which "focused on military and political matters" and were "restricted to a few members on each side" including Grechko, it could hardly have been unilateral.⁴⁴

Vinogradov himself related that Sadat "suddenly and without any provocation, very irritably, declared to me that he was giving up altogether the service of the Soviet military personnel." However, the envoy never confirmed that this was on 8 July, or indeed on any date that month. In reminiscences that were not included in his widely published memoirs, he states that this conversation took place in *June* 1972.⁴⁵ This is not the only Russian source to claim that "in *June* 1972 … Sadat invited the USSR's Ambassador in Egypt and the Chief Military Adviser … and declared that the Soviet advisers and specialists … were … no longer needed, and the time had come to bid farewell."⁴⁶ This is echoed by Kapitanets, the deputy commander of the Mediterranean

269

eskadra: "In *June* ... Sadat decided to forgo our advisers, and demanded in ultimative form that they leave the country within two days."[47]

These versions all retain the unilateral-expulsion line, which may have been either the only one handed down to the operational echelon, or the official version adopted later. But either way, the June date appears to reveal that Heikal's 8 July version concealed earlier communication with the Soviets, and to confirm that Sidqi's talks were aimed at final coordination to announce a previously agreed move that was already in progress.

When Sadat dropped his bombshell on 17 July, Soviet embassy official Akopov—who had long argued for a withdrawal—describes Vinogradov as furious. It can only be guessed whether this was mere pretense (like Kissinger's response), or genuine anger that *Moscow* had informed the ambassador so late about the adoption of his own proposal. But given Vinogradov's own mention of Sadat's notification in June, the latter seems unlikely. At any rate, Akopov soothed his boss: "Here we have Sadat ... facilitating the task for us to withdraw the Soviet specialists and advisors ... he played in our favor."[48]

In Moscow, Chernyaev too considered, or was told: "Sadat ordered our military personnel out of Egypt after all. It may be for the best—we will not be liable when he tries to wage war against Israel and gets smacked once again. As for our 'superpower prestige' ... in our time, it is not so precious." He listed the event as second in importance that week, after a huge fodder-grain deal with the United States, one of the Soviets' main objectives at the summit.[49] As this, like the other responses to Sadat's move, can be interpreted in several directions, the ultimate test must be what actually occurred both before and after his announcement.

D. *The pilots leave first*

The Soviet MiG-21 fighter squadrons had not gone into action against Israel since the ceasefire of August 1970; the only air engagement reported in this period was on 13 June, when two Egyptian MiG-21s were shot down as they tried, unusually, to attack Israeli planes northeast of Port Said.[50] The Soviet airmen therefore could be gradually and unobtrusively withdrawn before Sadat's declaration. As the aircraft had always borne Egyptian markings, they were not easily distinguishable from EAF MiG-21s. A pilot and political officer of the Soviet aviation group in Egypt, probably reflecting the line he was instructed to propagate, wrote that "in *June* 1972, our units became redundant, and they returned to the USSR."[51] The same timing appears in memoirs of other Soviet airmen.[52] One of them gives the exact date of 3 June.[53] At least some of the planes were handed over to the Egyptian Air Force.[54] But as both Sadat and Gromyko had stressed, the training of Egyptian pilots by Soviet instructors continued.

In contrast, the high-profile part of the Soviet airmen's departure was made only the day before Sadat's announcement. This was the cessation of MiG-25 reconnais-

THE DEAL AT THE SUMMIT AND THE "EXPULSION" MYTH

sance flights, which had been performed *only* by Soviet pilots. The detachment that operated them was actually the last of the Soviet air formations to be withdrawn from Egypt, and the only case in which real or staged discord has been reported. Several post-Soviet sources indicate at least a partial withdrawal of the craft earlier.[55] But there are more detailed testimonies that the flights ceased, and the last planes were flown back to the Soviet Union, on 16 or 17 July 1972.[56] This change would certainly have been noticed immediately by Israel, which was "painfully" aware of the MiG-25 intrusions because it still had nothing to counter them.[57]

The Egyptians' demand to acquire the planes had not yet been resolved. When, in a discussion with Ivliev after Sadat's announcement, Urwick referred to "the very high-performance aircraft used for reconnaissance over Sinai," the Soviet attaché replied that their sale to Egypt "was under consideration and he did not yet know … but added that he privately thought the aircraft would be returned to the USSR."[58] Evidence from 2008 shows that this had in fact already been decided. The urgency to get the Foxbats out of Egypt was reflected by inter-agency competition in Moscow. Abramov, the Air Force colonel on the *Kavkaz* staff, estimated that dismantling and crating the planes would take a week, which caused his boss Krivoplyasov some embarrassment: the aviation industry minister had told Grechko it could be accomplished in two days. Abramov pointed out that the faster process would require sending twenty to thirty factory experts to Egypt, which would add an extra burden to the transport flights (another indication that a mass repatriation was already being planned). Krivoplyasov went back to Grechko, and the 63rd's own ground crews were given the week they needed—which indicates the timing of the original order.[59]

One of the group's pilots, V. Gordienko, related (and evidently was told at the time) that after Sadat ordered a halt to the Foxbats' reconnaissance flights, Moscow issued an "ultimatum" to fly them back immediately, but Egyptian tanks blocked the runways before the An-22s could take off; "the crisis was solved by diplomatic means."[60] Bezhevets claims that the pilots were feted and decorated by Mubarak to acknowledge the completion of their task to map out Israel's defenses.[61]

E. The field advisers: mass recall, gradual redeployment

An even more blatant exercise was timed for the days immediately before Sadat's announcement, in order to create the semblance of a sudden expulsion. This was a sharp and obtrusive break in routine for the Soviet military advisers attached to Egyptian ground units. An Egyptian document bearing the significant date of *16* July 1972 confirms that the 112th Infantry Brigade's four Soviet "experts" and their interpreter "have handed over everything they had in their possession and are now unattached."[62] These "marching orders"—which must have followed previously issued instructions—are exceptional in that all the brigade's advisers departed simultaneously; their rotation was normally staggered.

271

This was not the only measure taken after the Moscow summit to create the appearance of an abrupt recall. As the anti-aircraft adviser Murzintsev relates, routine repatriation of advisers whose tour of duty had ended was *delayed* for over six weeks up to mid-July, with no reason provided. "His" battalion had been holding a forward position in Port Fuad since November 1971, and he was able to move with his wife into one of the comfortable beach cabins formerly used by Suez Canal Company personnel.

> I had already hoped to serve out my term in this Egyptian paradise, but it was not to be. ... On 2 June 1972, my tour of duty was to end, but I received no notice about my replacement. On one of my trips to Cairo ... I was told that my replacement was being delayed somewhat. ... On 19 July, I was in Cairo. Early the next morning, I was getting ready to leave for Port Said but a visit from Yavorsky disrupted all plans.

Col. Gennady Yavorsky, another anti-aircraft adviser, had arrived in Egypt together with Murzintsev and so was likewise awaiting replacement.

> "Do you know why all the advisers are being assembled in Cairo?" he asked. "I'm hearing about this for the first time. I leave for Port Said tomorrow." "I wanted to leave too, but there's talk that everyone has been summoned here." At the meeting we were told about the order: in three days, be ready to fly back to the Motherland. [Our] bewildered questions how to explain our sudden departure to our advisees and friends were answered curtly: "We have accomplished the assigned mission. [Make] no comments and certainly no assumptions or speculations." Those whose tour of duty in Egypt had ended were to leave in the first plane. The same day, Mister Usama [Murzintsev's advisee] showed up at my apartment. He looked worried and bewildered. "Why, Mister Vasily? Why?" What could I answer him? I asked myself the same question and found no answer.

So far, Murzintsev's account might be consistent with a sudden and unexpected expulsion of the Soviets. But he goes on:

> my thoughts were confused by the new advisers who were arriving. We were packing our bags, while for some [of us] replacements arrived from Moscow. Those who arrived swore that they knew nothing about a withdrawal of advisers and troops. The very fact of their arrival aroused distrust about what was going on.

The planes that were to evacuate the "expelled" advisers were bringing in their replacements—on 19 July, that is, after Sadat's public announcement and at least twelve days after the Soviets were supposedly informed that the advisers were no longer welcome.[63]

"Lt Smirnov," the "radio-technical" expert, was assigned besides maintenance of Soviet hardware to train Egyptian personnel in its use. In "late July" 1972, on

> an ordinary workday ... a call came from the office of our ambassador, Vinogradov: "Everyone is to stay at his workplace, but not to start working." ... Suddenly, another call came with a new order: "... The Soviet military experts' mission is being terminated. ...

THE DEAL AT THE SUMMIT AND THE "EXPULSION" MYTH

Gather all documents, papers, and property ... by the end of the day, prepare lists of those to be evacuated."[64]

There was, then, an extraordinary, conspicuous and sudden recall of the military advisers to Cairo in mid-July. The "most unusual" disappearance of Soviet advisers from the canal zone was noted by an informant of the French embassy even before Sadat's order was made public.[65] The display was further amplified by including the Soviet civilian advisers. On 21 July, the British agent Urwick cabled to London "the Spanish M[ilitary] A[ttaché] ... says he has reliable information that the Soviet engineers helping to run the generating plant etc. at Aswan have left. The head of the attachés branch, Col. Ezzy, also said that all the Russians, including civilian technicians, were leaving."[66] The Western defense attachés in Cairo thus operated as an echo chamber, amplifying and mutually corroborating meager information from the same limited and tendentious sources.

24

WITHDRAWN REGULARS CONCEAL "BANISHED" ADVISERS

A. The numbers add up—or not

Late on 19 July 1972, a TASS report mentioned only that "a certain number of Soviet military personnel" would return "shortly" to the USSR after completing their "temporary assignment to teach Egyptian forces" how to "master Soviet equipment"— thus maintaining the image of "advisers."[1] To this day, no official Soviet or Russian figure has been given for the number and breakdown of servicemen who left Egypt in the summer of 1972. The closest thing was provided by Dobrynin: "about 17,000."[2] A former KGB officer in Egypt states that "in half a month about 20,000 of our advisers left."[3] Another Russian account puts the number as high as 21,000.[4] An article in the Russian armed forces newspaper puts the number of evacuees at 15,000.[5] The official Russian military history oddly quotes only Western publications and Sadat's memoirs, which "average out" at the same.[6]

Although even the smallest of these figures was much higher than the greatest estimate of Soviet advisers to Egyptian formations, a consensus formed in Western and Israeli intelligence that it was these advisers who were expelled. Within two days of Sadat's speech, Israeli intelligence had concluded that Soviet advisers were "being withdrawn from GHQ down to unit level" but *not* "at this stage ... the Soviet strategic units nor 'experts' attached to air defense units."[7] This was evidently the idea that the Israeli ambassador in Washington, Rabin, had when, a week later, he estimated that "while some advisors remain in headquarters, advisors are gone from units in field. ... [The] bulk of the advisory personnel (4–6,000) have left or will leave Egypt." The State Department rather pathetically passed this on to Kissinger.

Rabin did suggest that "Soviet forces tied into Egypt's air defense (10–12,000) have been asked to leave. Rabin was not sure if this applied to all or most of the air defense personnel."[8] US Defense Secretary Melvin Laird, on the other hand, concluded "that the Egyptian order ousting Soviet military personnel was limited to advisers, and did not apply to the Soviet military forces stationed in Egypt, who were flying and operating sophisticated weapons themselves."⁹ This was almost the exact opposite of the situation on the ground. The back-channel agreement was thus effectively camouflaged even within the US administration.

Uninformed about Kissinger's moves, the CIA too continued for some time to refer to an unilateral, comprehensive "ouster" of the Soviets from Egypt resulting from Soviet reluctance to supply offensive weapons, even while the agency registered specific exceptions and reservations to both elements. Ultimately, this would feed into the CIA's failure to foresee an Egyptian offensive. CIA Director William Colby (1973–6) admitted as much after the Yom Kippur War: "over a period of time many of our Middle East analysts apparently developed a conceptual framework that simply did not allow them to accept what in retrospect turned out to be fairly good evidence of impending hostilities."

While offering praise for Kissinger's performance, Colby slipped in a jab at his secretiveness—and, subtly, at its results. "It is clear that the back channel in many instances is becoming the main channel, causing lost and even counterproductive motion, aside from anguish, among many not in the circuit." Colby suggested that at least *he* should be informed and consulted.¹⁰

The widespread misperception of the "expulsion" is all the more notable because, despite Kissinger's best efforts, even at the time there were indications of the withdrawal's actual character and scope. *Al-Ahram* stated explicitly that "instructors needed to support Egyptian military forces" would stay on, which a leading Israeli commentator calculated to mean at least a third of the total Soviet manpower in Egypt.¹¹ Such distinctions were largely lost in the sweep of generalizations that *all* the Soviets were being ejected. At best, the prevailing, erroneous notion was that the expulsion pertained chiefly and definitely to advisers, with the withdrawal of integral units only a possible complement. The question of how the estimated count of evacuees could consist only or mainly of advisers, whose number was a fraction of the total figure, was hardly addressed.

Over time, the conventional description became that the Soviets "complied, indeed over-complied immediately" with Sadat's order within one week of 17 July, "withdrawing personnel beyond the advisers sent with the air-defense system in 1970, so that *even* Soviet instructors working in Egyptian military institutions were withdrawn. They took with them all their SAM equipment and refused to sell any of the systems to Egypt."¹² This distortion was facilitated by the previous references to the regular Soviet formations as "experts," "technicians," or "advisers." TASS was quite truthful when it "announced that Soviet forces in Egypt had 'completed their functions' and would 'shortly return' to the USSR ... These forces were intended to remain in Egypt for only a 'limited period' and ... both sides had 'deemed it expedient' to bring them home." But as intended, the CIA read this as making the best of a setback: "the Soviets have chosen conciliatory language in order to minimize the damage."¹³

WITHDRAWN REGULARS CONCEAL "BANISHED" ADVISERS

B. The zenitchiki's *actual departure*

The air defense division, which actually accounted for most of the repatriated Soviet personnel, left only gradually. A third round of deployment, headed by Maj.-Gen. Nikolay Rytov, theoretically took over from SAM division chief Boshnyak in June, which appears to indicate preparation for the regulars to stay for at least another year. But unlike his predecessors, Rytov was not replaced at his former command (the 19th Air Defense Division, a post he had held from 1966), and he returned there in August 1972, to remain through 1975. This division's highly detailed history on the 8th Air Defense Corps' veterans' website does not so much as mention Rytov's brief mission in Egypt.[14]

A photo contributed to the history web page of *Kavkaz*'s 18th Division by Rytov's family shows the general addressing a parade of regulars at an unspecified desert location, on the morning of Sadat's announcement, 18 July 1972. But there is no other record there or elsewhere of Rytov's activity in Egypt, and little about new manpower that came with him.[15] His dispatch appears, then, to have been intentionally temporary, and possibly even part of the effort to create an illusion that it was unexpectedly terminated. An exceptional account by Lt Semen Luk'yanov, of a technical support unit serving two SAM-3 *divizyons* near Mersa Matruh, describes his dispatch among 400 air defense personnel on board the liner *Rossiya* in May 1972 but adds that many of their functions on the ground had already been transferred to Arabs.[16]

In fact, the *second* round's planned tour of duty had been extended, apparently in order to avoid sending another full complement of Soviet replacements and to enable a handover to Egyptians instead. This was already in progress when Rytov arrived—as already noted in respect of the fighter squadrons. In the SAM units, the troops' normal rotation order was routinely staggered, and this was maintained in the summer of '72. Col. Linkov's *divizyon* served in Egypt for well over a year. The first half of its manpower returned to Sevastopol on the *Rossiya* on 3 June. On this voyage or another one in June, the liner also took the entire *Strela* platoon of the SAM *divizyon* protecting Helwan, after its men were rousted out at 2 a.m. and informed they were going home.[17] The rest of Linkov's outfit was flown out to Kiev by An-22s on 3 August, leaving all its weaponry behind.[18]

In some cases, the order of evacuation was apparently determined by the visibility factor: "the Soviet forces deployed around Cairo were withdrawn within 24 hours," but one brigade—apparently the first—shipped out of Alexandria only on 31 July, after being bivouacked for some time on the local university campus:

> On the evening of 30 July the men were playing cards as usual when the ship [the liner *Pobeda*] arrived. The Arabs allotted 15 trucks and transported all the brigade's manpower in two rounds. The men brought along only their personal weapons. The Egyptian leadership had barred the complexes [hardware] of 22 *Pechora* [SAM-3] *divizyons* from leaving [or so the head of the missile-experts delegation, Nikiforov, was told].

THE SOVIET–ISRAELI WAR, 1967–1973

Nikiforov's own contract was to expire only on 18 August, but the Egyptians—despite the supposed expulsion—actually wanted to extend it for another two months. When Nikiforov reported this by telephone to Moscow, he was told that "under the conditions of withdrawal" that Sadat had ordered this would not be possible. As his group had arrived without visas, they could not leave by civilian airliner, and had to join the missilemen on the *Pobeda*. Up to the last moment, the advisers' "curator" Col. Bardisi and generals from the Egyptian General Staff tried to persuade Nikiforov *not* to leave, but he told them Moscow was adamant. "The ship was overloaded; the soldiers slept crowded on deck. Some were diagnosed with dysentery and quarantined" en route to Sevastopol.[19]

Shazly, Egyptian chief of staff, stated in 1990 that it was only "by the end of 1972" that "we were able to replace the Soviet military specialists on fifteen SAM missile [*divizyons*]." But "most of the Soviet advisers [again, loosely used for the SAM operators] didn't leave till October 1972."[20] Two former servicemen with air defense units in the canal zone give their departure dates as 2 August and 12 September.[21] The handover continued at least until March 1973, when "every one [of the Soviets] who had a suitable military specialty was sent 'into the field' to break in [Egyptian] air defense men, who arrived after having finished their training in the [Soviet] Union."[22]

Like the pilots, the Soviet missilemen left *without* much of their hardware. Vsevolod Veligosha, a cook and paramedic, was posted with his SAM detachment in Alexandria. He does not give the precise date when, "after Nasser's death ... we were asked to leave," but relates that the Soviet personnel "left all their equipment to Arabs whom we had urgently taught; every one of us prepared a replacement for himself."[23] Lt Luk'yanov's unit was flown back to Lvov in An-22s in October or November 1972, after handing over their gear to Egyptians. Although they had heard of Sadat's decision, they sensed no change in the attitude of the locals and continued to visit Mersa Matruh cafes together until their departure.[24] Maj. Yury Makarenko had arrived with his "*spetsnaz* radio-technical" outfit in early May 1972 to replace a Lt-Col. A. Mavrin and his men, but Mavrin left only in August and Makarenko himself on 27 October. He was transferred to Iraq to complete his two-year contract in a similar capacity.[25]

C. The internatsionalisty's homecoming: quarantined and silenced

An official Russian history also describes the bulk of personnel who returned from Egypt to the USSR in July–August 1972 as "soldiers"—that is, regulars—who were "sent out by planes ... and cruise liners to Sevastopol and Odessa."[26] What befell them also bespeaks a deliberate effort to obscure both their deployment itself and how it ended, from the Soviet public as well as Western eyes:

> The soldiers and officers expected a festive reception. ... But ... the ports were surrounded by a chain of armed men in civilian clothes. It was forbidden to make telephone calls, to go to the toilet without an escort, or to share any impression from the foreign tour of duty

with local personnel. Only on the fourth day, after appropriate instruction was conducted by officers of the special department, a start was made at sending the internationalist soldiers to their permanent stations.[27]

This is echoed, often bitterly, by the veterans themselves:

> For 40 days we were kept in quarantine, after which all kinds of bizarre occurrences began. We were given our military papers ... but nothing was written in them. Where had we been all that time? Unknown. When we said in the recruiting office [at our discharge] that we had been in Alexandria, we were laughed at: "Is that near Kiev?" ... We also signed a pledge not to talk [about our service in Egypt] for 25 years. I kept my word.[28]

Radio specialist Pechenkin was told that the details of his foreign service need not be listed in his papers "for all to see," but he could rest assured that they were entered in his military dossier—a promise that often turned out to be unfounded.[29]

Even in the late 1980s, with their oath of silence about to expire and their campaign for recognition as combat veterans already rewarded with some material benefits, the *Kavkaz* old-timers had difficulty in obtaining official confirmation of their war record in Egypt. Lt Bebishev, the diver who did two tours of duty in Alexandria, applied several times to the Navy and the Defense Ministry for certification of his "internationalist soldier" status, but was told as late as 1999 that between the dates he provided "your outfit was in Sevastopol."[30] A *Shilka* radar operator who had been promoted to staff sergeant while on duty in Egypt was busted back to private, "since no one had ordered him to Egypt," and his papers were inscribed "departed in June 1971, reported [back] in September 1972"—with nothing about the interim.[31]

The *Kavkaz* officers' career progress was, if anything, held up by their combat experience. The SAM brigade commander Zhayvoronok met his fellow colonel, who had evaded going to Egypt. "He was already a general, having served within the USSR, while all the recommendations for medals that were submitted for my boys can't be found to this day."[32] Gen. Smirnov complained in 2001 that many more of his men were recommended for Soviet medals than the 166 who actually received them.

> Many of my comrades ask me how to get justice restored, and I haven't found an answer yet. Those who are still in the armed forces received a certificate from the Supreme Soviet of the USSR and an "internationalist soldier" pin. It's much harder to solve the problem of conferring this decoration on those who have retired or left the service. The local military authorities are in no hurry, in fact they refuse to handle this on various pretexts. All our comrades-in-arms ought to receive the Motherland's recognition as soon as possible.[33]

By mid-August 1972, the CIA had taken note of the Soviet regulars' withdrawal, even assuming it was already complete, but began to interpret it in the way that would remain prevalent till October 1973:

THE SOVIET-ISRAELI WAR, 1967-1973

The departure of Soviet missile crews, five squadrons of fighter aircraft and other air defense personnel sharply reduce[s] Egypt's capability to defend itself against Israeli air attack. The Egyptians may have deluded themselves into believing that they can somehow get along without Soviet help in this area. ... The Egyptians have no capability to put forces across the canal and hold territory for more than a day or so. ... The chances of Egypt's initiating any major military action have become even smaller than they were before Sadat's 17 July announcement. Thus it is unlikely that there will be a cross-canal assault or a "war of attrition."[34]

Likewise, "from 17 July onwards, few indeed were the military experts in Israel ... who believed that Egypt was capable of going to war." But the predominant concept remained that this was because the Soviet *advisers* had left, and the carefully cultivated confusion between them and the regulars now paid off. Calculating *down* from a total "Soviet contingent" of 15,000–20,000 before 17 July, and following "some sources" whereby "about ten per cent stayed behind," Sella estimated a decade later that only "about 1500 to 2000 advisers were left in Egypt."[35] But at about the same time, calculating *up* from "the size of local armed forces and intensity of advisory mission penetration," Efraim Karsh estimated that in 1970, at the height of Soviet involvement, there had been 2,300 Soviet advisers (as distinct from troops).[36] Since only the advisers remained, there was little change in their number, but in view of the supposed mass "exodus" it now seemed like a mere remnant.

The "expulsion" was thus used to end the direct Soviet military intervention in Egypt without admitting that it ever took place. The deception that enabled this may have been designed also to prevent Israel from taking advantage of the transitional period until Egyptian units completed their takeover of the anti-aircraft array. This illusion, first created by the mass, simultaneous recall of the advisers to Cairo, would then hardly be dispelled when the advisers trickled back, unnoticed, to "their" units. Asked thirty years later how there were advisers' dependents to be evacuated from Egypt in October 1973 if they had been expelled the previous summer, Gen. Gareev obfuscated: "everyone cannot leave in one day. In those months, a planned evacuation went on. Every day someone arrived in Egypt, and someone else left. Military–technical cooperation went on."[37]

Unlike Rytov, the advisers' boss Okunev completed his two-year tour and was then replaced by Lt-Gen. Petr Samokhodsky, who also retained the title of "head of the Soviet forces group." As will be seen, this title was not empty even after the main body of *Kavkaz* troops departed—indeed, it involved considerable activity during the Yom Kippur War and after.[38]

25

DECEPTION-ON-NILE, JULY 1972

A. Marwan feeds disinformation to Britons, too

As incredibly early as the morning of 22 July—even before the *Pobeda* sailed—an Egyptian source told Urwick "in strict personal confidence" that "*all* the Soviet military advisers had now left Egypt."[1] The MI6 operative hastened to report this at face value, without questioning how such a logistical feat could have been completed within four days. Urwick's proviso that his source "should be fully protected" now seems risible, since he named the informant as none other than Ashraf Marwan, "Sadat's secretary for information."[2] In London, doubts soon arose about the veracity of this claim; in cabinet on the 27th, Foreign Secretary Alec Douglas-Home stated: "it appears that Soviet personnel manning SAM-3 missile sites and instructors engaged in MiG training were still there."[3]

Both the credulous MI6 agent and his superiors tended more to believe Marwan's sweetener: that Egypt would now switch its military procurement from Soviet back to British weapons. A few days later, the foreign secretary told the cabinet "we were considering how far we might be able to take this opportunity to establish a position of greater influence in Egypt *without* inheriting the responsibility of the Soviet Government as her principal supplier of arms."[4]

Like Marwan's reports to the Mossad, this mostly false promise was supported by some nucleus of truth. Egypt did put out feelers for the Rapier SAM system, which had just entered service with British forces.[5] But the purchase never materialized, and besides disinformation the talks may have served to gain data on the brand-new British missile that was shared with the Soviets.[6] By December, NATO sources reported that as London had refused to sell long-range missiles and bombers, "the Egyptians were about to renew negotiations for more Soviet arms," and "the Soviets were not taking the Egyptian–British talks seriously."[7] A month earlier, the *New York Times* had already quoted military and diplomatic sources that "the Egyptians were unsuccessful in negotiations with Britain to purchase the Rapier" and had received advanced Soviet SAMs instead.[8] Some minor purchases of British electronic equipment were made, but nothing that approached a radical shift.[9]

THE SOVIET–ISRAELI WAR, 1967–1973

Marwan was only one player in the disinformation campaign. An American diplomat learned that the UN observer chief Ensio Siilasvuo was "highly puzzled" when on 4 September, in Cairo for a routine call, he "was entertained at an elaborate dinner instead of the usual lunch." The mystery was resolved when "his hosts asked him ... as a high Finnish military officer ... whether he knew of any method of obtaining a steady flow of spare parts for Russian-built aircraft without going through USSR government channels." The Finnish general replied that there was no such way.[10]

Thus, as described by Sadat's confidant Abdel Satar al-Tawila, the war correspondent of *Rose el-Yussef* magazine, "various government agencies spread rumors and stories that were exaggerated, to say the least":

> habitués of Egyptian and Arab coffee houses ... turned into arms experts and babbled ... about the question of offensive and defensive weapons, inventing arbitrary differences between them while ... defensive anti-aircraft weapons actually played an offensive role during the war of October 6. Moreover, the Egyptian press gave prominence to an inclination to seek arms in the West ... [which] would mean, simply, that the date of the expected battle is far off.

Spreading the version about the advisers' immediate and complete "expulsion" was thus "a strategic cover ... a splendid distraction for our going to war": "It raised questions about the genuineness of the regime's threats to resort to war. After all, how would the Egyptian army be able to fight without the presence of thousands of Russian experts ... to train [it] ... and even to operate some of this hardware themselves?"[11]

On 22 July, the day Marwan claimed all the Soviets were gone, the interpreter Igor' Vakhtin relates that he was among the *first* to leave, on a scheduled Aeroflot flight, as his *komandirovka* was over anyway. It was only in the morrow, Egypt's Revolution Day, that Murzintsev's group flew home, and his final recollection from Egypt hardly reflects any hostility or resentment on the part of local officialdom: "we are drawn up for a parade at the airfield. The deputy defense minister of Egypt decorates us with medals and thanks us for our help." Vakhtin heard similar descriptions from colleagues who were repatriated only in August, by military aircraft.

> A bus with our advisers would drive up to the plane. They would be awaited by an Egyptian general holding a cardboard box with a pile of Egyptian decorations made of yellow metal in the form of the Arab eagle, or as it was known colloquially, "the chicken." At the ramp, an Arab would hand each one his "chicken," with thanks and a strong handshake. ... The foremost question that came to the mind of our guys who were honored with this distinguished award, was absolutely mercenary: was it gold, and could it be used for dental crowns? Some of them, to the Arabs' great astonishment, tried to test the "chicken" with their teeth.

They had reason for suspicion: operations officer Podalka, who was awarded "a distinguished" Egyptian medal, was dismayed to discover that it was gilded rather than solid gold as promised.¹² Vakhtin reckoned in retrospect that "the Egyptians were trying 'to sweeten the pill,'" but his account hardly reflects any bitterness at the time beyond the Soviets' usual contempt.

Once flown back home, the advisers and interpreters received somewhat more welcome and recognition than the mass of *Kavkaz* regulars who would form the bulk of the withdrawal and return by ship. Murzintsev received the Order of the Red Banner. Vakhtin, a recent alumnus of the Military Languages Institute, wrote that his entire group of interpreters who had served from 1970 to 1972, forty officer graduates and fifty noncoms who were still students, were nominated for the somewhat lower Order of the Red Star, "the biggest mass award in the history of the institute."¹³ But those advisers and interpreters who were not due to be relieved were not withdrawn at all.

On Egypt's Revolution Day, four SAMs were fired at Israeli planes flying east of the canal and Egypt claimed a Phantom shot down (the IAF denied it). This first cross-canal SAM launch since the Stratocruiser downing was ascribed in Israel to a demonstration of the Egyptians' capability to operate the "missile shield" on their own. It underlined Sadat's Revolution Day speech, in which he drew applause by declaring "I am not a Soviet agent ... I will never be a Marxist."¹⁴

This was exactly the spin propagated by the Cairo gossip mill, which now applied it also retrospectively to the previous, pre-"expulsion" incident. As the CIA reported in hindsight, the dogfight on 13 June was now "rumored to have been the result of an attempt by Egyptian pilots to intercept an Israeli flight against Soviet orders or advice, and the incident is said to have become another point of friction" between them. The agency conjectured that "Israeli political leaders may be restrained from retaliating for fear of the effect ... on the Soviet evacuation."¹⁵ In Langley, then, Sadat's "expulsion order" was accepted by way of "no sooner said than done."

B. Kissinger's feigned surprise

Chapter XXX of Kissinger's memoirs is entitled "Sadat *Expels* the Soviets." After omitting the essential antecedents, Kissinger claims that Sadat's announcement came "as a complete surprise" to him—pretending that it was all Sadat's doing, at Kissinger's own behest but without his being notified, and hiding his role in negotiating it with the Soviets:

> To be sure, my strategy had sought to induce Cairo to lessen its reliance on the Soviet Union. I had expected that at some point ... Sadat would be prepared to offer to trade Soviet withdrawal for progress with us. But ... I never guessed that he would settle the issue with one grand gesture, and unilaterally ... for no return.¹⁶

Contemporary accounts describe his rhetorical display of astonishment: "'Why has Sadat done me this favor?' he asked his aides. 'Why didn't he get in touch with me? Why didn't he demand of me all kinds of concessions first?' For in a curious intelligence failure, Kissinger learned of the expulsion from news dispatches."[17]

Some who took Kissinger's reaction at face value accounted for it by "a quid pro quo known only to a few in the CIA," whose "direct payments" Sadat "had been apparently receiving ... since the late 1960s ... contacts known to only a very few in Washington." For this description, Kenneth Stein relied on several US officials (including Quandt) who claimed to have been surprised, but only on a single *Washington Post* report for Sadat's purported recruitment by the CIA.[18]

No further evidence of such collusion has emerged. If Sadat was in US pay, explaining the Americans' surprise at the launch of his cross-canal offensive would require an even more elaborate conspiracy theory whereby Kissinger was the sole US party to the plot (which has indeed been suggested, with no more evidence).[19] Rather, the shoe appears to have been on the other foot: as late as March 1972, the CIA itself was still leaning only on "the Middle East press" for predictions "that some or all Soviet personnel will be expelled from Egypt."[20] Aleksey Volovich, the interpreter for Lt-Gen. Lev Gorelov, chief adviser at the Cairo Military District, entered in his diary on 16 July 1972, just before the general gathered his staff to announce their repatriation, that "rumors" were circulating whereby Kissinger himself, in a clandestine visit to Cairo in April 1972, had offered Sadat $3 billion a year in aid in exchange for expelling the Soviets.[21] When Sadat did break with Moscow after the Yom Kippur War, Soviet sources took up this canard as fact, adding that Sadat may also have been bribed personally.[22]

The back-channel papers now do show that Kissinger's surprise was feigned. He could have been surprised only that the Soviets and Egyptians had forced his hand on the interim settlement ahead of the US election, by carrying out the part he had most desired, before he produced Israeli compliance—which he was incapable of delivering. Kissinger's memoirs claim he went so far as to accuse Brezhnev of "amazing chutzpah" when, on 20 July, the general secretary wrote to Nixon that the Soviet departure was "a down payment, as it were, on the offer to withdraw Soviet forces" that Gromyko had made in September 1971.[23] However, Kissinger's report on the meeting in which Dobrynin handed him this letter reads quite differently. "We were not aware of these events beforehand," he told the Soviet ambassador:

> We had not yet fully understood their significance. Nor did we know the extent of Soviet withdrawal. In any event, I wanted Dobrynin to know that the President had issued the strictest orders that there would be no U.S. initiatives toward Cairo and that we would not try to gain unilateral advantages. On the contrary, we would proceed within the letter and spirit of my conversations with Gromyko in Moscow ... Dobrynin said he appreciated this and that now ... it was up to us to take some reciprocal action. I said we would study the letter and no doubt there would be some formal response.

None came. The next day, "Dobrynin ... asked a number of questions about what approaches we had made to Egypt, and I assured him that we had not made any. But he seemed very uncertain. This conversation, like the one the day before, ended on an extremely cordial note."[24] If Nixon himself was incensed at the Soviet claim, he hid it in a press conference a week later. Asked about the impact of the withdrawal, the president fudged: "It might exacerbate the problem by trying to evaluate what happened between Sadat and the Soviet leaders."[25] By 1981, Nixon was taking credit for the achievement when "Soviet advisers were thrown out of Egypt in 1972."[26]

Kissinger thus came full circle from his declared goal to expel the Soviet military formations from Egypt, while the individual advisers might stay—although this was what he actually achieved. His political motivation now required that he advertise the opposite: that he had reached no agreement for withdrawal of the Soviet troops, much less granted the concessions at Israel's expense that the Soviets had demanded in return. But he was also eager to prove that his efforts to promote détente had caused a Soviet setback as a by-product, which could only be done by establishing the misnomer "expulsion of advisers" and depicting it as a bolt from the blue rather than the outcome of extended negotiation. By Nixon's next meeting with Brezhnev, on 14 June 1973, Kissinger was proudly advising the president: "the one area where Soviet policy seems most confused and uncertain is the Middle East. The abrupt dismissal of Soviet *advisers* from the UAR last summer may well have been the highwater mark for the Soviet offensive. ... Their influence with Sadat has declined."[27]

In this, he had the willing cooperation of the Egyptians and the Soviets, for their own motives. Kissinger consistently perpetuated this line in subsequent publications—from his 1979 description of Sadat's "bombshell" move as terminating "the mission of the more than 15,000 Soviet military advisers and experts" to a sweeping statement twenty years later: "In 1972 ... Sadat dismissed all his Soviet military advisers and asked Soviet technicians to leave the country."[28] How pervasive this version became even in recent studies is illustrated by an authoritative overview of the Cold War ("Sadat expelled some 15,000 Soviet advisers from Egypt") and a history of the Palestinian–Israeli conflict ("to the world's surprise, he evicted the Soviet Union's 15,000 military advisers.")[29] Neither writer saw need to provide a reference.

One of the first analyses, by Walter Laqueur in 1974, in referring to the "exodus" as "unexpected and startling," relies mainly on Egypt's "semiofficial version" and Sadat's public statements. Laqueur accepted the subsequent disinformation described below whereby the "expulsion" was later reversed. But his evaluation is actually one of the most accurate to date, in stating that the expulsion was partial, and concealed the effectiveness of war preparations.[30] Other early studies, while accepting the claim of a full expulsion, pointed out that "the rift did not last long ... and the Soviet withdrawals had in fact paved the way for re-establishing military relations on a more stable basis," including supplies specifically aimed at enabling a war.[31] But few have acknowledged that neither rift nor reconciliation ever happened; rather, the bulk of genuine advisers in Egypt resumed their work soon after their mass recall to Cairo in mid-July.[32]

THE SOVIET–ISRAELI WAR, 1967–1973

C. "But the Russians are leaving!" "Well, we have arrived."

"Radio-technical" expert "Smirnov" relates that after about ten days of idling at headquarters in Cairo, which began to cause some drinking problems, "our superior suddenly appeared. ... 'The Arabs have asked us to help them. We have decided to send you out on assignments.'" "Smirnov" and a colleague were sent to Alexandria. At the Hyde Park Hotel where the Soviets were routinely quartered, they noticed that a large portrait of Lenin was still on display. The Egyptian floor manager was, however, surprised to see them, because—he said—"the Russians are leaving." But after reporting their arrival and receiving instructions, he became even more cordial, "addressing us as ... 'comrades-in-arms.' ... This was repeated the next day, when we reported to regimental headquarters ... 'But the Russians are leaving!' 'Well, we have arrived.'" The commanding officer, "without any comment on the supreme leadership's decision to banish all the Soviets to the USSR, declared that he was delighted to see Soviet specialists in his unit again."[33]

This conforms with Kapitanets's account that in August 1972 he "received an order to come to Alexandria for a meeting with the new commander of the Egyptian Navy. ... The admiral stated [that] relations between our fleets remained without any change," despite the discontinuation of the Soviet naval-aviation base in Egypt.[34] The latter, along with the recall of the MiG-25s, was indeed a significant change. But either the introduction of longer-range surveillance aircraft, reliance on other bases (now in Libya too, in addition to Algeria and Syria), or improvement of satellite reconnaissance appear to have made this price acceptable, if not desirable. There is no evidence that Sixth Fleet vessels reported their Soviet shadowing diminished.

Returning to Cairo later in August, "Smirnov" was told that repatriation flights to Russia had ended "as all the nonessentials had already been sent home." He was reassigned to a radar plant, where his Egyptian superior "was not surprised at our appearance." Maj. Baranov explained that "after the first feverish days of evacuation had passed, the command decided to delay whomever they could ... so as not to transport people unnecessarily back and forth." They were henceforth taken to work in a civilian bus. "Morale was not bad ... and billeting was much improved, as many apartments had been vacated."[35]

In Egyptian ground units, the Soviet advisers' presence was likewise renewed—to the extent that it was interrupted at all. Another captured Egyptian document, which was composed about ten months after the "marching orders" issued to the advisers of the 112th Brigade, lists the same number and ranks of Soviet advisers, with an "English" interpreter, as still serving with another infantry brigade, the 2nd. Two of these advisers had arrived before the supposed expulsion (one as early as January 1971 and one in April 1972); they were still on duty in May 1973. The other two advisers and the interpreter are listed as having "arrived in the brigade" in September–October 1972. One of the latter two is the "armored forces adviser" Vladimir Alekseyevich

Nualov, who had been suspected of distributing Soviet literature in the same brigade in *June* 1972; he was, then, relieved before the "expulsion" but reassigned to the same unit afterward.[36] Continuous service before and after 18 July 1972 is also confirmed by Viktor Yakushev, an interpreter, who lists his tour of duty in Egypt from 1971 through 1973.[37] Another linguist, Mikhail Ryabov, was sent to Egypt in 1971 for a second hitch and "returned home" only in August 1973.[38]

The domestic advantage of the withdrawal from Egypt, when presented as a Soviet initiative, is illustrated by a note in Chernyaev's diary from 11 August: with the drought worsening, food shortages growing and Moscow choking on smoke from forest fires, he consoled himself that at least "it's a good thing that we freed ourselves politically from the Middle East, which was dangerous for us!"[39] But the actual continuity in the Soviets' presence is reflected in an annual work plan (December 1972–November 1973) for the advisers of yet another Egyptian brigade.[40] This plan focuses, among other objectives, on "offensive action against a well-fortified enemy"—illustrating that the advisers remained committed to implementing the offensive, for which Moscow had supposedly withdrawn its support. Previous such plans had tasked the advisers with training Egyptian battalions for "crossing water obstacles and securing a bridgehead."

Israeli military historian Dani Asher, who first published this work plan, describes it as representing a "reduction of [the advisers'] activity to a minimum," because the training exercises they supervised were now "only from the individual soldier up to company level." However, it was precisely the advisers' penetration of the Egyptian army *down* to this level that had previously been seen as a measure of their increased influence. Asher stresses that the Egyptian plan for a cross-canal offensive, even after the change of strategic concept that was attributed to Sadat in October, was modeled on Soviet military doctrine and made possible by the advisers' efforts.[41] An IDF study of captured Egyptian documents found that the operational orders were drawn up precisely according to Soviet procedures—detailed plans for the initial phases and only general outlines for the following ones, to permit battleground flexibility.[42]

What definitely was lowered after 17 July was the Soviets' visible profile. Culling the "unessentials" and minimizing the *oboz* (camp follower and baggage) problem, which had increasingly clouded Egyptian–Soviet relations at least since the ceasefire, was clearly both a purpose and a result of the "expulsion." Likewise the issue of off-duty behavior by the advisers themselves, as the GRU station chief in Cairo, Ivliev, admitted when Urwick "suggested to him that whatever he thought about the decision officially, privately he was probably quite glad to be relieved of ... sorting out the problem of advisers who got drunk or who had car accidents. He laughed and nodded."[43]

"Smirnov" now noticed that "no toddlers played any longer in the sand under the eyes of their mothers, officers' wives; no off-duty men sat in the shade smoking their favorite Nefertiti cigarettes and turning the pages of week-old Soviet newspapers."[44] But however dramatic this outward change may have seemed, enough dependents remained (or arrived with newly stationed advisers) for their evacuation in October 1973 to require a massive sea- and airlift. The interpreter Vakhtin, who was then in a group reposted urgently to Egypt, found the advisers' quarters in Nasser City to be just as when he left in July 1972; even the same Egyptian mess hall attendants were on duty, which bespoke unbroken operation.[45]

D. "The biggest canard": denial of offensive aircraft

The extent and success of the Soviet–Egyptian deception was particularly pronounced in respect of Soviet arms shipments. As Rubinstein termed it not long after the "expulsion," "the biggest canard in all Western reporting on the affair was the prevailing uncritical acceptance ... of Sadat's claim" that supplies had been slashed. "Excluding nuclear weapons, of course, no other weapons in the Soviet arsenal were denied the Egyptians."[46] Stein, writing twenty-two years later, also pointed out the "virtually uninterrupted military supply flow from Moscow," which "lends support to the notion that Brezhnev wanted to repatriate Soviet advisers and ... sustain some leverage over Cairo."[47] And thirty years after the event, a Russian diplomat in Israel confirmed: "Sadat's rift with the Soviet Union was more of a theatrical gesture than a serious policy turnaround: the flow of Soviet arms and military equipment to Egypt never stopped."[48]

Several hours before Sadat's announcement, the CIA reported it had learned that he "has ordered a sharp reduction in the Soviet military presence ... apparently as a demonstration of Egypt's independence of great power influence." But the agency listed this development beneath an illustrated report that in late May—that is, after the summit—"Cairo has received a second shipment of T-62 tanks ... indicating Moscow's willingness to meet some of President Sadat's request," noting that this shipment of "advanced" tanks was "the first delivered outside the Warsaw Pact."[49] By 1984, a US military study resorted to prepositional harmonization: "*Despite* the ejection of the majority of the Russian advisors in June of 1972, the Soviet Union not only maintained, but increased the flow of military equipment to Egypt. Clearly, the 1973 war would not have been fought without this support."[50]

After the war, Heikal confirmed that there had been no substantial hiatus in Soviet weapons supplies to Egypt, and in fact some additional and distinctly offensive systems were provided after the alleged rift. Tawila even dates the effort to spread reports about "deficiencies" of Soviet weapons "*at the very time* when the two parties—Egypt and the USSR—had reached agreement about the supply of quantities of arms during the second half of 1973—weapons which in fact, were beginning to arrive." The informants deployed to spread the bluff, "speaking in the jargon of the scientist and the expert, ... would say that the Soviets ... were even cutting off the supply of spare parts in such a manner that our planes had turned into useless scrap."[51]

DECEPTION-ON-NILE, JULY 1972

Actually, the supply continued not only of spares for existing models but of entire and increasingly advanced aircraft, with the attendant instruction by Soviet advisers. Andrey Yena, the deputy commander of a fighter regiment, was abruptly ordered to Egypt in the first week of June, that is, after the Moscow summit and just before the withdrawal of the Soviet MiG-21 squadrons. He was sent on a six-month *komandirovka* at the head of an eleven-man team, whose mission was to oversee the assembly of Su-20 planes. This was the stripped-down export version of the swing-winged Su-17 attack bomber, which besides Egypt and Syria was being supplied only to Poland. The kits were already en route, and once they were put together Yena's group was to instruct Egyptian pilots in their operation.

Yena submitted his work plan directly to EAF Commander Mubarak. He relates that about six weeks into this program, after being told of Sadat's "agreement" with Vinogradov (which establishes the date of Yena's dispatch), his entire group—except the flight instructors—was notified that they were to go home. But within two more weeks, the Egyptians requested that the technical advisers remain too. Yena recounts that while the Cairo media trumpeted the "expulsion," the attitude of his Egyptian counterparts was only slightly more reserved than before, and his trainees politely sidestepped the subject. His mission not only went on to its planned conclusion in November but was even extended for another two months in order to assist in the introduction of the fully equipped Su-17s, which then began to arrive; altogether, Egypt acquired forty craft. By June 1973, the CIA was aware that this model was being supplied, but stated that only seventeen planes had been delivered since the "expulsion," and did not judge that this answered Sadat's demand for offensive air power.[52]

Some of the Soviet squadrons' MiG-21s were said to have been transferred to Syria, and evidently this was the case with part of the advisers—including Yena's superior and Mubarak's personal adviser, Gen. Vagin. The latter's planned two-year stint in Egypt was reduced to eleven months after "relations between the USSR and Egypt cooled off and instructions came from Moscow to leave." Following a short break in Moscow, "toward the end of 1972" Vagin was attached to Mubarak's Syrian counterpart, Jalil Naji—a red-headed Chechen whose family had settled in Syria in the 1920s. Naji evidently needed professional advice: Israeli experts considered him more a politician than a soldier or pilot, whose incompetence impaired the capability of his force.[53] Vagin won his confidence, which would gain the Soviet inside information in the run-up to the 1973 war.[54]

The Soviet presence also continued, or was soon resumed, with the Tu-16s in Upper Egypt. According to Igor' Trofimov, a radio-technician with the aviation arm of the Baltic Fleet, in late 1972 or early 1973 two squadrons of its Badgers were actually flown on short notice *to* Asyut, where they were painted in Egyptian markings; he served there "till the summer of 1973."[55] A history of these Tu-16s' parent formation confirms the stationing of such missile-carrying bombers in October–November

1971, with the primary mission of training the Egyptians. By June 1972, ten Egyptian crews had completed their courses, and in July "an order came to terminate the group's mission." The planes were handed over, but it soon transpired that the Soviets' repatriation was premature. "The EAF command needed the assistance of the Tu-16 experts again. In December 1972 a group of so-called 'instructors' from the same unit of the Baltic fleet arrived in Egypt," including missile experts. They had a six-month contract, but "the missile men stayed ... till October 1973."[56] There was, then, at least some Soviet involvement when these planes would fire twenty-three Kelts at Israeli targets in the Yom Kippur War.[57]

At the EAF's Inshas airbase, Col. Rubtsov's ten-man instructor team continued its activity into August; during the last two months, they were only limited to joint flights in two-seater training craft rather than solo demonstrations. They were seen off cordially, and Rubtsov received both Egyptian and Soviet decorations—the latter from Grechko in person.[58]

E. From canard to "Concept"

Tawila's stress on the aircraft aspect of the deception exercise, and Yena's disclosure about his mission's continuity, are of special importance as they pertain to a central tenet of the evolving Israeli "Concept." It held that Egypt would not initiate even a limited war for lack of fighter-bombers capable of striking at Israel's hinterland, mainly its airbases; and that these would not be forthcoming as a result of the supposed rift with Moscow. This assumption rested, among other sources, on reports received from Ashraf Marwan in 1971–2, whereby regardless of any offensive plans and exercises, the Egyptian military did not regard a cross-canal attack as feasible without such air capability.[59] The IDF chief of staff, Elazar, reckoned as late as 17 September 1973 that the main reason for the improbability of war was the Arabs' own assessment of their planes' inability to reach IAF bases with a sufficient payload.[60]

However, the new Egyptian Sukhois' range, from bases west of the canal, did cover nearly all of Israel. Syria's easily covered the rest—indeed, they were sent on such missions in the 1973 war.[61] But although Israeli military analysts were aware of the Sukhoi deliveries "about a year before the [Yom Kippur] war," they did not consider these planes equal to the task.[62] The head of MI research claimed that though the Egyptians once considered the Su-17 as adequate, "we concluded that when they got to know it they would understand it wasn't, and that's exactly what happened."[63] But on the very eve of the war, MI chief Ze'ira himself voiced concern over the arrival of an Su-20 squadron in Egypt, describing even this export model's specifications as "approaching those of the Phantom." He estimated that the Su-20 and the "MiG-23" were capable of attacking the IAF and thus of deterring it from resumption of its depth bombings.[64]

DECEPTION-ON-NILE, JULY 1972

Still, Ze'ira considered that the Arabs were counting mainly on future supply of Western craft. There was much debate whether Mirage V planes transferred from Libya would fulfil this requirement—and *when* this would happen, the estimate being that their numbers (five squadrons) and integration would be sufficient only in 1975–6. Justifying this assessment after the war, Ze'ira did not even mention the Sukhois.[65] The Libyan Mirages' transfer was negotiated by Marwan as Sadat's envoy, and was reported by him to the Israelis—which may explain the overrated significance they ascribed to it.[66] In the Yom Kippur War, Libyan Mirages were sighted bombing Israeli positions along the canal but were not used for long-range attacks.[67] Neither, for that matter, were the Egyptian Sukhois. The "Concept" turned out to be entirely wrong on this matter, evidently at least in part as a result of disinformation.

Like the other advisers, Yena noted an effort to minimize public awareness of their presence. "Our multi-storey hotel in Nasser City was emptied. The Soviet headquarters was transferred to a private villa. Now we lived in a three-floor villa not far away from headquarters."[68] As their posting to Egypt was for less than one year, Yena and his crew were not entitled to bring their families along, so they created no *oboz* problem.

On 11 August 1972, as Kissinger reported, Dobrynin handed him another letter from Brezhnev "urging a resumption of bilateral Middle East negotiations." But this time the Soviet ambassador "eschewed the pretense that the Soviet withdrawal represented an advance payment on the offer of last October." Rather, Dobrynin admitted that "Sadat had miscalculated. He had thought the request to leave would produce negotiations. Instead, the Soviet Union had pulled everybody out"—as sweeping an exaggeration as Marwan's.[69]

26

THE SOVIETS "RETURN" IN OCTOBER

Primakov at last met Israeli Atomic Energy Commission head Freier again at a Pugwash conference in Oxford, 7 to 12 September 1972.[1] The Soviet emissary's account—the only one available from this meeting—appears to reflect Israeli acceptance of the "expulsion" as fact. "[Freier] stressed the Israeli assessment that the departure of Soviet personnel from Egypt should impact positively on mutual relations," and even said that Israel was planning to propose resumption of diplomatic relations. It was Primakov who downplayed the withdrawal's significance: "the USSR as before has a strong position in Egypt, other Arab states and the Palestinian movement, and Soviet policy remains a central factor." He warned against "using contact with us to press the United States, which is flirting with Egypt, to complicate Soviet–Arab relations." Primakov's report claimed that Freier agreed; it was relayed by Andropov to the Central Committee, where it was endorsed by head of state Podgorny, Premier Kosygin and the Party's ideologue Mikhail Suslov. But no further action was taken.[2] In February 1973, Brezhnev told the Politburo that "Andropov and Gromyko are assigned to look for new ways to establish contact with Israel," but acknowledged that "past attempts were unsuccessful."[3]

The Israelis evidently felt no urgency. They took Primakov's remarks as putting the best face on a Soviet setback, and the developing "Concept" was not affected; if at all, it was reinforced. On 20 January 1973, the semiannual estimate from IDF intelligence held that the prospect of an Egyptian cross-canal offensive was "more remote than ever." The main reason given was that Egypt had been weakened by the expulsion of the Soviet SAM division.[4]

The day after the Pugwash conference ended—13 September—Kissinger was back in Moscow to prepare a visit by Brezhnev to the United States, in effect another summit. The Middle East was broached by the Soviet leader as the last item in their discussion: the transcript shows little rancor on either side. Kissinger, far from his charges of "chutzpah," now appeared to believe that he had engineered a Soviet–Egyptian rift as a Soviet concession in return for the benefits of détente, and complimented Brezhnev for it. The general secretary made no attempt to correct him, and even appears to have uttered some expletive about the Egyptians:

> *Dr Kissinger*: ... Some of the charges made by the Egyptian leaders against you reflect the serious and responsible role you have played. ... [It] puts on us a certain responsibility to deal towards you in the same spirit.
>
> ... *Mr Brezhnev*: That is ... a logical and absolutely correct analysis.
>
> ... *Dr Kissinger*: That does not mean that the people we are dealing with are always logical. (Brezhnev makes off-record remark.) ... this area is a good test of our relations. ... We will take no major initiative in this area except in full consultation and discussion with you.

They agreed that the situation was actually worsening and blamed the regional actors, but saw little urgency in acting on it before the US election—a marked change from Brezhnev's message two months earlier.[5] This appeared to bear out a CIA analysis presented the same day, which connected the expulsion with a weakening of Brezhnev's domestic standing and predicted he would respond "in a measured manner": "The crucial questions are ... how Brezhnev will react if he feels his own position is threatened. ... We expect the Soviet leaders to fight to limit their losses, to attempt to consolidate and play up their 'victories' and to avoid the dramatic."[6]

A major setback dealt to the USSR by its "ouster from Egypt" was thus accepted as fact by Western intelligence professionals, as well as possibly biased political players.

Field reports whereby Soviet advisers had actually remained in Egypt tended to minimize both their numbers and significance. A British assessment "as of 0600 hours, Thursday 5 October" states that "*only* about 1,000 [Soviet military personnel] are left ... mainly technicians and military advisers."[7] This British document quotes an unaccountably high figure of 20,000 Soviet servicemen in Egypt "as at 29 July." Marwan's claim that all were gone a week earlier had apparently been dismissed by now; the remaining number appeared small by comparison. But given the previous total for Soviet *advisers*, as distinct from troops, even if this estimate had been accurate it was quite significant—and definitely should not have corroborated the Soviets' sweeping expulsion. As Asher quotes exactly the same figure for the remaining Soviet advisers, it appears to have been accepted by the IDF as well.[8]

These observations of an unbroken Soviet presence have now been amplified by the Soviets' own accounts, but both at the time and in subsequent historiography they were belittled if not ignored. When the evacuation of Soviet advisers' dependents in October 1973 demonstrated the advisers' own continued presence, a widespread version developed that it had been *re*established, after a complete or near-complete break. Herzog's widely acclaimed 1975 history of the Yom Kippur War first describes Sadat's "decision to ask the Soviet Government to remove its forces and advisers," then asserts a Soviet–Egyptian agreement in October to "arrest the process of deterioration in the relationship." Herzog goes on to claim that "soon after, Soviet

THE SOVIETS "RETURN" IN OCTOBER

military officers *returned* to Egypt," but admits that "these were in addition to those advisers and instructors who had remained after July 1972."[9] Even if accepted as valid, this gloss would drastically reduce the significance of the original "expulsion"; but the actual activities of the advisers show that there was no need for such a reversal.

The supposed *re*stationing of Soviet advisers and other personnel was accounted for by hypothesizing that the expulsion forced Moscow to accept Sadat's demands for weaponry in order to maintain a vestige of influence. Conversely, it has been suggested that the weakness and political unrest exposed in the Egyptian military by the expulsion compelled Sadat to scale down his war plans in order to regain Soviet support. Asher puts the finalization of this supposed change in October 1972. The official Egyptian military history of the war puts the decision to undertake a "military effort at a higher level than a renewed war of attrition" in concert with Syria at "the end of 1972."[10] This was exactly when both Egyptians and Soviets began to plant a second round of press reports about a Soviet return, which once denied would reinforce the overall illusion of an irrevocable rift.

The Middle East was again the last item discussed by Foreign Minister Gromyko and Kissinger when they met in Washington on 2 October. They did little but restate their previous positions (the Soviet insisting again on a comprehensive settlement including all the Israeli-occupied territories and the Palestinian refugees):

> *Gromyko*: What should I report to the General-Secretary on your views?
>
> ... *Dr Kissinger*: On some of the proposals you have suggested, we disagree. On others we agree; on others we should discuss.
>
> *FM Gromyko*: When?
>
> *Dr Kissinger*: Early November, after the election. ...
>
> *Amb. Dobrynin*: You will need one week after the election for celebration![11]

But as they spoke, a rapid succession of indications strengthened the impression that the Soviets were taking advantage of the interim to regain the standing they had supposedly lost in Egypt.

On 3 October, Vinogradov returned to Cairo, which he had left shortly after the "expulsion" order for a longer absence than the usual summer vacation.[12] After a call in Moscow by Egypt's information minister, it was reported that a "reconciliation" visit there by Prime Minister Sidqi had been arranged by Syrian President Assad. Heikal (who had been rebuffed by Kissinger when he asked to meet in Europe) called for a rapprochement with the USSR, because "even if the Soviets give us 50 percent of what we asked for," that would be more than the Europeans and Americans would provide. Sadat himself reiterated that the main dispute with Moscow was over the "means to strike at the Israeli hinterland."[13] Following an Israeli raid in Lebanon, Sadat claimed that "if I had had 'MiG-23s' ... I would have attacked Israel"; Sidqi was reported to be bearing a renewed demand for supply of Foxbats.[14] Before returning to Cairo on the 19th, Sidqi reportedly received a "Soviet promise to resume deliveries of spare parts and replacements for Soviet weapons now in Egypt."[15] On 10 October, for the first time since 23 July, SAMs were fired—again from the Ismailia sector—at Israeli aircraft east of the canal, and this time Cairo claimed one shot down.[16]

On 26 October, Defense Minister Sadiq resigned following reports of a botched coup attempt by field-unit officers, who reportedly had plotted to put him in charge of a military junta to replace Sadat and Sidqi.[17] It soon transpired that the mutiny, and the subsequent arrests among the officer corps, had more to do with criticism of the revived federation plan with Libya than with a direct Soviet context, but this did not prevent suggestions of a pro-Soviet about-face in Cairo.[18] Ahmed Ismail, who had accompanied Sidqi to Moscow, was credited with "stifling" the coup, and replaced the "anti-Soviet" Sadiq as minister of defense and commander in chief.[19] In Israel, Dayan opined that Ismail's reinstatement signaled an improvement of relations with the USSR and resumption of arms deliveries, but he "hoped and assumed" that "as before" there would be no direct Soviet involvement in combat.[20] The Israelis had evidently begun to believe, or at least continued to propagate, their own public downplaying of the Soviets' role less than three years earlier.

In retrospect, Israeli historians would point to the Egyptian government reshuffle as a turning point toward finalization of Sadat's revised war plan. Much has been made of an abrupt change that Sadat reportedly announced to the supreme military council on 24 October: that he had given up on obtaining either US political support *or* the Soviet offensive weaponry essential for recapturing all of Sinai. Instead, Egypt would pursue total war but for a limited objective, with the arms it already had. Sadiq—it was now claimed—was one of the officers who objected and were dismissed.

This is the version that Ashraf Marwan has been credited for relaying to his Mossad handlers, by means of a radio transmitter they had equipped him with "for brief messages when necessary." Even Marwan's strongest Israeli advocate, Bar-Joseph, admits that as in other cases the Israelis received the same information from additional sources too.[21] The list of IDF intelligence-gathering objectives for 1973–4 did include monitoring "the USSR's ... intentions toward the region and Israel." But the news that Sadat had effectively accepted Moscow's line, while the USSR continued its military support, was ignored in MI's aforementioned semiannual estimate on 20 January 1973.[22] Asher has traced Israel's unpreparedness for the Yom Kippur War to its failure to appreciate this change in Sadat's strategy.[23]

Contrary to Marwan's message, one component of the "essential offensive weaponry"—attack aircraft—was already in the process of induction into the EAF by Soviet advisers, and the other—Scud missiles—would soon follow. At the time, correct perceptions of continuing, or at most reactivated, Soviet military support were scotched by the appearance and prompt discrediting of inflated, and apparently planted, reports that a complete rupture had been reversed. A report from the

THE SOVIETS "RETURN" IN OCTOBER

Telegraph's John Bulloch on 30 October, headlined "Russians Return to Egypt," caused a stir as high up as the British foreign secretary:

> Russian military advisers are quietly moving back to Egypt to man the air defenses along the Suez Canal and around Cairo. At least 400 are already in the country. Plane loads of technicians are arriving every day to replace the men expelled by President Sadat last July. The new Russian Advisers clearly expect to remain this time. Wives and children have also been arriving, and a Russian club closed three months ago has reopened. ... Sadat's policy ... was reversed.

Bulloch described the dismissal of the "violently anti-Russian" Sadiq as "the price the Russians demanded for renewed aid," and claimed that Sidqi was "selected by Moscow as its man in Cairo" who might even depose Sadat himself if necessary to forestall an anti-Soviet countercoup.[24]

This report, and a similar item in the *Financial Times* the same day, were soon discredited.[25] The British ambassador in Cairo, Richard Beaumont, responded to urgent inquiries from London that he had "no (repeat no) evidence whatever" for such daily planeloads of advisers. "Our strong impression is that Bulloch came to Cairo ... to find Russians under every stone. ... He may have succeeded in picking up just enough clubroom gossip to make this thesis look plausible."[26] Sir Richard's counterpart in Beirut was finally "able to tackle Bulloch" a week later, and reported that the journalist admitted his claims were based on "a general consensus of well-informed opinion"; the ambassador was impressed that Bulloch "did not appear to have checked his 'facts.'"[27] The *Financial Times* writer who had also referred to a "return of advisers" told the Foreign Office that "he set very little store by this report but used it merely as a peg" for his story.[28]

Consulted about the *Telegraph* article, the British defense attaché in Tel Aviv also reported that the Israelis "did not believe it to be true," and estimated that Bulloch "had read into the removal of Sadek ... more than was justified." Meeting a new British ambassador, Israeli Foreign Minister Eban "raised on his initiative the *Daily Telegraph* story" and proceeded to dismiss it:

> neither the Israelis nor Washington had any confirmation. ... He thought that the Russians probably did not want to return to the positions they had held in Egypt before 18 July. It was too close to confrontation with the Americans, and the presence of large numbers of Russians was bound to irritate Egyptian nationalist sentiments.

The Briton cautiously (and as it now appears, correctly) noted "there may be a touch of wishful thinking in what Mr Eban said."[29] In Cairo, Beaumont was entirely confident that "General Ahmed Ismail is *not* pro-Soviet. There is strong resistance in the Egyptian Army and Air Force to the return of any Soviet advisers, and Sadat would have difficulty in overcoming it."[30]

A month later, Beaumont did admit that, after all,

some Soviet experts may well ... have returned recently from their summer holidays and of course, as Sadat has always said, a number of technicians particularly on the air defence side have a continuing job to do under arrangements pre-dating the Soviet withdrawal. ... To the best of our knowledge, the Russian club mentioned by Bulloch never closed.

Some of the Soviets had returned with families—indicating long-term postings. Still, he was "pretty convinced that the current Whitehall estimate of between 400 and 1200 Soviet military advisers/technicians in Egypt is much too high"—which actually confirmed Bulloch's *lower* figure.[31] Beaumont aptly noted that "the Egyptians themselves have not done much to help matters by consistently blurring the distinction between 'advisers' and 'experts.'" But he was evidently taken in himself, since he described the advisers as formerly constituting "the bulk of the Soviet military presence here." His "considered view" was still "that there are no Russians attached in any capacity to the Egyptian navy, and probably few Russians, if any, attached to the army."

Though Beaumont confirmed that Soviet technicians were *maintaining* the SAM array, he reported no Soviet personnel involved in *operating* the SAM-3 batteries that were handed over to Egypt.[32] The Soviets themselves hardly made such a distinction. Mikhail Ryabov, a military interpreter, had returned to Egypt for a second tour of duty before the "expulsion" and remained there until August 1973 with a SAM maintenance outfit. It was attached to the Egyptian III Army Corps "in the trenches on the Suez Canal, engaged in improving the combat readiness of the troops and planning an offensive operation across a water obstacle ... as part of the strategic objective which they accomplished in the October 1973 War."[33]

Beaumont insisted that, as a Beirut paper had claimed, all the Soviet SAM-6 missiles had been removed from Egypt and that none had been returned. But the *New York Times* soon reported from US "military and diplomatic sources" that "the Soviet Union has recently shipped about 60 advanced surface-to-air missiles to Egypt."[34] Israeli intelligence also reported that SAM-6 deliveries to Egypt (as distinct from deployment of Soviet-manned batteries), which had been agreed upon in February 1972, actually *began* in August. But this was not considered to have replaced attack aircraft as the "key" element that Egypt still lacked for an offensive.[35]

Beaumont's assessment whereby *all* Soviets were gone from the Egyptian Navy went further than GRU station chief Ivliev volunteered to the British naval attaché on 13 November: "all advisers and all specialists ceased duties with the Egyptian Navy on seventeenth July and have subsequently gone home," *except* for "a few solely concerned with liaison duties ... Ivliev was insistent that the Soviet government would not (not) allow advisers to return ... and did not expect an invitation."

But the British attaché's report listed several major aspects of continuing Soviet naval presence: "Soviet warships still use Alexandria for self-maintenance," supported by "a resident depot ship ... two Soviet submarines were in Alexandria on 12 November ... the numbers of Soviet engineers and technicians in the ship repair

THE SOVIETS "RETURN" IN OCTOBER

yard have not yet been reduced." Ominously, Port Said still "provided a haven for Soviet commando units as a counter to marine forces of the Sixth Fleet"—so that not even all regular Soviet formations had been withdrawn. Ivliev confirmed in effect that the main change was in visibility: "Soviet ratings are still forbidden to go ashore in uniform."[36] This time, Whitehall's reading was quite correctly that Ivliev's aim was "to convince us that the Soviet naval presence ... was smaller than it really is."[37]

Overall, whether or not the reports of a Soviet return were intentionally floated by the Egyptians and/or Soviets in order to shoot them down, the end result was to further belittle if not to entirely negate *any* Soviet presence. This hardly changed even when Sadat declared a few weeks later that he had promised the Soviet Union continued use of naval facilities *even after a settlement with Israel*, and that he intended to keep Soviet advisers attached to the Egyptian Army "because war is a science now."[38] This promise has been cited as prompting the Soviet military's supposed reconsideration of its earlier supposed refusal, and its resulting decision to provide Egypt with the weapons Sadat desired. But as already seen, the naval bases' use was continuous and the arms transfers had never stopped anyway.[39] In February 1973, Dayan was unimpressed by recurring talk in the United States that if nothing were done (usually meaning that if Israel did not show flexibility toward a settlement), the Soviets were *liable* to return to Egypt.[40]

PART 4

"WE PREPARED THE WAR"

This point on the timeline—late 1972 or very early 1973—is where scrutiny must begin in order to answer another question that has been as vexing for historians as it was for national actors at the time. This is whether and to what extent the Soviet Union colluded with Egypt, as well as Syria, in initiating, timing and conducting the Yom Kippur War. The following chapters seek to delineate the continuity to this war from the various elements of previous Soviet involvement. Discussion will center, therefore, on the opening phases of the war and those subsequent features of Soviet action that clearly cannot be attributed to *ad hoc* response to unforeseen developments.

In Putin's Russia, it has become politically correct to describe the October 1973 surprise attack as "one of the most brilliant operations conceived by Soviet military advisers and their Arab friends."[1] But most Western scholarship has been slow to abandon the official Soviet line, as laid down by Brezhnev at the CPSU CC plenum in September 1974. "The speech was read out at Party assemblies ... He criticized Sadat and explained that the USSR did not know about Sadat's planned operation."[2]

Even semi-official Russian histories have conceded by now that in fact "the USSR was informed about its Arab allies' intent."[3] Assad's sympathetic biographer Patrick Seale went a step further: "did the Soviets know the October War was coming? Obviously, yes. Did they help in its planning? The answer must also be yes, to the extent that Arab arms requirements were worked out with Soviet experts on the basis of specific military plans."[4] The questions of general foreknowledge and essential material support have, then, become moot. What must still be addressed are the issues of practical collusion in preparing the war—by both military moves and deception efforts—and direct participation in its conduct.

The usual focus on the very last days before the Egyptian–Syrian attack on 6 October necessarily highlighted the mass evacuation of Soviet civilians, including the dependents of military advisers, from Egypt and Syria that was ostensibly improvised on the shortest notice on the 4th. It was taken to indicate that Moscow was previously unaware at least of the zero hour for the offensive, and that it was so reluctant to get involved that it was willing even to compromise the advantage of surprise

301

for its allies. Therefore, while Soviet propaganda justified the Arabs' "liberation" campaign, Western leaders (followed by historians) tended—or pretended—to believe Moscow's protestations that its clients had acted against Soviet advice.

Doubts were already expressed in real time. As Israeli Foreign Minister Eban testified shortly after the war (12 December):

> I think the jury is still out ... whether they [the Soviets] desired it. My impression is that they did ... Dr Kissinger ... [considered that] they certainly knew there would be a war, and even if they did not want it—they did not consult with the US, as required by the Détente idea ... that they were unrestrained with the armament, that they incited other Arab states to take part in the war, and afterwards brought America to the brink of confrontation—but I never heard the Americans say that the USSR desired and initiated this war.[5]

Three weeks into the war, columnist Joseph Alsop asserted flatly that "the Soviet Union sponsored the Egyptian and Syrian attack on Israel. In view of the massive Soviet supplies poured in before the attack, and the undoubted Soviet advance knowledge of the attack itself, 'sponsorship' is a most conservative word."[6] But Alsop, as already seen, was discounted as "a militant cold warrior perennially sounding the tocsin against the worldwide Kremlin conspiracy."[7] Such a determination—essentially, that Moscow *deliberately* jeopardized global détente by putting it to such a severe test—was rarely made either in contemporary pronouncements or in subsequent histories.

This meant that the USSR's support of the Arab side after the outbreak of war, both politically and by means of a massive military resupply effort, had to be considered as practically imposed upon the Soviets by their clients as the price for maintaining regional influence. Such perceptions persisted even when at a critical juncture, when Israel threatened to reverse the initial Arab gains, the Soviets were believed to have thrown their own nuclear capability into the equation, triggering a commensurate US response. When Egypt did switch to the US camp after the war, this was taken retrospectively to prove its intentions going in, and to confirm that this reluctant Soviet effort had been forlorn to begin with.

Tracing the antecedents largely obviates detailed analysis of the climactic first week of October 1973 in order to resolve the issues of Soviet complicity. The questions have to be rephrased: *Given* Soviet collusion, how and why were the evacuation and other Soviet moves made in the ultimate run-up to the war and its initial phases? Shortly after Alsop's column, and with the even greater passion of a convert from communism, Theodore Draper pointed out that the distinction between passive acquiescence and active connivance was in effect a quibble:

> If the "basic principles" of Détente had been respected, the Egyptian–Syrian attack should not have taken place. ... The Soviets encouraged it by acquiescing, and they would have discouraged it by refusing to acquiesce. ... In fact, the vast and expensive effort the Russians

PART 4: "WE PREPARED THE WAR"

must have made to render this war possible required a major decision on the part of the Soviet leadership many months ago.[8]

With the proviso that *both* parties to détente often preferred their interests over its declared principles, newly emerged evidence has borne out both Alsop and Draper. The proud claims of Soviet veterans that "we prepared" the Yom Kippur War refer as much to the post-"expulsion" phase as to the previous stages.[9] They add convincing evidence that besides weapons supply and strategic advice, Soviet personnel and weapons took an active, if limited and undisclosed, part in the actual fighting.

27

"WE CAN'T CONTROL THE ARABS BUT MUST SUPPORT THEM"

A. "Peace" in Vietnam obscures war preparations in Egypt

On the very day of the government shakeup in Cairo, 26 October 1972, Kissinger announced that a breakthrough in the Paris talks had put "peace at hand" in Vietnam, and although this proved premature it helped Nixon to a landslide election victory on 7 November. The two main obstacles that Kissinger had cited for making good on his share of the Moscow summit's Middle East understandings—Vietnam and the US election—were ostensibly removed.

Briefly, Egyptian statements appeared to reflect expectation of a superpower accommodation. The usually "snake-eating and fire-spitting" Chief of Staff Shazly was quoted that five more years of preparation were needed before a war could be launched. EAF chief Mubarak returned from an "arms-shopping" trip to Moscow, which was noted as "the first visit by a top-level Egyptian military delegation to the Soviet Union since President Anwar Sadat ousted 10,000 Soviet military personnel," but he reportedly had little to show beyond continued supply of spare parts.[1] Sadat again justified the Soviets' "expulsion," as they were "arrogant and didn't deliver." He told US columnists Evans and Novak that he hoped to reconstruct relations with Moscow.[2] But for the Soviets détente with the Americans now overshadowed all else, and there was no way to know how far Brezhnev would support Egypt at the approaching second summit with Nixon.

Before the Vietnam accord was finalized, US bombing raids were intensified. On 22 November 1972, North Vietnamese SAM-2s scored their first shootdown of a B-52 strategic bomber. The Vietnamese claimed downing thirty-one more B-52s between 12 and 29 December.[3] They acknowledged that "a major contribution ... was made by Soviet military specialists in Vietnam, the personnel of Soviet design bureaus, and factory workers."[4]

Tabulation of the downed (American) bombers in Vietnam was held up to the advisers in Egypt as a challenging example, with the implied suggestion that on their

305

front too, the Americans or Israelis might attempt to force a more favorable settlement. "Smirnov," the radio-technical expert, recorded that "the Egyptian leadership was concerned, though this was a completely different war ... that Israel was about to land a blow."[5] The Israelis felt a similar threat from Egypt, but on 1 December, Meir still stated she did not expect Soviet combat involvement. "If the Russians didn't do that at the time of their massive presence in Egypt ... they can't be assumed to do so now, under fundamentally changed circumstances, when ... the Russians ... are literally dependent upon the West."[6]

An Egyptian attack was now deemed possible nonetheless, based on information from Marwan and others. Israel's concern was communicated to Nixon, Kissinger and CIA Director Helms.[7] The tone of Egyptian statements indeed changed abruptly, in a matter of weeks. Shazly told *Al-Ahram* that war was near and "Egypt must make do with the arms it has."[8] Sadat, in parliament, repeated more than a dozen times that war was inevitable, and announced "practical measures" to prepare it. Friendship with the Soviet Union, he said, was still "a major factor, though the limitations of every friend must be understood."[9]

These "practical measures" were soon noticed by "Lt Smirnov": "they moved all the combat equipment from its permanent storage facilities to the desert and deployed it in hardened positions. ... 'Our' [superior] Baranov was summoned 'upstairs.' He returned unusually grim," and announced a 24/7 alert. When asked against what emergency it was aimed, "he barked back" that there might be a need for "repair of radio-location equipment"—that is, an attack on the SAM array was expected. "After cooling off a bit, he added more softly: 'God forbid.' In those days, hearing such words from an atheist and communist was simply extraordinary."[10]

This account corresponds with "tentative indications of Egyptian intent to reopen fire" that were detected by Israeli intelligence in December.[11] It would be the first of several false alarms that contributed to dulling Israeli readiness. Then, "Smirnov" relates, "everything settled down. After completing the bombings, the Americans returned to the table and concluded the Paris talks [on Vietnam]. Nobody attacked Egypt, the equipment was brought home from the desert, all the radar stations remained intact and Western tourists again calmly posed for photos at the pyramids."[12] Both superpower leaders declared to their entourages that they would now more actively seek political progress in the Middle East. On 2 February, Chernyaev of the Central Committee International Department noted a statement by Brezhnev in the Politburo: "let Sadat think about what the end of the war in Vietnam means for him. Andropov and Gromyko are assigned to look for new ways to establish contact with Israel."[13]

But there was little change of tone toward Israel in a note that Dobrynin handed to Kissinger on 28 January—one day after the formal signing of the Paris accords. Convinced that Kissinger was not about to deliver on the summit deal, Dobrynin

"WE CAN'T CONTROL THE ARABS BUT MUST SUPPORT THEM"

handed him a reminder that his excuses had expired, and a warning of the consequences for détente:

> Time is passing while the situation in the Middle East remains complicated and dangerous. If effective measures are not taken the events there can get out of control. ... Further existence of the deadlock in the settlement, for which Israel is to blame, cannot but force the Arab countries to seek a way out along the lines of using military methods ... no matter what would be the attitude of others to it.[14]

This would become the consistent Soviet line: Moscow could not control its Arab allies, but would be constrained to support them if Israeli intransigence compelled them to fight. The "expulsion" had thus absolved the Soviets of responsibility without weakening their commitment to an Arab military option.

King Hussein of Jordan said as much to Kissinger:

> the Egyptians' expulsion of the Soviet advisors ... removed the Soviet presence from possible direct involvement in any resumption of armed conflict between the Egyptians and the Israelis, [but] it also increased the danger of President Sadat perhaps heating up the situation on his own. ... Indeed, we have heard from President Sadat himself that such are his intentions. ... The Soviet policy in the area, following the relative deterioration of their position in Egypt, appears to be one of ... saving what they could of their presence in Egypt.[15]

Hussein thus helped to propagate the "dualistic" view of "reluctant" Soviet support for Sadat's war aims. The asymmetry in superpower–client relations was exemplified when Rogers told the Jordanian king—rather pathetically—that the "only problem we have in our relations with Arabs is Israel. Otherwise, we get along fine with Arabs ... much better than Soviets do."[16]

B. Watergate foils Nixon's plot against Kissinger

Nixon claimed in his memoirs that at this point "I spoke to Henry about the need to get going on the Mideast."

> What he's afraid is that Rogers, *et al.* will get ahold of the issue and ... that it will break down. ... Henry has constantly put off moving on it ... but I am determined to bite this bullet ... because we just can't let the thing ride ... providing a fishing ground not only for radicals but, of course, for the Soviets.[17]

Nixon's Oval Office tapes confirm that the president considered removing Kissinger entirely from the Middle Eastern brief. Speaking with the White House chief of staff, Kissinger's former NSC deputy Alexander Haig, Nixon objected mainly to "Henry's" reluctance to confront Israel and its US supporters, which might encourage Meir to attack Egypt:

> Henry's filibustered the Mideast for almost four years too, because he is totally attacking what the Jewish agenda wants. ... We've got to take it. We can't let State handle the

Mideast; they'll screw it up. But I just can't see Henry doing it. ... Right after the election ... I said, "Henry, the time has now come ... to squeeze the old woman."[18]

But within a week, the first convictions in the Watergate affair were handed down, Nixon's standing deteriorated rapidly, and no move was made to dislodge Kissinger or to alter his approach. On the contrary, his grip intensified until he achieved an unprecedented monopoly by retaining his position as national security adviser when he replaced Rogers as secretary of state on 22 September 1973. The State Department could not be blamed when two weeks later, Kissinger's policy at least failed to prevent the Yom Kippur War.

While the war was in progress, Kissinger and his Vietnamese opposite number were awarded the Nobel Peace Prize for the Paris accords. Le Duc Tho declined the prize, as the pact had not yet been implemented, and it never was. A quarter-century later, a reassessment published by the Norwegian Nobel Institute concluded that in the Middle East no less than in Vietnam, "the Soviet–American summits of 1973–74 increasingly represented a public façade; underneath that façade the search for unilateral advantages continued. ... All said, the 'performance' hardly merited a prize."[19]

For now, in early 1973, the US embassy in Israel confirmed that "today, with what Israelis consider to be [the] de-Sovietization in large degree of [the] Middle East conflict and U.S.–Soviet rapprochement, they think that U.S. fears of global confrontation no longer will lead to U.S. pressure."[20] Hopes of a radical pro-American shift in Cairo were raised by feelers toward Washington from Sadat's envoy Hafez Ismail, but dampened by continuing signs of a Soviet–Egyptian reconciliation. The CIA saw a silver lining in terms of renewed Soviet pressure for a settlement:

> the meeting in Cairo on 25 January between President Sadat and the Soviet Ambassador ... who had just returned from consultations in Moscow ... was their first meeting in six months. ... In his 1 February 1973 message, Hafiz Ismail ... noted that the present state of Egyptian–Soviet relations is more favorable than that of Egyptian relations with the US. ... Moscow may be preparing for or even stimulating a revival of interest in a Middle Eastern settlement, now that a Vietnam peace agreement has been signed. The Soviets ... could have made this point so strongly to Sadat that he now feels more restricted and inhibited.

This reading of a Soviet–Egyptian rapprochement as aimed mainly at promoting a Soviet-backed peace initiative was unchanged even in an updated postscript: "Vinogradov received a Soviet military delegation from Moscow ... on 1 February 1973"—that is, the delegation's dispatch had been coordinated before he returned to Cairo.[21] It spent at least twelve days in Egypt.

C. Lashchenko returns to coordinate offensive plans and armament

This military mission was described as "relatively low-level ... discussing routine maintenance and spare-parts supply." But it was received by both Ahmed Ismail and Sadat

"WE CAN'T CONTROL THE ARABS BUT MUST SUPPORT THEM"

himself.[22] Retrospectively, Egyptian sources attached great importance to this delegation as a milestone in preparations for war: it was led by none other than Lashchenko, the original architect of the cross-canal offensive plan. No Western reports mentioned his presence, but Lashchenko "left with an agreed list of our armament needs" for the operation—"The Final Deal."

On documents later captured by Israel, the earliest date of an operational plan is 14 January 1973—a date also claimed by Sadat in several retrospective interviews.[23] According to Heikal, Lashchenko arrived the day after a top-secret meeting (on 31 January) of the Egyptian and Syrian military chiefs, who set up a unified command and determined that only their armies (not other potential partners, such as Libya) would take part in the offensive.[24] The Soviet general was thus presented with a specific blueprint, and endorsed it along with the associated requests for materiel, which Moscow would formally approve the next month.

Reports reaching Israel soon verified the delivery of at least two essential items on this list: water cannon and large quantities of *Malyutka*s. For now, their significance was dismissed; one Israeli general was quoted by a colleague as boasting: "put all the Egyptian paratroops on a hill with Saggers, and I'll wipe them out with a couple of tanks."[25] MI chief Ze'ira admitted after the war that "in hindsight he realized that Sadat changed his concept sometime in spring or summer 1973." The Agranat Commission found that the evidence at the time already indicated this change occurred at the beginning of the year, when the Egyptians resolved to fight Israel "with whatever military resources they had, even without fulfillment of the condition of acquiring long-range fighter-bombers."[26] In fact, however, even this condition was already being fulfilled. Within two weeks, "Israeli and Egyptian planes fought a brief air battle over the Gulf of Suez ... breaking eight months of silence" since the "expulsion."[27]

These developments were eclipsed by a supposed diplomatic breakthrough when Hafez Ismail consented to visit Washington (after standing for some time on meetings in Europe). Much has been made, most recently in a book by Yigal Kipnis, of a peace initiative that Ismail floated on behalf of Sadat. Disagreement centers on whether it was sidetracked by Kissinger himself or disregarded by Meir and her cabinet, thereby missing an opportunity to avert war and leading Sadat to settle on war preparations only in July 1973.[28]

The IDF's voluminous official history of the Yom Kippur War suggests the opposite: that "in the fall of 1972, or at the latest in the spring of 1973"—that is, by the time of Lashchenko's visit and Ismail's mission—Sadat had already abandoned "hopes that the powers would impose [an Israeli] withdrawal ... without a military move."[29] This might be construed as retrospective apologetics, but the following survey of Soviet and Egyptian activity hardly indicates that in 1973, any more than at any time since the summer of 1967, they were genuinely open to any option but a military one. What might have followed a complete Israeli acceptance of Sadat's terms—including the Palestinian non-starter—or a full, unilateral Israeli withdrawal is a matter of counterfactual speculation. Even if in view of the horrendous Israeli losses in October such possibilities ought to have been explored, the record suggests that neither Cairo nor Moscow expected or desired it.

Ismail came to the United States only after "three days of intensive consultations in Moscow." His Kremlin talks included another post-"expulsion" first, a "marathon" five-hour session with Brezhnev as well as three meetings with Foreign Minister Gromyko to "coordinate policy ahead of an expected US initiative."[30] As an East German official was told in Moscow, Ismail stated that an Israeli withdrawal could be achieved only through military means. Brezhnev responded that "the Egyptians are their own masters and control their army. If they deem themselves ready, [they] are welcome to consider it. We think that Egypt is not yet ready for it. We think that reactionary forces in Egypt are trying to blame their weakness on Soviet military technology." Brezhnev pointed to the huge US losses of planes and tanks in Vietnam to prove that the problem was not in the Soviet weapons but in their Egyptian operators. Briefing his East German guest on the talks, Ponomarev's deputy for developing countries stressed that "while aspiring to a political solution, the Soviet Union is reinforcing Egypt's military potential. ... Now the Egyptians are leaning toward the Soviet Union again."[31]

On 18 February, Soviet chargé d'affaires Yuly Vorontsov "hand carried" to Nixon a letter from the "Soviet leadership," whereby "we have got an impression from our talks with Mr Ismail that, if at this time also no progress is reached towards political solution ... the Arabs can turn to the use of ... other methods of struggle. ... They simply will have no other alternative."[32] Arriving in Washington in the last week of February, Ismail heard from Nixon himself about his post-election determination to achieve a *pax Americana*, starting with a "Middle East month" to include visits by Hussein and Meir; the Soviets were to be dealt out.[33] Kissinger, summing up two days of talks with Ismail, determined that the latter "did not change Egypt's position on any basic issue."[34]

Kissinger was still in no hurry to press forward. He told Dobrynin, when the latter asked "how the talks with Ismail had gone," that "there was no possibility of a settlement along the lines of the paper that Gromyko had given me during my visit last April. ... As long as I was negotiating with the Egyptians I saw no point in our [US–Soviet] discussions going beyond the statement of general principles."[35]

In the US and Western media, the novelty of a ranking Egyptian envoy at the White House (to be followed by Foreign Minister Ismail Fahmy), and even more so Israel's horrible blunder when on 21 February it shot down a Libyan airliner that strayed over Sinai, overshadowed the military preparations that were the order of the day in Moscow. The world press almost entirely ignored the arrival of Defense Minister Ahmed Ismail in Moscow on 26 February—with the unexpected distinction of flying in on board a VIP transport of the Soviet Air Force.[36]

"WE CAN'T CONTROL THE ARABS BUT MUST SUPPORT THEM"

His talks were described as following up on those of Lashchenko's delegation, which was now openly reported to have discussed the details of a new arms deal. To the extent that Ahmed Ismail's mission was covered in the more attentive Israeli press, it revived speculation that

> some Soviet advisers are expected to return to Egypt ... to handle the maintenance of delicate and highly sophisticated equipment that Egypt will apparently receive. ... The USSR and Egypt will be checking close up some severe logistical problems [that may arise] in case an "interim" political settlement permits Egypt to send troops across the canal.[37]

But the specific Egyptian desiderata were more in line with a hostile crossing. The Soviets were correctly reported as still refusing Egyptian demands to acquire Foxbats, but contemplating an offer of some other new model instead; this possibly referred to the Su-17s whose supply had already begun. Incorrectly, as it soon transpired, the Soviets were still supposed to be withholding Scud missiles.[38] Some Egyptian sources date the Soviet agreement to provide Scuds and even the start of their delivery at "the beginning of 1973"—that is, Ahmed Ismail did clinch this deal in Moscow.[39]

Even the proud official Egyptian military history of the October War concedes that the technical efforts of Egyptian industry only provided half the volume of equipment that was now received from the USSR.[40] As radio-technical expert "Smirnov" noted, in early 1973 "the Arabs began to get serious about integrating the new Soviet weapons. ... They also had a self-produced submachinegun called the Port Said, a crude wood-and-metal contraption that our specialists ridiculed: 'perhaps it can kill at 30 meters but the maximum range is 50.'" He observed that "more and more often, among the desert dunes soldiers could be seen drilling, with the stress on storming an enemy strongpoint in rough desert surroundings. They all had new Kalashnikovs, and every third man had an RPG"—an emphasis on infantry anti-tank capability that would have momentous impact in October. "The shooting attested that they were not sparing ammunition," "Smirnov" observed, adding that similar preparations were under way in other Egyptian services.[41]

Israel learned "in early 1973" that the new arms deal had been made and that it included bridging and fording equipment, additional SAMs (mainly SAM-6s) and electronics.[42] Egyptian air defense—as one of its Soviet advisers relates—had since the "temporary peace in 1971," when "the issue of liberating Sinai came onto the agenda," begun preparations to advance the SAM array across the canal.[43] However, the dismissive attitude in Israel was reflected by the head of MI research when he claimed, even after the 1973 war, that "in February the Egyptians didn't even know what plane to ask for ... they didn't know what types of plane existed in the USSR."[44]

On Ahmed Ismail's way back to Cairo, it was announced that he stopped in Damascus.[45] Other sources put this visit in mid-February—that is, *before* Ismail's visit to Moscow—and claim that he then proposed three dates for war with Israel, of which Assad preferred October over the earliest option, in May.⁴⁶ According to Syrian military documents recently published in Russia, the decision to launch a joint attack on Israel was reached by Sadat and Assad on 25 February, at an otherwise unreported meeting in Alexandria, to which Assad brought preliminary plans that his generals had submitted two weeks earlier. Ahmed Ismail—as commander of the Egyptian–Syrian–Libyan federation's united forces—was informed; that is, he arrived in Moscow with the joint decision already made.⁴⁷ This would put the determination of date and the finalization of arms supply as the main items that he arranged in Moscow and relayed back to the Syrians, who were already "elaborating the details" of the operational plan.

The Syrian documents state that this plan was completed on 31 March, but the General Staff in Damascus decided on 18–19 April to postpone implementation "to the autumn, in order to improve preparation and complete induction of equipment newly arrived from the USSR."⁴⁸ Accordingly, as the US embassy in Rabat reported, although a delegation from Morocco visited Syria on 19–20 March to arrange the dispatch of troops, no date was set; they ultimately would be sent in August.⁴⁹

Bar-Joseph's *The Angel* cites an earlier version whereby the Alexandria summit was on 23 *April* and Assad then went again to Moscow for more aircraft and air defense systems, returning to Damascus with Soviet Air Force chief Kutakhov.⁵⁰ Bar-Joseph's purpose was to show that a warning by Ashraf Marwan on 11 April, whereby a war was to be launched in May, was genuine, as the postponement to the fall had not yet been agreed. But the evidence now indicates that the Soviets clearly knew by the end of April that the offensive was *not* going to be launched that spring, which casts new light on the accepted view that it was postponed after preparations on the ground were already begun and detected.

Brezhnev did not mention any arms deal when, on 14 March, he wrote to Nixon that Ahmed Ismail "had expressed the Egyptian Government's serious concern with the absence of any progress toward a peace settlement. ... The Egyptian Government was coming to the conclusion that military confrontation with Israel might become unavoidable. Therefore, Egypt had to prepare itself." Again, "Brezhnev concluded his message by saying that he wanted to draw the President's attention to the necessity of taking constructive steps in order to prevent such a confrontation."⁵¹ Testifying before the Israeli commission of inquiry after the Yom Kippur War, Foreign Minister Eban effectively blamed the Americans for taking such statements at face value and pushing the Israelis in the same direction:

> since we were cut off from [the USSR] due to the Six-Day War, I must say that the general opinion in our quarters was undoubtedly influenced by those who had more contacts there. It was that because of Détente ... the Soviet Union would identify 100% with the Arabs, arm them subject to certain limitations, [but] wouldn't give them any weapons of which the very receipt would tempt them toward war ... [as] it did not desire a war. This was first and foremost an American chorus ... We helped to convene some seminars of

"WE CAN'T CONTROL THE ARABS BUT MUST SUPPORT THEM"

Kremlinology experts. The brunt of opinion before the war was that the Soviet Union has no interest in a war, because if there were to be one, Egypt would be routed and [the Soviets] would be faced with a very painful choice.[52]

The lack of formal relations did not prevent "Soviet low-level approaches to Israeli representatives in various capitals ... continuing roughly once a month." On 21 March, the Foreign Ministry's Soviet affairs director, Avigdor Dagan, told a US "embassy official" that these "approaches invariably were clumsy and pointless ... Soviets involved all seemed to be KGB agents." The Israelis were puzzled. Dagan "could not discern any serious line currently in USSR's posture," except "warning to the Arabs not to trust Washington," and possibly an attempt to discourage "flirtation with Peking."[53]

This assessment hardly changed after Primakov again met Gazit and Baron of Prime Minister Meir's office on 22–6 March 1973, at a house arranged by the Israelis in the outskirts of Vienna. This time he was accompanied or minded by Yu.V. Kotov, "a top foreign intelligence analyst."[54] Primakov reported home that the Israeli leadership was approaching acceptance of an interim solution to include the canal opening, and was even ready to accept withdrawal to "interim positions." However, the Israelis still rejected a prior timetable for complete withdrawal from all the territories, and wanted the Americans to arrange direct talks with Sadat. "Gazit tried to display disinterest in any Soviet role in an interim settlement," which Primakov claims he knew had already been agreed with Washington. Most importantly, he reported, "the Israelis are completely confident of their military superiority, do not expect any Arab operations, and envisage an extended period to exploit Arab divisions in order to maintain their own negativism."

Primakov's memoir implies that internal Soviet rivalries doomed the option he explored of resuming diplomatic relations, and the Israelis did not press for it urgently. "No Soviet leader would risk a personal decision to change the formula," which allowed for resumption only after the reasons for the 1967 rupture were removed: the territories restored and Palestinian rights upheld including a state. Compromise might mean being charged with "acquiescence in assisting the aggressor." Andropov and his foreign intelligence supported resuming relations (which would permit the return of "legal" agents to Israel), Gromyko vacillated, and Brezhnev "didn't oppose" it, but others were against. So while a report by Andropov and Gromyko included a proposal "to tell the Israelis that we might consider their suggestion to enlarge their interests section at the Dutch embassy," even this gesture was dropped from the ultimate Politburo resolution on 18 April. The Israelis, for their part, as Primakov complains, dragged their feet on a proposal for another round of talks in Vienna in June.[55]

Gazit was now director-general of the Prime Minister's Office, replacing Simcha Dinitz, who left for Washington to take up Rabin's post as ambassador. In his first meeting with Kissinger, Dinitz "surprised" the latter with a report on the "new"

THE SOVIET–ISRAELI WAR, 1967–1973

Soviet–Israeli back channel—which indicates that the Israelis had not shared the previous meetings. Amnon Lord, based on Dinitz's reports, categorizes Primakov's mission as straight disinformation by a past master of the art. Primakov's advice was that "the Israelis should not be too impressed by, or overestimate the importance of, the expulsion of experts in July '72," because the Soviets actually "are still strongly in Egypt, with friends and weapons." If this typical arrogance of Primakov's was indeed disinformation, it was of an unusual variety: truth that is intended to be taken as empty bluster. Whether or not this was Primakov's intent, the Israelis indeed perceived his "veil of threats" as masking Soviet discomfiture.[56]

28

"WE WILL BE TWO ISMAILS"

A. The "Blue-White" scare

While Primakov's talks with the Israelis were in progress (on 25 March), Sadat himself took over as prime minister from the Soviets' reputed point man Sidqi. Ahmed Ismail remained defense minister in a new cabinet dedicated "to prepare the country for a total confrontation with Israel."[1] "Political sources" specified even before the announcement that this meant preparations for war.[2] At the new cabinet's first session, Sadat also appointed himself military governor-general, with emergency powers in case of national crisis.[3] His move could be, and was, still interpreted as aimed at quelling domestic dissent, with "continuity in foreign affairs."[4] But the Soviets took part in the accelerated military activity that followed.

In March, the manpower of Baranov's technical-adviser outfit was abruptly cut by two-thirds, but not for repatriation. As his subordinate "Smirnov" relates,

> all those whose military specialty was suited for combat were sent into the field, to handle the induction of Egyptian air defense men who were returning from their training course in the USSR. These soldiers already left a completely different impression from those we met a year or year and a half before. They were more self-confident, nimbler, and enjoyed demonstrating the skills and knowhow that they had learned.

They spoke Russian, if heavily accented, and showed photos of Russian girlfriends. "Our women apparently left an indelible impression on these soldiers of Allah, and thus contributed more than a little to strengthening Soviet–Arab friendship." In trial launches of SAMs, Egyptian crews now acquired the targets on their own and followed "successfully" through the entire procedure.[5]

Meanwhile, Nixon's "Middle East month" was getting nowhere. By mid-April, "once again Mrs Meir, that singleminded lady of unbending conviction, appears to have triumphed—she came, received new promises of Phantom jets, and convinced Nixon nothing need be done" on the diplomatic front. "In the White House, a mood of frustration is rampant. Surveyors of the scene tend to throw up their hands with plague-on-both-your-houses disdain ... Neither antagonist seems willing to fit into the Nixinger model of realpolitik."[6] Any remaining intention to detach Kissinger from Nixon's Middle East policy (or foreign policy in general) had gone by the board as Watergate escalated. After 30 April, when the president's top aides resigned or were deposed, he was not about to cut loose from his main untainted retainer, and Kissinger's hegemony remained unchallenged. In Moscow, by contrast, Brezhnev's loyalists Andropov, Grechko and Gromyko were appointed to the Politburo on 27 April. Only Andropov had previously been even a candidate member.

In mid-April, Israel received the first definite indications of Egyptian intent to resume hostilities. This was based apparently on observation of the intensified activity described by "Smirnov," but also on the same signal that would be repeated in October: the repatriation of twenty-eight families of Soviet advisers from Egypt.[7] In the previous alerts (at end of the 1971 "year of decision" and in November–December 1972), Israeli military intelligence had downplayed the Egyptian moves as maneuvers and was seemingly borne out when no offensive materialized; it now repeated the same estimate. IDF Chief of Staff Elazar and Defense Minister Dayan were more apprehensive, and after an inner-cabinet meeting on 18 April, the IDF enacted a plan codenamed "Blue-White" to improve readiness for war that summer. The cost of about $15 million, a hefty outlay in Israeli terms, was criticized when the summer passed uneventfully, but was credited in hindsight for providing the wherewithal to contain the Egyptian offensive in October.[8] On the other hand, this third ostensible vindication of MI's reassuring estimation that Sadat would relent from war reinforced its disastrously erroneous repetition six months later.[9]

Bar-Joseph holds that a warning from Ashraf Marwan on 11 April was instrumental in causing the Israeli decision, and presents it as evidence of Marwan's genuine value for Israel.[10] When his warning was received in October, it was taken seriously *despite* his handlers' recollection that he had "cried wolf" in the spring.[11] Moreover, the aforementioned evidence whereby the postponement of the Egyptian–Syrian offensive to the autumn had already been decided by April (which, if Marwan was indeed privy to Sadat's closest secrets, he should have known), calls his motives into even greater question.

It also casts doubt on the widespread assumption that a genuine Arab decision to attack was postponed at Soviet behest after an earlier timing had been set; this is usually connected with the preparations for the San Clemente Summit or with these talks themselves. Lower-level Soviet officials, such as Akopov, were indeed told that "Brezhnev visited the United States and Sadat was told to wait a bit after the visit was over, not to weaken our position."[12] But this time, Kissinger's aides were closer to the mark in evaluating "indications of Arab intentions to initiate hostilities," when they suggested that these were part of "an effort to arouse international concern and put psychological pressures on Israel and the US."[13] Sadat himself (among several rationales that he gave for the postponement) claimed that *he* had preferred to await the summit's outcome.[14]

"WE WILL BE TWO ISMAILS"

Israel received several suspiciously "identical" tips that Egypt and Syria had acceded to Soviet requests to delay the war until after the summit, in the hope that the talks would produce a desirable settlement.[15] However, shortly after the Yom Kippur War, Israeli commanders testified that they also had reports whereby, regardless of political developments, "Assad had decided to postpone the offensive from May to September, on the grounds that the Syrian army was not ready, mainly in aerial defense and also in tanks." These reports were followed by Syrian deployment of a "dense air defense array on the Golan, which made it taboo for [our] planes and raised the question of offensive intent."[16] A Soviet serviceman recently confirmed that he was in a large contingent of air defense advisers that was dispatched to Syria in April, and instructed how to act when—rather than if—hostilities erupted.[17] On 30 April, the Israeli Foreign Ministry's research department endorsed a Mossad assessment that war was inevitable *by* October.[18]

Kissinger was allowed to indulge in the conceit that Soviet concern for the summit and prior detection of preparations for a spring offensive had enabled him to scotch it. Meeting Brezhnev at the latter's *dacha* on 7 May, he ran through a detailed list; Brezhnev responded with the Soviets' information about "Blue-White":

> *Kissinger*: We have some military information ... of various movements in the Arab world. ... Airplanes, military forces.
>
> *Brezhnev*: Yes.
>
> *Kissinger*: Within Egypt, they have moved what we call SA-6 surface-to-air missiles to within 20 miles of the Suez Canal. They have received 30 Mirage fighters from Libya. They have moved Tu-16 bombers, which you gave them, from Aswan to Cairo. There is a high state of alert in the Egyptian Air Force, and reservists have been recalled. They have moved some commando units closer to the Suez Canal. ... We do take it very seriously, and there is a possibility that there is a plan to do something before the summit to force us into joint action. ...
>
> *Brezhnev*: That's not bad intelligence. Israel also is recalling its reservists and has banned holidays and vacations for doctors. And they have deployed advance hospitals with a capacity for 1,000 wounded.

He persisted with the Soviet line that détente notwithstanding, the Soviets could not restrain the Arabs if a settlement were not reached that met their demands—which he knew Kissinger could not deliver:

> all good things done by us... at the Summit of achieving Détente and avoiding a confrontation will all be scrapped. ... So where do we go from here?
>
> *Kissinger*: Well, of course, we have your proposed principles. And I will see—I expect—Mr Ismail the end of the next week.
>
> *Brezhnev*: I too have met our Ismail, another Ismail. I will probably become an Ismail too. And you too will become an Ismail. And then we will be two Ismails.[19]

There is no indication that Kissinger sensed Brezhnev's sarcasm or the significance of his allusion to two Ismails, one of whom (Ahmed, Egyptian Chief of Staff) elaborated war plans and procurement in Moscow while the other (Hafez, Sadat's envoy) floated a peace initiative in Washington. Even recent American and Israeli studies still took the statements at face value: Brezhnev, fearful that the Egyptian–Syrian determination to fight would wreck détente, was sincerely urging the Americans to secure a settlement. Kissinger, confident in US intelligence assessments that any Arab offensive would fail, resisted any pressure for concessions.[20]

On 20 May, Hafez Ismail again met Kissinger, who had obtained Nixon's approval first and foremost to prevent war before the summit, and to "buy ourselves a year."[21] It was, then, hardly a disappointment when after the talk Kissinger concluded: "in short, Ismail came to this meeting to probe White House intentions further—not to discuss concrete elements of a possible Egypt–Israel agreement."[22] In his memoirs, Kissinger was harder on Ismail: "he ... said he would check with Sadat and let me know. I never heard from him. ... Ismail knew that Sadat was determined on war. ... We did not know it."[23]

When this was published (1982), accusations were already rife that Kissinger himself had been party to a conspiracy to enable a "small victory" for Sadat, and the memoir appears to reflect his effort to refute the allegations. But unlike his performance in respect of the "expulsion" a year before, documentation that has since emerged does not entirely contradict his claim. Eban recalled after the war an "explicit" assessment by the State Department's Middle East specialists in May '73 that Sadat was not about to launch a war at all, as his chances were better on the political front. In particular, he could achieve more, after a rapprochement with the Saudis, by utilizing the oil weapon—but not against the United States. Another "agency" predicted war within one to one and a half months, others disagreed. "The President and Secretary of State adopted the more reassuring version."[24] Publicly at the time, Eban appeared to take the same position when he told the Knesset on 28 May "in the defense arena we must prepare ... but also not ignore the possibility that this is just an international intimidation campaign."[25]

By then, on 17–23 May—according to the recently published Syrian documents—Egyptian and Syrian Air Force commanders had met in Cairo to assign targets and timing for a coordinated offensive. The joint command asked the Syrians to present their detailed plan at another meeting in Cairo on 6 July—that is, after the summit.[26]

Returning to Israel on 15 June, just before the summit, the KGB-linked Soviet journalist Victor Louis gave Gazit the same warning that Brezhnev had given Kissinger: the USSR would willy-nilly have to support an Egyptian attack when it came, even though Moscow estimated it had little chance: "*VL*: The Russian military information is that you would win this war. ... Unfortunately Russia still sticks to the idea that we have to support Egypt because otherwise the Arab world [would turn against the Soviet Union] ..."[27]

Contrary to his previous visit and despite his bad back, this time Louis requested, and was treated to, a tour of Sinai—the first Soviet to visit this "occupied territory," which underlined his "unofficial" capacity. This even allowed him to go as far as "suggesting" to his Israeli hosts that they should extend their conquest west of the canal—presumably in order to test their response.

Louis may or may not have been honest about Soviet intentions and assessments—depending on what he actually knew—but he certainly helped to establish the misleading impression that the Soviets were neither confident in, nor supportive of, Arab military capability. Eban was clearly referring to him, to Primakov or to both when he testified shortly after the October war: "there were also signals from Soviet personalities—hard to tell how authoritative they were, but they took care to spread [this notion], and it was accepted almost without reservation worldwide, that ... the Soviet Union does not want war."[28]

B. Brezhnev's insomnia at San Clemente

At the "Western White House," Kissinger and Gromyko had a long preliminary session to wrangle over a rephrasing of the Moscow "principles." As before, contention centered on Resolution 242 and whether full peace following an Israeli–Egyptian settlement should be linked to a comprehensive regional one (i.e., including the Palestinians).[29] As in Moscow a year before, this remained the main unresolved issue going into the top leaders' talks.

On the final night (23 June), as Kissinger would write, they had all gone to bed early when

> at ten o'clock my phone rang. It was the Secret Service informing me that Brezhnev was up and demanding an immediate meeting with the President, who was asleep. It was a gross breach of protocol ... a transparent ploy to catch Nixon off guard and with luck to separate him from his advisors. ... It transpired that Brezhnev had been seized with an all-consuming desire to discuss the Middle East.

Dr Chazov, who accompanied Brezhnev to San Clemente, has provided a differing explanation for this sleepless night: in the spring of 1973, Brezhnev began to display symptoms of atherosclerosis of brain blood vessels, "the first harsh experiences with his health which affected his nervous system. This in turn caused insomnia."[30]

As Nixon would describe it, Brezhnev was in top form, trying "to browbeat me into imposing on Israel a settlement based on Arab terms. He kept hammering." Kissinger holds that

> The Soviet leader made his most important proposition of the entire trip: that the United States and the Soviet Union agree then and there on a Middle East settlement, based on

total Israeli withdrawal to the 1967 borders in return not for peace but an end to the state of belligerency. Final peace would depend on subsequent negotiations with the Palestinians. ... Brezhnev must have understood—and if he did not, Gromyko was much too experienced not to know—that there was no chance whatever ... of reaching any such agreement in the remaining few hours.

The record indeed shows Brezhnev threatening the entirety of détente: "I am categorically opposed to a resumption of the war. But without agreed principles ... we cannot do this."[31] Nixon proudly related displaying "firmness": "I pointed out that there was no way I could agree to any such 'principles' without prejudicing Israel's rights."

A few hours later, the communiqué "emphasized areas of agreement while glossing over differences in such areas as achieving a Middle East settlement."[32] On this issue, it said only that "each side set forth" its views.[33] To reporters covering the conference, this topic was listed above "European security matters" as "the most difficult" in the talks.[34] As Chazov felt in the Soviet entourage, Brezhnev "returned as a victor."

Unlike the Moscow summit, there could be no claim that he had let Egypt down, and by setting demands that the Americans and Israelis clearly would not meet he had supplied the legitimacy for war. Nixon wrote in hindsight: "whether he already had a commitment to the Arabs to support an attack against Israel is not clear." The United States could not take credit for foreseeing, let alone preventing, the Soviet-supported offensive in the first place. But as consolation, Nixon claimed: "I am confident that the firmness I showed that night reinforced the seriousness of the message I conveyed to the Soviets when I ordered a military alert four months later during the Yom Kippur War."[35]

As after the Moscow summit, after San Clemente too the prevailing interpretation, as stated by the Israeli Foreign Ministry, was that Sadat had hoped for a settlement but was again disillusioned. Now, however, he blamed mainly the United States rather than the Soviet Union, and after a nonaligned initiative "to distort the correct meaning of Resolution 242" (as the Israelis called it) was foiled by a US veto on 26 July, he bitterly and publicly attacked the Americans.[36]

C. The final precondition: the Scuds arrive

In "early July," data was again received in Israel about intensive Syrian–Egyptian coordination to resume hostilities.[37] This may reflect some information about a Syrian–Egyptian consultation in Cairo—the one originally scheduled for 6 July. It took place "from 3 to 5 July," and the main issue was now the zero *hour* for the joint offensive, which had been a matter of some contention as the Egyptians would be attacking eastward, the Syrians westward, and both preferred to have the sun in the enemy's eyes. It was now set for midday, in order "to achieve the first targets by dark." The preceding air and artillery strikes were timed accordingly, and on 1–2 August

"WE WILL BE TWO ISMAILS"

operational orders were issued to the top echelons. The *date* would be pinpointed a few weeks later.[38]

An Egyptian military circular on 12 August reminded field units of standing orders that visits by Soviet advisers had to be pre-authorized and escorted. Besides confirming the advisers' continued presence, the perceived need to refresh the procedure may have stemmed from stepped-up Soviet activity.[39] Moscow's support for the intensifying war preparations is borne out by Bulgarian documents whereby "despite the disagreements in the period August 1972–July 1973," delivery of Ahmed Ismail's desiderata continued apace. "On the eve of the October War against Israel," the Soviet Union supplied Egypt with (among other armaments) 100 MiG-21 fighters, ten Tu-16 bombers, 150 T-54/55 tanks, ninety of the latest T-62 model, and most obtrusively, sixty SAM-6 missile launchers.[40] By early October, the Israelis estimated the Suez missile shield to consist of 150 "batteries"—i.e., *divizyons*—forming a "severe obstacle" to IAF reconnaissance as well as operational activity 20 kilometers east of the canal.[41]

Allowing for the unclear definition of "eve of the war," this was quite closely approximated by the CIA's estimate in June, except that it modified the numbers with deprecating qualifiers and an emphasis on the lasting mark of the Soviets' "ouster":

> sixty MiG-21s that had been operated by the Soviets in Egypt were turned over to the Egyptians following the expulsion. Since then, *only* seven MiG-21s, 15 Su-17 fighter bombers, and two helicopters have been delivered. Although the Soviet-manned SA-6 missile equipment defending the Aswan Dam was shipped back to the USSR ... SA-6s for Egyptian units started arriving in Alexandria last September. Other identified cargos have included T-62 medium tanks, armored personnel carriers, artillery, vehicles, and support equipment.

Despite the new models it listed such as the Su-17s, T-62s and SAM-6s, the memorandum considered these shipments as "designed to maintain Cairo's arms inventories rather than to introduce new weapons systems." Dualistic harmonization was resorted to again: "this outward cooperation between the two countries has not been matched by the restoration of mutual confidence."[42]

Neither list even mentioned the second key for Egypt's offensive capability, according to the Israeli "Concept": the Scud ballistic missile. Several dates have already been quoted for Moscow's agreement to supply the Scuds, but its delivery is now documented from the Soviet side as beginning shortly after the California summit. "In the middle of July [1973], together with the hardware for deployment of an Egyptian operative-tactical brigade, a group of Soviet missile specialists arrived in Cairo under command of Colonel Sal'nikov," as recorded by an interpreter with the outfit, which was sent on a six-month mission "to train the Egyptians."[43]

The interpreter of the Scuds' fueling platoon wrote anonymously in February 2009 that the missiles were of a new and advanced variant, R-17E (*Elbrus*), which would

321

be put to its first operational test in the war.⁴⁴ Israeli military intelligence (as claimed by its then-chief, Ze'ira) first detected the missiles' arrival on 24 August 1973—upending a previous estimate that they would not be supplied before 1976.⁴⁵ Ze'ira's deputy gave a differing version: that the first reports of the Scuds' delivery were initially dismissed, because MI believed up to that point, "on good evidence," that the Egyptians had given up entirely on obtaining the missiles.⁴⁶ Perhaps this disparity is because only Ze'ira himself was privy to the dispatches of Ashraf Marwan, who had reported the Scud sale on 20 May. According to an MI document from September 1973, Marwan reported in late July that "the *Soviet* ground-to-ground missiles would be deployed" by the end of September.⁴⁷ If, as now seems probable, the deal was in the works since Ahmed Ismail's visit in February, Marwan's message was late, but came just long enough before the missile's expected detection in Egypt to "prove" his value.⁴⁸ The same would apply to Marwan's fateful warning in October.

It was now assumed that training Egyptian crews would take at least until the following year (estimates ranged from February to April). This disregarded the possibility that the Egyptians had been trained in advance; and while "theoretically, the Soviet instructors themselves could fire the missiles at targets in Israel, based on past experience it could be concluded that this prospect was remote." Therefore, Israeli intelligence appraisals up to the war's outbreak doubted that the Scuds' delivery had fulfilled Sadat's requirement for long-range offensive capability. Even the more alarmist officers admitted that this detracted from their suspicion that the "Concept" had become outdated.⁴⁹

Despite the missiles' categorization as offensive weapons, the Israelis defined the prospect of their use as defensive: the Soviets were perceived as drawing their tripwire for approving an Egyptian launch at the ceasefire line, that is, at the canal. Possibly because ballistic missiles came under the purview of IAF intelligence, this was perceived by the Israelis mainly as applying to any new attempt at "depth bombings" (which indeed were not attempted in Egypt, unlike Syria, throughout the 1973 war). The official IDF history confirms that the Scuds indeed deterred Israel from attacking the Egyptian hinterland during the war—which, it claims, was Sadat's main motive, rather than initiating launches against Israeli targets.⁵⁰ But the tripwire function could equally apply to a ground crossing of the canal—which in the event did trigger the Scud launches.

Evidence presented to the Agranat Commission that was released only in September 2012 shows Mossad chief Zamir telling Meir on 23 August 1973—a day before the date given by Ze'ira for detection of the missiles' arrival—that according to information received from the CIA, the Soviets had deployed in Egypt a brigade of Scuds "which have nuclear and chemical warheads." Either Zamir or the meeting's note-taker misunderstood "nuclear-capable" as meaning "nuclear-armed," or the US agency was frightening the Israelis with information that it did not have.⁵¹ On the day of the war's outbreak, the CIA was still not sure that Scuds had reached Egypt at all, or at least professed so.

Colby told the Washington Special Actions Group: "we have been unable to confirm the story about the SCUD missiles being delivered. ... Some of the ones we saw are still on the docks [in the USSR]." He went on: "if they have the Soviet SCUD missile, its range is 160 miles with an 1100 pound bomb"—that is, he envisaged no nuclear potentiality.[52] Stationing nuclear weapons in Egypt, let alone handing them over to Egyptian control, would have constituted such a radical change in Soviet doctrine that Israel would hardly have let it pass. But when on 1 October Israeli Ambassador (and Meir's confidant) Dinitz invoked the "theoretical" Scud threat to Israeli cities in a talk with Sisco, he too mentioned no non-conventional capability.[53]

D. A council of war at Alexandria

The Scuds' arrival in Egypt (or the Israelis' first information about it) coincided with the finalization of the Arab offensive's date. An Egyptian–Syrian protocol, quoted by a Syrian intelligence officer studying at a Soviet military academy, is one of the sources that date this decision "between 11 and 26 August 1973, [when] the supreme council of the Egyptian and Syrian armed forces conducted meetings at navy headquarters in Alexandria."[54] Given the continuing presence of Soviet advisers at Egyptian naval headquarters and of Fifth *Eskadra* ships in Alexandria, this gathering could hardly have been concealed from them. But the Soviets' role in convening the council has been confirmed by General Baheiddin Noufal, Egypt's chief of operations for the "Federal" Command, who also narrowed down the dates for the conclusive session to 20–3 August.

Noufal related that this meeting posed a logistical nightmare: how to camouflage the arrival of six top Syrian officers—including Defense Minister Mustafa Tlas. Tlas himself described to an interviewer in the 1990s how the Soviets were involved in accomplishing this. "We traveled on board a Russian ship, wearing civilian clothes. The Soviet Ambassador accompanied us and told the captain: 'this ... is the Syrian Minister of Defense. Protect him during the journey and don't tell anyone who he is.'"[55]

At Alexandria, the Syrians once again requested a three-month postponement "to complete induction of new weaponry" and a rescheduling of the attack to daybreak, but were overruled by Ismail. Midday on 6 October was finally determined, and a plan for "strategic deception" outlined.[56] Sadat visited Syria on 25–7 August, after obtaining in Riyadh a Saudi commitment to "use the oil weapon" in case of an extended war; in Damascus, he ratified the target date with Assad and Tlas (who had by then returned from Alexandria).[57]

Deception indeed appears to have been the purpose, and certainly was the effect, of Ashraf Marwan's warning at 1 a.m. (Israel time) on 6 October, whereby the offensive would begin the same day, just before dark. If the Syrian documentation is authentic as to the date when the earlier hour was fixed, the explanation by Marwan's Israeli advocates that it was changed after he transmitted his message is spurious. While Egyptian field commanders were informed of the date on 1 October, the zero hour was not divulged to them until a day before the attack. But at the level to which Marwan's access made him so highly trusted, the hour was determined long before.[58]

At any rate, the Israelis had already been deceived—among others, by Marwan, when he reported in late July that Sadat had told Assad during a visit to Damascus on the 14th–16th that Egypt would go to war in late September or early October, with or without Syrian participation. But, as the MI documentation of this report added, "the source doubts whether Egypt will actually go to war at the time the president specified; ... this date too will pass without a war, as the previous dates did."[59] Marwan thus provided himself with a retrospective alibi that he had given correct and timely warning, while portraying *Sadat* as again crying wolf, which would discredit genuine alerts from other informants about Egypt's real intentions (as indeed happened on 1 October). Evidently, Marwan was believed, as ironically and fatefully, on 12 August—as the Alexandria council began—the "Blue-White" alert was relaxed.[60] It was not reinstated even when, despite the Soviets' precautions, Israel did receive from other sources some inkling of the council-of-war at Alexandria, including the Soviets' role.

Zubok's 2007 history acknowledges the revision necessitated by new sources including the veterans' memoirs, but still maintains ambivalently that Sadat "kept the Politburo and Soviet representatives in Egypt in the dark, although the KGB and military must have known about the preparations. ... The Kremlin leaders could not control or restrain their foreign clients."[61] But did they even try, or did they rather encourage those clients? Among the recently declassified testimonies before the Agranat Commission, several top Israeli officers mentioned an intelligence report whereby the "Russians ... convinced them [the Syrians] that from the balance-of-power viewpoint, Syria was able to capture the Golan Heights." Deputy Chief of Staff Yisra'el Tal, from memory, put this report "between May and September."[62] Reading from a file of reports from a source whose identity is censored (but is clearly distinct both from Marwan and from the source of the 1 October warning that will be discussed presently), Commission member and former Chief of Staff Yiga'el Yadin quoted a dispatch from September. It stated that "the Soviet [sanitized] said in late August that if Syria and Egypt attacked Israel simultaneously, the Syrian army can capture 100 percent of the Golan within 36 hours."[63]

In this context, more attention is warranted to a heretofore little-noticed statement that former US ambassador in Egypt, Hermann Eilts, made in 1998: "As far as I know, nobody has mentioned that in the weeks before the 1973 war, Marshal Grechko ... came to Egypt and was taken around the military installations. It was apparently suggested to him that the Egyptians might attack, not with any indication of date."[64]

"WE WILL BE TWO ISMAILS"

Eilts arrived in Egypt only after the war, to take charge of the US interests section and reconstitute it as an embassy. He did not clarify whether the section had learned of Grechko's visit and supposed remarks in real time or only in retrospect. Either way, Eilts's comment that "nobody has mentioned" the visit still holds true to the best of *our* knowledge too—with one exception.

This is Grechko's senior adjutant, Viktor Minin, who in his memoir describes a reception thrown by Sadat for Grechko in a marquee at the pyramids "in 1973, when Egypt was fighting Israel," a frame narrowed down by Eilts's statement; no other visit by the defense minister in 1973 has been recorded. Minin recalls that the lights suddenly went out, and he covered his boss with his body—no small feat, given Grechko's height—"in case of an Israeli attack."[65] At the conference where Eilts referred to it, none of the Egyptian or Soviet participants is recorded as challenging his statement. Given the disclosure of the Alexandria council, within the same time frame and at Grechko's level of defense ministers, his presence would strongly corroborate Soviet complicity in the Egyptian–Syrian offensive.

An uncommon veteran's testimony from Syria illustrates the Soviets' participation in preparing the offensive. Senior Sgt Mikhail Mikhailovich, who was serving in a *Grad* rocket-launcher unit in Hungary, relates his mission:

> in the summer of 1973, 33 men of our battalion were summoned to the 'Lenin Room' and issued an order: we were being urgently transferred for implementation of a responsible mission. But where and what for they didn't say. ... Under the command of five officers, for a total of 38 men ... the convoy comprised two APCs and six *Grad* systems.

They went through Yugoslavia to a Bulgarian port, where they were awaited by what Mikhailovich describes as "a *desant* [landing] ship designed to appear as a merchant-marine freighter." The men were dressed in "Arab" uniforms with flak jackets. Though they were not allowed to go on deck, conditions in the hold were "luxurious" and the chow included delicacies that

> we never saw in civilian life. Only on shore did it become clear that we were in Syria and would have to fight a bit. There were hostilities between Syria and Israel, and we had to give military support to the Syrians, but clandestinely. ... As I understood, our outfit was to land an unexpected lightning blow on concentrations of military equipment, and just as quickly and covertly to disappear.

Four *Grad* salvos were fired, from rapidly changed positions. They were not told of the results, but as the crews with the best training scores had been selected, they were certain that they hit the targets. They were evacuated by the same ship the next day.[66]

As Israel reported no such rocketing on the Syrian or Egyptian front before the surprise offensive on 6 October, unless Mikhailovich misdated the event (which seems unlikely as other details in his account place it around July–August), his mission was a demonstration in preparation for the war. According to the Syrian documents, the joint Egyptian–Syrian command went on to promulgate its directive (on 15 September), and reserve mobilization was begun (two days later).[67] Operational coordination "was completed at the army level" on 13 September. The same day, an Israeli air patrol west of the Syrian ports of Latakiya and Tartus (which also housed Soviet naval facilities) spotted Soviet ships unloading tanks, artillery and missiles. A Syrian attempt to intercept the patrol triggered a massive dogfight, in which the Syrians lost thirteen planes to Israel's one.[68]

Perhaps in order to dodge responsibility for the disastrous engagement of 13 September, the Soviet adviser to the Syrian Air Force chief, Gen. Vagin, claims that his advisee Naji did not seek his counsel in advance. But afterward, Vagin "was entrusted even with absolutely secret information":

> I knew the date for launching military operations against Israel two weeks in advance. Naji told me: "but you must tell no one." But how could I tell no one? Of course I reported to the chief adviser, but stressed that the source should not be exposed. Every one of ours understood at the time how important this was. ... Why did he tell me? A plan had to be developed for air strikes. For two weeks I wrangled with him which targets should be struck and what order of forces should be involved. Finally he did see reason, and the plan turned out successful.

Or at least more successful than on 13 September; Vagin argued against an attack on Israeli airbases, where he reckoned that interceptors on thirty-second alert would already be airborne, and instead suggested targeting air defense control centers on the Golan Heights.[69] Even in the unlikely case that the Soviets were not informed at a higher level about the Alexandria council's decision, this source puts them in the know on 22 September at the latest.

One consequence of Syria's temporizing on the date might have worked in Israel's favor: it delayed the war until after the IDF had completed, in September, the development and fabrication of one improved and one completely new bridging system. However, a training facility on the Mediterranean coast was not yet ready, the equipment and personnel were untried, and these innovations were of little effect when they were needed. The ultimate Israeli canal crossing that determined the war's outcome was accomplished only thanks to "heroic" improvisation.

29

THE ULTIMATE TEST OF ASHRAF MARWAN

A. An embarras de richesse *for Israeli intelligence*

Soviet foreknowledge of impending war is further attested by an unprecedented reinforcement of the Fifth *Eskadra* that began before the first shots were fired. The same technique that had been used in the run-up to the Six-Day War was employed again: ships were sent into the Mediterranean as though for normal rotation, but the ships they were slated to replace stayed put.[1] According to Vladimir Zaborsky, one of the squadron's officers, by the outbreak of war its order of battle was raised to a record 120 units. Lyle Goldstein and Yury Zhukov, working from Soviet naval documents, arrived at lower figures: fifty-two units on 4 October, eighty-eight on the 24th and ninety-six by the 31st, but this too surpassed the Sixth Fleet in numbers and approached it enough in firepower to leave either fleet the only option of a first strike if it was to survive a confrontation. As described to the skippers, some of their activity was directly linked to preparations for war: "At the end of August 1973," Capt. Zaborsky writes, the *Eskadra* "according to the plan to assist Syria at preparing a war with Israel, in an atmosphere of the strictest secrecy ... carried out an operation to transport a brigade of Moroccan troops from Algeria to Syria ... under cover of supposedly conducting landing maneuvers."[2]

In 1967, CIA Director Helms had held that there were no nuclear weapons in the arena. This time there was no doubt that the Soviets had nuclear-missile submarines in the Mediterranean (at least two at the outset of the crisis, seven by its end), as well as nuclear-armed surface vessels.[3] An entire "brigade" of ten diesel submarines, with their tender ship, were dispatched from the Northern Fleet early enough to pass Gibraltar on 3 October, the earliest date conventionally given for Sadat's alert to Moscow—without the previous Mediterranean "garrison" being withdrawn. According to naval historian Rozin, the submarine captains were puzzled by some of the orders that the fleet commander gave them in person. Two of the submarines were to take up positions off the Israeli coast and "upon the outbreak of hostilities" to search for and destroy enemy vessels approaching or leaving Israeli ports. One of these submarines was positioned "south of Cyprus and west of Haifa" to "protect

[Soviet] transports." The brigade commander received angry responses when he asked for further clarification.⁴

On 28 September, the Soviet Baltic Fleet's marine force was put on alert. Part of its complement, under Lt-Col. V.I. Gorokhov, was flown in transport planes to Sevastopol with personal arms only. There it was loaded, with full battle gear and weapons borrowed from the Black Sea Fleet's counterpart regiment, onto a large landing vessel (BDK). Additional units followed the same day by train, to embark on two medium landing ships (SDKs); all of them set sail for the Mediterranean. Another reinforced marine battalion steamed on the same day to the Mediterranean directly from Baltiisk, on the Baltic Fleet's own BDK *Krasnaya Presnya*. The Baltic Fleet marines' rotating presence at Port Said had been maintained even after the "expulsion," as Cairo station chief Ivliev indicated in 1972. But the urgency and mode of the additional *desantniki*'s dispatch indicates preparation for a highly extraordinary development. The then-lieutenant who recorded it notes that his men's "combat service," until they landed at Tartus on 7 December, was "very difficult."⁵

The MI sigint chief, Col. Ben-Porat, had since 24 September been receiving reports of preparations for an Egyptian exercise, which included marshaling of bridging equipment. As Ben-Porat "knew everything about the source and his quality, ... I was stunned" at his positive warning that the exercise would turn into an offensive, and ordered an immediate alert in his array's forward listening bases against physical attack. According to the newly released testimony of Brig.-Gen. Yisra'el Li'or, Meir's adjutant, before the Agranat Commission, the Mossad was alerted on 30 September by "one of its important sources" (also described as an "agent") that an Egyptian war game would start the next day, to disguise preparations for launching a war, together with Syria, a week later.

The source's Mossad handler asked him repeatedly through 3 October whether he was certain of this, and the source replied time and again that he was. Still, Mossad chief Zamir did not refer the report immediately and directly to the political leadership but passed it on to MI, which in turn buried it in its daily digest. Zamir disparaged both the source's credibility and the likelihood that he was right. So did MI chief Ze'ira, though he qualified the source as "good." He did point out—in one of the few references to the USSR in these deliberations—that the Soviet doctrine, "which the Syrians have learned well," called for launching offensives from out of a defensive array.⁶

Since all agents' identities were sanitized in the commission's declassified papers, some press reports about the new release identified this source as Ashraf Marwan. But these versions were soon retracted, because the context, as well as testimonies about Marwan's subsequent, notorious warning, show that the early warnings came from other sources—who were discounted so long as he did not confirm them.⁷ As lamented by a senior MI officer at the time, Marwan created an *embarras de richesse*: "the intelligence officers had a super-source who provided authentic material, from the horse's mouth, but also drew them into a blind dependence ... which overshad-

THE ULTIMATE TEST OF ASHRAF MARWAN

owed and sidelined any other information, including evidence that obviously pointed to a war."[8]

B. 4 October: dependents out, advisers in

All the above tends to obviate the ongoing debate whether Sadat specified the exact date and hour of the attack to the Soviets on 3 or 4 October, and how this notice was transmitted. However, the notion that the Soviets were first informed on either of these days has become so firmly fixed, in even the most recent and reputable reference works, that uprooting it seems next to impossible.[9]

Low- and mid-level Soviet officials and officers may be entirely truthful in attesting that *they* were first warned of the impending war less than two days in advance, that is, on 4 October, after Sadat served notice on Ambassador Vinogradov the day before. Sadat himself related retrospectively that he did give Vinogradov a *general* warning on the 3rd, without stating the precise time.[10] Vinogradov—as he did in respect of Nasser's "secret visit in January 1970"—describes this in even vaguer terms: "Sadat raised the possibility that Egypt might take retaliatory action against a big Israeli provocation, and promised to inform the USSR when this came about."[11] Vinogradov's deputy, Akopov, did not clarify the issue much when he stated in a retrospective interview that Sadat disclosed the exact date "two or three days before the war started."[12]

According to Sadat, the precise zero hour was divulged to the Soviets by Syrian President Assad on the 4th, as the two Arab leaders had prearranged. Assad's biographer Seale also maintains that the Soviets were not told "officially" until 4 October, though as already mentioned they were privy to the preparations.[13] In the best-known Soviet "insider" account, Victor Israelyan maintained that the Soviet ambassador in Damascus, Nuritdin Mukhitdinov, did meet Assad on the 4th—but received the same general declaration as his counterpart in Cairo, and was finally told about the zero hour only on the morning of the 6th.[14]

But given what is now known about Mukhitdinov's role in the council-of-war at Alexandria in August, either these meetings or the accounts about their content seem like a choreographed charade. Israelyan admits that he failed to find the crucial information in any diplomatic dispatches from Cairo or Damascus; he concluded that the Soviet leadership must have received it through "special channels," and "its 'special connection' in Cairo or Damascus remains undisclosed." He stresses that this does *not* allude to KGB representatives in either Arab capital reporting to Moscow without informing the ambassadors.

This was aimed specifically against a claim by the KGB's Cairo *rezident* Kirpichenko that his agency had, on its own evidence, "predicted the outbreak of a war in the first days of October."[15] But at a conference in 1998, three years after Israelyan's book was published, Kirpichenko stood on his version that "we learned

329

the date of the military action about five or six days in advance."¹⁶ In 2000, this version was adopted in an official Russian history, which stated that on 4 October, Moscow was not notified by the Egyptians at all, but rather learned about the impending war from its own intelligence.[17] At any rate, Soviet actions make it unnecessary to sort out what looks like rather pathetic retrospective inter-service bickering in Yeltsin-era Moscow. What matters is that on 4 October, Soviet action shifted from a military buildup that could at least partly be concealed to high-profile moves that had to be detected—indeed, were intended to be.

By 7 p.m. on 4 October, when Gromyko convened senior Foreign Ministry officials to tell them that "the Egyptian and Syrian leaders had made their final decision to attack Israel," he could state that "the matter had already been discussed at the 'highest level' in the Kremlin," and "steps were being taken to evacuate Soviet civilian personnel and their families." It makes little difference whether this move was initiated by Moscow or, as Akopov stated, it was prompted by Sadat: "it is my duty to warn you because you have too many people and specialists here." The former variant seems more plausible, as upon receiving the order from Kosygin, Vinogradov (as Israelyan claims the ambassador told him) tried to object, out of anxiety that such an overt measure would give away the Arab plan. But he was denied his usual direct access to Brezhnev—on the grounds that "such apprehensions had been thoroughly considered by the Politburo." The target date for evacuation was thus set in advance, and disclosed to both Egyptians and Soviets at various levels on a need-to-know basis—which explains the conflicting versions given to researchers by former Soviet officials as to whether the evacuation was intended as a warning to the United States or was undertaken *despite* this predictable effect.[18]

Gromyko evaded a question about the elimination of the surprise factor when one of his aides dared to pose it, and would not instruct them how to explain the evacuation if asked. He laid down the official Soviet line by repeating several times that the war would start on Saturday, 6 October, at 2:00 p.m. and that "neither [he] nor Brezhnev supported the Arab decision. ... The Soviet leadership had done everything it could to talk Sadat and Assad" out of it.[19] The military history also attributes to Gromyko an angry response: "they didn't listen to us! They're rushing ahead without knowing themselves what for!"[20] His performance is about as credible as Kissinger's surprise at the "expulsion."

This line, rather than the overwhelming evidence against it even at the time, established itself in Western historiography in such formulations as "the Soviet Union repeatedly warned Sadat against the use of military force."[21] It is just barely possible that there was time to convene the Politburo following an out-of-the-blue message from Cairo, to conduct "thorough consideration" and take extensive practical measures within a few hours. But the evacuation clearly could not have been implemented on 4 October if it had been ordered only on the same day.

THE ULTIMATE TEST OF ASHRAF MARWAN

Prior anticipation of the evacuation is borne out by a professor of medicine from Kiev. On 3 October 1973, he was unable to reserve a room at any hotel in town for a subordinate, who was about to arrive for a weekly tutorial. When the professor tried to invoke his connections, a friend told him in strict confidence that "there was an order to clear all hotels from 4 October, for imminently arriving evacuees from the Middle East."[22] In Syria, as Air Force adviser Vagin recalled, his advisee "Naji did ask me afterward, 'how did you manage to evacuate the families a day before the war?' I said: 'Apparently some signal was received, but not necessarily from you.'"[23]

In Cairo, as Akopov let slip, there already were fewer Soviet civilians than usual to look after, as "we had already sensed" the incipient war and "limited the number of tourists to Egypt." Akopov—who was charged with organizing the evacuation—related that, within a day and a half, 1,700 people were sent home by planes alone. The rest—Israelyan quotes a total of 3,700—were driven to Alexandria, and there boarded naval vessels, including even submarines, "for Odessa."[24] At least part of the evacuees were transshipped to civilian liners that met the naval vessels midway; the latter's return would be noticed soon.

An airlift might conceivably have been mounted within a few hours, but the presence of adequate ships on such short notice is more noteworthy. The Fifth *Eskadra*'s commander, Vice-Admiral Evgeny Volobuyev, is reported to have received his instructions before 01:00 hours on 4 October—that is, several hours before his superiors in the Kremlin supposedly ordered the evacuation. He then commanded all available craft to head for Egyptian and Syrian ports—which indicates that the requisite ships were already within a few hours' sailing distance, if not in harbor.[25]

The initial reports that Ze'ira had from Damascus as early as 4 October held that "last night an order was given to evacuate women and children. ... They got buses from the Syrians, with the intent to send them to Latakiya to get there by 1200 today for evacuation by sea."[26] He was therefore stumped by the arrival, a few hours later, of six Aeroflot airliners in Cairo and five in Damascus. Apparently because the Soviet dependents had been limited to 30 kilograms of baggage each, he now reckoned that "the planes came to evacuate the dependents"—even though the Soviet airliners were estimated to have a capacity of 750 and 600 passengers respectively, far less than the number of actual evacuees. "It's our impression that the Russians, at least at intermediate level, were astonished and also that the plane business was hastily done. There's no information why." He could offer only varying speculations: (1) the Soviets believed their own warning that Israel was about to attack; (2) "the Russians came to the conclusion that Syria and Egypt are about to attack, and in order to take no risk or to demonstrate dissociation from this step, they are evacuating"; (3) a full-fledged Russian–Egyptian/Syrian dispute.[27]

Once the aircraft were detected, the Israelis no longer connected the Soviet naval move with the evacuation, even when the ships left port with the evacuees on board, and some other explanation had to be found.[28] As Ze'ira reported to a council of

331

ministers on 5 October, it was only the ships' departure, rather than their arrival, that was noticed by Israeli intelligence: "[last night,] almost all the Soviet vessels that were in Alexandria left port, which has never happened except once, when there was anxiety that the Egyptians would carry out what was called the year-of-decision war—that was in 1971." He now leaned toward the second scenario of the three he had listed: the ships' departure was "a move that means Soviet reservation about an Egyptian offensive. ... The USSR is trying to influence both Syria and Egypt not to launch an attack on Israel. Yet we estimate that the USSR's power to influence these two countries is a) small b) steadily decreasing." A briefing sent to Eban for US consumption went so far as to adopt the third contingency: it read the "predictable" departure of ships "as a consequence of a crisis in Soviet relations with Egypt and Syria [as] the result of a Soviet assessment that hostilities may break out"—even though both Dayan and Chief of Staff doubted it.[29]

The CIA arrived at the same "tentative" conclusion: the evacuation was, "as in July 1972 ... a sign of a crisis in Arab–Soviet relations."[30] This interpretation was reinforced when Israeli sigint reported intercepting an Egyptian message "clearly indicating" that the Russians were evacuating "their advisers" themselves as well as the latter's dependents. The original description of Soviet "families" had already been modified to that effect—even to "all" the advisers—by Ze'ira and a senior MI research officer, Yonah Bendman.[31] This was precisely what the Soviets were trying to achieve. As the Arab attack began on 6 October, Quandt still affirmed that some advisers as well as 1,000 dependents were evacuated, and possibly even expelled; therefore

> the effectiveness of an Arab attack is likely to be somewhat degraded and the risks of Soviet involvement will lessen ... [but] our intelligence services have continued to downplay the likelihood of an Arab attack on Israel. ... They appear to favor the alternative explanation of a crisis in Arab–Soviet relations.[32]

Regarding deniability of the Soviets' complicity, the evacuation thus succeeded more than they could have expected. In operational terms, it was designed to trigger a call-up of Israeli reserves only when it was too late to meet the offensive at full strength—a matter that Lashchenko had identified as critical from the outset. As Heikal relates—in this case, quite credibly—at the early planning stage, Minister Ahmed Ismail estimated that shorter notice than four or five days in advance—preferably, three—would suffice to preclude a full IDF mobilization. On 2 October 1973, Egyptian Chief of Staff Shazly opined that it was already too late for Israel to mobilize ahead of an attack on the 6th.[33] Sadat echoed this on 3 October, as "it would be impossible for Israel to mobilize armored formations and deploy along the Canal in less than 72 hours, [nor] for the entire mobilized strength of Israel to be deployed ... in under five to six days."[34]

To meet the same timetable, it was also on 4 October that the Soviet media began "disseminating an increasing number of reports of an alleged Israeli military buildup."

THE ULTIMATE TEST OF ASHRAF MARWAN

Manufacturing a provocation that could legitimize the offensive was almost an exact replay of preparation for war in May 1967. The preplanning of this propaganda campaign—as with the Kiev hotels—is illustrated by advance instructions to the Soviet media "to keep space available for stories on the Middle East."[35] The Israeli aerial victory over Syria on 13 September was held up as "a provocation to prepare an Israeli attack."[36] As Kissinger would later claim, Egyptian Foreign Minister Mohammed el-Zayyat informed him on 6 October that "the Russians were telling us there was a concentration [of Israeli forces] on the Syrian front."[37] Given the Soviet awareness of Egyptian–Syrian plans, even if they were informed only on the 4th, this fabrication was even more egregious than in 1967, and just as obviously coordinated. It tends to confirm our finding that the Soviet warning in '67 too was an agreed signal and propaganda cover rather than a deliberate misleading of Moscow's allies or mere error.[38]

Repeating its erroneous interpretation of the Soviet warning in May 1967, Israeli intelligence construed the Soviet charges as disinformation aimed at Moscow's Arab clients: "the Soviets are conducting unusually great political activity in Egypt these days." They were judged as still "fearful of an Egyptian rapprochement with the United States," but military intelligence interpreted Brezhnev's omission of the Middle East in a speech in Tashkent as "reliably reflecting the issue's low priority." Large concentrations of Syrian troops, artillery and tanks were detected, but were attributed to Syrian "apprehensions about us, which apparently were fed by the Russians," rather than offensive intent. This was also the rationale given for similar preparations that were observed in Egypt, although such a response to an alleged Israeli threat hardly conformed to the description of the Egyptian "big troop concentrations" as "a large-scale exercise for capturing Sinai."

Eban claimed (after the fact) that when he met Kissinger on 4 October, "the US was unaware of any impending crisis." The "main point of the talk" was the secretary's suggestion that after the Israeli election scheduled for 30 October, Eban should come again to America "to get a negotiating procedure in motion," hinting that their Egyptian counterpart would be there too and joking that Sisco had "drawers full of plans." Although by then they both had reports about Egyptian as well as Syrian troop concentrations—the Americans had requested an urgent Israeli assessment on 1 October—Eban said these were not discussed "because there had already been false alarms on six occasions since 1970."[39]

Despite some dissenting opinions, neither the Soviet evacuation nor the Arab military buildup, much less the other indications, were thus taken by the top leadership in Jerusalem or Washington as conclusive evidence of a looming war until after midnight (Israel time) on the night of 4–5 October. Zamir's office then received, and relayed to his assistant Alfred Eini, a telegram from Marwan in London. As revealed by Eini's testimony before the Agranat Commission (with Marwan's name still excised), this cable not only included a code word that "the angel" had set in a meet-

333

ing with Zamir a month earlier; bizarrely, the cable also explicitly specified the code word's significance: an imminent war.

Eini's disclosure caused one of the commission members to point out that Marwan could safely do so only if, being a double agent, interception of the cable would not compromise him. Eini responded with the unconvincing suggestion that if Marwan had been working for the Egyptians, he would have relayed no warning at all. Marwan insisted that he would give further details only to Zamir in person. Asked whether Marwan could have been unaware what damage might be caused by the resulting delay, Eini replied only that the agent "did not take [this] into consideration."[40]

Zamir grasped the import of the message only after Ze'ira shared with him the incoming reports about the Soviet evacuation. Still, Zamir awaited the first commercial flight to London on the morning of the 5th. Some three hours after he took off, the Israeli leadership considered requesting the United States to "ask the Russians why they are going home." Ze'ira, certain that the Americans were still unaware of this, objected that it would give away Israel's sources. He still considered that "if the Russians think the Arabs are going to war, that is against the Russians' advice and it proves they have no influence."[41]

Meanwhile, based only on "the telegram" (Marwan's original message), Eban was alerted in New York to arrange an urgent meeting with Kissinger, but most of the day had elapsed by the time he received a new "briefing" for the secretary. Eban was to ask Kissinger to tell the Arabs and Soviets that any expectation of an Israeli offensive was unfounded, but that Israel would respond forcefully to any attack. Kissinger's deputy at the NSC, Brent Scowcroft, responded gladly to Israel's "reassuring" estimate, and said the Americans concurred. "I heard after the fact that they thought, 'it's May 1973 all over again,'" Eban told the Agranat Commission, "Then we went to pray Kol Nidre [the opening prayer on Yom Kippur eve]." Eban didn't believe Kissinger passed the requested message on to either the Arabs or the Soviets, as it was not considered immediately urgent. Kissinger confirmed after the war that the overall tone of the Israeli warning was "unemphatic" and he felt safe to delay contacting the Soviets until the next day.[42]

Zamir finally met Marwan only at 10 p.m. that night, and by the time "the angel's" most famous and controversial message was coded, transmitted and delivered in Israel, it was 3:40 a.m. on Saturday, Yom Kippur. Besides a positive assertion that a war was imminent, the message included what was by this time disinformation, whether Marwan knew it or not: that the attack would begin "before sunset," which was interpreted in Israel as meaning 6 p.m. If this had been correct, it would have given the Israelis less than twenty hours' warning; in the event, the attack was four hours closer. This discrepancy might perhaps be explained as reflecting older information about the Syrians' preferred zero hour—in which case the question arises of why Marwan didn't volunteer it earlier.

THE ULTIMATE TEST OF ASHRAF MARWAN

Bar-Joseph glosses over the tardiness of Marwan's warning with a suggestion that his original message was only a general alert, and he happened to find out the final timetable for the Arab offensive only from a friend in London while Zamir was en route there. Besides stretching credibility (e.g., how, in his first cable, Marwan could have promised data he did not yet have, or how "a friend in London" might have it), this reduces Marwan's importance and access to information to near-trivial—certainly not worth the $100,000-plus that he was paid in this case alone.[43]

In what concerns this study most directly, Marwan took care to tell Zamir that "the Russians will take no part in the war."[44] If the wrong zero hour that he provided can somehow be excused, the following pages will show that this statement was utterly false—and suggests strongly that, as before, Marwan served as a disinformation conduit for the Soviets as well as the Egyptians. It corresponds so neatly in content and timing with the other, simultaneous measures described above that discerning an overall deception pattern is hardly escapable. Marwan's message, like the dependents' evacuation, succeeded beyond any reasonable expectation: the Russians were provided with deniability, without compromising the Egyptian operation by a timely call-up of Israeli reserves.

C. 6 October: zero hour for Arab offensive and Soviet resupply

Reading "the cable from Tzvika [Zamir]'s guy" Marwan before an urgent ministerial consultation that was convened at 8:05 a.m on 6 October, even the "previously skeptical IDF Chief of Staff Elazar concluded that it was 'authentic'"—and that the ten hours' notice was "'very short for us.'" Defense Minister Dayan reported that "this business of the Russians' departure has already become large-scale. It's ongoing. Thousands are leaving." He did, however, speak of "panicked" evacuation of "Soviet families" alone, and considered that "it's essential for us to try and settle this intelligence-wise with the Americans." The latter, Dayan said, "so far have stated that they see no preparations for war. They can't explain the withdrawal of the Russian dependents" or "a lot of other things." Among these other concerns, Dayan raised the specter of attacks with Scud and Frog missiles.[45] A partial call-up of reserves was begun, but Meir took care to assure US Ambassador Kenneth Keating that a full mobilization was not under way and Israel had no offensive intent.[46]

Eban received the alarming report of Marwan's message at 5:30 a.m New York time and informed Kissinger within half an hour. Within another hour, Kissinger reported back that he had spoken with Egyptian Foreign Minister Zayyat, who claimed that Israel had launched an air and naval attack, and with Dobrynin, who—as Kissinger told Eban—was "evasive."[47] The latter term—indeed, both conversations with Eban—do not appear in the blow-by-blow account of that day that Kissinger published in 2003, where he claims to have been awoken by Sisco with Keating's report.

THE SOVIET–ISRAELI WAR, 1967–1973

These transcripts show that Kissinger confessed to Dobrynin that "until an hour ago I did not take this seriously"—and Dobrynin's actual response shows that "evasive" was quite an understatement. It was 6:40 a.m. His monosyllabic replies to most of the American's dramatic statements were understood by Kissinger that he was "obviously waking him up." This, however, can hardly explain part of the exchange: "*K*: ... 'this is very important for our relationship, that we do not have an explosion in the Middle East right now.' *D*: 'What is our relationship?'"

Kissinger let pass this disavowal of any mutual commitment, personal or official. The Soviet ambassador did not even bother to mention the Soviet accusations about Israeli concentrations, much less an actual Israeli attack. He promised only to relay Meir's reassuring message, but Kissinger told the Israeli Deputy Chief of Mission Mordechai Shalev a few minutes later, with no apparent basis, that Dobrynin "said they will cooperate with us."

Later that morning, asked by White House Chief of Staff Alexander Haig about the Soviet attitude, Kissinger still held "that they are trying to keep it quiet and they are surprised." He told Dobrynin that charges of Israeli attacks were "baloney," but did not confront the ambassador over Soviet complicity—which he suggested to Nixon five minutes later. Barely an hour after the shooting started, Kissinger was aiming to "get the fighting stopped and then use the opportunity to see whether a settlement could be enforced" with Soviet cooperation. Within another few minutes he was offering "to take a neutral position" in the UNSC, as "we don't know who started but are in favor of the status quo ante," and to proceed according to his and Nixon's agreement with Gromyko.[48]

Late on the second day of the war, Kissinger still professed to believe a "friendly message" from Brezhnev that "the Russians pulled out all their advisers against the wishes of the Arab governments," as "we have confirmed this through our sources." The Soviets, he estimated, "quite honestly ... were taken aback by what the Arabs did. They knew about it two days in advance. So there are no Russians involved."[49] It was only when Kissinger briefly left a Washington Special Action Group (WSAG) meeting the same evening that the others dared to second-guess this sweeping exoneration:

> *Mr Sisco*: I've heard Henry say that all the Soviet advisers are out, and I thought some were still there. We need a clarification of that ... I thought there was a residue of Soviet advisers still there.
>
> *Mr Colby*: They have some people working on the Helmand [*sic*; he must have meant Helwan] plant.
>
> *Mr Sisco*: I thought they still had some involved in radar and some training.

Then Kissinger returned, and no one pressed the issue.[50] But his colleagues' doubts were actually underestimated. Not only was it never the case that all the advisers left Egypt; more had actually arrived in the run-up to the war, and yet more—as well as Soviet regulars—were to follow.

30

IN THE THICK OF THE YOM KIPPUR WAR

A. *The singing general's canal crossing*

In 1988, Lt-Gen. and Hero of the Soviet Union Anatoly Pushkin, president of the Interregional Association of Internationalist Soldiers, greeted the conference of Soviet and Egyptian veterans to mark the twenty-fifth anniversary of the Yom Kippur war. He recognized in the audience "direct participants in the events of October 1973. ... The Soviet military contingent—advisers and experts, independent operative groups, technical and armaments [specialists] took an active part in the October epic. We join in tribute to these participants. ... Their combat experience is still relevant today."[1] The following year, the manpower chief of the Soviet Army published an article in its official organ to honor soldiers who had taken part in "combat operations abroad." He listed "Egypt, 5 October 1973–1 April 1974" as one such operation.[2] "The grandson of a Soviet admiral" declared in 2004, referring to the Yom Kippur War: "no less than 5,000 Soviet military advisers took part in the operation itself. Of these, 1,500 took part in combat, especially pilots and anti-aircraft defense experts."[3] This is the only source for such figures, but multiple testimonies from individual participants bear out his general claim.

Giving 5 October as the start of Soviet combat operations in Egypt, rather than the 6th when hostilities actually began, is hardly coincidental. It took until 10 October for any Western assessment even to speculate that the Soviet airliners presumed to have been sent to fetch Soviet nationals from Egypt and Syria did not go there empty, but carried hardware deliveries of some kind.[4] Preoccupied with the meaning of the Soviet dependents' departure, no one in Israeli and Western intelligence is recorded as asking whether there were any incoming passengers. It would take almost thirty years to reveal that far from removing Soviet personnel from the war zone, the planes actually brought in a fresh contingent just before the Arab offensive was unleashed—that is, when Moscow was admittedly aware of it. The recurring Israeli denial, true or not, that the IDF encountered a single Soviet adviser on the battlefield does not reflect the extent of their activity.[5]

THE SOVIET–ISRAELI WAR, 1967–1973

In May 2001, about a year after Putin was first elected president, a leading Russian literary weekly published an unusual text entitled "Dust over the Suez Canal." This was one of the first examples of veterans turning from documentation to "fiction." It also dealt with a chapter that the copious veterans' literature had almost entirely sidestepped: the long-denied direct and active role of the Soviet military not only in preparing but finally in implementing Egypt's cross-canal offensive. "Dust" was exceptional also in respect of its author's rank and renown. He was Maj.-Gen. (retired) Viktor Kutsenko, "who has already published in these pages materials about Afghanistan"—where he served for three years as the revered commander of engineers.

Kutsenko gained fame afterward as "the singing general": a guitar-strumming bard performing his own protest songs, as well as a talented painter dedicated to protesting the *Afgantsy*'s plight and supporting their struggle by depicting the horrors of the war. "But," the newspaper now added, "only recently we learned that Kutsenko was also a witness, and to some degree a participant, of the Arab-Israeli war in 1973. The general has written a story about it—a *story*, not a documentary study." The author himself explained that even if he could still be held to the pledge of secrecy that he signed at the time, "how can counter-intelligence press charges against a fictitious story?!"[6]

What factual credibility can be attached to Kutsenko's account, which is vividly narrated in the third person about a "Col. Vasily Bodrov?" Besides the editors' note, there were at first only vague hints that Kutsenko had been in Egypt. A decorated hero, he was eminently respectable, with a sterling record of fearless struggle for truth. His formal biography left a gaping blank between 1965 and 1980, mentioning only that he "took part in the conflict in Egypt"—but this was put in red letters to indicate combat, like his subsequent service in Afghanistan.[7] After he died in 2008, a eulogy in the official army newspaper added that the record of "this gifted military engineer" included "throwing bridges across water obstacles in Egypt, which aided the success of the Egyptian army during Arab–Israeli hostilities."[8]

That still might be construed as referring to practice exercises in training grounds such as Wadi Natrun, leaving room for doubt whether "Bodrov's" role in the actual canal crossing was by way of eyewitness testimony. But in 2013, someone posted on YouTube an old amateur video of a "concert" that was held in 1992, at the height of post-Soviet latitude, to celebrate Kutsenko's sixtieth birthday. It was mostly devoted to his songs about Afghanistan, but toward the end his former commander took the floor to say: "not all of you know that Viktor Pavlovich first experienced the whistle of bullets, the blast of shells and shrapnel" as early as the Middle East of the '60s and '70s. "He did not observe the events from the sidelines, but took a direct part"—among other actions, "in overcoming a water obstacle and storming enemy fortifications that had been considered impregnable."[9] So Kutsenko had to be taken literally when, two years after "Dust" appeared, he told the house magazine of his civilian employer that before Afghanistan, in Egypt too "I never put

IN THE THICK OF THE YOM KIPPUR WAR

down my notebook. During the brief moments of rest, the poems and sketches just begged to be put on paper."[10]

Kutsenko's timeline clarifies that "Bodrov's" dispatch to Egypt was on 4 October, on board an Il-18 airliner—that is, one of the six planes that were spotted landing in Cairo. He was among "60 officers of the Moscow military district" who were "rousted out at 6 am. By 8 they were at Chkalovsky military airport and by 8 pm had already reached a briefing room in Cairo." Their operational action began the next day—5 October. Given the time difference between Cairo and Moscow, the Politburo decision to select and send such a group had to be made before Sadat's supposed tipoff, even if it was delivered on the 3rd.[11] The mission entrusted to Kutsenko's alter ego is of special significance: "Bodrov" was to replace the chief engineering adviser to one of the Egyptian army corps, who had suddenly fallen sick. Advisers who were already attached to Egyptian formations might perhaps have been caught up willy-nilly in the operation—but if Moscow had disapproved of it, a substitute would hardly have been posted so urgently for a key adviser, whatever the reason for his absence, or sent specifically for the canal-crossing assignment.

What follows is a detailed account of the Soviet engineer's role in the crossing. Much of it conforms to descriptions of the Egyptian operation that Kutsenko might theoretically have gleaned from literature about the war or from his own professional knowhow—for example, the model (*Moskva*) of the outboard motors on the inflatable dinghies that were used for the initial infantry assault. The claim that pontoon bridges for armored vehicles were constructed within thirty-five minutes is actually modest compared with Israeli estimates.[12] Attributing the use of high-pressure water jets rather than explosive charges to breach the Israeli earthwork to a last-minute suggestion from Bodrov appears inflated too, especially since Soviet-made water cannon were already supplied in January 1973 and their use in the war was widely described.[13] But Kutsenko's known figure and reputation bolster his own hedged claim of authenticity and warrant further inquiry in those cases where the substance is new.

One such case is the otherwise uncorroborated claim that "Bodrov" commandeered civilian fire engines and floated them on makeshift ferries built of two pontoons each: the Israeli side just described these as "water-jet barges," so the fire-engine version is not entirely implausible.[14] His charge that the army corps commander and his Soviet adviser, "Gen. Trofimov," abandoned "Bodrov" and his advisee, "Col. Yahya," and they had to flee their headquarters south of Ismailia under heavy Israeli fire that killed "Yahya," fits in with the record of the Israeli crossing, which took place south of the city and reached its outskirts. On the other hand, decades of controversy and research on this hallowed chapter of IDF annals have not confirmed that Israeli tanks drove across "Bodrov's" bridges, after his repeated calls to dismantle them went unheeded.

THE SOVIET–ISRAELI WAR, 1967–1973

B. Prepositioning of the Soviet resupply

The wealth of detail in Kutsenko's "fiction" is, then, of varying factual credibility—but he undoubtedly was *there*, along with dozens if not hundreds of colleagues flown in on 4 October. This is of momentous significance as it clarifies more oblique allusions to the sensitive issue in previous accounts. Ambassador Vinogradov's deputy Akopov, for instance, mentioned that together with "military officers who flew from Moscow we organized the airlift" of military materiel that began soon after the outbreak of war, as "the Egyptians could not cope."[15]

The Soviet resupply effort was quite correctly perceived at the time as a "smoking gun" in respect of Soviet collusion. A panel of experts led by the former US ambassador in Moscow, Foy Kohler, pointed out that Assad disclosed within days of the war's end that he and Sadat had planned it to last ninety days:

> Could the Arab leaders have risked planning on a 90-day campaign if they had not had prior Soviet assurance of receiving additional munitions ... or conversely, if the Soviet Union had limited the amount ... in order to maintain control over ... its clients, why did this control prove ineffectual?[16]

This question would be as cogent if the war were planned for thirty days or less, and it has remained cogent despite the prevailing trend in Western historiography to portray the Yom Kippur War as one that "the Soviet Union did not want."[17]

The question has been underlined by new evidence that clarified the timing of the resupply operation. The starting date of the airlift component was "the subject of some controversy," with the earliest date given as 7 October.[18] This was in a report by Quandt three years after the war; in real time, in an 8 October memo to Kissinger, Quandt counseled against compliance with Israeli resupply requests for "larger items," because of "the signal it would send to the Soviets and Arabs ... There are some grounds for thinking the Soviets may be more restrained this time than in 1967"—indicating that the United States was not yet aware that major Soviet shipments had begun.[19] The same evening—that is, past midnight in the Middle East, when the IDF's situation on the canal front looked bleakest—Kissinger still saw "no chance of its going like 1967 with the Soviets ... They're making no threatening noises, no military moves. ... If we wind up with the Arabs and the Soviets stay with us, we'll be doing very well." His only anxiety was "if we brief the Hill, some jackass will run out and say something pro-Israel. Then we've had it."[20]

Two days later (10 October), when the Soviet airlift was no longer in doubt, in Washington its motivation was open to conflicting interpretations—whether the Soviets were responding to heavy Arab losses in the first days of fighting, or as Sonnenfeldt suggested, they "were somewhat surprised by the extent of Arab successes." He noted that "the air supply operation got going when the odds for a status-quo-plus end to the war for the Arabs were rising." The Soviets, then, might "have become infected with the optimism of the Egyptians ... they may smell victory and the credit that comes with it." This supposed euphoria was held to explain "apparent Soviet violations of the Greek and maybe Turkish air control zones," which Moscow had avoided at considerable cost in 1967.

The next day (11 October), Sonnenfeldt told Kissinger: "that there was Soviet foreknowledge of the imminence of military action seems beyond dispute."[21] By 13 October, he was more specific: the Soviets had "foreknowledge at least by October 3, but probably in late September."[22] This was apparently based on a fresh report from the US interests office in Cairo that the local "TASS agency rep ... told us that Soviets first learned of Egyptians' plans for attack across canal at end of September."[23] US assessments were thus conditioned by leaks from the Soviets themselves. By then, the Soviet resupply effort's early start had discredited any claim that Moscow was notified just several hours before the dependents' evacuation began. Moving the line back by a few days was now the best option to obscure Soviet collusion that went back at least a few more months. A "reliable" informant of Israeli intelligence reported "on the eve of the war" that the Egyptians could hardly believe their vaunted adversaries had not seen through "their deception and camouflage."[24] The same could be said of the Americans.

The preplanning of the resupply effort's sea component is even clearer-cut than that of the airlift. Post-Soviet Russian sources put the departure of the first cargo ships from the Black Sea ports of Ilyichevsk and Oktyabrsky also as early as (Sunday) 7 October—barely twenty-four hours after the first shots were fired.[25] Each of these ships was by then laden with up to ninety-two armored vehicles. It stretches the imagination to suppose that such a mass of armor was marshaled from scratch, moved and loaded from one day to the next. An Israeli intelligence report on the evening of 8 October already mentioned a Soviet ship carrying aircraft ("at least five on deck") and bridging equipment passing through the Dardanelles.[26] The contrast with previous Western perceptions and official Soviet/Russian statements, which put the first ships' departure on 9 October, is thus highly significant.[27]

In Syria, according to the historian Aleksey Vasiliev who was serving there as an interpreter, the ships were met by "Soviet military personnel [who] unloaded the tanks in port, transferred them to the front, operated the radar systems, [and] repaired tanks and other technical equipment."[28] Once the Politburo approval required for transfers of such magnitude is factored in, dating the first shipments to the 7th puts the resupply commitment even earlier—indeed, before the outbreak of war.

It is remotely possible, though highly unlikely, that this complex operation was authorized only when "the matter was discussed at the 'highest level' in the Kremlin" in the afternoon of 4 October (as Israelyan attributes to Gromyko)—that is, the Politburo decision was taken within a few hours and carried out within two days. This too would belie Soviet dissociation from the offensive. But it seems a safe assumption that the transports were standing by well in advance, ready to go as soon as this easily detectable measure could be presented as response to a *fait accompli*. All the more so if, as Quandt reported in 1976 from Israeli sources, some of the equipment captured during the war came from Warsaw Pact stocks in Eastern Europe, which must have been readied in advance.[29]

C. Advisers and spetsnaz *in action across the canal*

The influx of Soviet personnel continued on the morrow of the war's outbreak: the attaché Ivliev has attested that a dozen senior officers arrived in Cairo, and he led five of them across the canal on the same day, in order to tour the battlefield as the Egyptian forces advanced.[30] One of these officers was apparently Robert Bykov, a GRU operative and missile expert with special-operations experience worldwide, who is also described as "a veteran of the 1967–1976 Egyptian campaign." Bykov, who retired as a colonel of the General Staff, told a Russian television interviewer in 2003 how in the Yom Kippur War he was tasked to oversee the use of the *Malyutka* in its first massive combat test. As Bykov narrated—probably with a touch of dramatization: "we took a poorly trained peasant ... gave him 10 of these *Malyutkas* and left. The Israeli tanks could be heard from far away. Later ... we arrived there and saw the peasant literally clapping his hands ... [he] showed us six destroyed Israeli tanks in the distance."[31]

Chief of Staff Shazly lists only fifty Saggers among the weapons whose supply was agreed upon with Lashchenko in February 1973 and finalized by Defense Minister Ismail in Moscow the next month.[32] But either this was just one of several shipments, or its quantity was much greater. The Soviets may have somewhat exaggerated the *Malyutka*'s success when they credited it for bagging 800 Israeli tanks, but it did take a lethal toll—as well as starting a controversy within the IDF over its relative importance and the Israeli response.[33]

"Egyptian ambushes destroyed entire [tank] companies" using, besides the *Malyutka*s, which were ineffective after dark, RPG-7s with night-vision sights at very close range, and even mines laid by hand in front of the tanks. The forward Israeli division lost two-thirds of its tanks in the first day of fighting, mainly to infantry before major Egyptian tank forces were introduced.[34] The missiles flew so thick that even when they missed, Israeli tank turrets got enmeshed in the guide wires.[35] Still, the first mention of Saggers in an Israel intelligence report was almost a day into the fighting, and then too as an expected threat rather than an already observed reality; it took MI almost twenty-four hours to conclude that the initial Egyptian crossing was mainly by infantry rather than armor.[36]

Meanwhile, Marwan's belated warning had an extra, probably unpredicted effect when the hastily mobilized IDF armored formations, believing that they would face a tank force, gave their own tanks first priority for transport to the front. They arrived, and were thrown into combat, without artillery cover and infantry support against the Egyptian soldiers, who quickly dug in according to the doctrine that Zakharov had inculcated. Gen. Sharon also noted that the Israeli

IN THE THICK OF THE YOM KIPPUR WAR

tanks had been mostly stripped of machineguns, which would have been effective against infantry.

Sharon was among the few who downplayed the effect of the Saggers relative to the rocket-propelled grenades (RPGs), and the Soviets themselves were not entirely content with the *Malyutka*'s performance either.[37] "Despite the overall success, the war in Egypt uncovered a serious flaw of the new weapon. The missile was too slow." The designer Nepobedimy set about developing the next generation.[38] The Egyptian arena thus continued to function as a proving ground for Soviet weapons, as well as a source for captured US hardware.

Ivliev stated in an interview that he was charged with collecting samples of Israeli- and US-made armaments. He is credited for sending exemplars of several dozen weapons to Moscow during the war. The Soviets took some of the Egyptians' booty, but also made sure to get the most sought-after items themselves. Among their best prizes, Ivliev reports, were a downed unmanned aerial vehicle and a brand-new M-60 Patton tank with only 100 kilometers on the odometer, which Ivliev's group took immediately after crossing.[39]

Another testimony reveals that such feats were accomplished by specially assigned Soviet *spetsnaz* (special ops) detachments. Such units were either drawn from among those who were already posted in Egypt (e.g., to guard such sensitive elements as the Scuds and, later, a redeployed MiG-25 outfit), or were specially dispatched for the purpose. In the first few hours of the war, it was reported to Moscow—evidently by Ivliev's advisers—that Egypt's newly supplied T-62 amphibious tanks were unexpectedly vulnerable to the cannon of presumably outdated Israeli Centurions.[40] Soviet commandos twice went behind Israeli lines to obtain these British-made tanks for study of their Israeli-upgraded gun.

In raids on 8 and 9 October, the *spetsnaz* teams succeeded in killing two Centurion crews while disabling the vehicles only in such a way that they could still be driven back over the pontoon bridges to Cairo for air transport to Moscow. The *Komsomolskaya Pravda* report about this exploit backed it up with a facsimile of one plane's flight log. But for anyone with a military background this account is further authenticated by an anecdote that rings unmistakably true. The first tank's turret was immobilized with the cannon pointing sideways, and it wouldn't go through the cargo plane's back door. After hours of vain attempts, an Egyptian begged "Mr Officer, just cut it off!" to which *spetsnaz* Major "Ivanov" replied: "I'd sooner cut off my you-know-what." Finally, both Centurions were loaded and flown to the USSR. One was used as a target for weapons development and the other is still exhibited at the Kubinka proving ground near Moscow.[41]

A Soviet "air group" was set up in Cairo under the command of Maj.-Gen. M.S. Dvornikov "on the war's sixth day, when luck turned against the Egyptians." It was attached to the Soviet embassy in Cairo to prepare an air intervention on the Arabs' behalf. The air group's "full deployment" never materialized, except for the redeployment of MiG-25s.⁴² There are several indications that Soviet combat pilots already in Egypt as advisers, or instructors inducting new aircraft, were expected to go into combat and possibly even did. MI had prior information whereby the Egyptians were instructed that "in the event that the Soviet pilots do not wish to fly in the war, the Egyptians will fight without them"—that is, they were expected to fight.⁴³ Toward the end of the war, the State Department recorded "a report from an Israeli Air Force pilot that the IAF had captured two Soviet MiG pilots."⁴⁴

This is one of several references to Soviet POWs being taken by the IDF, which—as in 1967—were never officially confirmed. A reserve paratrooper in the Israeli force that closed in on Suez City from the southwest in the final stage of the war related that in one of the bunkers his unit mopped up,

> I moved a big curtain aside with the barrel of my Uzi, and there were about 15 men, Egyptian soldiers and four or five Soviet officers, in Soviet uniforms with insignia. I'm not sure whether they were armed—maybe with pistols. They all surrendered quietly. The Soviets tried to speak with us in English. ... As best I know, they were in command of missile batteries. Later, in beach villas on the outskirts of Suez that looked like fancy living quarters, we found radios that were constantly receiving signals in Russian. We only understood some Russian curses.⁴⁵

This account conforms to those of Soviet signal- and missilemen—regular crews as well as advisers—who were sent to Egypt and Syria just before the war or at its outbreak. Israeli field officers reported extreme difficulty in command and control due to much-improved jamming of their units' frequencies. They attributed this to the Soviets.⁴⁶ This was evident from the very outset, as the head of the IDF's Southern Command testified: "on Saturday [6 October, there was] very little, on Sunday very much, and on Monday nearly everything" was jammed, even systems that were considered relatively immune.⁴⁷

C. Zenitchiki *redeployed*

As for air defense units, about 18 October, "Kosygin, in Cairo, ordered 300 Russians to fly immediately to Egypt to stiffen the air defense barrier, as he feared Israeli raids."⁴⁸ But there is convincing evidence that this partial reprise of *Kavkaz* began well before the reversal of the Egyptian offensive occasioned the Soviet premier's concern. Vladimir Agafonov, who was already in Egypt with the Scud advisers, noted the arrival "at the beginning of hostilities ... for defense of Cairo, [of] an air defense SAM battalion at full combat complement under Col. Bryantsev."⁴⁹

This narrows down the time frame of a testimony from Valentin Sapizhenko, whereby "in October 1973" a battalion was assembled from units of the 8th Air Defense Army, put under Bryantsev's command and "sent to take part in hostilities in the Egyptian Arab Republic." He speaks specifically of a SAM-2 *divizyon*, implying that

IN THE THICK OF THE YOM KIPPUR WAR

he served in it.⁵⁰ One can only speculate whether it was these *zenitchiki* (anti-aircraft operators), Soviet advisers guiding Egyptian crews, or newly resourceful Egyptians on their own who on 18 October put their missiles to an extraordinary improvised use. When Israeli mechanized infantry attacked two missile bases on the west bank of the Bitter Lake, "the defenders fired SAM-2s directly at us. One exploded 10 meters behind the company commander's APC, but no one was injured."⁵¹

Whether other SAM models were included in Bryantsev's outfit is unclear, but seems likely. Despite the retrospective stress on the air defense belt that was composed mainly of SAM-2 and -3s and remained west of the canal, the Israelis attributed the bulk of their aircraft losses to newer, mobile SAM-6s. Ambassador Dinitz told Kissinger two days into the war "we suffered very heavy casualties ... from the SAM-6s which were very effective against our planes." Kissinger took this up with US Chief of Naval Operations Moorer, who admitted "yes, for two reasons. They're mobile and [the Israelis] can't find the launchers. Also, we have never been able to get sufficient information about them to develop any good countermeasures."⁵² Some of them crossed the canal, extending the danger zone for Israeli aircraft. A SAM-6 radar system was destroyed by Israeli tank fire near the IDF's counter-crossing point, to the dismay of the IAF, which wanted to study it.⁵³ The SAM-6 had previously been operated in Egypt only by Soviet crews and was supplied to Egyptian forces only after Ahmed Ismail's visit to Moscow in March 1973.⁵⁴ It therefore seems likely that at least Soviet advisers, if not regular crews, were involved.

In Syria, they certainly were, from the very outbreak of war. *Politruk* Gumar Sagdutinov from Kazan, then stationed near Lvov on the Polish border, was summoned urgently "in early October 1973" and attached, with ten of his comrades, to a brigade of *Kub* (SAM-6) missiles, which—complete with *Strela* and *Shilka* defenses—was dispatched by freighter (the *Ho Chi Minh*) with a warship escort to Syria. When they arrived in Latakiya, "there were already burnt and sunken ships in the harbor"—the aftermath of an Israeli naval attack on the first night of the war.

After the Soviet freighter *Ilya Mechnikov* was sunk in Tartus on 11 October, the Soviet news agency TASS issued a warning that the USSR could not remain indifferent to Israeli action that caused Soviet casualties in Syria *or* Egypt (thereby confirming the presence of military personnel in both), and if it continued this would lead to severe consequences for Israel. Dayan, always the most apprehensive among Israeli leaders about Soviet intervention, accused the IAF of disobeying instructions not to bomb Latakiya "if Russians were there," to which IDF Chief of Staff Elazar responded that there was no bombing; the ship was hit in an exchange between Syrian missile boats berthed next to it and Israeli ones.⁵⁵

Sagdutinov's SAM-6s took up positions in olive groves around Latakiya, but only the *Shilka*s got to fire at suspected Israeli helicopters. After a week, the outfit moved to Damascus, where it stayed for fourteen months. "Soviet military advisers openly told" the interpreter Vasiliev, "who was in Damascus at the time," that

Soviet officers sat at the command tables of the Syrian air defense array, which was reinforced immediately after the Israeli attacks on the Syrian capital. "I can attest that after serious losses were inflicted on the IAF there were no more attacks on Damascus." Before their return, the *zenitchiki* handed over most of the hardware but kept the secret systems.[56]

Vasiliev "has no information that any advisers took part in battles at the front." However, Dudchenko (in one of his documentary publications) hedges this somewhat: there were "no authorized figures of Soviet military personnel in combat, [but this] almost certainly occurred." Mikhail Razinkov, the interpreter for air defense advisers who were posted in April, reports that his group of advisers was instructed that "upon the start of combat activity, all Soviet military specialists are to stay at their workplace, always with their *posdovetny* (advisee)."[57] This is further confirmed by Soviet casualties: Razinkov recalls three "compatriots" killed, one missing, and many injured. The MIA can perhaps be added to unconfirmed reports of Soviet prisoners taken by the IDF; Dudchenko cites a 1974 Knesset statement by Shim'on Peres, by then the defense minister, whereby during the war several high-ranking Soviet officers were killed on the Golan Heights.[58] The veterans' memorial list includes two officers killed "in combat operations" in Syria: Lt-Col. Aleksandr Sipakov, adviser to the headquarters of a mechanized brigade, as early as 6 October, and two days later the adviser to the commander of such a brigade, Lt-Col. Vyacheslav Golovkin.[59]

The influx of Soviet personnel increased "when one Egyptian army [corps] was already surrounded and another, defending Cairo, was demoralized." KGB Col. (then Capt.) Stanislav Leshchuk was sent to Syria in October 1973, decorated for combat service and reposted to Cairo in a civilian airliner. He was one of a group of officers, "every one of whom was a first-class specialist in his field—artillerymen, intelligence operatives, tankists, engineers and signalmen. They worked around the clock, sometimes risking their lives." Suddenly, in a marked change, "besides their combat missions" the officers were ordered—for the first time—to don Soviet dress uniforms and parade through the most teeming areas of Cairo in groups of four to six. "The rationale was simple: at the Peace Congress that was then convened in Moscow, the USSR declared that it had fulfilled its commitment to an ally to extend all support, including military."[60]

31

THE SOVIET NUCLEAR THREAT AND KISSINGER'S DEFCON-3

> The Middle East is the worst place in the world for the US to get engaged in a war with the Soviets ... the $64,000 question [is]: "If the Soviets put 10,000 troops into Egypt what do we do?" ...
>
> Adm. T.H. Moorer, 24/25 October 1973[1]

When put to the test in October 1973, the assumption that an Arab offensive aimed only at regaining territory lost in 1967 would not trigger an Israeli nuclear response proved unexpectedly risky. Documents published in Israel as well as the United States in 2013 confirmed longstanding reports that the Egyptian–Syrian offensive's initial success *was* briefly seen in Israel as an existential threat, and a nuclear response was at least contemplated—mainly by Dayan—if not actually readied. Soviet accounts of preparations for a nuclear counterstrike from Egypt (by means of Scud missiles as suspected by the Americans or, more plausibly, MiG-25 aircraft) claim they were undertaken not only after but *because* such Israeli plans were found out. Bar-Lev's diary records that Dayan proposed a "let me die with the Philistines" option (the biblical source for "Samson" in Hersh's title).[2] In an oral testimony recorded in 2008 and published by Avner Cohen, a ministerial aide in 1973 related witnessing this statement, on the morning of 7 October.

At that point, the most pressing concern was on the Syrian front, where the initial Syrian breakthrough seemed about to progress into the Jordan Valley. Razinkov, the interpreter then stationed with Soviet air defense advisers, attests that they were instructed to advance with the Syrian forces, but only "to go as far as the 1967 lines." The Israelis evidently disregarded or disbelieved Primakov's assurances that this was the limit of Soviet support, and therefore of Arab advance; indeed, Razinkov admitted, "true, no one knew exactly how to determine those borders and what to do when they were reached."[3] Cohen's informant stressed that Dayan suggested carrying out not a targeted strike but rather a nuclear "demonstration." Cohen interprets this as bombs dropped from aircraft to detonate in air over desert areas close enough to

THE SOVIET–ISRAELI WAR, 1967–1973

Cairo and/or Damascus for the flash to be visible there at night. The idea was received "uncomfortably" by Atomic Energy Commission head Freier, totally rejected by Meir and other ministers, and never implemented.[4]

Hersh's widely accepted version puts this discussion a day later, when the situation on the Egyptian front was at its bleakest following a failed Israeli counterattack. One of the present authors (Remez) was told by a staff officer in the Southern Command forward headquarters late in the night of 8–9 October that "we have only 50 tanks left between the Egyptian Army and Tel Aviv." Cohen dates Hersh's account, which he rejects, more plausibly to the following morning when Dayan was at his most despondent. Hersh holds that an Israeli nuclear strike was indeed readied—besides aircraft, by ground-based missiles, whose silo covers were opened and detected by both US and Soviet satellites, as well as Soviet "operatives" in Israel.[5]

The versions that either Meir rejected Dayan's idea *or* that she did brandish the nuclear option in what Hersh calls "nuclear blackmail" to accelerate vital US resupply have been described as mutually exclusive.[6] But that is not necessarily the case. Such signals as opening silos might have been made without the missiles actually being armed. The impression that a nuclear option was under consideration, or even being readied, could have been transmitted to Kissinger (who could be trusted to tell the Soviets), or intentionally conveyed by the Israelis to Moscow, or gathered by Soviet informants in Israel. The latter is precisely the interpretation proposed in 2001 by a senior Russian defense analyst.[7] It may explain the orders issued to Soviet submarines at the start of the war to prepare a nuclear counterstrike.

Leonid Tikochinsky, then a rare if not singular Jewish officer on a Soviet nuclear submarine, related that his boat had been patrolling the Mediterranean since 1972, "including Israeli waters, well aware that we might be taking decisive action against that country." After the outbreak of the Yom Kippur War, he was instructed by the fleet admiral: "when you receive the order you are to fire missiles at Israel." As in the Six-Day War, it was specified that this would be only as a second strike, but now it was assumed that Israel had both weapons and delivery systems. "The order would be given only if Israel dared employ its nuclear weapons at Arab states. The Soviet submarines were to deter Israel from firing its nuclear missiles." Tikochinsky noted that the usual procedure was to give captains only geographic coordinates of their land targets; this time, he was explicitly assigned Israeli objectives, and in hindsight suspected that this was done intentionally to test his loyalty.[8]

Shortly afterward, on 11 October, "Special Air Detachment 154" was alerted for deployment to Egypt. This formation consisted of four MiG-25s, this time all of the reconnaissance bomber (RB) variant, with seven pilots, ground crews and support staff totaling over 220 men. Beginning on 13 October, twelve An-22 and seventy-two An-12 sorties were needed to fly the outfit to Cairo-West. The men were stripped not only of documents and insignia, but of any item identifiable as Soviet, from wristwatches to matches. The planes' Soviet military markings were painted over. But

THE SOVIET NUCLEAR THREAT

unlike the MiG-25s' previous stint in Egypt in 1971–2, the red stars were not replaced with Egyptian marks "as no one would believe it anyway." Once reassembled, the Foxbats carried out four "uniquely important" reconnaissance sorties by the war's end; the product was flown to Moscow within hours.

The flight dates are not specified in the main Russian account of this episode. In the afternoon of 22 October, Ze'ira reported, in a briefing for Kissinger by IDF officers, that "he had just learned that two Foxbat photoreconnaissance planes are flying in the canal zone ... flown by Russian pilots. That morning they overflew the Western Desert and now they are flying over the canal."[9] On 24 October, a report to the US chief of naval operations listed, among other indications that Moscow was preparing to follow up on the threat of intervention that Brezhnev made the same day: "Soviet pilots flying (possibly) Foxbats in Egypt. (If Soviets were going to introduce troops, they would want their own people doing reconnaissance in advance)."[10] The Soviets were, indeed, releasing their observations to the Egyptians only after vetting in Moscow, and this applied to satellite images as well. Vafa Guluzade, then an interpreter at the Soviet embassy in Cairo, puts it around this time ("after the III Army Corps was surrounded") that

> Sadat asked the USSR to give him aero-cosmic intelligence about the positions of Israeli forces ... Moscow complied and sent to Egypt two GRU operatives at the rank of colonel, who brought photos ... made from space. I was tasked to escort them to Sadat and to help transfer [the data] from the photos onto the Egyptians' military maps.[11]

Unlike the satellites, the MiG-25s had another potential function. The aviation writer Viktor Markovsky, based on participants' accounts, claims that when dispatched to Egypt, the pilots of the 154th were instructed to prepare for *both* uses of the RB version.[12] He states that the RB's bombing function, which had been readied but not used in 1971, was now close to implementation. GRU units began practical training for "another insane plan" to "land" in Israel's Negev desert (presumably by helicopter or parachute; there were a series of attempted helicopter-borne raids by Egyptian commandos in Sinai during the opening phases of the war). The Soviet commandos were to set up radio beacons to guide aircraft for an attack on the Israeli nuclear complex at Dimona with burrowing missiles that would destroy the site's underground facilities.

Markovsky notes that the planes were designed, and the pilots thoroughly trained, to launch standoff nuclear weapons from a range of 40 kilometers. Whereas at the start of the war Israeli anti-aircraft defenses successfully intercepted some of the "winged missiles" (i.e., Kelts) fired by Egyptian Tu-16s, the Israelis still had nothing that could cope with the MiG-25s' altitude and speed or intercept their nuclear weapons once launched. Markovsky even claims that "as the military situation changed daily against the Arabs, an attack on Tel Aviv ... was seriously considered." He does not specify if the requisite nuclear weapons were actually delivered to Egypt,

349

nor whether their use was contemplated as a nuclear first strike—contrary to the USSR's longstanding doctrine—or only in response to an Israeli nuclear blow.

Professor Aleksandr Minayev of Moscow State University clarified this point in a 2008 article. Minayev's elder brother Alexey (the deputy minister for the aircraft industry, who had accompanied the Foxbats' previous deployment in Egypt) convened a consultation to determine whether the MiG-25s could safely overfly Tel Aviv. The context was "the eventuality of an Israeli air strike on the Aswan Dam ... which might cause a nuclear war. ... It was rumored in the highest corridors of power in Moscow that in response to such a development, our air force would have to land a nuclear blow on Israel."[13]

How seriously the nuclear option was considered is illustrated by a memoir of Zinaida Freydin, the widow of physicist Ilya Livshits. In a volume commemorating the thirtieth anniversary of his death in 1976, she related that in October 1973 his colleague and close friend, the nuclear weapons developer Yakov Zeldovich, left a note with Livshits (both Jews), to be opened if the USSR launched a nuclear attack on Israel—in which case Zeldovich intended to commit suicide.[14]

Minayev and other ex-Soviet writers have asserted that the Israelis' awareness of this threat and of their inability to counter the Foxbats is what *prevented* the use of Israeli nuclear weapons.[15] This claim seems dubious, as by 13 October the Syrian advance had been reversed, a renewed Egyptian thrust into Sinai was repulsed, and the US airlift to Israel was finally under way, so that any Israeli doomsday scenario was by then obviated. In the event, the MiG-25 detachment carried out only reconnaissance sorties, including at least one over Tel Aviv. But precisely the turning of the war's tide lends credibility to the offensive plans, conventional if not nuclear, that are now attributed to the Soviet MiG-25s. The strategic significance of their deployment to Egypt, regardless of détente commitments, is illustrated by the simultaneous dispatch of a Foxbat squadron to Poland.

The nuclear option associated with the MiG-25s adds a new twist—but not much more credibility—to the much-debated reports that US intelligence identified emissions from Soviet nuclear weapons on board a ship headed for Egypt. This was retrospectively cited as the climactic motivation for Kissinger's decision to declare a worldwide Defcon-3 alert during the night of 24 October, that is, on the 25th (Middle East time). So far, these putative nuclear weapons were held to have been warheads for the Scud missiles based in Egypt.[16]

On 16 October, the day of the IDF's counter-crossing of the canal, Sadat threatened publicly to launch missiles "at the very depths of Israel any minute" if Israel attacked the Egyptian hinterland. He specifically mentioned the *el-Zafar* missile whose development had begun in the early 1960s by German experts and was later abandoned. If it had been a serious threat to Israel, the repeated Egyptian demand for Scuds would have been gratuitous.[17] The next day, the Americans were still not sure

THE SOVIET NUCLEAR THREAT

at all of the Scuds' arrival in Egypt (though this had been communicated to them by the Israelis in August) and did not envisage any nuclear use for them:

> *Adm. Moorer*: ...The Israelis think the Soviets have given them some SCUDs, and we have seen some on the docks at Nicolai [*sic*], but we have no proof that there are any in Egypt. ... It's a terror vehicle. ... It would have no really serious effect but it would scare hell out of the Israelis. It's an expensive way to deliver a 1000-pound bomb.[18]

Five days later, on the 22nd, as the first ceasefire was about to go into effect, conventionally tipped Scuds were fired at the Israelis' canal counter-crossing point. Moorer was right as to the effect on the Israelis: in 1993, Bar-Lev—as Israel's ambassador to post-Soviet Russia—still claimed to Israelyan that the Scuds were very inaccurate and did not damage Israeli targets, but admitted that "it was a big excitement."[19]

It was such an excitement that the Israelis suppressed the news at the time and never officially confirmed the missile hits nor the Soviet connection. An IAF publication disclosed in 2006 that "one of about three missiles" struck a convoy of ammunition trucks, killing seven soldiers.[20] This article cited a study by the IDF History Department, but five years later the department's own detailed compilation of command deliberations during the war does not mention that Scud impacts were identified or reported among "Egyptian violations of the ceasefire that caused Israeli casualties."[21] The IDF memorial site still lists none of the fatalities on that day as a victim of a Scud strike; one is described as "a driver in an ammo convoy" in the same sector.[22]

Any suggestion that Egyptian operators alone were involved is negated by the testimony of the interpreter Agafonov, who came with the advisers that accompanied the missiles' arrival in July. He related that at the outbreak of war, "the Egyptian Scud brigade was urgently supported by a group of specialists and regulars-instructors, and brought up to battle readiness." Israelyan adds that the missiles were also "guarded by a Soviet military unit," like the *spetsnaz* detachment that guarded the MiG-25s in 1971–2 and during their wartime redeployment. Although the training course that Agafonov's team had been assigned to give the Egyptians was not yet completed, he states that the latter "pressed the button," after Sadat obtained Moscow's consent.

According to Israelyan, the required authorization was given by Defense Minister Grechko. He describes the marshal's order as an offhand response to Vinogradov's repeated badgering from Cairo, in contravention of official Kremlin policy (which aroused the ire of Gromyko, who tried belatedly to prevent it).[23] This account seemed suspicious to begin with: Grechko could hardly have undertaken such an escalation of the direct Soviet role without at least some backing at Politburo level—presumably, including Brezhnev.

Chernyaev's diary has now confirmed that Grechko not only had such approval, but that he was instructed to initiate the Scud launches. On 1 December, Chernyaev wrote that he had "found out from the documents" that Brezhnev, contrary to the line spread in Moscow, had not at all displayed "anger against our own extremists," who proposed a crackdown against Israel. On the contrary,

> during the peak of the war in the Middle East ... when Israel violated the ceasefire agreement ... seized a large piece of territory on the west bank of the Suez and moved tanks towards Cairo, Brezhnev did two things: a) he wrote a letter to Nixon with a proposal to send Soviet–American troops into Egypt together; or if Nixon did not want to do that, Brezhnev would do it alone. That is why the Americans announced defense readiness condition 1 [*sic*].

Allowing for the inaccuracies (Brezhnev's note was sent three days later), this much was known before Chernyaev's journal was published. However, he also found that

> b) Brezhnev wrote a note to Politburo members, suggesting to do "something" immediately—to bring the Soviet fleet to Tel Aviv or allow the Egyptians to strike Israel with our medium-range missiles (but not Tel Aviv or Jerusalem), or something else. Two things remain a mystery—why have Nixon and Kissinger not leaked [this] information ... [and] why did Brezhnev's note to the PB not have any consequences. Who stopped this initiative and how.

It attests once more to the compartmentalization of knowledge in the Soviet hierarchy that over a month after the fact, Chernyaev (the deputy director of the Party Secretariat's international department) was not aware that Scuds had already been launched. Chernyaev's following statement is even more revealing: "it is astonishing that the letter has not been confiscated. Even some staff in our department have read it, and are still reading it, when everything turned out differently."[24] In other words, "confiscation" and elimination of potentially embarrassing documents was the rule rather than the exception—yet another illustration that absence of archival evidence cannot in itself disprove otherwise reliable reports.

The ship supposedly emitting radiation was first spotted on 22 October entering the Mediterranean from the Black Sea. It docked on the 25th at Port Said—an unlikely destination, unnecessarily close to the combat zone if it carried warheads for the Scuds *or* the Foxbats, both of which were stationed near Cairo. Rather, this ship was probably escorted by, or was an auxiliary of, a Soviet flotilla of five warships that was ordered into Port Said on the 24th.

According to Capt. Zaborsky, as early as 17 October (that is, after the Israeli canal crossing), "preliminary plans for a limited 'demonstration' landing of Soviet naval infantry on the west bank of the canal were drafted ... One large and six medium landing ships were already in the region but they were all being used for equipment transport"—that is, the resupply sealift. "Subsequently ... Gorshkov ordered the already deployed landing ships to be used for troop transport and a landing force to be assembled of 'volunteers' from the crews of all combatant and auxiliary ships." Capt. Evgeny Semenov, then the *Eskadra*'s chief of staff, wrote in his journal that

THE SOVIET NUCLEAR THREAT

"some thousand men signed up." Goldstein and Zhukov, quoting from Semenov's unpublished manuscript, conclude that "this resort to volunteers is a sign that the *eskadra* was to some extent in over its head." But as in 1967, the "volunteer" character of the force is risible.[25] Although, as Zaborsky states, "the bulk of the naval infantry force was still in Sevastopol preparing for deployment into the Mediterranean," the landing ships would have carried their routine complement of marines, unless they had disembarked at Port Said before the ships left harbor around 3–4 October.

Finally ordered to carry out the mission at the height of US–Soviet tension on 24 October, Capt. Semenov wrote: "Seems we're going to save Port Said from the Israelis." Like the routine Soviet "garrison" there in previous years, the force now included three SAM destroyers, a BDK (large landing vessel) and two SDKs (medium landing vessels). An Israeli advance on Port Fuad, which had first been proposed by the IDF and supported by Dayan as early as 7 October "because the Soviets have evacuated Port Said," was repeatedly postponed and finally ruled out by the prime minister on the 22nd. This was after a meeting with Kissinger, and partly out of fear that it would trigger the missile launch at Israel that Sadat had threatened.[26] Whether or not the Soviets were aware of this, their landing was called off "at the last minute," but the ships apparently returned to Port Said as others did to Alexandria.[27]

No evidence has emerged so far that the "nuclear warheads" ship's detection was so much as mentioned in any of the discussions that led to the declaration of Defcon-3—or for that matter, that the United States was aware of any other Soviet nuclear preparations, such as the Foxbats'. Kissinger's virtually singlehanded initiation of the alert quickly became public and highly controversial; while its genesis is beyond the scope of this study, it can be assumed that Kissinger—under heavy criticism for supposedly political motivation, three days after the "Saturday Night Massacre"—would have cited such a very apt motive as a Soviet nuclear threat, had it really led to his decision. Even in retrospect, he mentioned only the menace of intervention by Soviet conventional forces, "the ... sense of impending crisis" when "eight Soviet An-22 transport planes each capable of carrying 200 or more troops were slated to fly from Budapest to Egypt."[28] The much closer marine landing went either unknown or unmentioned. In this case, contemporary documents published in 2008 bear out Kissinger's memoirs. More than a month later, he maintained in a briefing to the congressional leadership "we don't think the Soviets have put them [nuclear weapons] in." He also came as close as a US official ever did both to confirming that Israel possessed nuclear weapons, and to admitting he had been informed that their use had been contemplated: "should Israel brandish nuclear weapons, the Soviets would counter it and it would be very dangerous for Israel."[29]

But on the night of 24–5 October, Kissinger's statements, as recorded by Adm. Moorer, reflect no concern about a Soviet nuclear danger to Israel. Rather, they reflect his discomfiture both at Nixon's weakened position and at the apparent unraveling of his own policy linchpin:

353

"*If the Democrats and the US public do not stop laying seige [sic] to their government ... sooner or later, someone will take a run at us.* Friday the PresUS was in good shape domestically. Now the Soviets see that he is, in their mind, non-functional ... *So far the Congress has had a great time enjoying Détente, wrecking Defense and destroying the President.* ... It appears now that the hawks prevailed over Brezhnev." ... He [Kissinger] was still puzzled by the action taken by the Soviets.

CIA Director Colby

noted that the Soviets can recoup with the Arabs if they placed a major force in Cairo. ... HAK asked "*What does 5,000 men in Cairo really mean?*" It means that the Soviets want a challenge and that, if they get in, they'll never get out. ... *If we do put Marines or troops into the Middle East it will amount to scrapping Détente.* ... HAK asked "*What did we do wrong?*"[30]

Taken separately, each of these cases might be construed as a *post facto* attempt by the Soviets to make the best of an undesired predicament. But cumulatively, the facts as they have now been fleshed out definitely narrow down the spectrum of tenable hypotheses by ruling out the possibility that an unwitting and unwilling Kremlin merely tried to cope with a war it had tried to avoid.

EPILOGUE

SO WHAT WENT WRONG, AND WHEN?

If at least the opening surprise of the Yom Kippur War went according to a joint Soviet–Egyptian plan, why did it all end so badly for the mutual relationship? The cliché that Egypt needed the Soviets for the war, but the Americans for the peace seems closer to reality than some other widely held notions about the interwar years that have been reassessed in the present book. We found the Soviets to have been aware of this impending liability, but their attempts to offset it with overtures toward Israel were even more inept than the much-overrated American outreach toward Egypt.

A detailed study of the interrelated military and diplomatic moves will be needed to judge whether it was the relatively reserved US support for Israel compared with the USSR's for Egypt, more than any American blandishments toward Cairo, that gained Washington the peace broker's function. Whereas in the War of Attrition it was the direct Soviet intervention that ensured Egypt of gaining its war goals, in 1973 the United States enjoyed the extra advantage of never having to "put boots on the ground" and thus did not intensify Arab enmity and distrust. Or was it Israel's costly, hard-fought and narrow edge in the field that gained its unenthusiastic patron this benefit?

Further study may perhaps enable a judgment whether Egypt—that is, Sadat—premeditated his conversion to "no more war" from the time he came to power, as he claimed in hindsight when this became advantageous; or (as seems likelier from our examination of the interwar period) he changed course only in response to unforeseen developments in the latter phases of the 1973 war and afterward. If, after all, the former possibility is borne out, it would mean the Soviets knowingly maintained their support in an ultimately doomed effort to keep Sadat in the fold. Otherwise, they simply squandered the return on the persistent, conscientious and dedicated effort by 50,000 of their men, besides the enormous material cost.

There is little confirmation—in the post-Soviet and other sources that we have reviewed—for the variety of theories that put a major breakdown in Soviet–Egyptian relations at some point during the Yom Kippur War itself or soon after. One such supposed breaking point merits discussion here, as it stems from the Soviet involvement in the years preceding the war. This is the Egyptians' armored thrust, on 14 October, beyond the original bridgeheads and out of the safety provided by the static SAM array west of the canal. Israel defeated this thrust in what has been called the greatest tank battle since Kursk in the Second World War.

Heikal is one of several Egyptian sources who blamed this move on a direct and explicit demand from Moscow, including personal appeals from Brezhnev and Grechko (though Heikal admits he too favored the idea). Although the Soviet leaders asserted, and Ambassador Vinogradov constantly urged Sadat, that such an advance would maximize Egypt's gains and improve its position, the Soviets' main motive and argument was to divert Israeli attention and forces from the northern front, where the Syrians were already being beaten back.[1] The Egyptian attack's repulse with heavy losses opened the way for the Israelis' counter-crossing of the canal, and Egyptian resentment at being thus sacrificed was a leading harbinger of the ultimate break with Moscow—thus Heikal.

The official Egyptian military history completed soon after the war does give the reason for the move "to reduce pressure" on Syria as well as to "strengthen [Egypt's] hold on the bridgeheads." It makes—as usual—no mention of any Soviet input, while blaming the Egyptian failure on a US spy plane that on 13 October "revealed our plans to develop the attack."[2] Chief of Staff Shazly (as he claimed, along with both the army corps' commanders) opposed the "blunder from which all other blunders followed," and was cashiered for it even though he carried out Sadat's order. His memoir, which is often critical of the Soviet role on other points, does not mention them at all in this context. Ironically, it is Shazly who took credit for devising the fictitious "Operation 41" plan, which called for precisely such an advance to the passes, for presentation to the Soviets to justify larger demands for weapons, while the Egyptians (as he claimed) intended only to carry out the more modest "High Minarets."

But at least those Soviets who had taken part in the planning expected the Egyptians to deliver on the plan they had been equipped for. Malashenko—who had personally advised Shazly, and credited his own 1968 blueprint for originating the offensive plan—was in October 1973 back in the USSR and reassigned. He was evidently referring to "Operation 41" when he complained that "after crossing the Suez Canal, the following operations did not carry out the recommendations that called for rapid expansion of effort by introducing armored and reserve divisions to develop the attack, which caused a crisis in the course of the operation."[3]

Shazly's main motive was to blame Sadat, but he is also the only source for a significant instance of continuity in Soviet participation from 1967 through and after the 1973 war: "A month after the war General Lashnekov [Lashchenko] ... came to Egypt to be briefed on the military situation." Shazly attended, in one of his last acts as chief of staff. His resentment of Lashchenko's attitude reflects years of previous experience: "the Russians remained resolutely Russian, which is to say ... as harsh and obstinate as ever." This, however, referred to the Soviet general's response to the Egyptians' specific battlefield lessons for improving Soviet hardware, mainly the anti-tank weapons (which Shazly praised overall):

EPILOGUE

Lashnekov was brusque: "Russian scientists calculate everything and do not need such ideas," he said. "Soviet weapons are excellent. We made them and we know it." "You may have made them," I said. "We have fought with them. If you know everything why are you here questioning us?"

The Minister [Ahmed Ismail] stepped in to cool the situation. But a few minutes later Lashnekov was making equally blunt and ill-formed criticisms of the deployment of our air force.

In sum, though, Shazly—who opposed the ultimate peace treaty with Israel, and the US patronage that enabled it—justified the alliance with Moscow:

All debate about the wisdom of Egypt's relationship with the Soviet Union boiled down to a single question: "Is there any other country in the world which in the past, present or near future could or would supply Egypt with sufficient arms to give her the local superiority over Israel to liberate her territories?" The answer is no.[4]

An official Russian military history likewise takes credit for a mission well accomplished.

The October War marked the success of Soviet policy in the Middle East: the Arab–Israeli military confrontation ended in a tie. Under the conditions then prevailing, the lack of an Israeli victory was in fact a defeat at the hands of Arab armies equipped with Soviet weapons and trained by Soviet instructors. ... But immediately after the War, there began a rapid process of squeezing the USSR out of active positions in the Middle East.[5]

If the Soviets' "expulsion" from Egypt in 1972 was mostly a feint, after 1973 it became a reality.

Tracking this gradual process from the Soviet viewpoint merits a separate study. It obviously was not abrupt: not only did Egypt (as well as Syria and the Arabs in general) continue to enjoy Soviet political backing well after the Yom Kippur War; even the military relationship went on. Lt-Gen. Samokhodsky, who served as the chief adviser during the war, was replaced in 1974 by Maj.-Gen. E. Bokovikov, who remained on duty until 1978—a significant date, as will be suggested.[6] Though the rank of the chief adviser was thus somewhat lowered, he did retain the title of "head of the Soviet forces group," and he had plenty of activity to oversee. To cite two examples, Soviet naval ships did take part in the canal reopening when it began; arms shipments not only replenished Egyptian losses but included new systems, such as the real MiG-23 (Flogger) that was provided in 1974.

The Soviets secured co-sponsorship of the first postwar effort at a settlement, the Geneva Conference in December 1973. Partly for that very reason, the conference was as ineffectual as the various incarnations of prewar talks. When in 1978 Oleg Grinevsky was appointed to head the Middle East Department of the Soviet Foreign Ministry without any previous exposure to the region, he was told by Gromyko that this would remain an arena for superpower confrontation, indeed the only area where bloc alignments were still fluid. Therefore, Soviet policy was built on the assumption that "as long as *hostility* dominates in the Middle East, we are needed there."[7] The USSR, then, was not merely unable to deliver a settlement with Israel; it had no perceived interest to do so, and proceeded to hinder the process wherever it could.

The ensuing changes in Soviet attitudes toward Ashraf Marwan exemplify the gradual turnaround in Moscow–Cairo relations. Despite his last-minute tipoff to the Israelis or—more plausibly—thanks to its judicious timing and preparation, Marwan continued to be entrusted with top-level missions for Sadat. Ironically, this would include escorting Mrs Kissinger and arranging the secretary's own itinerary when he finally did make his first visit to Egypt in 1974. Marwan himself was welcomed in Washington the same year.[8] That November, Marwan's wife, "Mona G.A. Nasser," was along with her mother Tahiya the guest of the prestigious Artek children's camp in Crimea.[9]

The first Egyptian–Israeli agreement (the Sinai interim accord) was signed in September 1975 in Geneva, but it was the product of Kissinger's "shuttle diplomacy" rather than the Soviet-backed Geneva Conference (which never resumed). It gave the United States alone a monitoring and policing role that for the first time did put US boots on the ground. As it involved a return of Egyptian territory, it could be countenanced by Moscow as embodying some return on its military investment in Egypt, but the trend was unmistakable. In March 1976, Sadat abrogated the friendship and cooperation treaty five years into its fifteen-year term, and the KGB initiated "active measures" against him in response.

A letter was forged on French Foreign Ministry paper,

> emphasizing that the Egyptian president's steps were apparently made with the direct participation of the United States to open up further prospects for US capital in Middle Eastern nations and assist in turning Egypt into an active conduit for US interests in oil-producing countries. The document is brought to the attention of Syrian President Assad through *agentura* channels.[10]

Evidently some of the blame was put on Marwan, as by May 1976, his "anti-Soviet attitude" had become so irksome for the Soviets that the KGB "implemented a complex operation" to compromise him by revealing his "contacts with US special services" and embezzlement of Saudi funds allocated for purchase of US weapons. Reports were even circulated that he had "intimate relations" with Sadat's wife, Jehan. The KGB gave this operation partial credit for Sadat's subsequent dismissal of Marwan (but he retained his lucrative position heading the Egyptian arms industry).[11] Sadat himself was, then, not yet targeted; the Soviet purpose was still to halt his pro-US tilt, not to remove him.

The breaking point appears to have been Sadat's celebrated visit to Jerusalem. According to Oleg Grinevsky, the KGB knew of this dramatic move two days in

EPILOGUE

advance—which coincides with Sadat's prior call on Assad in Damascus. Grinevsky asserts that the Syrian president tricked Sadat by encouraging him to call Israel's bluff. Actually, Assad foresaw, correctly, the isolation of Sadat and Egypt by his separate-peace initiative—and considered, less accurately, that it would elevate Syria to a leadership position in the Arab world. It did leave Syria as the main base for Soviet, and then Russian, military and intelligence operations in the region. This would be endangered only by the uprising against Assad's son and heir Bashar in 2011, which at its peak triggered Putin's direct military intervention in 2015 that displayed marked similarities to Brezhnev's forty-odd years before. But following Egypt's defection, Moscow's policy of maintaining "no war, no peace" as enunciated by Gromyko put an increasing emphasis on the Palestinians.

It was at this point, following Sadat's peace initiative, that the Soviet ideologues Suslov and Ponomarev began to demonize him as a counterrevolutionary, and the KGB to characterize him as "a braggart, a poseur, inexperienced in any field essential for national politics," who from his accession "began to signal the Americans: you hold the key to a Middle Eastern settlement"—as Primakov and others had charged before but were overruled. As Grinevsky describes it with a measure of apologetics,

> [Israeli Prime Minister Menahem] Begin and Sadat got the peace train moving without the United States or the USSR, but the crafty Americans jumped onto it when it was already in motion. Common sense dictated that we should do the same, but Gromyko knew his Politburo colleagues too well. The only remaining option was to poke spokes in the wheels, but would that stop the train?

Gromyko dictated that

> our course must be to prevent any separate accord. ... We must get the entire Arab world from Syria to Saudi Arabia up on its hind legs. The only unifying factor in the Arab world is not Sinai or the Golan Heights, but the Palestinian problem, and it should be the focus of our attention.

Grinevsky still concludes that "we did right to condemn the nascent Egyptian–Israeli connection, otherwise our Arab friends would have felt that we betrayed them like the Americans."[12] Both before and after the Egyptian–Israeli peace treaty was signed in March 1979, Soviet propaganda denounced it as an American ploy to gain "deeper military and political influence" and "to safeguard American interests in the Middle East after the Iranian revolution."[13]

Soviet invective against Egypt in general and Sadat in particular reached heights never seen during the supposed rift of July 1972—thus demonstrating in hindsight that it hadn't taken place. "Angry criticisms" in the Soviet media accused him of "a sellout, blackmail, 'a plot behind the back of the Arabs,' a fake peace." TASS news agency charged him with "capitulation to Israeli demands," although the treaty regained every inch of Sinai.[14] A KGB agent, "Bristol," arranged the publication in Damascus of "a history of Sadat's betrayal."[15]

Subversion efforts went beyond mere words in December 1977: the KGB *rezidentura* (embassy station) in Damascus "registered no objection" when it was informed of a Syrian–PFLP plan to "physically eliminate" Sadat and Marwan.[16] Whether this ultimately led to Soviet sponsorship of Sadat's actual assassination, on the eighth anniversary of the October War, by such unlikely allies as the Muslim Brotherhood, remains a major question for research of the post-1973 phase. But Sadat himself evidently suspected this was afoot: a few weeks earlier, he had expelled the Soviet ambassador, Vladimir Polyakov, and his staff for "involvement in a plot to destabilize the country."

In the unkindest cut of all, Sadat also disclosed that since the Soviet invasion of Afghanistan in December 1979, he had been selling his now-surplus stock of Soviet-made weapons to the United States for supply to the mujahideen, and training the anti-Soviet fighters. The *Afgantsy* thus faced the same weapons and knowhow that their older colleagues had provided to Egypt. The USSR was for almost three years in the anomalous situation of no diplomatic relations with Israel *or* Egypt, until a "thaw" initiated by Sadat's successor—the Soviets' old friend Husny Mubarak—culminated in the Cairo embassy's restoration in July 1984.[17] It was only in the final days of December 1991 that Aleksandr Bovin, Brezhnev's former speechwriter, became the last Soviet ambassador anywhere to present his credentials—in Jerusalem. His Soviet diplomatic corps' gold-braided dress uniform had become so obsolete that an American reporter wondered, "Did they bring the hotel doorman too?"[18]

Bovin later remarked to the authors: "Do you know why Russia is so big? Because it never gave back anything." How post-Soviet Russia, especially under Putin, moved to reclaim its standing as a Middle Eastern power, by backing "traditional allies" such as Syria and the Palestinians, fostering new ones (like Iran), mending fences with erstwhile clients like Egypt and—not least—by maximizing its nuisance value against US hegemony was the focus of our journalistic work for years, and merits yet another book. Suffice it for now to say that the sense of *déjà vu* is overpowering.

NOTES

Testimonies before the Israeli Commission of Inquiry on the Yom Kippur War (the Agranat Commission, AC), all in Hebrew, are accessible from the list on the IDF Archive website, http://www.archives.mod.gov.il/pages/Exhibitions/agranat2/exb.asp. Page numbers are in the pdf versions, not the original typescripts, where the pagination is erratic. The commission's reports, accessible from the list at http://www.archives.mod.gov.il/pages/Exhibitions/agranat/agranat_commission.asp, are referred to by the pagination in the text. The Commission's Additional Partial Report is abbreviated here to APR.

Documents from the Israel State Archive are cited by division (HZ-), box/file (4082/7).

Documents from NA(PRO)—National Archive (formerly Public Records Office), London—are in file FCO 39/1265, unless otherwise indicated.

Documents in *Foreign Relations of the United States* (*FRUS*) are cited by administration (J=Johnson, N=Nixon), volume (XIX) and document number (no. 491), rather than page number, to facilitate location in the e-book versions.

All references to the Mitrokhin Archive (MA) are to file MITN 2/24, "Near and Middle East," by page and item number.

Two frequently cited works are *The Rise of Detente: Document Reader* (M. Munteanu et al., eds), abbreviated to DR, and David C. Geyer and Douglas E. Selvage's *Soviet-American Relations: The Détente Years, 1969–1972*, abbreviated to SAR.

FOREWORD

1. AC, Tal Testimony, Part 1, p. 27.
2. Akopov, transcript, p. 27; Vladimir Voronov, "Zhara, klopy i 'stingery,'" *Sobesednik* (Moscow), reprinted in *Ekho* (Tel Aviv), 13 September 1999, p. 42. Col.-Gen. Boris Utkin of the Military History Institute put the figure at "15,000–20,000 at the end of 1971," in Valery Vartanov et al. (eds), *Rukopozhatie cherez chetvert' veka, 1973–1998: Materialy nauchno-prakticheskoy konferentsii* (Russian and Arabic), Moscow: Institute of Military History, Council of Veterans of War in Egypt and Attaché Office of Egyptian Arab Republic, 1999, p. 12. A total figure of 60,000 was recently calculated, based on Russian sources, as against 26,000 in Korea, 43,000 in Cuba and over 6,000 in Vietnam; Evgeny Platunov, "Provaly v pamyati," *Altaiskaya Pravda*, 30 May 2007, http://www.ap.altairegion.ru/158-07/10.html. The strength of Soviet air defense units in Vietnam has been estimated at a total of 10,000 men throughout the war, three *divizyons* at a time (as against dozens in

Egypt), in addition to air force instructors who also flew combat missions (as against regular Soviet squadrons in Egypt); Jerrold Schecter and Leona Schecter, *Sacred Secrets: How Soviet Intelligence Operations Changed American History*, Washington, DC: Brassey's, 2002, pp. 279–80.

3. An admittedly incomplete list compiled by a veterans' website names fifty-eight fatalities, including victims of disease and accidents. "Kniga Pamyati," http://www.hubara-rus.ru/heroes.html

4. Review of *Foxbats* by Lawrence Freedman, *Foreign Affairs* (September–October 2007), https://www.foreignaffairs.com/reviews/capsule-review/2007-09-01/foxbats-over-dimona-soviets-nuclear-gamble-six-day-war

5. It is, for example, treated as a connecting section between the two wars in George W. Gawrych, *The Albatross of Decisive Victory: War and Peace Between Egypt and Israel in the 1967 and 1973 Arab–Israeli Wars*, Westport, CT: Greenwood, 2000.

6. A recent volume of conference proceedings (Nigel Ashton (ed.), *The Cold War in the Middle East: Regional Conflict and the Superpowers 1967–73*, London: Routledge/LSE, 2007), which was aimed at refocusing attention on the subject, lists (p. 4) only three previous books devoted to the 1967–73 period, all at least fifteen years old: David Korn, *Stalemate: The War of Attrition and Great Power Diplomacy in the Middle East*, Boulder, CO: Westview, 1992; Yaacov Bar-Siman-Tov, *The Israeli–Egyptian War of Attrition, 1969–1970*, New York: Columbia University Press, 1980; and Lawrence Whetten, *The Canal War: Four-Power Conflict in the Middle East*, Cambridge, MA: MIT, 1974. To these should be added the main work that concentrated on the Soviet role, Alvin Z. Rubinstein, *Red Star on the Nile: The Soviet–Egyptian Influence Relationship since the June War*, Princeton: Princeton University Press, 1977, as well as a previous volume of conference proceedings: Itamar Rabinovich and Haim Shaked (eds), *From June to October: The Middle East between 1967 and 1973*, Piscataway, NJ: Transaction, 1978. Other studies, which appeared in Hebrew, had little impact on international academic discourse, e.g., Dan Schueftan, *Attrition: Egypt's Post-war Military Strategy, 1967–1970*, Tel Aviv: Ministry of Defense, 1989, and Dima Adamsky, *Operation Kavkaz*, Tel Aviv: Ministry of Defense, 2006.

7. Igor' Plugatarev, "Pamyati ne vernuvshikhsya s kholodnoy voyny," *NVO*, 25 April 2014, www.ng.ru/nvo/2014-04-25/14_monuments.html

8. Vladimir Vinogradov, *Diplomatiya: Lyudi i sobytiya, iz zapisok posla*, Moscow: ROSSPEN, 1998, pp. 12–13.

9. Viktor Karyukin, "Kak soyuz Izrail' nakazyval: Neizvestnye podrobnosti ob uchastii sovetskikh voysk v arabo–izrail'skom konflikte," *Stolitsa*, 8 (1992).

10. Mohamed Hassanein Heikal, *The Road to Ramadan*, London: Collins, 1975, p. 7.

11. Vinogradov, *Diplomatiya*, pp. 7–8.

12. James Cable, *Gunboat Diplomacy: Political Applications of Limited Naval Force*, London: Institute for Strategic Studies, 1971, p. 153.

13. Richard Ned Lebow and Janice Gross Stein, *We All Lost the Cold War*, Princeton University Press, 1994, pp. 165, 168.

14. Galia Golan, *Soviet Policies in the Middle East: From World War II to Gorbachev*, Cambridge University Press, 1990, p. 86.

15. George W. Breslauer, *Soviet Strategy in the Middle East*, London: Routledge, 1990, p. 41.
16. Amnon Sella, *Soviet Political and Military Conduct in the Middle East*, London: Macmillan, 1978, pp. 78–9.
17. Korn, *Stalemate*, p. 189; emphasis added.
18. Lebow and Stein, *We All Lost*, pp. 158, 452n44
19. Ibid., pp. 160–3.
20. David Kimche, *The Last Option: After Nasser, Arafat and Saddam Hussein; The Quest for Peace in the Middle East*, London: Weidenfeld and Nicholson, 1991. However, as noted about other studies, this is only an introductory chapter of a book devoted to a later period. It is unsourced, and when we inquired in the early 2000s, the late Dr Kimche could state only that this chapter was derived from the archive of his brother, the British journalist Jon Kimche, who by then was deceased. But David Kimche himself, a former senior Mossad operative and director-general of the Israeli Foreign Ministry, undoubtedly based his assessment also on his own experience.
21. In the author's (Remez) personal experience, such releases were often dictated over the phone directly to media newsrooms from the IDF spokeman's office, beginning with such formulas as "our military correspondent learned that ..." These semi-official communiqués can be distinguished from the correspondents' genuine contributions by the absence of their names in the by-lines, as well as the identical text in various media. Likewise, reports credited to an unnamed "Arab affairs correspondent" were routinely disseminated by MI's open-source unit "Hatzav"; "political correspondent" by the Prime Minister's Office, etc.
22. Gerhard L. Weinberg, "Some Myths of World War II," The 2011 George C. Marshall Lecture in Military History, *Journal of Military History*, 75 (July 2011), p. 707.
23. Even the IDF's official history of the Yom Kippur War (Elchnan Oren's *The History of Yom Kippur War*, Tel Aviv: IDF History Department, 2013), lists the memoirs of Kissinger and Nixon as its sole sources for "the impact of Détente," the "expulsion of Soviet advisers from Egypt," the "feelers by Sadat toward the United States," the San Clemente summit, etc.; p. 60n12.
24. To Brezhnev, in "Memorandum of Conversation," Moscow, 13 September 1972, *FRUS* N-XV, no. 44.
25. Aleksandr Kiknadze, *Taynopis': Sobytiya i nravy zashifrovannogo veka*, Moscow: Sovetsky Sport, 1998, p. 24.
26. See, e.g., Vitaly V. Naumkin et al. (eds), *Blizhnevostochnyy konflikt, iz dokumentov arkhiva vneshney politiki Rossiyskoy Federatsii*, Moscow: Materik, 2003, which was co-published by Yale University Press as part of a series, "Russia in the 20th Century: Documents," but appeared only in Russian. For a particularly revealing example, see our analysis of document 263, vol. 2, pp. 577–8, in Isabella Ginor and Gideon Remez, "Un-Finished Business: Archival Evidence Exposes the Diplomatic Aspect of the USSR's Pre-Planning for the Six-Day War,'" *Cold War History*, 6, 3 (2006), pp. 377–95.
27. For example, the "Annals of Communism" series of Yale University Press.
28. Rudolf Pikhoya, *Sovetsky Soyuz: Istoriya Vlasti, 1945–1991*, Novosibirsk: Sibirsky Khronograf, 2000, p. 651.

29. Among the most prominent examples: the Vasily Mitrokhin Archive (MA) and Aleksandr Vassiliev's Notebooks, published by the Woodrow Wilson Center (http://digitalarchive.wilsoncenter.org/collection/86/Vassiliev-Notebooks).
30. Shimon Golan, *Decision Making of Israeli High Command in Yom Kippur War*, Tel Aviv: Ma'arakhot (IDF publishing) and Modan, 2013, and Oren, *History*, "clarify" (both on p. 4) that the: "IDF documents that this book rests upon are internal documents which are not necessarily open for study to the general public."
31. Many of these, which were first published in *DR*, are cited here from subsequent and more easily accessible publications, particularly *FRUS* and *SAR*.
32. In the most flagrant case, *FRUS* J-XIX, no. 75, of which no content, nor even a title, date or origin is reproduced, we concluded that such a non-document could have been included only as a veiled protest by the editors at excessive sanitizing. One of the editors confirmed to us that this was indeed their intent. Isabella Ginor and Gideon Remez, "Too Little, Too Late: The CIA and US Counteraction of the Soviet Initiative in the Six-Day War," *Intelligence and National Security*, 26, 2–3 (2011), p. 302n41–2.
33. *SAR*, English (Geyer and Selvage) and Russian (Lavrov) editions.
34. Pikhoya, *Sovetsky Soyuz*, p. 652.
35. Isabella Ginor and Gideon Remez, *Foxbats over Dimona: The Soviets' Nuclear Gamble in the Six-Day War*, New Haven: Yale University Press, 2007, pp. 3–4, 50–1.
36. Lawrence Stone, untitled 1985 lecture in Douglas Greenberg and Stanley Katz (eds), *The Life of Learning*, Oxford: Oxford University Press, 1994, p. 24.
37. Schecter and Schecter, *Sacred Secrets*, pp. 171–2.
38. Pikhoya, *Sovetsky Soyuz*, pp. 647–8.
39. Karyukin, "Kak Soyuz Izrail' nakazyval"; emphasis added.
40. Col. Boris Syromyatnikov, "'Shestidnevnoy voyny' moglo ne byt,'" *Voenno-Promyshlenny Kur'er*, 28 (25 July 2007), p. 9, http://www.vpk-news.ru/sites/default/files/pdf/issue_194.pdf
41. A. Smirnov, "'Operatsiya 'Kavkaz': V gushche sobytiy,'" in M.S. Meyer et al. (eds), *Togda v Egipte*, Moscow: Moscow State University and Council of Veterans of Combat Operations in Egypt, 2001, pp. 36–7.
42. "Egipet: Neizvestnaya voyna," *Sputnik*, January 1991.
43. B. Zhayvoronok, "Vozvrashchenie k proshlomu," in V.Z. Safonov et al. (eds), *Grif "sekretno" snyat*, Moscow: Council of Veterans of Hostilities in Egypt, 1998, p. 45.
44. Maj.-Gen. Artem Khandanyan, "Zharkoe nebo Egipta," *VKO*, http://www.vko.ru/biblioteka/zharkoe-nebo-egipta, referring to the same year. A career *politruk*, then a colonel, he served as the 18th Division's chief political officer in Egypt in 1971–2.
45. N. Solov'eva, "Poyushchy general," *Metrostroyevets*, 3, 13077, 24 January 2003, http://udarnik-m.narod.ru/2003/13077.htm. The "singing general" is Viktor Kutsenko; see Chapter 30.
46. "Spravka-kontekst o veteranakh lokal'nykh voyn v SSSR," Gazeta.ru, 16 October 2002; text of law and list of recognized combat operations, http://base.garant.ru/10103548/3/
47. An applicant from Kazakhstan waited a year and a half, and once he received the certifi-

cate from Moscow, he waited even longer to enjoy such benefits as "a modest apartment"; Sergey Tereshchenko, "Egiptyanin," *Novy Vestnik* (Karaganda, Kazakhstan), 20 July 2005, http://www.nv.kz/2005/07/20/2767/. A veteran in Ukraine was still unrecognized and "living in poverty" when interviewed in January 2004, and had given up on demanding his rights as he feared "Soviet secrecy" might be imposed on him; Andrey Potyliko, "Uspeshno obstrelyav pozitsii izrail'tyan, boevye raschety taino pribyvshikh v Siriyu sovetskikh reaktivnykh ustanovok 'Grad' zatem ushli ot pogoni amerikanskogo esmintsa," *Fakty i kommentarii* (Kiev), 16 January 2004, http://fakty.ua/68364-uspeshno-obstrelyav-pozicii-izrailtyan-boevye-raschety-tajno-pribyvshih-v-siriyu-sovetskih-reaktivnyh-ustanovok-quot-grad-quot-zatem-ushli-ot-pogoni-amerikanskogo-esminca

48. "Russia Is Not a Piece of Furniture," *The Economist*, 22 April 2006, p. 29. The service in question was "off the coast of Lebanon" during the 1980s.
49. Vasily Murzintsev, *Zapiski voennogo sovetnika v Egipte*, Kaluga: MRIP, 1995, http://militera.lib.ru/memo/0/pdf/russian/murzintsev_v01.pdf, p. 134.
50. Fredrik Logevall, "Innocents Abroad: A Choice of Enemies: America Confronts the Middle East [New York: Public Affairs, 2008] by Lawrence Freedman," *Washington Post*, 3 July 2008, http://www.washingtonpost.com/wp-dyn/content/article/2008/07/03/AR2008070302734.html
51. Isabella Ginor, "'Under the Yellow Arab Helmet Gleamed Blue Russian Eyes': Operation Kavkaz and the War of Attrition," *Cold War History*, 3, 1 (October 2002). After this paper appeared in 2002, Dima Adamsky principally used the former Soviet sources that we had introduced for his 2006 book *Operation Kavkaz*, as well as his paper "How US and Israeli Intelligence Failed to Estimate the Soviet Intervention in the Arab–Israeli War of Attrition." The latter was presented at the same conference in 2006, and published in the same volume of proceedings, as our chapter about the end of *Kavkaz* (Ginor and Remez, "The Origins of a Misnomer: The 'Expulsion of Soviet Advisers' from Egypt in 1972," in Ashton, *The Cold War in the Middle East*, pp. 136–63). A related paper of Adamsky's, "The Seventh Day of the Six-Day War: The Soviet Intervention in the War of Attrition (1969–1970)," illustrated the tendency to treat this war as a postscript to the 1967 conflict when it appeared as a chapter in Ro'i and Morozov, June 1967.
52. Vladislav M. Zubok, *A Failed Empire: The Soviet Union in the Cold War from Stalin to Gorbachev*, Chapel Hill: University of North Carolina Press, 2007, p. 238.
53. David Lowenthal, "Archival Perils: An Historian's Plaint," *Archives*, xxxi, 114 (2006), pp. 51–4.
54. Rachel Donadio, "The Iron Archives," *NYT Book Review*, 22 April 2007, http://www.nytimes.com/2007/04/22/books/review/Donadio.t.html
55. "Putin: Rosarkhiv budet perepodchinen napryamuyu prezidentu," TASS, 4 April 2016, http://tass.ru/politika/3174626
56. Soon after the publication of *Foxbats*, Russian Foreign Minister Sergey Lavrov declared in a joint briefing with his Israeli counterpart Tzipi Livni that, in view of "Israeli researchers' interest" in the 1967 war, a new joint project would be launched to publish documents about it; Herb Keinon and Etgar Lefkovits, "Russia to Open Archives on Israel Ties,"

Jerusalem Post, 20 March 2008, http://www.jpost.com/landedpages/printarticle. aspx?id=95723. Since then, nothing has come of this project. Another example is the discrepancy between the titles of the English and Russian versions of *SAR* in respect of the period to be covered. The Russian edition, of which Lavrov is titular editor-in-chief, is designated as vol. 1; an editorial note (p. iv) specifies the intent to publish another volume reaching to 1976, but the English edition does not promise it and it has not materialized. Kissinger's reports have been included unilaterally in *FRUS* volumes for the post-1972 period.

57. Igor' Meyden, "Na rasstoyanii udara," *Vesti Segodnya*, 288 (Riga), 13 December 2008.
58. Resolution of the State Duma no. 1923-IV, 27 May 2005, "O popytkakh falsifikatsii istorii," http://russia.bestpravo.com/fed2005/data07/tex23894.htm
59. John Wendle, "Russia Moves to Ban Criticism of WWII Win," *Time*, 8 May 2009, http://content.time.com/time/world/article/0,8599,1896927,00.html
60. Facsimile of decree no. 549, 15 May 2009, http://www.dezinfo.net/foto/16114-popytka-ne-pytka.html; Andrew Osborn, "Medvedev Creates History Commission," *Wall Street Journal*, 21 May 2009, http://online.wsj.com/article/SB124277297306236553.html; Pavel Felgenhauer, "Medvedev Forms a Commission to Protect Russian History," *Eurasia Daily Monitor*, 6, 98 (21 May 2009), http://www.jamestown.org/single/?no_cache=1&tx_ttnews[tt_news]=35018&tx_ttnews[backPid]=13&cHash=6729b2258e
61. Reuters, "Putin Passes Law Banning Nazi Crime Denial," *Times of Israel*, 5 May 2014, http://www.timesofisrael.com/putin-passes-law-banning-nazi-crime-denial/
62. Federal law no. 128-fz, passed by State Duma on 23 April 2014. Text at www.rg.ru/2014/05/07/reabilitacia-dok.html
63. Announcement at http://www.hubara-rus.ru/meeting2014.html
64. Maj.-Gen. Viktor Kutsenko, "Pyl' nad Suetskim Kanalom," *Literaturnaya Rossiya*, 18 (4 May 2001), http://old.litrossia.ru/archive/38/soul/900.php
65. Igor' Kvasyuk, "Snova na front," n.d., website of Union of Veterans of Military Languages School, http://www.vkimo.com/node/2463. The author was an older graduate of the Military Languages School (class of '53), who had served in Egypt during the 1956 Suez crisis and was reposted there in 1969.
66. Anatoly Z. Egorin, *Egipet nashego vremeni*, Moscow: Institut vostokovedeniya, 1998, p. 179.
67. March 2014, http://www.perewod.ru/competition2/terms.php. One of the participants whose stories are cited below, Boris Vakhtin, states that he used fictitious names and the details might not be accurate "as he kept no notes at the time."
68. See, e.g., Odd Arne Westad, *The Global Cold War: Third World Interventions and the Making of Our Times*, Cambridge: Cambridge University Press, 2005, pp. 198–9, 431n62; Zubok, *Failed Empire*, pp. 397n36, 427.

1. RESCUING AND REARMING THE USSR'S ALLIES IN JUNE 1967

1. "Polish Record of Meeting of Soviet-Bloc Leaders (and Tito) in Budapest, 11–12 July 1967," in James G. Hershberg (ed.), *The Soviet Bloc and the Aftermath of the June 1967 War: Selected*

Documents from East-Central European Archives, Washington, DC: Cold War International History Project, 2004, p. 36.
2. Egorin, *Egipet*, p. 185.
3. Yury Nastenko, "Aviatsiya v Egipte," in Safonov et al., *Grif*, pp. 55–7.
4. Vladimir Semenov, "Ot Khrushcheva do Gorbacheva: Iz dnevnika Chrezvychaynogo i Polnomochnogo posla, zamestitelya ministra inostrannykh del SSSR," *Novaya i Noveyshaya Istoriya*, 3 (May–June 2004), p. 131.
5. Russian air historian Mikhail Zhirokhov adds that the putative intervention "would have been supported by no less than twelve fighter regiments commanded by ... Vybornov. But the idea proved impractical." Mikhail Zhirokhov and David Nicolle, "The Unknown Heroes: Soviet Pilots in the Middle East 1955–1970," Group 73 Historians, Part 1, http://group73historians.com/group73historians/2013–03–16–12–04–49/190. He dates this "immediately after the June War," but Vybornov's own statements prove that he was already in Egypt in the run-up to the war.
6. Report of July 2006 interview with Vybornov by a researcher for television documentary in which Ginor served as adviser, in authors' possession. He evidently referred to Cairo-West airbase.
7. Mordechai Altshuler, "Daat hakahal vehateguva hayehudit bi-Brit ha-Mo'atzot le-milhemet sheshet ha-yamim: Ti'ud hadash," *Contemporary Jewry: Zionism, the State of Israel, and the Diaspora* (Jerusalem and Haifa), 11–12 (1998), pp. 241–62; Yeshayahu Nir, *The Israeli–Arab Conflict in Soviet Caricatures, 1967–1973*, Tel Aviv: Tcherikover, 1976, pp. 58, 101, 103, 109.
8. Aleksandr Lokshin, "Shestidnevnaya voyna i sovetskaya propaganda," *Lekhayim*, 159 (Moscow), July 2005, http://www.lechaim.ru/ARHIV/159/zavesa.htm
9. Leonid Mlechin, *Zachem Stalin sozdal Izrail'?*, Moscow: Yauza-Eksmo, 2005, p. 436.
10. Ro'i and Morozov, *June 1967*, pp. 20–1, 319.
11. Lt-Col. Anatoly Isaenko, "Polety na Blizhniy Vostok," *NVO*, 15 December 2006. http://nvo.ng.ru/history/2006–12–15/5_polety.html. In this comment on V. Sochnev, "My byli pervymi," Isaenko specified that his group of linguists was recruited early enough to be "sitting in the planes" at Chkalovsky military airport near Moscow by 9 June; http://vkimo.com/node/1755#comment-1243
12. Egorin, *Egipet*, pp. 174–5.
13. Ro'i and Morozov, *June 1967*, p. 320.
14. Egorin, *Egipet*, p. 202.
15. CIA Directorate of Intelligence, "Intelligence Report: Leonid Brezhnev, the Man and His Power" (CAESAR XXXVII), 5 December 1969, pp. 9–12, https://www.cia.gov/library/readingroom/docs/DOC_0001408620.pdf
16. *Ma'ariv*, 11 October 1967, p. 16.
17. E.g., "there were indications the military aid was promised before the war broke out." UPI, "Reds Pledge Food, Planes to Egypt," *Vancouver Sun*, 24 June 1967, p. 11; "US sources ... said the volume was not especially large and could be a carry-over of material en route before the war started"; AP, "Russia Rebuilding Egyptian Forces," *Leader-Post* (Regina, SK), 21 June 1967, p. 1.

18. Whetten, *Canal War*, p. 59.
19. Sochnev, "My byli pervymi."
20. Zhirokhov states that each An-12 carried only *one* "MiG-17, a MiG-21 or a Su-7B." Zhirokhov and Nicolle, "Unknown Heroes," Part 1. Thus the claim that the first two An-12 flights brought twenty fighters to Egypt (Ro'i and Morozov, *June 1967*, p. 21) is clearly inaccurate.
21. Following quotations from Brezhnev's speech are from Hershberg, *Aftermath*, document no. 2, pp. 14ff. The figures included shipments to Syria and Iraq, as well as Algeria, to offset its transfers to Egypt.
22. Interviewed in Elena Pavlova, "Spetszadaniya s peresecheniem gosgranitsy," *Vitebsky Kur'er*, 2 September 2005. Dikusarov was later appointed political officer of his "battalion."
23. Isaenko, "Polety." This corresponds with reports that a paratroop division had been training in Crimea (and another in Azerbaijan) for a month before the Six-Day War for a drop in Israel, and kept in readiness on the runways for its duration. Isabella Ginor and Gideon Remez, "The Six-Day War as a Soviet Initiative: New Evidence and Methodological Issues," *Middle East Review of International Affairs* (MERIA), 12, 3 (2008), http://www.gloriacenter.org/2008/09/remez-2008-09-02/#_ednref20
24. Sochnev, "My byli pervymi"; "Veteran G.A.," posting from 25 September 2007 on http://www.avia.ru/forum/8/3/62742171210130298099811753321 83_17.shtml
25. Rubinstein, *Red Star*, p. 14. Podgorny's official title was chairman of the Supreme Soviet Presidium.
26. Richard Eder, "Yugoslavs Confirm Soviet Replacement of 100 MiG's Egyptians Lost in War," *NYT*, 18 June 1967, p. 24.
27. [Simha] Dinitz, Rome, to director-general, Foreign Ministry, 19 June 1967, ISA HZ-4083/2.
28. Anatoly Z. Egorin, "Iz-pod arabskoy zheltoy kaski sineli russkiye glaza," *Trud-7* (Moscow), 6 March 1998, p. 22.
29. Handwritten glossary of Arabic terms in Russian transliteration, http://www.hubara-rus.ru/index.html
30. Semenov, "Ot Khrushcheva," entry for 6 June 1967, Part 1, pp. 130–1.
31. Petr Lashchenko, "Zapiski Glavnogo Voennogo Sovetnika," *Voenno-Istorichesky Zhurnal*, 11 (November 1996), p. 49.
32. AP, "Airliner Departs from Cairo," *News-Press* (St. Joseph, MO), 17 June 1967, p. 7.
33. John A. Callcott, UPI, "Egypt Today Is a Land of Uncertainty and Fear," *News and Courier* (Charleston, SC), 18 June 1967, p. 6C.
34. Dennis Neeld, AP ("Based in Cairo during the Arab–Israeli war, [now] reports from Greece ... on Egyptian developments"), "Ex-prisoners Detained," *Leader-Post* (Regina, SK), 22 June 1967, p. 16.
35. Gaven Hudgins, AP, "War Fever Weeks an Eternity," *Morning Herald* (Daytona Beach, FL), 13 June 1967, pp. 1, 8.
36. Don McGillivray, Southam News Service, "After Noisy Defiance, a Stunned Silence," *Edmonton Journal*, 9 June 1967, p. 1.

37. McGillivray, "17 Hours of Terror in Mob-Ruled Cairo," an "uncensored story following his return from a month in Cairo," describes Westerners being attacked on the night of Nasser's resignation. *Edmonton Journal*, 20 June 1967, p. 22.
38. For a detailed analysis of CIA performance, see Ginor and Remez, "Too Little."
39. Fred S. Hoffman, AP, "Reds Give Egypt 50 MiGs since War," *Hopkinsville Kentucky New Era*, 21 June 1967, p. 7; "Soviets May Send Newer Arms to Help Rebuild Egypt Forces," *CSM*, 23 June 1967, p. 5.
40. Marquis Childs, United Features Syndicate, "Johnson–Kosygin Summit Results Not Productive," *Daily Times* (Watertown, NY), 28 June 1967, p. 6.
41. John F. Walsh, executive secretary, Control Group, to McGeorge Bundy, White House, 15 June 1967. LBJ, box 15: Memos to President and White House. Emphasis in original.
42. Col. Yury Makarenko, interviewed in Meyden, "Na rasstoyanii."
43. Interviewed in Viktoriya Gefele, "Napishi ty mne, mama, v Egipet," *Podrobnee* (Yaroslavl'), 23 March 2003. Similar figures and descriptions are given by Viktor Rogozhinsky in "Kak nash zemlyak v Egipte sluzhil," *Pavlogradskie Novosti* (Ukraine), 14 November 2004, http://pavlonews.info/news/categ_2/6218.html
44. Voronov, "Zhara"; Irina Temirova and Vladimir Shunevich, "Vo vremya voyny na Sinaye, izrail'tyanye menyali egipetskikh plennykh na arbuzy," *Fakty i komentarii* (Kiev), 26 December 2000. For comparison, a more modest Zaporozhets (the Soviet version of a Fiat 600), cost 3,500 rubles or 700 foreign currency certificates; to save that much, an interpreter had to forgo luxuries in Egypt. Petr Stavitsky, "Krylataya fraza," website of Military Language School alumni, 18 March 2011, http://www.clubvi.ru/news/2011/03/18/bayki/6/. Lt-Col. Gumar Sagdutdinov, then a junior political officer who served fourteen months in Syria including the 1973 war, saved enough to buy the export version of the Moskvich. Timur Latypov, "O druzhbe, voyne i nefti," *Vremya i Dengi* (Kazan), 23 February 2006, www.e-vid.ru/index-m-192-6-63-article-12275
45. Col. Linkov in Aleksandr Bondarenko, "Kak mariupol'tsy zashchishchali nebo Egipta," *Priazovsky Rabochy* (Mariupol, Ukraine), 4 March 2008, www.pr.ua/news.php?new=5251&num=101
46. Evgeny Lashenko interviewed in Sergey Komlev, "Voyna u Piramid," *Rech'* (Cherepovets, Russia), 30 September 2005.
47. Mlechin, *Stalin*, pp. 437–8.
48. Anatoly Chernyaev, *The Diary of Anatoly S. Cheryaev, 1972*, Washington: National Security Archive, 2012, http://www2.gwu.edu/~nsarchiv/NSAEBB/NSAEBB379/1972%20as%20of%20May%2024,%202012%20FINAL.pdf, p. 23.
49. Walsh to Bundy, 15 June 1967.
50. Rubinstein, *Red Star*, pp. 13–14.
51. Hal Ford, chief DD-I Special Research Staff, CIA, "The Growth of the Soviet Commitment in the Middle East (Reference Title ESAU-XLIX)," January 1971, CIA FOIA website, http://www.foia.cia.gov/sites/default/files/document_conversions/14/esau-48.pdf, summary at http://www.foia.cia.gov/sites/default/files/document_conversions/89801/DOC_0000501068.pdf, p. 32 (in the summary).

52. Walsh to Bundy, 15 June 1967.
53. Lord Chalfont, "How Israel Fits in to the Jigsaw of Soviet Power," *Times* (London), 4 August 1975, p. 12.
54. This turned out to be fighting yesterday's war, as the Israelis never repeated the attack on active airbases. But the hardened shelters' strength was proved when a fully armed aircraft exploded inside and caused only minor structural damage. Col. Boris A. Abramov, *Goluboe nebo Egipta*, Moscow: Patriot, 2008, pp. 36–7.
55. Lt-Col. K.M. Molodtsov, "Opyt boevogo primeneniya RTV PVO Egipta v 1968–1972gg," *VKO*, 2005, http://www.vko.ru/biblioteka/opyt-boevogo-primeneniya-rtv-pvo-egipta-v-1968-1972-gg
56. Egorin, *Egipet*, p. 175.
57. Interview with former Engineer-Major Mikhail Rozman, Nahariyya, Israel, 24 January 2008. He related that a general who visited his base connected the alert with Israel's victory in "the *three*-day war," indicating that the Soviets considered Egypt the main arena.
58. Mission at the United Nations to the Department of State, 26 October 1967, *FRUS* J-XIX, no. 491. Either Eban or US Ambassador Arthur Goldberg, who reported the statement, may have confused "the Swedes" with Finland, which represented Soviet interests in Israel after the severance of relations on 10 June.
59. These bombers were erroneously identified as Tu-95s in *Foxbats* (p. 136). For a correction and additional sources, see Ginor and Remez, "Soviet Initiative."
60. Maj.-Gen. Vladimir A. Zolotarev et al. (eds), *Rossiya (SSSR) v lokal'nykh voynakh i voyennykh konfliktakh vtoroi poloviny XX veka*, Moscow: Institute of Military History, 2000, p. 185. Unless this reference misdates the Soviet Tu-16s' publicized arrival on 3 December, it is the first disclosure of this earlier visit. It was not announced, and as the nearby Cairo International Airport was still closed, it was not observed by the Western press.
61. Mikhail Zhirokhov and David Nicolle, "The Unknown Heroes: Soviet Pilots in the Middle East 1955–1970," Group 73 Historians. Part 2, http://group73historians.com/group73historians/2013-03-16-12-04-49/189. The English version on an Arabic website is extremely garbled. A shorter version of the same account that appears in Ostroumov's own book, Lt-Gen. Nikolay Ostroumov, *Ot letchika-istrebitelya do generala aviatsii: V gody voyny i v mirnoe vremya 1936–1979*, Moscow: Tsentrpoligraf, 2010, accessible at http://bookz.ru/authors/Nikolay-ostroumov/ot-let4i_786.html (p. 10 of the online text), also seems confused; he was almost 100 at the time of publication.
62. Heikal (*Road to Ramadan*, p. 43) states incorrectly that "Zakharov had arrived with Podgorny," and this appears to have been copied widely even though some contemporary reports did distinguish between their delegations; UPI, "Soviet Prexy in Cairo for Military Talk," *News-Sentinel* (Lodi, CA), 22 June 1967, p. 21.
63. Akopov, transcript, p. 9.
64. Circular from Gromyko to ambassadors in several People's Democracies for verbal relay to the heads of state, 13 June 1967. Naumkin et al., *Blizhnevostochnyy konflikt*, vol. 2, document no. 258, pp. 581–6.
65. Henry Shapiro, UPI Moscow, "Kosygin Woos Charlie's Aid in Fight on Israel," *Mid-Cities Daily News* (Texas), 16 June 1967, p. 2.

66. Lyndon B. Johnson, *The Vantage Point: Perspectives of the Presidency, 1963–1969*, New York: Holt, 1971, p. 483.
67. Following quotations of Shelest are from *Spravzhniy sud istorii shche poperedu*, Kiev: Geneza, 2003, pp. 241–2.
68. Mlechin, *Stalin*, pp. 437–8.
69. Documentation of the deliberations and proposal were formally released only in June 2012; ISA dossier at http://www.archives.gov.il. Communicated to the United States for transmittal to Egypt and Syria, the proposal went unanswered and was implicitly rejected by the Arab summit conference at Khartoum on 2 September. It was formally superseded when the Israeli cabinet on 31 October 1968 resolved that in any accommodation with Egypt it would retain Sharm el-Sheikh and a strip connecting it with Eilat.
70. Kimche, *Last Option*, p. 9.
71. Galili to Levavi, 20 June 1967, ISA HZ-4083/2.
72. Dev Murarka, "Another Time ...," *Spectator*, 19 June 1967, p. 701.
73. "Tomas Schuman," *World Thought Police*, Los Angeles: Almanac, 1985, pp. 36–8, https://archive.org/stream/BezmenovWorldThoughtPolice1986/World_Thought_Police-Tomas_Schuman-1986-68pgs-SOV-POL.sml_djvu.txt. The actual writer was Yury Bezmenov, a former press officer of the Soviet embassy in India, who defected to the West in 1970; http://uselessdissident.blogspot.co.il/2008/11/interview-with-yuri-bezmenov.html
74. *Foxbats*, pp. 77, 100, 171, 172, 198, 210.
75. Aleksandr Bovin, *XX vek kak zhizn'*, Moscow: Zakharov, 2003, p. 160.
76. *The Economist*, translated in *Ma'ariv*, 3 July 1967, p. 9.
77. V. Yu. Markovsky, "'My gotovili voynu,'" first published in *Aerohobby* magazine before 2001, reproduced at www.foxbat.ru/article/mig25/mig25_1.htm
78. Francis Fukuyama, "Soviet Military Power in the Middle East," in Steven L. Spiegel, Mark A. Heller, and Jacob Goldberg (eds), *The Soviet–American Competition in the Middle East*, Lexington, MA: Lexington Press, 1988, pp. 163–4.
79. According to Czechoslovak General Maj.-Gen. Jan Šejna, who defected in 1968. Lord Chalfont, London *Times*, 4 August 1975, p. 12.
80. The Grechko–Amer plan was first described in 1975, in a brilliant analysis of the sources then available, by Avraham Ben-Tzur in *Gormim Sovietim*, which is widely quoted in *Foxbats*.
81. *Foxbats*, pp. 95–7.
82. Israelyan, in Richard Parker (ed.), *The Six-Day War: A Retrospective*, Gainesville: University of Florida Press, 1996, p. 61.
83. Unattributed assertion in Michael Oren, *Six Days of War: June 1967 and the Making of the Modern Middle East*, New York: Oxford University Press, 2002, p. 299, contradicted by Chuvakhin's biography at http://www.proza.ru/2009/03/28/326. The two ambassadors' "ouster" was interpreted at the time as part of a move by Kosygin to take advantage of their failure and regain control of the diplomatic service from KGB operatives. *Der Spiegel*, translated in *Ma'ariv*, 4 July 1967, p. 9. Former KGB General Pavel Sudoplatov names Pozhidaev as attached to the Paris *rezidentura* as early as 1940. *Raznye dni taynoy*

voyny i diplomatii 1941 god, Moscow: Olma-Press, 2001, Chapter 8, http://www.pseudology.org/Abel/Sudoplatov1941/index.htm
84. Richard Parker, *The Politics of Miscalculation in the Middle East*, Bloomington: Indiana University Press, 1993, p. 21. The former ambassador was in fact alive enough to be interviewed by Ginor a year later, from his Moscow home. *Ha'aretz*, 5 July 1991.
85. Kimche, *Last Option*, pp. 16–17.
86. Egorin, *Egipet*, p. 114.
87. Yossef Govrin, Israeli embassy, Buenos Aires (formerly in Moscow) to East European Department, Foreign Ministry, 4 September 1967. ISA, HZ-4048/18. In France, Vinogradov for years cultivated the retired Charles de Gaulle, thus gaining unequalled access in Paris (and standing in Moscow) when the general returned to power (Boris Kudaev, *Perevodchiki*, now inaccessible; the book text is accessible at http://www.e-reading-lib.com/chapter.php/1001592/0/Kudaev_-_Pule_perevodchik_ne_nuzhen.html). Vinogradov likewise foresaw the rise of Nasser's underling Sadat when no one else considered the latter a likely successor (Akopov, transcript, p. 19).
88. "Polish Record," in Hershberg, *Aftermath*, p. 11.
89. Andropov and Gromyko to CPSU Central Committee, 10 June 1968. Boris Morozov (ed.), *Evreyskaya emigratsiya v svete novykh dokumentov*, Tel Aviv University: Cummings Center, 1998, p. 62; Committee resolution, ibid., p. 63.
90. CIA Intelligence Information Cable 65699, 6 October 1967; CIA Office of National Estimates Special Memorandum 10–67, 21 November 1967, CIA FOIA website, https://www.cia.gov/library/readingroom/docs/DOC_0000109059.pdf.

2. HOLDING THE LINE ON THE SUEZ CANAL

1. Korn, *Stalemate*, pp. 54–5.
2. Naumkin et al., *Blizhnevostochnyy konflikt*, vol. 2, document no. 275, pp. 597–8.
3. A Mirage-III shot down at night over Sinai on 8 June. List of IAF air crew killed in action, http://www.sky-high.co.il/image/users/134771/ftp/my_files/KIA/KIA%20date.pdf?id=3269650
4. Korn's erroneous statement (*Stalemate*, p. 167) that in 1967 "Israel's air victory was so quick and so complete that no surface-to-air missiles were fired" may reflect Heikal's earlier, unfounded claim that "in the surprise of the Israeli air-strike they [the SAM-2s] were never fired" (*Road to Ramadan*, pp. 79–80).
5. "What Happened to Egypt's Rockets?," *Canadian Jewish Chronicle Review* (16 June 1967), p. 14; Danny Shalom, *Like a Bolt Out of the Blue: "Moked" Operation in the Six-Day War, June 1967*, Rishon le-Zion (Israel): Bavir, 2002, pp. 215–18.
6. Naumkin et al., *Blizhnevostochnyy konflikt*, vol. 2, document no. 275, pp. 597–8.
7. "Polish Record," in Hershberg, *Aftermath*, pp. 9, 16.
8. Ford, "Growth of the Soviet Commitment," p. 118.
9. Naumkin et al., *Blizhnevostochnyy konflikt*, vol. 2, document no. 275, pp. 597–8.
10. Vadim A. Kirpichenko, *Iz arkhiva razvedchika*, Moscow: Mezhdunarodnye Otnosheniya, 1993, pp. 94–5.

11. Naumkin et al., *Blizhnevostochnyy konflikt*, vol. 2, document no. 275, pp. 597–8.
12. Shelest, *Spravzhniy*, p. 244; Mlechin, *Stalin*, pp. 437–8. This statement's attribution to Pokryshkin adds to its credibility: the USSR's leading fighter-pilot ace in the Second World War and thrice HSU had a reputation for fearless honesty. Ironically, the following year he was promoted to deputy commander of the entire Soviet air defense arm, a position he held until 1972. Thus he at least formally oversaw a far greater deployment to Egypt than the one he protested in June '67.
13. Hershberg, *Aftermath*, p. 29.
14. Ibid., pp. 16–17.
15. A *divizyon* in this Soviet air defense context is not to be confused with a ground-forces division (*diviziya*). Closer to a Western battery, it consisted of four SAM launchers with their radar system, anti-aircraft cannon and shoulder-fired missile defenses, with about 100 men. Aleksandr Okorokov, *Sekretnye voyny Sovetskogo Soyuza: Pervaya Polnaya Entsiklopediya*, Moscow: Yauza-Eksmo, 2008, p. 74.
16. Vladimir Shirin, "Pomogali Egipetskoy Armii," in L.I. Sannikov et al. (eds), *Internatsionalisty: Sbornik vospominanii voinov-internatsionalistov*, Smolensk: Smyadyn', 2001, pp. 107–8.
17. Dennis Neeld, AP, "Ex-prisoners Detained," *Leader-Post* (Regina, SK), 22 June 1967, p. 16.
18. "US, Israel Blamed by De Gaulle," *Milwaukee Journal*, 21 June 1967, p. 3.
19. AP, *Ma'ariv*, 26 June 1967, p. 1.
20. "Memorandum for the Record: Meeting with Brigadier General Mordecai Hod," 13 January 1968, IRISNUM #01024071. Released by USAF at authors' request, 6 April 2012.
21. Vladimir Maurin, "V tel'nyashke i skafandre," *Kuzbass Daily* (Kemerovo, Russia), 19 March 1999, http://viperson.ru/uploads/attachment/file/425503/kz93j010.txt; Anzhero-Sudzhensk Regional History Museum, "Meropriyatie 'Morskaya dusha: Tel'nyashka,'" 18 February 2011, http://as-museum.ucoz.ru/publ/4–1–0–59
22. Viktor Volodin, "Na Izrail' my zakhodili so storony morya," *Vremya Novostey* (Moscow), 5 June 2007, http://www.vremya.ru/2007/96/13/179605.html
23. "Egypt and the Warsaw Pact," *Jewish Observer and Middle East Review* (22 December 1967), p. 3.
24. "Report by the Bulgarian Foreign Minister on the Ministerial Meeting in Warsaw," 4 January 1968, CWIHP Digital Archive, http://digitalarchive.wilsoncenter.org/document/113426
25. Semenov, "Ot Khrushcheva," p. 135.
26. On 20 June, in an otherwise remarkably prescient analysis, the head of the Israeli Foreign Ministry's East European Department estimated: "it cannot be ruled out that the Soviets will try to provide the Arabs not only with weapons but also with volunteers—not from the USSR but from other East European countries such as Bulgaria." Aryeh Ilan to Teko'a, ISA HZ-4083/2. This may have been based in part on a report from 11 June that "in the last two days numerous Bulgarian army units have moved south, destination unknown." Israel Legation, Sofia, to East European Department, ISA HZ-4090/27. If true, the report

appears to reflect heightened tension along the Warsaw Pact–NATO front as the Six-Day War approached its climax, rather than preparations to transfer Bulgarian troops to the Middle East—for which they would have to move *east* to Black Sea ports. In August, according to recently released Bulgarian documents, "the largest operational and tactical exercise in the Balkans area in the 1960s was carried out ... with a code name 'RODOPI' ... The exercise was not planned in advance, and was intended ... as a 'reaction' to the newly established Middle East situation." Jordan Baev, "Bulgaria and the Middle East Conflict during the Cold War Years," Washington: CWIHP, 2006, pp. 25–6, http://lib.sudigital.org/record/503/files/SUDGTL-BGCW-2010-294-ENG.pdf

27. Baev, "Bulgaria and the Middle East," p. 28. By January 1968, NATO discerned a "fairly clear Soviet tendency to leave physical presence [in Egypt] to Soviet advisers and experts alone." Wolfgang Behrends, NATO department head, West German Foreign Ministry, quoted in Nitzan Hadas, Israel embassy, Bonn, to Research Department, Foreign Ministry, 26 January 1968, ISA HZ-4095/20.

28. Egorin is identified by Vladimir Sakharov, a KGB operative in Alexandria at the time, as an agent of GRU (military intelligence) and its top authority on Egypt. Vladimir Sakharov, *High Treason*, New York: Ballantine, 1980, pp. 230–1, 246.

29. Egorin, *Egipet*, p. 178.

30. AC, Sharon testimony, Part 1, pp. 54–5.

31. Egorin, *Egipet*, p. 178.

32. Ivan Lyutkin, "40 let nazad ...," *Krasnaya Zvezda*, 16 June 2007.

33. Egorin, *Egipet*, p. 178. "Plugging into the lightning rod" is a euphemism for heavy drinking.

34. Lashchenko, "Zapiski," p. 45.

35. Zolotarev et al., *Rossiya*, p. 185; *Encyclopedia of the Black Sea Fleet*, http://flot.sevastopol.info/software/index.html. Likewise, *Krymsky Komsomolets* was "based in Egyptian ports in June 1967," http://flot.sevastopol.info/ship/desant/krimsk_komsom.htm

36. A similar raid on Alexandria failed, too, but stories spread after the war that the Egyptian Navy had been "devastated" by these operations; *Sunday Times* service, "Daring Israeli Frogman Tactics Outlined," *Calgary Herald*, 27 June 1967, p. 9.

37. Aleksandr A. Kharchikov, "Na moryakh sredi zemli," *Sovetskaya Rossiya*, 26 July 2003, http://www.sovross.ru/old/2003/081/081_4_1.htm. Kharchikov, in post-USSR times a "bard" with a strong Russian-nationalist bent and nostalgia for the Soviet period, did three Mediterranean tours.

38. Alexandr Rozin, "Sovetsky VMF v sderzhivanii i prekrashchenii 'chestidnevnoy voiny' v 1967g.," in A.O. Filonik (ed.), *Blizhniy Vostok: Komandirovka na voynu, Sovetskie voennye v Egipte*, Moscow: Academy of Sciences and Moscow State University, 2009, p. 188. This account puts the marine unit on board the *Krimsky Komsomolets*. "BDK-6," on which it is located in Zolotarev's list, was the appellation of this ship until 1970.

39. *Foxbats*, pp. 176, 257n46.

40. A.B. Morin, "Bol'shye desantnye korabli tipa 'Voronezhsky Komsomolets' pr. 1171," *Taifun*, 47 (2005); Arkhiv fotografiy korabley russkogo i sovetskogo VMF, http://navsource.narod.ru/photos/07/383/index.html

41. "Zabvenye korablya 'Voronezhsky Komsomolets' na nashey sovesti," *Kommuna* (Voronezh), 20 May 2005, http://www.communa.ru/news/detail.php?ID=10500&print=Y
42. Col. V[alery] Mallin, "Boevye sluzhby baltiyskoy morskoy pekhoty," website of the Baltic Fleet marines, http://belostokskaya.ru/BS/f_service. A similar account by Mallin, "V ryadakh morskoy pekhoty," was published in *Morskaya Pekhota* in 1997 and reproduced in abridged form in Filonik, *Komandirovka*, pp. 143–51.
43. Kimche, *Last Option*, pp. 11–12. He cites "Admiral Fahmy," apparently Mahmud Abdel Rahman Fahmy, who became commander of the Egyptian Navy in 1969.
44. "A. Smirnov," *Arabo-Izrails'skie voyny*, Moscow: Veche, 2003, p. 298, http://militera.lib.ru/h/smirnov_ai/index.html; Boris Krokhin, "Dubl: Kak dva molodykh rossiyskikh leytenanta byli ochevidtsami egipetsko-izrail'skoy voyny," http://www.hubara-rus.ru/double.html. Egypt's Home Guard was formally organized only after an Israeli raid in November 1968.
45. CIA Directorate of Intelligence, "Arab–Israeli Situation Report," 2 July 1967, http://www.foia.cia.gov/docs/DOC_0000234136/DOC_0000234136.pdf
46. Yitzhak Rabin, with Dov Goldstein, *Pinqas sherut*, Tel Aviv: Ma'ariv, 1979, 1:209. Moshe Dayan's *Story of My Life*, Jerusalem: Edanim, 1976, omits the incident.
47. Hassan al-Badri et al., *The Ramadan War*, Dunn Loring, VA: T.N. Dupuy, 1978, pp. 15–16.
48. Alieddin Hilal, "Triumph of the Will" and Gihan Shahine, "From Suez to Shanty Towns," *Al-Ahram Weekly On-line*, 8–14 October 1998, http://weekly.ahram.org.eg/1998/398/oct20.htm and http://weekly.ahram.org.eg/1998/398/oct04.htm; Ibrahim Nafie, "The October Generation," *Al-Ahram Weekly On-line*, 15–21 October 1998, http://weekly.ahram.org.eg/1998/399/op1.htm
49. AP, quoting MENA, "Egyptians Order Consulates Closed," *Morning Record* (Meriden, CT), 30 June 1967, p. 11.
50. Lyutkin, "40 let nazad ..."
51. CIA, "Arab–Israeli Situation Report," 2 July 1967.
52. Lashchenko, "Zapiski," p. 45, puts the second arrival of his delegation on 11 July; Brezhnev puts its departure on 10 July, indicating a routine stopover in Hungary.
53. Shmu'el Segev, *Ma'ariv*, 22 June 1967, p. 3. Two Egyptian commando battalions were flown to Jordan before the war and positioned in the West Bank for a mission against Israeli airfields, which failed with the loss of most of their personnel. Oren, *Six Days*, p. 203.
54. Eli Landau, *Ma'ariv*, 2 July, pp. 1, 3, and 3 July 1967, p. 3. Maj.-Gen. Evgeny Malashenko, *Vspominaya sluzhbu v armii*, Moscow: General Staff, 2003, p. 281.
55. Israeli Foreign Ministry research department, "Ha-hadirah ha-Sovietit la-Mizrah ha-Tikhon," 7 June 1970, ISA HZ-4605/2, p. 16.
56. Egorin, "Iz-pod arabskoy zheltoy kaski," p. 22.
57. Youssef H. Aboul-Enein, "Learning and Rebuilding a Shattered Force: Memoirs of Pre-Yom Kippur War Egyptian Generals, 1967–1972," *Strategic Insights*, IV, 3 (March 2005), https://www.hsdl.org/?view&did=453698. The article is a review and summary of Mohammed Al-Jawadi, *Fee Eikaab Al-Naksah*, Cairo: Dar-Al-Khiyal Press, 2001.

58. Hershberg, *Aftermath*, pp. 16–17, emphasis added.
59. Two reports in *Ma'ariv*, 9 July 1967, p. 3.
60. Personal communication from a former Israeli naval officer who requested anonymity, 4 July 2011. While the Soviet military routinely excluded anyone registered as Jewish from any mission to Arab countries, some individuals did serve there who had a Jewish grandparent or later married Jewish women, and thus qualified for immigration to Israel.
61. *Foxbats*, pp. 86–7, 149.
62. Capt. Vladimir Zaborsky, "Sovetskaya Sredizemnomorskaya Eskadra," *NVO*, 13 October 2006, http://nvo.ng.ru/history/2006–10–13/5_eskadra.html
63. Shelest, *Spravzhniy*, p. 242.
64. TASS, quoted by UPI, "Soviet Warships to Visit Egypt," *Sarasota Herald-Tribune*, 10 July 1967, p. 5.
65. E.g., photo caption in the Monmouth County, NJ, *Daily Register*, 11 July 1967, p. 1; "Russ Send Warships to Port Said," *Bee* (Modesto, CA), 10 July 1967, p. 2. The error was repeated in Cable, *Gunboat Diplomacy*, p. 146.
66. Australian Associated Press, "Russian Ships, Top Envoy Go to Egypt," *The Age* (Melbourne), 12 July 1967, p. 2; Agencia EFE report, *ABC* (Madrid), 12 July p. 46. As the reports are virtually identical and both name the admiral as "Igor' Nikolay Molotsov," they evidently originated from the same reporter.
67. AP, "Israelis Down Egyptian Jet, Agree on Suez," *Utica Observer-Dispatch*, 11 July 1967, p. 1.
68. UPI, *Pittsburgh Press*, 12 July 1967, p. 1. The Israeli force was led by the destroyer *Ellat*, which would allow its sinking in October to be described as retaliation.
69. AP, "Israelis, Arabs in New Battles," *Spokane Spokesman-Review*, 16 July 1967, p. 1.
70. "Memorandum for the Record: Meeting with Brigadier General Mordecai Hod," 13 January 1968.
71. Zaborsky, "Sovetskaya Sredizemnomorskaya Eskadra."
72. John K. Cooley, "Soviet Naval Visit Reassures Egypt," *CSM*, 12 July 1967, p. 1.
73. UPI, "Israel Prepared to Fight to Defend Boats in Suez," *News and Courier* (Charleston, SC), 19 July 1967, p. 4; Hershberg, *Aftermath*, p. 22.
74. At Qantara, other advisers told Egorin that Israeli fire had intensified once *their* presence became known. *Egipet*, pp. 180–1.
75. Willam R. Frye, *CSM*, "Kremlin's Gunboat Diplomacy Reminds Israel of War Limit," *Star-Phoenix* (Saskatoon, SK), 18 July 1967, p. 11.
76. Cable, *Gunboat Diplomacy*, p. 14, illustrating his point that the Soviet Mediterranean *eskadra* was intended to perform such missions *because* it was so inferior to the Sixth Fleet. He defines "purposeful" intervention as one that "induces someone else to take a decision which would not otherwise have been taken" (ibid., p. 39).
77. Vice-Adm. A[leksandr] A. Tatarinov et al. (eds), *Shtab Rossiyskogo Chernomorskogo Flota: 1831–2001; Istorichesky ocherk*, Simferopol: Tavrida, 2002, p. 81.
78. Admiral of the Fleet Ivan Kapitanets, *Na sluzhbe okeanskomu flotu 1946–1992*, Moscow: Andreevsky Flag, 2000, p. 177. He commanded a group of three destroyers that was en

route from the Northern Fleet to the Black Sea in May 1967, when it was ordered to remain in the Mediterranean, and took on board a landing party of naval cadets from the *Eskadra*'s flagship.
79. Reuters, in *The Phoenix* (Saskatoon, SK), 8 July 1967, p. 2 (an AP report on the same page tells of Eshkol denigrating Dayan and praising Rabin).
80. Yosef Harif, *Ma'ariv*, 10 July 1967, p. 3.
81. [Gideon] Rafael, Israel UN Mission, to Foreign Ministry, 9 July 1967, ISA HZ-4078/7
82. [Moshe] Bitan, Foreign Ministry Jerusalem to [Avraham] Harman, ambassador in Washington, 10 July 1967, ISA HZ-4078/7.
83. Dan Pattir, Israeli embassy, Washington to Foreign Ministry, 11 July 1967, ISA HZ-4083/8.
84. *Ma'ariv*, 21 July 1967, p. 1; emphasis added. The ninth vessel, listed elsewhere as a maintenance ship, evidently was detached from Kasatonov's command near Crete to ferry a group of staff officers to Egypt.
85. UPI, "Soviets Beef Up Middle East Navy," *Star-News* (Wilmington, NC), 22 July 1967, p. 1.
86. Horst Pommerening, West German delegate at a NATO Middle East experts' meeting, quoted in Nitzan Hadas, Israeli embassy, Bonn, to Foreign Ministry, 27 May 1968, ISA HZ-4221/17.
87. R.W. Daly (ed.), *Soviet Sea Power*, Washington: CSIS and New York: Dunellen, 1969, pp. 3, 59; emphasis added. "LSM (landing ship, medium)" is the US appellation of the Soviet SDK. The book presents the conclusions of a panel, which were clearly aimed to support US Navy lobbying for newer ships and reinforcement of the Sixth Fleet. Not all the panelists agreed; e.g. Curt Gastgeyer (p. 112) suggested that the Soviet goal was 'establishing a presence' rather than 'control.'"
88. Zaborsky, "Sovetskaya Sredizemnomorskaya Eskadra"; Mallin, "Boevye sluzhby."
89. Telephone interview with Yury Khripunkov, Donetsk (Ukraine), August 1999. Khripunkov, in 1967 a lieutenant and the gunnery officer of a frigate (SKR) in the Mediterranean, was tasked with leading a landing party into Haifa port as part of the Soviets' abortive intervention during the Six-Day War (*Foxbats*, pp. 83–4, 150–2). Later promoted to gunnery officer of a three-ship flotilla, he spoke of several subsequent tours of duty in Port Said. His description here clearly refers to the immediate postwar period, as there is daylight at 03:45 only around the summer solstice on 21 June.

3. THE SOVIET PRESENCE IS FORMALIZED AND EXPANDED

1. Hershberg, *Aftermath*, pp. 15, 18; Lashchenko's name is garbled to "Moshchenko." Following quotations of Lashchenko are from "Zapiski," pp. 44–52; emphases added.
2. V.P. Klimentov, "God s tankistami vtoroy polevoy armii," in Meyer et al., *Togda*, pp. 194–5; Mark Kramer, "New Evidence on Soviet Decision-Making and the 1956 Polish and Hungarian Crises," *Cold War International History Project Bulletin*, 8 (1996), pp. 358–75, http://www.wilsoncenter.org/sites/default/files/CWIHPBulletin8-9_p6.pdf
3. Nikolay Ufarkin, "Lashchenko, Petr Nikolaevich," http://www.warheroes.ru/hero/hero.asp?Hero_id=1881; "Lashchenko, Petr Nikolaevich," The Great Soviet Encyclopedia

(1979), http://encyclopedia2.thefreedictionary.com/Lashchenko,+Petr+Nikolaevich. The latter entry omits his service in both Hungary and Egypt.

4. Klimentov, "God s tankistami vtoroy polevoy armii," pp. 194–5.
5. CIA, "Views of Deputy UAR Prime Minister Zakariyah Muhiy al Din on His Power Status," 31 July 1967, http://www.foia.cia.gov/sites/default/files/document_conversions/89801/DOC_0000095042.pdf. The assessment was repeated in "Comments by Soviet Official on the Possible Renewal of Arab–Israel Hostilities," 14 February 1968, http://www.foia.cia.gov/sites/default/files/document_conversions/89801/DOC_0000126888.pdf
6. Following quotations of Malashenko are from *Vspominaya*, pp. 227–67.
7. Among others, between July and October the Egyptian Army chief of staff and foreign minister were in Moscow, and a Soviet deputy foreign minister in Cairo (Daniel Dishon et al. (eds), *Middle East Record, 1967*, Jerusalem: Israel Universities Press, 1971, p. 25).
8. Christopher Andrew and Vasili Mitrokhin, *The Mitrokhin Archive: The KGB in Europe and the West*, London: Penguin, 2000, p. 17), identified Primakov as a KGB "co-optee" codenamed Maksim. He later served as Middle East envoy for Gorbachev, then head of foreign intelligence (SVR, 1991–6), foreign minister (1996–8) and prime minister (1998–9) in post-Soviet Russia.
9. Ro'i and Morozov, *June 1967*, p. 353; emphasis added.
10. The last sentence reproduces almost verbatim Lashchenko's previously published memoir ("Zapiski," p. 45).
11. "The June Challenge," *Al-Ahram* Weekly, 7 June 2007, http://weekly.ahram.org.eg/2007/848/sc4.htm
12. Mohsen had been the field commander of Egyptian forces in Sinai up to and during the war; Gen. Mohamed Fawzi (called Muhammad Fawzy in this book), "Reflections on Mistakes Made in Planning, Training, Equipping, and Organizing Egyptian Combat Formations prior to the 1967 Six-Day War," Part III, http://www.thefreelibrary.com/Egyptian+General+Mohamed+Fawzi%3A+part+III%3A+reflections+on+mistakes...-a0314564926
13. Badran was still imprisoned in December 1970, close to the cell where ten Israeli POWs were held. He was allowed a radio receiver, which they were denied, and used to tune in loudly to Israel Radio for their benefit. Amia Lieblich, *Seasons of Captivity: The Inner World of POWs*, New York: New York University Press, 1994, p. 127.
14. Howeidy denied to the last that Amer had been assassinated, as persistent versions have charged.
15. Semenov, "Ot Khrushcheva," p. 133.
16. "More on the Cairo Plot," *Jewish Observer and Near East Review* (8 September 1967), p. 4.
17. G.V. Karpov, "Vospominaniya sovetskogo voennogo sovetnika v Egipte," in Filonik, *Komandirovka*, p. 71.
18. There was speculation that Sokolov was intended to replace the older, unhealthy Zakharov as chief of staff, but the date of the former's promotion indicates that this was not a result of the fiasco in the Six-Day War. When Zakharov was dispatched to Egypt on 16 June, Sokolov

was sent to Syria on an identically defined mission and joined Podgorny when the latter visited Damascus after Cairo. Zakharov remained chief of the General Staff until his retirement in September 1971, and Sokolov (who died in 2012, aged 101) never served in that capacity, though he was made a marshal and commanded the Soviet invasion of Afghanistan. Hershberg, *Aftermath*, p. 15; AP, "Podgorny Opens Talks In Syria," *Press* (Binghamton, NY), 1 July 1967; bios of Zakharov and Sokolov, http://www.warheroes.ru

19. S. Vinogradov, report of conversation with Nasser, 21 October 1967. Naumkin et al., *Blizhnevostochnyy konflikt*, vol. 2, document no. 299, pp. 641–4.
20. *Al-Ahram*, 23, 25 and 27 October 1967, quoted in Dishon et al., *Middle East Record 1967*, p. 25. The anniversary of groundbreaking for the dam was approaching in January, and there was talk about a festive visit by Brezhnev. Sokolov could have discussed the dam's defense against air attack, but this was not announced.
21. AP photo of Zakharov captioned "arrived in Cairo unannounced in the midst of an Israeli–Egyptian controversy" over the *Eilat* sinking; *Citizen-Advertiser* (Auburn, NY), 23 October 1967, p. 1.
22. The first *Komar*s were provided to Egypt in 1962.
23. Cable, *Gunboat Diplomacy*, p. 133.
24. AP and UPI, "Soviets Rush Military Chief to Cairo: Kremlin Concerned about Sinking of Elath" and Reuters, "'What You Deserved': Moscow," *Montreal Gazette*, 24 October 1967, p. 21.
25. AFP, Moscow, *Journal de Genève*, 25 October 1967, p. 5. Zakharov had concluded a ten-day visit to France and returned to Moscow on Wednesday, 18 October. Shirokorad's account states that after prior orders were received from naval headquarters, the boats were ordered out at 17:00, "assumed combat course" at 17:10, and fired the first missile at 17:19; Aleksandr B. Shirokorad, *Rossiya na Sredizemnom more*, Moscow: AST, 2008, p. 330.
26. Telegram to the White House, 3 November 1967, *FRUS* J-XIX, no. 500.
27. Naumkin et al., *Blizhnevostochnyy konflikt*, vol. 2, document no. 299, pp. 641–4.
28. Daniel El-Peleg, "Ihui Shevarim," *Ba-Mahaneh* (IDF weekly), 7 April 2009, quoting Egyptian general and military historian Gamal Hammad; cf. "Sinking *Eilat*, the Destroyer," http://yom-kippur-1973.info/eng/before/Eilat.htm, excerpted from Mohamed Abd Al-Ghany Al-Gamasy, *The October War 1973*, 2nd edn, 1998.
29. AP, "Egyptian Forces Open Fire in Suez," *Leader-Herald* (Gloversville, NY), 24 October 1967, p. 1.
30. Yossi Melman, "The Destroyer's Last Secret," *Ha'aretz* English edn, 11 March 2005.
31. Shalom Rosenfeld, *Ma'ariv*, 27 October 1967, p. 9.
32. Walter Logan, UPI, "Clash Raises Fear of Mideast War," *Citizen-Advertiser* (Auburn, NY), 23 October 1967, p. 1.
33. Uri Dann, *Ma'ariv*, 23 October 1967, p. 2.
34. Nitzan Hadas, Israeli embassy, Bonn, to Ze'ev Dover, East Europe Department. Foreign Ministry, 31 October 1967. ISA HZ-4049/6.
35. Alfred Vestring, personal assistant to parliamentary secretary for foreign affairs, quoted in Hadas to Foreign Ministry, 19 December 1967, ISA HZ-4049/6. The Israeli official

with whom this information was shared noted that the West Germans had undertaken a special intelligence effort to ascertain it, out of concern that their own outdated destroyers faced the same Soviet-made missile boats in the Baltic Sea.
36. Zolotarev et al., *Rossiya*, p. 186.
37. J.P. Marriott, naval attaché, Cairo to MOD, 14 November 1972. NA (PRO).
38. Shirokorad, *Rossiya*, pp. 330–1.
39. Vice-Adm. Vitaly Zub, "Sovetskie moryaki: Voiny-internatsionalisty v OAR-Egipet," in Safonov et al., *Grif*, pp. 73–4.
40. Marriott, naval attaché, Cairo to MOD, 14 November 1972. NA (PRO).
41. "Whether the incident would have occurred if Soviet ships had been present ... is an open question. But many observers ... both Egyptian and foreign, believe it would not have happened." Joe Alex Morris Jr., *Los Angeles Times*, "Soviet Navy Flexes Its Muscles," *Times* (Geneva, NY), 15 May 1968, p. 2.
42. Dishon et al., *Middle East Record 1967*, p. 26.
43. Whetten, *Canal War*, p. 61, citing Cable, *Gunboat Diplomacy*, p. 146—though the latter does not mention the ships' leaving harbor at all.
44. Anatoly Usikov and Valery Yaremenko, "Flot kak instrument politiki," *NVO*, 29 August 2003, http://nvo.ng.ru/forces/2003–08–29/3_flot.html
45. Kharchikov, "Na moryakh sredi zemli."
46. Amos Eran, embassy in Washington, to Foreign Ministry, 24 October 1967, ISA HZ-4048/27. The informant was Jay Lovestone, a former Communist who at the time was director of the AFL-CIO's International Affairs Department and a contact of the CIA's point man on Israel, James Angleton.
47. Kharchikov, "Na moryakh sredi zemli."
48. Israeli minister, Paris, to director, Middle East Department, Foreign Ministry, 11 December 1968, ISA HZ-4221/17.
49. Posted on 10 January 2003, http://www.bigler.ru/printable.php?story_id=A1301
50. Reproduced in Russian by "Kollezhsky Sovetnik," 27 March 2010, http://tsushima.su/forums/viewtopic.php?id=3310
51. S.V. Baranova (ed.), "Zashchitniki Otechestva," *Nasha Gazeta* (Belgorod), February 2004.
52. "Memorandum of Conversation," *FRUS* J-XIX, no. 482. In the course of this talk, Eban was notified that "the" Soviet deputy defense minister had "just arrived" in Cairo; the minutes do not clarify whether this referred to Zakharov or Sokolov, nor whether either side in the discussion was aware that *two* such officials were in Egypt.
53. AP, "Egyptian Forces Open Fire in Suez Area," *Leader-Herald* (Gloversville, NY), 24 October 1967, p. 1.
54. "Notes of Meeting," *FRUS* J-XIX, no. 483.
55. McPherson to Johnson, 31 October 1967, *FRUS* J-XIX, no. 494n3.
56. Mitchell G. Bard, "The 1968 Sale of Phantom Jets to Israel," http://www.jewishvirtuallibrary.org/jsource/US-Israel/phantom.html; UPI report, *Davar*, 25 October 1967, p. 1.
57. In this case, the Soviets appear to have palmed off old hardware. The Tu-16T was one of the earliest variants, developed in the mid-1950s, and by 1965 was being phased out by Soviet Naval Aviation.

58. I.A. Slukhay, *General Ivan Katyshkin*, Moscow: Patriot, 2008. Excerpted at http://www.mkvv.ru/memory3.html; Egorin, *Egipet*, p. 179, quoting this figure from the London annual *The Middle East and North Africa*: "I won't claim that their number was more or less; I doubt we will ever know the precise number."
59. A. Yu. Dashkov and V.D. Golotyuk, "Arabo-Izrail'skiy konflikt: Boevye deystviya sovetskoy aviatsii i PVO v Egipte," www.airaces.ru/stati/arabo-izrailskijj-konflikt-boevye-dejjstviya-sovetskojj-aviacii-i-pvo-v-egipte.html#identifier_2_4428; excerpted from their book, *100 let Voenno-vozdushnym silam Rossii* (1912–2012 gody), Moscow: Fond "Russkie Vityazi," 2012. Katyshkin was promoted to colonel-general a few days after arriving in Egypt.
60. Bardisi, a counter-intelligence officer, is described in Igor' Kubersky's, *Egipet-69*, St. Petersburg: Gelikon-Plus, 2010, as charged with surveillance of the Soviet advisers. Serialized in *Zvezda* (St. Petersburg), January 2011, http://zvezdaspb.ru/index.php?page=8&nput=1534, and February 2011 http://zvezdaspb.ru/index.php?page=8&nput=1557
61. Col. Vladimir T. Serkov, *Liniya fronta: Suetsky kanal; Dnevnik voennogo sovetnika*, Kurtamish (Russia): GUP Kurtamishskaya tipografiya, 2007, pp. 16–17.
62. Zub, "Sovetskie moryaki: Voiny-internatsionalisty v OAR-Egipet," pp. 73–4.
63. Personal communication from Zekharia Chesno, Jerusalem, 13 December 2000.
64. Telephone interview with Zardusht Alizadeh, 16 February 2001, when he was co-chairman of the Social Democratic Party of Azerbaijan. Alizadeh's entire class of ten in the Oriental Studies Faculty of Azerbaijan State University was recruited as interpreters. He was attached in 1969 to the Soviet adviser to the chief of staff of Egyptian Air Defense.
65. Maj. Yury Gorbunov, "Napishi mne, mama, v Egipet: Vospominaniya voennogo perevodchika," Military Krym website, 2013, http://military.sevstudio.com/napishi-w-egipet/
66. Egorin, *Egipet*, p. 178.
67. The edition from 1988, quoted by Zub, "Sovetskie moryaki: Voiny-internatsionalisty v OAR-Egipet," p. 68; emphasis added.
68. Karpov, "Vospominaniya," pp. 71, 84.
69. Gorelov, a combat ace and HSU from the Second World War, was another of Lashchenko's Ciscarpathian subordinates whom he recruited for Egypt, where he served from November 1967 to May 1969; "Gorelov, Sergey Dmitrievich," http://www.warheroes.ru
70. Karpov, "Vospominaniya," p. 75.
71. Shimshon Ofer, *Davar*, 28 August 1967, p. 2; Eli Landau, *Ma'ariv*, 27 August 1967, p. 2.
72. IAF website, http://www.iaf.org.il/3579-6841-he/IAF.aspx
73. Harold H. Saunders, "Memorandum of Conversation," 26 February 1968. NARA, National Security File, Country File Israel, vol. 8, box 141. Amit "felt that we [Americans] should do 'much more' to block the Soviets. ... General Amit and Mr [Walt] Rostow agreed ... that perhaps the Soviet influx into Egypt was directed more at establishing a base for activities beyond the UAR in Africa rather than against Israel."
74. Naumkin et al., *Blizhnevostochnyy konflikt*, vol. 2, document no. 299, pp. 641–4.
75. Christel Steffler, Soviet Affairs Department, West German Foreign Ministry, quoted in

Hadas to Ze'ev Dover, West Europe Department, Foreign Ministry, 12 December 1967, ISA HZ 4049/6; emphasis added.

76. Editorial note, *FRUS* J-XIX, no. 541. The Russian language has no definite article, and thus is inherently ambiguous; the UN Russian translation did not specify "all." Shabtai Rosenne, "On Multi-lingual Interpretation," *Israel Law Review*, 6 (1971), http://www.mfa.gov.il/mfa/foreignpolicy/peace/guide/pages/on%20multi-lingual%20interpretation%20-un%20security%20counc.aspx

77. Mohammed Al-Gawady, *Al-Shaheed* (the martyr) *Abdel-Moneim Riad*, Cairo: Dar-Al-Atebaa, 1984, cited in Youssef H. Aboul-Enein, "Egyptian General Abdel-Moneim Riad: The Creation of an Adaptive Military Thinker," *Infantry Magazine* (March–April 2004), https://www.thefreelibrary.com/Egyptian+General+Abdel-Moneim+Riad%3A+the+creation+of+an+adaptive...-a0118986343

78. Danny Shalom, *Phantoms over Cairo: Israeli Air Force in the War of Attrition 1967–1970*, Rishon le-Zion: Bavir, 2007, vol. 1, pp. 131–4; military correspondent, *Davar*, 3 December 1967, pp. 1–2; *Ma'ariv*, 3 December 1967, p. 2.

79. The Vautour pilot Aki Artzi's widow Ya'el describes this incident and her efforts to establish his fate in her book *Missing in Action*, Tel Aviv: Miskal, 2001. She confirmed to the present authors that the other helmet was washed up later on the Israeli-held shore of the gulf. Both were unfastened, indicating that they had been taken off either by the airmen themselves or by others.

80. *Jewish Observer and Near East Review* (8 December 1967).

81. Col. G. P. Roshchin, "1962 god, Egipet," on www.egyptstyle.ru (now inaccessible). In 2011, Steven A. Cook claimed retrospectively that "although he perfected his Russian, the two years in the Soviet Union were not happy ones for Mubarak, who disliked his Russian instructors and colleagues, derided Soviet-built military equipment, and openly criticized Communism." Steven A. Cook, *The Struggle for Egypt: From Nasser to Tahrir Square*, Oxford: Oxford University Press, 2011, p. 156. If he harbored such sentiments in 1967–73, no contemporary reports or veterans' memoirs reflect it, and several examples to the contrary follow.

82. Rubtsov, memoir.

83. Anatoly Z. Egorin, "Zapiski korrespondenta APN," http://www.clubvi.ru/news/2011/04/07/ppl/egorin/zap/

84. Pavel Mel'nik, "Zvezdy nad Nilom: Kak eto bylo," *Aviapanorama*, 2 (200), http://www.aex.ru/fdocs/1/2007/5/18/10299/. In addition to his father, Mel'nik interviewed Gennady Kvakin, another co-pilot of the same rank. Both later rose to Lt-Col.

85. K.C.Thaler, UPI London, "SU Widens Its Aid to Egyptians," *Times-News* (Henderson, NC), 7 December 1967, p. 3.

86. "Memorandum for the Record: Meeting with Brigadier General Mordecai Hod," 13 January 1968, IRISNUM no. 01024071. Released by USAF at authors' request, 6 April 2012.

87. Dov Sattat, acting director, East Europe Department Foreign Ministry, to Hadas, 7 December 1967, ISA HZ-4049/6. Sattat allowed that the Soviets might not appreciate adequately that they were encouraging the Arabs toward acts that might endanger peace.

88. Aleksey Vasiliev, *Rossiya na Blizhnem i Srednem Vostoke: Ot messianstva k pragmatizmu*, Moscow: Nauka, 1993, pp. 96–7.
89. Semenov, "Ot Khrushcheva," p. 135; Baev, "Bulgaria and the Middle East," pp. 32–3.

4. FRAMING THE CROSS-CANAL GOAL AND THE ATTRITION STRATEGY

1. Semenov, "Ot Khrushcheva," p. 135.
2. Naumkin et al., *Blizhnevostochnyy konflikt*, vol. 2, document no. 299, p. 642.
3. Abramov, *Goluboe*, pp. 35–6.
4. Hershberg, *Aftermath*, p. 14.
5. Nikolay Ufarkin, "Lashchenko, Petr Nikolaevich," http://www.warheroes.ru/hero/hero.asp?Hero_id=1881
6. Lt-Col. Avi Shai, "Mitzrayim liqrat milhemet yom ha-kippurim," *Ma'arakhot*, 250 (July 1975), p. 38n72, http://maarachot.idf.il/PDF/FILES/8/108768.pdf
7. Following quotations of Malashenko are from *Vspominaya*, pp. 244–93. Lashchenko actually *overestimated* the Israeli force; the front line was routinely held by two or three battalions, that is, the equivalent of one brigade or less. In early 1968, the Israelis did begin preparing a canal crossing of their own, for preemption of an Egyptian attack or as a counterstrike, but made little progress. According to Maj.-Gen. Yisra'el Tal, until June 1972 (when he took over as deputy chief of staff), despite a prodigious investment, no practical crossing capability had been achieved and "the IDF couldn't cross a sewage ditch." AC, Tal testimony, Part 1, p. 38, and Part 5, pp. 3–5.
8. Following quotations of Karpov are from "Vospominaniya," pp. 83–100; of Serkov, from *Liniya fronta*, pp. 18, 31, 123; "Afanasyev, Pavel Aleksandrovich," in *Znamenitye lyudi Vologdy*, http://www.nason.ru/znamenit/2095. Abu Ghazala would command Egyptian artillery in the 1973 war and later become field marshal and minister of defense.
9. "Azovkin, Yury Petrovich," http://www.warheroes.ru/hero/hero.asp?Hero_id=4320
10. Hulda Kjeang Mørk, "The Jarring Mission: A Study of the UN Peace Effort in the Middle East, 1967–1971," master's thesis, University of Oslo, 2007, *passim*.
11. "Comments by Soviet Official on the Possible Renewal of Arab–Israeli Hostilities and Soviet Intentions," CIA Intelligence Information Cable, 5 February 1968, https://www.cia.gov/library/readingroom/docs/DOC_0000126888.pdf
12. AC, testimony of Brig. Gen. Aryeh Shalev, p. 17.
13. Kharchikov, "Na moryakh sredi zemli."
14. Charlie Charalambous, "Israeli Sub to Be Salvaged," AFP, 5 October 1999; Amos Har'el, *Ha'aretz*, 12 October 2000; Amir Rappaport, *Ha'aretz*, 25 January 2002, pp. 12–16.
15. "Soviet and Russian Navy ASW and AAW Ships," http://www.hazegray.org/features/russia/destroy.htm. A Black Sea Fleet website states that, throughout 1968, the *Soobrazitel'nyy* was "in a zone of military actions, [and] carried out a battle task of rendering assistance to the armed forces of Egypt"; http://flot.sevastopol.info/eng/ship/largeaswdestroyers/soobrazitelny.htm
16. On 4 February 1968, Erell's subordinate and successor Avraham Botzer told a Knesset committee that the Navy by then doubted the authenticity of both messages and attrib-

uted their identification with the *Dakar* to a signalman's wishful thinking. Transcript of Defense and Foreign Affairs Committee session, [misdated] 6 January 1968, ISA, http://www.archives.gov.il/archives/#/Archive/0b0717068001c167/File/0b07170684cc4835/Item/0907170684ee6b50

17. Several Egyptian claims were listed by Shlomo Abramovich in *Yedi'ot Ahronot*, 19 April 1996, p. 20. The most recent—that an "alien" submarine hit the shallow sea bed off Alexandria when it made a "hasty" dive after his ship gave chase—was made by an Egyptian naval officer, Mohamed Azab, to *al-Sharq al-Awsat* in 2005, http://www.aawsat.com/details.asp?section=4&issueno=9713&article=309359&feature=#. This was disproved when the *Dakar*'s remains were located elsewhere. An Israeli marine biologist, Asher Gitai, has claimed, based on crustaceans that grew on the *Dakar*'s buoy, that the submarine sank in shallow water near the Egyptian coast and was later moved, which would lend credence to the Egyptian claims with or without Soviet assistance. Gitai, lecture abstract, 21 May 2002, in authors' possession; his theory was angrily rejected by the Israeli Navy. Shmu'el Me'iri, *Zeman Haifa*, 24 May 2002, p. 10.
18. Mike Eldar, *Dakar ve-sippurah shel shayyetet ha-tzolelot*, Tel Aviv: Nir, 1997, pp. 64–7.
19. Transcript of cabinet session, 28 January 1968, ISA, http://www.archives.gov.il/archives/#/Archive/0b0717068001c167/File/0b07170684cc4835/Item/0907170684ee6b4b
20. ISA release,10 March 2013, dossier on ISA website, http://www.archives.gov.il
21. Dayan elaborated: "The Americans said they were taking it upon themselves to contact the Russians, but afterward they notified us that they were unsuccessful in this. They asked us to find another way to contact the Russians, and we did so." Transcript of Defense and Foreign Affairs Committee session, [misdated] 6 January 1968. If the Americans gave this weak excuse, it conforms with their reluctance to get involved, as described by Erell.
22. Vinogradov's return was announced only on 21 April, after Gromyko's Egyptian counterpart Riad had been received in Moscow (which was announced at the time). Reuters and UPI, *Davar*, 22 April 1968, p. 1.
23. Reuters, Cairo, quoted in *Davar*, 3 April 1968, p. 1.
24. An Israeli intelligence officer noted in the margin of Malashenko's book, next to Kirichenko's name, "PGU?" (the KGB First Directorate). Grechko also had a sister, Pavla, who was married to a division-level artillery adviser, Nikolay Gontarev, and apparently accompanied him in Egypt.
25. Zub, "Sovetskie moryaki: Voiny-internatsionalisty v OAR-Egipet," pp. 78–9.
26. *Foxbats*, pp. 131–2; for the establishment of an advanced Soviet air base in Yemen, see Jesse Ferris, "Soviet Support for Egypt's Intervention in Yemen, 1962–1963," *Journal of Cold War Studies*, 10, 4 (2008), p. 28. http://acepilots.com/vietnam/olds_bolo.html
27. Reports from Paris by Uri Dann, *Ma'ariv*, 3 April 1968, p. 4 and 14 April, p. 2; Soviet press reports quoted in Dishon et al., *Middle East Record 1968*, p. 35.
28. L. Zakharov, "Komandirovka v Egipet," *Mir Aviatsii* journal, 5 (2005), pp. 24–39.
29. National Intelligence Estimate 11–06–67, "Soviet Strategy and Intentions in the Mediterranean Basin," 16 May 1968, p. 1, https://www.cia.gov/library/readingroom/docs/DOC_0000278476.pdf. In October 1968, Allon referred in the Knesset to a "squad-

ron of Soviet-manned Tu-16 *bombers* permanently stationed in Egypt" but was clearly referring to these TU-16Rs. *Ma'ariv*, 31 October 1968, p. 1.
30. Gorbunov, "Napishi mne." Kudaev, *Perevodchiki*, describes the US carrier as just having undergone capital refitting, which dates his account during the ship's later tour in the Mediterranean from April 1968 to January 1969. On the other hand, Kudaev (now a professor of English at Nalchik in the North Caucasus) confirmed in response to the present authors' query that a Tu-16 crash with loss of all hands, which he describes as having occurred while buzzing the *Independence* in the Mediterranean, actually involved a plane of the "same regiment, same squadron" and the USS *Essex* in the Norwegian Sea the same year. "I adapted ... this episode into my book for the sake of making my narrative more interesting" (personal communication, 30 December 2011)—an illustration of the caution with which this "fiction" genre must be treated. Kudaev did not respond to follow-up questions.
31. Harold H. Saunders, "Memorandum of Conversation," 26 February 1968, NARA National Security File, Country File Israel, vol. 8, box 141.
32. Dashkov and Golotyuk, "Arabo-izrail'sky konflikt."
33. Zakharov, "Komandirovka v Egipet," pp. 24–5; A.N. Zabolotsky and A.I. Sal'nikov, "Samolet Amfibiya Be-12," http://aviation-gb7.ru/Be-12.htm
34. Ray Moseley, UPI, translated in *Ma'ariv*, 4 November 1968, p. 2.
35. Arnold Sherman, *Ma'ariv*, 18 November 1968, p. 9.
36. Israeli minister, Paris, to Middle East Department, Foreign Ministry, 11 December 1968, ISA HZ-4221/17.
37. Sherman, *Ma'ariv*, 18 November 1968, p. 9. A report by CSIS shortly afterward suggested that "the Soviets could augment their Mediterranean fleet by bringing in ... for *air cover* ... squadrons of their more modern fighters and fighter bombers, for example the Foxbat, in local Arab states." A contemporary map of ranges for Soviet aircraft models based in Egypt includes the "MiG-23 Foxbat." Daly, *Soviet Sea Power*, pp. 58, 61; emphasis added. There was confusion at the time about the permanent Soviet appellation of the Foxbat—as it was dubbed by NATO—which was still known by several Soviet and Egyptian code names. In the West, it was expected to become the MiG-23, but this appellation was ultimately given by the Soviets to a swing-wing fighter (NATO reporting name Flogger). The latter model was never posted in, or supplied to, Egypt before 1974. In the following account, the Foxbat is anachronistically referred to by its ultimate appellation, MiG-25, except in quotations from contemporary sources, whose erroneous mentions of "MiG-23" are therefore put in quotation marks.
38. Mir M. Hosseini, "Phantoms Arrive in Iran," http://www.fouman.com/Y/Get_Iranian_History_Today.php?artid=1099
39. Elena Lange, "Voinov, Alexander Ivanovich," Borisoglebskoye Flight School website, http://www.bvvaul.ru/profiles/1111.php
40. Maj. Valery El'chaninov, "Dan prikaz yemy ... v Egipet," *Soldat Udachi*, 2 (Moscow) (2001). The accident is dated only July–August 1971.
41. According to Serkov, sidearms were issued only to the Soviet advisers posted on the canal and only in late 1969, after "the Israelis had made a sortie onto the west bank."

42. Gorbunov, "Napishi mne."
43. Dev Murarka, "The Ghost of Hollybush," *Spectator*, 7 July 1967, p. 4. Israeli Foreign Ministry official Ilan had earlier suggested—apparently based in part on Murarka's 7 July report, as quoted by Galili—that East European volunteers would begin "organization, planning and direct assistance for a war of harassment" (*milhemet hatradah*, as distinct from *milhemet hatashah*—the harsher term that would become standard for "war of attrition"). Ilan to Teko'a, 20 June 1967, ISA HZ-4083/2
44. Bar-Siman-Tov, *War of Attrition*, pp. 145–6, 232n1.
45. *Foxbats*, pp. 18, 34–5, 141, 208.
46. Y. Agmon, Foreign Ministry security officer, to director, East Europe Department, 12 June 1968, ISA, HZ-4221/4.
47. Nikolay Dolgopolov, "Bezvestnost': Luchshaya nagrada," *Trud*, 27 September 2001, http://www.trud.ru/article/27-09-2001/30439_bezvestnost—luchshaja_nagrada.html; Ilya Kuksin, "Legenda Rossiyskoy razvedki," http://www.berkovich-zametki.com/2009/Zametki/Nomer15/Kuksin1.php; *Foxbats*, pp. 43–4.
48. Morozov, *Evreyskaya emigratsiya*, pp. 62–3.
49. The covert agency known as *Lishkat ha-Qesher* (Liaison Bureau) and later as *Nativ* (Trail), which was aimed at alleviating the plight of Soviet Jews and enabling their immigration to Israel, took care to distance itself from the CIA and to avoid any activity that could be construed as espionage. Its "clientele" by definition had little access to privileged political or military information. Nechemia Levanon, *Code Name: "Nativ"*, Tel Aviv: Am Oved, 1995, pp. 270, 472 (Levanon headed the agency from 1970).
50. Golan, *Decision Making*, pp. 284–5. Other instances in this book describe reports from the USSR as received indirectly through US intelligence.

5. THE NUCLEAR NON-ISSUE

1. Department of State to embassy in Israel, 28 April 1968, *FRUS* J-XX, no. 155. Johnson rejected Rusk's suggestion that he sign the letter himself.
2. Telegram from Department of State to embassy in Israel, 6 June 1968, *FRUS* J-XX, no. 189.
3. Telegram from embassy in Israel to Department of State, 2 July 1968, *FRUS* J-XX, no. 205.
4. *Foxbats*, pp. 49–57.
5. Seymour M. Hersh, *The Samson Option*, New York: Random House, 1991, pp. 186–7, quoting the estimate's author Carl Duckett. This is, almost verbatim, the only source that Primakov (*Konfidentsial'no: Blizhniy Vostok na stsene i za kulisami*, Moscow: Rossiyskaya Gazeta, 2006, p. 343) quotes, without attribution, for Israeli possession of nuclear arms in 1968. He does assert that "the USSR knew too" about Israeli nuclear preparations during the October 1973 war. Primakov does not mention the NPT at all.
6. In contrast to the Soviet nuclear "umbrella" over Egypt (and Syria), this study urged that "the US should *not* ... extend ... bilateral guarantees to potential nuclear states ... setting us against the Soviets." State Department Policy Planning Council study "After NPT, What?", 28 May 1968. NSA, *Impulse*, no. 27.
7. [Michael] Comay, Israel mission, New York, to Foreign Ministry, 26 November 1968, ISA HZ-4221/5.

NOTES pp. [68–70]

8. Department of State, Memorandum of Conversation, "Nonproliferation Treaty," 17 May 1968, NSA, *Impulse*, no. 24. A year later, Kissinger reported to Nixon that Kosygin "asks us to press the Germans and other countries allied with us (presumably meaning Japan and, *by Soviet definition*, Israel)"—though Kosygin's message did not name either one. Kissinger to Nixon, 28 May 1969, *FRUS* N-XII, no. 51, emphasis added.
9. Savita Pande, *The Future of NPT*, New Delhi: Lancer, 1995, pp. 53–4.
10. Primakov, *Blizhniy Vostok*, p. 342. His main evidence is the reported Israeli diversion of uranium from the ship *Scheersberg A* in November 1968, but while this uranium was bought in Belgium by an Israeli shell company based in Germany, not even the wildest accounts have connected it with the German government. Primakov claims this purchase was partly in exchange for Israeli supply of "laser technology for uranium enrichment," which rests on even slimmer Western evidence (Peter Vincent Pry, *Israel's Nuclear Arsenal*, Boulder, CO: Westview, 1984, p. 27).
11. Dishon et al., *Middle East Record 1968*, p. 32. State Department analysis concluded that "although initially Soviets may have conceived of NPT as primarily [aimed at] controls on FRG, [we] believe ... Soviets have come to develop a broader view ... Chicom nuclear developments, ME war etc. surely had part." State Department cable 107235 to US embassy, Bonn, 30 January 1968, NSA, *Impulse*, no. 11.
12. Telegram from Department of State to embassy in Moscow, July 4, 1968. Months later, the Soviet ambassador in London told Lord Sieff and Israeli official Yaacov Herzog, "*pro forma*," that Israel's two "sins" were "threatening to blow up the Aswan Dam" and non-accession to NPT, but voiced interest in maintaining contact anyway. [Aharon] Remez, Israel ambassador, London, to Foreign Ministry, 20 December 1968. ISA HZ-4221/5.
13. *FRUS* J-XX, no. 315.
14. Heikal, *Road to Ramadan*, pp. 74–5. He dates the visit shortly after the Libyan revolution, which began on 1 September 1969.
15. Shlomo Aronson, *Nesheq gar'ini bamizrah hatikhon: Mi-Ben Gurion uve-hazara*, Jerusalem: Academon, 1995, vol. 2, pp. 124–6; quoted in Hersh, *Samson Option*, p. 177.
16. "Summary of the Situation and Issues," attached to Kissinger to President, "Israeli Nuclear Program," 19 July 1969, pp. 1, 3, National Security Archive "Nuclear Vault," http://nsarchive.gwu.edu/nukevault/ebb485/docs/Doc%2010%207-19-69%20circa.pdf
17. Shmu'el Segev, *Ma'ariv*, 26 July 1970, p. 9. In August 1970, shortly after the ceasefire on the canal, the Soviet ambassador in Nepal warned his Israeli counterpart that "if Israel does not withdraw and forces Egypt into another war, this might be an atomic war." M. Avgar, ambassador in Kathmandu, to Foreign Ministry, 17 August 1970, HZ-4604/5. In November 1971, a Soviet diplomat in Vienna—the IAEA seat—attempted to contact the Israeli embassy through local journalists for details of Israel's atoms-for-peace activity, purportedly in order to *counter* Egyptian pressure for nuclear weapons. Israel rejected the feeler. Y[itzhak] Patish, ambassador in Vienna, to Foreign Ministry, 24 November 1971, ISA HZ-4604/7.
18. In December 1971, according to a newly arrived interpreter and liaison officer with the Soviet top brass in Cairo, "Egyptian military circles ... were insulted by the USSR's refusal

to give them so much as a single nuclear warhead, in order to put pressure on Israel." Viktor Borodin, interviewed in Andrey Chernitsyn, "Mirovaya ekspansiya," *Noril'sky Nikel'*, 5, 36 (August–September 2007). But as the Egyptians still had not received the only vehicle they would ultimately have for such weapons—Scud missiles—this unique version seems more like a rationale for the Soviets' "expulsion" a few months later.

19. Vice-Admiral Nikolay Shashkov, formerly captain of K-172, interviewed in Nikolay Cherkashin, "On dolzhen byl unichtozhit' Izrail," *Evreyskie Vesti* (supplement of *Golos Ukrainy*) (Kiev), 17–18 (September 1996), and quoted in Aleksandr Mosyakin, "Mesyats Nisan," *Chas* (Riga), 70, 489 (25 March 1999).

20. Although some Egyptian figures have denied it, Syrian counterparts confirmed a similar nuclear-umbrella arrangement with their country. Shai Feldman, *Israeli Nuclear Deterrence: A Strategy for the 1980s*, New York: Columbia University Press, 1982, pp. 68–9.

21. Gorbunov, "Napishi mne."

22. Ariel Levite and Emily Landau, *Israel's Nuclear Image: Arab Perceptions of Israel's Nuclear Posture*, Tel Aviv: Papyrus, 1994, pp. 42–3. See also Avner Cohen, *Israel and the Bomb*, New York: Columbia University Press, 1998, pp. 289–90.

23. *Foxbats*, pp. 142–4.

24. Large-scale maps in Russian that were produced by the Soviet Defense Ministry in the late 1980s show the armistice line of 1949 as the border between Israel and the "Palestinian Territories," which are described as "occupied by Israel since 1967." The 1947 partition boundaries are not marked; http://www.finkel.tribune.co.il/IS_MAP_1987/index.html

25. CIA Intelligence Information Cable 49185, 14 February 1968.

26. Transcript of Primakov–Eban conversation, 29 August 1971, ISA A-7037/17.

27. Summary of talk between Primakov and unnamed Israeli official, apparently Hanan Baron, 30 August 1971, ISA A-7037/17.

28. Col. V. Larionov, "New Weapons and Strategy," translated in "Lt-Col. L. Merhav" (ed.), *Mahshava tzeva'it Sovietit ba-idan ha-gar'ini*, Tel Aviv: Ministry of Defense, 1969, p. 41. Heikal confirmed to Hersh (*Samson Option*, p. 235n**) that Soviet information about Israel's nuclear capability was "taken very seriously [but] had no impact on the overall Egyptian military operations."

29. As P.R. Kumaraswamy concluded in 2000 (*Revisiting the Yom Kippur War*, London: Frank Cass, 2000, p. 9), there is still no evidence to back converse speculation whereby Egyptian offensive plans were at any time after 1967 more ambitious (i.e., included an invasion of Israel), but were scaled down because of Israeli nuclear deterrence or Soviet warnings thereof.

30. Karen Dawisha, *The Kremlin and the Prague Spring*, Berkeley: University of California Press, 1984, p. 172. After the Soviet invasion, there were US speculations that "Japan and the FRG probably would have signed ... except for the Czech events ... other nuclear-capable countries, which have been hanging back, such as Israel ... would presumably have begun to feel isolated." William C. Foster, director, US Arms Control and Disarmament Agency, to Executive Secretary Benjamin H. Read, "Basic Issues Regarding NPT and Timing of Ratification," 22 November 1968, NSA, *Impulse*, no. 34. In the case of Israel at least, this appears far-fetched. West Germany signed the NPT on 28 November 1969.

31. The unofficial Soviet triumvirate, which included the heads of the party (Brezhnev), government (Kosygin) and parliament (Podgorny).
32. Dishon et al., *Middle East Record 1968*, p. 18.
33. Moshe Zak, *Ma'ariv*, 5 July 1968, p. 42.
34. Shalom Rosenfeld, *Ma'ariv*, 5 July 1968, p. 9.
35. AC, Dayan testimony, Part 2, p. 35. A potential attack on the USSR could hardly refer to anything *but* nuclear weapons, presumably missile-launched. The sanitized transcript records no comment from the commission members, and none of its released papers mentions the term "nuclear." Nor does S. Golan's official 1,350-page survey (*Decision Making*) of the Israeli leadership's consultations during the 1973 war.
36. Hersh, *Samson Option*, pp. 139, 174–9. See discussion in *Foxbats*, p. 33.

6. "YELLOW ARAB HELMET, BLUE RUSSIAN EYES"

1. Nitzan Hadas, Israeli embassy Bonn, to Foreign Ministry, Jerusalem, 15 July 1968, ISA HZ-4221/17; Richard Beeston, *Sunday Telegraph*, translated in *Ma'ariv*, 3 July 1968, p. 1. Reports about "a long shadow" thrown over the talks (London *Times*), and mutual disappointment (*Frankfurter Allgemeine Zeitung*, both on 11 July) appear to have rested on the phrase "frank views were exchanged" in the final communiqué; Dishon et al., *Middle East Record 1968*, p. 32; Whetten, *Canal War*, pp. 67–8.
2. Gottfried Albrecht, head of Middle East Research Department, and Christel Steffler of Soviet Affairs Department, quoted in Hadas, Israel embassy Bonn, to Foreign Ministry, 15 July 1968, ISA HZ-4221/17; Alfred Vestring, personal assistant to parliamentary secretary for foreign affairs, Albrecht and Steffler quoted in Hadas to Ministry, 15 July 1968, ISA HZ-4221/4.
3. Dishon et al., *Middle East Record 1968*, p. 32.
4. Rubinstein, *Red Star*, pp. 63–4, citing BBC/ME/2830/ p. A9, 25 July 1968.
5. Bar-Siman-Tov, *War of Attrition*, pp. 145–6, 232n1. However, this conclusion is hardly supported by the sources cited, such as Yaacov Ro'i (ed.), *From Encroachment to Involvement: A Documentary Study of Soviet Policy in the Middle East, 1945–1973*, New York: Wiley, 1974, p. 514.
6. Evgeny Chazov, *Zdorov'e i vlast'*, Moscow: Novosti, 1992, pp. 41–7.
7. Yury Makarenko, who took over in May 1972, interviewed in Meyden, "Na rasstoyanii." His formation sent out patrols to the canal bank to locate and monitor Israeli stations. "Under my command were three such groups who together covered the entire length of the Suez Canal." Ivan Skobanev, in "Raketny zaslon: Iz dnevnika starshego leytenanta Ivana Skobaneva," *Krasnaya Zvezda*, 14 January 2000, www.pvo.su/news/n000114_2.htm, apparently refers to such a detachment in describing his "radio-technic" unit numbering some thirty men.
8. Nehemia Bergin, who was soon after appointed head of the Russian-language monitoring unit Masregah, quoted in Adamsky, *Kavkaz*, p. 136.
9. Lt-Col. Anatoly Isaenko, "Nash chelovek v Egipte," *NVO*, 21 October 2005.
10. Gorbunov, "Napishi mne."

11. Klimentov, "God s tankistami vtoroy polevoy armii," pp. 191–2. The bikinis seem at first blush like a flight of fancy, as was definitely the case with a "bloodcurdling" legend among the Soviets about "Israeli female commandos who landed in the rear of Egyptian forces and butchered hundreds of sleeping soldiers" (Viktor Moiseenkov, "Soldat iz Kazakhstana v strane pyramid," *Karavan* (Almaty), 12 April 2002). Likewise, a SAM systems specialist who arrived in Egypt in March 1971 heard stories about raiding Israeli tanks "with half-naked women in the turrets" that put the "pious Moslem" Egyptian soldiers to flight— a myth that apparently developed around the only Israeli armored raid, on 9 September 1969, in which no women actually took part. Oleg Khitrov, chairman of the internationalist veterans' council, Minsk, interviewed in Maksim Lobzhanets, "Voeval v peskakh Egipta i Sirii," *Borisovskie Novosty* (Belarus), 6 September 2007, http://borisovcity.net/index.php?act=news&id=285. But Israeli accounts confirm there were female conscripts in such functions as communications in the IDF's front-line units well into the War of Attrition, and they regularly visited the forward outposts. Ezra Yanuv, *Ma'ariv*, 18 April 1969, p. 51. Even after the artillery duels in September and October 1968, a battalion commander used to bring one of these women with him to outposts on the canal "on calm days," and had her display herself to the Egyptians—who would come out of their trenches to ogle her and thus expose their positions. Ehud Michalson, *Abirei lev: Gedud 184*, Tel Aviv: Ministry of Defense, 2003, p. 22.
12. Following quotations of Serkov are from *Liniya fronta*, pp. 38–46.
13. Eli Landau, *Ma'ariv*, 10 September 1968, p. 3.
14. Klimentov, "God s tankistami vtoroy polevoy armii," p. 191. Sikstulis also said that several of the Israeli soldiers were immigrants from the USSR, which explained the signs in Russian. In 2002, Sikstulis, then a lecturer in Hebrew and later dean of the Theology Faculty at the University of Latvia, Riga, declined the authors' request for further details.
15. Lieblich, *Seasons*, pp. 23, 47, 52, 57.
16. Isaenko, "Nash chelovek."
17. David Moshayov, *Davar*, 4 October 1968, p. 3.
18. Arnold Sherman, *In the Bunkers of Sinai*, New York: Sabra Books, 1971, p. 22; Hebrew version, *Me'uzei Sinai*, Tel Aviv: Ma'ariv, 1972, p. 18.
19. For example, Brig.-Gen. Dani Asher, *Breaking the Concept*, Tel Aviv: Ministry of Defense, 2003 (has appeared in English as *The Egyptian Strategy for the Yom Kippur War: An Analysis*, Jefferson, NC: McFarland, 2009), p. 65.
20. Following quotations of Malashenko are from *Vspominaya*, pp. 278–98. The jetty held by Israel was across the canal from the town of Port Tawfik, the eastern part of Suez City.
21. Following quotations of Karpov are from "Vospominaniya," pp. 96–8. The visit to the canal by Dayan and Bar-Lev is confirmed by Israeli reports: *Davar*, 10 September 1968, p. 1.
22. David Moshayov, *Davar*, 4 October 1968, p. 3.
23. Gorbunov, "Napishi mne."
24. "Republican Decree No. 199" subordinated the Air Defense Forces directly to the minister of defense. Hanan Khairy, "Air Defence Forces on Target," *Middle East Observer* (Cairo), 24 July 2015, http://www.meobserver.org/air-defence-forces-on-target/

25. Shmu'el Segev, *Ma'ariv*, 16 September 1969, p. 9.
26. Dishon et al., *Middle East Record 1968*, pp. 263–7.
27. V.I. Popov, "Desantnye korabli osvaivayut Sredizemnoye more," *Taifun*, February 2002, p. 45, cited in Lyle J. Goldstein and Yury M. Zhukov, "A Tale of Two Fleets: A Russian Perspective on the 1973 Naval Standoff in the Mediterranean," *Naval War College Review*, 57, 2 (Spring 2004), pp. 49, 62n154, http://scholar.harvard.edu/files/zhukov/files/2004_GoldsteinZhukov_NWCR.pdf. Popov's account of a landing, if correct, apparently refers to events preceding the incident on 30 January. On 25 January, a "friendly visit" to Port Said by a Soviet cruiser, destroyer and landing vessel was announced by MENA, after Western agencies reported the ships' passage through the Turkish straits. Reuters and AFP, *Davar*, 26 January 1968, p. 1. Throughout the month, there were Egyptian warnings that Israel might intervene to prevent the extrication of ships from the northern sector of the canal (political correspondent, *Davar*, 4 January 1968, p. 1), but there is no record of an actual Israeli advance.
28. *Davar*, 4 July 1968, p. 1; Jay Bushinsky, *Chicago News*, "Mysterious Soviet Dredge," *Daily Freeman* (Kingston, NY), 11 July 1968, p. 4; Lawrence Martin, *The Spectator*, translated in *Ma'ariv*, 9 October 1968, p. 9.
29. "The Middle East: Restraint Running Out?," *Time*, 8 November 1968, http://www.time.com/time/magazine/article/0,9171,902496,00.html#ixzz1XJF1LhlA
30. Political correspondent, *Davar*; Uri Dann, *Ma'ariv*, both 18 June 1968, p. 1.
31. Eric Pace, "Cairo Is Said to Favor Israeli Use of Canal if Troops Pull Back," *NYT*, 9 July 1968, p. 1.
32. "The Middle East: Restraint Running Out?"
33. Chaim Herzog, *Ma'ariv*, 13 October 1968, p. 10.
34. Wolfgang Behrends, NATO Department head, West German Foreign Ministry, quoted in Hadas to Research Department, Foreign Ministry, 26 January 1968, ISA HZ-4095/20.
35. Alvin J. Cottrell, "Yahasei Mitzrayim-Brit ha-Mo'atzot," *Ma'arakhot*, 208 (July 1970), pp. 22–3; translated from the US Army's *Military Review*; http://maarachot.idf.il/PDF/FILES/6/108236.pdf.
36. Cottrell in Daly, *Soviet Sea Power*, p. 120.
37. Adm. Elmo R. Zumwalt, *On Watch: A Memoir*, New York: Quadrangle, 1976, pp. 361–8.
38. "The Suez Canal," vice director of the Joint Staff (Freeman) to Secretary of Defense Laird, 1 May 1971, *FRUS* N-XXIV, no. 30.
39. Zumwalt, *On Watch*, pp. 367–8.
40. Marshall I. Goldman, "The Oil Crisis: In Perspective," *Daedalus* (Fall 1975), pp. 129–43.
41. This widely reproduced claim (e.g., Peter Mangold, *Superpower Intervention in the Middle East*, London: Croom Helm, 1978, p. 136n37) is based on a report in *CSM*, 25 September 1972.
42. Department of State to the embassy in Jordan, 9 February 1973, FRUS N-XXV, no. 15.
43. George Weller, *Chicago Daily* News Service, "Soviets Want Suez Reopened to Link Powerful Naval Units," *Herald-Statesman* (Yonkers, NY), 16 October 1968, p. 37.

44. Dean Rusk, "Briefing on the World Situation," 9 September 1968, in US Senate, *Executive Sessions of the Senate Foreign Relations Committee (Historical Series)*, vol. XX, 1968, Washington, DC: Government Printing Office, 2010, p. 1001.
45. AP, "Russians Outnumber 6th Fleet in Mediterranean Ship Buildup," *Gazette* (Schenectady, NY), 20 August 1969, p. 38.
46. Cottrell in Daly, *Soviet Sea Power*, pp. 119–20.
47. AP, "Soviets Beef Up Offensive Punch in Mediterranean," *Observer-Dispatch* (Utica, NY), 25 September 1968, p. 17.
48. William Beecher, *NYT*, "USSR Counters Polaris Threat," *Observer-Dispatch* (Utica, NY), 25 September 1968. This too, however, caused "some talk in US naval circles of withdrawing US Polaris submarines from the cramped Mediterranean because of potential counter by ... future Soviet helicopter carriers and submarines." Daly, *Soviet Sea Power*, p. 43.
49. In a map of Russia's presence in Egypt on 6 June 1970, *Newsweek* marked "Russians dredging harbor" at Mersa Matruh.
50. Egyptian newspaper *Al-Masa*, quoted in *Davar*, 27 October 1968, p. 2.
51. Diver Yury Bebishev, quoted in Maurin, "V tel'nyashke i skafandre." His group was the second to make a six-month tour of duty at Alexandria.
52. J[oseph] Finkelstone, *Ma'ariv*, 17 November 1968, p. 1, quoting *The Sunday Telegraph*.
53. Shirokorad, *Rossiya*, pp. 331–2. A report about such a port call in "early 1969" might refer to this visit or another in a series; it reportedly took place "with no prior notice, as if this was her home port, and without taking the regular precautions against radiation," which increased resentment against "the Soviet takeover of Egypt." *Sunday Telegraph*, 9 March 1969, quoted by UPI, *Davar*, 10 March 1969, p. 7.
54. Norman Polmar, *Guide to the Soviet Navy*, 3rd edn, Annapolis, MD: Naval Institute Press, 1983, pp. 110, 368–9.
55. This report dated the visit to early January. "Visit by a Russian Submarine to Egyptian Port Is Reported," *NYT*, 17 March 1969, p. 3.
56. Ya'el Vered, director, Middle East Department, Foreign Ministry Jerusalem, to Hadas, 1 November 1968, ISA HZ-4221/17.
57. Bejamin Welles, "Reports of a Moscow–Cairo Deal on Arms Dismay U.S. Officials," *NYT*, 13 October 1968, p. 1.
58. Moshe Zak, *Ma'ariv*, 13 September 1968, p. 9.
59. Lucius D. Battle (assistant secretary of state and former ambassador to Egypt), "Middle East Situation: Phantoms for Israel," 9 September 1968, *FRUS* J-XX, no. 247.
60. "Notes on President Johnson's Meeting with Congressional Leaders," 9 September 1968, *FRUS* J-XX, no. 248.
61. Sevinc Carlson, in Daly, *Soviet Sea Power*, p. 119.
62. Nasser returned from Moscow on 17 August. Dishon et al., *Middle East Record 1968*, p. 34.
63. *Der Spiegel*, quoted in *Ma'ariv*, 10 September 1968, p. 3.
64. AC, Ben-Porat testimony, pp. 46–8.
65. Malashenko, *Vspominaya*, pp. 281, 282–3, 298.

66. Bar-Siman-Tov, *War of Attrition*, pp. 43–4.
67. Dmitri Makarov, "Rezident GRU vspominaet: Pozvol'te mne vas zaverbovat'," *Argumenty i Fakty* (Moscow), International Edition, 7 June 2000, p. 16.
68. Zhirokhov and Nichol, "Unknown Heroes," part 2. The IAF has confirmed putting its first reconnaissance UAVs into service only in early 1972, and their first combat use in the 1973 war; IAF website, http://www.iaf.org.il/4968-33518-HE/IAF.aspx. As Tsoy's account is dated before the ceasefire of August 1970, the "enemy" drone might have been American.
69. Telephone interview with Valery Yaremenko (Moscow), 21 January 2001. Yaremenko was a Middle East specialist at the Russian Defense Ministry's Institute of Military History. As a military interpreter attached to a SAM unit, he witnessed the Israeli attack on Iraq's nuclear reactor in 1981.
70. The source, Nurtay Kniazov, is described and pictured as an anti-aircraft gunner, who would hardly qualify for such missions, and other features of his account are clearly imaginary. Moiseenkov, "Soldat iz Kazakhstana."
71. US officials were deliberating at this time whether to press Israel on its plans to acquire "medium and short-range surface-to-surface missiles," but this referred to such nuclear-capable weapons as the French MD-660, which had been contracted for before 1967. Battle, "Israel and the MD-620 Missile," 20 June 1968, *FRUS* J-XX, no. 196. There is no indication that the United States was aware of the Israeli rocketing on the canal until Egypt publicized it.
72. Michalson, *Abirei lev*, p. 23.
73. He came very close: the scant information released later in Israel puts the *Ze'ev*'s payload at 70 kilograms and its range at 4.5 kilometers. There was a heavier variant, with a 170 kilogram warhead that could fly for only 1 kilometer, but it is not clear whether it was used at this stage. Zeev Schiff and Eitan Haber (eds), *Israel, Army and Defence: A Dictionary*, Tel Aviv: Zmora-Bitan-Modan, 1976, p. 196. For comparison, the Soviet M-24 240mm *Katyusha*, of which several mobile multiple launchers were captured by Israel in 1967 and put into IDF service, carried half the payload but to more than twice the range. The M-466 130mm cannon, the mainstay of Egypt's artillery, could lob a 30 kilogram shell for over 27 kilometers.
74. The IDF Ground Forces website lists the *Ze'ev* launch that killed Riad "and several of his senior officers" as (still) experimental; http://mazi.idf.il/5221-6394-HE/IGF.aspx. Asher's recent English version (*Strategy*, p. 28) mentions "Israeli rocket fire" as killing Riad, correcting the earlier Hebrew version that credited "mortar fire" (*Concept*, p. 48).
75. News agencies, *Davar*, 10 September 1968, p. 1. The observers heard, at night, sounds that they attributed to rockets.
76. V.I. Ryabukhin, "V Egipte," in I.V. Shishchenko and A.P. Glazkov (eds), *Smolyane-internatsionalisty*, Smolensk: Smyadyn', 2000, pp. 177–8; Malashenko, *Vspominaya*, p. 293.
77. Rusk, "Briefing on the World Situation," 9 September 1968, in US Senate, *Executive Sessions*, pp. 1000–1.
78. Bard, "Phantom Jets."
79. Arab affairs correspondent, *Davar*, 27 October 1968, p. 1. We found no other references

to the rockets in the contemporary Israeli press, which indicates that this one slipped through a censorship blackout.
80. The official Egyptian history claims that "the Israeli short-range missile batteries" were destroyed by Egyptian artillery as early as September 1968, but this is obviated by Riad's fate and other later uses of the *Ze'ev*. Badry, *Ramadan War*, p. 16.
81. Dishon et al., *Middle East Record 1968*, pp. 360–1.
82. Michalson, *Abirei lev*, p. 21.
83. Uri Dann, *Ma'ariv*, 28 October 1968, p. 2.
84. Yehoshu'a Bitzur, *Ma'ariv*, 31 October 1968, p. 3.
85. Shimshon Ofer, *Davar*, 27 October 1968, p. 1. The article features several blanks that are clearly results of censorship. Michalson, *Abirei lev*, p. 17.
86. Karpov's efforts, if not publicly acknowledged by the Egyptians, were highly appreciated by his Soviet superiors; he is among a handful of advisers singled out by Malashenko for special praise for rehabilitating Egyptian forces through long and arduous field work (*Vspominaya*, p. 284).
87. Michalson, *Abirei lev*, pp. 16, 18–19, 37.
88. *Davar*, 9 September 1968, p. 1.
89. Military correspondent, *Davar*, 28 October 1968, p. 1.
90. Shmu'el Segev, *Ma'ariv*, 28 October 1968, p. 9.
91. "The Middle East: Restraint Running Out?"
92. The mythical Second World War hero Gen. Ivan Panfilov encouraged his hastily organized division in the 1941 defense of Moscow to initiate skirmishes with the Germans and thus overcome their awe of the enemy's invincibility. Shimshon Ofer, *Davar*, 13 September 1968, p. 3; Eli Landau, *Ma'ariv*, 28 October 1968, p. 9; Uri Dann, *Ma'ariv*, 7 May 1970, p. 9. The use of this comparison by several military and other correspondents appears to reflect grudging admiration in the IDF, as Panfilov was iconic in the Israeli military from its pre-state underground days.
93. Uri Dann, *Ma'ariv*, 28 October 1968, p. 2
94. "The Middle East: Restraint Running Out?"
95. As disclosed by the IDF four years later. *Davar*, 30 May 1973, p. 6, quoting *ba-Mahaneh* (IDF magazine).
96. Eli Landau, *Ma'ariv*, 28 October 1968. Landau, like Dann, was considered a proponent of Ariel Sharon and the latter's "mobile" strategy against Bar-Lev's "static" approach.
97. According to a Soviet adviser, the electric facility (which he locates at Asyut, north of Nag Hammadi) had been constructed by Soviet and Czechoslovak experts, was damaged beyond repair, and had to be rebuilt. Molodtsov, "Opyt."
98. Mikhail Zhirokhov, *Rozhdennye voynoy: Istoriya VVS Izrailya*, Chapter 6, http:www.air-war.ru/history/af/iaf/stati/born5.html

7. FACING THE BAR-LEV LINE

1. Maj.-Gen. Avraham Adan, *On the Banks of the Suez: An Israeli General's Personal Account of the Yom Kippur War*, San Francisco: Presidio Press, 1980, p. 43.

2. Serkov, *Liniya fronta*, pp. 46–7.
3. Korn, *Stalemate*, p. 107.
4. Following quotations of Malashenko are from *Vspominaya*, pp. 269–99.
5. Vinogradov, *Diplomatiya*, p. 245. Eitan Haber, Ze'ev Schiff and Dani Asher, *The War: Yom Kippur War Lexicon*, revised edn, Tel Aviv: Kinneret, Zmora-Bitan, Dvir, 2013, p. 14.
6. Interviewed in *Vo slavu rodiny* (Minsk, Belarusian Defense Ministry daily), 20 February 2003.
7. Badry, *Ramadan War*, p. 16.
8. Heikal, *Road to Ramadan*, pp. 44, 78, 110, 182 ("Lashinkov"); Gen. Sa'ad el-Shazly, *The Crossing of the Suez*, revised English edn, San Francisco: American Mideast Research, 2003, pp. 197–8, 277–8 ("Lashnekov").
9. Katyshkin was promoted to colonel-general a few days after arriving in Egypt.
10. For example, naval adviser Vladimir Kryshtob, "I eta voyna," who also describes similar opinions of Katyshkin among colleagues in the ground forces.
11. Gennady Goryachkin, "Sud'ba voennogo perevodchika v Egipte," in Meyer et al., *Togda*, p. 72.
12. 112th Infantry Brigade, "Instructions concerning *modus operandi* of experts in the Armed Forces," 29 January 1969, CDE-IHC, 367/12.
13. Shmu'el Segev, *Ma'ariv*, 9 July 1968, p. 9.
14. Herzog, *Ma'ariv*, 13 October 1968, p. 10.
15. Uri Dann, *Ma'ariv*, 28 October 1968, p. 2.
16. William Beecher, "Role of Egypt's Russian Advisers Is Worrying U.S.," *NYT*, 22 October 1968, p. 12; Shalom, *Phantoms*, vol. 1, p. 200.
17. AP, "Israel, Egypt Jets Dogfight over Canal," *Post-Gazette* (Pittsburgh); UPI, "Israel, Arabs Edgy over New Flareups," *Press* (Pittsburgh), both 24 October 1968, p. 1.
18. *Ma'ariv*, 4 October 1968.
19. Eli Landau, *Ma'ariv*, 28 October 1968.
20. Brig.-Gen. Iftach Spector, *Loud and Clear*, Tel Aviv: Yedi'ot Ahronot, 2008 (has appeared in English as *Loud and Clear: The Memoir of an Israeli Fighter Pilot*, Minneapolis: Zenith, 2009), pp. 145–6; *Davar*, 4 November 1968, p. 1. The Egyptian claims are reflected in David Nicolle and Tom Cooper, *Arab MiG-19 and MiG-21 Units in Combat*, London: Osprey, 2004, p. 25.
21. The chronology in the official "victory album" *1,000 ha-Yamim* omits these incidents entirely, as does the IAF history website.
22. Shalom, *Phantoms*, vol. 1, pp. 203–5.
23. Department of Defense Memorandum of Conversation I-359993/68, Rabin and others with Assistant Secretary Paul C. Warnke and others, 4 November 1968, p. 3. Kindly shared by Michael Oren. IAF chief Hod was present and had certainly been informed about the previous day's action.
24. Memorandum of Conversation, "Negotiations with Israel: F-4 and Advanced Weapons," 4 November 1968. Lucius Battle had urged at least to demand straight answers from Israel on its missile development program, but this was not pressed. "Israel and the MD-620

Missile," memorandum from Battle to Rusk, 20 June 1968, *FRUS* J-XX, no. 306 and no. 196.
25. Robert J. Murray, "Negotiations with Israel: F-4 and Advanced Weapons," 5 November 1968; Harry Schwartz, "F-4 Negotiations with the Israelis," 9 November 1968. *FRUS* J-XX, no. 308 and no. 311.
26. Benjamin Welles, "U.S. Will Sell Israel 58 Phantom Jets," *NYT*, 7 November 1968, p. 2; Hedrick Smith, "U.S. Will Start Delivering F-4 Jets to Israel in 1969," *NYT*, 28 December 1968, p. 1. The Americans told Egyptian Foreign Minister Riad that the promise was leaked by "someone in the aircraft industry," but did not deny it. *FRUS* J-XX, no. 314.
27. *Ma'ariv*, 25 October 1968, p. 1.
28. Mohamed Hassanein Heikal, *The Sphinx and the Commissar: The Rise and Fall of Soviet Influence in the Middle East*, New York: Harper and Row, 1978, p. 154.
29. Department of State Memorandum of Conversation 7725942, Gromyko and Vance, 30 September 1977. Kindly shared by Michael Oren.
30. Leonid Nikolaev: "Arabsky Ace #1," *Ekho Stolitsy* (Moscow), 9 July 1999.
31. Egorin, *Egipet*, p. 185.
32. Dashkov and Golotyuk, "Arabo-izrail'sky konflikt," unpaginated, endnote 3.
33. Alizadeh, interview. This probably refers to the P-12 system that was "lifted" by the Israelis a year later; its usual description only as a "radar station" omits its other functions.
34. Egorin, *Egipet*, p. 185.
35. Foreign Ministry to mission in New York, 21 November 1968, ISA HZ-4221/5.
36. Victor Israelyan, *On the Battlefields of the Cold War*, University Park, PA: Penn State University Press, 2003, pp. 165–6.
37. Goldmann to Eshkol, 19 November 1968, ISA HZ-4221/5.
38. This comment was made to the director-general of the Austrian Foreign Ministry, who told the Israeli ambassador. Z[e'ev] Scheck, embassy in Vienna, to Foreign Ministry director-general, 13 January 1971 ISA HZ-4605/3.
39. Mordechai Gazit, "Conversation of M.G. with 'David' [Primakov] on 8 October [1971]," p. 7, ISA A-7037/17.
40. Teko'a to [Michael] Comay, Foreign Ministry, 25 October 1968, ISA HZ-4221/5. Teko'a too had stipulated confidentiality, but news of the meeting emerged on 19 December 1968, in *Ha'aretz* from its New York correspondent.
41. Israel Foreign Ministry Research Department, 7 June 1970, ISA HZ-4605/2.
42. Yehoshu'a Bitzur, *Ma'ariv*, 31 October 1968, p. 3. How Allon inferred this from his talks in Washington is unclear.
43. Herzog, *Ma'ariv*, 13 October 1968, p. 10.

8. A NEW PHASE FROM MARCH '69?

1. Badry, *Ramad an War*, p. 16.
2. For example, Bar-Siman-Tov, *War of Attrition*.
3. Henry Kissinger, *The White House Years*, Boston: Little, Brown, 1979, p. 1286.
4. For Sedov's role during the Six-Day War, see *Foxbats*, pp. 110, 200–3.

5. Later, Sedov contemplated recruiting a Kissinger aide at the NSC, but Kalugin claims to have overruled him. Oleg Kalugin, *Spymaster: My Thirty-Two Years in Intelligence and Espionage against the West*, New York: Basic, 2009, p. 123.
6. Marvin Kalb and Bernard Kalb, *Kissinger*, Boston: Little, Brown, 1974, pp. 21–6.
7. *SAR*, no. 4, p. 7.
8. UPI, "Israel Rejects Peace Plan," *St. Petersburg Times* (FL), 6 January 1969, p. 2. TASS UN correspondent Sergey Losev, who had previously been posted (and identified as a KGB operative) in Israel, argued to an Israeli diplomat that the Soviets' call for a full withdrawal in return for less than a peace treaty would be better for Israel. [Moshe] Leshem, New York, to director general, Foreign Ministry, 12 January 1969, ISA HZ-4221/9.
9. Reuters, *Davar*, 12 January 1969, p. 12; *Pravda* quoted in *Ma'ariv*, 12 January 1969, p. 3.
10. Kalb and Kalb, *Kissinger*, pp. 102–5. Nixon instructed Rogers that a decision about "talks on strategic weapons" should depend on "progress toward stabilizing the explosive Middle East situation." *SAR*, 4 February 1969, no. 1, pp. 3–4.
11. *SAR*, no. 3, pp. 5–6; emphasis in original.
12. *SAR*, no. 4, p. 7.
13. *SAR*, no. 11, p. 20 and no. 24, p. 66.
14. "Our superiors in Moscow" were especially "delighted" by the intercept of a talk between Kissinger and his then-fiancee. Kalugin, *Spymaster*, p. 102.
15. *SAR*, Kissinger Foreword, p. x; emphasis added.
16. *SAR*, no. 6, p. 15.
17. According to a former Indian military attaché who was a frequent guest in Egypt, this was also Nasser's main motivation for launching the War of Attrition. Maj.-Gen. D.K. Palit, *Return to Sinai: The Arab Offensive, October 1973*, New Delhi: Lancer, 1974; reprinted, 2002, pp. 10–11.
18. *SAR*, no. 8, pp. 20–1.
19. *SAR*, no. 11, pp. 31–2.
20. Memorandum of conversation, 1 March 1969, *DR* vol. 2, sec. VIII, no. 32, p. 4. De Gaulle "believed that the Soviets were not far" from his position, and Kissinger admitted to Dobrynin two days later that the United States might be outnumbered or tied in the four-power talks. *SAR*, 3 March 1969, no. 11, p. 31.
21. Zhirokhov, *Rozhdennye voynoy*, Chapter 6. Like most other histories, he adds inaccurately "Nasser declared the War of Attrition."
22. Cited in *Ma'ariv*, 19 February 1969, p. 2.
23. Haggai Eshed, *Davar*, 11 March 1969, p. 1; editorial in same issue.
24. Korn, *Stalemate*, p. 108. Contemporary press reports dated this visit, and the officers' clamor, on 1 March. The date given to Korn may have originated from a cabinet session chaired by Nasser on 16 February to discuss the sniping that had already begun and Israeli threats to retaliate.
25. Military correspondent, *Ma'ariv*, 13 February 1969, p. 1.
26. Paris correspondent, *Ma'ariv*, 16 February 1969, p. 2; Shimshon Ofer, *Davar*, 7 March 1969, p. 4.

27. Interview with Fred Friendly, *Ma'ariv*, 7 March 1969, p. 10.
28. Following quotations of Serkov are from *Liniya fronta*, pp. 52–78.
29. Bar-Siman-Tov, *War of Attrition*, p. 46.
30. IAF website for 3 March 1969, http://www.iaf.org.il/3590-6899-he/IAF.aspx
31. Shalom (*Phantoms*, vol. 1 p. 212) quotes an unsourced Israeli claim that several senior Soviet advisers were killed in Riad's party. Western histories also asserted more generally that "there were ... some casualties among Soviet military personnel." Nadav Safran, *Israel: The Embattled Ally*, Cambridge, MA: Belknap, 1978, pp. 262–3. Cf. Rubinstein, *Red Star*, p. 80. But no Soviet combat fatalities at this stage are mentioned in the veterans' detailed honor rolls.
32. Moshe Zak, *Ma'ariv*, 14 March 1969, p. 9. This reading is mirrored in later studies, e.g., "it is not at all certain that the Soviets had any interest in seeing belligerent action ... The Soviet political leadership judged that all the diplomatic means available should be tried first." Bar-Siman-Tov, *War of Attrition*, pp. 46–7.
33. Israeli accounts confirm that a SAM-2 shot down one of two artillery observation planes east of the canal. Avino'am Misnikov, "Happalat Piper 033," www.sky-high.co.il; IAF website, http://www.iaf.org.il/3590-he/IAF.aspx; Shalom, *Phantoms*, vol. 1, p. 239.
34. Jean Daniel, *Davar*, 22 May 1969, p. 6.
35. Nasser's speech to the ASU conference on 27 March; Israeli reports stressed his threat to strike at civilian targets within Israel proper. Arab affairs correspondent, *Ma'ariv*, 28 March 1969, p. 2.
36. Uri Dann, *Ma'ariv*, 8 March 1970, p. 9.
37. Badry, *Ramadan War*, p. 17.
38. This use of the rails was disclosed in Israel by leaking it to the *NYT* only after the results on 8–9 March proved its effectiveness. Hanson W. Baldwin, Tel Aviv, "Sinai Rail Tracks, Torn Up, Bolstering Israeli Bunkers," *NYT*, 11 March 1969, p. 6; *Ma'ariv*, 12 March 1969, p. 2. There is no evidence that the Egyptians or Soviets were aware of it earlier—possibly because the work was done at night due to Egyptian sniping.
39. Shmu'el Segev, *Ma'ariv*, 24 July 1969, p. 3; on the same page, the paper's "Arab affairs correspondent" again discerned "the USSR's restraining influence."
40. Vasiliev, *Rossiya*, pp. 89, 91–2.
41. Commander of 336th Infantry battalion, "Report on Experts' Activity," 7 November 1969, CDE-IHC, 367/12 p. 5. This adviser's name may have been garbled, as it has not appeared in the veterans' literature.
42. Upon his return in June 1972 he was rewarded with an appointment as dean of the Western Languages Faculty of the Military Languages School (under Katyshkin).
43. Serkov, *Liniya fronta*, entry for 18 March 1969, pp. 65–8.
44. Ibid., entry for 13 March 1969, pp. 63–5. The term "special operations" (*spetznaz*) may indicate that the eponymous Soviet units of this type, which Yaremenko reports as operating across the canal during the War of Attrition, were in place by this time and emulated by the Egyptians.
45. Nasser, according to Heikal, held that "missile cover" was essential for longer raids. *Road to Ramadan*, pp. 53–4.

46. Korn, *Stalemate*, pp. 175, 207.
47. Shimshon Ofer, *Davar*, 12 December 1969, p. 4. "Hatashah," the Hebrew term for "attrition," is still given in quotes as Egyptian parlance. "Egypt Reports 250 Men Staged Its Biggest Raid," *International Herald Tribune*, 8 December 1969, p. 1.
48. Michalson, *Abirei lev*, pp. 33, 358.
49. AC, testimony of Avraham Adan, Part 2, pp. 16–21.
50. Badry, *Ramadan War*, p. 17.
51. Kissinger briefing by IDF officers, 22 October 1973; Golan, *Decision Making*, p. 1146.
52. Gennady Goryachkin ("O voennykh perevodchikakh v Egipte," in Safonov et al., *Grif*, p. 175) mentions this team among the advisers on "short-term missions" in his hotel in August 1969.
53. Michalson, *Abirei lev*, pp. 27, 34, 36. Sharon confirmed that the first encounters with Saggers were during the War of Attrition, but claimed that most had been fired from across the canal. AC, Sharon testimony, Part 1, pp. 95–6.
54. Maj.-Gen. Ya'aqov Amidror, interviewed on Israel Army Radio, 6 October 2014, http://glz.co.il/1064-51308-he/Galatz.aspx, at 9'45". Amidror stated that in October 1973 the Sagger was already known to the IDF from *Syrian* use in an incident "half a year before the war. ... A lot of papers were issued but we didn't understand the significance until we encountered it on the battlefield."

9. WHAT TRIGGERED *KAVKAZ*? REFUTING HEIKAL'S VERSION

1. BBC transcript, 25 July 1970, cited in Rubinstein, *Red Star*, p. 107.
2. BBC Summary of World Broadcasts, 1 September 1971, quoted in Ilana Kass, *Soviet Involvement in the Middle East: Policy Formulation 1966–1973*, Boulder, CO: Westview, 1978, pp. 155, 263n2.
3. Ro'i, *Encroachment*, p. 52n3.
4. See pp. 78–86, 166–87. Heikal reiterated his versions of the two episodes in *Sphinx*, pp. 197–8, 242–55.
5. In effect, until the appearance of Victor Israelyan, *Inside the Kremlin during the Yom Kippur War*, University Park, PA: Pennsylvania University Press, 1997.
6. Ambassador Murad Ghaleb and Minister of Defense Fawzy. Their accounts first appeared in Arabic and thus took even longer to figure alongside Heikal's in Western scholarship. Laura James, "Egyptian Decision-Making during the War of Attrition," in Ashton, *The Cold War in the Middle East*, pp. 110–11n99.
7. Walter Laqueur, *Confrontation: The Middle East War and World Politics*, London: Abacus, 1974, p. 14n*.
8. The only exception discovered so far is the unsigned article in *Sputnik*, January 1991—one of the first to confirm the Soviet intervention at all, with a very confused timeline. This Soviet imitation of *Reader's Digest* may have copied Heikal's version with no reservation because no official Soviet one was yet available.
9. Col. V.E. Tkachev, "Pochemu Izrail' prekratil voennye deystviya na egipetskom fronte," *Voenno-Istoricheskiy Zhurnal* (Moscow), 6 (2005), p. 43.

10. V[ladimir] Vinogradov, "Sovetskie voiny v Egipte," in Safonov et al., *Grif*, p. 11; "K istorii Sovetsko-Egipetskikh otnosheny," in Meyer et al., *Togda*, pp. 14–15.
11. See, e.g., 18th Air Defense Division's history webpage, http://www.hubara-rus.ru/kavkaz.html#12.69, which dates the visit to early December and Grechko's order to commence *Kavkaz* later the same month; Zolotarev, *Rossiya*, p. 189; Gen. Aleksey Smirnov, interviewed in Andrey Pochtarev, "Kak podrezali kryl'ya fantomam," *Krasnaya Zvezda*, 14 January 2000; Col. Konstantin Popov, in Aleksey Galanin, "Boi nad piramidani," *Shchelkovo Vremya* (Russia), 19 December 2007; Valery Yaremenko, "Sovetsko-egipetskoe voennoe sotrudnichestvo nakanune i v khode oktyabr'skoy voyny 1973 goda," in Vartanov et al., *Rukopozhatie*, p. 44. For additional sources and a detailed discussion, see Ginor, "Arab Helmet."
12. Isaenko, "Eta vera," a review of Kubersky's "novel" *Egipet-69*.
13. Kubersky, *Egipet-69*, Part 1.
14. Col. Asher Snir, "Boom al-qoli be-Qahir," *Heyl ha-Avir* (IAF magazine), 54 (November 1986), pp. 12–15. Snir led the pair that was sent north of Cairo to overfly the nuclear reactor and air base at Inshas.
15. For example, "a pair of IAF Mirages ... flew over Nasser's Cairo home and Cairo-West airport, creating sonic booms ... Nasser was embarrassed and angry." Benny Morris, *Righteous Victims: A History of the Zionist–Arab Conflict, 1881–1999*, New York: Knopf, 1999, p. 350. "They were flying to photograph installations around Cairo, and to shake the capital with a sonic boom ... to deter the Egyptians." Col. Eliezer Cohen, *Israel's Best Defense: The First Full Story of the Israeli Air Force*, New York: Crown, 1993, p. 27.
16. Shalom, *Phantoms*, vol. 1, pp. 273–6. Col. Yury Makarenko, who in 1972 (as a major) commanded a *spetsnaz* radio-technical detachment in the top-secret Mt Muqatem facility, describes it as built underground in an artificially deepened crater. His outfit's function was to monitor and disrupt IDF signals; in 2008, he preferred not to discuss its equipment and capabilities. Interviewed in Meyden, "Na rasstoyanii."
17. UPI, London, "Unprecedented Reconnaissance," *News-Sentinel* (Lodi, CA), 28 June 1969, p. 2.
18. "Nasser has replaced the top two Egyptian Air Force officers, apparently in a move to improve standards." Paul Kidd, "Cairo Today," *Montreal Gazette*, 19 June 1969; "It was probably the Hamadi [air] raid [on 30 April] which led to the [dismissal of] two key EAF officers." Francis Ofner, Tel Aviv, "Semiwar," *CSM*, 26 June 1969, p. 1.
19. *NYT* Service, Beirut, "Israeli Planes Buzz Cairo, Draw No Egyptian Reaction," *Spokesman-Review* (Spokane), 30 June 1969, p. 12; UPI, "Mideast Clashes pose New Crisis," citing "Cairo reports," *Press* (Pittsburgh), 23 June 1969, p. 38.
20. Mikhail Zhirokhov, "Soviet Pilots in Egypt," *Aero Historian*, 38, 12 (December 2004), p. 6, http://www.airwar.ru/history/locwar/bv/sovegipet/sovegipet.htm. A history of Arab air forces doubts that the sonic boom affair caused Hinnawy's ouster: "[his] period as commander, focusing ... on reorganization and intensive training, had come to a close, and he was replaced by an aggressive leader." Nicolle and Cooper, *Arab MiG Units*, p. 2.
21. "Air Defense Forces Historical Background."

22. Kubersky, *Egipet-69*, Part 1.
23. Nicolle and Cooper, *Arab MiG Units*, p. 30.
24. Molodtsov, "Opyt."
25. The next day, Israel admitted one Mirage lost and another damaged in a dogfight, as against five Egyptian planes—the first IAF loss in air combat since 1967. Shalom, *Phantoms*, vol. 1, pp. 337–51.
26. UPI, "Guns and Tanks Battle across Suez Canal," *Eagle* (Reading, PA), 21 July 1969, p. 4.
27. See, e.g., Nicolle and Cooper, *Arab MiG Units*, p. 30: "Israeli commandos destroyed a radar position on Green Island to punch a breach in Egyptian radar coverage. Israeli fighters swarmed through."
28. Lecture by former Navy Commander Rear Admiral Ze'ev Almog, 12 September 2013; summary in authors' possession. A senior Soviet adviser to Egyptian Air Defense does not list Green Island among the radar stations that Israel destroyed in 1969–70; Molodtsov, "Opyt."
29. Shalom, *Phantoms*, vol. 1, pp. 328–30.
30. Bar-Siman-Tov, *War of Attrition*, pp. 57–8, 81ff.
31. Karpov, "Vospominaniya," p. 105.
32. Dmitriev's marine detachment arrived from the Black Sea Fleet on 19 May for a three-month tour of duty. It included two infantry companies (of which he commanded one), one each of amphibious tanks and of mortars, and a platoon of "shoulder-fired anti-tank missiles"—the earliest mention so far of *Malyutkas* in Egypt. They practiced, among other exercises, a tank-supported landing in Port Fuad to enable the evacuation of Soviet advisers in case of an Israeli incursion. On their return voyage in August, they took part in the Fifth *Eskadra*'s "first joint maneuvers" with the Egyptian and Syrian navies. V.I. Dmitriev, "Zapiski leytenanta morskoy pekhoty," in Filonik, *Komandirovka*, pp. 22–6.
33. Arab affairs correspondent, *Davar*, 23 July 1969, p. 1; Jean Daniel, translated in *Davar*, 22 May 1969, p. 6; Israel Foreign Ministry Research Department 7 June 1970, ISA HZ-4605/2. A biography of Kharchikov mentions that he was injured (and decorated for it) in 1968 in Port Said. Yury Belov, "Russky Bard," *Sovetskaya Rossiya*, 14 February 2008, http://www.sovross.ru/articles/142/2755
34. Shalom, *Phantoms*, vol. 2, p. 731. Shmuel Gordon (*Thirty Hours in October*, Tel Aviv: Ma'ariv, 2008, pp. 82–3) calculates a total of 120 deep-penetration sorties out of 10,520 combat sorties in the entire War of Attrition.
35. Alizadeh, interview. The first such casualty to be named and dated was a Col. Kolchenko from Kazakhstan, who was killed in a bombing on the II Army Corps headquarters at Tel el-Kebir on 20 July 1969; another adviser and their interpreter were injured. Klimentov, "God s tankistami vtoroy polevoy armii," p. 193.
36. Serkov, *Liniya fronta*, pp. 93, 121–3, 128–30.
37. V[ladimir] Dudchenko, "Voyna sudnogo dnya: krovavaya nich'ya," in Filonik, *Komandirovka*, p. 29. Palit (*Return to Sinai*, p. 30) lists Wadi Natrun among several such facilities.
38. AC, testimony of Siman-Tov Binyamin, p. 15.

39. Sherman, *Bunkers*, p. 28. This claim is made, almost verbatim, in the official "victory album" (Brig.-Gen. Yitzhak Arad et al., eds, *1000 ha-yamim: 12 yuni 1967–8 august 1970*, Tel Aviv: [IDF] General Staff Chief Education Officer and Ministry of Defense Publishing, undated [1970], p. 220), which confirms that Sherman's statement reflected the IDF's publicity line.
40. Alizadeh, interview.
41. Karpov, "Vospominaniya," pp. 105–6.
42. Serkov, *Liniya fronta*, entry for 1 August 1969, p. 91.
43. Badry, *Ramadan War*, pp. 121–4; the SAM-3s' subsequent success in shooting down six Phantoms is attributed to these Egyptian crews with no mention of the Soviets, though other sources clarify that the first Egyptian crews did not complete their training for this system until after the ceasefire of August 1970.
44. Heikal, *Road to Ramadan*, pp. 77–8.
45. Slukhay, *Katyshkin*.
46. Karpov, "Vospominaniya," pp. 105–7. He also mentions a high-ranking delegation from the Soviet Air Defense headquarters that inspected Egyptian air defense forces "before 9 September," but does not clarify whether it was connected with Savitsky's visit. Serkov, *Liniya fronta*, pp. 91–3.
47. Molodtsov, "Opyt."
48. Kubersky, *Egipet-69*, Part 1.
49. Alexey Chebotarev, "Ekskluzivnoe interv'yu sozdatelya 'Igly,'" *Solidarnost'*, 40 (29 October 2003), www.solidarnost.org/thems/sudba-cheloveka/sudba-cheloveka_247.html
50. Heikal, *Road to Ramadan*, p. 61. The visit ended on 2 February. UPI, "Diplomatic Door Opens," *Daily Times* (Watertown, NY), 2 February 1969, p. 1.
51. Malashenko, *Vspominaya*, p. 299.
52. CIA "Intelligence Memorandum: The Soviet 'Strela' System; A Man-Portable SAM," 21 July 1970, https://www.cia.gov/library/readingroom/docs/DOC_0000484030.pdf
53. Col. Viktor Tkachev, "'Strely' i 'shilki' v boyu," *VKO*, 6, 25 (25 July 2005), http://militaryarticle.ru/voenno-kosmicheskaya-oborona/2005/12355-strely-i-shilki-v-boju
54. Interviewed in "TV Profiles, Shows Lifetime Work of Top Russian Missile Designer," Moscow Channel 1 TV, 23 May 2003; transcribed in English, Russian Military and Security Media Coverage 2326, 2 (17 June 2003), https://groups.yahoo.com/neo/groups/RMSMC/conversations/messages/2351
55. Shalom, *Phantoms*, vol. 1 p. 464.
56. Kubersky, *Egipet-69*, Part 1.
57. Yaremenko, "Sovetsko-egipetskoe voennoe sotrudnichestvo," pp. 45–6. A similar claim is made in Zolotarev et al., *Rossiya*, for which Yaremenko was the lead contributor on the Middle East (p. 189). It adds that Egyptians were trained to operate the *Strela* in the Orenburg region of Russia.
58. Schueftan, *Attrition*, p. 439.
59. Telephone interview with Yaremenko, 21 January 2001.
60. Viktor S. Logachev, "Eto zabyt' nevozmozhno," in Safonov et al., *Grif*, p. 153.

61. A. Smirnov, "Operatsiya 'Kavkaz': V gushche sobytiy," in Meyer et al., *Togda*, p. 31.
62. Yaremenko, "Sovetsko-egipetskoe voennoe sotrudnichestvo," pp. 45–6.
63. Kubersky, *Egipet-69*, Part 1.
64. Bar-Siman-Tov, *War of Attrition*, p. 147.
65. Philip Benn, *Ma'ariv*, 30 July 1969, p. 2.
66. Lewis W. Bowden, "Soviet Oral Statement on Suez Cease Fire," 1 August 1969. NARA, Nixon Presidential Materials project, NSC files, country files, box 710, USSR, vol. XXI.
67. Nastenko, "Aviatsiya v Egipte," pp. 55–7, 59.
68. Zhirokhov and Nicolle, "Unknown Heroes," Part 2.
69. Abramov, *Goluboe*, p. 47.
70. Zhirokhov and Nicolle, "Unknown Heroes," Part 2.
71. Alizadeh, interview.
72. Gordon, *Thirty Hours*, pp. 107–8.

10. DR CHAZOV'S "VACATION IN EGYPT"

1. Dobrynin's report was submitted by Gromyko to the Politburo only on 12 July. *SAR*, no. 24, pp. 66, 70n1.
2. By February 1970, Washington officials admitted that "they could not believe their ears" when the Soviets rejected the Rogers Plan in December, as this in effect tore up understandings that had been reached months before between Rogers and Gromyko as well as between Sisco and Dobrynin. They attributed the about-face to Nasser's "veto" over Soviet policy. Philip Benn, *Ma'ariv*, 27 February 1970, p. 10.
3. Kirk J. Beattie, *Egypt during the Nasser Years*, Boulder, CO: Westview, 1994, p. 225.
4. James, "Egyptian Decision-Making," p. 99.
5. Heikal, *Road to Ramadan*, p. 81.
6. This mention of the still-experimental MiG-25s appears to confirm the Foxbats' missions from Egypt over Israel in May 1967, as outlined in *Foxbats*—and Nasser's awareness of them.
7. Chazov, *Zdorov'e i vlast'*, pp. 47–55.
8. "Nasser Reported Fighting Soviet Ouster," *St. Petersburg Times* (FL), 18 September 1969, p. 3-A; AP and Reuters, "Nasser Fears Ouster; Purge of Reds Hinted," *Calgary Herald*, 8 Sept 1969, p. 1.
9. UPI, "Nasser Kicks Russian Advisor Out of Egypt," *Dispatch* (Lexington, NC), 20 September 1969, p. 1.
10. The Soviets also exploited the El-Aqsa arson: the KGB *rezidentura* in New Delhi spent 5,000 rupees to rent a crowd of "20,000 Moslems" for a protest outside the US embassy. Report by Andropov to the Central Committee, 25 August 1969, obtained by the authors in 1992.
11. Eliahu Salpeter, "Dateline Jerusalem," *Canadian Jewish Chronicle Review* (17 October 1969), p. 16.
12. UPI, "Soviet, Nasser Meeting Soon," *Press-Courier* (Oxnard, CA), 28 September 1967, p. 6.
13. UPI, "Nasser Reported Nearly Recovered," *Milwaukee Journal*, 24 September 1969, p. B-2.

14. Jack Anderson, "Nasser to Nixon," *Robesonian* (Lamberton, NC), 2 October 1969, p. 9: "Nixon's reply ... didn't go much beyond warm words and general assurances. Therefore Nasser let it be known that the US reply was completely unacceptable." No official record has emerged yet of this exchange.
15. "A Few Rays of Hope in the Middle East," *Miami News*, editorial, 26 September 1969, p. 14-A.
16. Chazov, *Zdorov'e i vlast'*, p. 51.
17. Sadat's speech at Tanta in the Nile delta on 4 January 1971, as reported by Shmu'el Segev, *Ma'ariv*, 5 January 1971, p. 2.
18. Reuters, "Nasser Pushes Purge," *Montreal Gazette*, 19 Sept 1969, p. 1. On Ahmed Ismail's Soviet training, see T.N. Dupuy, *Elusive Victory: The Arab–Israeli Wars, 1947–1974*, New York: Harper & Row, 1978, p. 388.
19. Kubersky, *Egipet-69*, Part 2, p. 41.
20. A list of Soviet casualties names a Col. Vasily G. Korneyev as killed on 9 September but describes him as the adviser to an air defense brigade; http://www.hubara-rus.ru/heroes.html
21. Dayan may have referred to this incident when he spoke in 1975 about "a Soviet delegation" that happened to be on the site of an Israeli raid in southern Egypt, and some of its members were hit. "There were other Soviet casualties elsewhere, but none ... were intentional." Moshe Zak, *Israel and the Soviet Union: A Forty Years' Dialogue*, Tel Aviv: Ma'ariv, 1988, pp. 179–80. The "radio-technical" adviser Molodtsov ("Opyt") confirms that Israeli tanks destroyed the installation, but does not mention Soviet casualties.
22. Platunov, "Provaly v pamyati." Maj. Mikhail Antonov witnessed the two coffins being loaded onto the transport plane that brought him to Cairo-West; Latypov, "O druzhbe." At the time, the Israelis counted over 100 Egyptians killed but mentioned no Soviet casualties. Only thirty years after the raid, its commander disclosed a "Russian colonel killed at Zaafrana." Col. Baruch "Pinko" Har'el in *Shiryon* (IDF Armored Corps Magazine), January 1999, pp. 18–19, http://www.yadlashiryon.com/vf/ib_items/164/Shiryon_03.pdf#page=18
23. Col. Avraham Zohar, "'Escort,' 'Raviv': Peshitot be-hof mifratz Suez, September 1969," *Ma'rakhot*, 297 (January 1985), pp. 15–23; http://maarachot.idf.il/PDF/FILES/8/109358.pdf. Har'el's article, whose title translates "we took no risks and destroyed everything," confirms that civilian or unidentified vehicles were also targeted—but does not specify a bus.
24. A Skyhawk was shot down by cannon fire and the pilot bailed out but was never found; his helmet later washed up on the Israeli-held shore. Shalom, *Phantoms*, vol. 1, pp. 428–30. The first Phantoms had been delivered on 5 September, but Israel announced their first combat action only on 22 October.
25. Parker, *Politics of Miscalculation*, p. 137 (unsourced).
26. Chazov, *Zdorov'e i vlast'*, p. 53.
27. Kirill Privalov, "Chelovek Kremlya," *Itogi*, 14 June 2010, http://www.itogi.ru/spetzproekt2/2010/24/153297.html

28. Nikolay Zubashenko, "Gennady Shishlakov: 'Egipetsky serebryany orden ya poluchil za to, chto podbil amerikansky samolet Mirazh,'" *Establishment* (Zaporozhe, Ukraine), 5 April 2006. The *Shilka* entered service in Soviet forces only in 1965, and in '67 was still in the process of replacing earlier models.
29. Lt-Gen. A.D. Sidorov (chief of cadres in the USSR Ministry of Defense), "Dlia tekh, kto voeval," *Krasnaya zvezda*, 12 October 1989, p. 2, quoted in Richard F. Staar, "Russia's National Security Concept," *Perspective*, 8, 3 (January–February 1998), http://www.bu.edu/iscip/vol8/Staar.html
30. Dashkov and Golotyuk, "Arabo-izrail'sky konflikt."
31. Slukhay, *Katyshkin*.
32. *Foxbats*, p. 167.
33. Reuters, *Davar*, 10 December 1969, p. 2.
34. Badry, *Ramadan War*, p. 149.
35. Shalom, *Phantoms*, vol. 1, pp. 557–8; Alizadeh, interview.
36. Arye Yodfat, *The Soviet Union and the Middle East*, Tel Aviv: Ministry of Defense, February 1973, p. 32.
37. Liad Barkat, "Nordim al ha-Nilus," *Heyl ha-Avir* (IAF Magazine), 126, April 1999, http://www.iaf.org.il/511-18975-HE/IAF.aspx
38. Smirnov, "Operatsiya 'Kavkaz': v gushche sobytiy," p. 26.
39. Ze'ev Schiff, "Ha-Hatashah," *Heyl ha-Avir* (IAF magazine), 91 (July 1973), p. 133.
40. Zub, "Sovetskie moryaki: Voiny-internatsionalisty v OAR-Egipet," pp. 77–9. Badry (*Ramadan War*, p. 17) describes the attack with no mention of Soviet participation.
41. The first group of F-4 pilots and WSOs, ten men in all including the two prospective squadron leaders, were trained in the US from January to February through July 1969. Ten additional crewmen were sent only in May 1970 for ten-day sessions on a simulator of the Iranian Air Force, which had received its first F-4s in September 1968. Shalom, *Phantoms*, vol. 1, pp. 394–406, vol. 2, p. 1098; Joe Baugher, "Phantom with Iran," http://www.joebaugher.com/usaf_fighters/f4_44.html
42. AP, "Nasser Aides in Moscow for Talks," *Daytona Beach Morning Herald*, 8 December 1969, p. 2.
43. Anthony Astrakhan (*Washington Post*, Moscow), "Kosygin outlines Soviet stand on Mid-East," *Times* (Geneva, NY), 11 December 1969, p. 33. Korn (*Stalemate*, p. 190) makes an unsourced claim that "in December, Soviet leaders made an in-principle commitment to Sadat, Fawzi and Riad for supply of the SA-3," but without Soviet personnel—which now appears to be an understatement.
44. Serkov, *Liniya fronta*, p. 119.
45. For example, A.V. Zhdanov, "Egipet, 1969–1970," in Safonov et al., *Grif*, p. 80.
46. Riad, *Struggle for Peace*, pp. 112–14; Gordon, *Thirty Hours*, p. 103.
47. Interview by Hayyim Tal, Israel Channel 1 Television, Moscow, August 2007.
48. See, e.g., Timur Latypov, "V efire obshchat'sya tol'ko po-arabski ..." *Vremya i Dengi*, 1 August 2006, www.e-vid.ru/index-m-192-p-63-article-14434
48. Evgeny Lashenko, interviewed in Komlev, "Voyna u piramid."

49. "Delegates Report to Nasser," *NYT*, 13 December 1969.
50. Heikal, *Road to Ramadan*, p. 79. The "motorcade took four hours to reach city center [of Benghazi]," Reuters, "Libyans Laud Nasser despite Talks Failure," *Calgary Herald*, 29 December 1969, p. 2. Nicholas Hagger's eyewitness account (*The Libyan Revolution: Its Origins and Legacy, a Memoir and Assessment*, London: O Books, 2009, p. 71) confirms the story.
51. Batitsky's standing in the Soviet establishment is illustrated by his having personally executed former NKVD boss Lavrenty Berya in 1953. Sergo Berya, *Moy Otets: Lavrenty Berya*, Moscow: Sovremennik, 1994, p. 380. He commanded a Soviet air defense expeditionary force in the Chinese Civil War in 1950. Zolotarev et al., *Rossiya*, pp. 63–4.
52. Interviewed in Karyukin, "Kak Soyuz Izrail' nakazyval."
53. Pochtarev, "Kak podrezali kryl'ya fantomam." Smirnov retired as deputy commander of air defense forces.
54. Abdel-Malek Khalil, "Building a Wall of Missiles," *Al-Ahram Weekly*, 8 October 1998. The interview was conducted in Moscow, evidently in connection with the veterans' conference on the 1973 war, the proceedings of which were published in Vartanov et al., *Rukopozhatie*.
55. Interviewed in Galanin, "Boi nad piramidani."
56. "18-ya (28-ya) Krasnoznamennaya diviziya PVO osobogo naznacheniya," http://www.hubara-rus.ru/18zrd.html
57. Zolotarev et al., *Rossiya*, pp. 190–1.
58. Abramov, *Goluboe*, p. 43.
59. Zhayvoronok, "Vozvrashchenie k proshlomu," p. 45. The designation of "brigade" for components of the air defense division—which in usual Soviet practice was composed of "regiments"—was adopted to match the Egyptian system and thus to mask the Soviet presence. See "18-ya (28-ya) Krasnoznamennaya diviziya PVO osobogo naznacheniya."

11. THE SOVIET REGULARS MOVE IN

1. Temirova and Shunevich, "Vo vremya voyny."
2. Logachev, "Eto zabyt' nevozmozhno," p. 143. According to Presnukhin, Jews in his outfit were permitted to decline the mission after they guessed its destination. Gefele, "Napishi."
3. Temirova and Shunevich, "Vo vremya voyny."
4. Galanin, "Boi nad piramidani."
5. V. Rakovsky: "Napishi mne, mama, v Egipet," *Melitopolskiye Vedomosti* (Ukraine), 5 October 1999, quoted in Yefim Segal and Zinovy Dubrovski: "Ne dolzhny molchat'," *Novosty Nedelyi* (Tel Aviv), 2 March 2000, p. 19.
6. Personal communication from Zekharia Chesno, Jerusalem, 13 December 2000.
7. "18-ya (28-ya) Krasnoznamennaya diviziya PVO osobogo naznacheniya" lists seven military districts from Kaliningrad to Baku that contributed *divizyons* or components. A year later, their replacements would be drawn from as far as the Far East.
8. Oleg Grachev, "Egipet: V pritsele—nebo," *Vecherny Chelyabinsk*, 27 May 1998.
9. Rakovsky, "Napishi mne."

10. Evgeny Poluektov, "Rabochaya situatsiya," http://www.clubvi.ru/news/2013/01/12/poluektov/. His account was submitted to a memoir competition held by the website of his school's alumni in 2012–13, and is written in the first person but subtitled "a story." As such, it might conflate several events and add fictionalized detail. For example, he describes the flights as taking off from a gigantic Soviet airbase in Hungary, but not Tököl; rather, he locates it at Székesfehérvár, southwest of Budapest. The only aviation site near this city was a heliport at nearby Seregélyes, which did not have runways for fixed-wing craft. Poluektov does refer to helicopters in numbers suitable for a heliborne *desantnik* (landing) regiment; http://wikimapia.org/27407007/Apron
11. Nastenko, "Aviatsiya v Egipte." Poluektov likewise describes landing at Cairo-West during an Israeli attack that he attributes to Skyhawks—which never operated around Cairo.
12. The altitude for the 4 November sortie is given as 700 feet. Cohen, *Best Defense*, p. 293.
13. Col. Shim'on Yiftah, "Al tilim be-Mitzrayim," *Ma'arakhot*, 217–18 (September 1971), http://maarachot.idf.il/PDF/FILES/9/108389.pdf.
14. Zhirokhov and Nicolle, "Unknown Heroes," Part 2.
15. Stavitsky, "Krylataya fraza." The author was of the class of '73, so was still in an early stage of his studies. In the summer of 1970 he spent several months at an Egyptian aircraft repair facility at Helwan.
16. AC, Ben-Porat testimony, p. 73.
17. Gordon, *Thirty Hours*, pp. 104–6.
18. Shalom, *Phantoms*, vol. 1, pp. 564–80.
19. Igor' Kulikov, "Kak izrail'tyane u egiptyan radar ukrali," *Soldat udachi*, 1 (Moscow) (2000). Kulikov was the interpreter for the Soviet adviser to the 3rd Mechanized Division, Maj. Taras Panchenko.
20. Interviewed in Latypov, "O Druzhbe." Antonov, a Second World War veteran, found his old tank model T-34 still in use with his Egyptian advisees.
21. Foreign Ministry Research Department to Europe 3 Department, Foreign Ministry, 25 January 1970, quoting US embassy official [H.H.] Stackhouse. ISA HZ-4604/5. Heikal first broke the story on 23 January; Korn, *Stalemate*, p. 176.
22. The Israelis' proud description of the P-12 as "state-of-the art" has been challenged in view of its original introduction in the 1950s. However, the model was continually updated into the 1970s, and the Ras Gharib station had continued functioning despite repeated IAF bombings. Uri Milstein, *Ma'ariv*, 27 December 2015, http://www.maariv.co.il/news/military/Article-519169
23. Molodtsov, "Opyt."
24. Alizadeh, interview.
25. Milton Friedman, a reporter with JTA "whose connections with the Israel Embassy are known to Sedov," reported their talk the same day and stressed that "Sedov repeated this sentence several times." Nir Baruch, Israel embassy, Washington, 6 January 1970, ISA HZ-4604/5.
26. Robert S. Allen and John Goldsmith, "Inside Washington: Soviet General Commands Egypt's Suez Canal front," *News-Tribune* (Rome, GA), 20 April 1970, p. 2. Allen was

recently exposed as a collaborator with Soviet intelligence in the 1930s and 1940s; Samuel Nicholson, "A Most Unlikely Agent: Robert S. Allen," *Washington Decoded*, 11 September 2010, http://www.washingtondecoded.com/site/2010/09/a-most-unlikely-agent.html; Thomas E. Ricks, "Patton's Third Army Deputy Intel Officer Briefly Was on the KGB's Payroll," *Foreign Policy* (1 December 2010), http://ricks.foreignpolicy.com/posts/2010/12/01/pattons_third_army_deputy_intel_officer_briefly_was_on_the_kgbs_payroll

27. Vladimir I. Kryshtob, "I eta voyna byla by zavtra ...," *Novaya Gazeta*, 26 July 2004, http://2004.novayagazeta.ru/nomer/2004/53n/n53n-s21.shtml
28. This source was a former Soviet serviceman living in Israel, who related to the authors that his non-Jewish classmate was sent with a tank unit to Egypt in 1971. Other references include the *Shilka* gunner Shishlakov, who mentioned "tanks" but gave no further detail; Zubashenko, "Gennady Shishlakov." The announcement in 2014 of a planned memorial for Soviet casualties in Egypt listed tankists among the "experts" who were repatriated in 1972.
29. Slukhay, *Katyshkin*.
30. Khalil, "Building a Wall of Missiles"; Zolotarev et al., *Rossiya*, pp. 190–1.
31. Interview in *Yedi'ot Ahronot*, 2 March 1990, quoted in Korn, *Stalemate*, p. 229. Korn reconciles this date with the SAM units' supposed dispatch after Nasser's appeal in January 1970 by referring to the *deployment* of Popov's outfit on the canal front in March.
32. A.G. Smirnov, "O podgotovke i provedenii operatsii '*Kavkaz*,'" in Safonov et al., *Grif*, pp. 19–21. This is evidently the delegation referred to by Katyshkin's biographer: "at the end of the 1960s, a Soviet military contingent arrived in Egypt ... [including] air force pilots, led by the famous ace from the Great Patriotic War, HSU Gen S[emen]. I. Kharlamov, an air defense division under General ... Smirnov, radiotechnic, engineering and other detachments." Slukhay, *Katyshkin*.
33. Kryshtob, "I eta voyna byla by zavtra ..."; Konstantin Popov ("Divizyony dayut ognya," in Meyer et al., *Togda*, p. 306), relates a similar *Strela* incident while his *divizyon* was stationed in Alexandria in March 1970. He describes the plane, however, as an Egyptian An-24 airliner.
34. Abraham Rabinovich, *Sefinot Cherbourg*, Re'ut (Israel): Meltzer, 2001, pp. 137, 138–9, 145.
35. V.M. Pak, "Vspominaya shtab flota," in Meyer et al., *Togda*, p. 277.
36. Kryshtob, "I eta voyna byla by zavtra ..."
37. G[avri'el] Strassman, *Ma'ariv*, 29 December 1969, p. 2, quoting Claire Hollingworth in the *Daily Telegraph* the same day.
38. L. Zakharov, "Komandirovka v Egipet," p. 31.
39. Vinogradov, "Sovetskie voiny v Egipte," p. 11.
40. Roy Macartney, "US Is Disillusioned over Middle East," *Sydney Morning Herald*, 30 January 1970, p. 2.
41. *SAR*, no. 42, pp. 110–12 and no. 43, pp. 112–13.
42. Sakharov, *High Treason*, p. 223; emphasis added.

43. Rubinstein, *Red Star*, p. 107.
44. Lt-Col. Aleksei Zhdanov, "Egipet 1969–70," in Safonov et al., *Grif*, pp. 80, 97. Zhdanov, an engineer, had previously been sent to Egypt in 1964.
45. Smirnov, "O podgotovke," pp. 21–5.
46. "Flight Log" for January 1970, IAF website, http://www.iaf.org.il/837-he/IAF.aspx
47. Shalom, *Phantoms*, vol. 2, pp. 649–51, 725–6.
48. Laqueur, *Confrontation*, p. 4. The anachronistic claim that Nasser's trip to Moscow *followed* the Abu Zaabal raid apparently originated in Sadat's 1971 speech at Tanta, when he also said that Nasser went despite being ill with the flu—a fabrication that will be discussed below. By then, the Israeli press had accepted Nasser's trip on 22 January as fact and Sadat was quoted only to explain the circumstances. Shmu'el Segev, *Ma'ariv*, 5 January 1971, p. 2.
49. "Further Background on the Kosygin Letter," memorandum for the president from Kissinger, 6 February 1970. NARA, NSC files, country files, USSR, vol. VII, box 711.
50. Serkov, *Liniya fronta*, p. 132. Vlasenko died in hospital on 30 January; NBC correspondent Wilson Hall, quoted in a *NYT* report, *Ma'ariv*, 30 January 1970, p. 1.
51. Sadat's aforementioned speech at Tanta, which was not witnessed by a single foreign correspondent. The initial version, distributed by MENA, was flashed worldwide as the first confirmation that Soviet personnel had manned Egypt's air defense (Reuters, "Sadat Reveals Israeli Raid Killed 6 Soviet Missilemen," *NYT*, 5 January 1971, p. 1). It quoted Sadat as referring to 28 January, when indeed Dahshur was struck in *Priha-5*. The attacking Phantom pilots reported evading missiles and scoring hits that caused massive explosions. Shalom, *Phantoms*, vol. 2, p. 629. This might account for the Soviet casualties mentioned in more recently emerged sources as reported to Brezhnev on that day. See Chapter 18, note 18.
52. Unlike the other targets of *Priha-1*, the headquarters of the Egyptian II Army Corps at Tel el-Kebir was only about 35 kilometers from the canal. Serkov, *Liniya fronta*, pp. 129–30, 132; Shalom, *Phantoms*, vol. 2, pp. 613, 625.
53. Chapter 9, note 35. Serkov, *Liniya fronta*, p. 136; "Kniga Pamyati," http://www.hubara-rus.ru/heroes.html. After this repeat attack, the II Army Corps HQ was pulled back to Kafr Abbas, closer to Cairo.
54. Gorbunov, "Napishi mne."
55. Interviewed in Baranova, "Zashchitniki Otechestva."
56. Kryshtob, "I eta voyna byla by zavtra ..."
57. Viktor Rogozhinsky, interviewed in "Kak nash zemlyak."
58. Presnukhin, interviewed in Gefele, "Napishi."
59. Amnon Sella, *The Value of Human Life in Soviet Warfare*. London: Routledge, 1992, p. i.
60. The closest target that Israel reported that day was at Maadi, just across the Nile from Giza. This upscale district was described, however, as the quarters of "most of the foreign advisers," and so was apparently where the 6th Division's advisers were billeted. This would also explain Brezhnev and Grechko's reference to "the advisers' house."
61. The third fatality may refer either to the second attack or to the adviser who died in hos-

pital after the first. By Goryachkin's reckoning, Soviet losses in Egypt for 1969–70 included thirty to forty killed, of whom about half were from the "advisers' *apparat*" and the rest from regular Soviet units. Goryachkin, "Sud'ba voennogo perevodchika v Egipte," pp. 175–80.
62. Serkov, *Liniya fronta*, p. 136.
63. Heikal, *Road to Ramadan*, p. 84.
64. *Ma'ariv*, 30 January 1970, p. 1.
65. Arab affairs correspondent, *Davar*, 30 January 1970, p. 1. Nasser had already met Vinogradov immediately after the 28 January air raid "to request urgent supply of means against air attack." Arab affairs correspondent, *Davar*, 29 January 1970, p. 1.
66. *NYT* Service, "Nasser Soviet Visit Bared," *St. Petersburg Times* (FL), 30 January 1970. The report quotes "diplomats in Cairo" that Nasser went primarily to request Soviet support in recapturing Shadwan Island in the Red Sea, which Israeli paratroops had raided the same day (22 January) and evacuated only while he was in Moscow; the air defense issue is listed among "other topics." This version was unlikely even at the time, given the sequence of events as well as the island's minor importance, and Heikal's account does not mention Shadwan at all—although he commented on it in *Al-Ahram* on 23 January, which casts further doubt whether he was then in Moscow with Nasser. But the theory that the visit was triggered by Shadwan rather than the depth bombings is still proposed (e.g., by Israeli military historian Avraham Zohar, "Ha'im levatze'a haftzatzot omeq be-milhemet ha-hatashah," in Yehudit Reifen-Ronen and Avraham Zohar (eds), *Yahasei medinah-tzava be-Yisrael 1948–1974*, Tel Aviv: Golda Meir Memorial Fund and Tel Aviv University, 2004, http://goldameir.org.il/archive/home/he/1/1133282899.html#a003
67. Department of State telegram 034236 from secretary of state to American embassy, Tel Aviv, 1 February 1970. NARA, NSC country files, ME–Israel, box 605.
68. Ronen Bergman and Gil Meltzer, *The Yom Kippur War: Moment of Truth*, updated edn, Tel Aviv: Yedi'ot Ahronot-Hemed, 2004, pp. 174–88.
69. Eliyahu Ze'ira, *Myth versus Reality: The October 1973 War; Failures and Lessons*, Tel Aviv: Miskal, 2004, pp. 112, 116, 145–63. Maj.-Gen. Shlomo Gazit, who succeeded Ze'ira as MI chief, conceded after Marwan's death that there were indications he was a double agent, but also alternative interpretations. Gazit, "Mot ha-Sokhen," *NRG* website, 4 July 2007, http://www.nrg.co.il/online/1/ART1/603/909.html. The latest publication supporting Ze'ira's position is former MI officer Shimon Mendes's *Sadat's Jihad*, Tel Aviv: Effi, 2015, which portrays Marwan as part of an elaborate Egyptian deception effort.
70. "A-G Closes Investigation into Former MI Chief Ze'ira," *Jerusalem Post*, 9 July 2012, http://www.jpost.com/NationalNews/Article.aspx?id=276764
71. Isabella Ginor and Gideon Remez, "Israel's Best Spy—Or a Master Double Agent? New Light from the Soviet Angle on the Mystery of Ashraf Marwan," in *Need to Know V: The Human Element*, Funen, Denmark: University of Southern Denmark Press, forthcoming.
72. Dudchenko, *Kanal*, Part 1, Chapter 2.
73. Uri Bar-Joseph, *The Angel: Ashraf Marwan, the Mossad and the Yom Kippur War*, Tel Aviv:

Zmora-Bitan, Dvir, 2010, pp. 55–62. He was granted exclusive access to "four thick binders" of documents on Marwan. Though the book is obviously aimed at clearing the Mossad and Zamir of falling for a double agent, it is authoritative as to the dates and places of Marwan's meetings with the Israelis.

74. Sharaf has been identified as a KGB contact since 1955 and later a full-fledged agent. Sakharov, *High Treason*, p. 193; John Barron, *KGB: The Secret Work of Soviet Secret Agents*, New York: Bantam, 1974, pp. 70–8.
75. Bar-Joseph gives no specifics of Marwan's reports until 27 April 1970. By then, the Soviet presence in Egypt had been detected, and Marwan expressed his "contempt and hatred" for the Soviets "who were taking over Egypt and its army." Bar-Joseph admits that such patriotism was rather rich, coming from an Egyptian who was ostensibly selling out to his country's arch-enemy. But this does not affect Bar-Joseph's certainty that Marwan was not being operated by his Egyptian superiors. Bar-Joseph, *Angel*, p. 88.
76. Dudchenko also relates (Chapter 8) that "Hassan" met his Mossad contact for the second time in late September 1969 and claimed (to the Israeli's disbelief) that Egypt was already negotiating the delivery of SAM-3s and the Soviets were already deploying troops there. If not fictitious, this message was clearly *not* disinformation, and was aimed to deter Israeli air raids *until* the Soviet-manned SAMs could be deployed. But, if so, it was ignored, which was unusual for the Israelis in respect of Marwan's reports.
77. Aviel Magnezi, ynet website, 8 July 2012, http://www.ynet.co.il/articles/0,7340, L-4252869,00.html; AC, Ze'ira testimony, pp. 60–2, 88.
78. Bergman and Meltzer, *Yom Kippur War*, p. 177.
79. There are indications that the Israelis already had additional sources inside the Egyptian government, or that Marwan was recruited earlier. For example, Amit (in Rabin's presence) claimed on 26 February 1968 that "he had documentary evidence of USSR Deputy Foreign Minister Semenov's talks in Cairo." Harold H. Saunders, memorandum of conversation, 26 February 1968. NARA, national security file, country file Israel, vol. 8, box 141.
80. Ronen Bregman, "Ashraf Marwan and Israel's Intelligence Failure," in Asaf Siniver (ed.), *The October 1973 War: Politics, Diplomacy, Legacy*, London: Hurst, 2013, p. 208.
81. [Aryeh] Levin, embassy in Paris to Foreign Ministry, 6 February 1970; embassy in Vienna to Foreign Ministry, 10 February 1970, both in ISA HZ-4604/5; Bergman and Meltzer, *Yom Kippur War*, p. 177.
82. Rubinstein, *Red Star*, p. 107.
83. Kissinger, memorandum for the president, 18 February 1970, NARA WSAG Mtg 2/11/70 USSR and Egypt, H-files, box H-72, folder 2.
84. Jacob D. Beam, *Multiple Exposure: An American Ambassador's Unique Perspective on East–West Relations*, New York: Norton, 1978, pp. 247, 249.
85. Parker, *Politics of Miscalculation*, pp. 145–6.
86. Sonnenfeldt to Kissinger, 5 February 1970; Kissinger to Nixon, [misdated?] 4 February 1970, both in NARA NSC files, USSR, vol. VII, box 711.
87. Cohen, *Israel's Best Defense*, p. 294. Rabin effectively accepted Heikal's version when he

reportedly admitted, after the 1973 war, that he had initiated the bombings, for which "the Americans were very supportive," and "the bombings obliged Nasser to enlist direct Soviet intervention." Tzvi Y. Kesseh, letter to *Ha'aretz*, 27 January 2002, p. B2. Rabin is said to have made a special home visit to convey US support for the raids as a means of toppling Nasser, whereas both Dayan and Eban reportedly opposed the bombings for fear of Soviet response but were outvoted. Maj.-Gen. Emanuel Sakal, *"The Regulars Will Hold!" The Missed Opportunity to Prevail in the Defensive Campaign in the Yom Kippur War*, Tel Aviv: Ma'ariv, 2011, p. 48.

88. Eric Downton, *Daily Telegraph* from Beirut, *Ma'ariv*, 4 January 1970, p. 4.
89. Yosef Harif, *Ma'ariv*, 6 February 1970, pp. 11, 22. Eban's talk with the ambassador is dated "a few days ago." Another *Ma'ariv* commentator, Shmu'el Segev, who was connected more with intelligence sources than political ones like Harif's, had suggested a more realistic reading: that the Soviets would concentrate on improving Egypt's air defense, including SAM-3s; 5 February 1970, p. 9.

12. OPERATION *KAVKAZ* IS FORMALLY ORGANIZED

1. Safran, *Embattled Ally*, pp. 264–5. Apparently, the ultimate source is Heikal's *Road to Ramadan*.
2. Yaremenko's version is supported by the memoir of former British Foreign Secretary George Brown (*In My Way*, London: Penguin, 1972, pp. 223–4). He met Nasser on 5 January— that is, before the first "depth bombing"—and found him "over-involved with the Russians." The Egyptian president told Brown that he had twice responded in kind when "Khrushchev attacked me in public," but "if Mr. Kosygin were to attack me now, I would not say a word." On the road to the canal zone the same day, Brown encountered "large SAM trailers," but his escort's notes do not specify of which model. Bronwen Maddox, "George of Arabia," *Prospect* (London), April 2013, p. 48.
3. Yaremenko, "Sovetsko-egipetskoe voennoe sotrudnichestvo," pp. 45–6; Telephone interview with Yaremenko, 25 October 2000. Zolotarev (*Rossiya*, p. 189) states that Nasser several times offered to adhere to the Warsaw Pact "even tomorrow," quoting an article by I. Morozov, "Egipet, 1970 god: Skhvatka bez rukopashnoy," *Vecherny Klub*, 13 August 1994.
4. Telephone interview with Karen Brutents (Moscow), 17 October 2000.
5. Telephone interview with Dobrynin (Moscow), 10 October 2000.
6. Rubinstein, *Red Star*, p. 149.
7. Yaremenko, "Sovetsko-egipetskoe voennoe sotrudnichestvo," pp. 44–5.
8. Kissinger, *White House Years*, p. 561.
9. Korn, *Stalemate*, pp. 193, 301n22.
10. *SAR*, no. 47, pp. 121–2.
11. *SAR*, no. 48, pp. 123–5.
12. Abramov, *Goluboe*, pp. 50–6.
13. Pochtarev, "Kak podrezali kryl'ya fantomam."
14. Smirnov, "O podgotovke," p. 22.

15. Zhirokhov and Nicolle, "Unknown Heroes," Part 2.
16. Temirova and Shunevich, "Vo vremya voyny." Mishchenko was a colonel when interviewed in 2001.
17. This interpreter was sent to Syria under similar procedures. Mikhail Razinkov, "Siriya: Goryachiy oktyabr' 1973 goda," 9 September 2009, http://artofwar.ru/r/razinkow_m_w/text_0020.shtml
18. Gefele, "Napishi."
19. "It was especially chic for majors and colonels to wear a Soviet-uniform shirt and tie under the tunic." Boris Krokhin, "Zapiski 'Khabira'. Blizhniy Vostok ot Voyny i do Voyny: Glazami Sovetskogo Ofitsera," *Argumenty Nedeli*, 45, 79 (7 November 2007), http://argumenti.ru/history/n106/36060
20. Igor' Vakhtin, "Simfonichesky kontsert s vostochnym aktsentom," http://clubvi.ru/news/2014/06/16/remember/75%20vahtin/
21. Zhirokhov and Nicolle, "Unknown Heroes," Part 2.
22. Interviewed in Tereshchenko, "Egiptyanin."
23. Ol'ga Il'inskaya, "Voyna prizrakov," *Prem'er*, 49 (Cherepovets, Russia) (5 December 2001).
24. As decribed both by an air defense serviceman (Moiseenkov, "Soldat iz Kazakhstana") and a ground crewman at Beni Suef airbase (Oleg Yur'ev, "Ogon' na blizhnem vostoke," *LG-Zarechny*, 23 (Kuznetsk, Russia) (2006).
25. Zolotarev et al., *Rossiya*, p. 193.
26. Col. Stanislav V. Gribanov, *Az vozdam*, Moscow: Voyennoye Izdatel'stvo, 1998, p. 309. This book is a virulent anti-Semitic tract published by a military institution.
27. Nastenko, "Aviatsiya v Egipte," pp. 58–9.
28. Gordon, *Thirty Hours*, p. 73: IAF website for February 1970, http://www.iaf.org.il/838-7142-he/IAF.aspx
29. Hagger, *Libyan Revolution*, p. 75. He dates his arrival in Egypt the same day as the factory bombing at Abu Zaabal, 12 February, and his missile incident a few days later. He was staying at "a cheap hotel" on the Alexandria waterfront where "all the other guests were Russians."
30. Smirnov, "O podgotovke," p. 41.
31. Lt-Gen. Alexey Y. Kostin, "Pamyat' khranit," in Safonov et al., *Grif*, p. 100.
32. Zolotarev et al., *Rossiya*, p. 192.
33. Interviewed in Il'inskaya, "Voyna prizrakov."
34. *Youngstown Vindicator* (OH), 2 February 1970, p. 11.
35. Korn, *Stalemate*, p. 181.
36. Dave McManis, "Mid-air Collision between US and Soviet Aircraft," 11 March 1970. NARA, NSC country files, USSR, vol. VII, box 711.
37. Neither was a fatal collision between two Soviet MiG-21s in March 1971, which is known only from the journal of Kutakhov's deputy. Col.-Gen. Nikolay Kamanin, *Skryty Kosmos*, Moscow: Infortekst-IF, 1995–7, 4 vols., vol. 4, p. 247, http://airport-krr.ucoz.ru/index/0-4465
38. *SAR*, 20 March 1970, no. 53, pp. 138–9. Dobrynin's report (no. 54, pp. 139–40) gives

the precise time ("the evening of March 17") when, according to Kissinger, the Americans "learned unexpectedly 'from a reliable source' about shipments of the very latest Soviet SAM-3 type missiles ... The Israeli Government learned about this after they [the Americans] did, but 'independently of them.'"

39. Heikal, *Road to Ramadan*, p. 88.
40. Shalom Rosenfeld, *Ma'ariv*, 2 March 1970, p. 9.
41. *Ma'ariv*, 22 March 1970, p. 2.
42. Smirnov, "O podgotovke," pp. 26–8. He does not give the location, but it was evidently at an airbase in the Egyptian interior.
43. Smirnov, interviewed in Khalil, "Building a Wall of Missiles"; Anatoly Podalka, interviewed in Il'inskaya, "Voyna prizrakov."
44. IAF website for February 1970, http://www.iaf.org.il/838-7142-he/IAF.aspx. Shalom, *Phantoms*, vol. 2, p. 715, quotes diplomatic exchanges in which the Nixon administration discouraged such a "token attack."
45. Smirnov, "O podgotovke," p. 29.
46. IAF website for February 1970, http://www.iaf.org.il/838-7142-he/IAF.aspx. The figures attributed to Egyptian sources—300 to 400 fatalities a day for a total of 4,000—look suspiciously like those given by Heikal for the bombings of SAM-2 sites in the summer and fall of 1969, but the description of the sites as built for SAM-3s establishes that this refers to a separate operation.
47. AC, Allon testimony, pp. 29–30. Allon stressed that he was speaking from memory, but repeated the date in March twice. He did not mention whether the missiles' Soviet identity was discussed. The cabinet session was held as a ministerial committee on defense, whose deliberations are classified.
48. *SAR*, no. 55–6, pp. 142–4.
49. *SAR*, no. 57, 9 April 1970, and no. 58, 10 April 1970, pp. 144–6.

13. THE SOVIET–ISRAELI BATTLE IS JOINED

1. Shalom, *Phantoms*, vol. 2, p. 727.
2. Special Action Group, "Increased Soviet Involvement in UAR Military Operations: Contingencies and Options," 16 February 1970. NARA, SAG Meetings 3/20/70, box H-043, folder 5. Emphasis added.
3. Nastenko, "Aviatsiya v Egipte," p. 60.
4. However, he misdates this development as "late February," whereas it actually occurred on 13 April.
5. IAF website pages for 8 April, http://www.iaf.org.il/839-7158-he/IAF.aspx, and 13 April 1970, http://www.iaf.org.il/839-7159-he/IAF.aspx. Emphasis added.
6. Sherman, *Bunkers*, p. 28; emphasis added.
7. Heikal, *Road to Ramadan*, p. 85.
8. Kass, *Soviet Involvement*, pp. 162–3.
9. Dishon, *Middle East Record 1969–1970*, Part 5, p. 1275.
10. Amir Rappaport and Omri Essenheim, *NRG* news site, 13 August 2005, http://www.nrg.co.il/online/1/ART/969/882.html

11. Zhirokhov and Nicolle, "Unknown Heroes," Part 2. He lists such encounters on 13, 18 and 29 April, in all of which "when Soviet aircraft rose to meet them, [the Israelis] obeyed their orders and broke away."
12. "Policy Background: The Soviet Union Assumes Com[b]atant Role Against Israel," embassy in Washington to Foreign Ministry, 28 April 1970, p. 3; Information Department to all [Israeli] missions, 6 May 1970, both in ISA. HZ-4605/2.
13. William B. Quandt, *Decade of Decisions: American Policy toward the Arab–Israeli Conflict, 1967–1976*, Berkeley: University of California Press, 1977, p. 95. He attributes the Heikal version only to "Egyptian sources" and concedes that "evidence in support" of the Israeli view that the Soviet decision was taken by December 1969 "if not earlier" had already been presented by the time of writing, citing Uri Ra'anan, "The USSR and the Middle East: Some Reflections on the Soviet Decision-Making Process," *Orbis*, 17, 3 (Fall 1973). Quandt joined the NSC staff in 1972.
14. Ford, "Growth of the Soviet Commitment," p. 121.
15. Korn, *Stalemate*, p. 201.
16. Foreign Ministry to embassy in Washington, 28 April 1970, ISA HZ-4605/2.
17. Text at http://www.mfa.gov.il/MFA/Foreign+Relations/Israels+Foreign+Relations+since+1947/1947–1974/14+Soviet+Involvement+in+the+War+of+Attrition.+Gov.htm
18. Mordechai Gazit, "Conversation of M.G. with David [Primakov] 8 October [1971]," p. 9, ISA A-7037/17.
19. Personal, "top secret" letter from Arthur [Lurie], Foreign Ministry deputy director-general, to Aharon Remez (ambassador in London, father of the present writer), undated but before the latter's reply on 6 May 1970, both in authors' possession. Lurie's letter is handwritten, as "I'd rather not dictate [it] to a secretary." Their exchange followed Remez's formal protest to the ministry, 2 May 1970. ISA HZ-4605/2.
20. Sherman, *Bunkers*, pp. 103, 107.
21. Yodfat, *Soviet Union and the Middle East*, p. 91.
22. Arad, *1000 ha-yamim*, pp. 220–1.
23. Schueftan, *Attrition*, pp. 251, 254–9.
24. Korn, *Stalemate*, pp. 175ff, 190–2.
25. William B. Quandt, *Peace Process: American Diplomacy and the Arab–Israeli Conflict since 1967*, Washington, DC: Brookings Institute, 1993, pp. 85, 528–9n44.
26. Gawrych, *Albatross*, pp. 114–16, 125n49.
27. Badry, *Ramadan War*, p. 45.
28. For example, Maj.-Gen. N. Kupenko in *Krasnaya Zvezda*, 24 September 1969, quoted in Kass, *Soviet Involvement*, p. 221. Her study presents this as a retort to opposition from the "Strategic Forces" faction in the Soviet military, which belittled the importance of regional assets "in the era of ICBMs," in contrast to the "Theater Forces" group (which included Gorshkov, Kasatonov and even Grechko).
29. Col. Vladimir Akimov, "Zaboty komanduyushchego okrugom," http://www.vko.ru/biblioteka/zaboty-komanduyushchego-okrugom
30. Eli Landau, *Ma'ariv*, 15 May 1970, p. 1.

31. Military correspondent, *Ma'ariv*, 6 May 1970, p. 18.
32. Zhirokhov, *Rozhdennye Voynoy*, Chapter 6. He apparently misdates this operation: Israel reported an auxiliary naval vessel sunk and a landing craft damaged by Egyptian frogmen on 7 February 1970. Zhirokhov appears to suggest that the Soviets would never attack a civilian ship, which is borne out by Kryshtob, below. In a previous raid on Eilat on 16 November 1969, two merchant ships (claimed by the Egyptians as naval) were damaged.
33. *Ma'ariv*, 26 July 1970, p. 3.
34. Shalom, *Phantoms*, vol. 2, p. 1011. A Soviet rear-admiral's pennant was spotted on a landing vessel in Port Said on 10 June; [Shimshon] Arad, Israeli embassy, The Hague, to Foreign Ministry, 18 June 1970. Jerusalem responded that the officer might have come to survey the bombing damage. Yosef Hadas, Research Department, to Hague embassy, 19 June 1970, both in ISA HZ-4605/2.
35. Zak, *Forty Years' Dialogue*, p. 177. As 7 June was a Sunday when there are no plenary Knesset sessions, Eban's statement must have been made to the closed Defense and Foreign Affairs Committee. It was not reported in the next day's press. Evidently to sidestep censorship, on Tuesday Zak alluded in his column (*Ma'ariv*, 9 June 1970, p. 9) to such a warning over an incident in "an Egyptian harbor" and wrote that "Israel published nothing about it, trying to make the Russians understand we are not interested in a confrontation with them." Dayan's 1975 statement is quoted on p. 180.
36. Palit, *Return to Sinai*, p. 14.
37. *SAR*, no. 60, p. 152n1.
38. *SAR*, no. 62, p. 157n7.
39. *SAR*, no. 59 and no. 60n2, pp. 148–9, 152.
40. Kissinger, *White House Years*, p. 577.
41. *SAR*, no. 62, pp. 156–7.
42. *SAR*, no. 59, pp. 148–9n3.
43. *SAR*, no. 63, p. 162.
44. Radio Moscow program "This Week," quoted by Shmu'el Segev, *Ma'ariv*, 23 June 1970, p. 9.
45. Nastenko, "Aviatsiya v Egipte," pp. 58–9, 64; Zhirokhov, *Rozhdennye Voynoy*, Chapter 6.
46. Zhirokhov, "Soviet Pilots," Part 2.
47. Shalom, *Phantoms*, vol. 2, p. 1029. This may be the origin of a claim made in 1989 by a former Soviet pilot, who had served in Egypt in 1970, to an Israeli diplomat that "Soviet pilots had downed Israeli aircraft." Aryeh Levin, *Envoy to Moscow: Memoirs of an Israeli Ambassador 1988–92*, London: Frank Cass, 1996, p. 202.
48. Aleksandr Akimenkov, *Na poroge inogo mira*, Moscow: Aviko, 2002, p. 17.

14. "A FAMOUS INDISCRETION" AS THE AIR WAR PEAKS

1. John le Carré, *The Secret Pilgrim*, New York: Knopf, 1990 (p. 127, Ballantine paperback edition).
2. *Egyptian Gazette*, 19 July 1972, cited in Rubinstein, *Red Star*, p. 189.

3. For example, Quandt, *Peace Process*, p. 136.
4. Ibid.; Golan: *Soviet Policies*, p. 78; Rubinstein, *Red Star*, p. 190.
5. Kenneth W. Stein, *Heroic Diplomacy*, New York: Routledge, 1999, p. 65.
6. Quandt, *Peace Process*, p. 135.
7. *SAR*, no. 65, p. 168.
8. *FRUS* N-XII, no. 170, editorial note.
9. *SAR*, no. 64, p. 166.
10. E.R.F. Sheehan, *The Arabs, Israelis, and Kissinger: A Secret History of American Diplomacy in the Middle East*. New York: Reader's Digest, 1976, p. 22; Seymour M. Hersh, *The Price of Power*, New York: Summit Books, 1983, pp. 227–8.
11. Kissinger, *White House Years*, pp. 579–81; emphasis in original.
12. Kissinger, *Years of Upheaval*, Boston: Little, Brown, 1982, p. 202; emphasis added.
13. Marquis Childs, "Rogers Honeymoon Coming to End," *Times* (Geneva, NY), 21 July 1970, p. 9. Childs's report that Kissinger had gained the sobriquet "Nixon's grey cardinal" appears in a dispatch that Dobrynin sent to Gromyko the same day. *SAR*, no. 71, p. 182.
14. Debriefing report, quoted in Shalom, *Phantoms*, vol. 2, pp. 843–5. This and the corresponding page on the IAF website (http://www.iaf.org.il/840-7179-he/IAF.aspx) are the only references found so far to Bir Arida as an air base at this time. The location is on the road connecting Ras Zaafrana on the Gulf of Suez with Beni Suef on the Nile; a section of highway may have been used like Katameya as an "ambush" springboard for Soviet aircraft. Evgeny Groisman and Oleg Granovsky ("Spetsoperatsii: Ognevye nalety," *Bratishka*, April 2011, http://bratishka.ru/archiv/2011/4/2011_4_16.php) specify the Soviet planes were scrambled from Beni Suef.
15. Chazov, *Zdorov'e i vlast'*, p. 54. Besides Nasser's physical ailments, "in tête-à-tête meetings he did not hide his depressed mood and his concern about a [further] deterioration of his health."
16. Smirnov, "O podgotovke," pp. 29–30.
17. Eli Landau, *Ma'ariv*, 1 July 1970, p. 2. IAF website history page for 30 June 1970, http://www.iaf.org.il/840-7183-he/IAF.aspx, states the raid was aimed at "new SAM batteries," which were detected the same day after being advanced "up to the front line."
18. Smirnov, "O podgotovke," p. 31; personal communication to the authors from a Russian source who requested anonymity, 5 July 2001. The WSO of this Phantom was rescued by an IAF helicopter.
19. Heikal's weekly column in *Al-Ahram*, 9 July 1970, quoted in *Ma'ariv* the same day, p. 1.
20. Khandanyan, "Zharkoe nebo." Malyauka's competence and courage is likewise described by his superior, then-Maj. Ivan K. Kovalenko, in Boris Ershov, "Oni zashchishchali chest' strany, kotoraya ikh zabyvaet," *Karavan* (Tver, Russia), undated (2002?), http://www.karavan.tver.ru/html/n332/article5.php
21. Smirnov, "O podgotovke," p. 30.
22. Personal communication from Peer, 11 October 2000; Lieblich, *Seasons*, p. 68.
23. Lieblich, *Seasons*, p. 66.
24. Zubashenko, "Gennady Shishlakov." The veteran's claim of "shooting down an American

Mirage" refers to an engagement that occurred several months after his arrival in Egypt, when his *Shilka* was attached to Kutyntsev's SAM-3 *divizyon* in the canal zone. He correctly identified the plane as French-built, but described the pilot as American even though the latter bailed out over Israeli-held territory and was not captured; the claim presumably reflects the Soviet troops' indoctrination. Ironically, Shishlakov notes that the "highly literate" Kutyntsev "had fought in Vietnam."

25. Arieh O'Sullivan, "The Odd Bird," *Jerusalem Post*, 24 May 2000.
26. Zhirokhov and Nicolle, "Unknown Heroes," Part 2
27. Facsimile at http://www.hubara-rus.ru/foto/large/malauka000296.jpg.
28. Schueftan, *Attrition*, p. 354.
29. Shmu'el Segev, *Ma'ariv*, 24 December 1970, p. 9; Col. Shim'on Yiftah, "Al tilim be-Mitzrayim."
30. An Israeli intelligence report on 8 October 1973 listed "seven impacts in the Refidim area, possibly surface-to-surface missiles." The southern front commander, Shmu'el Gonen, stated that seven missiles struck his command post at Umm-Hashiba, west of Refidim. AC, Gonen testimony, Part 3, p. 47; Final Report, vol. 4, p. 1265.
31. Schueftan, *Attrition*, p. 354.
32. Interviewed in Komlev, "Voyna u piramid." Lashenko names the base as "Sahara," which is otherwise unknown; his description fits Luxor, where the IAF destroyed ten Tu-16s in 1967. Aleksandr Rodinov, a ground crewman who served at Beni Suef airbase from May 1971 to June 1972, described "Egyptian Tu-16s operated by Soviet pilots" as based there along with a Soviet MiG-21 squadron. Yur'ev, "Ogon'."
33. Schueftan, *Attrition*, pp. 349–51. He also cites Sadat's claim after Nasser's death that only the Soviet promises to Nasser in Moscow persuaded Sadat to accept the Rogers plan. Schueftan notes correctly that this was published in Sadat's 1977 autobiography, when he had no interest in highlighting his initial opposition to the US proposal.
34. In 1990, Elliott Richardson related to Korn (*Stalemate*, pp. 371–2) that at Nasser's funeral Sadat expressed his desire to improve relations with Washington.
35. *SAR*, no. 63, p. 165.
36. *SAR*, no. 66, pp. 168–9. Dobrynin's report of this meeting (no. 67) omits the matter entirely.
37. *SAR*, no. 66, p. 169n4.
38. IAF website, http://www.iaf.org.il/841-7199-he/IAF.aspx, attributes the loss to a missile. Shalom (*Phantoms*, vol. 2, pp. 924–5), quotes Levitov that this was the crew's impression because multiple missiles were fired at them, but concludes that the plane was actually struck by cannon shells.
39. Levitov is mentioned in Shalom, *Phantoms*, vol. 2, pp. 924–5, and Lieblich, *Seasons*, p. 38; Zamir is only mentioned in Lieblich, *Seasons*, p. 35.
40. Philip Benn (Washington), *Ma'ariv*, 7 July 1970, p. 1.
41. The accident was first disclosed in Shalom, *Phantoms*, vol. 1, p. 399, based on the squadron logbook. It occurred over water, as the two crewmen drowned after bailing out too low. IAF memorial pages on the two crewmen only give the date of their death "in the

course of duty" on 6 March 1970. Contemporary press reports about their funerals did not even mention their IAF affiliation; *Ma'ariv*, 8 March 1970, p. 3 and 9 March, p. 7. The IAF also withheld the model of the plane shot down on 2 April (as against three MiG-21s), but the Syrians exhibited an F-4 tail. Eli Landau, *Ma'ariv*, 3 April 1970, p. 2. The crewmwen were captured and not returned until 1974.

42. Spector, *Loud and Clear*, p. 198.
43. On 13 July, that is before the next Phantom was lost on 18 July, US intelligence was quoted that Israel had lost *five* F-4s in combat alone, two more than admitted by the Israelis. "Secret Jets to Israel Hinted," *Palm Beach Post*, 13 July 1970, pp. 1, 5.
44. Hod, interviewed by Yaqir Elqariv and Yaron Katz, *Heyl ha-Avir* (IAF Magazine), 140 (June 1984), p. 18.
45. Gordon, *Thirty Hours*, p. 87.
46. Korn, *Stalemate*, p. 247, based on an interview with Bergus.
47. Nixon approved supply of the EW pods two days after Meir requested them urgently on 2 July, that is, after the first two Phantoms were shot down. Quandt, *Decade of Decisions*, p. 101n43.
48. Gordon, *Thirty Hours*, p. 87.
49. *Ma'ariv*, 9 July 1970, p. 4.
50. *SAR*, no. 71, p. 182; emphasis added.
51. Embassy in the Soviet Union to Department of State, 11 July 1970, *FRUS* N-XII, no. 180. Note 1 clarifies that Kissinger approved the protest.
52. AP, "Nasser Flies Home after Soviet Talks," *Gazette* (Niagara Falls, NY), 17 July 1970, p. 1; *Davar*, 19 July 1970, p. 3.
53. He may have attempted to mislead the Soviets, assuming they would learn of his remark though the targets he mentioned were censored from local press reports. Naphtali Lau-Lavie, *Balaam's Prophecy: Eyewitness to History, 1939–1989*, Cranbury, NJ: Cornwall Books, 1998, p. 261; *Davar*, 17 July 1970, p. 1.

15. AN MIA MYSTERY AND SOVIET INTELLIGENCE METHODS

1. Charts, painting and photo of wreckage at http://www.hubara-rus.ru/kavkaz3.html#18.07.70
2. Lt-Gen. Dani Halutz, *Straightforward*, Tel Aviv: Yedi'ot Ahronot-Hemed, 2010, p. 63. A future IAF commander and IDF chief of staff, he was no. 4 in Hetz's formation.
3. *Ma'ariv*, 19 July 1970, p. 3.
4. Shalom, *Phantoms*, vol. 2, pp. 974–1002, 1144n42.
5. *Ma'ariv*, 20 July 1970, p. 3.
6. Menahem Eini, "Hetz Nafal," in Meirav Halperin and Aharon Lapidot (eds), *G Suit: Pages in the Log Book of the Israel Air Force*, Tel Aviv: Ministry of Defense Publishing, 1987, p. 68. Merom (*Ha-Hatashah*, p. 56) claims that Hetz tried to eject but was trapped in the cockpit. This agrees with the Russian version, but the account is unsourced and there is no indication how anyone but Hetz could provide it.
7. Valery Yaremenko, "Sovetsko-Egipetskoe voyennoe sotrudnichestvo nakanune i v khode

oktyabr'skoy voyny 1973 goda," in Vartanov et al., *Rukopozhatie*, pp. 52–3. Following the 18 July action, Heikal was quoted by TASS as calling the downed pilot "an American citizen" who "arrived in Israel early in 1967." *Krasnaya Zvezda*, 23 July 1970.

8. Lieblich, *Seasons*, p. 31.
9. Zolotarev et al., *Rossiya*, pp. 194–5.
10. According to Yaremenko. The *Kavkaz* veterans' website states that Tolokonikov was awarded the Order of the Red Banner, but the commander of Air Defense turned down a recommendation to make him an HSU.
11. Maj. Ranit Ron, Daily Press Department, IDF spokesman, to the authors, 22 January 2001, and verbal response to the authors' second questionnaire.
12. Isabella Ginor, "Ta'alumat ha-tayyas Hetz," *Yedi'ot Ahronot*, 25 April 2001, pp. 1, 5–7.
13. Sharon interview on Israel Radio, 24 April 2001.
14. Defense Department Prisoner of War/Missing Personnel Office (DPMO), "The Gulag Study: 2005 [Fifth] Edition," website of the National Alliance of Families for the Return of America's Missing Servicemen, now accessible at https://books.google.co.il/books?id =PJVB2sdI8bEC&printsec=frontcover#v=onepage&q&f=false. DPMO has since been reorganized as Defense POW/MIA Accounting Agency (DPAA).
15. Alexander Zuyev, *Fulcrum: A Top Gun Pilot's Escape from the Soviet Empire*, New York: Warner, 1993, Chapter 8; Zuyev defected with his MiG-29 in 1989.
16. Copy of the Russian document provided by Mr Kass. The authors thank him and Gen. Lajoie.
17. The Russian team was reconstituted by Medvedev in 2011, but the Joint Commission reconvened only in May 2016 after an eleven-year hiatus. Mr. Kass and Gen. Lajoie had by then retired. The Russians again denied that US personnel had been held in the Gulag, and were willing to conduct archival research only themselves, according to specific information to be provided by the Americans. "20th Plenum of the U.S.–Russia Joint Commission on POW/MIAs, May 23–24, 2016, Pentagon Conference Center, Washington, D.C.," pp. 33, 37–8, http://www.dpaa.mil/portals/85/Documents/ USRJC/20th_Plenum_Minutes.pdf. The minutes do not mention any discussion of an Israeli case.
18. Col.-Gen. Dmitry Volkogonov, *Etyudy o vremeni*, Moscow: ACT-Novosti, 1998, pp. 50–1; letter to Yeltsin, 5 September 1994, pp. 361–2.
19. Andropov to Brezhnev, 21 May 1970, marked "approve" with Brezhnev's signature, 25 May. The Sevier plot was evidently one of the "operations against US and Israeli personnel ... to obtain reliable information" that Andropov reported to Brezhnev in 1974. Isabella Ginor, *Ha'aretz*, 28 August 1992, p. 1.
20. Two downed Israeli pilots, Peer and Avino'am Kaldas, related trying to pose as Russians (Lieblich, *Seasons*, pp. 17–18, 32). Neither of them was believed, but this option appears to have been discussed by, or even prescribed to, IAF airmen.
21. WSO Moshe Goldwasser was killed and his pilot Yigal Shochat seriously injured by Egyptian soldiers after bailing out on 3 August 1970. Shalom, *Phantom*, vol. 2, pp. 1091–2. In the Yom Kippur War, a downed Phantom pilot was "nearly killed" by peasants with a pitchfork; Lieblich, *Seasons*, p. 229.

22. Dudchenko, *Kanal*, Chapter 13.
23. Posting no. 17, 21 January 2010, http://artofwar.ru/comment/d/dudchenko_w_a/text_0120?PAGE=2
24. Eduard Gavrilov (dir), *Verbovshchik*, Moscow: Mentor Cinema, 1991, accessible at numerous websites, e.g. http://filmix.net/boeviki/15826-verbovschik-1991.html
25. For the outstanding work done by the French activist Denis Sellem in this area, see the website of his Association Edouard Kalifat, http://aek.fr.free.fr/presentation.htm
26. Yiftah Spector, quoted in Shalom, *Phantoms*, vol. 1, p. 383.

16. SAM SUCCESSES AND A MIG DEBACLE

1. Lt. Presnukhin, who arrived in Egypt after the ceasefire, denied knowledge of such a practice but admitted hearing that certain parts of the *Shilka* had to be cleaned with alcohol "and maybe some of the boys lubricated their insides too." Gefele, "Napishi."
2. Skobanev, "Raketny zaslon."
3. Interviewed in Goryainov, "Prikazano zabyt'." The helicopters are described as heavy-lift Boeing Chinooks, which the IAF never operated.
4. Interviewed in "Kak nash zemlyak."
5. Korn, *Stalemate*, p. 254.
6. Memorandum of Conversation, 23 July 1970, *FRUS* N-XII, no. 184.
7. Shlomo Ginossar, London, *Davar*, 13 August 1970, p. 1.
8. Shmu'el Segev, *Ma'ariv*, 23 July 1970, p. 9.
9. Akimenkov, *Na poroge*, p. 17.
10. Eli Landau, *Ma'ariv*, 21 July 1970, p. 9.
11. For example, Skobanev, "Raketny zaslon," entry for 1 July 1970.
12. Krokhin, "Zapiski khabira."
13. Shalom, *Phantoms*, vol. 2, p. 1058.
14. Korn, *Stalemate*, pp. 252, 304n24. This may be either the source of, or confirmed by, Zhirokhov and Nicolle's unattributed account ("Unknown Heroes," Part 2): "On 25th July an Israeli Skyhawk was intercepted by two Soviet MiG-21s ... near the Suez Canal. The MiGs then pursued the Skyhawk across the canal, contrary to their standing orders. ... One of the MiG-21s launched an air-to-air missile which damaged the Israeli aircraft and obliged it to land." Whetten's earlier account (*Canal War*, p. 126) does not mention any damage to the Israelis, who "jettisoned their ordnance and withdrew."
15. Edward Kolcum, *Aviation Week*, translated in *Ma'ariv*, 12 January 1971, p. 16. This exclusive report dated the incident the day before the 3 August engagement. Shalom, *Phantoms*, vol. 2, pp. 1030–2; Gordon, *Thirty Hours*, p. 77.
16. "Lehappil et ha-Russim," IAF website for 30 July 1970, http://www.iaf.org.il/841-7201-he/IAF.aspx
17. Transcript of conversation between Dayan and "visitor" (Primakov), 31 August 1971, ISA A-7037/17, pp. 10–11. Dayan stressed that IAF planes were attacked "not in Cairo, or anywhere inside Egypt." He later corrected the date to "about 30 July," but if he was referring to the dogfight on that date his description was disingenuous: it did occur "inside

Egypt," and was initiated by the Israelis. Primakov answered only, "really, I don't know about this."
18. Shalom, *Phantoms*, vol. 2, p. 1039.
19. Eli Landau, *Ma'ariv*, 26 July 1970, p. 1. Russian accounts also mark a change in IAF tactics at this point, partly as apologetics for the Soviets' debacle on 30 July. The "aggressive and probably unauthorized action on the part of the Soviet pilots ... convinced the Israeli Air Force to cancel its existing unofficial 'truce' with the Soviet units [and] 'teach the Soviet pilots a lesson.'" Zhirokhov and Nicolle, "Unknown Heroes," Part 2.
20. Shalom, *Phantoms*, vol. 2, p. 742.
21. Akimenkov, *Na poroge*, p. 17: A largely corresponding Israeli account specifies that the clash took place at the northern end of the canal.
22. Lau-Lavi, *Balaam's Prophecy*, pp. 260–1; Mordechai Gazit, "Conversation of M.G. with David [Primakov] on 8 October [1971]," ISA A-7037/17, p. 9.
23. *Davar*, p. 1 and *Ma'ariv*, p. 3, 31 July 1970. Late editions of *Ma'ariv* on the 30th cited a report in the London *Daily Express* that Nasser had reported the Soviet planes' loss in a cabinet meeting.
24. *Ma'ariv*, 3 August 1970, p. 3.
25. For example, thirty-two pages in Shalom, *Phantoms* (vol. 2, pp 1039–72).
26. "Il diario del Colonel Ivlev," *JP4 Mensile di Aeronautica e Spazio*, January 1993, quoted in Shalom, *Phantoms*, vol. 2, Chapter 35. A detailed account in Zhirokhov and Nicolle, "Unknown Heroes," Part 2, is clearly derived mainly from Israeli and Egyptian sources. It does, however, name three of the four Soviet pilots killed (Zhuravlev, Yurchenko and Yakovlev), which had to come from Russian materials.
27. Zolotarev et al., *Rossiya*, p. 259.
28. Zhirokhov states that in the War of Attrition a total of "seven or nine Soviet pilots were killed, depending [on] which source is chosen." "Unknown Heroes," Part 2.
29. Platunov, "Provaly v pamyati."
30. Interviewed in Zhirokhov and Nicolle, "Unknown Heroes," Part 2.
31. Ze'ev Schiff (ed.), *The Might of the IDF: Military and Security Encyclopedia*, Air Force volume, Tel Aviv: Revivim, 1981, p. 143.
32. [Gen. William] Momyer, "Resume of My Conversations with Hod, October 27," 2 November 1971, IRISNUM 01011311. The Soviet pilots' tours of duty were actually for at least a year.
33. UPI and AFP, *Davar*, 4 August 1970, p. 1.
34. Kamanin, *Skryty Kosmos*, vol. 4, p. 116, http://airport-krr.ucoz.ru/index/0–4386. Kamanin was Kutakhov's deputy for space operations.
35. Akimenkov, *Na poroge*, p. 20.
36. Zhirokhov and Nicolle, "Unknown Heroes," Part 2. Unless the incident is misdated, this account indicates that the tactics and limitations described by Akimenkov remained in effect after 30 July. Tsoy's official biography states that "between February and December 1970, he participated in combat operations in Egypt, ... made 42 sorties in a MiG-21, and

took part in two air battles." He was awarded the Order of the Red Banner, went on to become deputy chief test pilot of the Sukhoi bureau, and was made a hero of the Russian Federation in 1992; http://warheroes.ru/hero/hero.asp?Hero_id=7749

37. Zhayvoronok, "Vozvrashchenie k proshlomu," p. 47. Linkov, who served in Egypt after the ceasefire, wrote apparently from word of mouth: "often, after launching a missile, the Egyptians would flee the emplacements and were of little use to the Soviet specialists, who were frequently killed with the untrained crews." Bondarenko, "Mariupol'tsy."

38. Konstantin Popov, "O vypolnenii internatsional'nogo dolga nashimi voinami PVO v ARE s marta 1970 po mart 1971g.," in Safonov et al., *Grif*, pp. 127–8.

39. The ballad was written by Evgeny Grachev, a journalism graduate from Moscow State University who served as an interpreter in the trenches of Qantara. Egorin, *Egipet*, pp. 182–3.

40. Viktor Logachev, "Eto zabyt' nevozmozhno," in Safonov et al., *Grif*, pp. 144–6. The writer was at the time of writing in 1998 a senior researcher at the Institute of Military History.

41. Volodin, "Na Izrail'."

42. Aleksandr Pechenkin, interviewed in Grachev, "Nebo."

43. Interviewed in Galanin, "Boi nad piramidami."

44. Khandanyan, "Zharkoe."

45. Interviewed in Aleksandr Chernushevich, "Ego nazyvali 'rusi khabar,'" *Minskiy Kur'er*, 1221 (12 June 2007). A fully equipped "Lenin Room" for Soviet personnel was discovered in a Syrian artillery headquarters when it was captured by the IDF in the Yom Kippur War. Prof. Omri Ronen, commenting in *Zvezda* Magazine, 5 (2013), http://magazines.russ.ru/zvezda/2013/5/e15.html

46. AC, Dayan testimony, pp. 67–8. Dayan still "believed" it was a SAM-6 battery; Commission member Lt-Gen. Hayyim Laskov, a former chief of staff, corrected him that it was an "advanced SAM-3."

47. Popov, "O vypolnenii internatsional'nogo dolga," p. 118. Lev Gromov was deputy for air defense to the chief adviser/commander of Soviet forces, and thus outranked Smirnov. Okorokov, *Sekretnye voyny*, pp. 72, 74; "18-ya (28-ya) Krasnoznamennaya diviziya PVO osobogo naznacheniya," http://www.hubara-rus.ru/18zrd.html

48. Shalom, *Phantoms*, vol. 2, pp. 1099–104.

49. AC, Dayan testimony, p. 68. Dayan may have meant that Ne'eman's plane was effectively put out of action.

50. Shalom, *Phantoms*, vol. 2, pp. 1071–2.

51. Smirnov, "O podgotovke," p. 33. Upon Smirnov's return to Moscow in February 1971, Grechko praised his outfit's performance and (as Smirnov recalled) related Nasser's exchange with Brezhnev as if it took place on 3 August 1970 rather than 30 June. Nasser was not in Moscow in August, and Heikal had already published the story in July. But this reflects the Soviets' pride in the engagement.

52. Logachev, "Eto zabyt' nevozmozhno," p. 158.

17. CEASEFIRE VIOLATION SEALS A STRATEGIC GAIN

1. Recorded testimony of an unnamed Israeli pilot, in film shown at an IAF Association event to mark the fortieth anniversary of the War of Attrition, 26 November 2009.
2. Yeshayahu Ben-Porat et al., *Kippur*, Tel Aviv: Special Edition, first published in Hebrew (as *Ha-Mehdal*), December 1973, p 13; Gordon, *Thirty Hours*, p. 81. Bar-Siman-Tov's otherwise perceptive *War of Attrition*, which was written after the effects of the ceasefire violation became evident, makes no mention of it and describes the United States and the USSR as partners in arranging the ceasefire; see pp. 185–92.
3. Hersh, *Price of Power*, pp. 229, 230n*.
4. UPI and AFP, *Davar*, 4 August 1970, p. 1.
5. K.V. Pirogov, "Egipet darit svoe serdtse," in Meyer et al., *Togda*, p. 300. This conforms to the mention by Kapitanets (*Na Sluzhbe*, p. 256) that, by September 1970, Nasser had authorized an R&R facility for Soviet submariners at Mersa Matruh, indicating preparations for an extended presence.
6. Ben-Porat, *Kippur*, p 13.
7. *Ma'ariv*, 12 August 1970, p. 2.
8. John L. McLucas, director of National Reconnaissance Office, to Secretary of Defense Melvin Laird, "Taking Stock of the National Reconnaissance Program," 18 December 1972, p. 12, http://www.nro.gov/foia/declass/GAMHEX/HEXAGON/9.PDF
9. Nixon and Kissinger blamed State for "failure to take proper photographs of Egyptian positions ... which led Washington mistakenly to deny that Cairo was violating the agreement." Barry Rubin, *Secrets of State: The State Department and the Struggle over US Foreign Policy*, Oxford: Oxford University Press, 1985, p. 164.
10. Norman Polmar (*Spyplane: The U-2 History Declassified*, Osceola, WI: MBI, 2001, pp. 166–7) attributes mediating the ceasefire itself entirely to Kissinger.
11. Yisra'el Landress, *Davar*, 2 August 1970, p. 1.
12. Beam, *Multiple Exposure*, p. 248. US and British veterans' websites clarify that the U-2s were posted to Akrotiri, Cyprus, stopping over at an RAF base in Britain; one of them dates the first monitoring flight as late as 11 August: "both the CIA (Det G) and the USAF set about planning a 'fast move' of a U-2 ... the CIA were quicker off the mark." Alan Johnson, "U-2 Dragon Lady, RAF Akrotiri," http://www.u2sr71patches.co.uk/1sters.htm; Louis E. Dye, "Brief Bio: U-2 Program," http://roadrunnersinternationale.com/dye_l.html
13. Jeffrey Richelson, *The Wizards of Langley: Inside the CIA's Directorate of Science and Technology*, Boulder, CO: Westwood, 2001, pp. 138–9.
14. But even the operation's codename was known by 1976, when it was given in Joseph S. Roucek, "Cyprus in the Mediterranean Geopolitics," *Il Politico* (Univerity of Pavia, Italy), 41, 4 (1976), p. 737.
15. That is, 1968–72, John L. McLucas's term as NRO director. McLucas to Laird in ibid.
16. Craig A. Daigle, "The Limits of Détente: The United States, the Soviet Union, and the Arab–Israeli Conflict, 1969–1973," PhD thesis, George Washington University, 2008, p. 188.

17. Polmar, *Spyplane*, p. 167.
18. A telegram from the embassy to the State Department on 13 August (*FRUS* N-E4, no. 274), is signed by Beam.
19. Dayan, *Story of My Life*, p. 522.
20. V. Vinogradov, *Diplomatiya*, pp. 147–8. "Going somewhere" is a Russian euphemism for going to the latrine.
21. The chargé's son, Ambassador Michael Klosson, told the authors that his late father left no papers that could throw light on the incident. Personal communication, 8 April 2013.
22. Shlomo Ginossar, London, *Davar*, 13 August 1970, p. 1.
23. Daigle, "Limits of Détente," pp. 185–90.
24. Dayan, *Story of My Life*, p. 522.
25. Korn, *Stalemate*, p. 267, based on an interview with the attaché, Owen Zurhellen.
26. Quoted by Haggai Eshed, *Davar*, 12 August 1970, p. 2.
27. Gil Kessari, *Ma'ariv*, 12 August 1970, p. 2.
28. "A Blow to the Mideast Truce," *Los Angeles Times*, 12 August 1970, p. C6.
29. Quandt, *Decade of Decisions*, p. 107.
30. Dayan, *Story of My Life*, p. 522. Israeli delegates returned to the Jarring talks only on 29 December.
31. A total of twenty-nine missions were flown through 10 November, when due to Egyptian protests the U-2s were replaced by less easily detectable SR-71s. The U-2 findings were complemented with data from US communications intercepts. Daigle, "Limits of Détente," p. 189; Polmar, *Spyplane*, p. 167.
32. Schueftan, *Attrition*, p. 354.
33. "Scope of Pullout in Egypt Hazy," *Milwaukee Journal*, 20 July 1972, pp. 1–2.
34. UPI, "Sergey Vinogradov, 62, Dead," *NYT*, 28 August 1970.
35. Beam, *Multiple Exposure*, p. 248; embassy in the Soviet Union to Department of State, 3 September 1970, *FRUS* N-XII, no. 201.
36. Department of State to embassy in the Soviet Union, 5 September 1970, ibid., no. 203.
37. Sonnenfeldt to Kissinger, 16 September 1970, ibid., no. 206.
38. The Palestinians were only certified as ideologically progressive national-liberation forces, and adopted as Soviet protégés and instruments, after 1967. This began with the declaredly Marxist–Leninist PFLP, whose co-founder Wadia Haddad was recruited by the Soviets shortly after its formation in December 1967. The Mitrokhin Archive (p. 81, no. 65) names him as a KGB agent "since 1968," as did a 1974 memo from Andropov to Brezhnev that was obtained and published by the authors; Isabella Ginor, *Ha'aretz*, 28 August 1992, pp. 1A, 2B. After Yasser Arafat's Fatah established its leadership of the roof body, the Palestine Liberation Organization (PLO), Moscow moved belatedly to hedge its bets and counter Chinese competition, availing itself of Romania's connections with Arafat. Lt-Gen. Ion Mihai Pacepa (former deputy head of Romanian foreign intelligence), "The Arafat I Know," *Wall Street Journal*, 1 January 2002. The mass of evidence indicates, however, that Moscow embraced Arafat only after Nasser brought him to Moscow in July 1968. His Moscow University-trained associate and future president of the Palestinian Authority

Mahmud Abbas (Abu Mazen) is listed by Mitrokhin (p. 47, no. 244) as a KGB agent (codename "Krotov"—mole), at least as of 1983.
39. *SAR*, no. 82, p. 192 (also *FRUS* N-XII, no. 218).
40. "Minutes of a Combined WSAG and Review Group Meeting," 9 September 1970, *FRUS* N-XXIV, no. 214.
41. *SAR*, no. 83, p. 193.
42. *SAR*, no. 84, pp. 194, 197.
43. *SAR*, no. 86, p. 201
44. Polmar, *Spyplane*, p. 167.
45. Daigle, "Limits of Détente," p. 196.
46. Arad, *1000 ha-yamim*, p. 273. As late as 1994, a prominent US study spoke of the "inconclusive termination of the war of attrition." Lebow and Stein, *We All Lost*, p. 163.
47. Sherman, *Bunkers*, p. 192; *Me'uzei Sinai*, p. 159.
48. Gordon, *Thirty Hours*, p. 89.
49. Edward Kolcum, *Aviation Week*, translated in *Ma'ariv*, 12 January 1971, p. 16.
50. Hod, interviewed by Yaqir Elqariv and Yaron Katz, *Heyl ha-Avir* (IAF Magazine), 140 (June 1984), p. 19.
51. Lieblich, *Seasons*, p. 41.
52. Interviewed, 2007, in Gordon, *Thirty Hours*, p. 81.
53. Spector, *Loud and Clear*, pp. 192–7; Gordon, *Thirty Hours*, p. 88. This constraint became acute in the Yom Kippur War: by 22 October 1973 the IAF had lost thirty-two F-4s and the United States had replaced them all, but as Elazar pointed out "the arriving Phantoms have no impact as as there are no pilots for them." The pilot/plane ratio for F-4s had declined to 0.9. Golan, *Decision Making*, pp. 1155–6, 1230.
54. Merom, *Ha-Hatashah*, pp. 57–8.
55. Military correspondent, *Davar*, 3 January 1971, p. 2.
56. Platunov, "Provaly v pamyati."
57. Bar-Joseph, *Angel*, pp. 94, 97. As he puts Nasser's death "within a month" of this meeting, it must have taken place on or shortly after 28 August.
58. The Soviet personnel in Egypt were told by their political officers that Nasser was poisoned "by the American *agentura* in the Spanish Embassy." Kvasyuk, "Snova na front."
59. The only mention ever made of Lashchenko by the *NYT* in an Egyptian context was to list him and Okunev among the signatories of a mourning statement for Nasser. Both are identified only by their other Soviet military titles. Bernard Gwertzman, "Moscow Affirms That It Seeks Political Settlement in Mideast," *NYT*, 30 September 1970, p. 1.
60. [Yosef] Ben-Aharon, Israeli embassy, Washington, to Foreign Ministry, 2 December 1970, ISA HZ-4605/3. The source was Walter Smith, Office of UAR Affairs, Department of State.
61. Vinogradov, *Diplomatiya*, pp. 205–6.
62. Vinogradov, "Sovetskie voiny v Egipte," p. 14. His appointment was not publicized until a week later; UPI, "Deputy Minister Is Named Soviet Ambassador to Cairo," *NYT*, 7 October 1970.

63. As in 1967, Zakharov complained that "he had seen signs of slackness among the sentries on roads and bridges." Heikal, *Road to Ramadan*, pp. 109–11.
64. Ben-Aharon, Israeli embassy, Washington, to Foreign Ministry, 28 August 1970, ISA HZ-4605/3. The report was distributed widely and as high up as the prime minister. The source was [Philip H.] Stoddard, Bureau of Intelligence and Research, Department of State.
65. "Kak nash zemlyak."
66. Heikal, *Road to Ramadan*, p. 118; Kapitanets, *Na Sluzhbe*, pp. 271–6.

18. SADAT PROVES HIS STABILITY AND LOYALTY

1. Viktor Zaytsev, "Pomnyu Egipet," in Grigory Abramov et al. (eds), *Smolyane v lokal'nykh voynakh XX veka: Sbornik vospominany*, Smolensk: Universum, 2006, p. 71.
2. Bondarenko, "Mariupol'tsy."
3. *Foxbats*, Chapter 13; further evidence in Ginor and Remez, "Soviet initiative."
4. Bard, "Phantom Jets." On the confusion between MiG-23 and 25, see Chapter 4, note 37.
5. *Davar*, 1 October 1968, p. 1.
6. Heikal, *Road to Ramadan*, p. 86, emphasis added. In retrospect, Israeli reports cited "increased rumors" in February 1970 that "'MiG-23s' would be activated in Egypt for defense against Israeli attacks." Eli Landau, *Ma'ariv*, 12 April 1971, pp. 9, 12. Shalom (*Phantoms*, vol. 1, p. 527, vol. 2, p. 1157n5) claims (unsourced) that the planes actually arrived in Egypt in 1970, but only "to serve the Russians' global interests ... and [were] not put at the Egyptians' disposal" until 1971.
7. Abramov, *Goluboe*, p. 56.
8. More than two months after the arrival of Soviet squadrons in Egypt, Reston took Nasser's word that "he is hesitating about asking for Soviet pilots." "Nasser, in Interview, Says He Is Seeking Soviet Weapons," *NYT*, 15 February 1970, p. 1.
9. Embassy Moscow to secretary of state, 19 February 1970, NARA NSC files, country files, USSR, vol. VI, box 711.
10. *SAR*, p. 140n2, citing Dobrynin's report to Foreign Ministry, 22 March 1970. There is no other record that Kissinger mentioned the "MiG-23," but the erroneous appellation indicates he cited a US source.
11. Vinogradov, "Sovetskie voiny v Egipte," p. 13.
12. Slukhay, *Katyshkin*. At this stage, "missile-bearing bombers" seems more applicable to the Tu-16s, but the experimental designation definitely refers to the future MiG-25.
13. V. Yu. Markovsky, "'My gotovili voynu,'" first published in *Aerohobby* magazine before 2001, reproduced at www.foxbat.ru/article/mig25/mig25_1.htm. The article provides copious technical details including the serial numbers of the four Foxbats that were eventually based in Egypt.
14. Volodin, "Na Izrail."
15. Memorial page for Lysenko at http://www.astronaut.ru (now unaccessible). William Stevenson's semi-fictional *Zanek: A Chronicle of the Israeli Air Force*, New York: Viking, 1971, pp. 39–48, 126, gives a bizarre account from April to May 1970 in which an IAF

Phantom nearly accomplishes an intercept of a high-altitude Soviet reconnaissance craft. It is "guessed" to be a Yak-25RV (Mandrake), an older Soviet model that was a rough counterpart of the U-2. There is no other evidence of this model's appearance over Israel, but as the book was completed before the 63rd was deployed to Egypt, it appears to indicate prior IAF awareness of Soviet spy planes.

16. Akopov, transcript, pp. 27–30.
17. "Ahmad Ismail," *Encyclopedia Britannica*, http://www.britannica.com/EBchecked/topic/930499/Ahmad-Ismail
18. In this speech, Sadat attributed the Soviets' dispatch of their SAM units to Nasser's visit in January 1970, but his statement that "Russian soldiers were killed alongside our boys" within a week of the visit in effect confirmed that Soviet missile crews had been in Egypt earlier. Could that have caused MENA's immediate retraction of the report? AP's Cairo bureau "indicated that its report had been censored" ("Russians Died at Missiles, Sadat Reports," *Toledo Blade*, 5 January 1970, p. 1); Reuters was approached to emend its version but refused. The *Daily Telegraph*'s John Bulloch reported that he had to fly to Cyprus to file his story, after—according to "western and Arab diplomats"—the Soviet embassy had prevailed on Egyptian authorities to censor the passage in question (Bulloch, quoted in *Ma'ariv*, 6 January 1971, p. 3). MENA and Cairo Radio then carried versions that omitted any mention at all of Soviet aid. Sadat spoke extemporaneously for two hours; no full transcript survived—if there ever was one. He was speaking on a tour aimed at whipping up support for a war; his thrust was strongly anti-American and pro-Soviet. See Chapter 4, notes 48 and 51.
19. War Ministry, Air Defence Forces Headquarters operations division, circular to formation commanders, 23 November 1970, CDE-IHC, 264/12.
20. Kapitanets, *Na Sluzhbe*, pp. 274–7.
21. Heikal in *Al-Ahram*, quoted by Arab affairs correspondent, *Davar*, 3 January 1971, p. 2.
22. Bergus, Cairo, to secretary of state, 8 February 1971. NARA, NSC H-files, box H-51, folder 5.
23. "We'll Replace War Loss," *Herald-Statesman* (Yonkers, NY), 18 January 1971.
24. Military correspondent, *Davar*, 4 February 1971, p. 1. Peres (then transportation minister) commented: "As long as the Russians protect Egyptian skies, as long as Egypt is a Soviet military protectorate, the temptation for Egypt will be too strong for her to make peace." *Davar*, 5 February 1971, p. 3.
25. Military correspondent, *Davar*, 10 May 1971, p. 1.
26. *SAR*, no. 115, pp. 278–9, 279n6.
27. *SAR*, no. 114, pp. 274–5, 275n4. The bracketed reference was penciled in. The editors provide no clarification for the otherwise unknown "Amin Channel." It might possibly be the "private channel" mentioned in the cable from Bergus to secretary of state, 8 February 1971. NARA, NSC H-files, box H-51, folder 5.
28. Primakov, *Blizhniy Vostok*, p. 139.
29. To Arnaud de Borchgrave of *Newsweek*. The interview appeared in the 22 February issue of the magazine, but its essence was released almost immediately.

30. James Reston, *NYT*, "Arab President Changes Tone," *Times* (Geneva, NY), 30 December 1970, p. 7.
31. Bergus, Cairo, to secretary of state, 8 February 1971. NARA, NSC H-files, box H-51, folder 5.
32. Harold H. Saunders, memorandum for Dr. Kissinger, "Review of US–USSR Positions on the Middle East," 19 February 1971, NARA SRG M ME 2–25 (71 [1 of 2]), H-files, box H-52, folder 4.
33. Joseph Alsop, "A Big Blink?," *Daily Times* (Watertown, NY), 17 February 1971, p. 6.
34. *SAR*, no. 125, p. 300n7, quoting Dobrynin cable to Foreign Ministry, 24 February.
35. Anthony Astrakhan, *Washington Post*, Moscow, translated in *Ma'ariv*, 1 March 1971.
36. AFP and AP, *Ma'ariv*, 8 March 1971, p. 1.
37. *SAR*, p. 305n6.
38. Kissinger, memorandum for the president, "NSC Discussion of the Middle East: February 26," 25 February 1971, NARA NSC Meeting ME and Laos 2/26/71, box H-030, folder 3, pp. 1, 5; emphasis added.
39. *SAR*, p. 304n6. The editors interpret "end of the ceasefire" as showing that Kissinger knew of Sadat's decision to terminate the ceasefire a day before it was announced. This does not conform to the other evidence cited here, including Dobrynin's remark.
40. AP, *Davar*, 8 March 1971, p. 1. This is another rare reference to Soviet tank units in Egypt.
41. Title of article by Yosef Harif, *Ma'ariv*, 8 March 1971, p. 3; exclamation point in original. Eban, for instance, held that the threat of war was meant to make the United States press Israel for concessions; he rejected UN Secretary-General U Thant's description of Sadat's reply to Jarring as positive.
42. *Ma'ariv*, 12 March 1971, p. 1.
43. The Israeli reading was that this actually reflected Sadat's reluctance to declare war, due to Egypt's failure to mobilize an eastern front against Israel, and that it was intended to pacify aggressive Egyptian officers. Shmu'el Segev, *Ma'ariv*, 15 March 1971, p. 9.
44. For example, *Le Figaro*, quoted in *Ma'ariv*, 9 March 1971, p. 2.
45. Shmu'el Segev, *Ma'ariv*, 7 March 1971, p. 9; this analysis commended Sadat for caution, and predicted that he would extend the ceasefire.
46. By US officials; *Ma'ariv*, 11 April 1971, p. 1.
47. Arab affairs correspondent, *Davar*, 3 January 1971, p. 2.
48. V. Vinogradov, "K istorii Sovetsko-Egipetskikh otnosheniy," in Meyer et al., *Togda*, pp. 18–19. Vadim A. Kirpichenko dates this meeting as 27 April 1971; *Razvedka i lichnosti*, Moscow: Geya, 1998, pp. 113–17.
49. Komlev, "Voyna u Piramid"; Vakhtin, "Simfonicheskiy kontsert." The Egyptian offer of "recreational programming" and the Soviet refusal were confirmed by "senior officers" to Mishchenko: "some desperate characters couldn't restrain themselves ... the next day it would be found out by the command, and within 24 hours the culprit would be sent home in disgrace." Temirova and Shunevich, "Vo vremya voyny."
50. Logachev, "Eto zabyt' nevozmozhno," pp. 156–7.
51. Interviewed in Tereshchenko, "Egiptyanin."

52. Khandanyan, "Zharkoe."
53. Akopov, transcript, pp. 27–30.
54. 16th Division headquarters to 3rd Infantry Brigade circular 71/8, "Re: Output Reports of Soviet Advisers," 28 March 1971, CDE-IHC., index no. 444006.
55. AP, *Davar*, 5 March 1971; *Daily Telegraph*, reproduced in *Ma'ariv*, same day.
56. *Newsweek*, quoted by Uri Dann, *Ma'ariv*, 15 April 1971, p. 17.

19. RETURN OF THE FOXBATS

1. The following account of the Foxbats' development and deployment, unless otherwise sourced, is based on: Vinogradov, "Sovetskie voiny v Egipte," p. 13; Lt-Col. A.M. Sinikchiyants, *Otechestva krylatye syny*, Moscow: Mozaika, 2002, pp. 341–50; adaptation of same in "63-y otdel'nyi aviaotryad: Boevoe primenenie MiG-25 v Egipte," www.testpilot.ru/russia/mikoyan/mig/25/r/63.htm; Volodin, "Na Izrail'"; Igor' Bysenkov, "V 20,000 metrakh nad zemley obetovannoy," November 2007, http://bratishka.ru./archiv/2007/11/2007_11_12.php; Georgy Baevsky, "Sekretnaya missiya v nebe Sinaya," *Vestnik vozdushnogo flota* (n.d., before 2001), www.foxbat.ru/article/mig25_2/mig25_2_1.htm; Abramov, *Goluboe*, pp. 71ff.
2. This is the date reported by Bysenkov. Bezhevets, in his earlier interview with Volodin, dated virtually the same account in mid-June 1970.
3. Vybornov has repeatedly related flying a dozen reconnaissance sorties over Israel before the 1967 war, including at least two in the aircraft later to be known as the MiG-25, which provided the title of our previous book; *Foxbats*, pp. 74–5, 85–6, 131–7. After *Foxbats* was completed, the Russian Air Force spokesman, Col. Aleksandr Drobyshevsky, confirmed MiG-25 flights over Israel in 1967, naming Bezhevets as the pilot although he is not recorded as being in Egypt at the time. Drobyshevsky's article was posted in October 2006 on the website of the Russian Ministry of Defense, but has since been removed; Ginor and Remez, "Soviet Initiative."
4. [Gen. William] Momyer, "Resume of My Conversations with Hod October 27," 2 November 1971, IRISNUM 01011311
5. Eli Landau, *Ma'ariv*, 12 April 1971, pp. 9, 12.
6. Secretary of state to US embassy, Tel Aviv, "Rabin and Sisco on MiG-23 Flight," 12 October 1971, marked as received in White House situation room; NARA NSC files, country files, ME–Israel, box 609. The number of twelve was given by *NYT* on 11 May 1971, quoted in *Davar* the next day (p. 3).
7. Arab affairs correspondent, *Ma'ariv*, 17 March 1971, p. 1.
8. V.B. El'chaninov, "Dan prikaz emu ... v Egipet!," in Meyer et al., *Togda*, pp. 89–90.
9. Arab affairs correspondent, *Davar*, 21 March 1971, p. 1.
10. *Ma'ariv*, 22 March 1971, p. 1.
11. Rabin to Foreign Ministry, 1 April 1971, ISA HZ-4549/7, quoted in Bo'az Vanetik and Zaki Shalom, "Helqo shel ha-bayit ha-lavan be-tirpud ha-hesder ha-helqi bein Yisra'el u-Mitzrayim bi-shenat 1971," *Yisra'el*, 17 (Spring 2010), p. 103; http://humanities1.tau.ac.il/zionism/images/stories/mahamar_ventick_vshalom.pdf

12. US embassy, London, to secretary of state, 11 November 1975, https://wikileaks.org/plusd/cables/1975LONDON17330_b.html
13. *Aviation Week*, quoted by Shimshon Ofer, *Davar*, 23 April 1971, p. 10.
14. UPI Cairo and *NYT*, in *Davar*, 26 March 1971, p. 1; Philip Benn, *Ma'ariv*, 25 March 1971, p. 1.
15. This is apparently a misidentification of the Su-15 "Flagon," possibly caused by the fact that this model, the MiG-23 and MiG-25 were all first displayed at the same air show in July 1967. *Ma'ariv*, 4 April 1971, p. 2.
16. Philip Benn, *Ma'ariv*, 11 April 1971, p. 1.
17. Eli Landau, *Ma'ariv*, 12 April 1971, p. 1.
18. *Ma'ariv*, 12 April 1971, p. 1. Similar report in *Davar*, p. 1, quoting *NYT* and AP from 11 April.
19. Uri Dann, *Ma'ariv*, 12 April 1971, p. 9.
20. Whetten, *Canal War*, p. 163.
21. Polmar, *Spyplane*, p. 167. He puts this proposal in the context of the U-2 flights, but Israel would hardly have proposed to the United States that it develop a counter to its own spy plane. Another version holds that Peace Jack was begun in conjunction with General Dynamics, but the State Department objected to developing and exporting an aircraft with performance similar to the the SR-71 and offensive capability beyond anything in the US inventory. The proposal was then modified to the unarmed RF-4X, but the USAF withdrew from the project because a high-performance Phantom might jeopardize funding for the anticipated F-15—which the IAF would indeed use in the first shootdown of a MiG-25 a decade later. But in the early 1970s, Israel settled for the conversion of several F-4Es to camera-bearing F-4E(S). Jay Miller, "Peace Jack: An Enigma Exposed," *Air International* (UK), 29, 1 (July 1985), pp. 18–23; Jewish virtual library: http://www.jewishvirtuallibrary.org/jsource/History/phantom.html
22. "Meeting between Ambassador Rabin and Dr. Kissinger," 12. April 1971, NARA, Alexander Haig's Memcons, box 978, quoted in Vanetik and Shalom, "Helqo shel ha-bayit ha-lavan," p. 104.
23. Rabin, *Pinqas sherut*, vol. 2, p. 351.
24. *SAR*, no. 143, p. 328.
25. *SAR*, no. 145, pp. 330–1.
26. *SAR*, no. 210, p. 490.
27. Secretary of state to US embassy Tel Aviv, "Rabin and Sisco on MiG-23 Flight," 12 October 1971, NARA NSC Files, country files, ME-Israel, box 609; Momyer, "Resume of My Conversations with Hod."
28. Rubtsov, memoir.
29. Konstantin Polyakov and Andrey Kulyasov, *Wings of Russia*, Episode 18, "Spies: Watching from Above," Moscow 2007, http://www.youtube.com/watch?v=w3TKjKDimIo (no longer accessible). The authors thank Dirk Pohlmann for bringing this documentary to our attention.
30. Bob Considine, "Russia's Foxbat," *Recorder* (Amsterdam, NY), 17 April 1971, p. 2.

20. TRIAL BALLOONS FROM BOTH SIDES

1. Recording of a conversation between Nixon and Rogers, 19 May 1971, Oval Office, Conversation 501–4, NARA, Nixon Presidential Materials, White House Tapes; quoted in Craig A. Daigle, "The Russians Are Going: Sadat, Nixon and the Soviet Presence in Egypt, 1970–1971," *MERIA*, 8, 1 (2004), pp. 1–15, http://www.rubincenter.org/meria/2004/03/daigle.pdf
2. Lau-Lavi, *Balaam's Prophecy*, p. 267.
3. Transcript of Rogers–Meir talk, 7 May 1971, ISA HZ-7031/1, pp. 16, 30; quoted in Vanetik and Shalom, "Helqo shel ha-bayit ha-lavan," pp. 112–13.
4. Nixon to Rogers, 26 May 1971, NARA Record Group 59, Lot Files, 71, Office Files of William P. Rogers, box 25. Quoted in Vanetik and Shalom, "Helqo shel ha-bayit ha-lavan," emphasis added.
5. Jean-Pierre Joulin, *Nouvel Observateur*, translated in *Davar*, 30 January 1971, p. 8. It has also been claimed that an officer of the KGB *rezidentura*, Vladimir Sakharov, who had been recruited by the CIA, informed the Americans about an impending coup against Sadat and *they* warned him, thus laying the foundations for his ultimate pro-US turn. Bar-Joseph, *Angel*, quoting Owen L. Sirrs, *A History of the Egyptian Intelligence Service*, New York: Routledge, 2010, p. 120. But Sakharov had been transferred to Kuwait several months before the coup. In *High Treason* and other publications aimed at highlighting his work for the CIA, he never took credit for such a major feat but claimed that he was surprised to hear about it.
6. Bar-Joseph, *Angel*, pp. 106–10.
7. James Reston, "Egypt's Power Struggle Far from Over," *Times* (Geneva, NY), 28 May 1971, p. 7.
8. Vinogradov, *Diplomatiya*, p. 227.
9. Sarah Yizre'eli, Davar, 13 October 1972, p. 13.
10. *SAR*, no. 163, p. 369.
11. *SAR*, no. 164, p. 374.
12. In October, speaking with Israeli officials, Primakov quoted Anderson to the effect that Rogers had rebuked Meir; he implied that Israel could not count on unconditional US support and would do better to hedge its bets with the Soviets. His Israeli interlocutor responded: "it went both ways. ... But it's all in the family." Mordechai Gazit, "Conversation of M.G. with David on 8 October," p. 10, ISA A-7037/17.
13. Primakov, *Blizhniy Vostok*, pp. 133–8, 141, 145.
14. Jay Axelbank, "Victor Louis: Soviet Mystery," *Daily Press* (Utica, NY), 27 August 1971, p. 6. Louis's host, Dr Aryeh Harel (Sternberg), director of Tel Aviv municipal hospitals, had served as ambassador in Moscow from 1958 to 1961. At that time, according to Louis's own accounts, he had just been released from a labor camp and was working for Western journalists and/or embassies, which would have been impossible without KGB clearance. Louis also claimed he had already been to Israel in 1963.
15. Schecter and Schecter, *Sacred Secrets*, pp. 226–60; quotes are from pp. 228, 233.
16. Dan Arkin, *Ma'ariv*, 29 June 1971, p. 2 (describing Louis as "head of the KGB psychological warfare department"); *Davar*, 29 June 1971, p. 1.

17. Andrey Vandenko, "Posledniy romantik," *Itogi*, 6 December 2010, http://www.itogi.ru/kultura/2010/49/159665.html, marking the publication of Kevorkov's biography *Viktor Lui*.
18. The *Coral Sea* was hit by several rockets and set on fire, but did not sink or blow up. It was only recently disclosed that its Greek captain saved the ship by fortuitously ordering the release of explosive fumes from the hold shortly before the attack. Former Mossad agent Gad Shimron, interviewed on Israel Radio, 25 March 2015.
19. Marcus Eliason, AP, "Israeli Tanker Hit by Bazooka from Passing Speedboat," *Gazette* (Schenectady, NY), 14 June 1971, p. 1.
20. MA, pp. 77, 80.
21. Political correspondent, *Davar*, 14 June 1971, p. 1, and 18 June 1971, p. 3.
22. AP, "Soviet Journalist Visits Israel," *Gazette* (Niagara Falls, NY), 28 June 1971.
23. UPI, "New Secret Talks Open," *Daily Times* (Watertown, NY), 30 June 1971, p. 8.
24. *St. Louis Post-Dispatch*, "Mr Helms' Journey," *Times* (Geneva, NY), July 9, 1971.
25. "CIA Head in Israel for Talks," *News* (Tonawanda, NY), 30 June 1971, p. 10; C.L. Sulzberger, *NYT*, "The Role of the Foreign Minister Is Declining," *Daily Times* (Geneva, NY), 14 July 1971, p. 8.
26. Dorothy Marks, North American Newspaper Alliance, "Wife of CIA Chief Leads a Demanding Social Life," *Daily News* (Watertown, NY), 12 August 1971, p. 4.
27. Transcript of talk between "SD" and "VL" (identified as "Mr Louis" on p. 8), 16 June 1971, ISA A-7037/17, pp. 21, 25. Louis referred to his reputation "as a KGB agent" and suggested "not to believe everything that was written about me, but a number of things are true" (p. 13).
28. Maj.-Gen. Adel Suleiman Yusry, "Planning the Operations of the 1973 October War" in Vartanov et al., *Rukopozhatie*, pp. 74–5.
29. Shazly, *Crossing*, pp. 27–32.
30. Transcript of talk between "SD" and "VL," 16 June 1971, ISA A-7037/17, pp. 9–10.
31. Shelepin's memo was relayed to the Politburo on 23 July. Primakov, *Blizhniy Vostok*, pp. 266–8.
32. Ponomarev had headed the International Relations Department of the CPSU CC since 1955 and would be appointed candidate member of the Politburo in May 1972.
33. The following account of Primakov's mission to Israel is based on his memoir, *Blizhniy Vostok*, and the Israel Prime Minister's Office file on "secret talks with the USSR," ISA A-7037/17. It includes a summary and transcript of Primakov's talk with Eban (29 August), summaries of a working lunch (30 August) and dinner (31 August) with an unnamed official, evidently Hanan Baron, and transcript of a talk with Dayan (31 August). The authors thank Bo'az Vanetik.
34. *SAR*, p. 431n2.
35. Sandra Ionno Butcher, "Herb York (1921–2009): On Pugwash History and a NWFW," Pugwash History Blog, 21 May 2009, http://pugwashhistory.blogspot.co.il
36. Emphasis added. This may have referred to an interview on Israel Radio, in which Dayan actually said he did *not* foresee Israeli accession to NATO, but pointed out the significance

of such Israeli bases as Refidim for NATO military planning. *Davar*, 11 July 1971, p. 3. The foreign press reported that he "seemed to be chiding Atlantic Alliance leaders for not allocating enough concern to Soviet 'expansionism' in the Mediterranean ... 'I find it unimaginable that those dealing with military issues in NATO do not perceive the new significance of Soviet consolidation here.'" "Dayan Says Egypt Hurts Peace Effort," *Herald-Statesman* (Yonkers, NY), 10 July 1971.

37. On 19 August, this statement by Dayan caused an uproar, protests in cabinet and a strong US response; he quickly clarified that he did not mean annexation. "Dayan View on Occupation Sharply Criticized by U.S.," *NYT*, 21 August 1971, p. 3.
38. On 1 August, the *NYT* reported that King Feisal of Saudi Arabia suggested this to Vice President Spiro Agnew; *Ma'ariv*, 1 August 1971, p. 1. This was denied by the Saudis; UPI, *Davar*, 12 August 1971, p. 2.
39. On the territories, "we have all the obligations and the duties that a government should have there ... we should not postpone to the indefinite future things that have to be done now ... [but] if at any time the Arabs want to ... negotiate the boundaries, we have ... to compromise with them." On NATO: "I've been asked several times whether NATO considers us as part of it, and I said no, but had I been asked whether Israel should join NATO if we were offered it, I would have said not."
40. *SAR*, no. 196, p. 442; p. 444n3.

21. FLEXING MUSCLES WHILE OFFERING A PULLBACK

1. Viktor Yakushev, "My—perevodchiki s Nila i s Volgi," 4 October 2012, http://artofwar.ru/j/jakushew_w_g/text_0020.shtml
2. AC, Tal testimony, Part 1, pp. 169–70; IDF archive, *Or Yeqarot* file. A captured Egyptian document recognized before the war that the system was obsolete; Haber, Schiff and Asher, *War*, p. 39.
3. This is the Soviet version as continued below; Israel stated that the pilot bailed out safely, which would have been remarkable at such low altitude but, as the Hetz-Eini case demonstrates, not impossible. IAF website entry for 11 September, http://www.iaf.org.il/3623-4950-he/IAF.aspx; "Egyptian Bomber Reported Downed," *NYT*, 12 September 1971, p. 11.
4. "Smirnov," *Arabo-izrail'skie voyny*, p. 277. He bought the *International Herald Tribune* to read about the death of Khrushchev on 11 September, and noticed in the report about the Sukhoi incident that the Israeli gunners wore no flak jackets or helmets, indicating that "no deterioration was expected in the canal zone." A Soviet pilot, Capt. Nikolay Filipenko, is named in the veterans' memorial list as killed in September 1971—the only case where no precise date is given; "Kniga Pamyati," http://www.hubara-rus.ru/heroes.html. The website of the flight school where he graduated in 1967 states only that he was killed in "combat operations in Egypt"; http://dev.topwar.ru/89170-35-ya-otdelnaya-razvedovatelnaya-aviacionnaya-eskadrilya-sovetskih-vvs-v-egipte-1970-72-gg.html. The fictional hero of the 1991 film *Verbovshchik* (Chapter 15, note 24) is also described as shot down east of the canal in 1971, when no other such incident is recorded.

5. In December 1971, Norman Anderson, a State Department specialist on Soviet–Middle Eastern affairs, told an Israeli diplomat that a Tu-16 base was "under construction" near Aswan, and that these planes, armed with Kelt missiles, would be an "unprecedentedly serious" threat to the Sixth Fleet. Anderson also claimed that a Soviet Su-7 squadron armed with anti-submarine weapons was based in northern Egypt. Y[osef] Ben-Aharon, Israeli embassy, Washington, to Foreign Ministry, 9 December 1971, ISA HZ-4605/3.
6. Zhirokhov and Nicolle, "Unknown Heroes," Part 2, which includes several details that do not appear in Mitrokhin's own published memoir, "Mysli vslukh gvardii mladshego serzhanta" in Safonov et al., *Grif*, pp. 197–98. He is not to be confused with Vasily Mitrokhin of the KGB archive.
7. Zhirokhov and Nicolle, "Unknown Heroes," Part 2.
8. Mordechai Gazit, "Conversation of M.G. with David on 8 October [1971]," p. 3, ISA A-7037/17.
9. "Smirnov," *Arabo-izrail'skie voyny*, p. 277. The IAF stated that of the crew of eight there was one survivor. All were named and described as Israelis.
10. Cohen, *Israel's Best Defense*, p. 317; Emad El-Sayed, "Securing Democratic Transition a Secondary Task of Air Defence Forces: Commander," *Daily News* (Cairo), 27 June 2015, http://www.dailynewsegypt.com/2015/06/27/securing-democratic-transition-a-secondary-task-of-air-defence-forces-commander/
11. Shazly, *Crossing*, Chapter 12.
12. Igor' Eliseev and Aleksei Tikhonov, "V teni pyramid," *Rossiskaya Gazeta*, 30 October 2010, http://www.rg.ru/2010/09/30/taina.html; Aleksey Tikhonov, "Vspomnim obo vsekh geroyakh," *Spravedlivaya Rossiya*, 30 September 2010; Yakushev, "My—perevodchiki."
13. US consent to supply the Shrikes was given to Rabin only on 14 August, in response to Israel's complaints of ceasefire violations. Quandt, *Decade of Decisions*, p. 107. Hod, interviewed by Yaqir Elqariv and Yaron Katz, *Heyl ha-Avir* (IAF Magazine), 39, 140 (June 1984), p. 19.
14. Arab affairs correspondent, *Davar*, 3 January 1971, p. 2.
15. Interview with Gareev, Moscow, 26 July 1996, in Jacob W. Kipp, "Confronting the RMA in Russia," *Military Review* (June–July 1997), http://fmso.leavenworth.army.mil/documents/confront.htm; Kipp and Grau, "Maintaining Friendly Skies: Rediscovering Theater Aerospace Defense," *Aerospace Power Journal* (Summer 2002), http://fmso.leavenworth.army.mil/documents/friendlyskies/friendlyskies.htm, quoting Gareev, *Esli zavtra voyna?*, pp. 142–3.
16. "Smirnov," *Arabo-izrail'skie voyny*, pp. 278–9. Smirnov's rank, function and dates of service in Egypt are similar to those of Boris Krokhin, and most of the eyewitness accounts in his book (this one excepted) are identical with those published under Krokhin's name—suggesting that "Smirnov" is a pseudonym. "Radio-technical" adviser Molodtsov admits that this single Shrike hit *destroyed* a P-35 radar station at Abu Suweir, but also credits the Soviet advisers for a major success in confusing the Shrikes by turning on every available radar system, including the *Shilkas*'. Molodtsov, "Opyt." Abu Suweir, a few miles west of Ismailia, had not been reactivated as an airbase since the Israeli bombing in 1967. Viktor

Rogozhinsky claims to have witnessed, on "a hot summer day" in 1971, a Phantom attack on Inshas airbase near Cairo that destroyed "with a single missile" an experimental precursor of the *Kolchuga* aircraft location system, killing his townsman Aleksey Avramenko (who does not appear on any list of Soviet casualties). The Shrike attack is the only Israeli air raid known that summer, but the Phantom is described as firing the missile point blank, which does not conform to the Shrike. See "Kak nash zemlyak."

17. Mordechai Gazit, "Conversation of M.G. with David on 8 October," p. 4, ISA A-7037/17.
18. Sadiq "issued an order to the armed forces to 'hit back immediately and violently and silence any Israeli attempt to fire at our positions' ... all units on the Suez Canal front ... should 'use all kinds of weapons.'" AP, "Middle East Uneasy: Egypt Gives Retaliation Order," *Times* (Geneva, NY), 20 September 1971, p. 3.
19. AP, "Rockets Are Fired in Suez Flare-Up," *Gazette* (Niagara Falls, NY), 18 September 1971, p. 1.
20. IAF website page for 18 September, http://www.iaf.org.il/3623-4952-he/IAF.aspx; UPI, "Missiles Fired in Israel Attack," *Milwaukee Sentinel*, 25 September 1971, p. 2.
21. Agassi, quoted in Gordon, *Thirty Hours*, p. 89; Cohen, *Israel's Best Defense*, pp. 317, 399, 471. An intercept of Egyptian signals on 7 October 1973 confirmed that they were prepared for a Shrike attack. AC Final Report, vol. 4, p. 1261.
22. [Gen. William] Momyer, "Resume of My Conversations with Hod, October 27," 2 November 1971, IRISNUM 01011311.
23. Remark by Yadin in AC, Dayan testimony, Part 2, p. 67.
24. "U.S. Disavows Plan to Send Lance Missiles to Israel," *NYT*, 9 August 1971. The sale was approved only after Soviet-operated Scuds were launched at Israeli forces during the Yom Kippur War, and it was delivered late in 1975. *The Economist*, "Missile Pledge Has Many Wondering," *Times* (Geneva, NY), 1 October 1975, p. 4.
25. AC, Tal testimony, Part 1, pp. 153–68; Golan, *Decision Making*, p. 709.
26. AC, final report, vol. 4, pp. 1205–6.
27. Alsop, "Egyptians Stockpile Weapons," *Herald-Statesman* (Yonkers, NY), 21 September 1971, p. 19.
28. Rubtsov, memoir.
29. Rubinstein, *Red Star*, pp. 156–7.
30. Kimche, *Last Option*, p. 19.
31. Kissinger, *White House Years*, p. 1286.
32. *SAR*, no. 198, p. 447.
33. *SAR*, no. 200, p. 452.
34. Primakov, *Blizhniy Vostok*, p. 277.
35. *Davar*, 26 September 1971, p. 2.
36. *SAR*, no. 201, pp. 452–3.
37. Recording of a conversation between Nixon and Gromyko, September 29, 1971, Oval Office, Conversation 580-20. NARA, Nixon Presidential Materials, White House Tapes.
38. Kissinger, *White House Years*, p. 1288.
39. *SAR*, no. 205, p. 478; no. 206, p. 482.

40. The apt characterization of Kissinger's "apologia" is by Theodore Draper, *Present History: On Nucler War, Détente, and Other Controversies*, New York: Random House, 1983, p. 216.
41. Kissinger's single mention of the issue during this period (*White House Years*, p. 1132) is discussed below.
42. Ibid., p. 1288.
43. Ibid., p. 1276; emphasis added.
44. *SAR*, no. 204, p. 475n3.
45. Mordechai Gazit, "Conversation of M.G. with 'David' on 7 October," pp. 1, 2, 7, 9–10, ISA A-7037/17; Primakov, *Blizhniy Vostok*, p. 279.
46. Shimshon Ofer, *Davar*, 12 October 1971, pp. 1–2.
47. Kimche (*Last Option*, pp. 20–4) points out that no account by Sadat of these talks exists, but the notes taken by Foreign Minister Riad contradict the "official" version, as published by Heikal in *Road to Ramadan*.
48. Shazly, *Crossing*, p. 29.
49. Bar-Joseph, *Angel*, pp. 126–7.
50. AC, Elazar testimony, Part 1, pp. 13, 23–4; the preferred source's identity is sanitized but the reference to Marwan is obvious.
51. Primakov, *Blizhniy Vostok*, pp. 278–80. The Israeli file does not include documentation of this meeting, but the minutes of the 10 October talk do refer to another session yet to be held.
52. [Gen. William] Momyer, "Resume of My Conversations with Hod October 27," 2 November 1971, IRISNUM 01011311.
53. *Davar*, 21 October 1971 p. 2.
54. Momyer, "Resume of My Conversations with Hod."
55. Shimshon Ofer, *Davar*, 8 November 1971, p. 7.
56. Ofer, *Davar*, 7 November 1971, p. 1.
57. JTA, *Davar*, 8 October 1971, p. 2. Senator Stuart Symington, a former secretary of the Air Force, championed supplying aircraft to Israel. US Senate, *Executive Sessions*, pp. 925–45.
58. *SAR*, no. 249, p. 557.
59. *SAR*, no. 251, p. 564.
60. *SAR*, no. 250, pp. 558, 562.
61. *SAR*, no. 255, p. 573; no. 256, pp. 575–6.
62. Rubinstein, *Red Star*, p. 170, citing FBIS/Egypt, 4 February 1972, G4.
63. UPI, "Moscow Veto of Middle East War Hinted," *Times Record* (Troy, NY), 7 February 1972, p. 1.
64. *Davar*, 13 January 1972, p. 2. Shortly before, US defense analyst Edward Luttwak alluded to the Foxbat's RB version as still under development, but deemed its bombing capability so limited that using it for this purpose "would be like having Brigitte Bardot over for the night and sending her to do the dishes." Luttwak, *Davar*, 3 December 1971, p. 9.
65. Abramov, *Goluboe*, p. 75.
66. Bar-Lev had in fact already stepped down on 1 January, after completing the maximum

four-year term, and was soon appointed to a ministerial position for the Labor Party. On 3 February, in London, he accused the Soviets of plotting the War of Attrition, but judged that they had learned from its "failure" and were now urging Egypt to avoid war. *Ma'ariv*, 31 January 1972, p. 3.
67. *Ma'ariv*, 20 January 1972, p. 3. Nixon had disclosed his decision in a television interview on 2 January, a few days after the F-4s topped the "shopping list" that Meir handed him.

22. JOCKEYING AND POSTURING

1. *SAR*, no. 266, p. 63.
2. Kissinger, *White House Years*, p. 1132.
3. *SAR*, no. 274, pp. 626–7. Kissinger reported (no. 272, p. 616) only warning against informing the Egyptians "since they were bound to be penetrated by the Israelis." But he noted that some of Dobrynin's claims about a potential "increase of military presence in Egypt ... seems confirmed by Israeli intelligence"—which indicates he was briefed about the Israelis' sources in Egypt.
4. Bar-Joseph, *Angel*, pp. 125–8.
5. State Department to Cairo, "Egypt through a Professor's Eyes," 9 March 1973, https://www.wikileaks.org/plusd/cables/1973STATE043758_b.html
6. CIA, Directorate of Intelligence, "Soviet–Egyptian Relations: An Uneasy Alliance," 28 March 1972, p. 6, https://www.cia.gov/library/readingroom/docs/CIA-RDP85T00875R001100130044-4.pdf; emphasis added.
7. V.B. Ivanov, "Egipetskie kontrasty," in Meyer et al., *Togda*, pp. 180–1.
8. [Capt.] N. Antropov, "Kod Pechora," in Abramov et al., *Smolyane*, p. 65.
9. AP, "Sadat Acts to Win Support at Home," *Daily Press* (Utica, NY), 21 February 1972, p. 48.
10. War Ministry, minister's directive 1972/4, 27 February 1972, CDE-IHC 320/12. A reminder was issued on 15 March to officers and noncoms of the 49th Infantry Brigade; CDE-IHC 479/1.
11. War Ministry Intelligence Directorate security circular no. 57, 12 April 1972, CDE-IHC.
12. Khandanyan, "Zharkoe." Bringing the gold into the USSR *was* illegal; an ocean-liner captain and several of his crew were jailed for smuggling gold from Alexandria for sale to dentists in Odessa. Sakharov, *High Treason*, p. 251.
13. Whetten, *Canal War*, p. 225; unsourced.
14. Primakov, *Blizhniy Vostok*, p. 280.
15. *SAR*, p. 627n3.
16. *SAR*, no. 288, p. 657.
17. Gefele, "Napishi." Presnukhin was tasked to convey secret documents to Okunev at a temporary command post near Aswan, which may have been connected with the following episode.
18. Interviewed by Andrey Marchenko "General-Mayor VVS Vagin: Vostok kak dal'ny tak i blizhniy; delo tonkoe," Part 2, *Avtodaydzhest-Online* (Minsk), 242, 8 November 2001,

and "Siriyskaya komandirovka," *Ekspress Novosti* (Minsk), 39, 26 September 2003, http://expressnovosti.narod.ru/39/za.htm

19. Vadim Udmantsev, "Bezvizovaya komandirovka," *Voyenno-promyshlenny Kur'er*, 23 (11 June 2008), http://vpk-news.ru/articles/5175. The account is based on documents and oral accounts provided by Nikiforov, then the director of the Almaz design bureau's museum. His allusion to faulty missiles may refer to their assembly under license at an Egypian plant, which is otherwise documented only later.
20. *SAR*, no. 300, pp. 673–5.
21. *SAR*, no. 301, pp. 675, 679.
22. Kissinger, *White House Years*, p. 1151.
23. *SAR*, no. 308, pp. 745–6.
24. Even to mid-ranking Soviet officials. On 25 April, Chernyaev wrote: "it was announced that Kissinger was in Moscow from April 20–24th, and Brezhnev and Gromyko received him." *Diary, 1972*, p. 14.
25. Ahron Bregman and Jihan El-Tahri, *The Fifty Years War*, London: Penguin and BBC, 1998, p. 111.
26. Mubarak's appointment was described as "hasty" to enable his inclusion in the party. News agencies, *Davar*, 28 April 1972, p. 1. He was "the first EAF commander who can be described without reservation as Soviet-trained, a fact that undoubtedly contributed to his promotion." Arab affairs correspondent, *Davar*, 25 April 1972, p. 2.
27. Laqueur, *Confrontation*, p. 15.
28. General Ahmed Fakher, a member of the military delegation that accompanied Sadat to Moscow, quoted in Bregman and El-Tahri, *Fifty Years War*, p. 111.
29. *SAR*, no. 346, p. 831. This refers to Brezhnev's "military policies" in general, but in view of Grechko's previous opposition to the withdrawal, he would hardly have been "used" if his position had not changed.
30. Kimche, *Last Option*, p. 22. Kimche was a senior Mossad official at the time; together with Whetten's aforementioned reference, this may indicate that some of the agency's informants—evidently *not* Marwan—reported preparation for an agreed Soviet withdrawal, but were discounted or ignored.
31. Foy D. Kohler, Leon Gouré and Mose L. Harvey, *The Soviet Union and the October 1973 Middle East War: The Implications for Détente*, Coral Gables: University of Miami, 1974, pp. 33–4, quoting *Pravda*, 30 April 1972.
32. War Ministry, "Instructions of the General Command of the Armed Forces," 8 May 1972, CDE-IHC.
33. Heikal, *Road to Ramadan*, pp. 156–65; Heikal, *Sphinx*, p. 238.
34. Egorin, *Egipet*, p. 202. This anecdote is dated after May 1971; Egorin left Egypt later that year.
35. The missiles demonstrated were the *Ametist* (Starbright), an improved submarine-launched version of the Styx, and the P-35 (Sepal) cruise missile. Capt. Yury Kruchinin, *Komanduyu korablem*, Sevastopol: L. Yu. Kruchinin, 2008, http://www.proza.ru/2010/02/27/1219. He commanded a BPK, *Krasny Kavkaz*, that accompanied the *Grozny* from Sevastopol

and took part in the exercise. Kruchinin also quotes a memoir by Adm. Igor' Kasatonov (son of Admiral of the Fleet Vladimir), *Flot vyshel v okean*, Moscow: Andreevsky Flag, 1996, p. 225.

36. Former first mate Anatoly Shevchenko, quoted in Vladimir Gundarov, "Geroy bez Zolotoy Zvezdy," *NVO*, 26 October 2007, http://nvo.ng.ru/history/2007-10-26/5_hero.html. The interview with Shevchenko, who rose to vice-admiral, states that the leak occurred "a few days after" the ceremony but does not specify whether the sub was still in Alexandria.

37. The flypast reportedly also exhibited "long-range bombers," which aroused speculation that Egypt was receiving the supersonic Tu-22 (Blinder). Ehud Ya'ari, *Davar*, 17 May 1972, p. 4. This never happened; though faster and newer than the Tu-16, the Tu-22 had proved problematic, and the Egyptian demand for bombing capacity against Israel was already being met by supply of Su-20 attack bombers, which began within a month. The bombers referred to on 16 May may have been the two MiG-25RBs then in Egypt.

38. The channel for this false Egyptian claim was again the *Telegraph*'s John Bulloch. *Yedi'ot Ahronot*, 17 May 1972, p. 1.

39. Pochtarev, "Kak podrezali kryl'ya fantomam"; Evgeny Pavlov and Lev Berne, "Pravda o MiG-25: Istoriya sozdaniya," *Kryl'ya Rodiny*, 2–5 (1990), http://techno-story.ru/articles/aircrafts/448-mig-25

40. [Uri] Ya'ari, posting on 26 August 2007 on http://www.fresh.co.il/vBulletin/showthread.php?p=161208&mode=threaded#post2355000. Ya'ari calls the intruding Foxbats "*efrohim*" (fledglings), which had been the IAF code name for the "mysterious" overflights of Israel in May 1967. This tends to confirm our attribution of these flights to Soviet MiG-25s.

41. Spector, *Loud and Clear*, p. 217. Hod had told Momyer that the Foxbat sorties were made by "a very loose formation of two aircraft." Both IAF pilots mention briefly sighting only one MiG-25 on 16 May 1972. One explanation offered for the IAF's failure was that "the proximity fuses on the AIM-7E missiles could not cope with the Mach-3 closing speed of the Foxbat and by the time they detonated, the aircraft was out of their lethal radius." "Foxbats over Sinai," http://www.spyflight.co.uk/foxbats.htm (which dates the episode to 6 November 1971).

23. THE DEAL AT THE SUMMIT AND THE "EXPULSION" MYTH

1. *SAR*, no. 367, p. 942.
2. Kissinger, *Years of Upheaval*, p. 204.
3. Anatoly Dobrynin, *Sugubo doveritel'no: posol v Vashingtone pri shesti prezidentakh SShA*, Moscow: Avtor, 1997, p. 238.
4. Kissinger, *White House Years*, pp. 1247–8. The declassification, for Kissinger's use only, of inherently secret papers was a controversial issue. Draper, *Present History*, pp. 246–7 (written in 1980).
5. Quandt, *Peace Process*, 539n46.
6. *SAR*, no. 374, p. 981.
7. *SAR*, no. 375, pp. 987, 989–90.

NOTES   pp. [265–268]

8. Kirpichenko, *Razvedka*, p. 318.
9. Sella, *Soviet Political and Military Conduct*, pp. 78–9.
10. Rubinstein, *Red Star*, pp. 198–9, quoting TASS, *Pravda* and other contemporary Soviet publications.
11. Maj.-Gen. Adel Suleiman Yusry, "Planirovanie operatsii oktyabr'skoy voyny 1973 goda," in Vartanov et al., *Rukopozhatie*, pp. 74–5.
12. Lebow and Stein, *We All Lost*, pp. 155–6, 449n29, quoting Brezhnev's commentary in an ideological periodical, *Leninskim kursom*, 21 December 1972.
13. Lt-Col. "Hayyim," "Mifgash ha-tzameret bein Nixon veha-hanhagah ha-Sovietit," *Ma'arakhot*, 225 (September 1972), pp. 31, 35, http://maarachot.idf.il/PDF/FILES/8/108478.pdf
14. Interview on 19 June 1991, Lebow and Stein, *We All Lost*, pp. 180, 460n177.
15. After the attack by "Japanese Red Army" terrorists on Lod (Lydda, later Ben-Gurion) Airport on the day the summit ended, 30 May 1972, the Soviet media dissociated from the group by giving its name only in transliterated Japanese and ignoring its cooperation with the Soviet-supported PFLP. Dov Appel, *Davar*, 7 August 1973, p. 6. A book by a former Romanian foreign intelligence chief (Ion Mihai Pacepa and Ronald Rychlak, *Disinformation*, Washington, DC: WND Books, 2013) has claimed, however, that the KGB took "secret credit" for this attack among eleven such incidents, allegedly as part of Andropov's revenge for the Soviet humiliation in 1967. David Martosko, "New Book Reveals How KGB Operation Seeded Muslim Countries with Anti-American, Anti-Jewish Propaganda," *Daily Mail*, 25 June 2013.
16. Rubinstein, *Red Star*, p. 212; Lebow and Stein, *We All Lost*, pp. 164, 455n87, based on an interview with a "senior official in Sadat's office," May 1977.
17. Security officer, 2nd Brigade, to 19th Division headquarters, 17 June 1972, CDE-IHC, 282/12.
18. Rubinstein, *Red Star*, p. 187n57; Golan, *Soviet Policies*, p. 79.
19. Rubinstein, *Red Star*, pp. 186–7n56.
20. Heikal, *Road to Ramadan*, pp. 170–5 and Heikal, *Sphinx*, pp. 241–4; Anwar el-Sadat, *In Search of Identity: An Autobiography*, London: Collins, 1978, pp. 228–31.
21. Chernyaev, *Diary 1972*, p. 25.
22. Irina Zvyagel'skaya et al., *Gosudarstvo Izrail'*, Moscow: Institute of Oriental Studies, 2005, p. 197.
23. Central Intelligence Bulletin, "Arab States–Israel," 18 July 1972, http://www.foia.cia.gov/sites/default/files/document_conversions/1699355/1972-07-18.pdf
24. UPI, *Davar*, 17 May 1971, p. 3.
25. Vinogradov, *Diplomatiya*, pp. 207–8.
26. *Davar*, 18 March 1971, p. 1.
27. Ehud Ya'ari, *Davar*, 14 May 1971, p. 1.
28. *Davar*, 16 January 1972, p. 1.
29. "By the time of his mission in July 1972, Sidqi was known to have strong pro-Soviet sympathies"; Rubinstein, *Red Star*, p. 165. Defense Minister Sadiq was described as more mod-

erate and favoring a compromise with pro-Americans like Vice-President Hussein Shafei; Jean-Pierre Joulin, *Nouvel Observateur*, translated in *Davar*, 30 January 1971, p. 8.
30. *Davar*, 8 March 1972, p. 1.
31. UPI, *Davar*, 31 March 1972, p. 1.
32. UPI, *Davar*, 9 April 1972, p. 1.
33. Yisra'el Landress, *Davar*, 6 June 1972, p. 2.
34. Sergey Krakhmalov, *Zapiski voennogo attashe: Iran–Egipet–Iran–Afganistan*, Moscow: Russkaya Razvedka, 2000, p. 128. Ghaleb had replaced Mahmud Riad when Sidqi became prime minister in January 1972.
35. Arab affairs correspondent, *Davar*, 27 July 1972, p. 2. Beirut newspapers wrongly predicted that Sidqi would be replaced by Hafez Ismail, "Egypt's Kissinger" and Sadat's liaison with Washington, and held that Sidqi's ouster was due to a dispute with Defense Minister Sadiq about the expulsion of Soviet advisers.
36. Rubinstein, *Red Star*, pp. 187–8.
37. Reuters, "Second Lead Sadat, Cairo," 18 July 1972, take 3, quoting "informed sources." Copy in NA(PRO).
38. Abramov, *Goluboe*, p. 109.
39. [Alan B.] Urwick to MOD, 21 July 1972, 1230 GMT, NA(PRO). Urwick later headed the MI6 station in Jordan (Nigel West, "Obituary for Sir David Spedding," *The Independent*, 15 June 2001) and (as Sir Alan) served as ambassador in Cairo from 1985 to 1987. His MI6 affiliation was confirmed to the authors by a former colleague.
40. Telegram 1065, Cairo embassy to FCO, 22 July 1972, NA(PRO).
41. Golan, *Soviet Policies*, p. 79.
42. Rubinstein, *Red Star*, p. 188 (citing *Egyptian Gazette*, 19 July 1972); p. 189n62.
43. Chernyaev, *Diary 1972*, pp. 27–8.
44. *Al-Ahram*, 16 July 1972, cited in Rubinstein, *Red Star*, p. 188n60.
45. Vinogradov, "K istorii Sovetsko-Egipetskikh otnosheniy," p. 19. This account was originally published in 1998, the year of Vinogradov's death, in another anthology, published by the Council of Combat Veterans in Egypt (Safonov et al., *Grif*, pp. 5–18). Both books were meant for distribution among the veterans only. The passage is conspicuously absent from Vinogradov's book *Diplomatiya*.
46. Ivanov, "Egipetskie kontrasty," p. 184.
47. Kapitanets, *Na Sluzhbe*, pp. 321–2.
48. Akopov, transcript, pp. 27–30.
49. Chernyaev, *Diary 1972*, p. 25.
50. IAF website page for 13 June 1972, http://www.iaf.org.il/3633-4958-he/IAF.aspx
51. El'chaninov, "Dan prikaz emu ... v Egipet!," p. 110.
52. [Col.] Porfiry Kuleshov, "V zone Suetskogo kanala," in Sannikov et al., *Internatsionalisty*, p. 116; N.R. Yakushev, "Eto bylo, bylo, bylo ..." in Meyer et al., *Togda*, p. 386; Ground crewman Aleksandr Rodionov, interviewed in Yur'ev, "Ogon'."
53. [Maj.] Gennady Lozynin, "Na zashchite Asuana," in Sannikov et al., *Internatsionalisty*, p. 106.

54. A later British assessment held that around twenty of the sixty Soviet MiG-21s were "handed over to the Egyptians." "Military Implications for NATO of the Soviet Withdrawal from Egypt," undated but giving estimates for 5 October 1972, NA(PRO).
55. The Israeli record of a flight on 16 May disproves the claim that "in March '72 two planes were ordered back with first group of personnel, and the rest in April"; Bysenkov, "V 20,000 metrakh." More plausible but apparently inaccurate is the version that "MiG-25 flights continued till June 1972," in "MiG-25 i modifikatsii," http://www.aviation-gb7.ru/MiG-25_01.htm
56. Andrey Pochtarev, "Blizhnevostochny triumf 'letuchikh lisits,'" *Krasnaya Zvezda*, 17 August 2002, http://old.redstar.ru/2002/08/17_08/4_01.html;V. Yu. Markovsky, "MiG-25 nad Sinaem," in Markovsky, "Idite v zemlyu egipetskuyu: Uchastie sovetskikh MiG-25RB v arabo-izrail'skoy voyne Sudnogo dnya 1973g."
57. N[o'am] Ofir, *Heyl ha-Avir* (IAF Magazine), 118 (December 1997), http://www.iaf.org.il/463-18650-he/IAF.aspx
58. Urwick to MOD, 21 July 1972, 1230 GMT, NA(PRO).
59. Abramov, *Goluboe*, p. 54
60. Vladimir Babich, "Kak MiG-25 ushel ot 'oblavy' bolee 10 'Fantomov,'" *Krasnaya Zvezda*, 24 February 1996, www.soldiering.ru/avia/airplane/25arabian.php
61. Volodin, "Na Izrail.'"
62. Authorization signed by the acting commander of the 112th Infantry Brigade, 16 July 1972, CDE-IHC 48/11.
63. Murzintsev, *Zapiski*, pp. 6, 135–8.
64. "Smirnov," *Arabo-izrail'skie voyny*, p. 282. Cf. Krokhin, "Dubl."
65. FCO telegram 1031, British embassy, Cairo, to FCO, 0900 GMT, 18 July 1972, p. 2, NA(PRO).
66. Urwick to MOD, UK; unnumbered FCO telegram, 21 July 1972, 1230 GMT, NA(PRO).

24. WITHDRAWN REGULARS CONCEAL "BANISHED" ADVISERS

1. Truthfully enough, but in what seemed at the time as covering up a unilateral expulsion, the report attributed their repatriation to mutual agreement. Roger Leddington, AP Moscow, "Job Done in Egypt, as Tass Explains It," *Yonkers Herald-Statesman*, 20 July 1972, p. 2.
2. Dobrynin, *Sugubo doveritel'no*, p. 244.
3. Lev Bausin, *Spetssluzhby mira na Blizhnem Vostoke*, Moscow: OLMA-Press, 2001, p. 207.
4. Markovsky, "My gotovili voynu."
5. Pochtarev, "Blizhnevostochny triumf."
6. Zolotarev et al., *Rossiya*, pp. 197, 519n357.
7. FCO telegram D14, British defense attaché, Tel Aviv, to MOD, 20 July 1972, NA(PRO), based on talk with Col. Reuter, a liaison officer of the IDF spokesman.
8. "Sisco–Rabin Conversation on Expulsion of Soviet Advisors," Department of State telegram 135853, secretary of state to embassy Tel Aviv (and others), 27 July 1972, NARA, NSC Files, country files, ME–Israel, box 609.

9. [Lord] Cromer, ambassador in Washington to FCO, 21 July 1972, NA(PRO).
10. Colby to Kissinger, "Critique of Middle East Crisis," 27 October 1973, http://www.foia.cia.gov/sites/default/files/1973-10-27-CIA.pdf
11. Ehud Ya'ari, *Davar*, 20 July 1972, p. 1.
12. Golan, *Soviet Policies*, p. 79; emphasis added.
13. Central Intelligence Bulletin, "Arab States–Israel," 20 July 1972, http://www.foia.cia.gov/sites/default/files/document_conversions/1699355/1972–07–20.pdf
14. Veterans' site of 8th Air Defense Corps, http://8oapvo.net/
15. "Third Round, June 1972-August 1972," 18th Air Defense Division history page, http://old.hubara-rus.ru/18zrd.html
16. Luk'yanov, who retired as a lieutenant-colonel, interviewed in Latypov, "O druzhbe."
17. Zaytsev, "Pomnyu Egipet," p. 72. He states that of the *vzvod's* sixteen men, fifteen returned as "we lost one and sent him back as 'cargo 200,'" the code for shipping coffins. As Helwan was not bombed during Zaytsev's service in Egypt, this must have been due to illness or accident.
18. Bondarenko, "Mariupol'tsy"; "Egipet: Neizvestnaya voyna."
19. Udmantsev, "Bezvizovaya komandirovka."
20. Bregman and el-Tahri, *Fifty Years War*, p. 112. This book was published to accompany the eponymous television series, which was first broadcast in the spring of 1998.
21. [Capt.] N. Antropov: "Kod *Pechora*," in Sannikov et al., *Internatsionalisty*, p. 120; Valery Serdyuk, a former *Shilka* radar operator, in Yosif Kalyuta, "Dialog ob internatsional'nom dolge s neozhidannym prodolzheniem," *Narodnaya gazeta* (Belarus), 22 October 1999. The date he provides, 12 September, refers to his unit's withdrawal from the canal, after a period of confinement to its positions with no town leaves, "as students were demonstrating against the 'Russian occupiers'"; it arrived in the USSR "by the end of the month."
22. "Smirnov," *Arabo-izrail'skie voyny*, p. 307.
23. Interviewed in Vladimir Shunevich and Nadezhda Shunevich, "Sumev pomoch' armii Egipta izbezhat' porazheniya, na Rodine nashi voiny edva ne ugodili pod tribunal," *Fakty i kommentarii* (Kiev), 22 March 2002, http://fakty.ua/91191-kogda-vernuvshiesya-v-marte-1971-goda-s-arabo-izrailskoj-vojny-sovetskie-soldaty-pytalis-obyasnit-chinovnikam-chto-voevali-v-rajone-aleksandrii-te-sprashivali-quot-eto-gde-pod-kievom-quot
24. Latypov, "O druzhbe."
25. Meyden, "Na rasstoyanii." Lt. Mishchenko, who was posted to Egypt in May 1971, also departed in August 1972 and thus was evidently in Mavrin's unit. Temirova and Shunevich, "Vo vremya voyny."
26. Several Russian sources claim that the withdrawal was carried out by aircraft as well as ships, which began to arrive within a day or two of Sadat's declaration. See, e.g., "Smirnov," *Arabo-izrail'skie voyny*, p. 283. This may refer to the planes that brought incoming advisers, as mentioned by Murzintsev, or to the removal of the Foxbats.
27. Zolotarev et al., *Rossiya*, p. 198.
28. Shunevich and Shunevich, "Sumev pomoch' armii Egipta."
29. Grachev, "Nebo."

30. Maurin, "V tel'nyashke i skafandre." By 2011, however, Bebishev was honored at a local ceremony for—among other achievements—his service in Egypt. Anzhero-Sudzhensk Regional History Museum, "Meropriyatie 'Morskaya dusha: Tel'nyashka.'"
31. Valery Serdyuk, as reported in Kalyuta, "Dialog."
32. Zhayvoronok, "Vozvrashchenie k proshlomu," p. 45.
33. Il'inskaya, "Voyna prizrakov." In a "stop press" postscript to "Egipet: Neizvestnaya voyna," *Sputnik* reported in January 1991 that noncommissioned officer Ivan Ivichuk, who had served in Egypt from early 1971 to July 1972 and was still in uniform, had just received his citation and pin.
34. Office of National Estimates, "The Russian Ouster: Causes and Consequences," 22 August 1972, http://www.foia.cia.gov/sites/default/files/document_conversions/1699355/1972-08-22.pdf
35. Sella, *Soviet Political and Military Conduct*, p. 77.
36. Efraim Karsh, "Soviet Arms Transfers to the Middle East in the 1970s," Jaffee Center Paper no. 22, Tel Aviv University, December 1983, p. 27.
37. Interviewed by Elena Suponina, *Vremya Novostei*, 6 October 2003, www.vremya.ru/print/81683.html
38. A. Yu. Dashkov and V.D. Golotyuk, "Arabo-Izrail'skiy konflikt: Boevye deystviya sovetskoy aviatsii i PVO v Egipte," www.airaces.ru/stati/arabo-izrailskijj-konflikt-boevye-dejj-stviya-sovetskojj-aviacii-i-pvo-v-egipte.html#identifier_2_4428

25. DECEPTION-ON-NILE, JULY 1972

1. Embassy Cairo to MOD, 22 July 1972, "Secret: UK Eyes Only," NA(PRO); emphasis added.
2. On the significance of this document for evaluating Marwan's function, see Ginor and Remez, "A Hidden Alley in the Arab-Israeli Maze," *NYT*, 30 July 2007, in response to Howard Blum, "Who Killed Ashraf Marwan?," *NYT*, 13 July 2007.
3. "Conclusions of a Meeting of the Cabinet," 27 July 1972, NA(PRO), CAB 128/50/39.
4. "Conclusions of a Meeting of the Cabinet," 1 August 1972, p. 3, NA(PRO) CAB 120/50/40.
5. AP, "Egypt Might Buy System from Britain," *Recorder* (Amsterdam, NY), 6 October 1972.
6. Likewise, if there was any basis to reports in December 1972 "that Egyptian pilots were undergoing familiarization courses in Kuwait on [British-made] Lightning aircraft." Sella, *Soviet Political and Military Conduct*, p. 179n15.
7. UPI, *Davar*, 11 December 1972, p. 2.
8. "Egypt Is Reported to Get Advanced Soviet Missile," *NYT*, November 12, 1972, p. 2.
9. AC, APR, vol. 1, p. 8.
10. "Egyptian Search for Alternate Source of Arms," Day, US consulate Jerusalem, to secretary of state, 11 September 1972, NARA, NSC files, country files, ME–Israel, box 609.
11. Sadat interview on Cairo Radio, 24 October 1975 and Tawila article on the anniversary of the war in *Rose el-Yussef*, 7 October 1974. Together with the relevant parts of Tawila's book *The Six-Hour War According to a Military Correspondent's Diary*, they were first

brought to wide Western attention by Uri Ra'anan in testimony before a congressional committee in March 1976 and in Uri Ra'anan, "The Soviet–Egyptian 'Rift,'" *Commentary*, 61, 6 (June 1976), pp. 30–2. They were reproduced, and Ra'anan's interpretation echoed, both by journalists, e.g., NBC and *Washington Post* correspondent Alvin Rosenfeld (*The Plot to Destroy Israel*, New York: Putnam, 1977, pp. 111–14), and scholars, e.g., Samuel Katz (*Battleground*, updated edn, Tel Aviv: Steimatzky, 1985, pp. 217–21, http://www.ourjerusalem.com/series/story/battleground040.html). Katz, like other right-wing Israeli historians, retained this interpretation ("The Man with a Plan," *Jerusalem Post*, 24 October 2003, http://www.saveisraelcampaign.com/atad/Articles.asp?article_id=1630). But when the Egyptian–Soviet rift after 1974 turned out not to have been a ruse, most mainstream historiography gratuitously discarded this characterization of Sadat's prewar moves as well. In the most notable exception, David Kimche asserted that the "expulsion" was "done in collusion with the Soviet Union" as a joint deception move, part of a strategy developed by Brezhnev himself (*Last Option*, p. 22).

12. Il'inskaya, "Voyna prizrakov."
13. Murzintsev, *Zapiski*, p. 138; Vakhtin, "Simfonicheskiy kontsert."
14. But he also lashed out against US policy; the same day, Egypt reported exposing an American subversion plot. Reports by David Moshayov, Ehud Ya'ari and AP, *Davar*, 25 July 1972, pp. 1–2.
15. The agency noted that Sadat's speech was "replete with references to firm US ... aid to Israel ... [which was] implemented 'automatically and most enthusiastically and violently,' in contrast to the limited Soviet response to Egypt's pleas ... the speech seemed primarily designed to salve some of the wounds in Moscow." Central Intelligence Bulletin, "Arab States–Israel," 25 July 1972, http://www.foia.cia.gov/sites/default/files/document_conversions/1699355/1972-07-25.pdf
16. Kissinger, *White House Years*, pp. 1276, 1295–6; emphasis added
17. Sheehan, *Arabs, Israelis, and Kissinger*, p. 22.
18. Stein, *Heroic Diplomacy*, p. 65.
19. The never-solved murder of Israeli Air Attaché Col. Joe Allon in Washington in July 1973 has been construed, most recently in an Israel TV "documentary," as aimed to suppress his knowledge of a conspiracy between Sadat, Kissinger and Dayan to "allow Egypt a small victory." No substantive evidence has ever been offered. Bar-Joseph, *Ha'aretz*, 12 April 2011, http://www.Ha'aretz.co.il/opinions/1.1170857
20. CIA Directorate of Intelligence, "Soviet–Egyptian Relations: An Uneasy Alliance," no. 0847/72, 28 March 1972, p. 6.
21. Aleksey Volovich, "Sovetskie voyska v Egipte," *Odesskie Izvestiya*, 14 February 2013, http://izvestiya.odessa.ua/ru/2013/02/16/sovetskie-voyska-v-egipte. This Gen. Gorelov was a paratroop commander and not to be confused with the air force general who served in Egypt earlier.
22. Vinogradov, *Diplomatiya*, pp. 220, 226–38; Kirpichenko, *Razvedka*, pp. 124–7; Ivanov, "Egipetskie kontrasty," p. 184.
23. Kissinger, *White House Years*, pp. 1297–8.

24. *FRUS* N-XV, no. 16–17.
25. As cabled to London by Lord Cromer, Washington, 28 July 1972, NA(PRO).
26. Richard Nixon, *The Real War*, New York: Warner Books, 1981, p. 327.
27. Memo for the president from Kissinger, 14 June 1973, *FRUS* N-XXV, no. 70.
28. Kissinger, *White House Years*, p. 1295; Henry Kissinger, *Diplomacy*, New York: Simon and Schuster, 1994, p. 739.
29. John Lewis Gaddis, *The Cold War: A New History*, New York: Penguin, 2005, p. 204; Gershom Gorenberg, *The Accidental Empire: Israel and the Birth of the Settlements, 1967–1977*, New York: Holt, 2006, pp. 232–3.
30. Laqueur, *Confrontation*, p. 19.
31. Mangold, *Superpower Intervention*, p. 126.
32. Quandt endorsed our thesis about the "expulsion" when it first appeared: "where I am most willing to cede ground to a new interpretation is on the issue of the 'expulsion' of Soviet military advisers ... [Ginor and Remez] convincingly show that the Soviet personnel who left Egypt were the combat troops that had come during the War of Attrition, not the advisers. The latter remained and were present at the time of the October 1973 war. This seems like a useful correction to conventional accounts." Review of Ashton, *The Cold War in the Middle East*, in *Journal of Cold War Studies*, 1, 1 (Winter 2009), p. 159. In his 2006 study, Dima Adamsky agrees with our previously published finding: "to this day, scholars mistakenly define Sadat's July 1972 step as 'an expulsion of Soviet advisers,' when in fact the advisers remained in Egypt." But he retains the concept of a unilateral Egyptian move. Dima Adamsky, "'Zero Hour for the Bears': Inquiring into the Soviet Decision to Intervene in the Israeli–Egyptian War of Attrition, 1969–1970," *Cold War History*, 6, 1 (2006), p. 129.
33. "Smirnov," *Arabo-izrail'skie voyny*, p. 284. Cf. Krokhin, "Dubl."
34. Kapitanets, *Na sluzhbe*, pp. 322–3.
35. "Smirnov," *Arabo-izrail'skie voyny*, pp. 282–301.
36. Operations officer, 2nd Infantry Brigade, to Operations Branch, 19th Infantry Division, 28 May 1973, CDE-IHC 295/12. A routine timetable of the same advisers' activities for the entire month of July, as for the previous months since January, had been issued on 26 June; 112th Brigade headquarters to Operations Department, 16th Division, "Activities Plan for the Soviet Advisers, July 1972," 22 June 1972, CDE-IHC 48/11.
37. http://artofwar.ru/j/jakushew_w_g/
38. [Lt-Col.] M[ikhail] Ryabov, "Ne zabud', stantsiya Khatatba," in Meyer et al., *Togda*, p. 330.
39. Chernyaev, *Diary 1972*, p. 28.
40. "Work Plan for Soviet Advisers in Training Year 1973," (n.d.), CDE-IHC 784/6. The previous plans are listed in doc. 367/12.
41. Asher, *Breaking the Concept*, pp. 113, 163–8.
42. Shai, "Mitzrayim," p. 35n35.
43. Urwick to MOD, 21 July 1972, 1230 GMT, NA(PRO).
44. "Smirnov," *Arabo-izrail'skie voyny*, p. 300.
45. Igor' Vakhtin, "Gusinaya pechenka na pistoletnom shompole," 17 April 2014, http://clubvi.ru/news/2014/06/16/remember/75%20vahtin/

46. Rubinstein, *Red Star*, pp. 192–3.
47. Stein, *Heroic Diplomacy*, p. 65, citing Mohamed Hassanein Heikal, *Autumn of Fury: The Assassination of Sadat*, London: Andre Deutsch, 1983, p. 46; for contemporary sources on the continuing supply of Soviet arms to Egypt, see Ra'anan, "Rift," p. 33n.
48. Vladimir Marchenko, "Voyna sudnogo dnya i amerikano-izrailskie otnoshennya: Tridtsat' let spustya," *Vestnik* (Cockeysville, MD), 22–9 October 2003, www.vestnik.com/issues/2003/1029/win/marchenko.htm
49. Central Intelligence Bulletin, "Arab States–Israel," 18 July 1972, http://www.foia.cia.gov/sites/default/files/document_conversions/1699355/1972-07-18.pdf. The T-62s would be among the first sent across the canal, but despite their "more powerful gun than the T-55s that now make up the bulk of Egyptian armor," they would be effectively countered by antiquated Israeli Sherman tanks refitted with even better guns.
50. Maj. Richard Owen, "Operational Valiant: Turning of the Tide in the Sinai 1973 Arab–Israeli War," Marine Corps Command and Staff College, 1984, http://www.globalsecurity.org/military/library/report/1984/ORL.htm
51. Ra'anan, "Rift," p. 31.
52. "Intelligence Memorandum Prepared in the Central Intelligence Agency," June 1973, *FRUS* N-XXV, no. 66.
53. Amir Oren, *Devar ha-Shavu'a*, 16 November 1979, p. 4.
54. Interviews in Marchenko, "General-Mayor VVS Vagin" and "Siriyskaya komandirovka." Vagin said that after the 1973 war, Mubarak on a visit to Syria "observed the results of our work" training Syrian pilots and invited him back to Egypt, as "everything has changed."
55. Interviewed in D. Belebentsev, "V poletakh nad piramidami," *Gazeta Sovetskaya Chuvashiya*, 4 February 2005.
56. "9-y gvardeyskiy minno-torpedy Kirkenesskiy Krasnoznamenny aviatsionny polk," http://www.airaces.ru/stati/9-jj-gvardejjskijj-minno-torpednyjj-kirkenesskijj-krasnoznamjon-nyjj-aviacionnyjj-polk-9-jj-gv-mtap-vvs-sf.html
57. Two missiles were fired at Tel Aviv in the first hours of the war: one malfunctioned and the other was shot down just off the city's waterfront by a Mirage. Ro'i Mandel, ynet news website, 17 September 2010, http://www.ynet.co.il/articles/0,7340,L-3955622,00.html. Of the other missiles, which were fired at military targets in Sinai, most were shot down by anti-aircraft cannon, but one destroyed a radar station near Sharm-el-Sheikh, killing five of its operators. Haggai Huberman, Channel 7 (Israel), 20 September 2010, http://www.inn.co.il/News/News.aspx/209414. The Soviets accounted for the Kelts' "low efficacy" by pointing out they were of an old variant, which was not adequately equipped against electronic countermeasures. "Na voennoy sluzhbe," in S.V. Ivanov (ed.), *Voyna v vozdukhe*, no. 26 (Tu-16), 2004?, http://betta.vlz.ru/il2/AirWar/26/04.htm
58. Rubtsov, memoir.
59. Bar-Joseph, *Angel*, pp. 133–6.
60. AC, final report, vol. 4, p. 1488.
61. Three were shot down while attacking IDF installations on Mt Miron, northern Israel. Golan, *Decision Making*, p. 442.

62. Bar-Joseph, *Angel*, p. 140; p. 191 states that the planes' arrival was detected only in "early 1973."
63. AC, Shalev testimony, Part 2, pp. 101–2.
64. AC, APR, vol. 1, p. 7, quoting Ze'ira at an ambassadors' conference, 21 September 1973; final report, vol. 4, p. 1493, quoting Zei'ra on 17 September.
65. AC, APR, vol. 1, pp. 60–1, 88–92.
66. Bar-Joseph, *Angel*, pp. 168–9.
67. Yoav Efrati, "1/72 AML Mirage IIIC: Israeli Recon," Air Resource Center, http://www.aircraftresourcecenter.com/Gal6/5001-5100/gal5049_Mirage_Efrati/00.shtm; Bar-Joseph, *Angel*, p. 192. At least two were shot down by IAF counterparts during an Israeli attack on their base at Mansura.
68. A.V. Yena, "Zashchishchaya nebo nad Egiptom," in Meyer et al., *Togda*, p. 136.
69. *FRUS* N-XV, no. 25.

26. THE SOVIETS "RETURN" IN OCTOBER

1. The meeting was a few days after the Palestinian attack on the Israeli team at the Munich Olympics. The Soviets in Egypt felt "there was some concern—someone high up in the Egyptian leadership feared Israeli retaliations, which was nonsense as Egypt had nothing to do with it." "Smirnov," *Arabo-izrail'skie voyny*, pp. 304–5.
2. Primakov, *Blizhniy Vostok*, pp. 280–1.
3. Chernyaev, *Diary 1973*, pp. 6–7.
4. Bar-Joseph, *Angel*, p. 189; Bar-Joseph, *The Watchman Fell Asleep: The Surprise of Yom Kippur and Its Sources*, Tel Aviv: Zmora-Bitan, 2001, p. 166.
5. Memorandum of conversation, Moscow, September 13, 1972. *FRUS* N-XV, no. 44.
6. Intelligence memorandum, "The View from the Kremlin Three Months after the Summit," 13 September 1972. *FRUS* N-XV, no. 45.
7. FCO, "Military Implications for NATO of the Soviet Withdrawal from Egypt," undated but giving estimates for 5 October 1972, NA(PRO).
8. Asher, *Breaking the Concept*, p. 113; unsourced.
9. Chaim Herzog, *The War of Atonement*, London: Greenhill Books, 1998, pp. 21, 23; emphasis added.
10. Asher, *Breaking the Concept*, pp. 93–101. Badry, *Ramadan War*, pp. 19–20.
11. Memorandum of conversation, Washington, 2 October 1972, *FRUS* N-XV, no. 55.
12. *Davar*, 4 October 1972, p. 1.
13. *Davar*, 1 October 1972, p. 1. On the same page, a first major Chinese loan to Egypt was reported.
14. Interview for *Al-Hawadess*, Beirut, reported in *Davar*, 6 October 1972, p. 1; Yisra'el Landress, Washington, *Davar*, 15 October 1972, p. 1.
15. Henry Tanner, Cairo, "Soviet Reported to Pledge Some Arms Aid to Egypt," *NYT*, 20 October 1972, p. 2. The day before, the *NYT* had reported from Moscow that Sidqi returned "without any new public pledges of Soviet military or economic aid." "Egypt's Premier Ends Soviet Talk," *NYT*, 19 October 1972, p. 7.

16. Shimshon Ofer, *Davar*, 11 October 1972, p. 1.
17. UPI, "Cairo Sources Deny Plot against Sadat," *Union-Sun Journal* (Lockport, NY), 20 November 1972, p. 1.
18. "Egypt's Arms Chief Quits After Leaders Back Sadat," *NYT*, 27 October 1972, p. 3. Kass, in 1978 (*Soviet Involvement*, pp. 205–15), still believed that Sadiq's ouster was due to his "pronounced anti-Soviet stance," and that it marked the success of the Soviet military's effort to restore relations with Egypt, against the political leadership's desire. Most of this was admittedly speculative.
19. "Ahmad Ismail," *Encyclopedia Britannica*, http://www.britannica.com/EBchecked/topic/930499/Ahmad-Ismail
20. Television interview on 27 October, quoted in *Davar*, 29 October 1972, p. 1.
21. Hanoch Bartov, *Dado: 48 shanah ve-od 20 yom*, vol. 1, Tel Aviv: Ma'ariv, 1978, p. 231; Bar-Joseph, *Angel*, pp. 185–6, 189.
22. Document cited by Justice Agranat, AC, Eban testimony, Part 2, p. 7.
23. Asher, *Breaking the Concept*, pp. 93–101.
24. Clipping in NA(PRO).
25. FCO telegrams: embassy Tel Aviv to FCO, 1 November 1972; defense attaché Tel Aviv to MOD, 2 November 1972; embassy Cairo to FCO, 2 November 1972; embassy Beirut to FCO, 9 November 1972; letter, A. J[ames] M. Craig to Beaumont, 3 November 1972, all in NA(PRO).
26. Beaumont was an eminent "Arabist," a fluent Arabic speaker and promoter of British–Arab relations. Obituary in the *Daily Telegraph*, 28 January 2009, http://www.telegraph.co.uk/news/obituaries/4376028/Sir-Richard-Beaumont.html.
27. [Ambassador Paul] Wright, Beirut to FCO, 9 November 1972, NA(PRO).
28. A.J.M. Craig, FCO, to Beaumont, Cairo, 3 November 1972
29. [Ambassador Bernard] Ledwidge, Tel Aviv to FCO, 2 November 1972.
30. Beaumont, Cairo to FCO, 2 November 1972, emphasis added.
31. Beaumont to FCO, 2 December, 1972, NA(PRO).
32. Beaumont to FCO, 2 November 1972, NA(PRO); emphasis added.
33. Ryabov, "Ne zabud'," p. 138.
34. "Egypt Is Reported to Get Advanced Soviet Missile," *NYT*, 12 November 1972, p. 2. The story also repeated Bulloch's claim about "Russians returning to Egypt," although the British tended by now to dismiss it.
35. AC, Shalev testimony, Part 2, pp. 99–100; this is attributed to a "very good" source of Ze'ira's whose identity is sanitized—possibly another case in which misleading information from Marwan overrode accurate reports from other informants.
36. Beaumont to FCO, 13 November 1972, NA(PRO). The attaché, J.P. Marriott, expanded on this interview in a letter to the MOD ("Call on Admiral Ivliev," 14 November), noting that his Soviet interlocutor had been very forthcoming on all subjects except the matter of Port Said, on which Ivliev seemed uncomfortable.
37. D.A.S. Gladstone to A.J.M. Craig, Near East and North Africa Department, FCO, "Soviet/Egyptian Relations in the Military Field," 21 November 1972, NA(PRO). Gladstone

pointed out that Ivliev's "long and bleak history ... is not such as to inspire automatic confidence," having been expelled from both Britain and France for intelligence activities. The British official also noted Ivliev's "admission that there is something peculiar about the use to which the Russians put Port Said (we have always suspected this)."

38. C.L. Sulzberger, "Sadat Says Soviet Will Retain Use of Bases in Egypt," *NYT*, 13 December 1972, p. 1.
39. Lebow and Stein, *We All Lost*, quoting interview with Vadim Zagladin, deputy director of CC International Relations Department in 1973, on 18 May 1989; pp. 170, 457n122.
40. Bartov, *Dado*, vol. 1, p. 234, citing joint interview for three Israeli papers, 2 February 1973.

PART 4: "WE PREPARED THE WAR"

1. Yuliya Latynina, "Armiya, kotoraya proigryvaet i zhaluetsya na zhenshchin," *Novaya Gazeta*, 25 October 2004, http://2004.novayagazeta.ru/nomer/2004/79n/n79n-s02.shtml
2. Posting by "Mir Vam," in *Novaya Gazeta* readers' forum, 27 October 2004, responding to the Latynina article.
3. Zvyagelskaya et al., *Gosudarstvo Izrail'*, p. 201.
4. Patrick Seale, *Asad: The Struggle for the Middle East*, London: Tauris, 1988, p. 193, citing Shazly, *Crossing*, p. 202.
5. AC, Eban testimony, Part 2, pp. 72–3.
6. Joseph Alsop, "Columnist's Scenario: Russians 'Blinked,'" *Herald-Statesman* (Yonkers, NY), 27 October 1973. Quandt (*Peace Process*, p. 165), quotes a similar estimate by Alsop on 15 October as well founded, while Kissinger was still "suspicious, but ... felt the Soviets were still interested in a diplomatic settlement."
7. David C. Hendrickson, review of Edwin M. Yoder Jr., *Joe Alsop's Cold War: A Study of Journalistic Influence and Intrigue*, in *Foreign Affairs* (September/October 1995)
8. Draper, *Present History*, pp. 201, 276–7 (written December 1973). As the "general principles" for the Middle East had not yet been made public, his reference is to violation of the global "basic principles."
9. See, e.g., Markovsky, "My gotovili voynu."

27. "WE CAN'T CONTROL THE ARABS BUT MUST SUPPORT THEM"

1. AP, "Egyptian Shops for Arms in Soviet Union," *Times-Record* (Troy, NY), 29 November 1972, p. 32; editorial, *Davar*, 5 December 1972, p. 9.
2. Rowland Evans and Robert Novak, "Egypt's Sadat at Bay," *Daily Press* (Utica, NY), 4 December 1972, p. 6.
3. "Reds Down First B-52 of War," *Los Angeles Times*, 22 November 1972, p. 1.
4. Lt-Gen. Mark Vorobyov, "Dvina Guarding Vietnam's Skies," *Military Parade, the Magazine of the [Russian] Defense Industry Complex*, 28 (29 July 1998).
5. "Smirnov," *Arabo-izrail'skie voyny*, p. 304.
6. *Davar*, 5 December 1972, p. 9.
7. Bar-Joseph, *Angel*, p. 187.
8. Arab affairs correspondent, *Davar*, 21 December 1972, p. 1.

9. *Davar*, 29 December 1972, p. 1.
10. "Smirnov," *Arabo-izrail'skie voyny*, p. 305.
11. "Smirnov," *Arabo-izrail'skie voyny*, pp. 304–5. Cf. Krokhin, "Dubl."
12. Chernyaev, *Diary 1973*, pp. 6–7.
13. Message from Dobrynin to Kissinger, 28 January 1973, *FRUS* N-XXV, no. 9.
14. Memorandum for the president's file by Kissinger, 6 February 1973, "Meeting with King Hussein of Jordan," *FRUS* N-XXV, no. 14.
15. Department of State to embassy in Jordan, 9 February 1973, *FRUS* N-XXV, no. 15.
16. Richard Nixon, *RN: The Memoirs of Richard Nixon*, New York: Simon and Schuster, 2013, pp. 786–7.
17. Conversation between Nixon and army vice chief of staff (Haig), 23 January 1973, *FRUS* N-XXV, no. 6.
18. Jussi M. Hanhimäki, "A Prize-Winning Performance? Kissinger, Triangular Diplomacy, and the End of the Vietnam War, 1969–1973," *Norwegian Nobel Institute Series*, 2, 1, Oslo (2001), p. 40, http://www.nppri.org/pdf/Vol2_No1.pdf
19. Embassy in Israel to Department of State, "Meir Visit," 13 February 1973, *FRUS* N-XXV, no. 17.
20. CIA paper, "Comments on the Egyptian Government Message of 1 February 1973," *FRUS* N-XXV, no. 10. Vinogradov was back in Egypt by October and it seems unlikely that he did not see Sadat in the period that followed.
21. Jim Hoagland, *Washington Post*, Cairo, translated in *Ma'ariv*, 12 February 1973, p. 5.
22. Shai, "Mitzrayim," p. 35n31. The interviews were given in October 1974 (to a Beirut newspaper) and January 1975 (to *Rose el-Yussef*).
23. Heikal, *Road to Ramadan*, p. 2. The account is unclear whether the autumn timing for the offensive was determined at this meeting or at another such council in Alexandria in August, which is discussed below.
24. Zamir, quoted in Bartov, *Dado*, vol. 1, p. 236. The earlier testimonies to the appearance of *Malyutkas* on the canal front call into question Shazly's version that the March 1973 deal provided for supply of the *first* fifty.
25. AC, final report, p. 85.
26. Terence Smith, "Israeli and Egyptian Jets Clash at Suez," *NYT*, 16 February 1973, p. 3; Shimshon Ofer, *Davar*, 16 October 1973, p. 1. The IAF denied Egyptian claims that an Israeli fighter was shot down; Cairo admitted losing one. According to the IAF web page for 15 February 1973, it was a MiG-21 that crashed into the water "during a low-altitude chase."
27. Yigal Kipnis, *1973: Haderekh le-milhamah*, Tel Aviv: Kinneret, Zmorah-Bitan, Dvir, 2012. Conversely, West German Chancellor Willy Brandt has been accused of failing to relay *Israeli* peace feelers to Egypt in June 1973. Michael Wolffson, "Wie Willy Brandt die Friedenskarte verspielte," *Welt am Sonntag*, 9 June 2013, pp. 8–9, http://www.perfect-game.de/images/perfect-game/pdfs/130609%20wams%20miw.pdf. Published in Hebrew with attached documents by ISA, http://www.archives.gov.il
28. Golan, *Decision Making*, p. 1275. On pp. 1282–4, Golan's survey of the military and polit-

ical leadership's consultations found no evidence for Kipnis's thesis that Meir and Dayan doubted even the most reliable reports of Eygpt's impending offensive as they hoped Sadat was merely escalating pressure on Israel for a political settlement after the upcoming Israeli election.

29. AP report, *Palladium-Times* (Oswego, NY), 10 February 1973, p. 1; *Davar*, 9 February 1973, p. 1.
30. "Vermerk über des Gespräch mit Gen. R[ostislav] A. Uljanowski, Stellvertreter des leiters der Internationales Abteilung des ZK der KPdSU an 27 Februar 1973 in Moskau," *Stasi* archive IV, 212.035/55, pp. 18–19, kindly provided by Stefan Meining, Munich. To their East German allies, the Soviets maintained the appearance of an "expulsion" from Egypt but minimized its significance and stressed its "reversal." Ulyanovsky quoted Brezhnev: "Sadat acted under pressure from right-wing forces, particularly former war minister Sadiq. Now they regret this move ... we have once again regulated the advisers' work [and] military cooperation."
31. Soviet leadership to President Nixon, *FRUS* N-XXV, no. 20.
32. *Washington Post*, "Nixon Tells Egyptian Advisor: Our Goal—Snap Mideast Deadlock," *Times* (Geneva, NY), 24 February, 1973, p. 2.
33. This Egyptian position included, besides a full Israeli withdrawal from all occupied Egyptian territory, the non-starter of "Palestinian rights," which Ismail carried beyond Sadat's demand for return of the refugees: "this problem should be reduced to the size of Arab and Jewish communities within the area of mandated Palestine." Kissinger to Nixon, 25–6 February 1973, *FRUS* N-XXV, no. 28.
34. Memorandum of conversation, 8 March 1973, *FRUS* N-XXV, no. 81.
35. Press photos showed Grechko meeting Ismail at the ramp of this Il-18. Previously, an Egyptian announcement said that he would fly on a special Egyptian plane.
36. Gil Qesari, Paris, *Ma'ariv*, 27 February 1973, p. 1.
37. Oded Granot, *Ma'ariv*, 26 February 1973, p. 2.
38. E.g., Egyptian Lt-Gen. Bassam Kakish in Parker, *October War*, p. 92.
39. Badry, *Ramadan War*, p. 46.
40. "Smirnov," *Arabo-izrail'skie voyny*, p. 306. His alter ego Krokhin, who published a near-identical version, left Egypt only in June 1973, and—exceptionally—received in the same month a *gramota* (citation) for "internationalist service," though without mention of where it was. Certificate pictured in Krokhin, "Dubl."
41. AC, APR, 1 April 1974, vol. 1, p. 8.
42. Molodtsov, "Opyt."
43. AC, Aryeh Shalev testimony, Part 2, pp. 101–2.
44. Reuters, *Davar*, 4 March 1973, p. 2.
45. Moshe Maoz, *Asad the Sphinx of Damascus: A Political Biography*, London: Weidenfeld and Nicholson, 1988, p. 166: "There is no good information about contacts between Syria and Egypt in early 1973, but it is known that such contacts to coordinate war moves were already then in progress."
46. G. Pernavsky (ed.), *Arabo-izrail'skie voyny: Arabsky vzglyad*, Moscow: Eksmo-Yauza, 2008,

pp. 102–3, 106. The book claims to reproduce a thesis on Arab–Israeli wars to 1982, written for a Soviet military academy by an unnamed Syrian officer "who in September 1970 served as head of intelligence in the southern military district" (p. 141). It includes testimonies by other "Arab officers and generals who studied at Soviet military academies ... They were required to provide detailed descriptions of their combat experience" (p. 4).

47. Pernavsky, *Arabo-izrail'skie voyny*, pp. 104–6. The "elaboration" went on from 22 February to 7 March.
48. US embassy, Rabat to State Department, 20 March 1973, https://www.wikileaks.org/plusd/cables/1973RABAT01213_b.html
49. Bar-Joseph, *Angel*, pp. 192–4, unsourced (there may of course have been two such conferences). Kissinger shortly afterward claimed to Brezhnev, "we have information that at the Arab Chiefs of Staff meeting, April 21–25, there was an atmosphere of despair and foreboding because of the Egyptian determination to go to war." Memorandum of conversation, Zavidovo, 7 May 1973, *FRUS* N-XV, no. 109.
50. Editorial note, *FRUS* N-XXV, no. 38.
51. Eban recalled only one US "exceptional figure" who insisted that "you're all being deluded ... including our president, our government, our secretary of state. ... The Russians want not only 'controlled obtension'—I think I [Eban] coined that phrase—[but] war too." In the testimony, as declassified in autumn 2013, this US figure's identity was still sanitized, probably indicating an intelligence official. AC, Eban testimony, Part 2, p. 25. The official CIA position, as quoted by Kissinger to Nixon in mid-May, was that "substantial Egyptian–Israel hostilities appear unlikely in the next few weeks ... Arab–Israeli hostilities taking place in 1973 would not involve wide-ranging ground warfare on the Egyptian front." National Intelligence Estimate, 17 May 1973, *FRUS* N-XXV, no. 59.
52. Zurhellen to State Department, 21 March 1973, https://www.wikileaks.org/plusd/cables/1973TELAV02177_b.html
53. Primakov, *Blizhniy Vostok*, p. 281. Kotov is identified in the Mitrokhin Archive as a "legal" agent in the Soviet embassy, Tel Aviv, before the 1967 war. Ronen Bergman, "Secret Documents Expose Israeli Politicians, Senior Defense Officials as KGB spies," ynet news (English), 26 October 2016, http://www.ynetnews.com/articles/0,7340,L-4870386,00.html
54. Baron was now ambassador to the Netherlands. Primakov, *Blizhniy Vostok*, pp. 281–4.
55. Amnon Lord, *The Lost Generation: The Story of the Yom Kippur War*, Tel Aviv: Yedi'ot Ahronot, 2013, pp. 59–61. He claims that the Primakov "channel" was managed by Efraim Halevy, a senior operative (and later head) of the Mossad—the KGB's counterpart agency.

28. "WE WILL BE TWO ISMAILS"

1. AP, "Sadat Juggles His Cabinet," *Gazette* (Schenectady, NY), 28 March 1973, p. 7.
2. AP, "Sadat Issues Call for War with Israel," *News* (Tonawanda, NY), 24 March 1973, p. 4-B
3. Henry Tanner, "Sadat Broadens His Emergency Powers," *NYT*, 30 March 1973, p. 4.
4. "Sadat Appoints a New Cabinet," *NYT*, 28 March 1973, p. 5.
5. "Smirnov," *Arabo-izrail'skie voyny*, p. 307.

6. George Sherman, "Washington Close-up," *Times* (Geneva, NY), 20 April 1973, p. 7.
7. AC, Shalev testimony, Part 2, p. 136; he dates this one week after a dramatic Israeli raid on Beirut, which occurred on 9 April. The newly published Syrian documents mention "maneuvers" in March–April that were detected by the Israelis (Pernavsky, *Arabo-izrail'skie voyny*, p. 104).
8. AC, APR, vol. 1, pp. 6–7. The "Blue-White" plan was presented to the full cabinet on 9 May.
9. AC, final report, p. 66. Marwan's role in triggering "Blue-White" is indicated by Commission member Yadin, who mentioned "one of the important reports received on 27 April [passage sanitized] ... [and] relayed raw to the prime minister."
10. Bar-Joseph, *Angel*, pp. 197–200, 231.
11. Ro'i Mandel, ynet news, 20 September 2012, http://www.ynet.co.il/articles/0,7340,L-4282122,00.html
12. Akopov, transcript, p. 28.
13. "Paper Prepared by the National Security Council Staff, Probably in Early May," *FRUS* N-XXV, no. 59n2.
14. Parker, *October War*, p. 141. Ze'ira opined on 24 April that Sadat was feigning despair in order to influence the summit; AC, APR, p. 70.
15. AC, APR, p. 93.
16. AC, Tal testimony, Part 1, pp. 3–5. This refers to the eastern part of the Golan Heights, which was not occupied by Israel.
17. Mikhail Razinkov, "Siriya: Goryachii Oktyabr' 1973 goda," http://artofwar.ru/r/razinkow_m_w/text_0020.shtml
18. Comment by Yadin in AC, Eban testimony, Part 2, p. 17, quoting "exhibit 26," which has not been released.
19. Memorandum of conversation, Zavidovo, 7 May 1973, *FRUS* N-XXV, no. 53. The editors note that Brezhnev was referring to "Ahmed Ismail's visit to Moscow *following* Hafiz Ismail's "visit" to Washington. Actually, Ahmed arrived in Moscow on 26 February, when Hafez's US talks were still in progress.
20. Ehud Eran, "Kishlon kehillat ha-modi'in ha-Americanit be-ha'arakhat mitqefet ha-peta h-Mitzrit-Surit be-milhemet Yom ha-Kippurim," Center on Intelligence and Terrorism, Israel Intelligence Heritage Center, 3 September 2013, http://www.terrorism-info.org.il/Data/articles/Art_20569/H_138_13_1132530023.pdf; Daigle, "Limits of Détente," pp. 265–9.
21. Conversation between Nixon and Kissinger, 16 May 1973. *FRUS* N-XXV, no. 58.
22. Kissinger to Nixon, 20 May 1973, *FRUS* N-XXV, no. 63.
23. Kissinger, *Years of Upheaval*, p. 227.
24. AC, Eban testimony, Part 2, pp. 6–8, 22. Commission members mentioned another paper, the identity of whose author remains sanitized.
25. AC, Eban testimony, Part 1, p. 16.
26. Pernavsky, *Arabo-izrail'skie voyny*, p. 105.
27. "Excerpts from a Record of a Meeting between Soviet Journalist, Victor Louis, and General

Director of the Prime Minister's Office, Mordechai Gazit, 15 June 1973," CWIHP e-Dossier, no. 31, http://www.wilsoncenter.org/publication/e-dossier-no-31-secret-soviet-israeli-negotiations. Guy Laron's description of this document, "secret Soviet–Israeli negotiations," is overstated: unlike Primakov's visit, the arrival of "Louis who is said to have contacts in the Kremlin" was publicized before this talk; UPI, "Soviet Journalist Arrives in Israel," *Star-News* (Wilmington, NC), 14 July 1973, p. 10. The transcript confirms that Louis brought no specific message, and certainly did not conduct "negotiations." His claim that the Soviets discounted Arab prospects in a war conforms better to Lord's description of Louis's mission, like Primakov's, as deliberate disinformation (*Lost Generation*, p. 107).

28. AC, Eban testimony, Part 2, p. 26.
29. Memorandum of conversation, 23 June 1973, *FRUS* N-XXV, no. 72.
30. Chazov charges that the cures urged upon Brezhnev by non-medical well-wishers led to depression and lethargy. At the summit, the doctor claims he dealt with this problem without giving it away—that is, without these medications—so that his patient was anything but drowsy, as confirmed by the Americans' descriptions. *Zdorov'e i vlast'*, pp. 112–15, 119–23.
31. Memorandum for the president's files by Kissinger, 23 June 1973, *FRUS* N-XXV, no. 73.
32. AP, "US, Soviet Heads to Seek New Arms Curbs," *Leader-Herald* (Gloversville-Johnstown, NY), 25 June 1973, p. 1.
33. Bernard Gwertzman, "Brezhnev Leaves U.S. for France: Communique Cites Improved Relations," *NYT*, 26 June 1973, p. 1.
34. Hedrick Smith, "Nixon, Brezhnev End Summit," *NYT*, 25 June 1973, p. 69.
35. Kissinger, *Years of Upheaval*, pp. 297–8; Nixon, *RN*, p. 885.
36. This assessment was endorsed by the AC. APR, p. 9.
37. AC, APR, p. 9.
38. Pernavsky, *Arabo-izrail'skie voyny*, pp. 107–8.
39. Artillery headquarters of 16th Infantry Division to 395th Field Artillery Battalion, 12 August 1973, CDE-IHC 54/11. The document refers to previous directives dating back to 31 July. A similar order (288/12), requiring reports of unauthorized visits by advisers, was issued at the brigade level on 7 September.
40. Baev, "Bulgaria and the Middle East Conflict," p. 35.
41. AC, APR, p. 8.
42. "Intelligence Memorandum Prepared in the Central Intelligence Agency," June 1973, *FRUS* N-XXV, no. 66.
43. Vladimir Agafonov, "Kto ukryl Rossiyu 'teplym odeyalom neftedollarov'?," *Vremya Novostey*, 198, 22 October 2003. Other sources put the delivery of the Scud system earlier, e.g., Egyptian Lt-Gen. Bassam Kakish, who dates it at the beginning of the year. However, this may refer to the agreement for its sale; Parker, *October War*, p. 92.
44. The writer describes a long career in Arab countries, ending at the rank of Lt-Col. Posting in response to a 2007 TV serial, *Russky Perevod*, 8 February 2009.
45. AC, APR, pp. 8–9; Ze'ira and Tal, *Myth versus Reality*, p. 117.
46. AC, Shalev testimony, p. 17.

47. Golan, *Decision Making*, p. 145n12.
48. Most sources put the agreement in May, as reported by Marwan on 20 May (Bar-Joseph, *Watchman*, p. 147 and *Angel*, pp. 138, 201) and the delivery in July or August 1973.
49. AC, testimony of Albert Sudai, head of the political section, MI Egyptian branch, p. 85.
50. Golan, *Decision Making*, p. 1275n5.
51. Ronen Bergman and Moshe Ronen, *Yedi'ot Ahronot*, 21 September 2012, pp. 4–6. The note-taker was apparently Meir's adjutant Yisra'el Li'or, who also told the AC that Zamir repeated the report, including the nuclear warheads, to Meir on 21 September. This was after questions were received from [sanitized]—presumably the CIA, which was still uncertain—and the missiles' presence was confirmed, "possibly" by aerial photography. Zamir confessed he was surprised at this Soviet "escalation" at "this stage of their relations with the Americans." Most of the exchange with the other party is deleted; Li'or testimony, pp. 13–20. The US identity of the "foreign intelligence" agency that was censored throughout the AC papers is confirmed by one case where "the Americans" slipped through, on p. 67.
52. Minutes of WSAG meeting, Washington, 6 October 1973, *FRUS* N-XXV, no. 103.
53. Telegram from the Department of State to the embassy in Israel, 3 October 1973, *FRUS* N-XXV, no. 95.
54. Protocol of the meeting of the Supreme Council of Syrian and Egyptian forces, no. 6198, 29 August 1973, file no. 1, in Pernavsky, *Arabo-Izrail'skie voyny*, pp. 105–7.
55. Bregman and El-Tahri, *Fifty Years War*, pp. 116–17. Seale, *Asad*, pp. 193–4, mentions only "a Soviet passenger liner on its regular run to Alexandria." At the time, it was announced only that on 2 July the Syrian foreign minister visited Cairo; Whetten, *Canal War*, p. 237, lists eighteen mutual visits between April and September 1973 but notes no Soviet involvement.
56. Pernavsky, *Arabo-Izrail'skie voyny*, pp. 107–8.
57. Oren, *History*, pp. 74–5, 635, citing the IDF History Department archive, holds that Sadat and Assad "acted independently of the USSR," and that the zero hour was determined only afterwards.
58. Dr Abdel Monem Said, "one of Egypt's top national security experts," told CBS after Marwan's death: "he was working for the security establishment of Egypt. ... He gave us a number of hours before the Israelis started to mobilize ... and that was enough to make the difference." CBS News, "Was the Perfect Spy a Double Agent?," 12 May 2009.
59. Golan, *Decision Making*, p. 145n12, quoting an MI document from September 1973.
60. Bar-Joseph, *Angel*, p. 200.
61. Zubok, *Failed Empire*, p. 238.
62. AC, Tal testimony, Part 1, p. 6.
63. AC, Elazar testimony, Part 1, p. 68. The commission's report specifies the source of this opinion as "Soviet experts" (APR, vol. 1, p. 77). Tal, in repeating his recollection, referred to the sanitized identity of the Russian party "who convinced, or tried to convince" the Syrians, in the singular, but later stated that the context was "a discussion or symposium," which corresponds with the Alexandria meeting (Tal testimony, Part 1, p. 9, and Part 3, pp. 4–9). Yadin insisted that the original dispatch spoke of Soviet experts in general.

64. Parker, *October War*, p. 130.
65. Viktor Minin, *Ispytaniya zhizn'yu*, Moscow: OMR-Print, 2009(?). The "publisher" of this 148-page book is actually a Moscow print shop. It was apparently printed in a small run for private distribution, was not advertised for sale, and was mentioned only in a brief review in a local newsletter, *Tverskaya 13*, 15 August 2009, p. 12. The quotation is from an excerpt, "Adyutant Ministra Oborony SSSR," that appeared on a now-defunct page of chudovo.org.
66. Andrey Potyliko, *Fakty i kommentarii* (Kiev), 16 January 2004, http://fakty.ua/68364-uspeshno-obstrelyav-pozicii-izrailtyan-boevye-raschety-tajno-pribyvshih-v-siriyu-sovetskih-reaktivnyh-ustanovok-quot-grad-quot-zatem-ushli-ot-pogoni-amerikanskogo-esminca
67. Pernavsky, *Arabo-Izrail'skie voyny*, p. 107, quoting directives no. 500/13715, no. 73/6 and no. 47/73/201, "file #1."
68. Ben-Porat et al., *Kippur*, pp. 16–17. This encounter has been suggested as a trigger for the Syrian–Egyptian offensive, but the chronology shows that it occurred while preparations were well under way.
69. Marchenko, "General-Mayor VVS Vagin."

29. THE ULTIMATE TEST OF ASHRAF MARWAN

1. *Foxbats*, pp. 79–81.
2. Total of surface warships, submarines and auxiliaries; Zaborsky, "Sovetskaya sredizemno-morskaya eskadra." He puts the Sixth Fleet's strength at the time at 140 units. Previous estimates, apparently counting only combat ships, placed the Soviet strength at fifty-eight units (Bruce W. Watson, *Red Navy at Sea: Soviet Naval Operations on the High Seas, 1956–1980*, Boulder, CO: Westview, 1982, p. 87) as against the Sixth Fleet's forty-eight warships (Joseph F. Bouchard, *Command in Crisis*, New York: Columbia University Press, 1991, pp. 106–7).
3. Goldstein and Zhukov, "A Tale of Two Fleets."
4. Aleksandr Rozin, "Voyna 'sudnogo dnya' 1973g.: Protivostoyanie SSSR-SShA na more," http://alerozin.narod.ru/oktovr.htm; Vladimir Zaborsky, "Sovetskaya Sredizemnomorskaya Eskadra," *NVO*, 13 October 2006, http://nvo.ng.ru/history/2006-10-13/5_eskadra.html
5. Mallin, "Boevye sluzhby."
6. AC, Li'or testimony, pp. 61–6; APR, pp. 50, 73; AC, Ben-Porat testimony, pp. 48–55; Brig.-Gen. Yo'el Ben-Porat, *Ne'ila: Locked-on*, Tel Aviv: Edanim, 1991, pp. 23–5, 51–3; Ronen Bergman and Moshe Ronen, *Yedi'ot Ahronot*, 21 September 2012, pp. 6–7.
7. The sources of both telegrams were sanitized in AC papers, e.g. Alfred Eini's testimony, pp. 28–9. Gili Cohen, *Ha'aretz*, 20 September 2012, http://www.Ha'aretz.co.il/news/politics/1.1827203; Communication by Ms. Cohen to the authors, 5 October 2012.
8. Brig.-Gen. Aharon Levran, who in 1973 was operations assistant to the head of MI research, in *Roeim Malam* (Intelligence Heritage Center bulletin), 15 (October 2012), p. 3. Levran, however, denies that Marwan was a double agent.
9. E.g. Haber, Schiff and Asher, *War*, p. 74.

10. Sadat, *In Search of Identity*, p. 246.
11. Vinogradov, *Diplomatiya*, p. 239.
12. Akopov, transcript, p. 32.
13. Sadat, *In Search of Identity*, p. 246; Seale, *Asad*, pp. 192–3.
14. Israelyan, *Inside the Kremlin*, pp. 10–11.
15. Ibid., pp. 4, 16.
16. Parker, *October War*, p. 49.
17. Zolotarev, *Rossiya*, p. 199.
18. Lebow and Stein, *We All Lost*, pp. 165–166.
19. Israelyan, "Inside the Kremlin", pp. 2–3.
20. Zolotarev et al., *Rossiya*, p. 199; Yaremenko, "Sovetsko-egipetskoe voennoe sotrudnichestvo," p. 58, both citing an article in *Vremya MN*, 5 October 1998.
21. Lebow and Stein, *We All Lost*, p. 163.
22. Personal communication from Dr Yon Degen, June 2003.
23. Marchenko, "General-Mayor VVS Vagin."
24. Akopov, transcript, pp. 31–32; Israelyan, *Inside the Kremlin*, p. 4.
25. Goldstein and Zhukov, *A Tale of Two Fleets*, p. 44.
26. AC, APR, pp. 25–6.
27. Ibid., pp. 75–6, 124–6; Bergman and Meltzer, *Yom Kippur War*, p. 34. According to Ben-Porat (*Ne'ila*, pp. 58–61), the first report was received about 4 p.m. on 4 October. In his testimony to the AC (pp. 68, 106), he put the first intercept "in Russian" at 7 p.m., and stated that the planes had left from various airports in the USSR, including Moscow and Odessa, in what appeared to be intentional ostentation. First reports of the "aircraft heading for the Middle East" came in around 10 p.m., and spoke of sixteen planes, including six An-22s that did not appear in subsequent versions and could not be disguised as civilian.
28. This was not challenged even by the AC. APR, p. 131.
29. Ibid., pp. 78, 80, 126.
30. Quandt, *Peace Process*, p. 150.
31. Bergman and Meltzer, *Yom Kippur War*, pp. 31–2, 37. They put this intercept of an Egyptian signal at 11:00 on 5 October, by "Unit 848" at Umm-Hashiba. The Russian-specialist unit *Masregah* had been disbanded after the "expulsion," even though Soviet policy and intentions remained one of MI's main gathering priorities for 1973–4 (document quoted by Justice Agranat, AC, Eban testimony, Part 2, p. 70). A sigint department chief at the time, Lt-Col. Shunia Pacht, has claimed that its monitors had dozens of intercepts confirming that only the dependents of Soviet advisers and of "military personnel" were leaving, but the monitors were reprimanded for inserting this clarification into a report on 4 October, and the distinction was rejected. *Roeim Malam* (Intelligence Heritage Center bulletin), 15 (October 2012), p. 7.
32. Memorandum from Quandt to Scowcroft, 6 October 1973, *FRUS* N-XXV, no. 99.
33. Heikal, *Road to Ramadan*, pp. 6, 18.
34. Herzog, *War of Atonement*, pp. 37–8. Herzog, a former chief of Israeli military intelli-

gence, does not dispute this estimate but notes that Sadat underestimated the time Israel needed to detect his preparations. Sakal (*Regulars*, p. 82) quotes a range of Israeli estimates of necessary prior alert between "reasonable" (a week) and "absolutely minimal" (forty-eight hours).

35. Israelyan, *Inside the Kremlin*, p. 5.
36. "In late September," the Soviets flew six Tu-22s to Iraq (out of a total transfer of twenty-four). Turkey, which had denied overflight permission in June 1967, granted it this time—or the Soviets ignored its refusal. AC, Eban testimony, Part 1, pp. 5, 12. On 10 October, the Americans were still unsure about this: "apparent Soviet violations of the Greek and maybe Turkish air control zones will sooner or later become general knowledge, if that is what actually is happening." Sonnenfeldt to Kissinger, "The Soviet Role," 10 October 1973, FRUS N-XXV, no. 142.
37. Henry Kissinger, *Crisis: The Anatomy of Two Major Foreign Policy Crises*, New York: Simon and Schuster, 2003, p. 21.
38. *Foxbats*, pp. 88–95.
39. AC, Eban testimony, Part 1, pp. 2–5, 12, 20–1, 23; a sanitized passage refers to one of divergent US estimates at the time.
40. AC, Eini testimony, pp. 20–3. Eini added that if Marwan were not genuinely serving Israel he would never "have left his country" to relay his message. But Bar-Joseph states that Marwan did not come to London specially from Egypt; rather, he continued alone from a preplanned delegation to Paris.
41. Bergman and Meltzer, *Yom Kippur War*, pp. 36–7.
42. AC, Eban testimony, Part 1, pp. 49–50; APR, pp. 58, 59n.
43. Bregman calculates Marwan's total payments from the Israelis as over $1 million. "Ashraf Marwan and Israel's Intelligence Failure," in Siniver, *October 1973 War*, p. 301n8.
44. As Zamir's message was first passed orally to Eini, there are conflicting versions as to its exact content and when it was transmitted to the top leadership; Golan, *Decision Making*, pp. 249–50. This controversy has deflected attention from the element of Soviet non-participation, which is common to all the versions. Bergman and Meltzer, *Yom Kippur War*, pp. 40–1; Bar-Joseph, *Angel*, pp. 231–5.
45. Transcript of [ministerial] "consultation at the Prime Minister's," 6 October 1973 at 08:05, released by ISA 2012, http://my.ynet.co.il/pic/news/yk%206%2010%2008%2005%20.pdf, p. 2; AC, APR, pp. 44–5.
46. Kissinger, *Crisis*, p. 14.
47. AC, Eban testimony, Part 1, pp. 51–3.
48. This account is summarized from Kissinger's version in *Crisis*, pp. 16–18, 28, 34–7; transcript of his talk with Dobrynin also in *FRUS* N-XXV, no. 100.
49. According to Kissinger, Brezhnev also claimed (as is now clear, just as falsely), that the Soviet navy had been withdrawn from the eastern Mediterranean. Transcripts of conversations with Senator Mike Mansfield and President Nixon, 7 October 1973, in Kissinger, *Crisis*, pp. 108–9. *FRUS* N-XXV reproduces the latter transcript (no. 122) and a message from Brezhnev that was delivered shortly before (no. 120)—which does not mention the

advisers or the navy. It does state that "we have already expressed to you some of our own considerations," but the editors do not refer to any such previous document.

50. Minutes of WSAG meeting, 7 October 1973, 6:06–7:06 p.m., *FRUS* N-XXV, no. 121.

30. IN THE THICK OF THE YOM KIPPUR WAR

1. Opening remarks, Vartanov et al., *Rukopozhatie*, p. 5.
2. Lt-Gen. A.D. Sidorov (chief of cadres in the USSR Ministry of Defense), "Dlya tekh, kto voeval," *Krasnaya Zvezda*, 12 October 1989, p. 2, quoted in Staar, "Russia's National Security Concept." Syria is not listed for the same period.
3. Posting by "Lishenets" (disenfranchised) in *Novaya Gazeta* readers' forum, 27 October 2004, responding to the Latynina article.
4. Sonnenfeldt to Kissinger, "The Soviet Role," 10 October 1973, *FRUS* N-XXV, no. 142.
5. "In the last year before the war [the advisers'] areas of activity were apparently reduced to a minimum. Most of them left Egypt in the very last days before the war." Haber, Schiff and Asher, *War*, pp. 270–1.
6. Kutsenko, "Pyl' nad Suetskim Kanalom."
7. R.N. Bryukhovetsky, "Kutsenko, Viktor Pavlovich," *Alma Mater* (website of the Military Engineering Institute), http://viupetra.3dn.ru/publ/37–1–0–321; widely reproduced elsewhere.
8. Elena Kolosentseva, "Afganistan: Ty bol' dushi moey," *Krasnaya Zvezda*, 2 June 2009, http://old.redstar.ru/2009/06/02_06/4_01.html
9. "Yubiley Viktora Pavlovicha Kutsenko, 12.11.1992g.," posted 29 January 2013, https://www.youtube.com/watch?v=RgI1xREmor0, at 54'. Egypt was not mentioned in another celebration of Kutsenko's birthday ten years later; https://www.youtube.com/watch?v=-rjB8Y5cRk0
10. N. Solov'eva, "Poyushchiy general," *Metrostroyevets* (weekly of the construction directorate of the Moscow Metro), 3, 13077, 24 January 2003, http://udarnik-m.narod.ru/2003/13077.htm
11. Sidorov, "Dlya tekh, kto voeval."
12. Haber, Schiff and Asher, *War*, p. 93.
13. Janice Gross Stein, "The Failures of Deterrence and Intelligence," in Parker, *October War*, p. 80; Ben-Porat, *Kippur*, p. 50. Badry (*Ramadan War*, p. 37) describes the "improvement" of the cannon by Egyptian engineers in great detail, with no mention of their origin.
14. Oren, *History*, p. 125. Many crossing points were between Israeli strongpoints and were not observed.
15. Akopov, transcript, pp. 34–5.
16. Kohler, Gouré and Harvey, *Soviet Union*, pp. 39–40. Assad's statement is quoted from *The Economist*, 3 November 1973, p. 62.
17. Opening statement of G. Golan, "The Soviet Union and the Yom Kippur War," in Kumaraswamy, *Revisiting*, p. 127. In a similarly titled essay thirteen years later, Golan still held that the USSR was "juggling interests" between détente and maintaining regional

influence, with preference for the former. "The Soviet Union and the October War," in Siniver, *October 1973 War*, pp. 101–3.
18. Quandt, *Soviet Policy*, p. 19n17, giving detailed contemporary calculations of the flights and tonnage.
19. Quandt and Donald Stukel of the NSC staff to Kissinger, 8 October 1973. *FRUS* N-XXV, no. 129.
20. Minutes of WSAG meeting, 8 October 1973, *FRUS* N-XXV, no. 131.
21. Sonnenfeldt to Kissinger, 10 October 1973, *FRUS* N-XXV, no. 142.
22. Sonnenfeldt to Kissinger, "Aspects of the Middle East War," 13 October 1973, *FRUS* N-XV, no. 170. On 7 October, CIA chief Colby still considered that the Soviets' "pull-out instructions were issued on October 3. ... They were either told there was going to be trouble, or at least they got a very hard tip." Minutes of WSAG meeting, 7 October 1973, *FRUS* N-XXV, no. 121.
23. US Interests Section, Cairo to secretary of state, 11 October 1973, https://wikileaks.org/plusd/cables/1973CAIRO03054_b.html
24. AC, APR, p. 98.
25. Rozin, "Voyna 'sudnogo dnya' 1973g."; thesis, "Blizhnevostochnyi konflikt 1973 goda," submitted at Moscow State University by "Sergey" (surname withheld), undated (before 2001), p. 37. http://www.btvt.by.ru/73.htm (now inaccessible).
26. This document was issued at the level of the Southern Command and so reflects information gathered even earlier by Military Intelligence. AC, final report, vol. 4, p. 1265.
27. Golan, *Soviet Policies*, p. 87; Zolotarev et al., *Rossiya*, p. 201. Goldstein and Zhukov also put the beginning of resupply at 9 October, but this is based only on Zumwalt's earlier writing, and they reconcile it with the Israeli naval attack on 11 October that sank a Soviet freighter in a Syrian port by suggesting—also based on previous US sources—that it had sailed before the major resupply effort (at notes 119 and 132). The voyage to Syria took three days, to Egypt presumably somewhat longer; Latypov, "V efire."
28. Vasiliev, *Rossiya na Blizhnem i Srednem Vostoke*, pp. 111–12.
29. Quandt, *Soviet Policy*, p. 22n23. Such origin of some shipments is confirmed by Bulgarian documents that describe an "urgent sea and air bridge" to the Middle East codenamed "Operation Danube," beginning on 11 October. However, even if this date is accurate, delivery of "more than 5,000 tons of armaments, ammunition and equipment on behalf of Poland" via Bulgarian Black Sea ports indicates an earlier start. Baev, "Bulgaria and the Middle East Conflict," pp. 37–8.
30. Andrey Pochtarev, "Orden za 'amerikantsa,'" *Krasnaya Zvezda*, 28 February 2002, http://old.redstar.ru/2002/02/28_02/2_02.html
31. Bykov, interviewed in "TV Profiles, Shows Lifetime Work of Top Russian Missile Designer," Moscow Channel 1 TV, 23 May 2003; transcribed in English, Russian Military and Security Media Coverage 2326, 2 (17 June 2003), https://groups.yahoo.com/neo/groups/RMSMC/conversations/messages/2351
32. Shazly, *Crossing*, pp. 177–8.
33. AC, final report, Part 1, p. 136; testimony of Tzvi Bar, pp. 54–6, 59–60; testimony of Siman-Tov Binyamin, p. 19.

34. AC, final report, Part 1, pp. 210–12, 226, 233; testimony of Dan Shomron, p. 39.
35. Michalson, *Abirei lev*, pp. 93, 110, 165–6.
36. Intelligence report of 7 October 1973, 10:00 hours, quoted in AC final report, Part 4, p. 1250.
37. AC, Sharon testimony, Part 1, pp. 55–8.
38. "TV Profiles, Shows Lifetime Work of Top Russian Missile Designer," Moscow Channel One TV, 23 May 2003, Russian Military and Security Media Coverage, 2326 (17 June 2003), http://groups.yahoo.com/group/RMSMC/message/2351
39. Pochtarev, "Orden za 'amerikantsa.'"
40. Israeli reports credited the repulse of a T-62 formation's crossing of the Bitter Lake to the far more antiquated Sherman tanks, upgraded and refitted with heavier guns.
41. This and other captured Israeli armored vehicles were crudely painted in US colors and markings, and exhibited as booty from Vietnam (where only Australian forces operated Centurions, and none were reported lost). Sergey Prokopenko and Viktor Baranets, "Pokhishchenie 'Tsenturiona,'" *Komsomolsakaya Pravda*, 27 May 1999; Isabella Ginor, *Ha'aretz*, 10 June 1999.
42. Markovsky, *Idite v zemlyu egipetskuyu*.
43. AC, APR, p. 132.
44. "Israelis Capture Soviet Pilots," Department of State Operations Center, Middle East Task Force, Situation report no. 67 as of 18:00 EDT 26 October 1973, NARA Nixon Presidential Materials, National Security Council Files, POW-MIA, box 1175, 1973 M. East War, file 21. The authors thank Adi Frimark for sharing this document and her research on the POW issue (the IDF denied this report to her).
45. Interview with former IDF reserve paratrooper, 22 April 2008. Another soldier in the same unit to whom he referred us could not confirm this version.
46. IAF commander in briefing for Kissinger, 22 October 1973. Golan, *Decision Making*, p. 1146.
47. AC, testimony of Shmu'el Gonen, Part 4, pp. 26, 29.
48. Edgar O'Ballance, *No Victor, No Vanquished: The Yom Kippur War*, London: Barrie & Jenkins, 1979, p. 299.
49. Agafonov, "Kto ukryl?"
50. Posting on the 8th Army veterans' website, 25 January 2012, http://8oapvo.net/history-logs/128-894-iap. Nikolay Bryantsev went on to command Air Defense forces in the Moscow District, retiring as Lt-Gen. A recent interview mentioned only that "during hostilities in Egypt, he ensured air defense." Timur Suntsov, "General Bryantsev: Pervoe znakomstvo," 5 May 2012, http://www.stihi.ru/2012/05/05/7292 (no longer accessible).
51. Yisra'el Har'el (ed.), *Abirei ha-lev: Hativat ha-tzanhanim bi-qeravot tzelihat te'alat Suez ve-kibbush gedatah ha-ma'aravit*, Israel: Paratroop Brigade Foundation, 1974, p. 64.
52. Conversation between Kissinger and Dinitz; WSAG Meeting, both 8 October 1973, *FRUS* N-XXV, no. 126, 131.
53. Michalson, *Abirei lev*, pp. 257–8.
54. Shazly, *Crossing*, pp. 177–8.

55. Golan, *Decision Making*, pp. 709, 816. It later transpired that the ship had been hit in Tartus. Rozin, "Voyna sudnogo dnya," Chapter 8.
56. Latypov, "V efire"; Vasiliev, *Rossiya na Blizhnem i Srednem Vostoke*, pp. 111–12. IAF attacks on central Damascus began on 9 October, after Syrian Frog missiles hit an Israeli airbase; http://www.iaf.org.il/843-13289-HE/IAF.aspx
56. Evgeny Lashenko, interviewed in Komlev, "Voyna u piramid."
57. Razinkov, "Siriya: Goryachii oktyabr'."
58. Dudchenko, "Voyna Sudnogo dnya." Peres became defense minister on 3 June 1974. We have not found such a statement in contemporary publications or the Knesset record, but Israeli censorship may have deleted them.
59. "Sovetskie voennnye sovetniki, pogibshie v Sirii," http://www.hubara-rus.ru/heroes.html
60. Interviewed in Igor' Sofronov, "Kontrrazvedchik Leshchuk: Ot Sirii do Afgana," *Bol'shaya Volga*, 41, 22 November 2002.

31. THE SOVIET NUCLEAR THREAT AND KISSINGER'S DEFCON-3

1. NSC/JCS meeting, *FRUS* N-XXV, no. 269.
2. Excerpts published in *Yedi'ot Ahronot*, 12 September 2013; Bar-Lev's son Omer (a former colonel, now an educator and member of Knesset), stated on Israel Radio the same day that Dayan clearly referred to the use of a nuclear weapon.
3. Razinkov, "Siriya: Goryachiy oktyabr'."
4. Avner Cohen, "When Israel Stepped Back from the Brink," *NYT*, 3 October 2013, http://www.nytimes.com/2013/10/04/opinion/when-israel-stepped-back-from-the-brink.html?ref=opinion&_r=0; Cohen, "Arnan 'Sini' Azaryahu," http://www.wilsoncenter.org/arnan-sini-azaryahu.
5. Hersh, *Samson Option*, pp. 245ff.
6. E.g., Michael Karpin, *The Bomb in the Basement: How Israel Went Nuclear and What It Means for the World*, New York: Simon and Schuster, 2006, p. 324.
7. A[ndrey] Kokoshin et al., *"Sderzhivanie vo vtorom yadernom veke,"* Moscow: Institute for Problems of International Security, 2001.
8. Aharon Granevich-Granot, "Chain Reaction," *Mishpacha* magazine, 23 September 2009, p. 52. Tikochinsky's position as *commander* of this sub may have been overstated by himself or the interviewer. Since this is described as his first shipboard assignment after a mainly technical career on land in the nuclear-weapons field, his actual function may have been connected with the sub's armament.
9. Golan, *Decision Making*, p. 1145.
10. Report by Bill Cockrell, "a Sovietologist second to none," quoted in Zumwalt, *On Watch*, pp. 439–40.
11. Vafa Guluzade, *Sredi vragov i druzey*, Baku: Azeribook, 2002, Chapter 1, http://modernlib.ru/books/guluzade_vafa/sredi_vragov_i_druzey/read_1/
12. Markovsky, *Idite v zemlyu Egipetskuyu*. Except where otherwise sourced, the following account is based on this study.
13. Aleksandr Minayev, "Polet nad Tel'-Avivom" (flight over Tel Aviv: thirty-five years ago, a

MiG-25R sortie prevented nuclear war), *NVO*, 24 October 2008, http://nvo.ng.ru/history/2008-10-24/15_mig.html. Minayev quotes a book by the senior government aviation specialist Yevgeny Fedosov, *50 let v aviacii. Zapiski akademika*, Moscow: Drofa, 2004.

14. Zeldovich, who was no longer directly associated with the weapons program, had heard "rumors in the ministry" about an impending strike at Israel. Minayev, quoting *Ilya Mikhailovich Livshits: Uchenyy i chelovek*, Kharkov, Ukraine, 2008. Also quoted in Istvan Hargittai, *Buried Glory: Portraits of Soviet Scientists*, Oxford: Oxford University Press, 2013, p. 49.
15. B.L. Talov, "Yadernye raketonostsy—khraniteli mira," *Russky Dom*, 11 November 1998, http://rd.rusk.ru/98/rd11/home11_15.htm
16. Barry M. Blechman and Douglas M. Hart, "Nuclear Weapons and the 1973 Middle East Crisis," in Robert J. Art and Kenneth Waltz (eds), *The Use of Force: Military Power and International Politics*, 5th edn, Lanham, MD: Rowman & Littlefield, 1999, p. 243.
17. AP, "Egypt Warns Missiles Poised to Hit Israel," *Leader-Herald* (Gloversville-Johnston, NY), 16 October 1973, p. 1.
18. Minutes of WSAG meeting, 17 October 1973, *FRUS* N-XXV, no. 198. "Nicolai" is a corruption of Nikolaev—a surprising error for an admiral, perhaps made by the stenographer.
19. Israelyan, *Inside the Kremlin*, pp. 144–5.
20. No'am Ofir, *IAF Magazine*, 171, 25 October 2006, http://iaf.org.il/1779-26839-HE/IAF.aspx
21. Golan, *Decision Making*, p. 1263.
22. Memorial page for Cpl Albert Mish'ali, http://www.izkor.gov.il/HalalKorot.aspx?id=94247
23. Agafonov, "Kto ukryl?"; Israelyan, *Inside the Kremlin*, pp. 143–4 states that a previous request from the Egyptians, relayed by the Soviet military, to fire Scuds at El-Arish had been blocked by Gromyko (according to another Foreign Ministry aide, Evgeny Pyrlin). El-Arish, a small port in northern Sinai, is adjacent to an airbase where according to Arab charges "the U.S. had flown material directly"—whch might explain Gromyko's objection; minutes of WSAG Meeting, 9 November 1973, *FRUS* N-XXV, no. 336.
24. Chernyaev, *Diary 1973*, p. 69.
25. The raising of "volunteer" landing parties on the *Eskadra*'s ships duplicates the procedure that we described from former Soviet sources as followed in June 1967. *Foxbats*, pp. 149–51.
26. Golan, *Decision Making*, pp. 436, 453–4, 1146, 1150.
27. The above account of the *Eskadra*'s moves is based on Zaborsky, "Zapiski o neizvestnoy voyne," *Morskoy sbornik*, 3 (March 1999) and an unpublished journal by Semenov, both quoted by Goldstein and Zhukov.
28. Nixon, *Years of Upheaval*, pp. 588–9. This was when Israel encircled the Egyptian III Army Corps and Brezhnev called on Nixon to intervene with a joint force, else "we should be faced with the necessity urgently to consider the question of taking appropriate steps unilaterally." Brezhnev to Nixon, 24 October 1973, *FRUS* N-XXV, no. 267.

29. Minutes of bipartisan leadership meeting, 27 November 1973, *FRUS* N-XXV, no. 360.
30. NSC/JCS Meeting, 24/25 October 1973, *FRUS* N-XXV, no. 269; emphasis in original.

EPILOGUE: SO WHAT WENT WRONG, AND WHEN?

1. Heikal, *Road to Ramadan*, pp. 216–26.
2. Badry, *Ramadan War*, pp. 73, 94.
3. Malashenko, *Vspominaya*, p. 265. He may, however, have been out of the loop in respect of Egypt by 1973, when the Soviets were evidently aware at least of the ultimate operation's codename, if not its limited objectives. An intelligence report on 8 October stated that "At 1400 hours on 6 October, armed forces of the Arab Republic of Egypt started operation High Minarets." Presenter-read excerpt of a top-secret letter from the head of No. 3 Directorate to the head of the Main Intelligence Directorate, Moscow, General Staff, 8 October 1973. Quoted in "TV Profiles, Shows Lifetime Work of Top Russian Missile Designer," Moscow Channel 1 TV, 23 May 2003; transcribed in English, Russian Military and Security Media Coverage, 2326, 2 (17 June 2003), https://groups.yahoo.com/neo/groups/RMSMC/conversations/messages/2351
4. Shazly, *Crossing*, pp. 277–8.
5. Zolotarev et al., *Rossiya*, p. 202.
6. Dashkov and Golotyuk, "Arabo-izrail'sky konflikt."
7. Oleg Grinevsky, *Tainy Sovetskoy Diplomatii*, Moscow: Vagrius, 2000, pp. 11–12; emphasis added.
8. Embassy Cairo to State Department, 5 May 1974, https://www.wikileaks.org/plusd/cables/1974CAIRO02830_b.html; 1 June 1974, https://www.wikileaks.org/plusd/cables/1974CAIRO03775_b.html; MA, p. 10, no. 45.
9. "Artek-74," http://artek-romashka.ru/forum/viewtopic.php?f=30&t=1449 (no longer accessible).
10. MA, p. 100, no. 442.
11. MA, p. 104, no. 448. In February 1976, shortly before his service at the Egyptian presidency ended, Ashraf Marwan "as Syrians claim, lied to them about the contents of the Israeli–Egyptian negotiations." Embassy Damascus to State Department, 14 February 1976, https://www.wikileaks.org/plusd/cables/1976DAMASC00837_b.html
12. Grinevsky, *Tainy Sovetskoy Diplomatii*, pp. 52–3, 58–61.
13. "Commentator in Soviet Derides Carter's Effort" and David Shipler, "Soviet Says US is Using Treaty to Bolster Influence," *NYT*, 15 and 16 March 1979.
14. AP, "Soviets Blast Mideast Pact," *Daily Press* (Utica, NY), 15 March 1979, p. 2; AP, "Soviets Key to Mideast Settlement?," *Herald-Statesman* (Yonkers, NY), 25 March 1979, p. B1.
15. MA, p. 9, no. 42.
16. MA, p. 10, no. 45.
17. "Soviet Names Envoy to Cairo," *NYT*, 7 July 1984; "Sadat Says U.S. Buys Soviet Arms in Egypt for Afghan Rebels," *NYT*, 23 September 1981.
18. Authors' notes from the ceremony.

BIBLIOGRAPHY

* marks English titles given for Hebrew-language books when provided on title page.

Newspaper and magazine articles are listed here only when they are by nature of primary sources. Otherwise they are cited in the endnotes only.

Aboul-Enein, Youssef H., "Egyptian General Abdel-Moneim Riad: The Creation of an Adaptive Military Thinker," *Infantry Magazine* (March–April 2004), https://www.thefreelibrary.com/Egyptian+General+Abdel-Moneim+Riad%3A+the+creation+of+an+a daptive...-a0118986343

—— "Learning and Rebuilding a Shattered Force: Memoirs of Pre-Yom Kippur War Egyptian Generals, 1967–1972," *Strategic Insights*, IV, 3 (March 2005), https://www.hsdl.org/?view&did=453698

Abramov, Col. Boris A., *Goluboe nebo Egipta*, Moscow: Patriot, 2008.

Abramov, Grigory et al. (eds), *Smolyane v lokal'nykh voynakh XX veka: Sbornik vospominany*, Smolensk: Universum, 2006.

*Adamsky, Dima, *Operation Kavkaz*, Tel Aviv: Ministry of Defense, 2006.

—— "'Zero Hour for the Bears': Inquiring into the Soviet Decision to Intervene in the Israeli–Egyptian War of Attrition, 1969–1970," *Cold War History*, 6, 1 (2006).

Adamsky, Dima and Uri Bar-Joseph, "'The Russians Are Not Coming': Israel's Intelligence Failure and Soviet Military Intervention in the 'War of Attrition,'" *Intelligence and National Security*, 21, 1 (2006).

Adan, Maj.-Gen. Avraham, *On the Banks of the Suez: An Israeli General's Personal Account of the Yom Kippur War*, San Francisco: Presidio Press, 1980.

Agafonov, Vladimir, "Kto ukryl Rossiyu 'teplym odeyalom neftedollarov'?," *Vremya Novostey*, 198, 22 October 2003.

Akimenkov, Aleksandr, *Na poroge inogo mira*, Moscow: Aviko, 2002.

Akimov, Col. Vladimir, *Voyska PVO strany vspominayut veterany*, Moscow: Aviarus-XXI, 2005. Extract, "Zaboty komanduyushchego okrugom," in *VKO* at http://www.vko.ru/biblioteka/zaboty-komanduyushchego-okrugom

Akopov, Pavel, transcript of 1997 interview for *The 50 Years War: Israel and the Arabs*, a six part television documentary made by Brian Lapping Associates, 1998. Liddell Hart Centre for Military Archives, King's College, London. The authors thank Brook Lapping Productions and the Trustees of the Liddell Hart Centre for granting of access to, and permission to quote from, this material.

BIBLIOGRAPHY

Altshuler, Mordechai, "Da'at hakahal vehateguva hayehudit bi-Brit ha-Mo'atzot le-milhemet sheshet ha-yamim: Ti'ud hadash," *Contemporary Jewry: Zionism, the State of Israel, and the Diaspora* (Jerusalem and Haifa), 11–12 (1998), pp. 241–62.

Andrew, Christopher and Vasili Mitrokhin, *The Mitrokhin Archive: The KGB in Europe and the West*, London: Penguin, 2000.

Anzhero-Sudzhensk Regional History Museum, 'Meropriyatie 'Morskaya dusha: Tel'nyashka,'" 18 February 2011, http://as-museum.ucoz.ru/publ/4-1-0-59

Arad, Brig.-Gen.Yitzhak et al. (eds), *1000 ha-yamim: 12 Yuni 1967–8 August 1970*, Tel Aviv: [IDF] General Staff Chief Education Officer and Ministry of Defense Publishing, undated [1970].

Aronson, Shlomo, *Israel's Nuclear Programme: The Six-Day War and Its Ramifications*, London: Kings College Mediterranean Studies, 1999.

—— *Nesheq gar'ini bamizrah hatikhon: Mi-Ben Gurion uve-hazara*, Jerusalem: Academon, 1995.

Art, Robert J. and Kenneth Waltz (eds), *The Use of Force: Military Power and International Politics*, 5th edn, Lanham, MD: Rowman & Littlefield, 1999.

*Artzi, Ya'el, *Missing in Action*, Tel Aviv: Miskal, 2001.

*Asher, Brig.-Gen. Dani, *Breaking the Concept*, Tel Aviv: Ministry of Defense, 2003 (has appeared in English as *The Egyptian Strategy for the Yom Kippur War: An Analysis*, Jefferson, NC: McFarland, 2009).

Ashton, Nigel (ed.), *The Cold War in the Middle East: Regional Conflict and the Superpowers 1967–73*, London: Routledge and LSE, 2007.

Badry, Maj. Gen. Hassan al- et al., *The Ramadan War*, Cairo, 1974; citations are from the Hebrew translation, *Milhemet Ramadan*, IDF Intelligence Open Sources Unit (Hatzav), 1974. English edn, Hassan al-Badri et al., *The Ramadan War*, Dunn Loring, VA: T.N. Dupuy, 1978

Baev, Jordan, "Bulgaria and the Middle East Conflict during the Cold War Years," Washington: CWIHP, 2006, http://lib.sudigital.org/record/503/files/SUDGTL-BGCW-2010-294-ENG.pdf

Baevsky, Georgy, "Sekretnaya missiya v nebe Sinaya," *Vestnik vozdushnogo flota* (n.d., before 2001), www.foxbat.ru/article/mig25_2/mig25_2_1.htm

Baranova, S.V. (ed.), "Zashchitniki Otechestva," *Nasha Gazeta* (Belgorod), February 2004.

Bard, Mitchell G., "The 1968 Sale of Phantom Jets to Israel," http://www.jewishvirtuallibrary.org/jsource/US-Israel/phantom.html

*Bar-Joseph, Uri, *The Angel: Ashraf Marwan, the Mossad and the Yom Kippur War*, Tel Aviv: Zmora-Bitan, Dvir, 2010.

—— *The Watchman Fell Asleep: The Surprise of Yom Kippur and Its Sources*, Tel Aviv: Zmora-Bitan, 2001.

Barron, John, *KGB: The Secret Work of Soviet Secret Agents*, New York: Bantam, 1974.

Bar-Siman-Tov, Yaacov, *The Israeli–Egyptian War of Attrition, 1969–1970*, New York: Columbia University Press, 1980.

Bartov, Hanoch, *Dado: 48 shanah ve-od 20 yom*, Tel Aviv: Ma'ariv, 1978.

BIBLIOGRAPHY

Bausin, Lev, *Spetssluzhby mira na Blizhnem Vostoke*, Moscow: OLMA-Press, 2001.

Beam, Jacob D., *Multiple Exposure: An American Ambassador's Unique Perspective on East–West Relations*, New York: Norton, 1978.

Beattie, Kirk J., *Egypt during the Nasser Years*, Boulder, CO: Westview, 1994.

Belebentsev, D., "V poletakh nad piramidami," *Gazeta Sovetskaya Chuvashiya*, 4 February 2005.

*Ben-Porat, Yeshayahu et al., *Kippur*, Tel Aviv: Special Edition, first published in Hebrew (as *Ha-Mehdal*), December 1973.

*Ben-Porat, Brig.-Gen. Yo'el, *Ne'ila: Locked-on*, Tel Aviv: Edanim, 1991.

*Ben-Tzur, Avraham, *Soviet Factors and the Six-Day War*, Tel Aviv: Sifriyat Poalim, 1975.

*Bergman, Ronen and Gil Meltzer, *The Yom Kippur War: Moment of Truth*, Updated edn, Tel Aviv: Yedi'ot Ahronot-Hemed, 2004.

Berya, Sergo, *Moy Otets: Lavrenty Berya*, Moscow: Sovremennik, 1994.

Bondarenko, Aleksandr, "Kak mariupol'tsy zashchishchali nebo Egipta," *Priazovsky Rabochy* (Mariupol, Ukraine), 4 March 2008, www.pr.ua/news.php?new=5251&num=101

Bouchard, Joseph F., *Command in Crisis*, New York: Columbia University Press, 1991.

Bovin, Aleksandr, *XX vek kak zhizn'*, Moscow: Zakharov, 2003.

Bregman, Ahron and Jihan El-Tahri, *The Fifty Years War*, London: Penguin and BBC, 1998.

Breslauer, George W., *Soviet Strategy in the Middle East*, London: Routledge, 1990.

Bysenkov, Igor', "V 20,000 metrakh nad zemley obetovannoy," November 2007, http://bratishka.ru./archiv/2007/11/2007_11_12.php

Cable, James, *Gunboat Diplomacy: Political Applications of Limited Naval Force*, London: Institute for Strategic Studies, 1971.

Chazov, Evgeny, *Zdorov'e i vlast'*, Moscow: Novosti, 1992.

Cherkashin, Nikolay, "On dolzhen byl unichtozhit' Izrail'," *Evreyskie Vesti* (supplement of *Golos Ukrainy*) (Kiev), 17–18 (September 1996).

Chernitsyn, Andrey, "Mirovaya ekspansiya," *Noril'sky Nikel'*, 5, 36 (August–September 2007) www.nn.nornik.ru/DOC.aspx?ieid=&DocsID=882

Chernushevich, Aleksandr, "Ego nazyvali 'rusi khabar,'" *Minskiy Kur'er*, 1221, 12 June 2007.

Chernyaev, Anatoly, *The Diary of Anatoly S. Cheryaev, 1972*, Washington: National Security Archive, 2012, http://www2.gwu.edu/~nsarchiv/NSAEBB/NSAEBB379/1972%20as%20of%20May%2024,%202012%20FINAL.pdf

——— *The Diary of Anatoly S. Cheryaev, 1973*, Washington: National Security Archive, 2013, http://www.gwu.edu/~nsarchiv/NSAEBB/NSAEBB430/Chernyaev%201973%20with%20cover%20page.pdf

Cohen, Avner, *Israel and the Bomb*, New York: Columbia University Press, 1998.

Cohen, Col. Eliezer, *Israel's Best Defense: The First Full Story of the Israeli Air Force*, New York: Crown, 1993.

Cook, Steven A., *The Struggle for Egypt: From Nasser to Tahrir Square*, Oxford: Oxford University Press, 2011.

Cottrell, Alvin J., "Yahasei Mitzrayim-Brit ha-Mo'atzot," *Ma'arakhot*, 208 (July 1970); translated from the US Army's *Military Review*, http://maarachot.idf.il/PDF/FILES/6/108236.pdf, pp. 22–3.

BIBLIOGRAPHY

Daigle, Craig A., "The Limits of Détente: The United States, the Soviet Union, and the Arab-Israeli Conflict, 1969—1973," PhD thesis, George Washington University, 2008.

—— "The Russians Are Going: Sadat, Nixon and the Soviet Presence in Egypt, 1970–1971," *Middle East Review of International Affairs (MERIA)*, 8, 1 (2004), pp. 1–15, http://www.rubincenter.org/meria/2004/03/daigle.pdf

Daly, R.W. (ed.), *Soviet Sea Power*, Washington: CSIS and New York: Dunellen, June 1969.

Dashkov, A. Yu. and V.D. Golotyuk, "Arabo-Izrail'skiy konflikt: Boevye deystviya sovetskoy aviatsii i PVO v Egipte," www.airaces.ru/stati/arabo-izrailskijj-konflikt-boevye-dejjstviya-sovetskojj-aviacii-i-pvo-v-egipte.html#identifier_2_4428; excerpted from their book, *100 let Voenno-vozdushnym silam Rossii (1912–2012 godi)*, Moscow: Fond "Russkie Vityazi," 2012.

Dawisha, Karen, *The Kremlin and the Prague Spring*, Berkeley: University of California Press, 1984.

*Dayan, Moshe, *Story of My Life*, Jerusalem: Edanim, 1976.

Dishon, Daniel et al. (eds), *Middle East Record, 1967*, Jerusalem: Israel Universities Press, 1971.

—— *Middle East Record, 1968*, Jerusalem: Israel Universities Press, 1973.

Dobrynin, Anatoly, *Sugubo doveritel'no: Posol v Vashingtone pri shesti prezidentakh SShA*, Moscow: Avtor, 1997.

Draper, Theodore, *Present History: On Nuclear War, Détente, and Other Controversies*, New York: Random House, 1983.

Dudchenko, Lt-Col. Vladimir A., *Voyna na istoshchenie*, Moscow: Eksmo, 2010; online version, *Kanal*, http://artofwar.ru/d/dudchenko_w_a/text_0030.shtml

—— "Voyna Sudnogo dnya: krovavaya nich'ya," *Tayny sovetnik* (St. Petersburg), 41, 25 October 2004, www.prazdnikinfo.ru/5/30/i21_12956p1.htm

Dupuy, T.N., *Elusive Victory: The Arab–Israeli Wars, 1947–1974*, New York: Harper & Row, 1978.

"Egipet: Neizvestnaya voyna," *Sputnik*, January 1991.

Egorin, Anatoly Z., *Egipet nashego vremeni*, Moscow: Institut vostokovedeniya, 1998.

—— "Iz-pod arabskoy zheltoy kaski sineli russkiye glaza," *Trud-7* (Moscow), 6 March 1998.

—— "Zapiski korrespondenta APN," http://www.clubvi.ru/news/2011/04/07/ppl/egorin/zap/

El'chaninov, Maj. Valery, "Dan prikaz yemy ... v Egipet," *Soldat Udachi* (Moscow), 2 (2001).

Eldar, Mike, *Dakar ve-sippurah shel shayyetet ha-tzolelot*, Tel Aviv: Nir, 1997.

Eliseev, Igor' and Aleksei Tikhonov, "V teni pyramid," *Rossiskaya Gazeta*, 30 October 2010, http://www.rg.ru/2010/09/30/taina.html

Eran, Ehud, "Kishlon kehillat ha-modi'in ha-Americanit be-ha'arakhat mitqefet ha-peta ha-Mitzrit-Surit be-milhemet Yom ha-Kippurim," Center on Intelligence and Terrorism, Israel Intelligence Heritage Center, 3 September 2013, http://www.terrorism-info.org.il/Data/articles/Art_20569/H_138_13_1132530023.pdf

Ershov, Boris, "Oni zashchishchali chest' strany, kotoraya ikh zabyvaet," *Karavan* (Tver, Russia), n.d. (2002?), http://www.karavan.tver.ru/html/n332/article5.php

BIBLIOGRAPHY

Fawzi, Gen. Mohamed (Muhammad Fawzy), "Reflections on Mistakes Made in Planning, Training, Equipping, and Organizing Egyptian Combat Formations prior to the 1967 Six-Day War," Part III, http://www.thefreelibrary.com/Egyptian+General+Mohamed+F awzi%3A+ part+III%3A+reflections+on+mistakes...-a0314564926

Feldman, Shai, *Israeli Nuclear Deterrence: A Strategy for the 1980s*, New York: Columbia University Press, 1982.

Ferris, Jesse, "Soviet Support for Egypt's Intervention in Yemen, 1962–1963," *Journal of Cold War Studies*, 10, 4 (2008).

Filonik, A.O. (ed), *Blizhniy Vostok: Komandirovka na voynu, Sovetskie voennye v Egipte*, Moscow: Academy of Sciences and Moscow State University, 2009.

Ford, Hal, Chief DD-I Special Research Staff, CIA, "The Growth of the Soviet Commitment in the Middle East (Reference Title ESAU-XLIX)", January 1971; CIA FOIA website, http://www.foia.cia.gov/sites/default/files/document_conversions/14/esau-48.pdf, summary at http://www.foia.cia.gov/sites/default/files/document_conversions/89801/DOC_0000501068.pdf

Fukuyama, Francis, "Soviet Military Power in the Middle East," in Steven L. Spiegel, Mark A. Heller, and Jacob Goldberg (eds), *The Soviet–American Competition in the Middle East*, Lexington, MA: Lexington Press, 1988.

Gaddis, John Lewis, *The Cold War: A New History*, New York: Penguin, 2005.

Galanin, Aleksey, "Boi nad piramidani," *Shchelkovo Vremya* (Russia), 19 December 2007.

Gareev, Gen. of the Army Makhmut, *Esli zavtra voyna?*, Moscow: VlaDar, 1995. English edn, *If War Comes Tomorrow? The Contours of Future Armed Conflict*, London: Frank Cass, 1998.

Gawrych, George W., *The Albatross of Decisive Victory: War and Peace between Egypt and Israel in the 1967 and 1973 Arab–Israeli Wars*, Westport, CT: Greenwood, 2000.

Gefele, Viktoriya, "Napishi ty mne, mama, v Egipet," *Podrobnee* (Yaroslavl'), 23 March 2003.

Geyer. David C. and Douglas E. Selvage (eds), *Soviet–American Relations: The Détente Years, 1969–1972*, Washington: Government Printing Office, 2007. (Russian version: Lavrov, Sergey (ed.), *Soviet–American Relations: The Détente Years 1969–1976, a Document Collection*, Moscow: Foreign Ministry of Russian Federation and US State Department, 2007). The Russian-language documents are quoted in the US version's translation. Page numbers are for the English edition; the document numbers are the same in both.

Ginor, Isabella, "'Under the Yellow Arab Helmet Gleamed Blue Russian Eyes': Operation *Kavkaz* and the War of Attrition," *Cold War History*, 3, 1 (October 2002).

Ginor, Isabella and Gideon Remez, *Foxbats over Dimona: The Soviets' Nuclear Gamble in the Six-Day War*, New Haven: Yale University Press, 2007.

—— "Israel's Best Spy Or a Master Double Agent? New Light from the Soviet Angle on the Mystery of Ashraf Marwan," in *Need to Know V: The Human Element*, Funen, Denmark: University of Southern Denmark Press, forthcoming.

—— "The Six-Day War as a Soviet Initiative: New Evidence and Methodological Issues," *MERIA*, 12, 3 (2008), http://www.gloria-center.org/2008/09/remez-2008–09–02/#ednref20

BIBLIOGRAPHY

—— "Too Little, Too Late: The CIA and US Counteraction of the Soviet Initiative in the Six-Day War," *Intelligence and National Security*, 26, 2–3 (2011).

—— "The Tyranny of Vested-Interest Sources: Shaping the Record of Soviet Intervention in the Egyptian–Israeli Conflict, 1967–1973," *Journal of the Middle East and Africa*, 1, 1 (November 2010).

—— "Un-Finished Business: Archival Evidence Exposes the Diplomatic Aspect of the USSR's Pre-planning for the Six-Day War," *Cold War History*, 6, 3 (2006), pp. 377–95

Golan, Galia, *Soviet Policies in the Middle East: From World War II to Gorbachev*, Cambridge: Cambridge University Press, 1990.

Golan, Shimon, *Decision Making of Israeli High Command in Yom Kippur War*, Tel Aviv: Ma'arakhot (IDF publishing) and Modan, 2013.

Goldstein, Lyle J. and Yury M. Zhukov, "A Tale of Two Fleets: A Russian Perspective on the 1973 Naval Standoff in the Mediterranean," *Naval War College Review*, 57, 2 (Spring 2004), http://scholar.harvard.edu/files/zhukov/files/2004_GoldsteinZhukov_NWCR.pdf

Gorbunov, Maj. Yury, "Napishi mne, mama, v Egipet: Vospominaniya voennogo perevodchika," Military Krym website, 2013, http://military.sevstudio.com/napishi-w-egipet/

*Gordon, Shmuel, *Thirty Hours in October*, Tel Aviv: Ma'ariv, 2008.

Gorenberg, Gershom, *The Accidental Empire: Israel and the Birth of the Settlements, 1967–1977*, New York: Holt, 2006.

Goryainov, Sergey, "Prikazano zabyt," *Nedelya* (Moscow), 43, 24 November 1997.

Grachev, Oleg, "Egipet: V pritsele; nebo," *Vecherny Chelyabinsk*, 27 May 1998.

Granevich-Granot, Aharon, "Chain Reaction," *Mishpacha* magazine, 23 September 2009.

Gribanov, Col. Stanislav V., *Az vozdam*, Moscow: Voyennoye Izdatel'stvo, 1998.

Grinevsky, Oleg, *Tainy Sovetskoy Diplomatii*, Moscow: Vagrius, 2000.

Groisman, Evgeny and Oleg Granovsky, "Spetsoperatsii: Ognevye nalety," *Bratishka*, April 2011, http://bratishka.ru/archiv/2011/4/2011_4_16.php

Guluzade, Vafa, *Sredi vragov i druzey*, Baku: Azeribook, 2002, http://modernlib.ru/books/guluzade_vafa/sredi_vragov_i_druzey/read_1/

Gundarov, Vladimir, "Geroy bez Zolotoy Zvezdy," *NVO*, 26 October 2007, http://nvo.ng.ru/history/2007-10-26/5_hero.html

*Haber, Eitan, Ze'ev Schiff and Dani Asher, *The War: Yom Kippur War Lexicon*, Revised edn, Tel Aviv: Kinneret, Zmora-Bitan, Dvir, 2013.

Hagger, Nicholas, *The Libyan Revolution: Its Origins and Legacy, a Memoir and Assessment*, London: O Books, 2009.

*Halperin, Meirav and Aharon Lapidot (eds), *G Suit: Pages in the Log Book of the Israel Air Force*, Tel Aviv: Ministry of Defense Publishing, 1987.

*Halutz, Lt-Gen. Dani, *Straightforward*, Tel Aviv: Yedi'ot Ahronot-Hemed, 2010.

Hanhimäki, Jussi M., "A Prize-Winning Performance? Kissinger, Triangular Diplomacy, and the End of the Vietnam War, 1969–1973," *Norwegian Nobel Institute Series*, 2, 1 (Oslo) (2001), http://www.nppri.org/pdf/Vol2_No1.pdf

Har'el, Yisra'el (ed.), *Abirei ha-lev: Hativat ha-tzanhanim bi-qeravot tzelihat te'alat Suez ve-kibbush gedatah ha-ma'aravit*, Israel: Paratroop Brigade Foundation, 1974.

BIBLIOGRAPHY

"Hayyim", Lt-Col., "Mifgash ha-tzameret bein Nixon veha-hanhagah ha-Sovietit," *Ma'arakhot*, 225 (September 1972), http://maarachot.idf.il/PDF/FILES/8/108478.pdf

Heikal, Mohamed Hassanein, *Autumn of Fury: The Assassination of Sadat*, London: Andre Deutsch, 1983.

—— *The Road to Ramadan*, London: Collins, 1975 (citations are from the Ballantine Books edn, New York 1975).

—— *The Sphinx and the Commissar: The Rise and Fall of Soviet Influence in the Middle East*, New York: Harper and Row, 1978.

Hersh, Seymour M., *The Price of Power*, New York: Summit Books, 1983.

—— *The Samson Option*, New York: Random House, 1991.

Hershberg, James G. (ed.), *The Soviet Bloc and the Aftermath of the June 1967 War: Selected Documents from East-Central European Archives*, Washington: Cold War International History Project, 2004.

Herzog, Chaim, *The War of Atonement*, London: Greenhill Books, 1998 (first published by Weidenfeld and Nicolson, 1975).

Il'inskaya, Ol'ga, "Voyna prizrakov," *Prem'er* (Cherepovets, Russia), 49, 5 December 2001.

Isaenko, Lt-Col. Anatoly, "Eta vera ot puli menya pod Suetsom khranila ..." www.clubvi.ru/news/2010/12/14/i

—— "Nash chelovek v Egipte," *NVO*, 21 October 2005.

—— "Polety na Blizhniy Vostok," *NVO*, 15 December 2006, http://nvo.ng.ru/history/2006-12-15/5_polety.html

Israelyan, Victor, *Inside the Kremlin During the Yom Kippur War*, University Park, PA: Pennsylvania University Press, 1997.

—— *On the Battlefields of the Cold War*, University Park, PA: Penn State University Press, 2003.

Johnson, Lyndon B., *The Vantage Point: Perspectives of the Presidency, 1963–1969*, New York: Holt, 1971.

Kahana, Ephraim and Muhammad Suwaed, *The A to Z of Middle Eastern Intelligence*, Lanham, MD: Scarecrow Press, 2009.

"Kak nash zemlyak v Egipte sluzhil," *Pavlogradskie Novosti* (Ukraine), 14 November 2004 http://pavlonews.info/news/categ_2/6218.html

Kalb, Marvin and Bernard Kalb, *Kissinger*, Boston: Little, Brown, 1974.

Kalugin, Oleg, *Spymaster: My Thirty-Two Years in Intelligence and Espionage against the West*, New York: Basic Books, 2009.

Kalyuta, Yosif, "Dialog ob internatsional'nom dolge s neozhidannym prodolzheniem," *Narodnaya gazeta* (Belarus), 22 October 1999, http://press.promedia.by/?mod=p_ind&NPID=36&No=206&Date=22.10.1999

Kamanin, Col.-Gen. Nikolay, *Skryty Kosmos*, Moscow: Infortekst-IF, 4 vols., 1995–7, http://airport-krr.ucoz.ru/index/0-2826

Kapitanets, Admiral of the Fleet Ivan, *Na sluzhbe okeanskomu flotu 1946–1992*, Moscow: Andreevsky Flag, 2000.

Karpin, Michael, *The Bomb in the Basement: How Israel Went Nuclear and What It Means for the World*, New York: Simon and Schuster, 2006.

BIBLIOGRAPHY

Karsh, Efraim, "Soviet Arms Transfers to the Middle East in the 1970s," Jaffee Center Paper no. 22, Tel Aviv University, December 1983.

Karyukin, Viktor, "Kak soyuz Izrail' nakazyval: Neizvestnye podrobnosti ob uchastii sovetskikh voysk v arabo-izrail'skom konflikte," *Stolitsa*, 8 (1992).

Kass, Ilana, *Soviet Involvement in the Middle East: Policy Formulation 1966–1973*, Boulder, CO: Westview, 1978.

Katz, Samuel, *Battleground*, Updated edn, Tel Aviv: Steimatzky, 1985, http://www.ourjerusalem.com/series/story/battleground040.html

Kevorkov, Vyacheslav, *Viktor Lui, chelovek s legendoy*, Moscow: Sem' Dney, 2010.

Khalil, Abdel-Malek, "Building a Wall of Missiles," *Al-Ahram Weekly*, 8 October 1998.

Khandanyan, Maj.-Gen. Artem, "Zharkoe nebo Egipta," *VKO*, http://www.vko.ru/biblioteka/zharkoe-nebo-egipta

Kharchikov, Aleksandr A., "Na moryakh sredi zemli," *Sovetskaya Rossiya*, 26 July 2003, http://www.sovross.ru/old/2003/081/081_4_1.htm

Kiknadze, Aleksandr, *Taynopis': Sobytiya i nravy zashifrovannogo veka*, Moscow: Sovetsky Sport, 1998.

Kimche, David, *The Last Option: After Nasser, Arafat and Saddam Hussein; The Quest for Peace in the Middle East*, London: Weidenfeld and Nicholson, 1991.

Kipnis, Yigal, *1973: Haderekh le-milhamah*, Tel Aviv: Kinneret, Zmorah-Bitan, Dvir, 2012.

Kipp, Jacob W., "Confronting the RMA in Russia," *Military Review* (June–July 1997), http://fmso.leavenworth.army.mil/documents/confront.htm

Kipp, Jacob W. and Lester W. Grau, "Maintaining Friendly Skies: Rediscovering Theater Aerospace Defense," *Aerospace Power Journal* (Summer 2002), http://fmso.leavenworth.army.mil/documents/friendlyskies/friendlyskies.htm

Kirpichenko, Vadim A., *Iz arkhiva razvedchika*, Moscow: Mezhdunarodnye Otnosheniya, 1993.

—— *Razvedka i lichnosti*, Moscow: Geya, 1998.

Kissinger, Henry, *Crisis: The Anatomy of Two Major Foreign Policy Crises*. New York: Simon and Schuster, 2003.

—— *Diplomacy*, New York: Simon and Schuster, 1994.

—— *The White House Years*, Boston: Little, Brown, 1979.

—— *Years of Upheaval*, Boston: Little, Brown, 1982.

Kohler, Foy D., Leon Gouré and Mose L. Harvey, *The Soviet Union and the October 1973 Middle East War: The Implications for Détente*, Coral Gables: University of Miami, 1974.

Kokoshin, A[ndrey] et al., "Sderzhivanie vo vtorom yadernom veke," Moscow: Institute for Problems of International Security, 2001.

Komlev, Sergey, "Voyna u Piramid," *Rech'* (Cherepovets, Russia), 30 September 2005.

Korn, David, *Stalemate: The War of Attrition and Great Power Diplomacy in the Middle East*, Boulder, CO: Westview, 1992.

Krakhmalov, Sergey, *Zapiski voennogo attashe: Iran–Egipet–Iran–Afganistan*, Moscow: Russkaya Razvedka, 2000.

Kramer, Mark, "New Evidence on Soviet Decision-Making and the 1956 Polish and

BIBLIOGRAPHY

Hungarian Crises," *Cold War International History Project Bulletin* no. 8 (1996), http://www.wilsoncenter.org/sites/default/files/CWIHPBulletin8–9_p6.pdf

Krokhin, Boris, "Dubl: Kak dva molodykh rossiyskikh leytenanta byli ochevidtsami egipetsko-izrail'skoy voyny," http://www.hubara-rus.ru/double.html. See also "Aleksey I. Smirnov."

—— "Zapiski 'khabira,'" *Argumenty Nedeli* (Moscow), 45, 79, 7 November 2007, http://argumenti.ru/history/n106/36060

Kruchinin, Capt. Yury, *Komanduyu korablem*, Sevastopol: L. Yu. Kruchinin, 2008, http://www.proza.ru/2010/02/27/1219

Kryshtob, Vladimir I., "I eta voyna byla by zavtra ..." *Novaya Gazeta*, 26 July 2004, http://2004.novayagazeta.ru/nomer/2004/53n/n53n-s21.shtml

Kubersky, Igor', *Egipet-69*, St. Petersburg: Gelikon-Plus, 2010. Serialized in *Zvezda* (St. Petersburg), January 2011, http://zvezdaspb.ru/index.php?page=8&nput=1534, and February 2011, http://zvezdaspb.ru/index.php?page=8&nput=1557

Kudaev, Boris, *Pule perevodchik ne nuzhen*, Moscow: Eksmo, 2011. Quotations are from the 2007 online version, *Perevodchiki*, now inaccessible; the book text is accessible at http://www.e-reading-lib.com/chapter.php/1001592/0/Kudaev_-_Pule_perevodchik_ne_nuzhen.html

Kulikov, Igor', "Kak izrail'tyane u egiptyan radar ukrali," *Soldat udachi* (Moscow), 1, 2000.

Kumaraswamy, P.R., *Revisiting the Yom Kippur War*, London: Frank Cass, 2000.

Kutsenko, Maj.-Gen. Viktor, "Pyl' nad Suetskim Kanalom," *Literaturnaya Rossiya*, 18, 4 May 2001, http://old.litrossia.ru/archive/38/soul/900.php

Kvasyuk, Igor', "Snova na front," n.d., website of Union of Veterans of Military Languages School, http://www.vkimo.com/node/2463

Lange, Elena, "Voinov, Alexander Ivanovich," Borisoglebskoye Flight School website, http://www.bvvaul.ru/profiles/1111.php

Laqueur, Walter, *Confrontation: The Middle East War and World Politics*, London: Abacus, 1974.

Lashchenko, General of the Army Petr, "Zapiski Glavnogo Voennogo Sovetnika," *Voenno-Istoricheskiy Zhurnal*, 11 (November 1996), pp. 44–52.

Latypov, Timur, "O druzhbe, voyne i nefti," *Vremya i Dengi* (Kazan), 23 February 2006, www.e-vid.ru/index-m-192-6-63-article-12275.

—— "V efire obshchat'sya tol'ko po-arabski ..." *Vremya i Dengi*, 1 August 2006, www.e-vid.ru/index-m-192-p-63-article-14434

Lau-Lavie, Naphtali, *Balaam's Prophecy: Eyewitness to History, 1939–1989*, Cranbury, NJ, and London: Cornwall Books, 1998.

Lebow, Richard Ned and Janice Gross Stein, *We All Lost the Cold War*, Princeton: Princeton University Press, 1994.

*Levanon, Nechemia, *Code Name: "Nativ"*, Tel Aviv: Am Oved, 1995.

Levin, Aryeh, *Envoy to Moscow: Memoirs of an Israeli Ambassador 1988–92*, London: Frank Cass, 1996.

*Levite, Ariel and Emily Landau, *Israel's Nuclear Image: Arab Perceptions of Israel's Nuclear Posture*, Tel Aviv: Papyrus, 1994.

BIBLIOGRAPHY

Lieblich, Amia, *Seasons of Captivity: The Inner World of POWs*, New York: New York University Press, 1994.

Lobzhanets, Maksim, "Voeval v peskakh Egipta i Sirii," *Borisovskie Novosty* (Belarus), 6 September 2007, http://borisovcity.net/index.php?act=news&id=285

*Lord, Amnon, *The Lost Generation: The Story of the Yom Kippur War*, Tel Aviv: Yedi'ot Ahronot, 2013.

Lyutkin, Ivan, "40 let nazad ..." *Krasnaya Zvezda*, 16 June 2007.

Makarov, Dmitri, "Rezident GRU vspominaet: Pozvol'te mne vas zaverbovat'," *Argumenty i Fakty* (Moscow), International edn, 7 June 2000, p. 16.

Malashenko, Maj.-Gen. Evgeny, *Vspominaya sluzhbu v armii*, Moscow: General Staff, 2003.

Mallin, Col. V[alery], "Boevye sluzhby baltiyskoy morskoy pekhoty," website of the Baltic Fleet marines, http://belostokskaya.ru/BS/f_service.

Mangold, Peter, *Superpower Intervention in the Middle East*, London: Croom Helm, 1978.

Maoz, Moshe, *Asad the Sphinx of Damascus: A Political Biography*, London: Weidenfeld and Nicholson, 1988.

Marchenko, Andrey, "General-Mayor VVS Vagin: Vostok kak dal'ny tak i blizhniy—delo tonkoe," Part 2, Avtodaydzhest-Online (Minsk), 242, 8 November 2001.

—— "Siriyskaya komandirovka," *Ekspress Novosti* (Minsk), 39, 26 September 2003, http://expressnovosti.narod.ru/39/za.htm

Marchenko, Vladimir, "Voyna sudnogo dnya i amerikano-izrailskie otnoshennya: Tridtsat' let spustya," *Vestnik* (Cockeysville, MD), 22–9 October 2003, www.vestnik.com/issues/2003/1029/win/marchenko.htm

Markovsky, V. Yu., "Idite v zemlyu egipetskuyu: Uchastie sovetskikh MiG-25RB v arabo-izrail'skoy voyne Sudnogo dnya 1973g.," http://www.mig-25inegipt.narod.ru/index.htm

—— "'My gotovili voynu,'" first published in *Aerohobby* magazine before 2001, reproduced at www.foxbat.ru/article/mig25/mig25_1.htm

Maurin, Vladimir, "V tel'nyashke i skafandre," *Kuzbass* daily (Kemerovo, Russia), 19 March 1999, http://viperson.ru/uploads/attachment/file/425503/kz93j010.txt

Mel'nik, Pavel, "Zvezdy nad Nilom: Kak eto bylo," *Aviapanorama*, 2 (2007), http://www.aex.ru/fdocs/1/2007/5/18/10299/

*Mendes, Lt-Col. Shimon, *Sadat's Jihad*, Tel Aviv: Effi, 2015.

"Merhav, Lt-Col. L." (ed.), *Mahshava tzeva'it Sovietit ba-idan ha-gar'ini*, Tel Aviv: Ministry of Defense, 1969.

Merom, Col. Oded (ed.), *Ha-Hatashah: Milhemet 1000 ha-yamim, yuli 1967–august 1970*, Tel Aviv: Air Force Association (program for an event to mark the fortieth anniversary of the War of Attrition, 26 November 2009).

Meyden, Igor', "Na rasstoyanii udara," *Vesti Segodnya* (Riga), 288, 13 December 2008.

Meyer, M.S. et al. (eds), *Togda v Egipte*, Moscow: Moscow State University and Council of Veterans of Combat Operations in Egypt, 2001.

Michalson, Ehud, *Abirei lev: Gedud 184*, Tel Aviv: Ministry of Defense, 2003.

Minin, Viktor, *Ispytaniya zhizn'yu*, Moscow: OMR-Print, 2009(?).

Mlechin, Leonid, *Zachem Stalin sozdal Izrail'?*, Moscow: Yauza-Eksmo, 2005.

BIBLIOGRAPHY

Moiseenkov, Viktor, "Soldat iz Kazakhstana v strane pyramid," *Karavan* (Almaty), 12 April 2002.

Molodtsov, Lt-Col. K.M., "Opyt boevogo primeneniya RTV PVO Egipta v 1968–1972gg," *VKO*, 2005, http://www.vko.ru/biblioteka/opyt-boevogo-primeneniya-rtv-pvo-egipta-v-1968-1972-gg

Mørk, Hulda Kjeang, "The Jarring Mission: A Study of the UN Peace Effort in the Middle East, 1967–1971," Master's thesis, University of Oslo, 2007.

Morozov, Boris (ed.), *Evreyskaya emigratsiya v svete novykh dokumentov*, Tel Aviv University: Cummings Center, 1998.

Morris, Benny, *Righteous Victims: A History of the Zionist–Arab Conflict, 1881–1999*, New York: Knopf, 1999.

Mosyakin, Aleksandr, "Mesyats Nisan," *Chas* (Riga), 70, 489, 25 March 1999, www.chas-daily.com/win/1999/03/25/g_51.html

Munteanu, M[ircea] et al. (eds), *The Rise of Détente: Document Reader Compiled for the International Conference 'Nato, the Warsaw Pact and the Rise of Détente, 1965–1972,' Dobbiaco/Toblach, Italy 26–28 September 2002*, Washington and Florence: CWIHP, Woodrow Wilson Center and Machiavelli Center, 2002.

Murzintsev, Vasily, *Zapiski voennogo sovetnika v Egipte*, Kaluga: MRIP, 1995, http://militera.lib.ru/memo/0/pdf/russian/murzintsev_v01.pdf

National Security Archive, "The Impulse towards a Safer World": 40th Anniversary of the Nuclear Nonproliferation Treaty," Washington, 2008, http://www2.gwu.edu/~nsarchiv/nukevault/ebb253

Naumkin, Vitaly V. et al. (eds), *Blizhnevostochnyy konflikt, iz dokumentov arkhiva vnyeshney politiki Rossiyskoy Federatsii*, Moscow: Materik, 2003.

Nicolle, David and Tom Cooper, *Arab MiG-19 and MiG-21 Units in Combat*, London: Osprey, 2004.

Nir, Yeshayahu, *The Israeli–Arab Conflict in Soviet Caricatures, 1967–1973*, Tel Aviv: Tcherikover, 1976.

Nixon, Richard, *The Real War*, New York: Warner Books, 1981.

——— *RN: The Memoirs of Richard Nixon*, New York: Simon and Schuster, 2013.

O'Ballance, Edgar, *No Victor, No Vanquished: The Yom Kippur War*, London: Barrie & Jenkins, 1979.

Okorokov, Aleksandr, *Sekretnye voyny Sovetskogo Soyuza: Pervaya Polnaya Entsiklopediya*, Moscow: Yauza-Eksmo, 2008.

*Oren, Elchnan, *The History of Yom Kippur War*, Tel Aviv: IDF History Department, 2013 (posthumously published; original version for internal circulation, 1992).

Oren, Michael, *Six Days of War: June 1967 and the Making of the Modern Middle East*, New York: Oxford University Press, 2002.

Ostroumov, Lt-Gen. Nikolay, *Ot letchika-istrebitelya do generala aviatsii: V gody voyny i v mirnoe vremya 1936–1979*, Moscow: Tsentrpoligraf, 2010, text accessible at http://bookz.ru/authors/Nikolay-ostroumov/ot-let4i_786.html

Owen, Maj. Richard, "Operational Valiant: Turning of the Tide in the Sinai 1973 Arab–Israeli

BIBLIOGRAPHY

War," Marine Corps Command and Staff College, 1984, http://www.globalsecurity.org/military/library/report/1984/ORL.htm

Pacepa, Ion Mihai and Ronald Rychlak, *Disinformation*, Washington: WND Books, 2013.

Palit, Maj.-Gen. D.K., *Return to Sinai: The Arab Offensive, October 1973*, New Delhi: Lancer, 1974; reprinted, 2002.

Pande, Savita, *The Future of NPT*, New Delhi: Lancer, 1995.

Parker, Richard (ed.), *The October War: A Retrospective*, Gainesville: University of Florida Press, 2001.

—— *The Politics of Miscalculation in the Middle East*, Bloomington: Indiana University Press, 1993.

—— (ed.), *The Six-Day War: A Retrospective*, Gainesville: University of Florida Press, 1996.

Pavlov, Evgeny and Lev Berne, "Pravda o MiG-25: Istoriya sozdaniya," *Kryl'ya Rodiny*, 2–5 (1990), http://techno-story.ru/articles/aircrafts/448-mig-25

Pavlova, Elena, "Spetszadaniya s peresecheniem gosgranitsy," *Vitebsky Kur'er*, 2 September 2005.

Pernavsky, G. (ed.), *Arabo-izrail'skie voyny: Arabsky vzglyad*, Moscow: Eksmo-Yauza, 2008.

Pikhoya, Rudolf, *Sovetsky Soyuz: Istoriya Vlasti, 1945–1991*, Novosibirsk: Sibirsky Khronograf, 2000.

Platunov, Evgeny, "Provaly v pamyati," *Altaiskaya Pravda*, 30 May 2007, http://www.ap.altairegion.ru/158-07/10.html

Plugatarev, Igor', "Pamyati ne vernuvshikhsya s kholodnoy voyny," *NVO*, 25 April 2014, http://nvo.ng.ru/nvo/2014-04-25/14_monuments.html

Pochtarev, Andrey, "Blizhnevostochny triumf 'letuchikh lisits,'" *Krasnaya Zvezda*, 17 August 2002, http://old.redstar.ru/2002/08/17_08/4_01.html

—— "Kak podrezali kryl'ya fantomam," *Krasnaya Zvezda*, 14 January 2000.

—— "Orden za 'amerikantsa,'" *Krasnaya Zvezda*, 28 February 2002, http://old.redstar.ru/2002/02/28_02/2_02.html

Polmar, Norman, *Guide to the Soviet Navy*, 3rd edn, Annapolis, MD: Naval Institute Press, 1983.

—— *Spyplane: The U-2 History Declassified*, Osceola, WI: MBI, 2001.

Poluektov, Evgeny, "Rabochaya situatsiya," http://www.clubvi.ru/news/2013/01/12/poluektov/

Potyliko, Andrey, "Uspeshno obstrelyav pozitsii izrail'tyan, boevye raschety taino pribyvshikh v Siriyu sovetskikh reaktivnykh ustanovok 'Grad' zatem ushli ot pogoni amerikanskogo esmintsa," *Fakty i kommentarii* (Kiev), 16 January 2004, http://fakty.ua/68364-uspeshno-obstrelyav-pozicii-izrailtyan-boevye-raschety-tajno-pribyvshih-v-siriyu-sovetskih-reaktivnyh-ustanovok-quot-grad-quot-zatem-ushli-ot-pogoni-amerikanskogo-esminca

Primakov, Evgeny, *Konfidentsial'no: Blizhniy Vostok na stsene i za kulisami*, Moscow: Rossiyskaya Gazeta, 2006. All quotes are from the Russian original in the present writers' translation, rather than from the English version (*Russia and the Arabs: Behind the Scenes in the Middle East from the Cold War to the Present*, New York: Basic, 2009), which is often ludicrously erroneous—e.g., "the Holland Heights" for "Golan Heights" (p. 264).

BIBLIOGRAPHY

Pry, Peter Vincent, *Israel's Nuclear Arsenal*, Boulder, CO: Westview, 1984.

Quandt, William B., *Decade of Decisions: American Policy toward the Arab–Israeli Conflict, 1967–1976*, Berkeley: University of California Press, 1977.

—— *Peace Process: American Diplomacy and the Arab–Israeli Conflict since 1967*, Washington and Berkeley: Brookings Institute and University of California Press, 1993.

—— "Soviet Policy in the October 1973 War: A Report Prepared for the Office of the Assistant Secretary of Defense/International Security Affairs," Santa Monica, CA: Rand Corporation, May 1976, http://www.rand.org/pubs/reports/2006/R1864.pdf

Ra'anan, Uri, "The Soviet–Egyptian 'Rift,'" *Commentary*, 61, 6 (June 1976).

—— "The USSR and the Middle East: Some Reflections on the Soviet Decision-Making Process," *Orbis*, 17, 3 (Fall 1973).

Rabin, Yitzhak with Dov Goldstein, *Pinqas sherut*, Tel Aviv: Ma'ariv, 1979.

Rabinovich, Abraham, *The Boats of Cherbourg*, New York: Seaver-Holt, 1988. Hebrew version, *Sefinot Cherbourg*, Re'ut (Israel): Meltzer, 2001.

Rabinovich, Itamar and Haim Shaked (eds), *From June to October: The Middle East between 1967 and 1973*, Piscataway, NJ: Transaction, 1978.

Razinkov, Mikhail, "Siriya: Goryachii Oktyabr' 1973 goda," http://artofwar.ru/r/razinkow_m_w/text_0020.shtml

Riad, Mahmud, *The Struggle for Peace in the Middle East*, London: Quartet, 1981.

Richelson, Jeffrey, *The Wizards of Langley: Inside the CIA's Directorate of Science and Technology*, Boulder, CO: Westwood, 2001.

Ro'i, Yaacov (ed.), *From Encroachment to Involvement: A Documentary Study of Soviet Policy in the Middle East, 1945–1973*, New York and Jerusalem: Wiley and Israel Universities Press, 1974.

Ro'i, Yaacov and Boris Morozov (eds), *The Soviet Union and the June 1967 Six-Day War*, Washington: Wilson Center Press and Stanford University Press, 2008.

Rosenfeld, Alvin, *The Plot to Destroy Israel*, New York: Putnam, 1977.

Rosenne, Shabtai, "On Multi-lingual Interpretation," *Israel Law Review*, 6 (1971), http://www.mfa.gov.il/mfa/foreignpolicy/peace/guide/pages/on%20multi-lingual%20interpretation%20-un%20security%20counc.aspx

Rozin, Aleksandr, "Voyna 'sudnogo dnya' 1973g.: Protivostoyanie SSSR-SShA na more," http://alerozin.narod.ru/oktovr.htm

Rubin, Barry, *Secrets of State: The State Department and the Struggle over US Foreign Policy*, Oxford: Oxford University Press, 1985.

Rubinstein, Alvin Z., *Red Star on the Nile: The Soviet–Egyptian Influence Relationship since the June War*, Princeton: Princeton University Press, 1977.

Rubtsov, Col. P[etr]., memoir posted by his son ("Le2N"), 3 August 2007, http://kubersky.ru/publ/otzyvy_i_recenzii/otzyvy_i_recenzii/ehta_vera_ot_puli_menja_pod_suehcom_khranila_razmyshlenija_nad_romanom_egipet_69_igorja_jurevicha_kuberskogo/55-1-0-96

Sadat, Anwar el-, *In Search of Identity: An Autobiography*, London: Collins, 1978.

BIBLIOGRAPHY

Safonov, V.Z. et al. (eds), *Grif "sekretno" snyat*, Moscow: Council of Veterans of Hostilities in Egypt, 1998.

Safran, Nadav, *Israel: The Embattled Ally*, Cambridge, MA: Belknap, 1978.

*Sakal, Maj.-Gen. Emanuel, *"The Regulars Will Hold!"? The Missed Opportunity to Prevail in the Defensive Campaign in the Yom Kippur War*, Tel Aviv: Ma'ariv, 2011.

Sakharov, Vladimir, *High Treason*, New York: Ballantine, 1980.

Sannikov, L.I. et al. (eds), *Internatsionalisty: Sbornik vospominaniy voinov-internatsionalistov*, Smolensk: Smyadyn', 2001.

Schecter, Jerrold and Leona Schecter, *Sacred Secrets: How Soviet Intelligence Operations Changed American History*, Washington: Brassey's, 2002.

*Schiff, Ze'ev (ed.), *The Might of the IDF: Military and Security Encyclopedia*, Air Force volume, Tel Aviv: Revivim, 1981.

*Schiff, Ze'ev and Eitan Haber (eds), *Israel, Army and Defence: A Dictionary*, Tel Aviv: Zmora-Bitan-Modan, 1976.

*Schueftan, Dan, *Attrition: Egypt's Post War Military Strategy, 1967–1970*, Tel Aviv: Ministry of Defense, 1989.

"Schuman, Tomas" (Yury Bezmenov), *World Thought Police*, Los Angeles: Almanac, 1985, https://archive.org/stream/BezmenovWorldThoughtPolice1986/World_Thought_Police-Tomas_Schuman-1986–68pgs-SOV-POL.sml_djvu.txt

Seale, Patrick, *Asad: The Struggle for the Middle East*, London: Tauris, 1988.

Sella, Amnon, *Soviet Political and Military Conduct in the Middle East*, London: Macmillan, 1978.

——— *The Value of Human Life in Soviet Warfare*, London: Routledge, 1992.

Semenov, Vladimir, "Ot Khrushcheva do Gorbacheva: Iz dnevnika Chrezvychaynogo i Polnomochnogo posla, zamestitelya ministra innostranykh del SSSR," *Novaya i Noveyshaya Istoriya*, 3 (May–June 2004), and 4 (July–August 2004).

Serkov, Col. Vladimir T., *Liniya fronta: Suetsky kanal; Dnevnik voennogo sovetnika*, Kurtamish (Russia): GUP Kurtamishskaya tipografiya, 2007.

Shai, Lt-Col. Avi, "Mitzrayim liqrat milhemet yom ha-kippurim," *Ma'arakhot*, 250 (July 1975), http://maarachot.idf.il/PDF/FILES/8/108768.pdf

*Shalom, Danny, *Like a Bolt out of the Blue: "Moked" Operation in the Six-Day War, June 1967*, Rishon le-Zion (Israel): Bavir, 2002.

*——— *Phantoms over Cairo: Israeli Air Force in the War of Attrition 1967–1970*, Rishon le-Zion: Bavir, 2007.

Shazly, Gen Sa'ad el-, *The Crossing of the Suez*, revised English edn, San Francisco: American Mideast Research, 2003.

Sheehan, E.R.F., *The Arabs, Israelis, and Kissinger: A Secret History of American Diplomacy in the Middle East*, New York: Reader's Digest, 1976.

Shelest, Petro, *Spravzhniy sud istorii shche poperedu*, Kiev: Geneza, 2003.

Sherman, Arnold, *In the Bunkers of Sinai*, New York: Sabra Books, 1971; Hebrew version, *Me'uzei Sinai*, Tel Aviv: Ma'ariv, 1972.

Shirokorad, Aleksandr B., *Rossiya na Sredizemnom more*, Moscow: AST, 2008.

BIBLIOGRAPHY

Shishchenko, I.V. and A. P. Glazkov, *Smolyane-internatsionalisty*, Smolensk: Smyadyn', 2000.

Shunevich, Vladimir and Nadezhda Shunevich, "Sumev pomoch' armii Egipta izbezhat' porazheniya, na Rodine nashi voiny edva ne ugodili pod tribunal," *Fakty i kommentarii* (Kiev), 22 March 2002, http://fakty.ua/91191-kogda-vernuvshiesya-v-marte-1971-goda-s-arabo-izrailskoj-vojny-sovetskie-soldaty-pytalis-obyasnit-chinovnikam-chto-voevali-v-rajone-aleksandrii-te-sprashivali-quot-eto-gde-pod-kievom-quot

Sinikchiyants, Lt-Col. A.M., *Otechestva krylatye syny*, Moscow: Mozaika, 2002.

Siniver, Asaf (ed.), *The October 1973 War: Politics, Diplomacy, Legacy*, London: Hurst, 2013.

Sirrs, Owen L., *A History of the Egyptian Intelligence Service*, New York: Routledge, 2010.

Skobanev, Ivan, "Raketny zaslon: Iz dnevnika starshego leytenanta Ivana Skobaneva," *Krasnaya Zvezda*, 14 January 2000, www.pvo.su/news/n000114_2.htm

Slukhay, I.A., *General Ivan Katyshkin*, Moscow: Patriot, 2008. Excerpted at http://www.mkvv.ru/memory3.html

"Smirnov, Aleksey I." (presumed pen name of Boris Krokhin), *Arabo-Izrails'skie voyny*, Moscow: Veche, 2003, http://militera.lib.ru/h/smirnov_ai/index.html

Sochnev, V[italy M.], "My byli pervymi (O bortovykh perevodchikakh, leto 1967 goda)," http://vkimo.com/node/1755

Sofronov, Igor', "Kontrrazvedchik Leshchuk: Ot Sirii do Afgana," *Bol'shaya Volga*, 41, 22 November 2002.

*Spector, Brig.-Gen. Iftach, *Loud and Clear*, Tel Aviv: Yedi'ot Ahronot, 2008 (has appeared in English as *Loud and Clear: The Memoir of an Israeli Fighter Pilot*, Minneapolis: Zenith, 2009).

Staar, Richard F., "Russia's National Security Concept," *Perspective*, 8, 3 (January–February 1998), http://www.bu.edu/iscip/vol8/Staar.html

Stavitsky, Petr, "Krylataya fraza," website of military language school alumni, 18 March 2011, http://www.clubvi.ru/news/2011/03/18/bayki/6/

Stein, Kenneth W., *Heroic Diplomacy*, New York: Routledge, 1999.

Stevenson, William, *Zanek: A Chronicle of the Israeli Air Force*, New York: Viking, 1971.

Sudoplatov, Gen. Pavel, *Raznye dni taynoy voyny i diplomatii, 1941 god*, Moscow: Olma-Press, 2001, http://www.pseudology.org/Abel/Sudoplatov1941/index.htm

Syromyatnikov, Col. Boris, "'Shestidnevnoy voyny' moglo ne byt'," *Voenno-Promyshlenny Kur'er*, 28, (25 July 2007), p. 9, http://www.vpk-news.ru/sites/default/files/pdf/issue_194.pdf

Tatarinov, Vice-Adm. A[leksandr] A. et al. (eds), *Shtab Rossiyskogo Chernomorskogo Flota: 1831–2001; Istorichesky ocherk*, Simferopol: Tavrida, 2002.

Temirova, Irina and Vladimir Shunevich, "Vo vremya voyny na Sinaye, izrail'tyanye menyali egipetskikh plennykh na arbuzy," *Fakty i komentarii* (Kiev), 26 December 2000.

Tereshchenko, Sergey, "Egiptyanin," *Novy Vestnik* (Karaganda, Kazakhstan), 20 July 2005, http://www.nv.kz/2005/07/20/2767/

Tikhonov, Aleksey, "Vspomnim obo vsekh geroyakh," *Spravedlivaya Rossiya*, 30 September 2010.

Tokarev, A.A. (ed.), *Veterany lokal'nykh voyn v mirotvorcheskikh operatsy OON vspomimayut*, Moscow: I.B. Belin, 2010, http://militera.lib.ru/memo/0/pdf/russian/sb_oon-vets.pdf

BIBLIOGRAPHY

Udmantsev, Vadim, "Bezvizovaya komandirovka," *Voyenno-promyshlenny Kur'er*, 23 (11 June 2008), http://vpk-news.ru/articles/5175

US Senate, *Executive Sessions of the Senate Foreign Relations Committee (Historical Series)*, vol. XX, 1968. Washington: Government Printing office, 2010.

Vakhtin, Igor,' "Gusinaya pechenka na pistoletnom shompole,' 17 April 2014, http://clubvi.ru/news/2014/06/16/remember/75%20vahtin/

――― "Simfonichesky kontsert s vostochnym aktsentom," http://clubvi.ru/news/2014/06/16/remember/75%20vahtin/

Vanetik, Bo'az and Zaki Shalom, "Helqo shel ha-bayit ha-lavan be-tirpud ha-hesder ha-helqi bein Yisra'el u-Mitzrayim bi-shenat 1971," *Yisra'el*, 17 (Spring 2010), p. 117, http://humanities1.tau.ac.il/zionism/images/stories/mahamar_ventick_vshalom.pdf

Vartanov, Valery et al. (eds), *Rukopozhatie cherez chetvert' veka, 1973–1998: Materialy nauchno-prakticheskoy konferentsii* (Russian and Arabic), Moscow: Institute of Military History, Council of Veterans of War in Egypt and Attaché Office of Egyptian Arab Republic, 1999.

Vasiliev, Aleksey, *Rossiya na Blizhnem i Srednem Vostoke: Ot messianstva k pragmatizmu*, Moscow: Nauka, 1993.

Vinogradov, Vladimir, *Diplomatiya: Lyudi i sobytiya, iz zapisok posla*, Moscow: ROSSPEN, 1998.

Volkogonov, Col.-Gen. Dmitry, *Etyudy o vremeni*, Moscow: ACT-Novosti, 1998.

Volodin, Viktor, "Na Izrail' my zakhodili so storony morya," *Vremya Novostey* (Moscow), 5 June 2007, http://www.vremya.ru/2007/96/13/179605.html

Volovich, Aleksey, "Sovetskie voyska v Egipte," *Odesskie Izvestiya*, 14 February 2013, http://izvestiya.odessa.ua/ru/2013/02/16/sovetskie-voyska-v-egipte

Voronov, Vladimir, "Zhara, klopy i 'stingery,'" *Sobesednik* (Moscow), reprinted in *Ekho* (Tel Aviv), 13 September 1999, p. 42.

Watson, Bruce W., *Red Navy at Sea: Soviet Naval Operations on the High Seas, 1956–1980*, Boulder, CO: Westview, 1982.

Westad, Odd Arne, *The Global Cold War: Third World Interventions and the Making of Our Times*, Cambridge: Cambridge University Press, 2005.

Whetten, Lawrence, *The Canal War: Four-Power Conflict in the Middle East*, Cambridge, MA: MIT, 1974.

Yakushev, Viktor, "My: Perevodchiki s Nila i s Volgi," 4 October 2012, http://artofwar.ru/j/jakushew_w_g/text_0020.shtml

Yiftah, Col. Shimon, "Al tilim be-Mitzrayim," *Ma'arakhot*, 217–18 (September 1971), http://maarachot.idf.il/PDF/FILES/9/108389.pdf

*Yodfat, Arye, *The Soviet Union and the Middle East*, Tel Aviv: Ministry of Defense, February 1973.

Yur'ev, Oleg, "Ogon' na blizhnem vostoke," *LG-Zarechny* (Kuznetsk, Russia), 23, 2006.

Zaborsky, Capt. Vladimir, "Sovetskaya Sredizemnomorskaya Eskadra," *NVO*, 13 October 2006, http://nvo.ng.ru/history/2006-10-13/5_eskadra.html

*Zak, Moshe, *Israel and the Soviet Union: A Forty Years' Dialogue*, Tel Aviv: Ma'ariv, 1988.

BIBLIOGRAPHY

Zakharov, Leonid, "Komandirovka v Egipet," *Mir Aviatsii*, 2 (2005), pp. 24–39, http://www.hubara-rus.ru/files/MA-2005-2_24–39.pdf

*Ze'ira, Eliyahu, *Myth versus Reality: The October 1973 War; Failures and Lessons*, Tel Aviv: Miskal, 2004.

Zhirokhov, Mikhail, "Soviet Pilots in Egypt," *Aero Historian*, 38, 12 (December 2004), p. 6, http://www.airwar.ru/history/locwar/bv/sovegipet/sovegipet.htm

—— *Rozhdennye voynoy: Istoriya VVS Izrailya*, httpwww.airwar.ru/history/af/iaf/stati/born5.html

Zhirokhov, Mikhail and David Nicolle, "The Unknown Heroes: Soviet Pilots in the Middle East 1955–1970," Group 73 Historians, Part 1, http://group73historians.com/group73historians/2013-03-16-12-04-49/190; Part 2, http://group73historians.com/group73historians/2013-03-16-12-04-49/189

Zohar, Avraham, "Ha'im levatze'a haftzatzot omeq be-milhemet ha-hatashah," in Yehudit Reifen-Ronen and Avraham Zohar (eds), *Yahasei medinah-tzava be-Yisrael 1948–1974*, Tel Aviv: Golda Meir Memorial Fund and Tel Aviv University, 2004, http://goldameir.org.il/archive/home/he/1/1133282899.html#a003

Zolotarev, Maj.-Gen. Vladimir A. et al. (eds), *Rossiya (SSSR) v lokal'nykh voynakh i voyennykh konfliktakh vtoroi poloviny XX veka*, Moscow: Institute of Military History, 2000.

Zubashenko, Nikolay, "Gennady Shishlakov: 'Egipetsky serebryany orden ya poluchil za to, chto podbil amerikansky samolet Mirazh,'" *Establishment* (Zaporozhe, Ukraine), 5 April 2006.

Zubok, Vladislav M., *A Failed Empire: The Soviet Union in the Cold War from Stalin to Gorbachev*, Chapel Hill: University of North Carolina Press, 2007.

Zumwalt, Adm. Elmo R., *On Watch: A Memoir*, New York: Quadrangle, 1976.

Zuyev, Alexander, *Fulcrum: A Top Gun Pilot's Escape from the Soviet Empire*, New York: Warner, 1993.

Zvyagel'skaya, Irina et al., *Gosudarstvo Izrail'*, Moscow: Institute of Oriental Studies, 2005.

INDEX

Abbas, Mahmud (Palestinian leader), 425–6n38
Abramov, Boris (Soviet staff officer), 124, 153, 214, 253–4, 271
Abu Ghazala, Abdel Halim (Egyptian general), 54
Abu Suweir airbase, Egypt 244
Abu Zaabal, Egypt, 144, 167
Adan, Avraham (Israeli general), 111
Afanas'ev, Pavel (Soviet adviser), 41, 54, 62, 75, 109, 112
Afghanistan, xiii, 360; Soviet veterans of, xxv, 338
A–4 Skyhawk (Israeli aircraft), 23, 41, 117, 119, 121, 122, 131, 138, 145, 158,n170–1, 175, 191–2, 193, 206, 404n24, 407n11, 421n14
Agranat Commission (Israel), xiii, xxii, 25, 56, 71, 111, 138, 251, 309, 322, 324, 328, 333–4
Ahiqar, Eyal (IAF pilot), 250
Akhbar al-Yawm (Egyptian newspaper), 267
Akhtyubinsk (USSR test facility), 224
Akimenkov, Aleksandr (Soviet pilot), 190–194
Akopov, Pavel (Soviet diplomat), 12, 215, 219, 221–2, 270, 316, 329–31, 340
Al-Ahram (Egyptian newspaper), 41, 46, 114, 133, 146, 158, 176, 180, 244, 267, 276, 306
Al-Akhbar (Egyptian newspaper), 267, 269

Al-Jarida (Lebanese newspaper), 127–8
Algeria, 8, 10, 39, 61, 286, 327
Alexandria, Egypt, 8, 24, 28–9, 74, 82, 126, 130, 137, 140, 143, 155, 168, 199, 208, 213, 277–9, 285, 315, 317, 321–3, 332, 342; naval base 20, 24, 28–9, 31, 40, 58–9, 81–2, 121, 140–1, 143, 145, 158–9, 216, 225, 261, 279, 286
Ali, Ahmed Ismail (Egyptian General). *See* Ismail, Ahmed
Ali, Hassan Kamel (Egyptian official), 116
Alizadeh, Zardusht (Soviet interpreter), 139
Allen, Robert (US official), 102, 407–8n26
Allon, Yigal (Israeli minister), 82, 87, 96, 105, 159
Almog, Avraham (IDF officer), 110
Almog, Ze'ev (Israeli navy commander), 401n28
Alsop, Joseph (US journalist), 217, 245, 302
Amer, Abdel Hakim (Egyptian commander-in-chief), 15–6, 35
Ametist, Starbright (Soviet naval missile), 439n35
Amit, Me'ir (Israeli general and Mossad chief), 45, 60
An- (Antonov), Soviet transport aircraft:
An–12, 6, 11, 60, 135–7, 225, 348
An–22, 225, 271, 277–8, 348, 353
Anderson, Jack (US columnist), 404n14
Anderson, Norman (US official), 435n5

INDEX

Anderson, Raymond (US reporter), 233

Andropov, Yury (KGB chief), 14, 64, 126, 129, 186, 234, 237, 251, 293, 306, 313, 316

Angleton, James (American intelligence officer), 380n46

Antikythera (Soviet Mediterranean anchorage), 28, 30, 141

Antonov, Mikhail (Soviet adviser), 139

Arafat, Yasser (Palestinian leader), 199, 425n38

Aronson, Shlomo (Israeli historian), 69

Artzi, Aki (IAF pilot), 382n79

Asher, Dani (Israeli military historian), 287, 294–5

Ashqelon, Israel, 250

Assad, Bashar (Syrian president), 359

Assad, Hafez (Syrian president), 269, 295, 301, 312, 317, 323–4, 329–30, 340, 358–9

Associated Press (AP), 8

Aswan Dam, 36, 131, 155, 159, 178, 203, 216, 321, 350, 387n12

Aswan, Egypt, 88, 242, 273, 317, 435n5, 438n17

Arab Socialist Union (ASU, Egyptian party), 70, 74, 108, 127, 177–8, 257, 398n35

Asyut airbase, Egypt, 289, 394n96

Azovkin, Yury (Soviet adviser), 55, 77

B–52 (US bomber), 305

B–70 (US bomber), 223

Badran, Shams (Egyptian minister of war), 6, 35, 254, 378n13

Baevsky, Georgy (Soviet Air Force officer), 223, 225–6, 229

Baghdad, Iraq, 59

Baghdady, Ali Mustafa (EAF officer), 116, 260

Baltic Sea Fleet. *See* Soviet military formations

Baltiisk naval base, USSR, 23, 328

Baranov (Soviet adviser), 286, 306, 315

Barbour, Walworth (US diplomat), 164, 200

Bardisi (Egyptian liaison officer), 42, 220, 278, 381n60

Bareqet, Yeshayahu (IAF officer), 138

Bar-Lev, Chaim (IDF chief of staff), 76, 175, 244, 254, 347, 351

Bar-Lev Line, 76, 89, 93–4, 101, 103, 108, 110, 117–8

Baron, Hanan (Israeli official), 238–9, 249, 313

Bar-Siman-Tov, Yaacov (Israeli historian), 64, 105

Bar-Joseph, Uri (Israeli historian), 148, 207, 256, 296, 312, 316, 335

Bassiouny, Mohammed (Egyptian general), 158

Batitsky, Pavel (Soviet Air Defense commander), 133, 140, 143, 166, 177, 406n51

BBC, 9

Beriev Be–12 (Soviet aircraft), 61

Beam, Jacob (US diplomat), 149, 181, 200–1, 204–5, 214

Beaumont, Richard (British diplomat), 297–8, 450n26

Bebishev, Yury (Soviet navy diver), 20, 279

Beirut, Lebanon, 55, 127, 146, 186, 227, 233, 297-

Belousov, Vladimir (Soviet SAM officer), 196

Bendman, Yonah (Israeli intelligence officer), 332

Ben-Gurion, David (Israeli prime minister), 38, 67

Beni Suef airbase, Egypt, 61, 190, 192, 417n14

Ben-Porat, Yo'el (Israeli intelligence officer), 83, 328

Beregovoy, M.T. (Soviet air defense chief), 120

INDEX

Bergman, Ronen (Israeli journalist), 148
Bergus, Donald (US diplomat), 156–7, 180, 190, 216–7, 233, 235
Berlin, Germany, 33, 81, 228, 237, 253
Bezhevets, Aleksandr (Soviet pilot), 20, 195, 215, 223–5, 228–30, 252–4, 262, 271
Bin-Nun, Avihu (IAF officer), 163, 183
Bir Arida airbase, Egypt, 175, 417n14
Bir Gafgafa. *See* Refidim
Black Sea Fleet. *See* Soviet military formations
Bokovikov, E. (Soviet general), 357
Bondarchuk, Nikolay (Soviet airman), 242
Borba (Yugoslav party organ), 20
Borshchev, Nikolay (Soviet pilot), 224–5
Boshnyak, Yury (Soviet SAM commander), 196, 277
Boumedienne, Houari (Algerian president), 10
Bovin, Aleksandr (Brezhnev speechwriter), 360
Bregman, Aharon (Israeli/British historian), 148
Brandt, Willy (West German Chancellor), 452n27
Brezhnev, Leonid (secretary general), xxii, 48, 250, 360, 456n30; and advisers 43, 53; and bilateral Middle East negotiations, 291; and contacts with Israel, 237, 249, 293, 306, 313, 318; determines ME policy, xviii, 3, 5–9, 12–3, 15, 19, 301; and Egyptian leaders, 26–7, 73–4, 97, 126, 132–3, 143–4, 146, 148, 151, 250, 256, 260–1, 268, 306, 310; and Moscow summit, 240, 260–1, 263, 266; and Palestinians, 186, 420n19, 425n38; and San Clemente summit, 285, 293–4, 305, 312, 316–20; and Soviet intervention, 25–7, 33, 121, 133, 149, 152, 154, 161–2, 359, 409n51–60; and Soviet power structure, xviii, 14, 15–6, 237,
294, 316, 389n31; and withdrawal from Egypt, 219, 240, 247–8, 252, 260, 263, 267, 284, 288, 291, 293–4, 445–6n11, 453n30; and Yom Kippur War, 330, 333, 336, 349, 351–3, 356, 454n49, 465n28
Brog, Dave (USAF officer), 182, 203
Brown, George (British foreign secretary), 412n2
Brutents, Karen (CPSU official), 151
Bryantsev, Nikolay (Soviet SAM officer), 344–5, 463n50
Budapest, Hungary, 6–7, 12, 19, 25–6, 33, 353
Bulganin, Nikolay (Soviet premier), 67
Bulgaria, 20, 49, 321, 325, 373–4n26, 462n29
Bulloch, John (British reporter), 227, 297–8, 428n18, 440n38
Bundy, McGeorge (US official), 9
Bykov, Robert (GRU operative), 342

Cable, James (British naval historian), xvii, 30, 37
Cairo International Airport, 5, 8, 48
Cairo-West (Egyptian airbase), 5, 8, 12, 18, 41, 47, 60–1, 74, 81, 137–8, 142, 157, 225–6, 258, 348, 367n6, 400n15, 404n22
Central Intelligence Agency (CIA), 5, 9, 16, 18, 25, 33, 40, 55–6, 68, 71, 121, 149, 155, 164, 186–7, 200–1, 234–5, 256–7, 267, 276, 279–80, 283–4, 288–9, 294, 308, 321–3, 327, 332, 354, 369n38, 386n49, 432n5, 454n51, 457n51
Centurion (Israeli tank), 343, 463n41
Chazov, Evgeny (Soviet physician), 73–4, 125–34, 175, 319, 320, 417n15, 456n30
"Cherbourg boats," 58, 141–2, 150, 167
Chernobay, Grigory (Soviet naval officer), 215

487

Chernyaev, Anatoly (CPSU official), 267, 269–70, 287, 306, 351–2, 439n24
Chervinsky, K. B. (Soviet political officer), 185
China, 69, 103–4, 154, 234, 237, 254, 406n51, 425n38, 449n13
Chistyakov (Soviet adviser), 86
Chuvakhin, Dmitry (Soviet diplomat), 15, 371n83
Cohen, Avner (Israeli historian), 347–8
Colby, William (CIA director), 276, 323, 336, 354, 452n22
Communist Party of Soviet Union (CPSU), xvii, xxviii–xxiv, 4, 42, 105, 139, 195, 220, 301; Central Committee (CC), xviii, 33, 102, 151, 301, 433n32; CC Secretariat, xxiv, 5, 352; Control Committee, 33, 102, 301; Politburo, xvii–xviii, xxii–xxiv, 3–5, 12–15, 18, 27, 71, 113, 130, 133, 142–3, 152, 219, 234, 237, 247, 249, 260, 263, 293, 306, 313, 316, 324, 330, 339, 341, 351–2, 359, 433n32
Coral Sea (Israeli-operated tanker), 234, 433n18
Crete, 28, 57, 141–2, 377n84
Cyprus, 57–8, 201, 327, 424n12, 428n18
Czechoslovakia, xvi, xxiii, 9, 11, 62, 82–3, 99, 136, 154, 371n79, 388n30, 394n97

Dagan, Avigdor (Israeli diplomat), 31
Daigle, Craig (US historian), 20
Daily Telegraph (London), 142, 227, 296–7. See also *Sunday Telegraph*
Dakar. See submarines
Damascus, Syria, 9, 59, 311–2, 323–4, 329, 331, 341, 345–6, 348, 359–60, 378–9n18
Dayan, Moshe (Israeli defense minister), 4, 77, 235, 238, 316, 332, 404n21, 412, 416, 423n46, 49, 446; against Syria, 345; combat clashes with Soviets, 168, 175; Egyptian preparations for war, 335; Israeli political rivalries, 26, 30, 87, 377n79; meeting with Soviet emissaries, 192, 197, 239–40, 433n33; NATO, 238, 239, 249, 433n36; and military operations against Egypt, 25–6, 105, 182, 353; nuclear response, 347, 348, 464n2; occupied territories and peace agreement, 202–3, 216–7, 219, 421–22n12, 434n37; on sinking of *Dakar*, 58; relations with Soviet Union, 30, 296, 344n21; testimony before the Agranat Commission, 71–2; and US ambassador, 200; visit to the Suez Canal, 87, 390n21; weapons development, 245
De Gaulle, Charles (President of France), 104, 372n87, 397n20
Depth/deep penetration bombing. See *Priha*
Dikusarov, Boris (Soviet pilot), 6
Dimona (Israeli nuclear facility), xiii, 223–4, 254, 349
Dinitz, Simcha (Israeli official and diplomat), 235–6, 240, 313–4, 323, 345
Dmitriev, V.I. (Soviet marine officer), 118, 401n32
Dobrynin, Anatoly (Soviet diplomat), accused US of failing to respond to offer of bilateral talks, 174; "back channel" meetings with Kissinger, xxiii, 102–4, 125, 143, 152–3, 156, 169, 174, 178–79, 205, 216–17, 228, 232–3, 253, 255, 256, 258, 284, 397n20, 427n10; cease-fire offer, 157, 190, 201; communication through Nahum Goldmann, 98; comprehensive Middle East settlement, 295; concerning an Israel air and naval attack, 335–6; contrasting accounts of conversation with Kissinger, 238; forewarning to Kissinger about the Middle East issue, 101, 246, 247;

INDEX

introduction of SAM–3s to conflict, 159; Israeli proposal for interim settlement, 227–8; letter forwarded to Kissinger from Brezhnev concerning resumption of meeting in Moscow with Kissinger, 259–263; meeting proposed in Moscow, 252–3; meeting with Rodgers and Sisco, 168–9; meetings with assistant Secretary of State Sisco, 125, 157, 403n2; note to Kissinger, 306–7; number of Soviet servicemen expelled from Egypt, 275; objection of American policy in the Middle East, 218; question of Israel and the NPT, 69; reaction to extension of Warsaw Pact outside Europe, 151; reaction to Kissinger proposal for US-Soviet Union summit, 19–60; sense of US attempt to exclude the Soviet Union from Israel-Egyptian talks, 170; Soviet offer to withdraw from Egypt, 249; Soviet proposals for general principles of settlement, 216, 255; view of Kissinger's influence on Nixon, 180–1

Dol'nikov, Grigory (Soviet air adviser), 225

DRGs (*diversionnye-razvedyvatelnye gruppy*, sabotage-intelligence groups), 75, 87, 110

Draper, Theodore (US historian), 302–3, 437n40, 440n4

Dvina. See SAM–2

Drugatin, Andrey (Soviet adviser), 109

Duckett Carl (estimator of Israeli nuclear capacity), 386n5

Dudchenko, Vladimir (Soviet interpreter), 118, 148, 186–7, 346, 411n76

Dvornikov, M.S. (Soviet air force general), 343

Dzerzhinsky (Soviet navy cruiser), 22–3, 28

East Germany (GDR), 69, 258, 453n30. *See also* Nazi Germany; West Germany

Eban, Abba (Israeli foreign minister), 12, 40–1, 67, 104, 150, 164, 168, 238, 252, 297, 302, 312, 318–9, 332–5, 411–2n87

Edmundson, James (USAF general), 182–3

Egorin, Anatoly (Soviet journalist and intelligence operative), 21, 26, 29, 47, 96, 98, 114, 374n28

Egorychev, Nikolay (CPSU official), 14

Egyptian military formations:
II Army Corps, 42, 54, 55, 75, 76, 77, 78, 83, 85, 91, 92, 105, 108, 145, 401n35, 409n52, 53
2nd Infantry Brigade, 63
2nd Infantry Division, 42, 54, 75, 145, 286
2nd Mechanized Infantry Brigade, 267
III Army Corps, 91, 92, 118, 119, 298, 349, 465n28
4th Division, 146
5th Air Division, 139
6th Motorized Division, 144
16th Infantry Division, 222, 456n39
112th Infantry Brigade, 271, 286, 443n62
118th Infantry Brigade, 62, 76
336th Infantry Battalion, 109

Eilat (Israeli navy destroyer), 32, 36–41, 58, 97, 141, 168

Eilat, Israel, 168, 361n69; port and naval base, 416n32

Eilts, Hermann (US diplomat), 324–5

Eini, Alfred (IDF intelligence officer), 333–4, 458n7, 460n40, 460n44

Eini, Menahem (Israeli airman), 132, 183–5, 206, 438n3

El Alamein, Egypt, 33, 156, 228

El-Aqsa mosque, 403n10

El Arish port and airbase, Sinai 108, 465n23

Elazar, David "Dado" (IDF chief of staff), 250–1, 290, 316, 335, 345, 426n53

489

INDEX

Erell, Shlomo (Israeli navy commander), 38, 57–8
Eshkol, Levi (Israeli premier), 30, 96, 105
Evans, Rowland (US columnist), 156, 305, 273
Ezzy, Col. (Egyptian liaison officer), 273

F–4 Phantom (US/Israeli aircraft), 41, 96, 97, 131, 157, 163, 176, 180, 182, 183, 206, 242, 252, 405n41, 419n41
   F–4E(S), 431n21
   F–4E, 227, 31n21
   F–4X, 227
   RX–4X, 31n21
F–15 (US/Israeli aircraft), 227, 431n21
Fahmy, Ismail (Egyptian foreign minister), 310
Fahmy, Mahmud Abdel Rahman (Egyptian navy commander), 215, 375n43
Fahmy, Mohammad Ali (Egyptian air defense chief), 116, 258
Fakher, Ahmed (Egyptian military official), 439n28
Fawzy, Mahmud (Egyptian premier), 268
Fawzy, Muhammad (Egyptian defense minister), *Dakar* and, 58; deterrence" or "active defense strategy," 77–8; effective counterstrike at the IAF, 59; interview with Polish newspaper, 130–1; Nasser and, 56, 165–6; relieved of position, 236; Soviets and, 208, 232; Suez Canal crossing and, 168; use of small arms, 93; War of Attrition, 399n6
Federal Republic of Germany (FRG). *See* West Germany
Feinman, Tovia (Israeli intelligence officer), 163
Filonov, Mikhail (Soviet adviser), 92
Financial Times (London), 297
Finland, 168, 233, 239, 282, 370n58
Flogger. *See* MiG–23
Foreign Relations of the United States (FRUS), xxii, xxiii, 40, 202, 366n56

Foxbat. *See* MiG–25
France, 39, 45–6, 61, 69, 104–5, 149–50, 221, 273, 358, 372n87, 379n25, 393n71, 450–1n37
France-Soir, 38
Freier, Shalhevet (Israeli official), 237, 293, 348
Freydin, Zinaida (widow of Ilya Livshits), 350
Frog. *See Luna*
Frye, William (US journalist), 29
Fursov, V.I. (Soviet military attaché), 21–2, 83

Gabriel (Israeli naval missile), 167
Galili, El'azar (Israeli military historian), 13–14, 386n43
Galkin, A. D. (Soviet SAM officer), 199
Gamasy, Mohamed (Egyptian general), 92
Gareev, Mahmut (Soviet senior adviser), 225, 244, 280
Gaza, 57, 236
Gazit, Mordechai (Israeli official), 249–59, 313, 518, 432n12, 455–6n27
Gazit, Shlomo (Israeli intelligence officer), 410n69
German Democratic Republic (GDR). *See* East Germany
Ghaleb, Murad (Egyptian diplomat), 246, 268, 399n6
Gianaclis airbase, Egypt, 137–8, 140, 170
Giza, Egypt, 146, 409n60
Goldmann, Nahum (Zionist leader), 58
Goldstein, Lyle (US naval historian), 327, 353, 462n27
Goldwasser, Moshe (Israeli airman), 196, 420n21
Golovkin, Vycheslav (Soviet adviser), 346
Gomułka, Władysław (Polish leader), 19
Goncharov, V.A. (Soviet adviser), 38
Gorbachev, Mikhail (Soviet leader), 177, 378n8

490

INDEX

Gorbunov, Yury (Soviet interpreter), 60, 63, 70, 74–5, 78, 145
Gordienko, V. (Soviet pilot), 226, 271
Gordon, Shmuel (Israeli historian), 401n34
Gorelov, Lev (Soviet adviser), 284, 446n21
Gorelov, Sergey (Soviet air adviser), 45, 381n69
Gorokhov, V.I. (Soviet marine officer), 328
Gorshkov, Sergey (Soviet naval commander), 10, 28, 30, 261, 352
Goryachkin, Gennady (Soviet interpreter), 145–6
Grad–2 (Soviet rocket), 93, 325
Grechko, Andrey (Soviet defense minister), 316, 384n24; anti-Semitism, 15; and arms supply to Egypt, 59, 91, 121, 258; confers decorations for service in Egypt, 290; "Grechko doctrine," 14–5, 415n28; MiG–25 deployment in Egypt, 224–5, 253; nuclear guarantee to Egypt, 68; orders to Soviet personnel, 62, 130, 153, 155; and Six Day War, 15, 35, 371n80; and Soviet intervention in Egypt, 123, 142–4, 149, 153–4, 166, 423n51; talks with Egyptian leaders in Moscow, 85, 176; and visits in Egypt, 59–60, 62, 199, 257, 260–2, 269, 324–5; and withdrawal from Egypt, 219, 271, 439n29; and Yom Kippur War, 325, 351, 356
Greece, 6–7, 136, 167, 201, 341, 460n36
Green Island, Egypt, 28, 117, 123, 401n27
Grinevsky, Oleg (Soviet official), 357–9
Gromyko, Andrey (Soviet foreign minister), 127, 316; and Israel, 64, 234–5, 25, 293, 306, 313; and Moscow summit, 259–60, 263–4, 284; post-1973 policy, 357–59; response to Six Day War 12, 20; and San Clemente summit, 319–20; Soviet withdrawal from Egypt, 247–9, 252–3, 259–60, 263–4, 270, 284; and United States, 86, 98, 101, 149, 181, 246–9, 284, 295, 310, 403n2, 439n24; and Yom Kippur War, 310, 330, 336, 341, 351, 465n23
Grozny (Soviet navy cruiser), 261, 439n35
GRU (Soviet MI), xxii, 60, 84, 146, 148, 287, 298, 342, 349, 374n28
Guluzade, Vafa (Soviet interpreter), 349
Gurov (Soviet SAM officer), 176

Hadas, Nitzan (Israeli diplomat), 48, 82
Haddad, Wadia (PFLP operative), 425n38
Haifa, Israel, 13, 167, 327; naval base, 57, 141–2, 377n89
Hafez, Mustafa (EAF officer), 193
Haig, Alexander (US official), 307, 336
Hall, Wilson (US reporter), 146
Harel (Sternberg), Aryeh (Israeli physician and ambassador), 432n14
Harlev, Rafi (IAF officer), 180, 245
Hassan, Abdel Kader (Egyptian general), 246
Hawk (US/Israeli anti-aircraft missile), 158, 189, 230
Hawke, Bob (Australian politician), 237
Heikal, Mohamed Hassanein (Egyptian propagandist), xvi, xx-xxi, 17, 69, 78, 97, 104, 110, 113–5, 117, 119–121, 123, 125–6, 133, 138, 144, 146, 150–4, 157–8, 162, 165–6, 173, 175–6, 179, 208, 214, 217, 219, 254, 261, 267, 270, 288, 295, 309, 332, 356, 372n4, 387n14, 388n28, 398n45, 399n4, 6, 8, 407n21, 410n66, 411–2n87, 414n46, 415n13, 420n7, 423n51
Heliopolis, Egypt, 115
Helms, Richard (CIA director), 9, 200, 234–5, 256, 308, 327
Hersh, Seymour (US journalist), 22, 347–8, 386n5
Herzog, Chaim (Israeli commentator), 95, 99, 203, 214, 294
Herzog, Yaacov (Israeli official), 387n12

INDEX

Hetz, Shmu'el (IAF pilot), 132, 182–7, 189, 206, 419n2

Hinnawy, Shalaby (Egyptian Air Force chief), 48, 110, 400n20

Ho Chi Minh (Soviet freighter), 345

Hod, Mordechai "Motty" (IAF commander), 117, 395n23; acknowledged Soviet pilot's bravery, 194; admitted number of F–4 crews, 180; meetings with USAF officers on Soviet presence, 20, 29, 48, 245, 251–2, 254, 262, 440n41; sonic boom over Cairo, 116; Soviet SAMs, 158, 200, 206; use of Shrike missiles against SAMs, 243; Soviet MiG–25 tactics, 229

Howeidy, Amin (Egyptian defense minister), 35–6, 378n14

Hungary, 7, 33, 36, 46, 60, 62, 325, 375n52, 377–8n3

Hurghada, Egypt, 129

Hussein (king of Jordan), 80, 307, 310

Ignatieff, George (Canadian diplomat), 68

Il- (Ilyushin), Soviet aircraft:
Il–18 transport 258, 339, 453n35
Il–28 bomber 137, 141, 158, 197, 258–9
Il–38 anti-submarine warfare plane 60

Ilan, Arieh (Israeli official), 373n26, 386n43

Ilya Mechnikov (Soviet freighter), 345

Independence (US aircraft carrier) 60, 385n30

Indian Ocean, 80–1

Inshas airbase, Egypt, 208, 246, 290, 400n14, 436–7n16

Iran, 45–6, 61, 80, 234, 359–60, 405n41

Iraq, 45–6, 205, 278, 368n21, 393n69, 460n36

Italy, 6, 7, 80, 201, 136, 268

Isaenko, Anatoly (Soviet interpreter), 74–76, 106, 367n11

Ismail, Ahmed (Egyptian defense minister), 26, 54, 92, 128–9, 215, 296–7, 308–10, 311–12, 315, 317–8, 321–3, 332, 342, 345, 357

Ismail, Hafez (Egyptian envoy), 308–10, 317–8

Ismail, Hassan Kamel (Egyptian official), 116

Ismailia, Egypt, 23, 29, 31, 42, 44, 62, 75, 79, 108, 119, 145, 170, 183, 197, 296, 339

Israelyan, Victor (Soviet official), 351, 399n5

Ivan Franko (Soviet liner), 213

Ivanov, Vladimir (Soviet adviser), 256–7

Ivliev, Nikolay (Soviet naval officer and intelligence operative), 148, 268, 271, 287, 298–9, 328, 342–3

Ivry (Israeli rocket), 245

Izvestiya (Soviet government organ), 118

Jackson, Henry (US senator), 218

Jalloud, Abdel Salam (Libyan revolutionary), 69

Jarring, Gunnar (UN envoy), 55, 86, 98–9, 103, 169–70, 202–4, 206, 216–7, 425n30, 429n41

Jerusalem, Israel, 31, 48, 98, 127, 141, 150, 191, 233, 237, 264, 333, 352, 358, 360

Jews: American 41, 102, 139, 159, 177, 248, 255, 307; Israeli (as epithet) 56, 139, 167, 239, 376n60; Soviet 16, 135, 348, 350, 376n60, 386n49, 406n2

Johnson, Lyndon B. (US president), xviii, xxii, 386n1; appeal to Israel to sign NPT, 67; approval of negotiating Phantom fighter sale, 86, 96–7, 214; Glassboro summit, 13; letter to Kosygin, 40; rejection of story about 6th Fleet movement, 40–1; told that Suez situation was serious, 82

Kadomtsev, Anatoly (Soviet air defense general), 214

INDEX

Kafr Abbas, Egypt, 409n53
Kakish, Bassam (Egyptian officer), 456n43
Kalashnikov (Soviet rifle), 311
Kalchenko, Mikhail (Soviet adviser), 144
Kaliningrad, USSR, 6, 23–4, 406n7
Kalugin, Oleg (KGB operative), 102–3, 397n5
Kamanin, Nikolay (Soviet Air Force general), 194, 413n37, 422n34
Kapitanets, Ivan (Soviet naval officer), 30, 208, 215, 269, 286
Karasev, Pavel (Soviet adviser), 129
Karpov, G.V. (Soviet adviser), 36, 41, 44–5, 54–5, 62–3, 76–7, 83–7, 119, 394n86
Karsh, Efraim (Israeli historian), 280
Kashin-class BPK (large anti-submarine ship), 57, 58
Kasatonov, Vladimir (Soviet admiral), 28, 30, 167, 377n84, 415n28
Kass, Norman (US official), 185, 420n17
Katameya airbase, Egypt, 170, 182, 417n14
Katyshkin, Ivan (chief Soviet adviser), 41–2, 94, 120, 130, 140, 161, 207–8, 214, 381n59, 395n9–10
Katyusha (Soviet rocket), 88, 245, 393n73
Katz, Samuel (Israeli historian), 446n11
Kazakhstan, Soviet Union, 85, 365n47, 401n35
Kazan, Soviet Union, 345
Keating, Kenneth (US ambassador), 335
Kelt (Soviet missile), 178, 250, 290, 349, 435n5, 448n57
Kevorkov, Vyacheslav (KGB general), 234
KGB (Soviet intelligence and security agency), abduction of westerners, 186; archives, xii, xxiv; and Egypt, xvi, 18, 126, 129–30, 143, 189, 265, 275, 324, 329, 358–60, 374n28, 384n24, 411n74, 432n5; and foreign journalists, 14; and Israel, 64–5, 234, 247, 313, 318, 397n8, 403n10; and Palestinians, 234, 425–6n38, 441n15; and Soviet Jews 16, 64–5; and Syria, 329, 346, 358–60; and the United States, 102–3
Kharlamov, S. I. (Soviet officer), 408n32
Khandanyan, Artem (Soviet political officer), 221, 257
Kharchikov, Aleksandr (Soviet naval crewman), 23, 39, 56–7, 83, 374n37, 401n33
Khartoum, Sudan, 12, 150, 371n69
Khripunkov, Yury (Soviet naval officer), 31–2, 377n89
Khrushchev, Nikita (Soviet leader), 234, 412n2, 434n4
Kiev, USSR, 13, 20, 28, 138, 277, 279, 331, 333
Kimche, David (Mossad operative and diplomat), xviii, 13, 24, 203, 261, 363n20
Kimche, Jon (British journalist), 203, 363n20
Kipnis, Yigal (Israeli historian), 309, 452–3n28
Kirichenko, A. I. (Soviet diplomat), 59
Kirichenko (née Grechko), Tatiana, 59
Kirilenko, Andrey (CPSU official), 5
Kirpichenko, Vadim (KGB operative), 18, 265, 329
Kissinger, Henry (US statesman), as adviser to Rockefeller, 69, 101; back-channel talks, 101–4, 125, 142–3, 152–3, 157, 169–70, 174, 179–81, 205, 216–7, 228, 232–3, 238, 247, 252–3, 255–6, 284, 291, 306–7, 310; and ceasefire violations, 200, 202, 205, 217; and CIA, 257, 276, 284, 424n9, 454n51; declares Defcon-3, 348, 350, 353; and detente, 266, 293; and Egypt, 248, 253, 255–6, 264, 284, 295, 309, 310, 317–8, 333, 358; and Israel, 69–70, 111, 227–8, 252, 255–7, 264, 313, 318, 333–40,

INDEX

345, 349, 353; and KGB, 102; memoirs, xx-xxiii, 248–9, 263 283; and Moscow summit, 159, 168, 252–3, 258–60, 263–4, 320; and Nixon, 101–3, 169, 179–81, 247, 307–8, 315–6; and NPT, 387n8; and San Clemente summit, 293–5, 317–20; shuttle diplomacy, 358; and Soviet intervention in Egypt, 149, 152–3, 157–159, 169, 413–14n38; and US Jews, 159–60, 170; and USSR, 10; and Vietnam, 305–6, 308; and withdrawal, 169, 174–5, 178, 216, 218, 231–2, 246–8, 253, 258, 260, 263–5, 275, 276, 283–5, 291, 293; and Yom Kippur War, 111, 302, 308, 333–41, 345, 446n19, 454n49

Klimentov, Valery (Soviet interpreter), 75–6, 83

Klosson, Boris (US diplomat), 201–2

Kohler, Foy (US diplomat), 340

Kolchuga (aircraft location system), 436n16

Komar (Soviet missile boat), 37–9, 168

Komsomolskaya Pravda (Russian newspaper), 343

Kon'kov, Aleksander (Soviet serviceman), 9–10, 189

Kopylov, Viktor (Soviet adviser), 243

Korea, 112, 140, 186, 361n2

Korn, David (US diplomat and historian), xvii, 93, 104, 110, 152, 157, 168, 178, 191, 372n4, 397n24, 405n43, 408n31

Korneyev (Soviet adviser), 404n20

Korniyenko, Georgy (Soviet official), 264

Korotyuk, Konstantin (Soviet air officer), 163

Kosygin, Alexey (Soviet premier), xviii, 5, 12–4, 16, 40, 68, 71, 113, 132, 147, 149–50, 152, 157, 181, 207, 215, 237, 268, 293, 330, 344, 371n83, 387n8, 389n31, 412n2

Kotov, Yu. V. (KGB analyst), 313, 454n53

Kovalenko, Ivan (SAM officer), 417n20

Krasnaya Presnya (Soviet landing ship), 328

Krasnaya Zvezda (Soviet military organ), 48

Krasny Kavkaz (Soviet anti-submarine ship), 439n35

Krivoplyasov, S. G. (Soviet general), 84, 153, 271

Krokhin, Boris (Soviet radio expert; Presumed pen name: "Smirnov, Aleksey"), 191, 244, 272, 286–7, 306, 311, 315–6, 435n16, 453n40

Kruchinin, Yuri (Soviet naval officer), 439n35

Krymsky Komsomolets (Soviet landing ship), 22–3, 374n35

Kryshtob, Vladimir (Soviet naval advisor), 140, 142, 145, 147, 167–8

Kub. See SAM-6

Kubersky, Igor' (Soviet interpreter), 115, 117, 120–2, 129

Kudaev, Boris (Soviet interpreter), 60, 385n30

Kulikov, Igor' (Soviet interpreter), 138, 139, 407n19

Kunaev, Dinmukhamed (CPSU official), 143

Kutakhov, Pavel (Soviet Air Force chief), 194, 199, 224, 260–2, 312

Kutsenko, Viktor (Soviet engineer officer), 338–40, 364n45

Kutyntsev, Nikolay (Soviet SAM officer), 196–7, 417–8n24

Kuwait, 266, 432n5, 445n6

Kuznetsov, Vasily (Soviet official), 204

Laird, Melvin (US Defense Secretary), 275

Lajoie, Roland (US general), 185, 420n17

Lance (US tactical missile), 178, 245

Laqueur, Walter (historian), 114, 144, 260, 295

INDEX

Laron, Guy (Israeli historian), 455–6n27

Lashchenko, Petr (Soviet chief adviser), xviii, xxviii, 12, 22, 26, 33–6, 39, 41, 43–5, 53–4, 56, 59, 62–3, 70, 77–8, 83–6, 93–4, 109, 11, 120, 207–8, 303–11, 332, 342, 356, 426n59

Lashenko, Evgeny (Soviet radar expert), 178, 220

Latakiya, Syria, 58, 326, 331, 345

Lebanon, 245, 365n48

Leningrad (Soviet helicopter carrier), 80

"Lenin Room," 196, 325, 423n45

Leshchuk, Stanislav, (KGB officer), 346

Levavi, Arye (Israeli official), 13

Levitov, Amos (Israeli airman), 179

Libya, 23, 69, 132, 150, 226, 232, 286, 291, 296, 309–10, 312, 317

Linkov, Vasily (Soviet SAM officer), 213, 277, 423n37

Li'or, Yisra'el (Israeli officer and official), 328, 457n51

Lishkat ha-Qesher (Israeli agency), 386n49

Livshits, Ilya (Soviet physicist), 350

Logachev, Viktor (Soviet political officer), 122, 195–7, 220, 423n40, 433n27

Loginov, V.S. (Soviet Air Force general), 123

Lord, Amnon (Israeli journalist), 314

Louis, Victor (Soviet journalist), 233–8, 254, 318–9, 432n14, 456–7n27

Lovestone, Jay (US trade unionist), 380n46

Luk'yanov, Semen (Soviet SAM technician), 277–8

Luna (Frog, Soviet short-range missile), 107, 178, 335, 464n56

Luxor air base, Egypt, 418n32

Lysenko, Alexsandr (Soviet test pilot), 215

M–60 Patton (US/Israeli tank), 343

Makarenko, Yury (Soviet radio-technical officer), 278, 389n7, 400n16

Malashenko, Evgeny (Soviet senior adviser), 33–5, 41, 45, 53, 55–6, 59, 62–4, 70, 77–8, 83–8, 91–6, 106, 226, 356, 398n86

Malik, Yakov (Soviet diplomat), 98, 103

Mallin, Valery (Soviet marine officer), 23–4

Malyauka, Valeryanos Prano (Soviet SAM officer), 176–7, 417n20

Malyutka (Sagger, Soviet anti-tank rocket), 94, 111, 309, 342–3, 399n53–4, 401n32, 452n24

Mansura airbase, Egypt, 191, 449n67

Mansurov, Midskhat (Soviet SAM officer), 194

Markovsky, Viktor (Russian aviation writer), 214, 349

Marwan, Ashraf (Egyptian official and "Israeli spy"), 147–9, 207, 232, 250–1, 256, 281–2, 290–1, 294, 296, 306, 312, 316, 322–4, 327–9, 331, 333–5, 342, 358, 360, 410n69, 439n30, 450n35, 455n9, 457n48, 457n58

Marriott, J. (British naval attaché), 450n36

Mary (Merv) airbase, USSR, 124

Masregah (MI unit), 162–5, 175, 191, 389n8, 459n31

McCloskey, Robert (US official), 31, 40–1

McLucas, John (NRO director), 200, 424n8, 15

Medvedev, Dmitry (Russian president), xxix, 420n17

Meir, Golda (Israeli premier), 105, 163, 231, 233–6, 238–40, 251–6, 306–10, 313, 315, 322–3, 328, 325, 556, 348, 419n47, 432n12, 438n67, 452–3n28, 457n51

Mel'nik, Boris (Soviet airman), 48

Melzer Gil (Israeli journalist), 148

Mersa Matruh naval base, Egypt, 61, 155, 261, 277–8, 392n49, 424n5

Mers-el-Kébir (Algerian naval base), 10

495

INDEX

Mi-8 (Soviet helicopter), 222
MiG- (Mikoyan-Gurevich), Soviet/
  Egyptian/Syrian aircraft, 6–8, 9, 12, 60,
  116, 138, 155, 157, 344
  MiG-17, 95, 97, 116, 192, 194, 368n20
  MiG-21, 6, 20, 26, 45–6, 62, 85, 95–6,
    104, 113, 123–4, 131, 136, 155, 157
    161–3, 170, 175, 190, 192–4, 214,
    216, 222, 225–6, 229, 239, 246 254,
    270, 281, 289, 321, 368n20, 413n37,
    418n32, 421n14, 422n36, 443n54,
    452n26
  MiG-23 (Flogger), 357, 387n37,
    431n15
  MiG-25 (Foxbat), 61, 126, 140, 203,
    213–6, 223–230, 247, 251–4, 262
    268, 270–271, 286, 290, 295, 343–4,
    347–50, 385n37, 403n6 427n10,
    430n3, 431n15, 431n21, 440n37
  MiG-29, 420n15
Mikhailovich, Mikhail (Soviet *Grad* rocket
  crewman), 325
Mikoyan (Soviet aircraft design bureau),
  223–5
Military Institute for Foreign Languages
  (Soviet), 74–5, 283, 366n65, 398n42
Minayev, Alexey (Soviet aviation industry
  official), 214, 225, 228, 350
Minayev, Aleksandr (Russian academic),
  350
Minin, Viktor (Soviet officer), 325
Mirage III (Israeli aircraft), 45, 95–6,
  115–6, 124, 131, 167, 170, 192, 194,
  197, 230, 254, 372n3, 401n25, 448n57,
  449n67
Mirage V (Libyan aircraft), 150, 291, 317,
  449n67
Mitla Pass, Sinai, 92
Mitrokhin, Aleksandr (Soviet serviceman),
  242, 435n6
Mitrokhin, Vasily (defecting KGB
  archivist), 186, 234, 364n29

Mohsen, Saleh (Egyptian general), 35,
  378n12
Molodtsov, Igor' (Soviet naval officer),
  28–31
Molodtsov, K.M. (Soviet radio adviser),
  139
Momyer, William (USAF general), 245,
  251–2, 254, 262, 440n41
Moorer, Thomas (US admiral), 81, 205,
  345, 347, 351, 353
Morocco, 127–8, 133, 312, 327
Moskva (Soviet helicopter carrier), 80–82,
  339
Mossad (Israeli intelligence agency), 45, 60,
  147, 165, 203, 250–1, 256, 281, 296,
  317, 322, 328, 363n20, 410–1n73,
  454n 55, 459n31
Mubarak, Husny (Egyptian Air Force
  officer), 47, 256, 258, 260, 271, 289,
  305, 360, 382n81, 439n26, 448n54
Mukasei, Elizaveta and Mikhail (KGB
  operatives), 64
Mukhitdinov, Nuritdin (Soviet diplomat),
  329
Muqatem (Mt., Egyptian air defense HQ),
  115, 400n16
Murarka, Dev (Indian journalist), 14, 63
Murzintsev, Vasily (Soviet adviser), xxvii,
  272, 282–3

Nag Hammadi, Egypt, 88–9, 131–2, 258,
  394n97
Naji, Jalil (Syrian Air Force chief), 289,
  326, 331
Nasser, Gamal Abdel (Egyptian president),
  death and succession, 207–8, 214–5,
  426n58; and *Eilat* sinking, 37; and
  France, 150; and Libya, 69, 132–3, 142;
  and Marwan, 147; and 1970 ceasefire,
  178, 190, 199, 203, 205; and Non-
  Aligned Movement, 5, 17, 48; and
  nuclear weapons, 67–71; and planned

INDEX

offensive across canal, 53, 56, 84, 93, 142, 173; and Poland, 19; reshuffles of Egyptian government, 34–5, 127–8; and Scud missiles, 107; "secret visit" to Moscow, January, 1970, xv, 113–4, 122, 125–6, 131–2, 144, 146–53, 164–6, 410n66; and sonic boom incident, 115–6, 120–1; and Soviet advisers, 34–6, 42–3, 53, 93–4, 107; and Soviet aircraft, 45–7; Soviet airlift, 5; and Soviet bases in Egypt, 47; and Soviet intervention, xv, 26–7, 88, 113–4, 119–20, 130, 133, 140, 143, 147, 162, 166, 214, 424n5; Soviet medical treatment, 73–4, 125–6, 128; and Soviet military delegations, 24–6, 33, 37, 140, 143; and Tito, 7; and United States, 10, 36–7, 70, 128–9, 142, 156–7, 178, 404n14; and USSR, xiv, xvi, 3, 10, 17–8, 24, 59, 64, 82–3, 94, 105, 127–9, 142, 403n2, 412n2; visit to USSR, July 1970, 127, 175–8; visits to USSR, summer 1968, 67–9, 73–4, 425n38; and War of Attrition, xvi, 64, 70, 77, 88, 101, 104, 108, 110, 117–8, 138, 142, 158, 167, 397n17; and Warsaw Pact, 5, 17, 48, 151–2

Nastenko, Yury (Soviet air officer), 123–4, 137, 141, 155, 161–3, 170

Nastoychivy (Soviet navy destroyer), 30

National Reconnaissance Office (NRO, United States), 200–1, 424n15

Nativ. *See* Lishkat ha-Qesher

NATO, 7, 31, 61, 79, 81, 213, 238–9, 249, 281, 373–4n26–27, 377n86, 385n37, 433–4n36, 39

Nazi Germany, xxix, 4, 29, 54–5, 63, 154. *See also* East Germany; West Germany

Ne'eman, Ra'anan (IAF pilot), 196, 423n49

Nepobedimy, Sergey (Soviet weapon designer), 120–1, 343

New York Times (NYT), 10, 41, 95, 214, 233, 245, 281, 298

Nike-Hercules (US anti-aircraft missile), 230, 253

Nikiforov, Yevgeny (Soviet weapon designer), 258–9, 277–8, 439n19

Nikolaev, USSR, 136, 154, 156, 190, 208, 213, 351, 465n18

Nixon, Richard (US president), and Brezhnez, xviii, 240, 252, 263, 284–5, 305, 312, 319–20, 352, 465n28; and de Gaulle, 104; and Dobrynin, 103, 169 179, 180, 217, 228, 253; and Eban, 104; and Gromyko, 247, 249, 252, 336; and Hafez Ismail, 310; and "interim decision" not to rearm Israel, 158; and Kissinger, 10, 101–3, 125, 149, 152, 159, 169, 179–80, 200, 202, 216, 218, 247, 249, 252–3, 255, 259, 263–4, 305–6, 307–8, 316, 318, 336, 352–4, 387n8, 424n9, 453n33, 454n51; and Meir, 256, 315; memo from Sonnenfeldt, 149; message from Kosygin, 149, 152–3, 181; Moscow summit, 217, 263–4; and Nasser, 128, 404n14; on Soviet advance in Egypt, 161, 204; and pressure to demand Israeli withdrawal, 105; protest from Ambassador Beam, 181; and rearming Israel, 164, 180–1, 203, 352, 315, 419n47; and Rogers, 231–2, 397n10; and Rusk, 69; and Sadat, 233; and San Clemente summit, 293–5, 317–20; and Soviet Middle East initiative, 102; and State Department initiative, 232–3; and Strategic Arms Limitation Talks (SALT), 102; and surprise at Egyptian ceasefire decision, 218; and US Jews, 102, 248; and Vietnam, 305; and visit to China, 254; and Vorontsov, 310; and Watergate, 308

Non-Proliferation Treaty (NPT), 67–71, 97

497

INDEX

Noratlas (Israeli transport aircraft), 132

Northern Fleet. *See* Soviet military formations

Novak, Robert (US columnist), 156, 305

Novosti (Soviet news agency), 14, 21, 29, 41, 47, 98, 102, 114

Nualov, Vladimir (Soviet adviser), 267, 287

Nurgaliev, Danakan (Soviet SAM serviceman), 155, 221

Odessa, USSR, 221, 278, 331, 438n12, 459n27

Ogibenin, Ivan (Soviet adviser), 144

Okunev, Vasily (Soviet chief adviser), 207–8, 225, 229–30, 256–9, 280, 426n59, 438n17

Operation Even Steven (US, U-2 flights), 202–3

Operation 41 (Egyptian codename), 236, 356

Operation High Minarets (Egyptian codename), 236, 250, 356, 466n3

Operation *Kavkaz* (Soviet codename), xxviii, 3, 20, 89, 97–8, 114, 122–4, 126, 130, 133–4, 137, 142–3, 151, 153–7, 162, 166, 173, 177, 197, 208, 214, 219, 223, 225, 253, 271, 277, 279–80, 283, 344, 400n11, 420n20

Or Yeqarot (Israeli canal-ignition scheme), 241, 434n2

Orit (Israeli trawler), 167–8

Ossa (Soviet missile boat), 37, 40

Ostroumov, Nikolay (Soviet Air Force general), 12, 370n61

P-12 (Soviet radar station), 138–9, 193, 396n33, 407n22

P-35 (Sepal) (Soviet cruise missile), 439n35a

Pacepa, Ion Mihai (Romanian intelligence officer), 441n15

Pacht, Shunia (Israeli intelligence officer), 459n31

Pacific Fleet. *See* Soviet military formations

Palestinians, xiv, 205, 217–8, 285, 293, 295, 309, 313, 319–20, 359–60, 388n24, 425n38, 449n1, 453n33; Fatah 425n38; PFLP 186, 234, 360, 425n38, 441n15; PLO 425n38

Pak, V.M. (Soviet interpreter), 141–2

Polmar, Norman (US historian), 200, 431n21

Paris, France, 12, 15, 62, 87, 95, 150, 305–6, 308, 371n83, 372n87, 460n40

Parker, Richard (US diplomat and historian), 149

Pechenkin, Aleksandr (Soviet radio technician), 136, 279

Pechora. *See* SAM-3

Pe'er, Yitzhak (Jeff Peer, IAF pilot), 177, 184, 420n20

Peres, Shim'on (Israeli official and politician), 346, 428n24, 464n58

Persian Gulf, 80–1

Petrov, Boris (Soviet naval officer), 28–9

Phantom. *See* F-4 Phantom

Piper Cub (IAF aircraft), 89

Pirogov, K. A. (Soviet cultural-educational officer), 199

Pobeda (Soviet liner), 277–8, 281

Pecoctić, Kuzma (Yugoslav naval officer), 40

Podalka, Anatoly (Soviet SAM officer), 156, 282

Podgorny, Nikolay (Soviet head of state), 7–8, 12–3, 17–9, 21, 24, 143, 216, 232–3, 235, 293

Pokryshkin, Aleksandr (Soviet air defense general), 19–20, 225, 373n12

Poland, 15–6, 18–9, 55, 62, 81, 130, 289, 350, 462n29

Polaris. *See* submarines, US

Politburo. *See* Communist Party

Politruk (Soviet political officer, also

INDEX

politrabotnik), xxv, xxvii, 70, 83, 122, 135, 139, 153, 176, 185, 191, 195–197, 220–1, 224–5, 257, 270, 345, 364n44, 368n22, 369n44, 426n58
Poluektov, Evgeny (Soviet interpreter), 136, 407n10–11
Ponomarev, Boris (CPSU official), 237, 259, 433n32
Popov, Konstantin (Soviet SAM officer), 133, 135, 140, 195–7, 213, 243
Popov, V. I. (Soviet naval officer), 79, 391n27
Port Fuad, Egypt, 24–6, 29, 56, 272, 353, 401n32
Port Said, Egypt, 20, 22–4, 26–9, 31–2, 36, 38–9, 56, 59, 62, 74, 79–80, 82–3, 106, 108, 118, 141, 162, 167–8, 178, 270, 272, 299, 311, 328, 352–3, 377n89, 391n27, 401n33, 416n34, 450–1n36–37
Port Tawfik, Egypt, 77, 86, 390n20
Povelko, V. P. (Soviet adviser), 146
Pozhidaev, Dmitry (Soviet diplomat), 5, 15, 26, 371n83
Pravda (CPSU organ), 34, 102, 107, 195, 237, 254
Presnukhin, Vladimir (Soviet SAM officer), 154, 258, 406n2, 421n1
Primakov, Evgeny, (journalist and KGB operative), xxii, 378n8; and Israel, 68, 102, 237, 347; and Israeli nuclear project, 386n5, 387n10; and KGB abductions, 186; and Sadat, 232, 235, 237; and Six Day War, 34; talks with Israelis, 71, 99, 234, 237–40, 242–244, 247, 249–51, 258, 265, 293, 313–4, 432n12; and War of Attrition, 107
Peace Jack (US F-4 adaptation project), 227
Priha (IAF "depth bombings" in Egypt), xiv, 57, 76, 113–4, 116, 118–9, 129, 142–5, 144–5, 150, 156, 162–6, 170, 249, 290, 322, 409n51–52, 410n66, 412n2
Pushkin, Anatoly (Russian general), 337
Putin, Vladimir (Russian president), xxviii–xxix, 60, 115, 221, 301, 338, 359–60

Qaddafi, Muammar (Libyan revolution leader), 69, 261
Qantara, Egypt, 23–4, 108, 376n74, 423n39
Qassassin, Egypt, 62
Qawm Ushim airbase, Egypt, 62
Quandt, William (US official and historian), 164, 166, 264, 284, 332, 340, 342, 415n13, 447n32, 451n6
Qarun (lake in Egypt), 62, 197

R-17E *Elbrus. See* Scud
Ra'anan, Uri (US historian), 265, 445–6n11
Rabin, Yitzhak (IDF chief of staff and Israeli diplomat), 25–6, 30, 67, 97, 147–9, 203, 227–9, 275, 313, 411n79, 412–13n87, 435n13
Ras Banas naval base, Egypt, 168
Ras el-Ish, Egypt, 24–9, 33, 37, 63, 79, 97, 168
Ras Gharib, Egypt, 138–9
Razinkov, Mikhail (Soviet interpreter), 346–7
Redeye (US anti-aircraft missile), 121
Refidim (Bir Gafgafa) airbase, Sinai, 45, 96, 163, 183, 196, 418n30, 433–4n36
Remez, Aharon (Israeli ambassador), 165, 387n12, 415n19
Reston, James (US journalist), 214, 232
Riad, Abdel Moneim (Egyptian chief of staff), 43, 46–8, 53, 56, 85, 92, 106–8, 128
Riad, Mahmud (Egyptian foreign minister), 35, 128, 132, 175, 190, 234, 250, 384n22, 396n26, 437n47, 442n34

INDEX

Richardson, Elliott (US official), 418n34

Rockefeller, Nelson (US presidential candidate), 69, 101

Rogers, William (US secretary of state), 80, 104, 128, 133, 142–3, 150, 153, 158, 168–9, 174, 178–81, 190, 199–202, 206, 217, 228, 230–7, 251, 253, 258, 264, 307–8, 397n10, 403n2, 418n33, 432n12

Rogozhinsky, Viktor (Soviet serviceman), 190, 208, 369n43, 435–6n16

Romania, 16, 20, 49, 425n38, 441n15

Romem, Yoram (Israeli airman), 196

Rose el-Yussef (Egyptian magazine), 282

Rossiya (Soviet liner), 277

Rostow, Eugene (US official), 69

Rostow, Walt (US official), 381n73

Rozin, Aleksander (Soviet naval historian), 23, 327

RPG–7 (Soviet anti-tank rocket launcher), 311, 342–4

Rubinstein, Alvin (US historian), 149, 288

Rubtsov, Petr (Soviet pilot), 229, 246, 290

Rusk, Dean (US secretary of state), 36, 40, 67, 69, 81, 86

Ryabov, Mikhail (Soviet interpreter), 287, 298

Ryabukhin, Vladimir (Soviet adviser), 85, 87

Rytov, Nikolay (Soviet chief adviser), 277, 280

Sabry, Ali (Egyptian politician), 127–8, 162, 215–6, 232, 268

Sadat, Anwar (Egyptian president), abrogation of ceasefire, 218, 223, 225, 227, 243, 268; advisors, 219, 257, 261, 339; Arab Socialist Union (ASU), 257; and Assad, 312, 359, 457n57; assassination, 360; and break with Moscow, 256, 260; and Brezhnev, 256, 261, 301, 206; and cease-fire extension, 216–7, 245, 429n4; and CIA, 284, 288–9, 432n45; and continuity of Egyptian policy after Nasser, 215; coup, 232, 296–7; and Dayan, 446n19; expulsion of advisors, experts and troops, 114, 117, 203, 216, 232, 249, 263, 265, 267, 269–73, 276, 277, 278, 280, 282, 283–4, 285, 291, 294, 295, 297, 305, 307, 444n26; formal orders to start war, 236; Friendship and Cooperation Treaty, 152; and Grechko, 260–1, 262, 325; and Gromyko, 253; and Hafez, 318; and Hussein, 307; and Ismail, 442n35; and Jarring, 216–7, 429n41 and Jehan (wife), 358; and Kissinger, 248, 253, 255–6, 264, 284, 446n19; and Kutakhov, 262 and Lashchenko, 309; and Marwan, 256, 316, 324, 358, 360; message to Brezhnev, 148; message to Washington, 216; Moscow visit, 132–3, 218–9, 222, 248, 250, 253–4, 260–1, 439n28; and Nasser, 126, 128, 140, 372n87; and Nixon, 233, 235; peace initiative, 309, 320, 359; policy shift toward United States, 215, 257, 308, 265–6, 316, 318, 358, 363n23, 418n34;, preparation for war, 268–9, 287, 296, 306, 308–9, 312, 329, 330, 332, 340, 349, 350–1, 353, 355, 446n1, 460n34; reluctance to declare war, 429n43; Revolution Day speech, 283; and Rogers, 231, 232, 235 and Sabry, 215; and Sadiq, 453n30; and scud missiles, 322; settlement proposal, 217–8, 309; and Shazly, 356; Soviet arming, 288, 299, 405n43; Soviet relations with Israel, 237–8, 240; and the Soviet Union, 128, 215, 226, 233, 246, 269, 285, 296, 299, 324, 327, 330, 359, 360 446n15, 418n33; speech (January 1971), 144, 428n18; speech at Tanta (January 1971), 215, 409n48, 51;

INDEX

State Department negotiations, 247; Vienna talks, 250; and Vinogradov, 243, 267, 269, 289, 329, 356, 452n20; visit to Jerusalem, 358–9; visit to Syria, 323; War of Attrition, 64, 77

Sadiq, Mohammed Ahmed (Egyptian defense minister), 128, 158, 236, 250, 257, 261–2, 296–7, 436n18, 441n29, 442n35, 450n18, 453n30

Sagdutinov, Gumar (Soviet political officer), 345, 369n44

Sagger. *See Malyutka*

Sakharov, Vladimir (KGB operative), 374n28, 411n74, 432n5, 438n12

Salahiya airbase, Egypt, 182

Sal'nikov (Soviet pilot), 170

Sal'nikov (Soviet missile officer), 321

SAM (Soviet/Egyptian anti-aircraft missiles), 18–20, 46, 55, 74, 76, 106, 118, 119, 121–22, 129–33, 136, 139–40, 143–44, 146, 154–6, 161, 166, 182–3, 194, 197, 199–200, 203, 206, 213, 219, 221, 226, 236, 242–43, 245, 259–60, 276–79, 281, 283, 293, 298, 306, 311, 344–45, 353, 356, 373n15, 390n11, 393n69, 408n31, 412n2, 417n17, 488n18

SAM–2 (*Dvina*), 17, 20, 23, 46, 98, 106, 117–19, 121, 123, 126, 129, 131–32, 138, 175–76, 178, 201, 203, 243, 305, 344–5, 372n4, 398n33, 414n46

SAM–3 (*Pechora*), 20, 113–14, 119, 123, 126, 132–33, 136, 138, 156–160, 162, 164–66, 175–76, 179–80, 183, 189, 196, 201, 214, 219, 256–9, 261, 277, 281, 298, 402n43, 411n76, 412n89, 414n38, 414n46, 418n24, 423n46

SAM–6 (*Kub*), 178, 196, 203, 245, 298, 311, n321, 345, 423n46

SAM–7. *See Strela–2*

Sarig, Yossi (Israeli intelligence officer), 124

Saudi Arabia, 47, 127, 234, 266, 318, 323, 358, 434n38

Saunders, Harold (US official), 206, 217

Savitsky, Evgeny (Soviet air defense commander), 33, 120

Schueftan, Dan (Israeli historian), 178

Scowcroft, Brent (US official), 334

Scud (*Elbrus*, Soviet tactical missile), 148, 250, 296, 311, 320–3, 325, 343–4, 347, 350–2, 387–8n18, 436n24

Sedov, Boris (KGB operative), 102, 129

Sejna, Jan (Czechoslovak general), 371n79

Sella, Amnon (Israeli historian), 265–6, 280, 363n16, 445n6

Semenov, Evgeny (Soviet naval officer), 352–3

Semenov, Vladimir (Soviet diplomat), 4, 49, 53, 98–9, 411n79

Serkov, Vladimir (Soviet adviser), 42, 63, 75, 77, 79, 86–8, 91, 93, 105–9, 111–2, 118–9, 146, 386n41

Sevastopol naval base, USSR, 28, 30, 277–9, 328, 353, 439n35

Severomorsk (Soviet naval-base complex), 60, 178

Shadwan Island, Egypt, 410n66

Shafei, Hussein (Egyptian vice-president), 268, 441–2n29

Shagal', Vladimir (GRU "Arabist"), 146

Shalev, Mordechai (Israeli diplomat), 336

Shalom, Danny (Israeli aviation historian), 116, 191

Sharaf, Sami (Egyptian official), 148, 232, 411n74

Sharashkin (Soviet adviser), 106–7

Sharm el-Sheikh, Sinai, 371n69, 448n57; air base 115

Sharon, Ariel (Israeli general), 21, 185, 342–3, 394n96, 399n53

Shavit, Aharon "Yalu" (IAF officer), 206

Shazly, Saad-el-Din (Egyptian general), 56, 236, 243–4, 250, 278, 305–6, 332, 342, 356–7, 452n24

Shcheglov, Afanasy, (Soviet general), 12, 143

501

INDEX

Shelepin, Aleksander (Soviet official), 120, 237

Shelest, Petro (Ukrainian CP leader), 4, 10, 13–6, 19, 28

Shengelaya, P.G. (Soviet aircraft designer), 225

Sherman (Israeli tank), 448n49, 463n40

Sherman, Arnold (Israeli writer), 206

Shevchenko, Anatoly (Soviet naval officer), 440n36

Shevchenko, Viktor (Soviet marine officer), 23–4

Shilka (ZSU-23-4, Soviet anti-aircraft cannon), 130–1, 133, 136, 175, 189, 196, 208, 213, 222, 226, 279, 345, 421n1, 435n16, 444n21

Shirin, Vladimir (Soviet SAM officer), 19

Shirokorad, Aleksandr (Russian naval historian), 38, 81, 379n25

Shishlakov, Gennady (Soviet serviceman), 130–1, 408n28

Shmonov, Aleksandr (Soviet pilot), 47

Shohat, Yigal (IAF pilot), 196, 420n21

Sholokhov, Mikhail (Soviet author), 225

Shrike (US missile), 203, 206, 241, 243–5

Sidqi, Aziz (Egyptian prime minister), 267–70, 282, 295–7, 315

Siilasvuo, Ensio (UN Observers chief), 282

Sikstulis, Janis (Soviet interpreter), 76

Sisco, Joseph (US official), 104, 125, 142–3, 147, 149, 152, 157, 168–9, 179–80, 204–5, 228–9, 233, 253, 333, 335–6, 403n2

Skobanev, Ivan (Soviet electronic-warfare specialist), 189, 389n7

Skobanev, Valery (Soviet electronic-warfare specialist), 189

Skyhawk. *See* A-4 Skyhawk

Smal'ta (Soviet radio jammer), 189

Smirnov, Aleksey (Soviet SAM commander), xxv, 122, 133–4, 140, 142–4, 156, 158, 175–8196–7, 279, 406n53

"Smirnov, Aleksey," presumed pen name. *See* Krokhin, Boris

Sochnev, Vitaly (Soviet interpreter), 7

Sokolov, Sergey (Soviet defense official), 36, 41–2, 53, 378n18, 379n20, 380n52

Sonnenfeldt, Helmut (US official), 149, 205, 340–1

Soobrazitel'nyy (Soviet anti-submarine ship), 57–8, 383n15

Soviet military formations:
   5th *Eskadra* (formerly "combined *Eskadra*"), 27–8, 29
   8th Air Defense Army Corps, 277, 344
   18th Air Defense Division, 134, 143, 154, 277, 364n44
   63rd Air Group, 223, 224, 225, 226, 227, 229, 230, 271, 428n15
   90th Naval Aviation Reconnaissance Squadron, 142
   154th Special Air Detachment, 349
   309th OMBP (Marine Battalion), 22, 23
   Baltic Sea Fleet, 22, 23, 27, 289, 290, 328, 375n42
   Black Sea Fleet, 23, 27, 28, 61, 528, 383n15, 401n32
   Northern Fleet, 22, 27, 145, 178, 327, 377n78
   Pacific Fleet, 80

Spain, xxv, 140, 201, 273, 426n58

Special Forces (Egyptian), 25, 56, 236

Spectator (London newspaper), 63

Spector, Yiftah (IAF pilot), 96, 207, 262

Spetznaz (Soviet special forces), 74, 140, 154, 189–90, 208, 278, 342–3, 351, 400n16

SR-71 (US spy plane), 213, 425n31

SS-12 (Soviet submarine-launched nuclear missile), 70

Stavitsky, Petr (Soviet interpreter), 137–8

Stein, Kenneth (US historian), 284, 288

Strategic Arms Limitation Talks (SALT), 102–3, 125, 159, 233

INDEX

Stratocruiser (Israeli aircraft), 243–4, 283
Strela-2 (SAM–7, Soviet anti-aircraft missile), 94, 119–123, 133, 136, 141, 175, 179, 196, 213, 277, 345
Streletsky, Nikolay (Soviet political officer), 196
Styx (Soviet naval missile), 36–7, 167, 439n35
Su- (Sukhoi), Soviet aircraft:
  Su–7, 8, 45, 95, 137, 193, 216, 222, 242, 435n5
  Su–7B, 20
  Su–17, 267, 289, 290, 311, 321
  Su–20, 267, 289, 290, 440n37
Submarines
  Dakar (Israeli), 56–58, 384n16, 17
  Israeli, 141
  Polaris (United States), 61, 392n48
  Soviet, 27, 68, 81, 213, 298, 327, 331, 348, 458n2
  K–172 (Soviet nuclear), 70, 388n19
  K–181 (Soviet nuclear), 70, 81
  K–313 (Soviet nuclear), 261
Suez City, Egypt, 24, 26, 39, 48, 76, 106, 117, 220, 344, 390n20
Sunday Telegraph, 81. See also *Daily Telegraph*
Super-Mystère (Israeli aircraft), 121, 197
Suslov, Mikhail (Soviet ideologue), 293, 359
Sutyagin, Boris (Soviet naval officer), 42, 59
Syria: challenge to Hashemite regime, 205; coordination of 1973 offensive with Egypt, 295, 309, 311–2, 316–8, 320, 323–31, 332–3, 333, 337, 347401n32; current crisis, xxix; dogfight with IAF, 180; false report that Soviet experts banished on eve of Yom Kippur War, 65; federation with Egypt and Libya, 232, 312, 318; IAF depth bombings, 322; Moroccan troop support, 312, 327; refueling stop for MiGs, 45; Soviet advisers and, 65, 92, 95, 205, 289, 301–2, 317, 331, 341–2, 344–6, 369n44, 413n17, 423n45, 448n54, 454n46, 462n56; Soviet arms resupply, 5, 6, 8, 15, 30, 45, 147, 224, 341, 389; Soviet nuclear guarantee, 386n6, 388n20; Soviet pilots, 95, 448n54; Soviet political backing, 357; Su–17 use in 1973, 290; Yom Kippur War, xiv, xv, 178, 301–2
Sysoev, Viktor (Soviet naval officer), 27–9

Tal, Yisra'el (IDF general), xiii, 245, 324, 383n7
Talaat (Egyptian general), 43
Tanks, 112
  Egyptian, 26, 271, 342, 348
  Israeli, 16, 21, 25, 62, 75, 83, 108, 110, 111, 117, 118, 129, 309, 339, 342, 343, 346, 352, 356, 390n4, 401n32, 404n21, 408n28
  Sherman (Israeli), 448n49, 463n40
  Soviet, 6, 16, 22, 33, 44, 83, 94, 117, 120, 128, 129, 139, 140, 218, 260 326, 341, 356, 408n28
  Syrian, 25, 317, 333
  United States, 310
  PT–76 (Soviet, amphibious), 22–3
  T–34 (Soviet), 250, 407n20
  T54/5 (Soviet), 56, 321
  T–62 (Soviet), 288, 321, 343, 448n49, 463nm40
Tanta, Egypt, 215, 409n48, 51
Taran, Pavel (Soviet Air Force general), 153
Tartus, Syria, 153
TASS (Soviet news agency), 48, 102, 233, 275–6, 341, 345, 359, 397n8
Tawila, Abdel Satar (Egyptian journalist), 282, 288, 290, 445n11
Tbilisi, Georgia, USSR, 6
Teko'a, Yosef (Israeli diplomat), 98–9
Tel Aviv, Israel, 13, 57, 63, 76, 93, 167, 184,

INDEX

191, 202, 244, 230, 238, 245, 253–4, 297, 348–50, 352, 448n57, 454n53
Tel el-Kebir, Egypt, 145, 401n35
Tikochinsky, Leonid (Soviet naval officer), 348
Tito, Josip Broz (Yugoslav president), 7, 17, 74
Tkachev, Viktor (Russian military historian), 121–3
Tlas, Mustafa (Syrian defense minister), 323
Tököl, Hungary (Soviet airbase), 7, 60, 137, 225
Tolokonikov, Vasily (Soviet SAM officer), 184–5, 189–90, 195
Trofimov, Igor' (Soviet radio technician), 289
Tskhaltubo (spa in Soviet Georgia), 74, 126
Tsoy, Oleg (Soviet pilot), 85, 194
Tu- (Tupolev), Soviet aircraft:
    Tu-16 (Badger), 12, 41, 46–8, 60–1, 70, 74, 81, 142, 157, 178, 226, 242, 250, 289, 290, 317, 321, 349, 370n60, 380n57, 384–5n29–30 418n32, 427n12, 435n5, 440n37
    Tu-22 440n37, 460n36
    Tu-95 370n59
Turkey, 45, 46, 155, 341, 460n336
Turkish Straits (Bosporus and Dardanelles), 30, 79, 80, 136, 155–6, 341, 391n27

U-2 (US spy plane), 200–2, 206, 213, 424n12, 425n31, 427–8n15, 431n21
Umm-Hashiba, Sinai, 162, 418n30, 459n31
United Kingdom, 57, 130, 149–50, 156, 165, 343, 450–1n37; "expulsion of Soviets" from Egypt and, 268, 273, 281, 294, 297–8; U–2 flights and, 200–1, 424n12

United Nations General Assembly, 13, 67, 128, 246, 252
United Nations observers, 27, 29–30, 77, 85–6, 105, 108, 216, 393n75
United Nations Security Council, 29, 40, 46, 53, 336
United Press International (UPI), 8, 214, 231
United States Air Force (USAF), 7, 20, 29, 48, 177, 180–2, 200, 203, 424n12, 431n21
United States Navy Sixth Fleet, 24, 30, 40, 59–61, 80–1, 130, 242, 286, 299, 327, 376n76, 377n87, 435n5, 458n2
United States-Russia Joint Commission on POWs and MIAs (USRJC), 185–6
Urwick, Alan (British diplomat and intelligence officer), 268, 271, 273, 281, 287
Ustinov, Dmitry (Soviet munitions production chief), 120

Vagin, Aleksandr (Soviet air adviser), 258, 289, 326, 331
Vakhtin, Igor' (Soviet interpreter), 220, 282–3, 288, 366n67
Vartanov, Valery (Russian military historian), 132
Vasilenko, Viktor (Soviet naval missile specialist), 145
Vasiliev, Aleksey (Russian historian), 341, 345–6
Vautour (Israeli aircraft), 46
Veligosha, Vsevolod (Soviet serviceman), 278
Vietnam, 11, 79, 97, 103, 112, 125, 140, 159, 161, 177, 180, 182, 186, 195–6, 233, 244, 259, 263, 266, 305–6, 308, 310, 361n2, 417–8n24, 463n41
Vinogradov, Sergey (Soviet diplomat), 15, 35–7, 43, 45–6, 53, 59, 118, 127–8, 147, 204, 372n87
Vinogradov, Vladimir (Soviet diplomat),

INDEX

xvi, 114, 142, 201–2, 204, 207–8, 214, 219–20, 232–3, 243, 246, 257, 260, 267, 269–70, 272, 289, 295, 308, 329–30, 340, 351, 356, 452n20

Vlasenko, Nikolay (Soviet adviser), 144

Voice of America (VOA), 9

Voinov, Aleksandr (Soviet pilot-adviser), 61

Volkogonov, Dmitry (Soviet military historian), xxiv, 186

Volobuyev, Evgeny (Soviet naval officer), 331

Voronezhsky Komsomolets (Soviet landing ship), 22–3

Vorontsov, Yuly (Soviet diplomat), 205, 310

Vybornov, Aleksandr (Soviet pilot), 4, 8, 367n5–6, 430n3

Wadi Natrun (training facility), Egypt, 118–9, 163, 338, 401n37

Warnke, Paul (US official), 97

Warsaw Pact, xiii, xvi, xxii, 5, 16, 20, 49, 83, 99, 121, 151–2, 166, 288, 342, 373–4n26

Weizmann, Ezer (Israeli general), 117, 206

West Germany (FRG), 4, 38, 46, 48, 68, 73, 82, 387n10, 388n30. *See also* East Germany; Nazi Germany

Yakovlev Yak–25 (Soviet aircraft), 427–8n15

Yakovlev (Soviet pilot), 422n26

Yakushev, Viktor (Soviet interpreter), 241, 287

Yaremenko, Valery (Russian military historian), 85, 121–2, 151–2, 154, 184, 187, 393n69, 398n44

Yavorsky, Gennady (Soviet adviser), 272

Yefimov, A.N. (Soviet Air Force commander), 154

Yeltsin, Boris (Russian president), xxii, xxvi, 330

Yemen, 35, 47, 59, 79–80, 234

Yena, Andrey (Soviet air adviser), 289–91

York, Herbert (US disarmament activist), 237

Yost, Charles (US diplomat), 103–4

Yugoslavia, 5, 7, 17, 19–20, 40, 46, 49, 60, 74, 136, 325

Yurchenko (Soviet pilot), 422n26

Yusry, Adel Suleiman (Egyptian general), 266

Yusubov, Ziyaddin (Soviet interpreter), 144

Zaborsky, Vladimir (Soviet naval officer), 327, 352–3

Zafar (Egyptian missile), 350

Zakharov, Leonid (Soviet airman), 60–1, 142

Zakharov, Matvey (Soviet chief of staff), 12, 21, 24, 26, 36–8, 43, 73, 123, 153, 207–8, 342, 378n18

Zamir, Amos (IAF pilot), 179

Zamir, Zvi (Mossad chief), 147–8, 165, 251, 256, 322, 328, 333–5, 410–11n73, 457n51

Zamyatin, Leonid (TASS director), xvii, 233

Zavesnitsky, S.K. (Soviet SAM officer), 179

Zayyat, Mohamed (Egyptian foreign minister), 333, 335

Ze'ev (Israeli rocket), 85, 94, 106–8

Ze'ira, Eliyahu (IDF MI chief), 111, 147–8, 290–1, 309, 322, 328, 331–2, 334, 349, 455n14

Zeldovich, Yakov (Soviet nuclear weapons developer), 350

Zhdanov, Aleksey (Soviet SAM adviser), 143

Zhirokhov, Mikhail (Russian aviation historian), 89, 124, 137, 168, 367n5, 368n20, 421n14, 422n19, 26, 28, 36

Zhukov, Yury (Russian naval historian), 327, 353

505

INDEX

Zhuravlev (Soviet pilot), 422n26
Zhuravlev, Vladimir (Soviet naval officer), 193
Zolotarev, Vladimir (Russian military historian), 185–6

Zub, Vitaly (Soviet naval adviser), 42
Zubok, Vladislav (Russian/US historian), xxviii, 324
Zumwalt, Elmo (US admiral), 462n27
Zuyev, Alexander (Soviet pilot), 420n15

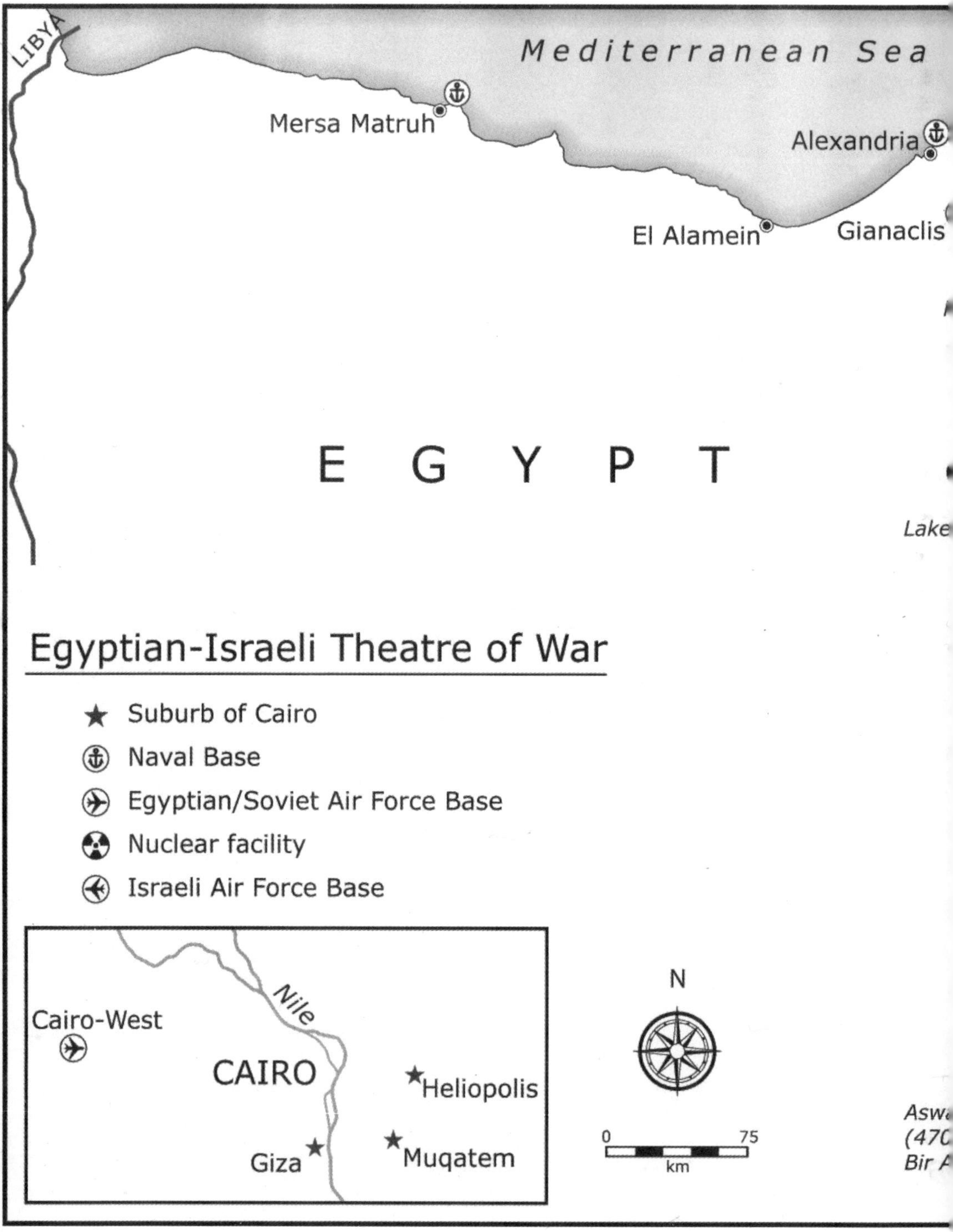

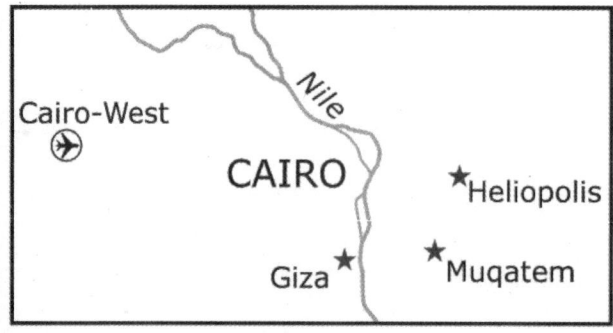